What They Said
in 1986

What They Said In 1986

The Yearbook Of World Opinion

Compiled and Edited by

ALAN F. PATER

and

JASON R. PATER

MONITOR BOOK COMPANY

To

The Newsmakers of the World . . .

May they never be at a loss for words

Preface to the First Edition (1969)

Words can be powerful or subtle, humorous or maddening. They can be vigorous or feeble, lucid or obscure, inspiring or despairing, wise or foolish, hopeful or pessimistic . . . they can be fearful or confident, timid or articulate, persuasive or perverse, honest or deceitful. As tools at a speaker's command, words can be used to reason, argue, discuss, cajole, plead, debate, declaim, threaten, infuriate, or appease; they can harangue, flourish, recite, preach, discourse, stab to the quick, or gently sermonize.

When casually spoken by a stage or film star, words can go beyond the press-agentry and make-up facade and reveal the inner man or woman. When purposefully uttered in the considered phrasing of a head of state, words can determine the destiny of millions of people, resolve peace or war, or chart the course of a nation on whose direction the fate of the entire world may depend.

Until now, the *copia verborum* of well-known and renowned public figures—the doctors and diplomats, the governors and generals, the potentates and presidents, the entertainers and educators, the bishops and baseball players, the jurists and journalists, the authors and attorneys, the congress-men and chairmen-of-the-board—whether enunciated in speeches, lectures, interviews, radio and television addresses, news conferences, forums, symposiums, town meetings, committee hearings, random remarks to the press, or delivered on the floors of the United States Senate and House of Representatives or in the parliaments and palaces of the world—have been dutifully reported in the media, then filed away and, for the most part, forgotten.

The editors of *WHAT THEY SAID* believe that consigning such a wealth of thoughts, ideas, doctrines, opinions and philosophies to interment in the morgues and archives of the Fourth Estate is lamentable and unnecessary. Yet the media, in all their forms, are constantly engulfing us in a profusion of endless and increasingly voluminous news reports. One is easily disposed to disregard or forget the stimulating discussion of critical issues embodied in so many of the utterances of those who make the news and, in their respective fields, shape the events throughout the world. The conclusion is therefore a natural and compelling one: the educator, the public official, the business executive, the statesman, the philosopher—everyone who has a stake in the complex, often confusing trends of our times—should have material of this kind readily available.

These, then, are the circumstances under which *WHAT THEY SAID* was conceived. It is the culmination of a year of listening to the people in the public eye; a year of scrutinizing, monitoring, reviewing, judging, deciding—a year during which the editors resurrected from almost certain oblivion those quintessential elements of the year's *spoken* opinion which, in their judgment, demanded preservation in book form.

WHAT THEY SAID is a pioneer in its field. Its *raison d'etre* is the firm conviction that presenting, each year, the highlights of vital and interesting views from the lips of prominent people on virtually every aspect of contemporary civilization fulfills the need to give the *spoken* word the permanence and lasting value of the *written* word. For, if it is true that a picture is worth 10,000 words, it is equally true that a verbal conclusion, an apt quote or a candid comment by a person of fame or influence can have more significance and can provide more understanding than an entire page of summary in a standard work of reference.

The editors of *WHAT THEY SAID* did not, however, design their book for researchers and scholars alone. One of the failings of the conventional reference work is that it is blandly written and referred to primarily for facts and figures, lacking inherent "interest value." *WHAT THEY SAID*, on the other hand, was planned for sheer enjoyment and pleasure, for searching glimpses into the lives and thoughts of the world's celebrities, as well as for serious study, intellectual reflection and the philosophical contemplation of our multifaceted life and mores. Furthermore, those pressed for time, yet anxious to know what the newsmakers have been saying, will welcome the short excerpts which will make for quick, intermittent reading—and rereading. And, of course, the topical classifications, the speakers' index, the subject index, the place and date information—documented and authenticated and easily located—will supply a rich fund of hitherto not readily obtainable reference and statistical material.

Finally, the reader will find that the editors have eschewed trite comments and cliches, tedious and boring. The selected quotations, each standing on its own, are pertinent, significant, stimulating— above all, relevant to today's world, expressed in the speakers' own words. And they will, the editors feel, be even more relevant tomorrow. They will be re-examined and reflected upon in the future by men and women eager to learn from the past. The prophecies, the promises, the "golden dreams," the boastings and rantings, the bluster, the bravado, the pleadings and representations of those whose voices echo in these pages (and in those to come) should provide a rare and unique history lesson. The positions held by these luminaries, in their respective callings, are such that what they say today may profoundly affect the future as well as the present, and so will be of lasting importance and meaning.

ALAN F. PATER
JASON R. PATER

Beverly Hills, California

Table of Contents

PART THREE: GENERAL

Editorial Treatment

ORGANIZATION OF MATERIAL

Special attention has been given to the arrangement of the book—from the major divisions down to the individual categories and speakers—the objective being a logical progression of related material, as follows:

(A) The categories are arranged alphabetically within each of three major sections:

Part One:	"National Affairs"
Part Two:	"International Affairs"
Part Three:	"General"

In this manner, the reader can quickly locate quotations pertaining to particular fields of interest (see also *Indexing*). It should be noted that some quotations contain a number of thoughts or ideas—sometimes on different subjects—while some are vague as to exact subject matter and thus do not fit clearly into a specific topic classification. In such cases, the judgment of the Editors has determined the most appropriate category.

(B) Within each category the speakers are in alphabetical order by surname, following alphabetization practices used in the speaker's country of origin.

(C) Where there are two or more quotations by one speaker within the same category, they appear chronologically by date spoken or date of source.

SPEAKER IDENTIFICATION

(A) The occupation, profession, rank, position or title of the speaker is given as it was *at the time the statement was made* (except when the speaker's relevant identification is in the past, in which case he is shown as "former"). Thus, due to possible changes in status during the year, a speaker may be shown with different identifications in various parts of the book, or even within the same category.

(B) In the case of a speaker who holds more than one position simultaneously, the judgment of the Editors has determined the most appropriate identification to use with a specific quotation.

(C) Nationality of the speakers is given only when it is relevant to the specific quotation.

THE QUOTATIONS

The quoted material selected for inclusion in this book is shown as it appeared in the source, except as follows:

(A) *Ellipses* have been inserted wherever the Editors have deleted extraneous words or overly long passages within the quoted material used. In no way has the meaning or intention of the quotations been altered. *Ellipses* are also used where they appeared in the source.

(B) *Punctuation and spelling* have been altered by the Editors where they were obviously incorrect in the source, or to make the quotations more intelligible, or to conform to the general style used throughout this book. Again, meaning and intention of the quotations have not been changed.

(C) *Brackets* ([ ]) indicate material inserted by the Editors or by the source to either correct obvious errors or to explain or clarify what the speaker is saying. In some instances, bracketed material may replace quoted material for the sake of clarity.

(D) *Italics* either appeared in the original source or were added by the Editors where emphasis is clearly desirable.

Except for the above instances, the quoted material used has been printed verbatim, as reported by the source (even if the speaker made factual errors or was awkward in his choice of words).

Special care has been exercised to make certain that each quotation stands on its own and is not taken "out of context." The Editors, however, cannot be responsible for errors made by the original source, i.e., incorrect reporting, mis-quotations, or errors in interpretation.

DOCUMENTATION AND SOURCES

Documentation (circumstance, place, date) of each quotation is provided as fully as could be obtained, and the sources are furnished for all quotations. In some instances, no documentation details were available; in those cases, only the source is given. Following are the sequence and style used for this information:

Circumstance of quotation, place, date/Name of source, date:section (if applicable), page number.

Example: *Before the Senate, Washington, Dec. 4/The Washington Post, 12-5:(A)13.*

The above example indicates that the quotation was delivered before the Senate in Washington on December 4. It was taken for *WHAT THEY SAID* from *The Washington Post*, issue of December 5, section A, page 13. (When a newspaper publishes more than one edition on the same date, it should be noted that page numbers may vary from edition to edition.)

(A) When the source is a television or radio broadcast, the name of the network or local station is indicated, along with the date of the broadcast (obviously, page and section information does not apply).

(B) An asterisk (•) before the (/) in the documentation indicates that the quoted material was written rather than spoken. Although the basic policy of *WHAT THEY SAID* is to use only *spoken* statements, there are occasions when written statements are considered by the Editors to be important enough to be included. These occasions are rare and usually involve Presidential messages and statements released to the press and other such documents attributed to persons in high government office.

INDEXING

(A) The *Index to Speakers* is keyed to the page number. (For alphabetization practices, see

Organization of Material, paragraph B.)

(B) The *Index to Subjects* is keyed to both the page number and the quotation number on the page (thus 210:3 indicates quotation number 3 on page 210); the quotation number appears at the right corner of each quotation.

(C) To locate quotations on a particular subject, regardless of the speaker, turn to the appropriate category (see *Table of Contents*) or use the detailed *Index to Subjects*.

(D) To locate all quotations by a particular speaker, regardless of subject, use the *Index to Speakers*.

(E) To locate quotations by a particular speaker on a particular subject, turn to the appropriate category and then to that person's quotations within the category.

(F) The reader will find that the basic categorization format of *WHAT THEY SAID* is itself a useful subject index, inasmuch as related quotations are grouped together by their respective categories. All aspects of journalism, for example, are relevant to each other; thus, the section *Journalism* embraces all phases of the news media. Similarly, quotations pertaining to the U.S. President, Congress, etc., are in the section *Government*.

MISCELLANEOUS

(A) Except where otherwise indicated or obviously to the contrary, all universities, organizations and business firms mentioned in this book are in the United States; similarly, references made to "national," "Federal," "this country," "the nation," etc., refer to the United States.

(B) In most cases, organizations whose names end with "of the United States" are Federal government agencies.

SELECTION OF CATEGORIES

The selected categories reflect, in the Editors' opinion, the most widely discussed public-interest subjects, those which readily fall into the over-all sphere of "current events." They represent topics continuously covered by the mass media because of their inherent importance to the changing world scene. Most of the categories are permanent; they appear in each annual edition of *WHAT THEY SAID*. However, because of the transient character of some subjects, there may be categories which appear one year and may not be repeated the next.

SELECTION OF SPEAKERS

The following persons are always considered eligible for inclusion in *WHAT THEY SAID*: top-level officials of all branches of national, state and local governments (both U.S. and foreign), including all United States Senators and Representatives; top-echelon military officers; college and university presidents, chancellors and professors; chairmen and presidents of major corporations; heads of national public-oriented organizations and associations; national and internationally known diplomats; recognized celebrities from the entertainment and literary spheres and the arts generally; sports figures of national stature; commentators on the world scene who are recognized as such and who command the attention of the mass media.

The determination of what and who are "major" and "recognized" must, necessarily, be made by the Editors of *WHAT THEY SAID* based on objective personal judgment.

Also, some persons, while not generally recognized as prominent or newsworthy, may have nevertheless attracted an unusual amount of attention in connection with an important issue or event. These people, too, are considered for inclusion, depending upon the specific circumstance.

SELECTION OF QUOTATIONS

The quotations selected for inclusion in *WHAT THEY SAID* obviously represent a decided minority of the seemingly endless volume of quoted material appearing in the media each year. The process of selecting is scrupulously objective insofar as the partisan views of the Editors are concerned (see *About Fairness*, below). However, it is clear that the Editors must decide which quotations *per se* are suitable for inclusion, and in doing so look for comments that are aptly stated, offer insight into the subject being discussed, or into the speaker, and provide—for today as well as for future reference—a thought which readers will find useful for understanding the issues and the personalities that make up a year on this planet.

ABOUT FAIRNESS

The Editors of *WHAT THEY SAID* understand the necessity of being impartial when compiling a book of this kind. As a result, there has been no bias in the selection of the quotations, the choice of speakers or the manner of editing. Relevance of the statements and the status of the speakers are the exclusive criteria for inclusion, without any regard whatsoever to the personal beliefs and views of the Editors. Furthermore, every effort has been made to include a multiplicity of opinions and ideas from a wide cross-section of speakers on each topic. Nevertheless, should there appear to be, on some controversial issues, a majority of material favoring one point of view over another, it is simply the result of there having been more of those views expressed during the year, reported by the media and objectively considered suitable by the Editors of *WHAT THEY SAID* (see *Selection of Quotations*, above). Also, since persons in politics and government account for a large percentage of the speakers in *WHAT THEY SAID*, there may exist a heavier weight of opinion favoring the philosophy of those in office at the time, whether in the United States Congress, the Administration, or in foreign capitals. This is natural and to be expected and should not be construed as a reflection of agreement or disagreement with that philosophy on the part of the Editors of *WHAT THEY SAID*.

Abbreviations

The following are abbreviations used by the speakers in this volume. Rather than defining them each time they appear in the quotations, this list will facilitate reading and avoid unnecessary repetition.

ABA:	American Bar Association
ABC:	American Broadcasting Companies
ABM:	anti-ballistic missile
ACDA:	Arms Control and Disarmament Agency
ACLU:	American Civil Liberties Union
AFL-CIO:	American Federation of Labor-Congress of Industrial Organizations
AIDS:	acquired immune deficiency syndrome
ANC:	African National Congress
ANZUS:	Australia, New Zealand, United States defense treaty
ASEAN:	Association of South-East Asian Nations
ASL:	Association of Soviet Lawyers
BBC:	British Broadcasting Corporation
CBS:	Columbia Broadcasting System (CBS, Inc.)
CEO:	chief executive officer
CIA:	Central Intelligence Agency
CNN:	Cable News Network
CPB:	Corporation for Public Broadcasting
DEA:	Drug Enforcement Administration
DH:	designated hitter
ERA:	equal rights amendment
FAA:	Federal Aviation Administration
FBI:	Federal Bureau of Investigation
FDA:	Food and Drug Administration
F.D.R.:	Franklin Delano Roosevelt
FMLN:	Farabundo Marti National Liberation Front (El Salvador)
FTC:	Federal Trade Commission
GNP:	gross national product
HEW:	Department of Health, Education and Welfare
HMO:	health maintenance organization
HUD:	Department of Housing and Urban Development

IAEA:	International Atomic Energy Agency
IBM:	International Business Machines Corporation
ICBM:	intercontinental ballistic missile
IMF:	International Monetary Fund
IQ:	intelligence quotient
IRA:	Irish Republican Army
IRS:	Internal Revenue Service
KGB:	Soviet secret police
L.B.J.:	Lyndon Baines Johnson
MGM:	Metro-Goldwyn-Mayer, Inc.
NASA:	National Aeronautics and Space Administration
NATO:	North Atlantic Treaty Organization
NBA:	National Basketball Association
NBC:	National Broadcasting Company
NEA:	National Endowment for the Arts
NEH:	National Endowment for the Humanities
NFL:	National Football League
NFLPA:	National Football League Players Association
NGO:	non-governmental organization
NOW:	National Organization for Women
NPA:	New People's Army (Philippines)
NRC:	Nuclear Regulatory Commission
NSC:	National Security Council
OAS:	Organization of American States
OPEC:	Organization of Petroleum Exporting Countries
OSHA:	Occupational Safety and Health Administration
PGA:	Professional Golf Association
PLO:	Palestine Liberation Organization
PR:	public relations
PTA:	Parent-Teachers Association
R&D:	research and development
SALT:	strategic arms limitation talks
SAT:	Scholastic Aptitude Test
SDI:	strategic defense initiative
SEC:	Securities and Exchange Commission
SWAPO:	South-West Africa People's Organization
TV:	television
UAW:	United Automobile Workers

ABBREVIATIONS

UN:	United Nations
UNCF:	United Negro College Fund
UNITA:	National Union for the Total Independence of Angola
U.S.:	United States
U.S.A.:	United States of America
USC:	University of Southern California
USFL:	United States Football League
U.S.S.R.:	Union of Soviet Socialist Republics
USTA:	United States Tennis Association
VCR:	video cassette recorder

The Quote of the Year

Indifference, to me, is the epitome of evil. The opposite of love is not hate, it's indifference. The opposite of art is not ugliness, it's indifference. And the opposite of life is not death. It's indifference. Because of indifference, one dies before one actually dies. To be in the window and watch people being sent to concentration camps or being attacked in the street and to do nothing—that's being dead.

—ELIE WIESEL,
Author, Historian
Interview, Oct. 27, 1986.

National Affairs

The State of the Union Address

Delivered by Ronald Reagan, President of the United States, at the Capitol, Washington, February 4, 1986.

Thank you very much. Mr. Speaker, Mr. President, distinguished members of the Congress, honored guests, and fellow citizens, thank you for allowing me to delay my address until this evening. We paused together to mourn and honor the valor of our seven Challenger heroes. And I hope that we are now ready to do what they would want us to do—go forward, America, and reach for the stars. We will never forget those brave seven, but we shall go forward.

Mr. Speaker, before I begin my prepared remarks, may I point out that tonight marks the 10th and last State of the Union Message that you've presided over. On behalf of the American people, I want to salute you for your service to Congress and country. Here's to you, Tip.

I have come to review with you the progress of our nation, to speak of unfinished work and to set our sights on the future. I am pleased to report the state of our union is stronger than a year ago, and growing stronger each day. Tonight, we look out on a rising America—firm of heart, united in spirit, powerful in pride and patriotism. America is on the move!

But it wasn't long ago that we looked out on a different land—locked factory gates, long gasoline lines, intolerable prices and interest rates turning the greatest country on earth into a land of broken dreams. Government growing beyond our consent had become a lumbering giant, slamming shut the gates of opportunity, threatening to crush the very roots of our freedom.

American People

What brought America back? The American people brought us back—with quiet courage and common sense; with undying faith that in this nation under God the future will be ours, for the future belongs to the free.

Tonight the American people deserve our thanks—for 37 straight months of economic growth; for sunrise firms and modernized industries creating 9 million new jobs in three years; interest rates cut in half, inflation falling over from 12 percent in 1980 to under 4 today; and a mighty river of good works, a record $74 billion in voluntary giving just last year alone.

And despite the pressures of our modern world, family and community remain the moral core of our society, guardians of our values and hopes for the future. Family and community are the co-stars of this great American comeback. They are why we say tonight: private values must be at the heart of public policies.

What is true for families in America is true for America in the family of free nations. History is no captive of some inevitable force. History is made by men and women of vision and courage. Tonight, freedom is on the march. The United States is the economic miracle, the model to which the world once again turns. We stand for an idea whose time is now: Only by lifting the weights from the shoulders of all can people truly prosper and can peace among all nations be secure.

Teddy Roosevelt said a nation that does great work lives forever. We have done well, but we cannot stop at the foothills when Everest beckons. It is time for America to be all that we can be.

We speak tonight of an agenda for the future, an agenda for a safer, more secure world. And we speak about the necessity for actions to steel us for the challenges of growth, trade, and security in the next decade and the year 2,000. And we will do it—not by breaking faith with bedrock principles, but by breaking free from failed policies.

RONALD REAGAN

Federal Budget

Let us begin where storm clouds loom darkest— right here in Washington, D.C. This week, I will send you our detailed proposals; tonight, let us speak of our responsibility to redefine government's role; not to control, not to command, not to contain us; but to help in times of need; above all, to create a ladder of opportunity to full employment—so that all Americans can climb toward economic power and justice on their own.

But we cannot win the race to the future shackled to a system that can't even pass a Federal budget. We cannot win that race held back by horse-and-buggy programs that waste tax dollars and squander human potential. We cannot win that race if we are swamped in a sea of red ink.

Now, Mr. Speaker, you know, I know, and the American people know—the Federal budget system is broken; it doesn't work. Before we leave this city, let's you and I work together to fix it— so that then we can finally give the American people a balanced budget.

Members of Congress, passage of Gramm-Rudman-Hollings gives us an historic opportunity to achieve what has eluded our national leadership for decades—forcing the Federal Government to live within its means.

Your schedule now requires that the budget resolution be passed by April 15th—the very day America's families have to foot the bill for the budgets that you produce.

How often we read of a husband and wife— both working, struggling from paycheck to paycheck to raise a family, meet a mortgage, pay their taxes and bills. And yet, some in Congress say taxes must be raised. Well, I'm sorry, they're asking the wrong people to tighten their belts. It's time we reduced the Federal budget and left the family budget alone. We do not face large deficits because American families are undertaxed; we face those deficits because the Federal Government overspends.

The detailed budget that we will submit will meet the Gramm-Rudman-Hollings target for deficit reductions; meet our commitment to ensure a strong national defense; meet our commitment to protect Social Security and the truly less fortunate; and, yes, meet our commitment to not raise taxes.

How should we accomplish this? Well, not by taking from those in need. As families take care of their own, Government must provide shelter and nourishment for those who cannot provide for themselves. But we must revise or replace programs enacted in the name of compassion that degrade the moral worth of work, encourage family breakups, and drive entire communities into a bleak and heartless dependency.

Line-Item Veto

Gramm-Rudman-Hollings can mark a dramatic improvement. But experience shows that simply setting deficit targets does not assure they'll be met. We must proceed with Grace Commission reforms against waste. And tonight I ask you to give me what 43 Governors already have— give me a line-item veto this year. Give me the authority to veto waste, and I'll take the responsibility, I'll make the cuts, I'll take the heat.

This authority would not give me any monopoly power but simply prevent spending measures from sneaking through that could not pass on their own merit. And you can sustain, or override, my veto—that's the way the system should work. Once we've made the hard choices, we should lock in our gains with a balanced-budget amendment to the Constitution.

Defense

I mentioned that we will meet our commitment to national defense. We must meet it. Defense is not just another budget expense. Keeping America strong, free and at peace is solely the responsibility of the Federal Government; it is Government's prime responsibility. We have devoted five years trying to narrow a dangerous gap born of illusion and neglect, and we have made important gains. Yet the threat from Soviet forces, conventional and strategic, from the Soviet drive for domination, from the increase in espionage and State terror remains great. This is reality. Closing our eyes will not make reality disappear.

We pledged together to hold real growth in defense spending to the bare minimum. My budget honors that pledge. I am now asking you, the Congress, to keep its end of the bargain. The Soviets must know that if America reduces her defenses, it will be because of a reduced threat, not a reduced resolve.

Keeping America strong is as vital to the national security as controlling Federal spending is to our economic security. But, as I have said before, the most powerful force we can enlist against the Federal deficit is an ever-expanding American economy, unfettered and free.

Tax Reform

The magic of opportunity—unreserved, unfailing, unrestrained—isn't this the calling that unites us? I believe our tax rate cuts for the people have done more to spur a spirit of risk-taking and help America's economy break free than any program since John Kennedy's tax cut almost a quarter century ago.

Now history calls us to press on, to complete efforts for an historic tax reform providing new opportunity for all and ensuring that all pay their fair share—but no more. We've come this far. Will you join me now and we'll walk this last mile together?

You know my views on this. We cannot and we will not accept tax reform that is a tax increase in disguise. True reform must be an engine of productivity and growth, and that means a top personal rate no higher than 35 percent. True reform must be truly fair and that means raising personal exemptions to $2,000. True reform means a tax system that at long last is pro-family, pro-jobs, pro-future, and pro-America.

Foreign Trade and the Dollar

As we knock down the barriers to growth, we must redouble our efforts for freer and fairer trade. We have already taken actions to counter unfair trading practices to pry open closed foreign markets. We will continue to do so. We will also oppose legislation touted as providing protection that in reality pits one American worker against another, one industry against another, one community against another, and that raises prices for us all. If the United States can trade with other nations on a level playing field, we can out-produce, out-compete, and out-sell anybody, anywhere in the world.

The constant expansion of our economy and exports requires a sound and stable dollar at home and reliable exchange rates around the world. We must never again permit wild currency swings to cripple our farmers and other exporters. Farmers, in particular, have suffered from past, unwise government policies; they must not be abandoned with problems they did not create and cannot control. We've begun coordinating economic and monetary policy among our major trading partners. But there's more to do, and tonight I am directing Treasury Secretary Jim Baker to determine if the nations of the world should convene to discuss the role and relationship of our currencies.

Confident in our future, and secure in our values, Americans are striding forward to embrace the future. We see it not only in our recovery, but in three straight years of falling crime rates, as families and communities band together to fight pornography, drugs and lawlessness, and to give back to their children the safe, and yes, innocent childhoods they deserve.

We see it in the renaissance in education, the rising S.A.T. scores for three years—last year's increase the greatest since 1963. It wasn't government and Washington lobbies that turned education around—it was the American people who, in reaching for excellence, knew to reach back to basics. We must continue the advance by supporting discipline in our schools; vouchers that give parents freedom of choice; and we must give back to our children their lost right to acknowledge God in their classrooms.

We are a nation of idealists, yet today there is a wound in our national conscience; America will never be whole as long as the right to life granted by our creator is denied to the unborn. For the rest of my time, I shall do what I can to see that this wound is one day healed.

5

Welfare Programs

As we work to make the American dream real for all, we must also look to the condition of America's families. Struggling parents today worry how they will provide their children the advantages that their parents give them. In the welfare culture, the breakdown of the family, the most basic support system, has reached crisis proportions—in female and child poverty, child abandonment, horrible crimes and deteriorating schools. After hundreds of billions of dollars in poverty programs, the plight of the poor grows more painful. But the waste in dollars and cents pales before the most tragic loss—the sinful waste of human spirit and potential.

We can ignore this terrible truth no longer. As Franklin Roosevelt warned 51 years ago standing before this chamber: He said welfare is "a narcotic, a subtle destroyer of the human spirit." And we must now escape the spider's web of dependency. Tonight, I am charging the White House domestic council to present me by December 1, 1986, an evaluation of programs and a strategy for immediate action to meet the financial, educational, social, and safety concerns of poor families—I am talking about real and lasting emancipation, because the success of welfare should be judged by how many of its recipients become independent of welfare.

Further, after seeing how devastating illness can destroy the financial security of a family, I am directing the Secretary of Health and Human Services, Dr. Otis Bowen, to report to me by yearend with recommendations on how the private sector and Government can work together to address the problems of affordable insurance for those whose life savings would otherwise be threatened when catastrophic illness strikes.

And tonight, I want to speak directly to America's younger generation—because you hold the destiny of our nation in your hands. With all the temptations young people face, it sometimes seems the allure of the permissive society requires superhuman feats of self-control. But the call of the future is too strong, the challenge too great, to get lost in the blind alleyways of dissolution, drugs and despair.

Never has there been a more exciting time to be alive—a time of rousing wonder and heroic achievement. As they said in the film, "Back to the Future": "Where we're going, we don't need roads."

Technology and Space

Well, today, physicists peering into the infinitely small realms of subatomic particles find reaffirmations of religious faith; astronomers build a space telescope that can see to the edge of the universe and, possibly, back to the moment of creation.

So, yes, this nation remains fully committed to America's space program. We are going forward with our shuttle flights. We are going forward to build our space station, and we are going forward with research on a new Orient Express that could, by the end of the next decade, take off from Dulles Airport, accelerate up to 25 times the speed of sound, attaining low-earth orbit or flying to Tokyo within 2 hours.

And the same technology transforming our lives can solve the greatest problem of the 20th Century. A security shield can one day render nuclear weapons obsolete and free mankind from the prison of nuclear terror. America met one historic challenge and went to the moon. Now, America must meet another—to make our strategic defense real for all the citizens of Planet Earth.

Soviet Relations

Let us speak of our deepest longing for the future—to leave our children a land that is free and just in a world at peace. It is my hope that our fireside summit in Geneva and Mr. Gorbachev's upcoming visit to America can lead to a more stable relationship. Surely no people on earth hate war or love peace more than we Americans.

But we cannot stroll into the future with childlike faith. Our differences with a system that openly proclaims, and practices, an alleged right to command people's lives and to export its ideology by force are deep and abiding.

Logic and history compel us to accept that our relationship be guided by realism—rockhard, cleareyed, steady and sure. Our negotiators in Geneva have proposed a radical cut in offensive forces by each side, with no cheating. They have made clear that Soviet compliance with the letter and spirit of agreements is essential. If the Soviet Government wants an agreement that truly reduces nuclear arms, there will be such an agreement.

Freedom and Peace

But arms control is no substitute for peace. We know that peace follows in freedom's path and conflicts erupt when the will of the people is denied. So we must prepare for peace not only by reducing weapons, but by bolstering prosperity, liberty and democracy however and wherever we can.

We advance the promise of opportunity every time we speak out on behalf of lower tax rates, freer markets, sound currencies around the world. We strengthen the family of freedom every time we work with allies and come to the aid of friends under siege. And we can enlarge the family of free nations if we will defend the unalienable rights of all God's children to follow their dreams.

To those imprisoned in regimes held captive, to those beaten for daring to fight for freedom and democracy—for their right to worship, to speak, to live and to prosper in the family of free nations—we say to you tonight: you are not alone, freedom fighters. America will support you with moral and material assistance your right not just to fight and die for freedom, but to fight and win freedom—to win freedom in Afghanistan; in Angola; in Cambodia; and in Nicaragua.

Central America

This is a great moral challenge for the entire free world. Surely, no issue is more important for peace in our own hemisphere, for the security of our frontiers, for the protection of our vital interests—than to achieve democracy in Nicaragua and to protect Nicaragua's democratic neighbors.

Now this year I will be asking Congress for the means to do what must be done for the great and good cause. As Scoop Jackson, the inspiration for our Bipartisan Commission on Central America, once said, "In matters of national security, the best politics is no politics."

What we accomplish this year, in each challenge we face, will set our course for the balance of the decade, indeed for the remainder of the century. After all we've done so far, let no one say that this nation cannot reach the destiny of our dreams. America believes, America is ready, America can win the race to the future—and we shall.

American Dream

The American dream is a song of hope that rings through the night winter air. Vivid, tender music that warms our hearts when the least among us aspire to the greatest things—to venture a daring enterprise; to unearth new beauty in music, literature and art; to discover a new universe inside a tiny silicon chip or a single human cell.

We see the dream coming true in the spirit of discovery of Richard Cavoli. All his life he's been enthralled by the mysteries of medicine and science. Richard, we know that the experiment you began in high school was launched and lost last week. Yet, your dream lives. And as long as it's real, work of noble note will yet be done—work that could reduce the harmful effects of X-rays on patients, and enable astronomers to view the golden gateways of the farthest stars.

We see the dream glow in the towering talent of 12-year-old Tyrone Ford. A child prodigy of gospel music, he has surmounted personal adversity to become an accomplished pianist and singer. He also directs the choirs of three churches and has performed at the Kennedy Center. With God as our composer, Tyrone, your music will be the music of angels.

We see the dream being saved by the courage of 13-year-old Shelby Butler—honor student and member of her school's safety patrol. Seeing another girl freeze in terror before an out-of-control school bus, she risked her life and pulled her to safety. With bravery like yours, Shelby,

7

America need never fear for our future.

And we see the dream born again in the joyful compassion of 13-year-old Trevor Ferrell. Two years ago, age 11, watching men and women bedding down in abandoned doorways, on television he was watching, Trevor left his suburban Philadelphia home to bring blankets and food to the helpless and homeless. And now, 250 people help him fulfill his nightly vigil. Trevor, yours is the living spirit of brotherly love.

Would you four stand up for a moment. Thank you. You are heroes of our hearts. We look at you and know it's true—in this land of dreams fulfilled where greater dreams may be imagined, nothing is impossible, no victory is beyond our reach; no glory will ever be too great. So now it's up to us, all of us, to prepare America for that day when our work will pale before the greatness of America's champions in the 21st century.

The world's hopes rest with America's future. America's hopes rest with us. So let us go forward to create our world of tomorrow—in faith, in unity, and in love. God bless you, and God bless America.

PART ONE

National Affairs

The American Scene

Corazon C. Aquino
President of the Philippines

1

What the U.S. does best is to afford equal opportunity. Anybody who is really talented can make it to the top. Social backgrounds do not matter, barriers are few. The American style gives almost everyone a chance to develop his full potential. In many nations around the world, and to some extent in my own country as well, one does not succeed if he has only talent and no connections. To me, such equal opportunity is a recognition of the innate dignity of man and his superiority over the circumstances that surround him. I hope the time will come when people elsewhere can be guaranteed the same liberty and opportunity.

Interview/Time, 6-16:52.

William J. Bennett
Secretary of Education of the United States

2

We know that in the real world the main alternative to the common culture of the U.S. is the common culture of [Libyan leader and suspected terrorist Muammar] Qaddafi and company. We know that our common culture is at once a precious historical legacy and a vulnerable one.

Before American Jewish Committee,
May 15/The Wall Street Journal, 5-27:28.

3

. . . running through our nation's history like a golden thread are certain ideals and aspirations. What are they? Well, we the people, all of us, believe in liberty and equality. We believe in limited government and in the betterment of the human condition. These truths underlie both our history and our society; they define us as a people; and while they may be self-evident, they are not spontaneously apprehended by the young. The young must be taught these things, and at the same time they should learn that a large part of the world thinks and acts according to other principles.

At University of Kansas,
Sept. 9/The New York Times, 9-23:14.

Robert Coles
Professor of psychiatry and medical humanities, Harvard University

4

This is a country that encourages people to express their opinions and doesn't clamp down on the rights of individuals to speak up. I've lived in every part of this country, and I've heard children from different regions and different backgrounds speaking their minds. What has amazed me is how true to the American tradition our children are: They do speak up! I think the diversity and intensity of that speaking up are a testimony to freedom in this country.

Interview/U.S. News & World Report, 2-17:62.

Nicholas S. Daniloff
Correspondent,
"U.S. News & World Report"

5

[On his release from Soviet arrest on spy charges, which he denies]: In the end, I think all of us have to think about this: Why does the whole government of the United States, why do 230 million Americans get [excited] about the outrageous kidnapping of a single American in Moscow? And to me, it is because in our country . . . the individual is a precious thing.

Moscow, Sept. 29/USA Today, 9-30:(A)5.

J. William Fulbright
Former United States Senator,
D-Arkansas

6

It's all right for a country to have self-esteem. You don't have to be a chauvinist to recognize the United States is a very powerful country. It's a big

(J. WILLIAM FULBRIGHT)

country; it has the best real estate in the world. Although there are many pockets of poverty, we are more affluent than anybody else in the world. We don't need to go around bragging all the time. It's perfectly obvious to any objective observer that we are big and powerful. Now, whether we are the best people, whether we have the best life, is a very big question . . . You cannot prove that by bragging about it. You can prove it only by your example, by the way people evaluate your society . . . I would say Holland is a great society. The ordinary citizens have a minimum of crime and pollution; their streets are immaculate. I was over in The Hague. I didn't see a pothole. There's almost no litter on the streets. All the public services, the trains, are very nice. Those citizens represent the right way to judge the quality of a society. So I don't think we should brag about being Number 1. What that actually means is we have more power to knock you down; we've got more missiles than anybody else.

Interview/USA Today, 8-1:(A)9.

Alan Garcia
President of Peru

1

The policy of the U.S. in Central America is excessive and wrong. This is why the government of Peru has made the decision to support the sovereignty of Nicaragua [in which the U.S. is backing rebels fighting the Sandinista government]. We understand that Nicaragua does not have a perfect democracy, but what is there today is better than what used to be there. There is no freedom of the press, which we demand; there is no pluralism of political parties. But this does not justify intervention by a great power . . . Nothing would justify any armed intervention or invasion of Nicaragua, much less by the most powerful nation in the world. And as we did in the case of the Malvinas [Falkland Islands] when Argentina suffered aggression [Britain's armed intervention to keep the Falklands British], we would sever relations with any power that invades Nicaragua.

Interview/
World Press Review, August:27.

Gerhard A. Gesell
Judge, United States District Court
for the District of Columbia

2

Do not be willing to leave government to others. Participate, demand competence in your leaders. Ours must be a vital, not a complacent, conforming, wholly materialistic society. Seek out the good, shun the bad. Vote. Work. Help others. Be useful. Obey the law. Speak out against intolerance. Get involved. Use your minds, not your fists. Your voice will be heard.

At naturalization ceremony for new U.S. citizens,
Washington, July 3/The New York Times, 7-4:30.

Ira Glasser
Executive director,
American Civil Liberties Union

3

[On the Bill of Rights]: [The Founding Fathers] recognized for the first time ever—and pretty much for the last time—that individual liberty, equal rights, etc., are not assured by democracy. The flaw in a democratic system is: What about the minority, whether religious, political, sexual or whatever—members of a class who would never win an election? The Bill of Rights says what the government cannot do. It is a set of negative limits.

Time, 6-16:29.

Bob Hawke
Prime Minister of Australia

4

The outstanding achievement of the U.S. has been to build a nation from the most widely disparate human resources. This summed up for me in such names as [film-maker] Steven Spielberg, [soprano] Jessye Norman, [Chrysler Corporation chairman] Lee Iacocca and [computer manufacturer] An Wang.

Interview/Time, 6-16:53.

Jesse L. Jackson
Civil-rights leader

5

[On the restoration of the Statue of Liberty and the re-opening party for it]: The state of lib-

(JESSE L. JACKSON)

erty in America is greater than any place else in the world. But liberty and justice must be indivisible, and today there is a tremendous focus on Miss Liberty, without her companion, Mr. Justice. The character of Lady Liberty historically has been to be welcoming hostess to the tired, the poor and huddled masses. Now they have lifted her face and tried to alter her character by making her the hostess for a party for the elite and the very wealthy. If the huddled masses would have gone to Ellis Island today, they would have been arrested trying to get there.

Newsweek, 7-14:33.

Sharpe James
Mayor of Newark, N.J.

1

Our society generally seems more violent, more drunk, more suicidal and more threatening of one another than generations past. Too many individuals are experiencing an ethical collapse, a spiritual withdrawal, and escaping reality through drugs, alcohol, sex-without-love, making unwanted babies, and turning on each other with violence. Drugs, especially crack, have reached epidemic proportions among our youth. We must crack down on crack. We must meet the challenge of raising the price and value of life everywhere. What difference does it make if the doors of opportunity swing wide open when you are too drunk or too high to go through? What difference does it make if you have an old schoolbook or a new book, if you open neither?

Inaugural address, July 1/
The Wall Street Journal, 7-25:18.

Elia Kazan
Motion-picture director

2

I think America is the most exciting, marvelous, mixed-up, chaotic, romantic, unusual place. America is the place where anything can happen. It's corny as hell to say it's the land of opportunity, but it's true.

U.S. News & World Report, 7-7:29.

Jack Kemp
United States Representative,
R-New York

3

I basically have a vision for the world and the country that is bigger than what I see coming out of other parts of the Washington political establishment. I think the potential of this country and our people is unlimited. I think that the Declaration of Independence was not written for white folks but for all folks, not just for one time in history but for all times, and not just for our continent but for all continents.

Interview/
The Washington Post, 9-2:(A)8.

Stephen King
Author

4

[On the U.S.]: I think the same thing about it that I have always thought: I think it's fantastic. We're killing ourselves; we're fiddling while Rome burns. I mean, while we've got enough explosives to turn planet earth into the second asteroid belt, the largest weekly magazine in the country is talking about where celebrities shop, and why people in Hollywood don't want to serve finger foods any more. It all seems really ridiculous to me, but I love it. I love everything about it.

Interview/American Film, June:47.

Helmut Kohl
Chancellor of West Germany

5

In recent years, the Americans have been pained and hurt in some of their experiences with the outside world and may have hardened somewhat. But still, after 200 or 300 years, they remain astonishingly young, occasionally naively so, but still sympathetically, truly young. European societies are much older, and their faces are often wrinkled. Yet, together with America, they make a nice combination.

Interview/Time, 6-16:52.

WHAT THEY SAID IN 1986

Charles Kuralt
Correspondent, CBS News

1

[On his long-time on-the-road reports for CBS]: One of the most encouraging things that's happened since I've started wandering around is that a national conscience has awakened [in the U.S.]. It's probably going to reassert itself one of these days. Someone is going to come along and say, "Look, we are not living up to our highest ideals; we are going to have to touch that sense of community." You see it in small towns: Let something go wrong, and you can be sure somebody will form a committee, somebody will hire a hall. The next thing you know, people are at work on the problem. You do find despair, but Americans have always believed that things will be better for their kids. It's in Americans' bones to be optimistic about the future.

Interview/U.S. News & World Report,
1-20:76.

Richard D. Lamm
Governor of Colorado (D)

2

[Saying many illegal immigrants do not assimilate into American society]: Today, they come and live their complete lives without learning English. Obviously, that is retarding their ability to compete in American society . . . America can and should accept people from many lands, but we have a great stake to make sure that they eventually become Americans. We have a great stake to see that they speak English, assimilate into our culture—even while changing it.

Before Congressional Joint Economic
Resources Subcommittee, Washington,
May 29/Los Angeles Times, 5-30:(I)4.

3

[Saying Americans take democracy too much for granted]: I think that democracy is going to go through a period of severe testing. I think those people who just blindly assume that democracy is a law of nature are going to be in for some surprises.

Interview, Denver/
The Christian Science Monitor, 8-18:21.

J. Anthony Lukas
Pulitzer Prize-winning author;
former reporter, "The New York Times"

4

Class [status] is an American reality. We have to deal with it but persistently fail to. Americans operate on the notion that mobility is so great it just doesn't make sense to talk about class. But I perceive a change in that. Look at the incredible attention given this past year to the under-class. That word . . . has connotations that made people feel very uncomfortable, but it has worked its way into the language, and people now say it without embarrassment.

Interview/U.S. News
& World Report, 4-28:75.

Norman Mailer
Author

5

[Saying the U.S. is unpopular in some quarters around the world]: In the eyes of foreigners, we're righteous, we're hypocritical. We're immensely powerful, we're immensely wealthy and, from a European and Third World point of view, we're filled with hideous contradictions . . . So I always take it for granted there'll be a lot of animosity toward Americans.

Interview, New York/
The New York Times, 1-27:17.

James A. Michener
Author

6

I've spent most of my life working abroad—in a lot of countries of the world—and wherever I went I'd have some people come to me at night on the street or in a bar and ask, "What are the chances of getting into the United States?" As a social critic, I know most of what's wrong with this country, but the balance is tremendously in our favor. We've put together a pretty strong country. Of all the forms of government in operation today, ours is the oldest. All the others have had to have radical changes, even Great Britain. Sweden changed, China and Russia changed dramatically, all the countries of South America.

(JAMES A. MICHENER)

We've found a way to survive—with our checks and balances—over a long period.

Newsweek, 7-14:33.

Akio Morita
Chairman, Sony Corporation (Japan)

1

What I like about Americans is their frankness, their openness. In America, I feel I can openly express whatever opinion I have, and it is welcomed, even if it conflicts with other opinions. In Japan, even among friends we can't have a difference of opinion—disagreement destroys friendship. But in America, a difference of opinion can make friends, bring people closer together. That open-mindedness and frontier spirit is why I am so comfortable in the U.S.

Interview/Time, 6-16:53.

Yuri Orlov
Exiled Soviet dissident

2

America is a very big village. That is my impression so far . . . In your suburbs, you have so many of these private homes, a lot of them two stories. The psychology of the Americans who live in these houses is very village-like, and to me that is nice. They have a certain naivete, a good-naturedness. On the streets, even people who don't know each other greet each other—as in my country, in the villages.

Interview, New York/
The Christian Science Monitor, 11-5:1.

Ronald Reagan
President of the United States

3

Some have called it mysticism or romanticism, but I've always thought that a providential hand had something to do with the founding of this country. That God had His reasons for placing this land here between two great oceans to be found by a certain kind of people. That whatever corner of the world they came from, there would be in their hearts a fervent love of freedom and a special kind of courage, the courage to uproot themselves and their families, travel great distances to a foreign shore and build there a new world of peace and freedom. And hope.

At Statue of Liberty centennial celebration,
New York, July 3/The New York Times, 7-4:10.

4

Believe me, if there is one impression I carry with me after the privilege of holding for five and a half years the highest office in the land, the office held by Adams and Jefferson and Lincoln, it is this: that the things that unite us—America's past, of which we are so proud, our hopes and aspirations for the future of the world and this much-loved country—these things far outweigh what little divides us.

At State of Liberty centennial celebration,
New York, July 4/The New York Times, 7-5:15.

5

. . . perhaps many years from now, when you have children or grandchildren of your own, one of them will ask about a November day long ago when a former sports announcer named "Dutch" Reagan came to town for "the last campaign" [for the forthcoming national elections]. And should that happen—since I won't be able to myself—I hope you'll tell them for me that I said it wasn't true, that there really are no last, no final campaigns; that each generation must renew and win again for itself the precious gift of liberty, the sacred heritage of freedom. Please tell them for me that I always thought being an American meant never being mean or small, or giving in to prejudice or bigotry; that it did mean trying to help the other fellow and working for a world where every person knows freedom is both a blessing and a birthright . . . That being an American also means that on certain special days, for a few precious moments, all of us—black or white, Jew or Gentile, rich or poor—we are all equal, with an equal chance to decide our destiny, to determine our future, to cast our ballot. Tell them, too, of my fondest hope, my greatest dream for them: that they would always find here in America a land of hope, a light unto the nation, a shining city on the hill.

At Republican rally, Costa Mesa, Calif.,
Nov. 3/The New York Times, 11-4:13.

WHAT THEY SAID IN 1986

Valentino
Italian fashion designer

1

We in Europe tend to create idols and then destroy them, whereas Americans go on supporting you. I'm struck by the way American actors and actresses continue working into their 80s and being showered with love and affection by their fans, even though they are no longer glamorous. Americans are the first to believe in you and the last to drop you.

Interview/Time, 6-16:52.

Eudora Welty
Author

2

The South is a nation of individualists if there ever was one. It's a place that feeds your imagination; there's no doubt about that . . . Everybody in the South tells things in a narrative style. They take you through their day when they really just want to tell you about one little thing that happened. There's always a kind of shared relish in what wonderful fools people can make of themselves. I remember one time [poet] Robert Penn Warren was at my house, and there was a bunch of us talking and telling old tales. When he left, he said: "I never had such a wonderful evening in my life, never laughed so hard. Not a serious word spoken all evening!" We were just talking about the foibles of human beings we all knew the likes of. That kind of attitude about human nature is common in the South.

Interview/U.S. News & World Report,
8-18:54.

Civil Rights • Women's Rights

Marion Barry
Mayor of Washington, D.C.

1

This history of the [black] civil-rights movement and this [Jewish] community go back a great deal. In 1964, when we were in Mississippi battling to get blacks registered to vote, some of our strongest allies were members of the Jewish community. There is a great history between those of us who are black in America and those of the Jewish faith. And if you look at our spirituals: "Go Down, Moses, tell Pharaoh, let my people go." So there is a parallel.

At Israeli Embassy ceremony honoring
the late civil-rights leader Martin Luther King, Jr.,
Washington, Jan. 15/The Washington Post, 1-17:(C)6.

Harry A. Blackmun
Associate Justice,
Supreme Court of the United States

2

[On abortion rights]: Our cases long have recognized that the Constitution embodies a promise that a certain private sphere of individual liberty will be kept largely beyond the reach of government. That promise extends to women as well as to men. Few decisions are more personal and intimate, more properly private, or more basic to individual dignity and autonomy, than a woman's decision—with the guidance of her physician and within the limits of *Roe [vs. Wade]*—whether to end her pregnancy. A woman's right to make that choice freely is fundamental. Any other result, in our view, would protect inadequately a central part of the sphere of liberty that our law guarantees equally to all.

Supreme Court opinion, Washington,
June 11/The New York Times, 6-12:13.

William J. Brennan, Jr.
Associate Justice,
Supreme Court of the United States

3

[The 14th Amendment is] the prime tool by which we as citizens can shape a society which truly champions the dignity and worth of the individual as its supreme value. Congress and the Federal judiciary have done much in recent years to close the gap between promise and fulfillment. But who will deny that, despite this great progress, the goal of universal equality, freedom and prosperity is far from won, and that ugly inequities continue to mar the face of the nation?

Before American Bar Association,
New York, Aug. 8/Los Angeles Times, 8-9:(I)21.

Gwendolyn Brooks
Poet; Poetry Consultant to the
Library of Congress of the United States

4

. . . I certainly have approved of the women's movement. It has changed everything, and I admire those women who were strong enough to go out there and make things easier for the rest of us, just as I admire the blacks who went out there and made things easier for the rest of us. But when I think of the women of the women's movement, I think of people like Gloria Steinem, Alice Walker and Betty Friedan. My part of modern rebellion is struggling for the survival of the black family, by which I mean the whole black family all over the world—people in South Africa, people in Brazil, people in East and West Africa. I want those people to feel that they're family and, when one contingent is suffering, I would like them to feel empathetic and do whatever they can to alleviate the woe.

Interview, Washington/
Washington Review, Feb.-Mar.:4.

Susan Brownmiller
Author

5

Pornography is virulent propaganda against women. It promotes a climate in which the ideology of rape is not only tolerated but encouraged.

Time, 7-21:18.

17

Patrick J. Buchanan
Director of Communications for the
President of the United States

1

[On the U.S. Supreme Court's favorable rulings on affirmative-action programs]: They said that sometimes discrimination is acceptable. I think that's dead wrong . . . And the Court will one day again say that all discrimination is wrong, whether done for benign or malevolent purposes; that you can't discriminate against the black kid going to school, and you can't discriminate against a white working guy simply because of what happened 100 years ago.

Interview/USA Today, 7-18:(A)9.

George Bush
Vice President of the United States

2

In his lifetime, many criticized [the late civil-rights leader] Martin Luther King's dedication to non-violence. They said it won't work; they said it was impractical. Well, I say that America today bears witness that Dr. King's faith in America was true faith. Love has overcome hate.

At observance of national holiday
in honor of Martin Luther King, Jr.,
Atlanta, Jan. 20/Los Angeles Times, 1-21:(I)1.

Sidney Callahan
Associate professor of psychology,
Mercy College

3

. . . am a pro-life [anti-abortion] feminist, and, as a feminist, I think the pro-life position is better for women. I can't see separating fetal liberation from women's liberation. Ultimately, I think the feminist movement made a serious mistake—politically, morally and psychologically—by committing itself to a pro-choice stance [on abortion], a stance which in effect pits women against their children . . . I think that the ideas of privacy and individual decision, which are so central to the pro-choice position, have been death to the feminist struggle for equality in the work force and in education. Women need social support in our society. But how are they going to get it if their attitude toward pregnancy is based on a cost-benefit analysis? "This baby is my private property," the pro-choice feminists say. "I have the choice to let it live or let it die." But if that's the case, why should a man support a child *he* doesn't want? And why should the society as a whole provide, say, day care? Or any of the other things that women need?

Panel discussion, New York/Harper's, July:36,37.

Henry G. Cisneros
Mayor of San Antonio

4

[On his being an Hispanic]: There's a point where you stop being a curiosity, an interesting novelty, and you are a person who has true power and resources to deliver. But you never lose some obvious attributes, such as your color and your cultural background. The minority community never stops seeing you as a minority Mayor. But once you get elected, your concerns suddenly are a lot larger than the minority community. For instance, you're very much concerned with economic development, which is not in any way a strictly Hispanic issue.

Interview/U.S. News & World Report, 4-7:32.

Barbara Corday
President, Columbia Pictures Television

5

A lot of us make a great point about how few women are heading major companies, but there aren't that many major companies to head. Then you have to get to the issue of how many women truly want to head major companies. It's not an issue of whether or not they want to be successful. Not everyone is cut out to be a corporate executive. Although I believe it's true that there are not enough women in these jobs and that not enough women are running companies, I also believe some percentage of the women choose not to do those jobs.

Interview/Emmy Magazine, Jan.-Feb.:51.

Wilhelmina Delco
Texas State Representative; Chair,
Texas House Higher Education Committee

1

Black teacher population is declining. If we don't do something, soon less than 5 per cent of the U.S.'s teachers will be black. That's not good for blacks or the nation. If black teachers are not out there as role models, communicating their own dedication and commitment, their own professional success, too many black kids won't have enthusiasm, excitement, even the motivation to come to school. It's one more element in creating a permanent social underclass.

Interview, Austin,
Texas/USA Today, 5-19:(A)12.

Ann Dummett
Director, Runnymede Trust (Britain);
Specialist in race relations

2

There is an enormous amount to be learned at a practical level from the American [civil-rights] experience. But Europeans are unwilling to do so, partly because there are important social and political differences, and partly because of a gut anti-Americanism. A typical example concerns affirmative-action programs. In Europe, any attempt to follow the U.S. approach tends to be labeled reverse discrimination and is felt to be undesirable.

Interview/U.S. News
& World Report, 3-31:27.

Don Edwards
United States Representative,
D-California

3

[Supporting affirmative-action programs that give special consideration to minorities in hiring]: To get beyond racism and sexism, we often must take race and sex into consideration. It's both silly and naive to think that we live in a color- and gender-blind society.

USA Today, 7-7:(A)8.

Jerry Falwell
Evangelist

4

The abortion issue is not going to be solved easily, because 1.5 million women have abortions annually, and the weight of the free-choice movement is strengthened with every passing year in that respect. However, I do think we are winning the ideological battle. We are educating the people. All the polls indicate that a majority of Americans believe that abortions are immoral. What we have learned is that there will be compromise when change eventually comes; that probably rape, incest, and where the physical life of the mother is threatened, will be exceptions. That doesn't bother me at all. That's less than 1 per cent of all abortions.

Interview, Lynchburg, Va. /
The Christian Science Monitor, 3-19:21.

5

[On the Attorney General's Commission on Pornography's report criticizing pornographic material]: I believe that it is a good and healthy report that places the United States government clearly in concert with grass-roots America. The recent move by retailers to eliminate pornography from their inventories is not a result of government intervention; it is a result of grass-roots repudiation of the garbage called pornography which has too long exploited the women and children of America.

July 9/The New York Times, 7-10:10.

Betty Friedan
Founder, National Organization for Women

6

We are seeing now, by a combination of court decisions, executive orders and willed Federal attrition, the gutting of the machinery for enforcement of the laws on sex discrimination. We lack the Constitutional guarantee the ERA would give us to fight this weakening.

USA Today, 3-24:(A)9.

7

It's really quite incredible to think how few we [in the women's movement] were in the be-

(BETTY FRIEDAN)

ginning, and that we somehow found each other. We can be proud of the work we did. We were ordinary American women and not so ordinary American women, in our feelings of injustice and of having to suppress thoughts of ourselves. We knew it would have to mean changes in the role of the family and changes in every institution. We've only just begun. The battle for ERA was lost. The laws we got on the books are being gutted, but women are not 4 per cent of the law schools and medical schools, they're 40 per cent. We have to encourage the mobilization of a generation that says, "I'm not a feminist but I intend to be a Senator, I intend to be a Supreme Court Justice, and I will have my 1.4 children when I want to!"

News conference, Washington/
The Washington Post, 10-27:(C)8.

Murray Friedman
Vice Chairman,
United States Commission on Civil Rights

1

The divisions that exist on the [Civil Rights] Commission are really divisions that exist across America. In some respects, I think we are worse off today than in the 1960s. Then we had a unified civil-rights movement. We have to learn how to return to that era of cooperation. I think of myself as a pragmatist. I'm committed to the original ideals of the civil-rights movement. Discrimination continues to exist. Racial violence continues to exist, and we need serious enforcement of the laws to root out racism. But having said that, there have to be new approaches. The problems facing minorities today are economic and their solutions require new strategies.

Interview, Washington/
The New York Times, 9-24:12.

2

My whole thesis is that in order to deal with the problems of minorities today and tomorrow, you have to go beyond the issue of discrimination. I would suggest that the central organizing principle of our thinking should be the interaction of economics and civil rights, and those strategies that can unite both the civil-rights community and liberals and conservatives behind commonly agreed-upon programs . . . It is probably no exaggeration to suggest that economics is the new frontier of civil rights. [As] we move toward the 1990s, we are going to have to think about issues involving inequality in a way we did not have to do as we sought to tear down those formal or institutional barriers that stood in the way of ethnic outsiders taking part in American life as full and equal partners.

Washington, Nov. 13/
The Washington Post, 11-14:(A)25.

Ellen V. Futter
President, Barnard College

3

Some young women honestly believe that those who have preceded them have opened all the doors and broken down all the barriers [for women], that from here on it will be smooth sailing. Please, please hear me now when I tell you that this is not so. Don't blithely believe that you will be able to be a Superwoman or that any other woman is or can be . . . The results are starting to come in now, and it is clear not only that women cannot have it all [a family and a successful business career], but that they and their children are paying a very steep price for even trying to have it all, a price that has both an economic and a psychological cost.

At Barnard College commencement,
May 14/The New York Times, 5-15:16.

Judy Goldsmith
Former president,
National Organization for Women

4

Somewhere down the road there is going to be the Equal Rights Amendment. The time frame is problematic at the moment, but the determination to have the amendment is not, for the very simple reason that it provides the Constitutional underpinning for legislation that protects women against discrimination.

The Christian Science Monitor, 12-1:14.

Linda Gordon
Professor of history,
University of Wisconsin
1

Abortion is a political issue. Indeed, for more than two centuries, reproductive issues have continued to emerge cyclically as social and political problems. Now, I don't deny that individuals may have deeply felt ethical differences over abortion. But the *social* problem of abortion has always divided people into two political camps, which might reasonably be called pro- and anti-feminist. I'm not sure, by the way, that we should spend our time debating the ethical points of abortion. A lot of political principles seem, to the people who hold them, extremely moral and ethical. So when I say "political," I mean simply that issues like abortion have to do with large social questions about who will have power and how power will be distributed . . . The ironic thing here is that the people who oppose abortion rights are in fact the people most firmly associated with what you call an individualistic attitude. Opponents of abortion rights are more likely to be against welfare, to support a military buildup, and to accept all of the political and economic implications of capitalism. It's the people who *support* abortion rights who are more likely to accept the communitarian philosophy . . . and it's been that way, I might add, since the late 18th century.

Panel discussion,
New York/Harper's, July:36,37.

Earl Graves
Editor and publisher,
"Black Enterprise" magazine
2

Ambitious blacks are making their fortunes in private enterprise; qualified blacks are finding success in some of the nation's *Fortune 500* corporations. That's just fine, until you look at the bottom line and read—black unemployment, twice that of whites; black teen unemployment, as high as 50 per cent in some areas; black college graduates earning less than white high-school graduates . . . My sense is that young people find entry-level jobs available, but they face frustration when they seek certain positions. At this point, racism dictates that they be held back.

Interview/
The Christian Science Monitor, 1-17:6.

Christie Hefner
President, Playboy Enterprises
3

[Criticizing the movement against pornography, including the Attorney General's Commission on Pornography's report calling for increased pressure against pornographic material]: The notion of citizen vigilantism against magazines, books, films or video cassettes is something I think conjures up visions of Nazi Germany, not of the United States.

July 9/The New York Times, 7-10:10.

Hugh Hefner
Founder, Playboy Enterprises
4

[On the closing of the Playboy Clubs and the current assault on *Playboy* magazine]: The Playboy Bunny was and is a symbol of a wonderful time of social and sexual change. A time of play and pleasure [that suggested] life could be more than a veil of tears. The lines are now very clearly drawn. For the better part of a decade, I've been fighting smoke. I've been fighting semantic confusions in which *Playboy* has been accused of exploitation by people [women's-rights activists] who, in every other area, have the same social-political views that I have. Finally, it all falls into place. [The Bunny has been done in by] authoritarian true-believers . . . fundamentalist and right-wing evangelists, [and] one limited, radical but very vocal part of the feminist movement. [These groups hold] a very old, very traditional, puritan view that the mind and body are in competition. It begins to sound like something I heard when I was a little kid: The devil is in the flesh.

Interview, Los Angeles/
The New York Times, 6-27:19.

WHAT THEY SAID IN 1986

Dorothy Height
President,
National Council of Negro Women

1

We [black women] suffer the double handicap of race and sex. Some things happen to black women because we are black. Many other things happen to us because we are women. We have a double jeopardy. As long as women earn less than men, and we are women, we earn what women earn. So long as blacks earn less than whites, and we are black, we earn less than what people of different races earn. And within our own group, black women earn beneath black men. We're at the bottom. Yet black women are the backbone of every institution in our community and have carried a major role since slavery in holding the family together. So we simply can't give up.

Interview/USA Today, 9-25:(A)7.

Jesse Helms
United States Senator,
R-North Carolina

2

[Criticizing the mandatory busing of children to achieve racial balance in schools]: Eighty per cent of the parents of America, black and white, are opposed to busing. It is an exercise in folly that has gone on too long.

Before the Senate, Washington,
June 3/Los Angeles Times, 6-4:(I)17.

Sylvia Ann Hewlett
Vice President, United Nations
Economic Policy Council

3

Many [American women's-rights] leaders in the late 1960s were fleeing the Norman Rockwell world of the '50s, and families were seen as the problem, not the solution. We attempted to be men much more aggressively than European women did. We forgot that 90 per cent of us have children and that, unless we help women resolve their double burden as mothers and workers, they are bound to remain second-class citizens . . . By largely ignoring working mothers and their

children, the women's movement has allowed the ultra-right to take over the family. Even the terminology—pro-life, pro-family—became rightist slogans. I think that's why the membership of NOW has dropped by one-third since 1980. I think it's because of the almost exclusive concentration on abortion rights and ERA. We should march for abortion rights, but also for pre-natal care and maternity benefits. We would get more support. I am a feminist. I would like to see the movement more vigorous.

Interview, New York/
The New York Times, 4-21:17.

4

Most women in our country are in lousy economic shape. They're squeezed between a rock and a hard place. They've lost the traditional protections of marriage because the divorce rate now approaches 50 per cent. At the same time, they've failed to gain significant earning power in the labor market. Despite our new access to high-level jobs—which clearly wasn't true 20 years ago—the gap between what men and women earn hasn't changed much in 50 years.

Interview/U.S. News & World Report, 5-12:70.

Arlie Hochschild
Sociologist, University
of California, Berkeley

5

One of the ironies of the women's movement is that women haven't made the same gains in their private lives as in their professional lives. The personal tensions are really the private expression of a social and public revolution that's gotten stuck midway.

Newsweek, 3-31:59.

Benjamin L. Hooks
Executive director, National Association
for the Advancement of Colored People

6

Today we [blacks] face a new struggle, against the negative, hostile attitude of the Reagan Administration toward affirmative action. [Reagan] chooses only to enforce laws he believes in. Our

(BENJAMIN L. HOOKS)

goal of equality is quite elusive in 1986. We can't smile and celebrate [the birth date of the late civil-rights leader Martin Luther King, Jr.] while the Administration ignores the rights he struggled to win for us. This is a meaningless holiday if we allow public officials to turn back the clock.

Interview/
The Christian Science Monitor, 1-17:6.

1

Yesterday we [blacks] fought for the right to check into the hotel. Today, we are fighting to have enough money to check out of the hotel.

At NAACP convention, Baltimore,
June 29/USA Today, 6-30:(A)3.

Jesse L. Jackson
Civil-rights leader

2

Why is it that so many politicians today emphasize that [the late civil-rights leader Martin Luther King, Jr.] was a dreamer and add, almost by accident, that, oh yeah, his dreams became reality? I submit that they want to project him as a dreamer because they wish us to remember this great leader as an idealist without substance, not as the concrete reality he was. Dr. King was a realist with ideals; he was not an idealist without reality . . . Dr. Martin Luther King, Jr., was not assassinated for dreaming. He was assassinated for acting and challenging the government. We honor Dr. King most by action for justice. His birthday should be celebrated by action, not just speeches and songs about action.

Before Federal Communications Commission
Bar Association of Washington, Jan. 12/
The New York Times, 1-15:8.

3

[Criticizing President Reagan on the occasion of the first national holiday honoring the late civil-rights leader Martin Luther King, Jr.]: Today, President Reagan went over [to a school] and held up little black children in his hands, rubbed his eyes and looked tearful. Same man [Reagan] that didn't march to Montgomery. He

was old enough. Same man. Same man that didn't support the march to Selma. Same man who implied that Dr. King was a Communist. The same man! [The press] will give him a free ride and project him as a kindly old man. [But] with all his power . . . even America will never have a national holiday named after Ronald Reagan!

At Ebenezer Baptist Church, Atlanta,
Jan. 15/The Washington Post, 1-16:(A)10.

4

[On President Reagan]: We have not had a President more insensitive racially and morally in at least a half century; we have not had the doors of the White House closed this tightly since Hoover. We [black leaders] cannot discuss with Reagan South Africa or job training; we cannot discuss anything. And [Reagan's aides] say, "If we have a press conference, blacks will criticize him." Well . . . *white* Democrats meet with Reagan and predictably have a different point of view. But the Congressional Black Caucus, the civil-rights leadership, the Conference of Black Mayors—no. That must be challenged . . . [Reagan] did not support any of the positions [the late civil-rights leader Martin Luther] King stood for. He did not support the Montgomery bus boycott, sit-ins . . . freedom rides, the right to vote, open housing . . . and he is trying to unravel everything he [King] achieved. And he gets a free ride of uncritical press observations.

Interview, Los Angeles, Jan. 16/
Los Angeles Times, 1-17:(I)23.

5

Do not underestimate the impact of 250 years of legal slavery followed by a hundred years of legal segregation. The damage it did to the minds of the oppressor and the oppressed must not be played down. When I grew up in South Carolina, I could caddy, but I couldn't play golf. That's why I can't play golf now; I could have been arrested for hitting a golf ball at the Greenville Country Club. I could shag balls, but I couldn't play tennis. I could shine shoes, but I couldn't sit on the stand and couldn't own a stand at the train station. I could wait tables, but I couldn't sit at them; and I could not borrow money to build a competing establishment . . .

WHAT THEY SAID IN 1986

(JESSE L. JACKSON)

Now, shagging balls and not playing tennis, caddying and not playing golf, not voting and seeing others vote—all of this had the cumulative effect of lowering people's ambitions and limiting their horizons.

Panel discussion,
New York/Harper's, April:38.

1

The same fervor with which we [blacks] marched for the right to vote, we must now march for enforcement of Section II [of the Voting Rights Act, which prohibits all forms of voter denial]. For, without voting rights enforcement, the right to vote is the hole of the doughnut.

Ebony, May:132.

John E. Jacob
President,
National Urban League

2

[Criticizing the Reagan Administration for wanting to cut affirmative-action programs and quotas]: If the Administration wants to be a "Rambo"-like destroyer of civil-rights gains, it should not pretend that its efforts are good for black citizens or that they reflect the color-blind society we have yet to become . . . The report we issue today accurately describes a black America excluded from the economic boom, excluded from full participation in job growth, and in danger of being excluded from tomorrow's economic mainstream . . . Black people today have jobs and opportunities they would not have had without the Executive order [of 20 years ago that mandated minority hiring goals and timetables for Federal contractors]. Companies that do business with the government have significantly better hiring and promotion records for women and minorities than those that don't have government contracts, and that is directly due to the Executive order the [current] Attorney General [Edwin Meese] wants revoked.

News conference,
Washington, Jan. 23/
Los Angeles Times, 1-24:(I)5.

John Paul II
Pope

3

[Condemning abortion and artificial birth control]: All human life is sacred from the moment of conception. It is the task of all mankind to reject whatever wounds, weakens or destroys human life—whatever offends the dignity of any human being . . . Suspension of procreation [cannot be achieved] by immoral and artificial checks . . . but by a life of discipline and self-control. Moral results can only be produced by moral restraint.

Mass, Bombay, India, Feb. 9/
Los Angeles Times, 2-10:(I)5.

4

[Criticizing abortion]: What a contradiction concerning the human truth of love, when one refuses to give life in a responsible way and when one consents to the death of a child already conceived. It is these that are the symptoms of a real sickness that touch a variety of people, couples, children, the society itself.

Mass, Paray-le-Monial, France, Oct. 5/
Los Angeles Times, 10-6:(I)13.

5

Today, the presence of women and mothers in almost every sector of the working world is a fact that has to be considered. They should be able to exercise their gifts and abilities in various forms of employment but, at the same time, due respect must be given to their obligations and aspirations. Work should be so structured that women do not have to bargain for their advancement at the expense of their own dignity or at the expense of their vital role inside the family.

Los Angeles Times, 11-27:(I)7.

Leanne Katz
Executive director, National
Coalition Against Censorship

6

[Criticizing the censoring of pornography]: I have been working in the anti-censorship cause for about 30 years, and I have never encountered a censorship controversy in which the other side

(LEANNE KATZ)

wasn't saying, "This isn't censorship." They also always argue that they are talking about harm. It's always harm to women, harm to children, harm to somebody. In truth, however, it is harm to our precious idea that all of us are supposed to be able to decide for ourselves what we can see and read and think.

Time, 7-21:15.

Coretta Scott King
Widow of the late civil-rights
leader Martin Luther King, Jr.

1

[On whether she considers the national holiday honoring her late husband to be a "black holiday"]: It's not promoted as a black holiday. We promote it as a holiday for people of all races and religions and color, that it should be an all-American holiday, and it should be celebrated as such. I would be disappointed if it turned out to be a black holiday. He was all-inclusive. As some people have said here in the South, he freed more white people than he did black people. I suspect that's true.

Interview/USA Today, 1-15:(A)11.

Edward I. Koch
Mayor of New York

2

We still have the cancer of racism. Anyone who says the country . . . is free of racism is not telling the truth or is simply an ostrich whose head is buried in the sand.

To reporters, New York, Dec. 28/
The Washington Post, 12-29:(A)3.

C. Everett Koop
Surgeon General of the United States

3

Today, hucksters of pornography have made an invasion into cable television, telephone communications and, unfortunately, the field of home videos . . . The issue we take with pornography has nothing to do with the First Amendment. It

seems to me that our country has never permitted or condoned speech that endangers the lives of others [as much of today's violent pornography does]. This material is blatantly anti-human. Its appeal is to a dark and anti-human impulse. We must oppose it as we oppose all violence and prejudice.

Before National Federation of Catholic
Physicians' Guilds, Chicago, Sept. 11/
The Washington Post, 9-12:(A)17.

William Kunstler
Civil-rights lawyer

4

I respected [the late civil-rights leader Martin Luther King, Jr.] highly [but] I dislike him being made into a God. He had weaknesses and failings . . . Too much reverence of Dr. King may make people think the struggle is over. I think virtually no progress had been made in the civil-rights movement since his death. Then the targets were clear-cut—voting and housing rights, school desegregation. Do you think a black kid in Harlem today is any better off than a black kid born in the slums of Atlanta 30 years ago?

USA Today, 1-20:(A)2.

Joyce Ladner
Professor of sociology,
School of Social Work,
Howard University

5

Blacks still experience a tremendous amount of racism. I feel very strongly that we can look at the high rates of unemployment as being one of the manifestations of racism. It is not an accident that we have upwards of 50 per cent of black youth unemployment. That's not accidental . . . Racial discrimination . . . is so deeply entrenched into the fabric of society that at the moment of birth a black child's life chances can be predictably less than [that] of a typical white child [even if the two are] born in a nursery alongside each other. That black child is much more likely to be born into poverty; and increasingly so these days, race determines class.

Interview/The Washington Post, 1-28:(A)9.

WHAT THEY SAID IN 1986

Celinda Lake
Political director,
Women's Campaign Fund

1

[On the fact that only one out of eight women running for state Governorships in the just-concluded elections won]: There are still barriers to seeing women as chief executives. Basically, women are seen as good listeners and as caring about people, so they are viewed as good at constituency service and legislative posts. They are not seen as good at budgets or managing on a macro level, things that people want in a chief executive.

The New York Times, 11-7:12.

Kate Rand Lloyd
Editor-at-large, "Working Woman"
magazine; Board member, National
Commission on Working Women

2

This has not been a very easy period for women, as the current [Reagan] Administration is not interested in implementing the laws and regulations that might support women as they try to get ahead in the work force. In spite of that, the sheer numbers of competent women who are coming into the work force every year are amazing. More women enter the work force every year than do men. That's why we are moving upward. Before the end of this century, there will be a 50-50 division between men and women in the work force.

Interview/USA Today, 5-21:(A)11.

Richard Long
Professor of English and
chairman, Afro-American studies
department, Atlanta University

3

The history of black people in this country occupies a unique niche. Black people are among the earliest settlers of this country from abroad, leaving aside the native Americans. Yet, because blacks were brought in—for the most part as uncompensated labor—it has been most convenient for the standard history of the country to overlook or under-value the contribution

that blacks have made. And because blacks themselves, without special effort, would not have access to this information, it's important both for blacks and whites that we pay some attention to [traditions such as Black History Month].

Interview/USA Today, 2-4:(A)7.

Barry W. Lynn
Legislative director,
American Civil Liberties Union

4

[Criticizing those who picket or boycott stores selling pornographic material]: It's unwise for pressure groups to force literature off the shelves, whether they are atheists trying to close down a Christian bookstore or pornography foes trying to get *Playboy* out of a convenience store. The First Amendment value of a free market of ideas is not possible if every group that dislikes a specific kind of literature forces it out of outlets where it is reasonable for it to be sold . . . Most studies show no connection between sexually oriented material and anti-social conduct. Some suggest that people who view large amounts of pornography may also be attracted to anti-social activities. But that's a long way from suggesting that, if you took those magazines away, the man would be in Sunday school instead of assaulting women.

Interview/U.S. News & World Report, 7-14:64.

5

Pornography does not create sex criminals. If it did, the members of the [Attorney General Edwin] Meese Pornography Commission, who wallowed in it for a year, would be on the road to incarceration themselves.

USA Today, 7-18:(A)4.

Roger M. Mahony
Roman Catholic Archbishop of Los Angeles

6

The sin of abortion is most deadly because it strikes at the very essence of God: creator and author of life. Once any person concedes that a particular life is vulnerable to extinction—whether in

(ROGER M. MAHONY)

the womb, in a glass container in some laboratory, in a hospital for the terminally ill—then all human life becomes vulnerable.

At prayer vigil against abortion,
Los Angeles, Jan. 22/
Los Angeles Times, 1-23:(I)26.

Norman Mailer
Author

1

I don't think that women have done much in developing their ideas. Can you tell me some new ones that have come out of women's liberation in the last decade or so? What are they saying now they weren't saying fifteen years ago? What astonishing new theses has *Ms.* magazine come up with lately? Many people respond supinely to totalitarian force. The women's movement at its worst is totalitarian—unforgiving, unfair, incapable of quoting accurately, and quick to distort the deeds of its adversaries.

Interview/Esquire, June:248.

Imelda Marcos
Wife of Philippine President
Ferdinand Marcos

2

[Saying women should not hold high political office]: I am well aware of my role as a woman. Women have their place, somehow, at home . . . Power is always the man. Power and strength is man. Beauty, inspiration, love is woman . . . Beauty is love made real, and the spirit of love is God. And the state of beauty, love and God is happiness. A transcendent state of beauty, love and God is peace. Peace and God is a state of beauty, love and God. Peace and happiness is a state of beauty, love and God . . . this is what we women have to bring about—to bring peace, bring order, bring harmony, bring discipline.

Interview, Manila, Jan. 22/
Los Angeles Times, 1-23:(I)1, 18.

Stanley Paytiamo
Governor, Pueblo de Acoma,
New Mexico

3

People say that the Indians are too lazy, that they don't have to work because they get funds from the Federal government every month. But we're not getting something for nothing. What the non-Indian world has to understand is that they stole our land.

Interview, Pueblo de Acoma, N.M./
The Christian Science Monitor, 6-25:16.

Clarence M. Pendleton, Jr.
Chairman, United States
Commission on Civil Rights

4

It has taken me four years to get to the right question that I think is on people's lips now: Is preferential treatment [for minorities] needed 20 years after the Civil Rights Act has been implemented? That is the Number 1 civil-rights question. If you give preferential treatment, does it eliminate discrimination or does it create more?

The Washington Post, 4-21(B)9.

5

I'm not against civil rights, but I believe the rights of the 21st century are moving us in a different direction from the past of the '60s. Black people can make good on their own without affirmative action, without welfare, without special favor.

Interview/
The Christian Science Monitor, 11-20:4.

Samuel R. Pierce, Jr.
Secretary of Housing and Urban
Development of the United States

6

I think the President [Reagan] is very sincere with respect to equality among people. I think sometimes people get mixed up because they think that the government should just give all the time—give people money, give them things. I think what a lot of people in the Reagan Admin-

27

WHAT THEY SAID IN 1986

istration feel is they want to help people, but they want people to help themselves.

At unveiling of bust of the late civil-rights leader Martin Luther King, Jr., at the Capitol, Washington, Jan. 16/The New York Times, 1-17:7.

1

What kind of liberty, what kind of justice, allows people, because of race, to deprive a family of the home they seek? This is not my kind of liberty, nor my kind of justice. The subtlety and sophistication of current discrimination render it no less demeaning or dispiriting to the people and communities involved, nor to any who consider themselves proud and loyal Americans.

Before National Urban League, San Francisco, July 21/ Los Angeles Times, 7-22:(I)15.

Ronald Reagan
President of the United States

2

Ultimately, the great lesson of [the late civil-rights leader] Martin Luther King, Jr.'s life was this: He was a great man who wrested justice from the heart of a great country—and he succeeded because that great country had a heart to be seized.

To black schoolchildren on the birthday of Martin Luther King, Jr., Washington, Jan. 15/The New York Times, 1-16:8.

3

[On his opposition to abortion]: I don't feel that I'm trying to do something that is taking a privilege from womanhood, because I don't think that a woman should be considering murder a privilege. The situation is, is the unborn child a living human being? Now, every bit of the medical evidence that I have come across says that it is. Then you're taking a human life. Now, in our society and under our law, you can only take a human life in defense of your own. And I would respect very much the right of a prospective mother if told that her life is in danger if she goes through with the pregnancy; then that is an entirely different situation. But until someone can prove medically that the unborn child is not a living human being, I think we have to consider that it is.

Interview, June 23/ Los Angeles Times, 6-24:(I)18.

4

[On his opposition to abortion]: I don't think that I'm trying to do something that is taking a privilege away from womanhood, because I don't think that womanhood should be considering murder a privilege.

Newsweek, 7-7:13.

William Bradford Reynolds
*Assistant Attorney General,
Civil Rights Division, Department
of Justice of the United States*

5

[On the busing of children to achieve racial balance in schools]: Busing is an available remedy. But if there is a better way to accomplish the end of [segregation] that is less burdensome on people in the school system, the fact that busing is available is no reason to reach for it.

Interview, Washington, May 22/ The New York Times, 5-23:9.

Rosalind Rosenberg
*Associate professor of history,
Barnard College*

6

[On criticism by feminists that her testimony on behalf of Sears, Roebuck & Co. helped that firm win a suit that had charged Sears with discrimination against women]: Scholars must not subordinate their scholarship to their politics, even if their scholarship appears to be heading in a politically dangerous direction. If the scholars allow their politics to drive their scholarship, they will be left with bad scholarship and misguided public policy.

Interview/The New York Times, 6-6:12.

Eleanor Smeal
President, National Organization for Women
1

My goal [for NOW] is a million members in the next decade. The National Rifle Association has a million members. Why shouldn't people who fight for women's rights, instead of gun rights, have more?

The Christian Science Monitor, 12-1:1.

Bruce Taylor
General counsel, Citizens for Decency Through Law
2

[Calling on citizens to picket or boycott stores that sell pornographic material]: The ACLU would like even child pornographers to enjoy First Amendment protection, but that's crazy. The Supreme Court has said obscene material is not protected by the First Amendment. People have a responsibility under the Constitution to make sure that their actions don't harm others. Pornography involves exploitation of young people, causes sex crimes and encourages organized crime, among other things . . . Since 1970, virtually all university and clinical researchers have found a link between pornography and callous attitudes of men toward rape, child abuse and subjugation of women . . . Studies in several cities have shown that there are four times as many sex crimes in areas near "adult" bookstores or theaters.

Interview/U.S. News & World Report, 7-14:64.

Agnes Varda
French motion-picture director
3

I'm a feminist, and I always have been; but when you dwell on that, it doesn't give credit to my work. Through my work, my way of living, my choices, my way of working with women, my respect for women, my subjects, and my point of view—all these show my attitude. We have to be proud to be women, and we have to be good artists. We help move the feminist goals forward by proofs of women's talent, friendship, respect, and all that.

Interview, Denver/
The Christian Science Monitor, 7-16:22.

George C. Wallace
Governor of Alabama (D)
4

[On his confrontations with Federal authorities over integration of schools in the 1960s]: We were going to integrate the University of Alabama the next year [1964]. *We* wanted to put the date on it, not the Justice Department. That's what the argument was—big government telling us what to do . . . The public-relations aspect of it was bad for me because it made it appear I was anti-black, when I was really anti-big government.

Interview, Montgomery, Alabama/
USA Today, 5-27:(A)2.

Lawrence Wilder
Lieutenant Governor of Virginia
5

Much has been written about my not being able to attend this university during my time [because of being black]. The fact that my son finished his undergraduate studies here and that my daughter is in this year's graduating class warms me with a poetic and ironic justice. We have come to see that this country's insistence on right can make a change . . . We've seen blacks rise to compete at every level, if given the opportunity to do so. But this did not just come about. Some people have to believe it so and fought for it to be—and it did.

At University of Virginia
commencement/Time, 6-9:63.

Linda F. Williams
Senior political analyst,
Joint Center for Political Studies
6

Blacks prefer a strong affirmative-action role for government in resolving the nation's social and economic woes, while whites are much more likely to say every individual should get ahead on his or her own . . . Sixty-five per cent of blacks, but only 24 per cent of whites, thought government should guarantee jobs . . . Eighty per cent of blacks, but only 27 per cent of whites, thought government should help minorities . . .

WHAT THEY SAID IN 1986

(LINDA F. WILLIAMS)

Eighty-six per cent of blacks, but only 55 per cent of whites, said government should spend more on social programs. Conversely, 53 per cent of blacks, but only 38 per cent of whites, thought government should spend less on defense. In short, blacks and whites may see common problems but they believe in different solutions. For most blacks, Federal programs remain key.

Oct. 14/The Washington Post,
10-15:(A)12.

Commerce • Industry • Finance

James T. Aubrey
Former president, CBS, Inc.;
Former president, Metro-Goldwyn-Mayer, Inc.

1

The thing that separates the men from the boys, in my opinion, the one thing in terms of leadership that stands out, is not intelligence or ability. Those who operate most effectively, those I respect most, simply are not afraid. And most people are afraid; they're scared of decisions. [CBS founder] Bill Paley could be ruthless, but he was not afraid of decisions. Everybody has a fear level, when you've gone as far as you can go, but you do have to go that far. Your *modus operandi* can't be, "What if it doesn't work?" I never really analyzed this, but maybe it's why I've taken the blame for many things. I was willing to take that blame.

Interview, Los Angeles/
Los Angeles Times, 4-27:(Calendar)23.

Malcolm Baldrige
Secretary of Commerce
of the United States

2

The ability of U.S. firms to combine [merge] and restructure domestically to meet the challenge of competition from abroad has been constrained by laws and regulations developed in the days when foreign competition was nil . . . Efficiency was not a primary concern. But today, in the global marketplace, there is almost universal agreement that efficiency is an important concern in antitrust enforcement.

Before National Association of Manufacturers,
Washington, May 30/The New York Times, 6-2:35.

George Ball
Chairman,
Prudential-Bache Securities

3

[On investigations into insider trading of stocks]: If people lose confidence in the integrity of the marketplace, then nice, plutocratic fat cats like me will lose their comfortable jobs.

Before House subcommittee, Washington/
U.S. News & World Report, 6-30:69.

Peter B. Bensinger
Former Administrator,
Drug Enforcement Administration
of the United States

4

[Supporting drug-testing of employees by their companies]: As a result of drug-testing in American industry, the number of job-related accidents is beginning to go down. Absenteeism is decreasing. Productivity is rising, and company medical costs are leveling off. It's saving money. It's saving lives . . . Drug-testing in and of itself is no magic wand. But it is a clear signal that the company is serious about addressing the hazards caused by drugs. Drug-testing used for pre-employment purposes, for example, sends a message to applicants and existing employees that people who are already in violation of a company policy will not be hired . . . Employers have a principal responsibility to have a safe work environment. Drug-testing is a means to provide a safer workplace.

Interview/
U.S. News & World Report, 3-17:58.

Zenas Block
Clinical professor of management,
Graduate School of Business,
New York University

5

Very many successful business starters are people with previous false starts. Among entrepreneurs there's a saying: "You really can't be successful until you've had at least one bankruptcy."

Nation's Business, January:59.

WHAT THEY SAID IN 1986

Kenneth E. Boulding
Professor emeritus of economics,
University of Colorado; Former president,
American Economic Association

1

There is a pathology of finance in this country. We have lost interest in production. In the United States [corporation] the finance manager has the highest job. In Japan, the production manager does.

> *The Christian Science Monitor,*
> *12-12:52.*

Leo Braudy
Professor of literature,
University of Southern California

2

The desire to be famous now is also infecting business executives. It used to be that, with the exception of an Andrew Carnegie or a John D. Rockefeller, money tended to be quiet. But in the 19th and early 20th centuries there was an effort to turn business into a spiritual calling. In 1925, Bruce Barton wrote *The Man Nobody Knows,* which essentially argued that Jesus was the world's greatest businessman. That was an early step toward the business executive presenting himself as a figure who ought to be admired for himself. To achieve that status, as [Chrysler chairman] Lee Iacocca has done, you cannot operate behind the scenes; you have to step on center stage and be a performer.

> *Interview/U.S. News & World Report, 10-6:86.*

Warren E. Burger
Chief Justice of the United States

3

[Saying the Federal Reserve Board does not have authority to regulate limited-service, or non-bank, banks]: Without a doubt, there is much to be said for regulating financial institutions that are the functional equivalent of banks. [But Congress] defined with specificity certain transactions that constitute banking subject to regulation. The statute may be imperfect but the Board has no power to correct flaws that it perceives in the statute it is empowered to administer.

> *Supreme Court ruling, Jan. 22*/
> *The Christian Science Monitor, 1-23:20.*

John J. Byrne
Chief executive,
Fireman's Fund Corporation

4

Insurance is an easy business to get into. There are no factories or plants or big distribution systems. So it's an industry that attracts a lot of dumb capital, which messes everything up.

> *The New York Times, 6-9:23.*

A. W. Clausen
President, International Bank for
Reconstruction and Development (World Bank)

5

[Criticizing developed countries for cutting back on their farm imports from poor countries]: Hardly a day goes by without new calls in the industrial countries for more restrictions on these developing-country commodities. It is true of the United States, the biggest agricultural exporter in the world. It is true of the European Economic Community, whose price supports and import controls greatly harm the interests of agricultural commodity exporters of the Third World, not to mention the interests of consumers of all nations.

> *Washington, March 14/*
> *Los Angeles Times, 3-16:(I)18.*

Norman Corwin
Visiting professor, School of Journalism,
University of Southern California;
Former radio dramatist

6

[Criticizing much of today's advertising]: I feel very strongly about the seeming need of the consumer and of the audience for kicks. It's not enough for a man simply to engage the viewer by earnest discussion [about a product or service]. He's got to run through an airport. And notice the square-shouldered, earnest, purposeful, *homus*

(NORMAN CORWIN)

americanus as he pedals his product. . . . corporate America smiles too much. When an airline paints a smile on its whole fleet and says, "We're the friendly skies" and "Service with a smile," that's all very pleasant. But there is a degree of trivialization that sets in. For example, these commercials where everybody's happy when they drink beer, smiling and happy when they eat Wheaties, and a daddy is very sweet and cuddly with his little girl while he tells her about some automobile. When material things, soups and soaps and automobiles, are equated with happiness-makers, then we are sending a very, very garbled, if not misleading, message.

Interview/USA Today, 8-18: (A)9.

William E. Dannemeyer
United States Representative,
R-California

1

[Saying such countries as West Germany and Japan have lower interest rates than the U.S.]: Our interest rates and unemployment figures are perfectly consistent with our trade deficit at $150-billion last year. As long as the cost of borrowing money to West German and Japanese producers is one-half of that to American producers, it is futile to expect that money will flow into productive enterprise and into stock, bond and foreign-exchange speculation. The stock market lives on its own dreams, dreaming that greenmail, leveraged buybacks and other incestuous practices can make for prosperity. The fact is that they can only make for the hollowing of American industry.

Before the House, Washington. March 18/
The Washington Post, 3-20: (A)22.

Richard G. Darman
Deputy Secretary of the Treasury
of the United States

2

The rising concern about the stewardship of America's great corporate bureaucracies is reflected in the media's increasing infatuation with characters like [financiers] Carl Icahn and T.

Boone Pickens, Jr. Once dismissed as corporate "raiders," they are gaining attention as a new kind of populist folk-hero—taking on not only big corporations, but the phenomenon of "corprocracy" itself.

Before Japan Society, New York, Nov. 7/
The New York Times, 11-21:30.

3

Much of corporate America remains parochial and knows far less about other cultures than foreign managers know about us. It is little wonder that the Japanese, Koreans and others can design and market state-of-the-art consumer products for our markets but that we are often inept at doing the reverse. Indeed, in many cases American managers are not even as adept as some foreigners in designing products, strategies and tactics for dealing with our own culture.

Before Japan Society, New York, Nov. 7/
Los Angeles Times, 11-16: (IV)3.

4

Some high-priced (big-business) managers seem to spend less time developing R&D budgets than they spend reviewing their golf scores.

U.S. News & World Report, 11-24:53.

Edward Donley
Chairman, Chamber of Commerce
of the United States

5

[The U.S.,] like the rest of the world, must be competitive. We must export or we won't have the funds we need to import, and our society won't survive. We must export, and we don't know how to do it. Yet the business people, the academic people, the Congress, the man in the street, aren't even aware that this is an important issue. So we've got a massive education program ahead of us.

Interview/USA Today, 4-28: (A)11.

Stanley Egener
President,
No-Load Mutual Fund Association

6

I think international investing is here to stay . . . Today, currencies are closely inter-

WHAT THEY SAID IN 1986

twined. There are many more multinational companies. The policies of one economy affect the policies of another. So I think that international investing will grow. Permanently. I find it very difficult to imagine how an investor, by himself, could invest internationally. There are all kinds of problems besides currency: lack of information and liquidity, for example. I think it's a perfect fit for the fund industry.

Interview, New York/
The Christian Science Monitor, 5-16:(B)3.

Robert Farrell
Chief stock-market analyst,
Merrill Lynch, Pierce,
Fenner & Smith, Inc.

1

[On the recent sharp rises in the stock market]: When you have a 600-point run-up in six months, as we had last fall and spring, you create excesses. You get stocks running way ahead of their fundamentals, and then you have a correcting period that makes people nervous before the next leg of the bull market.

Interview/U.S. News & World Report, 11-24:61.

Leon Febres Cordero
President of Ecuador

2

. . . I believe that businessmen must fulfill a social function, that through the workings of competition, free enterprise and free initiatives, entrepreneurs must not only look for their own benefit, but also search for the well-being of society. The lack of such an attitude is the most threatening danger that the market economy can face. Entrepreneurs are, within the structure of a society, organized around the market economy, an elite with more responsibilities than privileges, with obligations that mean much more than showing good balance sheets and income statements.

Before Chamber of Commerce
of the United States, Washington,
January/Nation's Business, Aug.:46.

Jerry Della Femina
Chairman, Della Femina,
Travisano, advertising

3

[On the trend of large advertising agency mergers and the resultant more business-like attitude in the advertising field]: Advertising guys used to try to look like bankers, and now they don't have to because they are bankers. It's not as much fun. I used to call it the business of [lighthearted actor] Tony Randall. Now it's the business of [serious dramatic actor] John Houseman . . . We can't concentrate on advertising any more. We're too busy looking at the paper to see which friend has become a zillionaire.

The New York Times, 5-20:13.

Daniel R. Fischel
Director, law and economics program,
University of Chicago Law School

4

[Saying some "insider" stock trading may be desirable]: It gives insiders incentives to do a good job and increase the value of the stock. But it is not desirable where trading·can be characterized as theft . . . I think the SEC makes a lot of moral statements which are gibberish. Their idea of the way the stock market should work is like a lottery. That's just ridiculous. It's extremely unrealistic and undesirable.

Interview/Los Angeles Times, 6-23:(IV)6.

John W. Gardner
Founder, Common Cause

5

The atmosphere today in the corporate world is piratical. All power overreaches if it is allowed to, and the corporate world is overreaching.

The Christian Science Monitor, 12-12:52.

Rudolph W. Giuliani
United States Attorney for the
Southern District of New York

6

[On insider trading in the stock market]: I don't think there is anything unique to Wall

(RUDOLPH W. GIULIANI)

Street about this. It is a reflection of our society. The same breakdown of honest, dishonest and somewhere-in-the-middle type people can be found in business communities elsewhere, in politics, in government, in the medical profession, in the legal profession. So it's not a special problem of Wall Street. It's a special problem of our society. We have a very serious ethical breakdown.

Interview/USA Today, 6-13:(B)4.

Ira Glasser
Executive director,
American Civil Liberties Union

1

[Opposing drug-testing of employees by their companies]: It is unfair to subject the innocent and the guilty alike to intrusive bodily searches in order to find those few who may be using chemical substances in a way that impairs job performance. The tradition in America is that you don't hang them all to get the guilty. You can search people, you can subject them to invasions of their privacy, but only if you have some reason to believe a specific individual is committing an offense.

Interview/U.S. News & World Report, 3-17:58.

Robert V. Goldstein
Vice president for advertising,
Procter & Gamble Company

2

My basic attitude toward [corporate] mergers . . . is that an acquisition which adds value to a firm, or to its capacity to serve its customers, has some merit. If the customers can be made happy and given better products, then society is better off, the company is better off, and they're going to prosper.

Interview/The New York Times, 8-21:43.

David Halberstam
Author, Journalist

3

[Comparing the Japanese auto industry with the U.S. auto industry]: They beat us by being really better at manufacturing. We [Americans] lost faith with what we had been. The manufacturing people lost power. Power moved to the financial people, the bean counters. That made it a stagnant industry creatively. Japanese manufacturing people are the true sons of the original Henry Ford. I think in American companies, comparably, we had people running the companies who were more committed, unconsciously, to profit than to product. They would never articulate it this way, but they believed, finally, in not just the bottom line, but in profit without risk. There's no such thing.

Interview/USA Today, 10-28:(B)7.

Gary Hart
United States Senator,
D-Colorado

4

We should resist what I think is the most isolationist aspect of foreign policy today—protectionism. We need to make this country more competitive by making it more productive. I advocate a program that includes re-evaluation of the dollar against other currencies, enforcement of current trade laws, reconstruction of the rules of international trade and an investment in the modernization of this country's economy.

Interview/U.S. News
& World Report, 6-23:23.

H. Erich Heinemann
Economist,
Ladenburg, Thalmann & Company

5

[On corporate mergers and take-over attempts]: [Congress should focus on] the truly critical issues—namely, the buildup of [corporate] debt and the restoration of the United States' competitive position in world markets. The toxic waste in most corporate takeover attempts is a mountain of debt which companies assume at the same time that they redeem large amounts of common stock. The totals run to the hundreds of billions of dollars.

The Christian
Science Monitor, 12-5:28.

WHAT THEY SAID IN 1986

William R. Hewlett
Vice chairman,
Hewlett-Packard Company

1

[Stressing the importance of research and development]: Industry is going to have to make some drastic changes in how it views the importance of the research-and-development program and the necessity of increasing productivity . . . Our company is so dependent on creativity that we are still emphasizing the recruitment of engineering graduates, even though a hiring freeze is in effect for the rest of the company. It may well turn out that the present period will be looked back on as one of unprecedented opportunity for the scientifically minded.

At Massachusetts Institute of Technology
commencement, June 2/The New York Times, 6-3:11.

Lee A. Iacocca
Chairman, Chrysler Corporation

2

[On his 1985 Chrysler compensation of over $1,600,000]: Well, I'm not a socialist, you know. I believe in our system. I probably should answer you by saying [that,] in salary and bonus, I'm probably over-paid. My board pays me and they think I'm worth that kind of money . . . But when you talk about stock options, I'm very candid about this. When we [Chrysler] were dying, they brought me into the company. I didn't know how bad off we were. I wouldn't have come—but I had to bring the people you see in this front row, plus a couple hundred others, into the company and I had nothing to offer them. They said we'll never have a bonus again—it looked like we would never do it—and our salaries were about two-thirds of the going rate of other auto company salaries. So I would issue paper. I would give them stock options at . . . $6, and most of them looked at me and said, "I've talked to my wife about leaving a good, cushy job and coming with you, and all you gave me was a lot of paper that she says that I will paper my room with some day." Now, they lived through this for five, six years and the stock went, on the pre-split basis, to $65. What the hell is wrong with that? Isn't that the American system? They grew with the company. We shouldn't feel ashamed about that part of it.

News conference, April 22/
The Wall Street Journal, 5-23:18.

Carl C. Icahn
Financier; Chairman,
Trans World Airlines

3

I think the managements in this country are sadly lacking; not all managements, I want to make clear—there are some very good managements. But, generally speaking, I think we have a great crisis managerially. What has developed is a sort of anti-Darwinian pattern where you have the survival of the unfittest. Just like college, where the president of the fraternity is a real likable guy, the president or the CEO of the company is usually a likable guy . . . But they're not the cleverest because clever guys, intelligent guys are often abrasive and they're not that well liked. It seems to go sort of hand in hand. A bit of creativity and a bit of abrasiveness. And what has happened in managements are the guys who got to the top are the guys that the board liked.

Interview/Newsweek, 10-20:52.

4

[On why he goes after control of major corporations]: I do it to make money. If there wasn't money there, I wouldn't do it. It's great to make money, but it's also a great source of satisfaction attempting to change something that's outrageous. [What's outrageous is that so many companies] are buried in a sea of bureaucracy today. If it doesn't stop, we will find ourselves in a critical situation because we won't be able to support our retirees. It's amazing, when you go into these companies, the number of people who are just shuffling papers around.

Interview/USA Today, 10-24:(B)2.

5

There's a corporate aristocracy that's very detrimental to the health of the economy. I don't blame individuals. I blame a corporate culture that builds layers and layers of management. It's almost like feudalism, and there's no answerabil-

(CARL C. ICAHN)

ity. The Japanese have two layers before the line, and we [in the U:S.] have 10. This is why we have problems with foreign competition. People are asking for protection, but the answer is to be more efficient.

Nov. 10/The New York Times, 11-11:27.

Michael H. Jordan
President, PepsiCo, Inc.

1

You can't look at the decline of international competitiveness [of U.S. companies] without seeing problems of efficiency. I would say there are a lot of companies which have done a good job of executing strategies that worked 10 years ago. But because of bureaucracy, or having too many layers of management, they get used to doing what they've always done—or fighting the last war. Certain large organizations tend to promote isolationism and to insulate top executives from what's going on around them.

Nov. 10/The New York Times, 11-11:27.

Herbert Kaufman
Former senior fellow,
Brookings Institution

2

When you compare organizations that expire with those that survive, you will find no correlation between ability, intelligence or leadership talents, on the one hand, and survival or extinction on the other. Thus, the differences in their fates must be the result of something else. I think that "something else" will prove to be a probability function. The survival of organizations is largely a matter of luck.

Interview, Washington/
The New York Times, 1-30:16.

Jack Kemp
United States Representative,
R-New York

3

I believe that, like tax reform—which was impossible up to the minute it happened—the ques-

tion of sound money ultimately will be decided in the political arena, not in gatherings of experts, important as they are. . . . problems such as fiscal disequilibrium and global debt and poverty are results of, not the cause of, monetary disorder, exchange-rate volatility and high tax rates. We need the spirit of democratic capitalism in the world . . . to pursue policies that will expand global wealth by liberating human capital and human potential, by providing a stable international unit of account with low, long-term interest rates, low tax rates on the factors of production and liberal trading policies.

Before Inter-Parliamentary Round
on Exchange Rates and Coordination,
July 1/The Wall Street Journal, 7-2:24.

Donald M. Kendall
Chairman, PepsiCo, Inc.

4

There's no place where success comes before work, except in the dictionary. You can't get to the top of any profession without a lot of hard work, and I don't care whether you're in art, music, in business, or in the academic world. Success at all levels requires tremendous effort . . . It also requires enthusiasm and excitement about what you're doing. If you're not happy every morning when you get up, leave for work, or start work at home—if you're not enthusiastic about doing that—you're not going to be successful. The other thing you need in probably equal proportion is a lot of luck, because there are a lot of people with the same ability who worked very hard, who haven't made it and who deserved to make it.

Interview/USA Today, 4-21:(A)13.

Lester Korn
Chairman, Korn/Ferry
International, executive-search firm

5

The social barrier is the single largest barrier to women reaching the top ranks [in American business]. The American executive is focused on his career—he lives it, he thinks it, he works at it and it's all-consuming to him. The male career in the family takes precedence and is oriented

WHAT THEY SAID IN 1986

frequently toward a social life. You do a great deal of business at black-tie affairs and over the weekends. [Ninety-four per cent of the respondents in a recent survey of senior executives] are presently married . . . In studying women, we find an astonishingly high divorce or unmarried rate. The women are just as dedicated, but they are not a part and parcel of the social fabric of the job—the country clubs, the golf clubs, the social gatherings that go on in many companies.

Interview/U.S. News & World Report, 4-14:52.

Paul Light
*Research director, National Academy
of Public Administration*

1

[Saying there is a national obsession with quick profits]: It's not so much greed as a short-term focus in the public and government and corporations to make your score quickly and get out . . . The old notion of investing and building over time is just as successful, but that's not where the corporate raiders or the politicians are coming from.

The Christian Science Monitor, 12-12:52.

Russell B. Long
United States Senator, D-Louisiana

2

[Arguing against reducing the tax deduction for business entertainment expenses]: I have often said that entertainment is to the selling business the same thing that fertilizer is to the farming business.

USA Today, 5-7:(A)5.

Henry Manne
*Dean, George Mason University
Law School*

3

Insider [stock] trading guarantees the market quickly and accurately reflects what's going on. No one is hurt by insider trading. Congress should be shooting at the SEC and at regulations curbing take-overs, not insider trading.

The Christian Science Monitor, 12-12:4.

John P. Mascotte
*Chief executive,
Continental Corporation*

4

[On multimillion-dollar judgments in liability cases]: Jury awards have a tremendous multiplier effect on the cases that do not go to trial. I don't think the real issue is whether there is a small surge in small jury awards or a large surge in large awards. What's important is whether the tort system is increasing the average payment in liability transactions, and evidence from industry files indicates that is the case. It's like an iceberg: The big hunk underneath is what's really creating the headache for insurance companies.

Interview/The New York Times, 8-5:30.

David Maxwell
*Chief executive officer,
Federal National Mortgage Association*

5

Chief executives who are my age [57], or even a little younger, still feel uneasiness dealing with women [executives]. They're much more comfortable dealing with other men. [Top executives are often] quick to feel the woman who is tough isn't being womanly, while the woman who isn't tough isn't worth having around.

Interview/The Wall Street Journal, 3-24:(D)1.

Robert E. Mercer
*Chairman, Goodyear Tire
& Rubber Company*

6

[Criticizing attempts by outside financiers to take over companies by stock purchases and then have the company buy them out at great company expense]: If you have the ability to come in and destroy a company, what's the difference if you do it with bombs or if you do it inside with a financial threat. The company gets destroyed one way or another. It's terrifying to see the lives of so many people affected drastically and permanently from a sneak attack that's done under the guise of protecting or enhancing shareholder value.

*Interview/
The Christian Science Monitor, 11-28:31.*

George J. Mitchell
United States Senator, D-Maine

1

America's trade deficit is now close to $150-billion a year. That's the biggest trade deficit ever run up by any country at any time in the entire history of the world. And every billion dollars of that deficit means thousands of jobs lost. These trade and budget deficits mean we are living on borrowed money, too much of it from foreigners. Living on borrowed money means living on borrowed time. The day of reckoning is not far off. We must respond now, before it's too late, by increasing American productivity, by competing aggressively in world markets and by insisting that fair competition is a two-way street.

Broadcast address to the nation,
Washington, Feb. 4/
The New York Times, 2-6:17.

Akio Morita
Chairman,
Sony Corporation (Japan)

2

I'm always criticizing management rather than the American work force. The American work force is very good. They can produce a good product. They have high morale, and they work hard. You [Americans] should give more incentive to management to run corporations with much longer viewpoints, instead of short-term profit. Give management more security to run companies. At the same time, you should discourage management from taking profit away.

Interview, Los Angeles/
Los Angeles Times, 11-1:(IV)1.

3

Right now in [the U.S.], service industries are booming. But if America goes to services and forgets production industries, you must not complain about imbalance of trade, because you are not producing . . . [And U.S. executives] are moving to the "money game"—buy a company, take over a company. If you continue this, American industry will completely deteriorate.

Interview, New York/
U.S. News & World Report, 11-17:57.

Joe C. Morris
Chairman-designate, United States
League of Savings Institutions

4

[On the financial health of savings institutions]: First, there is the 85 per cent of the business operating in the black. Of that, a minority—say, 40 per cent—is doing extraordinarily well. They are having record earnings, and they are growing quickly. The remaining institutions in this category are also doing well, and I would guess that if we had this kind of environment for the next year or two—low interest and low inflation—these institutions, too, would have record years. For the remaining 15 per cent, there is no question that a number of those institutions will fail.

Interview, Boca Raton, Fla./
The New York Times, 9-23:34.

Ralph Nader
Lawyer; Consumer advocate.

5

You can't deregulate the economic sector of an industry and at the same time allow the weakening of safety standards. Because of the deregulation—and they're cutting corners to compete—you cut corners on safety, so in that sense it's bad. But other than the safety and health area, it can be economically beneficial. [However,] deregulation, or taking the Federal cop off the corporate beat, can permit avoidable death, injury and disease to go unchecked. That's been [President] Reagan's trademark. His policy has been to ignore the need to enforce and keep up to date the safety and health standards for the American people. Loosened auto safety regulations, drugs, more pollution, unsafe drinking water—these are all examples of his government's indifference or outright antagonism. I think we're going to start hearing more about re-regulation.

Interview/Los Angeles Times Magazine, 2-16:18.

Yasuhiro Nakasone
Prime Minister of Japan

6

[Trade] protectionism not only saps the vitality of its users, it also begets further protec-

WHAT THEY SAID IN 1986

tionism, and ultimately the world economy will lapse into a coma.

USA Today, 1-9:(A)8.

John Nevin
Chairman, Firestone Tire
and Rubber Company

1

It was much more true 10 years ago than today that the mission of management was perpetuating or expanding the company. Managers are much more aware now than 10 years ago that they've got to generate wealth for their shareholders, or they will be in jeopardy of losing control of the corporations they run.

The New York Times, 11-24:24.

David Packard
Co-founder, Hewlett-Packard Company;
Former Deputy Secretary of
Defense of the United States

2

I see [international debt] more as a transient problem rather than a permanent [one]. The pressures of the stock market that encourage management to focus on short-term gains rather than the long-term [prosperity] of a company [are far more pressing]. I don't see any signs that this is clearing up. It will get worse before it gets better.

Interview, New York/
The Christian Science Monitor, 11-21:23.

H. Ross Perot
Financier; Chairman,
Electronic Data Systems Corporation

3

The general attitude [in American business management] is, whatever they teach you in the Harvard Business School is the one true path. Here's what they teach in the Harvard Business School: mergers, acquisitions, manipulations, leveraged buyouts. That has nothing to do with creating jobs. Go to Wall Street and make $500,000 a year just pushing numbers around. We need our best and brightest to go down on the factory floor and get dirty and find out how to make their products, how to serve the customers, how to beat the Japanese.

Interview, Herndon, Va.,
Nov. 18/USA Today, 11-19:(B)2.

4

In many of our huge corporations we treat people like commodities. And people cannot be managed. Inventories can be managed, but people must be led. And when people are reacting to being treated improperly, they are not doing their best work. And when they're not doing their best work, our international competitors can beat us. That is the core of our problem [in the U.S.]. It's not robots; it's not technology. It's how we treat our people.

Interview, Houston/Newsweek, 12-15:58.

John Phelan, Jr.
Chairman, New York Stock Exchange

5

You can't stop [corporate] take-overs, and you shouldn't be able to put up a [take-over] defense mechanism for management. [But] any guy who steps up—I don't care how much he thinks he's doing the U.S. a favor—and makes $95-million on a trade, the white begins to fall off his armor and it begins to get tarnished.

To reporters, Dec. 11/
The Christian Science Monitor, 12-12:4.

Joseph Pinola
Chairman, First Interstate Bancorp

6

Nationwide banking [by individual banks] is here in every way except legally. Advances in communications and technology have brought it about. Here and there, laws are starting to catch up.

U.S. News & World Report, 11-24:49.

Clyde V. Prestowitz
Counsellor to the Secretary of
Commerce of the United States

7

[On whether the large U.S. trade deficit with Japan is the result of unfair Japanese trade prac-

(CLYDE V. PRESTOWITZ)

tices]: I don't like to discuss it in terms of fair or unfair. The problem is that the nature of Japanese society is very different from American society. It's not that the Japanese are trying to cheat. It's that they have a differently structured economy and society, making it difficult to penetrate . . . I hesitate saying we ought to ban imports. The question is what do you want to get. In any negotiation there are carrots and sticks. Once you have determined what your objective is, then you want to have a few carrots and a few sticks and use a judicious mix of those to get your objective. So in some cases where our interests are being threatened by unfair trade activity, then I think it's legitimate to contemplate strong measures.

Interview, Washington/
The New York Times, 5-20:34.

William Proxmire
United States Senator,
D-Wisconsin

1

I think what we might do to limit "junk bonds" is to provide that margin requirements apply to junk bonds, which they don't now. If you or I want to go out and buy stock, we have to put up 50 per cent of our own money. On the other hand, some big wheeler and dealer can go out to [the securities firm of] Drexel Burnham [Lambert] and can borrow 3 or 4 billion dollars, putting up none of his own money. It can be junk bonds—high-interest-rate, high-risk bonds. He can bid for the corporation and maybe take over. It's ridiculous.

Interview, Dec. 3/
The Christian Science Monitor, 12-5:28.

Wayne Rasmussen
Chief historian, Department of
Agriculture of the United States

2

We're again considering doing away with all [farm] subsidies and price supports. That's fine in a true free market, where everybody plays according to the same rules. But if the farmer is

the only one out there as the lone free-market competitor, we aren't going to have many farmers left in this country . . . The only constant about agriculture is that it is cyclical. The crisis of over-supply we see today could end at any time. A crop failure in India, a drought in Australia, a heavy frost in Russia, a problem in the Middle West, could cause the huge surpluses of food to disappear. I'd much rather see us plagued with a surplus than fighting over food and Americans starving to death.

Interview, Washington/
The New York Times, 7-3:10.

Ronald Reagan
President of the United States

3

[Criticizing a House bill that would require Presidential retaliation against foreign trading partners that engage in trade subsidies, limitations on U.S. imports and other anti-U.S. trade actions]: This bill is so potentially destructive that even many of those who voted for it did so in the expectation it would be vetoed and so never become law. Well, if it comes to that, I assure them they will get their wish. The Democratic leadership may think this is clever politics in an election year, but the American people see this for what it is—kamikaze legislation that could take their jobs down in flames . . . [This] so-called omnibus trade bill is really an ominous anti-trade bill that could send our economy into the steepest nose-dive since the Great Depression. This reactionary legislation would force American consumers to pay billions in higher prices, throw millions of Americans out of work and strangle our economy as foreign markets slam shut in retaliation. This anti-trade bill isn't protectionism—it's destructionism.

Before National Association of Manufacturers,
Washington, May 29/The New York Times, 5-30:1,33.

4

[Arguing against trade protectionism]: America doesn't need to hide behind trade barriers. Given a level playing field, Americans can out-produce and out-compete anyone, anywhere on earth. That's why it's the policy of this Administration to open

(RONALD REAGAN)

markets abroad, not close them at home. We will bring the world with us into a new era of free trade. Free trade—with free traders—is our byword.

Before National Association of Manufacturers, Washington, May 29/The Washington Post, 5-30:(F)4.

1

A great many of the current problems on the farm were caused by government-imposed embargoes and inflation, not to mention government's long history of conflicting and haphazard policies. Our ultimate goal, of course, is economic independence for agriculture. And through steps like the tax-reform bill, we seek to return farming to real farmers. But until we make that transition, government must act compassionately and responsibly. In order to see farmers through these tough times, our Administration has committed record amounts of assistance, spending more in this year alone than any previous Administration spent during its entire tenure. No area of the budget, including defense, has grown as fast as our support for agriculture . . . The message in all this is very simple: America's farmers should know that our commitment to helping them is unshakeable. As long as I'm in Washington, their concerns are going to be heard and acted upon.

News conference, Chicago, Aug. 12/ The New York Times, 8-13:8.

Stephen Rhoades
Economist, Federal Reserve Board

2

[Saying corporate mergers do not necessarily produce strong companies]: You don't put two turkeys together and make an eagle. I don't think there is any significant evidence that permitting more mergers in industries that are hurt will help them a bit.

Time, 1-27:38.

James Rogers
Professor of finance, Graduate School of Business, Columbia University

3

[Saying there will be a bear market in 1987 and 1988]: In my view, this is going to be a real doozy—the worst bear market since 1937, during which the Dow Jones industrial average plunged 49 per cent. However, it's not going to be the end of the world. In fact, it should cleanse the system of a lot of those excesses. For example, a collapse in the junk-bond market means some of these guys are going to take a fall and that will stop the excesses we're seeing there. The point is that if the financial system does cleanse itself, the 1990s could be wildly prosperous.

Interview/U.S. News & World Report, 12-8:54.

Roy Rowan
Business journalist; Former editor, "Life" magazine

4

[On intuitive management and the "eureka factor"]: It's a sudden, illuminating, "I have found it" flash. Many executives will tell you that logic, analysis—the things they teach in business school—will only take you part way down the path to a decision. Finally, you have to make that intuitive leap using the cumulative knowledge, experience, taste, sensation that lies buried in your subconscious.

Interview/U.S. News & World Report, 5-12:52.

Fernand St. Germain
United States Representative, D-Rhode Island

5

[Criticizing banks for holding deposited checks too long before permitting withdrawals against them]: For the well-heeled with big balances in their checking account, the need for this legislation [to reduce the holding time] may indeed seem remote. But for the factory worker, the salaried employee, the retiree of modest means, and to others who must pay their basic living expenses out of their weekly or monthly income, these arbitrary check holds are a disaster.

Washington, Jan. 23/ Los Angeles Times, 1-24:(I)1.

Herb Schmertz
Vice president for public affairs,
Mobil Oil Corporation

1

[Criticizing press coverage of business matters]: The value system imposed on journalists by the structures of the organizations they work for, especially television, is a major problem. An even greater problem is incompetency. There is a high level of economic illiteracy among journalists. If I were business editor of a paper, the first thing I'd do would be to administer a questionnaire to reporters to find out what their economic literacy was, whether they can read balance sheets and know the difference between simple things like profits and profitability, revenue and income. Reporters also don't understand a lot of things that attract people to go into business—the tough negotiations, the competitiveness, the give-and-take. If they don't understand it, they don't identify with it. That causes them to report a lot of business conflict in a less than favorable light.

Interview/U.S. News & World Report, 5-26:62.

John Schnittker
Agricultural economist

2

[On government farm-price supports]: The program is not working. Every day we have more evidence of their malfunctioning. The law is expensive. The [crop] surpluses are getting worse. The payments being made are going mostly to well-off farmers. The situation is completely out of control.

The New York Times, 7-22:7.

Charles R. Schwab
Investment broker

3

In a bull [stock] market, greed and avarice are the emotional factors. In bear markets, fear takes over. I've seen people dump stocks at the worst time because they're afraid of going to zero. Buying when things are down and selling when they're up is wise, but contrary to human nature.

Interview/USA Today, 9-11:(B)2.

John S. R. Shad
Chairman, Securities and
Exchange Commission

4

Our nation's economic growth depends on investor confidence in the securities markets. People will be less willing to place their money at risk in securities if they believe that insiders, who have access to material non-public information, are using it to take advantage of them.

Interview, Washington, Nov. 20/
Los Angeles Times, 11-21:(I)1.

Irving S. Shapiro
Former chairman,
E. I. du Pont de Nemours & Co.

5

Getting the right information is a substantial part of the job [of being a chief executive]. The basic ground rule is that you can't be taken by surprise. You get lots of information and most of it is totally unnecessary. The organization tends to want to give you the good news and not cough up the bad news. But to manage well, you have to get the message across that, whatever the story is, let's get it on the table fast so there are no surprises. But it doesn't always happen that way.

Interview/The New York Times, 2-28:33.

George P. Shultz
Secretary of State of the United States

6

I don't think it's good for the United States to develop a system of [trade] protectionism . . . What I see is a sweep of protectionist sentiment in a variety of forms. The reasons I think this protectionist threat is so important right now are, of course, economic reasons . . . The lesson of history is that if we want to see our economies develop, open them up. And I say let's not turn our back on that lesson, even though for some people there may be difficulties.

Interview/USA Today, 8-5:(A)7.

Sanford C. Sigoloff
Chairman and president, Wickes Companies

7

There are two classes of people who save companies: People who talk about it and people

WHAT THEY SAID IN 1986

(SANFORD C. SIGOLOFF)

who have done it. And the number of people who've done it [with big companies], well, you can count those on your right hand after an accident.

Newsweek, 9-29:45.

Allen Sinai
Chief economist,
Shearson Lehman Bros., investment analysts

1

[On the large U.S. foreign-trade deficit]: Waiting for a turn in trade may be like waiting for Godot. The heart of the problem is that Americans just continue to buy so much from abroad.

Los Angeles Times, 8-30:(I)1.

Bruce Smart
Under Secretary for International
Trade, Department of Commerce
of the United States

2

Can the United States be sufficiently competitive [in foreign trade] to defend and advance a very high standard of living for its 200-and-some million people? Absolutely. Can the U.S. remain pre-eminent in essentially every area of commerce and industry as it was in the 1950s? Absolutely not . . . There's no way we can be best at everything.

Interview/USA Today, 1-30:(B)9.

3

It's a fact of life that changes in technology and demand affect an industry's ability to compete. Some people win, some people lose. Our role [in government] is to set rules to play fair, not to prevent there being winners or losers.

The New York Times, 7-28:26.

Roger B. Smith
Chairman,
General Motors Corporation

4

We have to watch the corporate raiders [those who attempt to buy out large companies]. They

destroy equity. They destroy jobs. They destroy communities. All for their own gain. That's not right and it should not be allowed in America. Legitimate take-overs, okay. Corporate raiders for their own profit, no good.

Newsweek, 12-1:52.

Ira Lee Sorkin
Director, New York office,
Securities and Exchange Commission
of the United States

5

[Criticizing "insider" stock trading]: The SEC is not looking to make a level playing field out of this—a lottery. There is no question that the rancher in Texas or the widow in Iowa are never going to be equal to the investment banker and the arbitrageur who work down on Wall Street, the people who interpret, analyze, digest, regurgitate and sniff around to make a decision as to whether to buy and sell. We're just trying to stop the use of non-public information.

Interview/Los Angeles Times, 6-23:(IV)6.

Michael Steinhardt
Investment analyst

6

There are two major factors that have accounted for the stock-market rise. First, there's a clear relationship between interest rates and stock prices, and interest rates have declined dramatically in this period of time. Second is what I like to call the "leveraging of America," the extraordinary explosion in use of debt on all levels of society. I think that will be the key issue in the economic future of the Western world.

At seminar sponsored by Columbia
University School of Business, New York/
The Christian Science Monitor, 5-27:24.

Laurence Tisch
Acting chief executive officer, CBS, Inc.

7

I am a firm believer that if you run a quality company . . . in the long run the financial performance will take care of itself . . . I have been

(LAURENCE TISCH)

in business for 40 years and have always followed that philosophy. Profits will follow from quality.

Interview/Newsweek, 9-22:59.

Alvin Toffler
Futurist

1

[On the wave of corporate mergers and takeovers]: If everything's getting bigger, bigger, bigger, that's a dangerous process. But I'd like to see an analysis in a year or two, to check whether companies, across the board, are bigger or smaller. Because one of the features of all this is disinvestment, and divestment. We acquire and then we strip away parts of the company. The result may be a set of flexible, more maneuverable, smaller companies. It's part of the economic restructuring that I call the transition to the Third Wave. It's busting up the old structures and trying to reconfigure them.

Interview/USA Today, 3-11:(B)4.

Leigh B. Trevor
Corporate-takeover defense lawyer

2

In the process by which hostile [corporate] takeovers are conducted in this country, nobody has time to think or plan or make the kind of judgments to deal adequately with the . . . lives involved . . . The process is absolutely undisciplined. We dispose of companies and lives on the basis of a 20-business-days minimum offering period. Hitler took Poland in 20 business days.

Interview/USA Today, 6-17:(B)2.

Michiyuki Uyenohara
Executive vice president,
NEC Corporation (Japan)

3

It takes 10 to 15 years for the fruits of basic research to appear on the market as a specific product. That's the period I call the pre-

competitive phase. Once the product appears, we are in competition with each other. Before that, though, there can be all kinds of international co-operation.

Interview, Tokyo/The Christian
Science Monitor, 11-24:20.

An Wang
Chairman,
Wang Laboratories, Inc.

4

It's my belief that there are no "secrets" to success. People fail for the most part because they shoot themselves in the foot. If you go for a long time without shooting yourself in the foot, people start calling you a genius.

USA Today, 8-20:(B)9.

Murray L. Weidenbaum
Director, Center for the
Study of American Business,
Washington University; Former
Chairman, Council of Economic
Advisers to President of the
United States Ronald Reagan

5

The newest fad among domestic policy-players in Washington is to attack "bloated, risk-averse, inefficient and unimaginative" [business] enterprises. Business-bashing has always been a popular parlor game, and serious shortcomings exist in every sector of human endeavor. But the current assault on business appeals to my sense of irony. It is led by people whose work experience extends all the way from Harvard to Federal agencies in Washington. "Bloated"? Isn't that the same government whose spending—and indebtedness—has been growing faster than that of the rest of the economy? "Risk-averse"? Isn't that the same government that just adopted a new Internal Revenue Code that reduces incentives to invest? "Inefficient"? Isn't that the same government whose civilian employment has been rising during the last half decade? And that maintains over 113,000 inspectors, rule-makers and regulators to second-guess the private sector? "Unimaginative"? Who else would recycle a term originated by one of

WHAT THEY SAID IN 1986

(MURRAY L. WEIDENBAUM)

[consumer advocate] Ralph Nader's former side-kicks? "Corpocracy" . . . rhymes with hypocrisy.

At meeting sponsored by
Chief Executive Magazine, Washington/
The New York Times, 12-26:24.

Hans Werthen
Chairman, Electrolux AB (Sweden)

1

[On what he likes about business]: I like the battles. Contrary to the military, industry is always at war. If industry does not have war, it's called a cartel, and for that you go to jail.

Interview, Stockholm/USA Today, 11-19:(B)7.

Martina Whitman
Vice president of public affairs,
General Motors Corporation

2

[For a company,] the profit is the ante. If you don't make profits you can't stay in the game and you can't do anything else useful. But it's also very clear that society does not regard that as the only goal. There is a kind of implicit social compact under which corporations, businesses, exist, in which they are expected to do a good deal more than that and are expected to fulfill a great many goals . . . If you ask me, as the person in charge of public affairs at General Motors who has come out of an economics background, what are the two big challenges confronting this corporation—and to some extent any corporation—it's the need to become and remain globally competitive, which is an absolute imperative, and to meet this plethora of social goals which are a part of this implicit compact with society.

Interview, Detroit/
The Christian Science Monitor, 12-23:15.

George F. Will
Political columnist;
Commentator, ABC News

3

Yes, [farm] price supports are expensive. In recent years they've been the fastest growing

major entitlement program. But look what we're getting for that. Three per cent of the American public is feeding the other 97 per cent of us and a good bit of the rest of the world as well. The farmers are feeding us so cheaply that we're spending an incredibly small percentage of our disposable income on our food. And furthermore, agricultural exports are keeping us from going absolutely off the brink with our trade deficits.

TV Guide, 1-25:8.

Michael Wilson
Minister of Finance of Canada

4

Our objective is to bring home to the United States the cost of [trade] protectionism. Nations which resort to unjustified protectionism must be made to realize that trade is a two-way street.

Before House of Commons, Ottawa,
June 2/The Christian Science Monitor, 6-4:9.

Charles L. Wingfield
Chairman, CIT Group

5

[On his firm's business of asset-based financing of companies that cannot obtain traditional bank financing]: Many of the middle-market companies, a potential market of more than 136,000 United States firms, are not companies that banks want to lend to on an unsecured basis. These are companies that have a need for funds beyond what they can justify purely on a balance-sheet basis, and banks are more inclined to lend traditionally on balance sheets. So they go to an asset-based financing company, where loans can be structured to meet the need for availability of cash based on the performance of the business and projected profits of the organization.

Interview/The New York Times, 12-9:34.

Frederick D. Wolf
Director, Accounting and Financial
Management Division, General Accounting
Office of the United States

6

[Criticizing Federal regulators for allowing troubled banks and savings-and-loans to use "ar-

(FREDERICK D. WOLF)

tificial accounting'' techniques to hide their financial problems]: [We should give] troubled institutions time to work out acceptable recovery programs with creditors. [But] we believe that accounting and public financial reporting should remain neutral and not become part of the mechanism intended to deal with troubled institutions or their problem debt . . . The United States has a vigorous system of both public and private security and financial markets . . . second to none in the world. These markets are based, to a very large degree, on the concept that full and fair disclosure provides the primary basis for investor protection.

Before House Oversight and Investigations
Subcommittee, Washington, April 10/
The Washington Post, 4-11:(B)9.

Thomas H. Wyman
Chairman, CBS, Inc.

1

A person who writes a thesis on Yeats, or majors in fine arts or specializes in French literature, ought to feel comfortable about a future in corporate life—at Citibank, at IBM or at CBS. And all of those companies ought to feel comfortable having such a person. But comfort is not enough. I am convinced that the future leadership of corporate America will depend on those who have experienced the varied rigors of a liberal-arts education as opposed to narrower, more specialized courses of instruction. I believe this on the basis of both common sense and self-interest. There is nothing that a chief executive likes less than to be surprised. But ours is an increasingly complex world characterized by frequent and accelerated change. Business decisions affect—and are affected by—many constituencies. Successful executives will be those who understand and interpret complex relationships. To be effective demands continual reconsideration of assumptions underlying old and familiar networks . . . as well as the gathering and sorting of new information. This puts a premium on managers with the ability to be flexible, critical and capable of continuous learning; managers with the skills to anticipate change . . . and not be surprised.

At Dickinson College/
The Wall Street Journal, 4-30:26.

Ted Zahavich
Director of Research,
Investment Canada

2

The U.S. is attractive to Canadian investors because there are limited opportunities in Canada for the big players. They've outgrown the playpen.

Time, 11-17:68.

47

Crime • Law Enforcement

Toney Anaya
Governor of New Mexico (D)

1

[Arguing against capital punishment]: Let us put an end to this macabre national death march. It is inhumane, immoral, anti-God—and is incompatible with an enlightened society.

News conference, Sante Fe, N.M.,
Nov. 26/Los Angeles Times, 11-27:(I)1.

Howard L. Berman
United States Representative,
D-California

2

[Arguing against a loosening of the exclusionary rule in drug-trafficking cases]: A "good-faith" exception [to the rule] . . . is not defined by any standard other than the subjective good-faith belief of the police officer. He [would] now [be] rewarded for un-Constitutional searches to the extent to which he testifies he does not know that the search was illegal. The court did not adopt the exclusionary rule because it loved to exclude evidence. It adopted it because there was no other effective and meaningful deterrent and remedy to deal with the problem of protecting our fundamental Constitutional rights.

Before the House, Washington, Sept. 11/
The Washington Post, 9-16:(A)13.

Rose Elizabeth Bird
Chief Justice,
Supreme Court of California

3

[On criticism that she and others on the California Supreme Court are against the death penalty and rule with that in mind]: My role is not to reflect what my personal view is. My role is to respect the people's view. The people voted for and wanted a death penalty. We in the Court are trying our very best to implement that within the restrictions of the Constitution and within the restrictions of due process. It is such an emotional issue that it's very difficult to have people see what the Court is trying to do—that it's trying to ensure that when you execute somebody here in California, you can sit there with a clear conscience and know that the person was executed not to re-elect a justice, not to ensure that the judicial branch of government is popular, but [that] the person was executed under a Constitutional law after a fair trial.

Before California Broadcasters Association,
Monterey, Calif., July 28/
Los Angeles Times, 7-29:(I)3.

Tom Bradley
Mayor of Los Angeles

4

[Saying he supports capital punishment]: I have seen far too many people killed. I have seen far too much violence in our society. I see some of it today with people who have no compassion, no concern, no idea of the consequence of their acts. So they would rather kill at the blink of an eye, go into a store and pull a robbery and when somebody doesn't move fast enough, they blow them away. I believe that the death penalty is necessary and I support it. There's got to be some way that we remove them, that we separate them from you and me and the rest of our society. Otherwise, all of us will be living in the jungle with no security, no protection. That's the only purpose of the death penalty.

To San Francisco County jail prisoners,
Jan. 8/Los Angeles Times, 1-9:(I)3.

William J. Brennan, Jr.
Associate Justice, Supreme
Court of the United States

5

Why do we have those protections for the accused in the Constitution? Obviously because we as a society have appreciated that a society's decency is best reflected in how it treats those who offend against its laws. That is not merely a mat-

(WILLIAM J. BRENNAN, JR.)

ter of compassion. It's a way of securing for every one of us guarantees which will protect us when we're prosecuted.

Interview, Washington/
The New York Times, 4-16:18.

William E. Brock
Secretary of Labor of the United States

1

[Calling on Teamsters Union members to rid the union of crime and corruption]: As Secretary of Labor, it isn't easy to hear about mobbed-up locals or pension-fund abuse—misuse of members' blood and sweat. It's impossible for me to ignore that. It is necessary for you to address it . . . Are there institutional processes which make it easy for some who want to exploit members to do so? If there are, change them. Are there locals where people are doing just that? Where crime interests reign and members' interests are ignored or trampled? If there are such locals, put them in trusteeship. Are there areas where good people have been silent too long— where it's just plain time to clean house? If so, do it. [The overwhelming majority of Teamsters Union members] are good, decent, honorable people. Be sure they run every local, that their issues are your agenda, that their values are reflected in your acts.

At Teamsters Union convention, Las Vegas,
Nev., May 19/Los Angeles Times, 5-20:(I)1,18.

Lee P. Brown
Chief of Police of Houston

2

We are going to have to come to the realization that there is a correlation—either direct or indirect—between socioeconomic problems and the crime problem in our society. We have to look at what is occurring in our cities. Where there is a cycle of what people are calling an underclass, we have to be concerned about breaking that cycle . . . I think what we have seen is a reaction to crime where we attempt to address it through things like burglar bars, or alarm sys-

tems . . . What we have done is reacted with stiff legislation and bigger prisons. What we have not done is to start looking at some of the causes of the problem and then doing what is necessary to address those causes.

The Christian Science Monitor, 10-31:18,19.

George Bush
Vice President of the United States

3

Liberal politicians . . . seem to think that our hearts should reach out to every two-bit punk with a knife or gun who mugs a cleaning lady waiting for the subway.

Before Conservative Party, New York/
The Christian Science Monitor, 2-3:44.

Mario M. Cuomo
Governor of New York (D)

4

[There] is no evidence the death penalty is a deterrent to crime. Violent crime has not uniformly decreased in states that have enacted capital punishment, nor has it increased in states that have abolished capital punishment.

Vetoing a death-penalty bill,
Albany, N.Y., March 17/
USA Today, 3-18:(A)3.

5

[Calling for a possible life sentence for anyone convicted of selling three or more vials of the drug "crack"]: The answer is not always the stiffest possible punishment. [But in the case of crack,] I think we need stiffer, sterner punishment— this is not Draconian. We will accept nothing less than the toughest penalties for those who would sell this addictive, destructive drug to our children.

Aug. 15/The New York Times, 8-16:1.

Wendell Foster
New York City Councilman

6

Instead of letting [drug] pushers go because we are told there is no jail space, they should be chained to fences or street lights on the street corners, or wherever apprehended, until there are jails to house them.

Newsweek, 8-18:11.

Willard Gaylin
Psychoanalyst

1

The inevitable result of most homicides is a constant erosion of the victim's image, of the respect with which he is held, of the memories . . . I'm saying that what happens ultimately is that the offenders appropriate and usurp the natural sympathy that ought to go to the victim, whether they intend to or not. We do not identify with a cadaver. We identify with a living, suffering person, and we ought to—that's the way we're built.

Interview/U.S. News & World Report, 8-18:52.

George W. Gekas
United States Representative,
R-Pennsylvania

2

[Calling for the death penalty in drug-trafficking cases]: The drug dealer will stop at nothing to further his enterprise. He would poison our populace; he would enslave our children; he would kill a judge; he would kill a prosecutor; he would kill a law-enforcement officer; he would kill anybody who would stand in his way . . . The amendment [calling for the death penalty] that is before us is society's response to this drug dealer, this czar of the most pernicious traffic ever known to mankind.

Before the House, Washington,
Sept. 11/The Washington Post, 9-16:(A)13.

Rudolph W. Giuliani
United States Attorney for the
Southern District of New York

3

As I understand it, the [New York] Governor's [Mario Cuomo] view is that the word "Mafia" should not be used as a generic term to describe all organized crime, because to do so reflects unfairly on Italians and Italian Ameri-

cans. I completely agree with that. There's no point in using terms like "Oriental Mafia" or "Israeli Mafia," though there are gangs who exploit immigrants of those nationalities. It is counter-productive, however, to avoid using "Mafia" where it properly applies—to the group of 24 or so families in the U.S. who have organized themselves along traditional Mafia lines. In Italy there certainly is no hesitation about using the word. In fact, there is a law known specifically as the anti-Mafia statute. So if a [U.S.] district attorney or a police official is afraid to use "Mafia," it looks to people on the street—the victims who are forced to pay money to the mob—as if the Mafia somehow has power over these officials.

Interview, New York/
U.S. News & World Report, 2-3:32.

Robert Graham
Governor of Florida (D)

4

[Criticizing courts for granting last-minute stays of execution to prisoners who bring up legal claims pertaining to their trials]: Again, we see people who have been on death row for many years wait until the last hour to raise claims. We've got to demand some changes at the Federal level that say a person only has a reasonable number of years after his trial to bring these claims. It's an abuse of justice to be questioning competency of counsel eight, 10, 12 years after the trials, when that issue was never raised [at the trial].

July 3/USA Today, 7-4:(A)3.

William W. Greenhalgh
Professor,
Georgetown University Law Center

5

[Criticizing proposals to do away with the exclusionary rule when police make a good-faith search]: All he [the law-enforcement officer] will have to do is say, "Gee, I thought I had sufficient probable cause." When you substitute subjectivity for objectivity, you can kiss the original understanding of the Fourth Amendment goodbye. They're

(WILLIAM W. GREENHALGH)

playing around with a concept that is not only mischievous but extremely dangerous.

The Washington Post, 9-17:(A)16.

Francis C. Hall
Commander, narcotics division,
New York City Police Department

1

The Federal government [anti-drug] effort has been a complete failure. I would rate it an F-plus. There is so much cocaine in New York City that you can buy it anywhere, even outside the [Catholic] Cardinal's residence on Madison Avenue.

At criminal-justice panel sponsored by
National Governors' Association, Hilton Head,
S.C., Aug. 25/The Washington Post, 8-26:(A)3.

Larry J. Hopkins
United States Representative,
R-Kentucky

2

I do not know how many states have the death penalty in our country, and I do not know how many people have been executed by these individual states, but I do know that not one of those persons has committed a single crime since then. So you be the judge as to whether or not the death penalty is a deterrent. I think that the record is very clear on that.

Before the House, Washington, Sept. 11/
The Washington Post, 9-16:(A)13.

Henry J. Hyde
United States Representative,
R-Illinois

3

[Calling for a loosening of the exclusionary rule in drug-trafficking cases]: If you really care about hitting drug trafficking where it hurts, never mind conferences, never mind scattering money as though it has bacteria on it. Do something substantial. Take that exclusionary rule, the criminal lawyer's best friend, and make it in-

applicable where a good-faith search and seizure has been made.

Before the House, Washington, Sept. 11/
The Washington Post, 9-16:(A)13.

Charles J. Hynes
New York State Special Prosecutor

4

[On police corruption]: You have to make people terrified of engaging in corruption. But until the day comes when police officers will turn in anybody who approaches them with a corrupt offer, you're always going to have a problem. There aren't a lot of lawyers who pick up the phone to report corrupt lawyers, or nurses or journalists who turn in their colleagues. But it's different for police officers. They're police officers. They've taken an oath to enforce the law. They have an obligation to be honest.

Interview/The New York Times, 11-10:15.

Arthur L. Kellermann
Assistant professor,
University of Tennessee, Memphis

5

The problem of firearms is not just a ghetto problem or a street problem. It's Ma and Pa America in their living-room getting in a fight and one of them picking up the family firearm. It's your next-door neighbor, in a fit of deep depression and possibly intoxicated, picking up a gun and ending his life. It's a problem we all share as Americans.

The Washington Post, 6-12:(A)3.

George L. Kelling
Research fellow, John F. Kennedy
School of Government, Harvard University

6

[Saying the first priority of the police is not to fight crime but to combat fear of crime in the community]: It's been a wholesale philosophical shift. You go back 15 years, ask police what their job is, and it's to fight crime. Now the function is to improve the quality of life . . . Fear can just gut a community. Fear debilitates cities

WHAT THEY SAID IN 1986

(GEORGE L. KELLING)

much more than serious crime. It's the signs of crime—disorderliness, etc.—that bother people and begin to undermine the normal community functioning.

Interview, Boston/
The Christian Science Monitor, 8-14:3.

Lane Kirkland
President, American
Federation of Labor-Congress
of Industrial Organizations

1

[On reports that organized crime has infiltrated labor unions]: If the labor movement is afflicted by racketeers, that points to a grievous failure by the law-enforcement authorities . . . Corruption and criminality are attributes of individuals, not of organizations.

March 7/The Christian Science Monitor, 3-10:7.

Edward I. Koch
Mayor of New York

2

[Saying illegal drug dealing should be subject to the death penalty]: What good does [just arresting dealers] do? You've got to take very drastic actions. Unless we do what I suggested, I do not believe we will ever have any major impact on the elimination of cocaine and heroin.

News conference/Los Angeles Times, 5-14:(I)2.

Eileen Luna
Director, International Association
for Civilian Oversight of Law Enforcement

3

The trend [for citizen review of police actions] is definitely up. Police officers are given far more power in this society than any other group. We [the people] give them that authority, that power, those weapons, but in return we expect them to wield that power in a way that is highly accountable to the public.

The Christian Science Monitor, 7-24:4.

Edwin Meese III
Attorney General of the United States

4

[On the use of the National Guard, and other forceful measures, to handle student anti-war protestors in California in the 1960s when he was involved as an official in the state government]: You couldn't allow sheer numbers of [protestors] to so overwhelm the system as to put it out of commission. It seemed to me there was a tremendous lack of gratitude and appreciation among the students for the benefits they had; this was an era of self-gratification and selfishness . . . I felt the same disgust as with other criminal behavior. The only difference was that these crimes were being committed by the most privileged people in our society.

Interview/
Esquire, July:83.

5

I would hope that ultimately we will reach a day when . . . the application of the "exclusionary rule" is unnecessary as a means of regulating police conduct and that it can thus be eliminated as an unneeded and undesirable interference with the truth-finding process that is inherent in the fair and impartial administration of justice.

At joint convention of U.S.
National District Attorneys Association
and Canadian prosecutors, Toronto/
The Washington Post, 8-7:(A)30.

6

To a large extent, the explosion of obscenity throughout our nation is the work of organized criminal enterprises that have taken over the large-scale production and distribution of obscenity on an interstate, multi-state and even international level . . . Victims of these crimes are plentiful—from the children exploited and molested, to the families destroyed by the sexual abuse of children and women, to the people intimidated by gangsters who line their pockets with profits from the manufacture and distribution of illegal obscenity.

News conference,
Washington, Oct. 22/
The Christian Science Monitor, 10-23:4.

James Mills
Author; Authority on
narcotics trafficking

1

[On the drug-trafficking problem]: The frustrating thing to me is that there is an answer. When you wait until the coca is made into cocaine, you can't stop it. Once the plants are harvested, and drugs are extracted from them, and they start their way toward a victim country like the U.S.A., then it becomes virtually impossible to stop them. It's like putting toothpaste back into a tube. The only ones who can do it are the local governments in those drug-producing countries, and they are the ones who are making all the money out of it.

Interview/USA Today, 7-8:(A)9.

2

[On the international drug-trafficking problem]: Our [U.S.] government has not wanted to come down on producing countries because, once you identify leaders of a foreign government as being criminals, you pretty well lose them as allies. You can no longer sit down with them and discuss trade agreements and military bases and political concerns. So, in order to maintain orderly foreign relations, we turn our back on the criminality of these nations, and of their leaders.

Interview/
USA Today, 7-8:(A)9.

Robert M. Morgenthau
District Attorney of Manhattan
(New York City)

3

We've got a serious drug problem here, and it's getting more serious day by day. We cannot cope with the level of drugs that is coming into the city at this time. Our citizens are angry and frustrated by the seeming inability of local law-enforcement officials to control narcotics trafficking. I share these emotions, although for different reasons. Once I thought we were treading water; now I feel we are drowning.

Los Angeles Times,
8-1:(I)1.

John J. Norton
Member, International Association
of Chiefs of Police

4

I have taken a stance supporting more effective handgun control. Specifically, I believe some citizens have the right to possess handguns—if they are competent in their use by training and knowledgeable in the legal aspects of their use. I believe that no felon, mentally disturbed person, drug or narcotic user, minor, infirmed person, or one incapable of accurately firing a handgun should be allowed to possess same; I feel that handgun owners should be as responsible for their weapons as they are for their automobiles. They should be required to keep them out of the hands of felons . . . I feel that a waiting period . . . is a valid restriction in the availability of handguns to first-time handgun owners . . . In this regard, law enforcement can and should do a better job of "screening" . . . prospective purchasers.

The Washington Post,
4-9:(A)22.

Nancy Reagan
Wife of President of the
United States Ronald Reagan

5

Today, there's a drug and alcohol abuse epidemic in this country, and no one is safe from it—not you, not me and certainly not our children, because this epidemic has their names written on it . . . There's no moral middle ground. Indifference is not an option. We want you to help us create an outspoken intolerance for drug abuse. For the sake of our children, I implore each of you to be unyielding and inflexible in your opposition to drugs. Our job is never easy because drug criminals are ingenious. For every door that we close, they open a new door to death. They prosper on our unwillingness to act. So we must be smarter and stronger and tougher than they are. It's up to us to change attitudes and just simply dry up their market.

Broadcast address to the
nation, Washington, Sept. 14/
The New York Times, 9-15:11.

Ronald Reagan
President of the United States

1

[On drug-abuse]: Our object is not to punish users but to help them, not to throw them in jail but to free them from dependency, not to ruin their lives by putting them behind bars but to prevent their lives from being ruined by drugs. Drug users can no longer excuse themselves by blaming society. The rest of us must be clear that, while we're sympathetic, we will no longer tolerate the use of illegal drugs by anyone.

To civic-group leaders, Washington,
July 30/The New York Times, 7-31:4.

Charles E. Schumer
United States Representative,
D-New York

2

[Opposing proposed drug-testing of Federal employees]: Trying to stop organized crime's multimillion-dollar drug business by creating a police state in Federal office buildings would be ineffective and would create one crime to stop another. Does this mean we're shifting away from going after crime syndicate kingpins and instead beginning to harass the average civil servant because he or she is easier to find?

March 4/The Washington Post, 3-5:(A)3.

3

The drug [abuse] boom is fueled by the demand of our children. Focusing on the supply side alone won't solve all drug problems. We must attack the demand side; we have to attack the ignorance that keeps demand sky high.

News conference, Washington, Aug. 5/
Los Angeles Times, 8-6:(I)13.

Larry Talley
Vice president of risk management,
Days Inns of America

4

[On companies that use lie detectors to screen employees for potential thieves]: Theft by employees is a tremendous drain on the American public, costing an estimated $40-billion a year—which is passed on to consumers in higher prices. In 1976, our company lost more than $1-million from employee theft. Since we started using the polygraph in 1977 as one of our loss-prevention tools, we've lost no more than $115,000 in a single year. Especially in the hotel, day-care and nursing-home industries, companies have been sued for hiring people who later committed crimes against a guest or a patient or someone in their care. If used properly, polygraphs help screen out such people.

Interview/U.S. News & World Report, 2-3:81.

Peter V. Ueberroth
Commissioner of Baseball

5

[The illegal-drug problem is] tearing this country apart . . . for future generations. If we declare war on the terrorists in Tripoli [Libya], when the hell are we going to declare war on terrorists bringing the [drug] poisons into our country? We seem to risk everything to stop these [Libyan] terrorists; but we seem to be unable to stop the terrorists who grow the drugs and the terrorists in this country who sell the drugs. We're not making the war on drugs a national priority.

At Congressional hearing, Washington,
May 7/USA Today, 5-8:(C)1.

William H. Webster
Director, Federal Bureau
of Investigation

6

The terrorist wins when he causes us to act totally from fear. The terrorist wins when he causes the government to act so repressively that it undermines confidence in government. The terrorist loses when citizens place their confidence in law enforcement and military defense mechanisms, when they go about their business in a prudent way, unaffected by the threats of terrorism and retaliation. [The terrorist also loses when] governments do their work quietly and effectively and without hyping the fear of the problem.

Before National District Attorneys
Association, Washington, May 6/
The Christian Science Monitor, 5-7:5.

(WILLIAM H. WEBSTER)

1

I came here [to the FBI] because I thought this institution was too important to lose. I was determined to see the institution viewed again as it had been in the past. We have been part of a post-Watergate period that included some very searching and at times devastating inquiries that affected not only us, but the other components of the intelligence community, and others in Federal law enforcement . . . We have a computer base of 12,000 qualified applicants for the FBI. They are coming in at 1,000 a month. They are coming in from major colleges and universities. They are coming in from the service academies, many already with decorations and achievements that are mind-boggling to me. And that's a good indication of how bright young people think of the FBI.

Interview, Washington/
The New York Times, 6-9:12.

2

[On the fight against drug trafficking]: There never has been a more mobilized effort by law enforcement at all levels, yet the price of cocaine is dropping and the supply rising. The most important contribution Congress made in the new anti-drug law was to appropriate hundreds of millions of dollars for drug prevention and treatment. We've got to bring down the demand for drugs. It's astonishing how much ignorance there is in key places. There's such a generation gap that parents could not accept until recently the idea of drugs in their children's schools because they hadn't experienced that during their childhood. Teachers are just as unaware, and

churches have taken no major steps.

Interview/U.S. News & World Report, 11-3:77.

Pat Williams
United States Representative,
D-Montana

3

[On the use of lie detectors by companies to screen employees for potential thieves]: They're convenient. They save employers money that otherwise would have to be spent creating good personnel practices and a good personnel department. It's a lot easier to give five dozen employees a lie-detector test than to do a good personnel check on them. There's a line in a song by the Western singer named Tom T. Hall: "If you hang 'em all, you'll get the guilty." Unfortunately, some American businesses have found that it's cheaper to hang them all than it is to really seek out the guilty.

Interview/
U.S. News & World Report, 2-3:81.

James Q. Wilson
Professor of government,
Harvard University

4

Crime statistics have so much noise in them and are responsive to so many random and unknown factors that year-to-year changes are almost meaningless. I think the only way to interpret city or national crime statistics is to take the figures for the last three years and plot them on a piece of paper and see if the line goes up, down or wiggles.

The New York Times, 5-24:9.

Defense • The Military

Morris B. Abram
Vice Chairman, United States
Commission on Civil Rights

1

There will be those who will say, dispense with anything but arms control. We must resist this and carry to the peace movement that if the Soviet Union is not trustworthy about [the human-rights accords of] Helsinki, then they are not trustworthy on arms.

Interview, Washington, Jan. 6/
The New York Times, 1-7:4.

Kenneth Adelman
Director, Arms Control and
Disarmament Agency of the United States

2

The history of arms control is a history of great visions eventually mugged by reality.

Newsweek, 12-1:37.

Les Aspin
United States Representative,
D-Wisconsin

3

[Criticizing President Reagan's opposition to Midgetman, a mobile single-warhead missile]: The President says "stability" every chance he gets. But does he know the meaning of the word? His proposed mobile ICBM ban rejects the only way on the books to protect these missiles, and suggests he does not. Maybe he does know what he's doing, but hasn't told us yet. Maybe he has an alternative to Midgetman and Soviet mobile ICBMs that will make the world more secure. Whatever the President has up his sleeve, I hope he'll tell us. Mr. Reagan can't sell his approach to the public, can't get the Congress to fund his buildup, and can't bargain effectively with [Soviet leader Mikhail] Gorbachev unless he's got a coherent policy to offer, tying together his strategic doctrine, forces and arms control. And for the moment, with his ban on mobile missiles,

how the pieces of the Reagan security puzzle fit together is a mystery to me.

Before World Affairs Council,
Feb. 12/The New York Times, 3-6:14.

4

[Calling for a reduction in military pensions after 20 years to discourage early retirement]: We want to encourage more people to serve longer. The current system has such generous benefits at the 20-year mark that it simply encourages them to get out at 20 years. In fact, there's a saying in the services that you're crazy to stay longer than 20 years because you're effectively working only for half pay after that.

News conference, Washington,
March 21/The New York Times, 3-22:8.

5

[On Reagan Administration criticism of the House Armed Services Committee's cut in the proposed defense budget]: We have a remarkably good defense budget, considering how much we had to take out due to Gramm-Rudman [Federal budget-balancing law]. I warned the Secretary of Defense and the President and anyone else who would listen that [Gramm-Rudman] would mean an unacceptable cut in the defense budget, but nobody was at home. They [the Administration] got themselves into this mess [by supporting Gramm-Rudman], but it's their own damned fault.

Washington, July 16/
The New York Times, 7-17:11.

6

[Criticizing the Reagan Administration for not consulting the Joint Chiefs of Staff on such matters as the secret U.S.-Iran arms deal and the U.S.-Soviet summit meeting in Iceland]: There has been a fundamental downgrading of the military in this consultation process. Everybody used to be scared of the Chiefs when it came to making arms proposals. I'm wondering what's happening to the Chiefs. They're not the players they once were. A Democratic Administration

(LES ASPIN)

wouldn't have dared treat them the way the right wing has treated them. It's just incredible what's happened.

Nov. 24/The Washington Post, 11-25:(A)14.

Thomas Barthelmey
United States delegate
to 40-nation disarmament
conference in Geneva

1

[On the U.S. decision to make public details of its chemical-weapons arsenal]: It is the hope of my delegation that the disclosure will encourage others, who have thus far manifested reluctance to accept prompt disclosure of stockpile locations, to show flexibility on this issue. Agreement on a chemical-weapons ban would be facilitated by confidence that the parties will comply with its provisions, and it would help build that confidence if the nation with the world's largest stockpile of chemical weapons, the Soviet Union, would be open and candid about possessing chemical-weapons stockpiles.

Geneva, July 10/
Los Angeles Times, 7-11:(I)4.

Aleksandr A. Bessmertnykh
Deputy Foreign Minister
of the Soviet Union

2

[Criticizing the U.S. decision not to be bound any more by the SALT II treaty]: The impact on the Geneva [arms-control] talks will be negative. It is difficult to believe in the sincerity of the other side's intent to seek new, far-reaching agreements when it violates the existing accords . . . The treaty represented a foundation on which it was possible to move forward with further reductions in strategic arms. Now this platform is being blown up.

News conference, Moscow, June 4/
The New York Times,
6-5:6.

Willy Brandt
Chairman, Social Democratic
Party of West Germany;
Former Chancellor of West Germany

3

This year a trillion dollars will be spent on arms [world-wide]. If just 5 per cent of that sum, or $50-billion, could be diverted into an aid fund, it would help the people in the developing world to emerge from at least a part of their misery. If that happened, a huge international plan could eliminate hunger in Africa. When I speak to young people, I sense that they feel as I do, that the present situation is unbearable. In a world where it is possible that people would no longer go hungry, the resources for this are instead wasted on needless arms.

Interview/World Press Review, January:14.

Harold Brown
Former Secretary of Defense
of the United States

4

[On being Secretary of Defense]: It's a taxing job . . . You need to be very close to the President. You need to have a common understanding as to what the nature of the task is . . . You need to be able to project at the same time to the uniformed military, which is another constituency, that you are a supporter but not an uncritical supporter, and indeed that you're in charge . . . You need to project to the Congress and to the public a correct image of knowledgeability, frankness and honesty. All of this gets harder as time goes by. And it is no accident that of the Secretaries of Defense who've stayed more than two years, almost all have either been fired by the President—or the American people—and/or have left with reputations somewhat clouded.

Interview/The Washington Post, 9-2:(A)17.

Patrick J. Buchanan
Director of Communications for the
President of the United States

5

[On President Reagan's recent meeting with Soviet leader Mikhail Gorbachev in Iceland]: From

WHAT THEY SAID IN 1986

(PATRICK J. BUCHANAN)

the early instant analysis [of the meeting in the U.S. press], all you got was that the summit collapsed because the President was intransigent on SDI [the proposed U.S. space defense system] . . . Basically, our story is this: The President made the most sweeping, far-reaching arms-control proposal in history. Gorbachev said "No." He made a non-negotiable demand that the President give up SDI and the President said "No." We do not believe it is a defeat for the U.S. when the President stands up and protects the national-security interests of the United States the way he did in Iceland.

Oct. 14/The New York Times, 10-15:7.

Joe Clark
Minister of External Affairs of Canada

1

[Criticizing the U.S. decision not to be bound any more by the constraints of the SALT II treaty]: We believe it is in the interests of arms control that the limits of SALT II be respected . . . It's premature to put it in a coffin until there's a corpse.

At NATO foreign ministers meeting, Halifax, Canada, May 30/The Washington Post, 5-31:(A)17.

John M. Collins
Senior military specialist,
Congressional Research Service

2

[In World War II, Korea and Vietnam,] I never looked up when I heard an aircraft and wondered whose it was—it was always ours. There is nothing more comforting to the guy on the ground than air superiority, not to mention air supremacy. We [the U.S.] have not got either any more.

The New York Times, 7-28:9.

Norman Cousins
Adjunct professor, School of Medicine,
University of California, Los Angeles;
Former editor, "Saturday Review"

3

The Number 1 problem in the world is not the presence of all this destructive weaponry—or the

emphasis on it and the organizations attached to it. That's the Number 2 problem. The Number 1 problem is the inability to recognize the Number 2 problem.

Interview, Beverly Hills, Calif./
The Christian Science Monitor, 11-12:28.

Dan Daniel
United States Representative,
D-Virginia

4

[The U.S. armed forces] for the last 40 years have concentrated on deterring nuclear conflict and the "big war" on the plains of Europe . . . We are well prepared for the least likely conflicts and poorly prepared for the most likely.

U.S. News & World Report, 11-3:42.

Thomas J. Downey
United States Representative,
D-New York

5

What the American people have been telling us is we want a strong defense, but we think we can have one—in fact, we know we can have one—by spending less money more wisely. Force-feeding the system [with money] has resulted in weapons systems that cost too much.

Before the House, Washington, May 15/
Los Angeles Times, 5-16:(I)1.

6

It is astonishing to see how the [Reagan] Administration is dropping the ball on national security. And it is even more astonishing to see how the pretense of interest in arms control is evaporating like the morning dew. For years, the Administration has been telling us it wants deep reductions in nuclear weapons. And it has been telling us how "Star Wars" [the proposed space defense system] is great bargaining leverage. So now the other side [the Soviets] says it wants to give us deep reductions in return for controls on "Star Wars." But the [Reagan] Administration says "nyet." So much for the pretense of deep reductions. It has been telling us it wants to move away from a world dominated by nuclear

(THOMAS J. DOWNEY)

weapons. So now the other side gives in to the policies of the past five Presidents and offers a comprehensive test-ban treaty on nuclear warheads. The other side even stops all [nuclear] testing for a year, unilaterally. But the [Reagan] Administration says "nyet." So much for the pretense of not liking nuclear weapons. Now comes the end to all pretense. Mr. Reagan says he wants to scrap SALT II. According to published intelligence estimates, this hands the Soviets another 5,000 nuclear warheads in the next decade alone. So much for the [Reagan Administration's] pretense of wanting to control nuclear weapons.

Before the House, Washington, June 4/
The New York Times, 6-7:7.

Alain C. Enthoven

Professor of public and private
management, Graduate School of Business,
Stanford University; Former adviser to the
Department of Defense of the United States

1

There is a widespread belief that, when in doubt, the safest thing is to over-estimate the enemy's strength. And yet, in this case, the over-estimation of Russian strength is counter-productive, because that's the reason we haven't increased the size, strength and readiness of our conventional [non-nuclear] forces. People believe the situation is hopeless because they've greatly over-stated the size of the Russian forces. Moreover, some people think that over-estimating the enemy is good because it's a way of getting more [U.S.] forces. And many people believe that if I'm saying the Russians aren't so big, it must be that I'm trying to disarm America. That is just wrong. I personally believed then, and still believe, that the Russians are extremely dangerous. They're a real menace to us and to our European allies. In fact, paradoxically, that's one of the costs of over-estimating them—they have more intimidating power if we over-estimate them. I think one of the reasons that [the late Soviet leader Nikita] Khrushchev, in 1961, was able to be so belligerent in the United Nations, and toward [the late U.S. President John Kennedy] and

so forth, leading up to the Cuban missile crisis, is that he perceived that we felt ourselves weak. And we felt ourselves weak because we were overestimating the Russians. I'm all in favor of a very strong national defense; I'm not particularly interested in seeing us cut defense spending now, but in seeing that we spend the money wisely and make decisions based on accurate information.

Interview/American Heritage, Feb.-Mar.:98.

Valentin Falin

Director, Novosti Press Agency
(Soviet Union); Former Soviet
Ambassador to West Germany

2

[Criticizing U.S. plans to abandon the limits set forth in the SALT II treaty]: As far as SALT is concerned, I don't know what we [Soviets] can do to satisfy the Americans—perhaps we should become the 51st state? Even if we should say we are ready to destroy all our missiles, the Americans would say, "Okay, that's fine," and then demand this or that additional step. What we are experiencing is a deterioration, and a premeditated deterioration, in the situation. We have reached the limits of our possibilities. There is no more room for one-sided concessions.

To journalists, Bonn, West Germany,
May 30/The New York Times, 5-31:2.

Thomas S. Foley

United States Representative,
D-Washington

3

[On President Reagan wanting a balanced budget but not wanting a cut in defense spending]: It's the same as saying you like the opera; you just don't like people dressing up and singing.

USA Today, 7-16:(A)4.

Norman Friedman

Authority on naval matters

4

When you use a [aircraft] carrier, you can operate unilaterally. The attitude of our allies shows that this capability is very valuable . . .

WHAT THEY SAID IN 1986

(NORMAN FRIEDMAN)

It's quite clear that, with the carriers we have, we are hard pressed to put up two in the Mediterranean. If you have a world with constant peacetime tensions, you need a large number of carriers.

The New York Times, 5-6:1,11.

J. William Fulbright
Former United States Senator,
D-Arkansas

1

At the beginning of U.S.-Soviet detente, we were much more powerful than they were. The Russians were determined to try to equalize. It's true the Russians sought to acquire parity. But so what? Did you expect the world to accept permanently, without doing anything about it, the superiority of the United States in the possession of weapons?

Interview/USA Today, 8-1:(A)9.

Frank J. Gaffney, Jr.
Deputy Assistant Secretary of
Defense of the United States

2

[Arguing against a moratorium on U.S. underground nuclear-weapons tests, saying they are important for checking and maintaining the reliability of such weapons]: Over one-third of all nuclear designs put into the U.S. stockpile since 1958, after what was considered to be adequate testing, required post-developmental testing to fix unexpected problems and restore confidence in the reliability of those weapons. The only way to have confidence [that] you really understand the vulnerability of these weapons is by exposing them to such effects from a nuclear-weapon assault.

Pentagon briefing, Washington, Sept. 24/
The Washington Post, 9-25:(A)31.

Barry M. Goldwater
United States Senator, R-Arizona

3

We are cutting too much from defense. Now, let's not kid ourselves. Anyone who thinks we can go on cutting the defense budget—to the point where we actually have declining growth rates of more than 3 per cent a year—without undermining our defense posture is indulging in a happy but unrealistic delusion. I have a terrible sense that we are returning to the irresponsible policies of the late 1970s.

Los Angeles Times, 10-16:(I)20.

4

I maintain . . . that the way to stay at peace in this world is to have a force so competent, so skilled and so strong that no other country or combination of countries will ever dare do anything to upset us. And I am proud to stand here today . . . and say that never in my life have I known such a high quality of enlisted men and officers as we have now.

At Pentagon ceremony honoring him,
Dec. 10/Los Angeles Times, 12-11:(I)28.

Mikhail S. Gorbachev
General Secretary, Communist
Party of the Soviet Union

5

[Proposing that his country and the U.S. should begin eliminating their nuclear weapons]: We propose that we should enter the third millennium without nuclear weapons, on the basis of mutually acceptable and strictly verifiable agreements. If the United States Administration is indeed committed to the goal of complete elimination of nuclear weapons everywhere, as it has repeatedly stated, it is being offered a practical opportunity to begin this in practice. Instead of wasting the next 10 to 15 years by developing new, extremely dangerous weapons in space . . . would it not be more sensible to start eliminating these arms and finally bring them down to zero? . . . It is absolutely clear to any unbiased person that if such a program is implemented, nobody would lose and everybody stands to gain. The sooner this program is translated into practical deeds, the safer will be life on our planet. It is time to abandon the thinking of the Stone Age, when the chief concern was to have a bigger stick or a heavier stone.

News broadcast, Moscow, Jan. 15/
Los Angeles Times, 1-16:(I)1,14.

(MIKHAIL S. GORBACHEV)

1

Since last summer we have been calling upon the United States to follow our example and stop nuclear explosions [testing]. Washington has not yet done that despite protests and demands on the part of the public, and contrary to the will of most states in the world. By carrying out more and more nuclear explosions, the U.S. side continues to pursue its elusive dream of achieving military superiority. This policy is futile and dangerous, a policy which is not worthy of the level of civilization that modern society has attained.

News broadcast, Moscow, Jan. 15*/
The New York Times, 2-5:5.

2

The cause of disarmament has not been advanced by a single millimeter because of the American Administration's open obstruction. Worse, Washington is destroying the remaining constraints containing the arms race—the SALT II treaty and other Soviet-American agreements. American officials are not short on eloquent statements about their desire for peace and disarmament, but they are doing just the opposite. We say to the West: Take seriously our proposal for the elimination of medium-range nuclear missiles, take seriously the proposal for the reduction of conventional armaments, and the possibility of easing tensions on the [European] continent will rise.

At Polish Communist
Party Congress, Warsaw, June 30/
The New York Times, 7-1:1.

3

[Saying the Soviet Union is extending its nuclear test moratorium until next January 1, and calling on the U.S. to join]: The Soviet Union has sufficient reasons for resuming its nuclear testing, yet we are convinced even now that the ending of nuclear testing, not only by the Soviet Union but also by the United States, would be a real breakthrough to arresting the nuclear arms race. The logic in this is simple: If there are no tests, the nuclear weapons, which both sides have stockpiled in abundance, will not be upgraded . . . Today it is simply suicidal to build

interstate relations on the illusion of attaining superiority in terrible means of destruction. Experts have estimated the explosion of the smallest nuclear warhead is equal in radioactivity to three Chernobyls [the Soviet nuclear power plant that recently experienced a serious radiation-emitting accident]. And if someone still dares to make a first nuclear strike, he will doom himself to agonizing death—not from a retaliatory strike but from the consequences of the explosion of his own warheads . . . On behalf of the Soviet people, I am appealing to the wisdom and dignity of the Americans not to miss another historical chance on the way to ending the weapons race.

Broadcast address to the nation, Moscow,
Aug. 18/Los Angeles Times, 8-19:(I)8.

4

[Criticizing SDI, the proposed U.S. space defense system]: I say this with confidence, since it is irresponsible to bluff in such matters: There will be a [Soviet] reply to SDI. An asymmetrical reply, but there will be a reply. And we shall not sacrifice much at that. But what is its danger? For one thing, there is a political danger. A situation is created right away that brings uncertainty and stirs up mistrust and suspicion of each other. Then the reduction of nuclear weapons will be put aside. In short, quite another situation is needed for us to take up thoroughly the question of reducing nuclear weapons. Second, there is a military aspect after all. The SDI can lead to new types of weapons. We also can say this with competence: It can lead to an entirely new stage of the arms race with serious, unpredictable consequences.

News conference, Reykjavik, Iceland,
Oct. 12/The Washington Post, 10-23:(A)22.

5

[Criticizing the proposed U.S. space defense system]: The SDI has become an obstacle to ending the arms race, to getting rid of nuclear weapons, and is the main obstacle to a nuclear-free world. When Mr. [George] Shultz, U.S. Secretary of State, tells the American people that the SDI is a sort of "insurance policy" for America, this is, to say the least, an attempt at misleading the American people. In actual fact,

WHAT THEY SAID IN 1986

(MIKHAIL S. GORBACHEV)

the SDI does not strengthen America's security but, by opening up a new stage of the arms race, destabilizes the military-political situation and thereby weakens both the United States security and universal [security].

Broadcast address to the nation, Moscow,
Oct. 22/The New York Times, 10-23:4.

Albert Gore, Jr.
United States Senator, D-Tennessee

1

The President [Reagan] has repeatedly assured the nation that SDI [the proposed space defense system] can be pursued without damage to existing arms-control agreements, and without prejudicing chances for agreements in the future. After all, it is only a research program, we are told. And yet, it is a curious and disquieting fact that SDI's most vehement supporters are veteran opponents of arms control. What is involved here is a conviction on their part that the United States-Soviet struggle will never yield to negotiations because the Soviet Union's underlying motives will not change. From this perspective, it is not in the U.S. interest to codify strategic nuclear equality, let alone stability, but, rather, to concentrate on recapturing our former nuclear dominance. And since the public will not support unlimited new deployments of strategic weapons, there must be another way: SDI. Not the President's SDI, of course, but the "real" SDI, whose most dedicated supporters mince no words. They want a major increase in U.S. hard-target forces, and they want those forces to be protected by some quick-and-dirty version of SDI.

The Washington Post, 5-20:(A)18.

Andrei A. Gromyko
President of the Soviet Union

2

[Criticizing the U.S. decision not to be bound by the limits of the SALT II treaty]: SALT II has been death blow after blow. The latest blow has a high explosive charge under it. This is undoubt-

edly a major blunder. We do not believe the American people want to bury this treaty. We make a distinction between the American people and the politicians.

To British lawmakers, Moscow,
June 2/The New York Times, 6-3:7.

Gary Hart
United States Senator, D-Colorado

3

A lot of money has been spent on the Pentagon without very much effect. The issue for the military—strength—is not measured by dollars . . . Strength is measured by effectiveness in combat, and there are very strong indications from recent history that we are not doing well in combat . . . In part because we are not buying the right kinds of weapons, because we're not training our troops properly, and because we're not pursuing the right kinds of tactics and doctrines—non-budgetary questions . . . The world changed, and we didn't change with it. In World War I and World War II, we were facing very easily identifiable nation-states—Germany, Japan. Since then, whether in Korea or Vietnam or guerrilla wars, we're not fighting states so much as we are fighting ideologies—and the kinds of weaponry we have and the way we fight have not adapted very well. We clearly were militarily superior in Vietnam, but we lost. So somebody ought to be asking themselves why? And no one in the Pentagon's asking themselves why, because they don't want to think that the world is changing.

Interview/USA Today, 5-8:(A)11.

4

As we pursue deep reductions in first-strike nuclear arsenals, we should make far greater use of asymmetrical agreements [with the Soviet Union]—asymmetrical, not in the benefit of each nation, but in the nature of weapons exchanged. The Soviets must agree to substantial cuts in offensive weapons, particularly their large ICBMs. We should agree to set limits on the testing and deployment of defensive systems.

At Georgetown School of Foreign
Service, Washington, June 11/
The Washington Post, 6-12:(A)9.

P. X. Kelley
Commandant, United States
Marine Corps

1

[Criticizing a Senate bill that would reorganize the armed forces, including giving the Chairman of the Joint Chiefs of Staff more power and authority over the services and the other Joint Chiefs]: If the draft bill were to be enacted in its current form, it would result in a significant degradation in the efficiency and effectiveness of the defense establishment—to the point where I would have deep concerns for the future security of the United States. In this regard, I know of no document which has concerned me more in my 36 years of uniformed service to my country.

Letter submitted to Senate Armed Services
Committee/The Washington Post, 3-7:(A)4.

Jack Kemp
United States Representative,
D-New York

2

[Supporting the proposed U.S. space defense system]: How do we threaten the Soviet Union by defending the United States? What is wrong with a defense that can save our lives and not kill a single Russian? It is preposterous for Soviet scientists, who have been feverishly working on their defense technologies for two decades, to condemn our SDI program in its infancy, lest it become "provocative and destabilizing" . . . This is the core question: to deploy or not to deploy. It is, I believe, the single most important national-security decision of the Reagan Presidency. I am convinced we must not only research, test and develop SDI, we must deploy it as soon as possible.

At Heritage Foundation, Oct. 8/
The Washington Post, 10-15:(A)18.

Donald M. Kendall
Chairman, PepsiCo, Inc.

3

We're throwing too much money at [defense]. The various military services are going up as though each one of them were going off to fight

the war themselves. Both the Soviet Union and the United States should be cutting back. What won World War II was our industrial economy. We can't destroy our industrial economy by spending so much money, creating so much debt that we have an economic crisis in this country. We've got social obligations that we have to take care of. We can't continue to spend money the way we have spent it on defense.

Interview/USA Today, 4-21:(A)13.

Edward M. Kennedy
United States Senator,
D-Massachusetts

4

[Criticizing President Reagan's decision not to be bound by the limits of SALT II]: The President's decision to repudiate the SALT II agreement is a triumph of ideology over common sense. The rabid right is spoiling for a new escalation of the arms race against the Soviet Union, and now their unrelenting, systematic anti-SALT campaign has finally won the acquiescence of the President.

Washington, June 2/
Los Angeles Times, 6-3:(I)16.

Neil Kinnock
Leader, Labor Party of Britain

5

For 26 or more years, I've had a moral conviction opposed to nuclear weapons. Ten years ago, it was necessary to dwell on the moral case, but the horror of Chernobyl [the recent Soviet nuclear power plant disaster] has made the moral argument less necessary.

Los Angeles Times, 11-29:(I)5.

Wayne Knudson
Brigadier General and
Director of Requirements,
United States Army

6

If you want a highly strategically deployable [infantry] force, you must give them the tools to meet a reasonably sophisticated enemy who is probably going to have some pretty well-heeled

(WAYNE KNUDSON)

armor protection on his primary combat systems. Unless we get something credible for our infantry, it's not going to play vitally in a future confrontation where modern-class tanks are to be attacked.

The Washington Post, 1-13:(A)8.

Helmut Kohl
Chancellor of West Germany

1

[Criticizing the Soviet handling of information about the recent nuclear power plant accident at Chernobyl in the U.S.S.R]: The Soviet leadership, in a completely inexplicable manner, elevated mistrust in the entire world by its information blockade. A major part of the problems we encounter in arms-control talks is that of verification, that is, the ability to confirm that disarmament is taking place. The Soviet side, since Chernobyl, has not reduced the West's concerns about verification, but rather increased them significantly.

Interview, Bonn, May 26/
The Washington Post, 5-30:(A)28.

2

[On U.S.-Soviet arms-control talks]: In Moscow you had one school of thinking that said, "Let's wait until after [U.S. President] Reagan is gone and we have a new President." I kept telling people from the Soviet Union that this is a foolish idea and that you should negotiate with this current President for two reasons: First, if you wait for the next President, you'll have lost time. Secondly, I told them that they should negotiate with a strong President. Whether or not you like the President, he is seen by the Americans as a man who will not just give away American interests. And that's very important.

Interview, Bonn, West Germany/
Newsweek, 10-27:25.

Robert W. Komer
Former Under Secretary of
Defense of the United States

3

[Saying the recent U.S. raid on Libya did not prove the general desirability of having aircraft

carriers]: In Libya, you are attacking a fourth-class target. It was not much of a test. Aircraft carriers are splendid for little wars; they are just not very good against Russia.

The New York Times, 5-6:11.

Curtis LeMay
General (ret.) and former Chief
of Staff, United States Air Force

4

[On whether nuclear war could be accidentally started by a computer mistake]: No. There have been a lot of movies made about that and, believe it or not, a Senator came up here to talk to me once. He asked if [then-] President Nixon were insane, could he start a war? Now, this was a Senator. There are so many built-in safeguards in this thing that my worry is, if we really wanted to start a real war, could we make it go? That's a little exaggeration, but that's my worry, more than if someone would go insane and start a war. That's impossible.

Interview/USA Today, 7-23:(A)9.

Richard G. Lugar
United States Senator, R-Indiana

5

[On President Reagan's proposal for a space defense system]: Most Europeans have been careful to draw a distinction between support for SDI research, in which they want to participate for economic and technical reasons, and post-research development and deployment phases of SDI, to which, at this point, they do not want to tie their political and security interests. While this cautious reaction is certainly understandable, it could give rise to an American perception of a rather "mercenary" approach to SDI . . . wherein allies desire to share in financial and technological benefits but none of the risks.

U.S. News & World Report, 1-20:28.

James A. Lyons, Jr.
Admiral and Commander-in-Chief
of the Pacific Fleet, United States Navy

6

[Former Congressman] Carl Vinson once said the most expensive thing in the world is a

(JAMES A. LYONS, JR.)

cheap Army and Navy. Weakness invites attack. I know the defense budget is under attack, but remember we suffered a 20 per cent decline in our budget during the 1970s. We're experiencing a repair job, not a buildup.

Interview/Los Angeles Times Magazine, 8-10:25.

Edward J. Markey
United States Representative,
D-Massachusetts

1

[Criticizing the Reagan Administration for not implementing a nuclear-weapons test moratorium to match the current Soviet moratorium]: Since the signing of the Nuclear Non-Proliferation Treaty in 1968, United States policy has been that the negotiation of a test ban would serve United States security interests by strengthening efforts to prevent nuclear proliferation. The Reagan Administration has turned that policy on its head. Apparently their visceral distaste for a comprehensive test ban is so great that they feel compelled to argue that a test ban will actually encourage proliferation. I have yet to see one shred of evidence that supports this patently ridiculous and Orwellian contention.

The New York Times, 4-22:3.

Sanford N. McDonnell
Chairman, McDonnell Douglas Corporation

2

[On reports of defense industry over-charging the Pentagon, such as the widely reported $435 hammer]: The $435 hammer wasn't really $435; it was $22. On the same invoice was engineering services for $413, entirely unrelated to the hammer. Now you say, $22 is pretty expensive for a hammer, but it wasn't $435. The press has given the impression that this is rampant throughout the industry, and that we're all a bunch of crooks waking up in the middle of the night thinking, "What can we get out of the Defense Department?" . . . Where the main potential payoff in savings is [is] in changing this unbelievably over-managed, over-controlled, over-regulated industry that we're in . . . The system is flawed,

and it needs to be overhauled—and I mean a major overhaul. I can say without hesitation that with a change in the system, 10 or 15 per cent worth of savings could be realized easily. And that's a big number.

Interview/USA Today, 5-27:(A)11.

Robert S. McNamara
Former Secretary of Defense of the United
States; Former President, International
Bank for Reconstruction and Development
(World Bank)

3

I think it's extremely dangerous to carry on our present [nuclear] strategy and our present weapons-development programs, in the direction they're headed, for another 40 years . . . We are in a world with 50,000 nuclear warheads—each one, on average, some 30 times the destructive power of that dropped on Hiroshima and Nagasaki. War plans covering their use are in existence—and there is, in effect, a mindset that would assure their use in the event of confrontation between East and West. And yet, no plan exists for initiating the use of nuclear weapons without the probable destruction of the civilization in the initiator.

Interview, New York/
The Christian Science Monitor, 12-16:20.

Seymour Melman
Professor of industrial engineering,
Columbia University

4

[Saying that military spending lowers the country's standard of living by diverting funds that could be used for consumer goods]: The nuclear submarine is marvelous, technologically. But you can't live in it, you can't consume it, and you can't make anything with it.

Newsweek, 3-24:52.

Richard M. Nixon
Former President of the United States

5

You've got our hawks who say [military] superiority is the answer. Not possible. Never go-

65

(RICHARD M. NIXON)

ing to happen. You've got others who say we will make nuclear weapons obsolete by substituting SDI [the proposed space defense system] for deterrents. I don't say it's not possible, but it's not until the next century, far into the next century. What must be avoided . . . is the broad, general statements that what we are searching for is a way to make nuclear war obsolete. I wish it were possible, but it is not going to happen.

Interview, Saddle River, N.J./Newsweek, 5-19:33.

Sam Nunn
United States Senator,
D-Georgia

1

[On the continuing confrontation between President Reagan and Congress on the defense budget]: The best case would be a flat defense budget protected for inflation—that's the best case I see for the next three years. Every year that the President lets go by without having a meeting of the minds . . . on how we're going to meet the [Federal] deficit totals, the defense budget is going to suffer more.

The Christian Science Monitor, 5-22:5.

2

[Criticizing the proposed U.S. space defense system]: The way a lot of well-meaning right-wingers describe it, is sort of like a candy store: We have that thing [the SDI] sitting there on the shelf, and all we have to do is pull it off and we can go out there and destroy all the Soviet missiles . . . We're going to be 10 to 15 years away from deciding whether the program will work. Then, we've got to decide whether it is cost-effective.

Washington, Oct. 13/
Los Angeles Times, 10-14:(I)10.

3

[Criticizing reported discussions between President Reagan and Soviet leader Mikhail Gorbachev about totally eliminating nuclear weapons]: If I were a Soviet General and were told that nuclear weapons were out of the pic-

ture, I would say, "Comrade, we would be in a dominant position in the world." We don't want to make the world safe for a massive conventional war.

U.S. News & World Report, 10-27:26.

4

[Criticizing President Reagan's decision to exceed the limits of SALT II]: I believe the President's decision . . . gives the Soviet Union a military advantage, with its near-term missile-production capabilities, as well as a substantial world propaganda advantage. It will cause our allies abroad considerable political discomfort, and it will now be much harder to reach a bipartisan consensus on strategic weapons and arms control here at home.

Nov. 28/The Washington Post, 11-29:(A)2.

David Packard
Chairman, President's Blue Ribbon Commission on Defense Management; Former Deputy Secretary of Defense of the United States

5

Our military forces are stronger today, and their spirit is higher. But there's no question that, because of long-term structural problems, we've wasted tens of billions of dollars out of the more than a trillion that's been spent. We think the American people deserve a better return for their money. With respect to weapons procurement alone, we start from a basic premise that here you have what's probably the largest management job in the world, and you don't really have anybody in charge of it. That's why we're recommending that a new post be established at the Number 2 level in the Pentagon for an under secretary who would have sole responsibility for acquisition.

Interview/U.S. News & World Report, 3-10:24.

Olof Palme
Prime Minister of Sweden

6

[On his campaign for nuclear disarmament]: To those who tell us we should mind our own business, I say: If the superpowers fight a nuclear war, we, too, will be wiped out. They won't con-

(OLOF PALME)

fine the war's consequences to their territories and to their people. Our security is involved and we have a right and a duty to speak out . . . The search for security [through arms] leads to even greater insecurity. We believe that security can only mean collective security. This means that a truly universal process of disarmament in both nuclear and conventional weapons must get started.

Interview, Stockholm/
The Christian Science Monitor, 2-27:11.

Linus Pauling
Winner, 1954 Nobel Prize in chemistry;
Winner, 1962 Nobel Peace Prize

1

[On the Reagan Administration's proposed space defense system]: I don't know any good, experienced scientist or physicist who thinks that there is any real chance of developing a 100 per cent-effective defense against a nuclear attack. If you do succeed in developing a system that would shoot down 95 per cent of incoming weapons, it is far cheaper for the Soviet Union to double the scale of the attack than it is to provide a defense. Laser beams, particle beams—this is just science fiction.

Interview/USA Today, 3-11:(A)7.

Javier Perez de Cuellar
Secretary General of the United Nations

2

[On the proposed U.S. space defense system]: SDI evidently is a defensive shield, but . . . the negative aspect is that the opposite side will try to find ways of making this device useless, which means they will have to develop their technology to create weapons which will defeat such a shield. It's a kind of—if you remember during the war—the famous Maginot Line, where the French spent lots of money on the Maginot Line and the Germans found a way of bypassing it through Belgium.

United Nations, New York, Oct. 14/
The Washington Post, 10-15:(A)25.

William Proxmire
United States Senator, D-Wisconsin

3

Barring women from combat has resulted in complex and arbitrary restrictions that limit our military flexibility. At the present time, each branch of the military has elaborate determinations for which specific assignments have high combat probability. These designations often change depending on the world situation, so that in the Navy, for example, all assignments of women to ships in the 6th and 7th fleets must be approved by the fleet commander. The fleet commander must review each case and use available intelligence resources to determine the likelihood of combat. Such time-consuming judgment calls may be manageable during peacetime, but they would be impossible in the crush of a war situation . . . Women soldiers make up roughly 10 per cent of our armed forces and are well integrated throughout. To keep tabs on all of them and try to restrict them from forward battle positions would not only be difficult, it would limit our flexibility and deprive the front line of skilled female specialists . . . The fact is that we cannot afford to encumber our military commanders with combat restrictions that affect a large fraction of their troops. We must open up our combat billets to all qualified soldiers in order to maximize our flexibility.

March 21/The Washington Post, 3-25:(A)16.

4

In peace or war, military procurement has never been efficient. It has never been truly competitive. It has consistently had one sure and predictable element: The cost rises.

The Washington Post,
4-17:(A)18.

Jean-Bernard Raimond
Foreign Minister of France

5

The human race has no vision of any alternative to nuclear deterrence. It has served the cause of peace well and should therefore continue to guarantee the security of our continent.

Time, 11-17:61.

67

WHAT THEY SAID IN 1986

Johannes Rau
Premier of North Rhine-Westphalia,
West Germany

1

This opinion that one could first begin with conventional weapons and then bring in A-weapons, this I consider highly dangerous . . . and I can only say that the only possibility for dealing with nuclear weapons is not to use them. And statesmen have always maintained this: It's a purely political weapon.

Interview, Dusseldorf, West Germany/
The Christian Science Monitor, 8-8:8.

Ronald Reagan
President of the United States

2

Millions of Americans actually believe we are now superior to the Soviet Union in military power. Well, I'm sorry, but if our country is going to have a useful debate on national security, we have to get beyond the drumbeat of propaganda and get the facts on the table . . . It is not just the immense Soviet arsenal that puts us on our guard. The record of Soviet behavior—the long history of Soviet brutality toward those who are weaker—remind us that the only guarantee of peace and freedom is our military strength and our national will . . . Let's maintain that crucial level of national strength, unity and purpose that has brought the Soviet Union to the negotiating table, and has given us this historic opportunity to achieve real reductions in nuclear weapons and a real chance at lasting peace. That would be the finest legacy we could leave behind—for our children and their children.

Broadcast address to the nation, Washington,
Feb. 26/The Washington Post, 2-27:(A)1,11.

3

George Washington's words may seem hard and cold today, but history has proven him right again and again: To be prepared for war, he said, is one of the most effective means of preserving peace. The past five years have shown that American strength is once again a sheltering arm for freedom in a dangerous world. Strength is the most persuasive argument we have to convince

our adversaries to negotiate seriously and to cease bullying other nations. But tonight, the security program that you and I launched to restore America's strength is in jeopardy—threatened by those who would quit before the job is done. Our adversaries, the Soviets—we know from painful experience—respect only nations that negotiate from a position of strength. American power is the indispensable element of a peaceful world—it is America's last, best hope of negotiating real reductions in nuclear arms. Just as we are sitting down at the bargaining table with the Soviet Union, let's not throw America's trump card away.

Broadcast address to the nation,
Washington, Feb. 26/USA Today, 2-27:(A)9.

4

Those who speak so often about the so-called arms race ignore a central fact. In the decade before 1981, the Soviets were the only ones racing.

Broadcast address to the nation,
Washington, Feb. 26/Los Angeles Times, 2-27:(I)14.

5

During the last decade, our government, paralyzed by uncertainty, permitted our defenses to erode and ignored a growing totalitarian threat. But the failures of the last decade should have taught us something. Crossing our fingers and hoping for the best is not the way to insure a more peaceful world. Peace through strength is a fact of life, and it's about time for America to leave uncertainty and indecision behind. It is time to grow up and face reality.

At Republican luncheon, New Orleans,
March 27/The New York Times, 3-28:3.

6

[On the U.S. soldiers who fought in the Vietnam war]: It was the unpampered boys of the working class who picked up the rifles and went on the march. They learned not to rely on us [at home]. They learned to rely on each other . . . They chose to be faithful. They chose to reject the fashionable skepticism of their time. They chose to believe and answer the call of duty. They had the wild, wild courage of youth. They seized certainty from the heart of an ambivalent age. They stood for something. And we owe

(RONALD REAGAN)

them something . . . first, a promise that, as they did not forget their missing comrades, neither ever will we.

Memorial Day address, Washington,
May 26/Los Angeles Times, 5-27:(I)6.

1

Some people will argue that strategic forces must take cuts along with everything else when budgets are tight. Those "spread the pain" theories are not only false, they are dangerous. Every dollar taken from our strategic programs is a victory for potential aggressors. Every cut or delay weakens our cause in [the arms-control talks in] Geneva and adds materially to the ultimate cost of deterrence.

Message to Congress, Washington,
June 3*/The New York Times, 6-4:6.

2

[Saying the U.S. will not be bound in the future by limitations of the SALT II treaty]: . . . this treaty was signed seven years ago, was never ratified . . . For seven years there was supposed to have been this restraint and . . . this observance of the treaty's terms. And for seven years this country has been doing that. The Soviet regime, for seven years, has been violating the restraints of the treaty . . . We're not seeking to achieve superiority over [the Soviets] but we're certainly not going to let them go on increasing their superiority over us . . . The treaty was really nothing but the legitimizing of an arms race. It didn't do anything to reduce nuclear weapons or the nuclear threat. All it did was regulate how fast and how much we could continue increasing the number of weapons. So I was always hostile to that particular treaty because it did not reduce weapons . . . We will observe the constraints to the same extent that the Soviet Union does, but we can't go on unilaterally observing this while they take off on their own with the violations that they've already made and probably more to come.

News conference, Washington, June 11/
The New York Times,
6-12:10.

3

Surely no man can have a greater goal than that of protecting the next generation against the destruction and pain of warfare that his own generation has known. There can therefore be no more important task before us than that of reducing nuclear weapons. I am committed—utterly committed—to pursuing every opportunity to discuss and explore ways to achieve real and verifiable arms reductions. What [the U.S. and the Soviet Union] do now in arms control will determine the kind of future that you—and, yes, your children and your children's children—will face.

Before graduating class of Glassboro (N.J.)
High School, June 19/The New York Times, 6-20:6.

4

[On his SDI space defense system proposal]: . . . there's one thing about SDI that I think all of us should look at. First of all, research is not violating any agreements or treaties. If research develops that there is such a weapon, wouldn't that be . . . a practical reason then to say to all the world, here it is and why don't we have this? . . . The world cannot forget that it knows how to make a ballistic missile. And, someday, there could be another madman . . . But if you've got this [SDI] and it's practical, then you can all go to sleep and rest easy at night, knowing that if somebody tries to cheat, it won't work because you have that system.

Interview, June 23/
Los Angeles Times, 6-24:(I)19.

5

. . . the United States has long urged radical, equitable, verifiable reductions in these offensive [nuclear weapons] systems. Note that I said reduction, for this is the real purpose of arms control—not just to codify the levels of today's arsenals, not just to channel their further expansion, but to reduce them, in ways that will reduce the danger of war. Indeed, the United States believes the prospect of a future without such weapons of mass destruction must be the ultimate goal of arms control.

At United Nations,
New York, Sept. 22/
The Washington Post, 9-23:(A)16.

WHAT THEY SAID IN 1986

(RONALD REAGAN)

1

[On the proposed U.S. space defense system]: SDI is America's security guarantee—if the Soviets should, as they have done too often in the past, fail to comply with their solemn commitments. SDI is what brought the Soviets back to arms-control talks at Geneva and Iceland. SDI is the key to a world without nuclear weapons. The Soviets understand this. They have devoted far more resources for a lot longer time than we to their own SDI. The world's only operational missile defense today surrounds Moscow, the capital of the Soviet Union . . . How does a defense of the United States threaten the Soviet Union or anyone else? Why are the Soviets so adamant that America [give up SDI and] remain forever vulnerable to Soviet rocket attack? As of today, all free nations are utterly defenseless against Soviet missiles—fired either by accident or design. Why does the Soviet Union insist that we remain so—forever?

Broadcast address to the nation, Washington,
Oct. 13/Los Angeles Times, 10-14:(I)5.

2

[On his recent arms-control meeting in Iceland with Soviet leader Mikhail Gorbachev]: I could see in Reykjavik that it came down to SDI [the proposed U.S. space defense system]. I made a proposal to [Gorbachev] that if we got the SDI shield then, with the Soviet Union sharing that, we could eventually sign a treaty to eliminate all ballistic missiles. But by the way he was hassling me, I could see he was trying to find a way to sink SDI. I tried everything I could think of, even a little Russian, an old Russian proverb that means "trust but verify." All the chips were on SDI. The restrictions that [Gorbachev] wanted would kill SDI. At the last, there were two places in the wording of the agreement that were left open. All of a sudden he is interrupting, and he says, "Why just ballistic missiles? What would you say if we included all of them, bombs, artillery shells, everything?" And I said, "Okay, we'll talk about everything, we can do that." But then he came back to SDI, and that was the end.

Interview/Time, 11-10:21.

Charles S. Robb
Chairman, Democratic (Party)
Leadership Council; Former
Governor of Virginia (D)

3

[As] a Marine Corps veteran, I believe America has to be strong enough to defend our basic values and our freedom. But money alone won't make us strong. It's time to focus on what we get for our money, not just on how much we spend. If defense spending has to be reduced, then let's reduce it. If domestic spending has to be cut, then let's cut it. If tax breaks have to be stopped, then let's stop them. It's going to take all of these steps, and all of us know it.

Broadcast address to the nation, Washington,
Feb. 4/The Washington Post, 2-5:(A)7.

Bernard W. Rogers
General, United States Army;
Supreme Allied Commander/Europe

4

Arms-reduction accords [between the U.S. and Soviets] are very high on the priority list of West Europeans. And therefore, if [the U.S. is] successful in negotiating those kinds of accords that are balanced and verifiable, a lot of other things that the United States might do, which cause umbrage on the part of West Europeans, might be ignored . . . because there is a perception on the part of many here in West Europe that the United States is not serious about arms-control.

Interview, Mons, Belgium/
The Christian Science Monitor, 7-14:9.

Andrei D. Sakharov
Soviet dissident physicist

5

[On proposals for a space defense system]: I do not think the Strategic Defense Initiative will ever be sufficiently effective to stop a powerful opponent. I am really negative about the Strategic Defense Initiative. I think that in the distant future this will be a technical possibility, but it will always be impossible from the military strategic point of view, since any strong opponent

(ANDREI D. SAKHAROV)

with a sufficiently high level of technology can always overcome the technical achievements of the other side at all stages. And he won't even have to invest as much or as many resources as are being invested by the creator of the SDI.

*Broadcast interview/"This Week
with David Brinkley," ABC-TV, 12-28.*

James R. Schlesinger
*Former Secretary of Defense
of the United States*

1

By asking the Soviets to reduce offense while we pose to them the possibility of greatly increased American defense, the [Reagan] Administration has created a situation in which the Soviets cannot accommodate the U.S. even if they wanted to.

Time, 6-23:22.

2

[On being Secretary of Defense]: The basic problem that you have is that you have to go to Congress and demand money under any circumstances, and that means either implicitly or explicitly taking it away from domestic programs. And you gradually wear out your welcome. Depending on one's personality, you wear it out more or less rapidly, but you wear it out because you're saying, "If you don't give me this money, you're endangering the national security." They know they can't give you the money, given budgetary pressures, and they don't like being accused of endangering the national security. Inevitably, in three or four years you begin to go downhill, just in terms of that key function of being able to extract money from the Congress.

Interview/The Washington Post, 9-2:(A)17.

Helmut Schmidt
*Member of West German Parliament;
Former Chancellor of West Germany*

3

At the moment, there is much more fuss and much more advertising about SDI [U.S. President Reagan's proposal for a space defense sys-

tem] than there is substance. SDI, more or less, is a perception or an idea in the minds of the American President and his aides. And it is a perception in the minds of the Russian beholders and SDI's opponents or adversaries. The hardware that already exists or that has been under development for the past 20 years—on the Russian side as much as on the American side—falls within the category of anti-ballistic systems. And there we have had a treaty since 1972, one negotiated between [then-U.S. and Soviet leaders] Richard Nixon and Leonid Brezhnev. In my mind, it's a good treaty. Now, during this so-called SDI period, there should be a mutual assertion by both sides that the ABM Treaty is going to stand in the future. On top of that, they should jointly interpret the limitations of that treaty so there would be no haggling about what would and would not be a violation. Then I would be totally satisfied.

Interview/U.S. News & World Report, 1-13:34.

Patricia Schroeder
*United States Representative,
D-Colorado*

4

[Criticizing the Reagan Administration's defense budget]: One would have thought the [White House] Office of Management and Budget tightwads could have located at least one Department of Defense program worthy of reform, termination or cutting. In my 13 years on the Armed Services Committee, I have seen evidence of many programs that are plagued by waste, fraud and abuse. The central idea behind a budget is to list priorities and to institute discipline. This is a defense budget with no priorities and no discipline. It's a Twinkie defense. It's like a child loose in a pastry shop. Even if one swallows hook, line and Trident the Reagan-Weinberger sermon on the national-security need for increased defense spending to meet the Soviet threat, the Administration still ought to be able to reform, terminate or cut those Department of Defense activities least useful to defending America in order to provide more money for those programs most useful to defending America.

Feb. 7/The New York Times, 2-17:8.

WHAT THEY SAID IN 1986

Eduard A. Shevardnadze
Foreign Minister of the Soviet Union

1

We [the Soviet Union] did not seek to acquire nuclear weapons, but ever since the time when we were compelled to develop them we have always been looking for ways to limit, reduce and eliminate them. Although we are not last among the members in the "nuclear club," we propose that it be disbanded. Let there be no mistake— we are as proud a nation as any other. But we associate the prestige and dignity of a great power with equivalent security for all . . . One can imagine the sigh of relief that people would have on hearing that in this year of peace the United States, too, has decided [as has the Soviet Union] to stop nuclear testing. This is what they had been expecting from the U.S. President. I have been authorized to state that the Soviet Union is prepared to sign at any time and in any place a treaty on a total prohibition of nuclear-weapons tests. We are prepared to do so here at the United Nations, so that the entire world community could become part of this great act, and a turning point in history is marked as a sign of respect for its will. Words not matched by deeds are a false value. But words supported by deeds are a country's gold reserve.

At United Nations, New York,
Sept. 23/The New York Times, 9-24:4.

2

[Criticizing U.S. plans for a space defense system]: Whatever is done to conceal it, the so-called defensive space shield is being developed for a first strike. The first strike may become the last one, and not just for the country which is attacked. Space weapons, like nuclear ones, do not choose whom to spare and whom to destroy.

At United Nations, New York, Sept. 23/
The Washington Post, 9-24:(A)17.

3

[Criticizing the U.S. position at recent arms-control talks with the Soviet Union in Vienna]: In Vienna, two conceptions, two diametrically opposed approaches, confronted each other. The Soviet Union was out to create the base for practical implementation of the agreements [re-cently] reached at [U.S.-Soviet mini-summit talks in] Reykjavik, while the United States tried to secure positions which lead to the erosion of the Reykjavik soil. [U.S. Secretary of State George Shultz is seeking] to replace the Reykjavik package with a Vienna package from which the key agreement was removed and other agreements were dissolved.

News conference, Moscow, Nov. 10/
Los Angeles Times, 11-11:(I)12.

George P. Shultz
Secretary of State of the United States

4

We have to remember that the Soviets have always been defense-oriented and very good at it, that they have deployed an ABM system around Moscow, and they've modernized it. We also know that they have been doing the kind of research that we are emphasizing in SDI [the proposed U.S. space defense system] for some time. So they are quite familiar with the concepts. They have an interest in this subject for their own sake. So the concept of SDI, assuming that you put it into effect not unilaterally but on some kind of agreed basis, has a lot of potential appeal . . . If we can get to the point where we're ready to talk about a concept of deterrence that has greater defense elements in it, and the importance of a transition to such a concept, then you lay the groundwork for a fruitful discussion about how you might do it [work with the Soviets on SDI], and "how" is not an easy problem. We made the suggestion of open laboratories, that we will allow Soviet scientists to come to our labs and get some sense of what we're doing, on the assumption that they will do likewise.

Interview, Washington, Feb. 3/
The New York Times, 2-10:12.

5

[Supporting the U.S. decision not to be bound by the limits of the SALT II treaty]: [The Soviets] have deployed a second [missile] system which is prohibited by the treaty, and they heavily encrypt their telemetry, which impairs verification under the treaty. So to imply . . . that somehow or other they are in conformance with

DEFENSE / THE MILITARY

(GEORGE P. SHULTZ)

it, and we may not be, is not correct. You have to take a treaty in all of its dimensions and not allow either side to decide, selectively, what it wants to conform to and what it doesn't.

Broadcast interview/
"Meet the Press," NBC-TV, 6-1.

1

Arms control cannot exist as a process in isolation from other sources of tension in East-West relations. When justice is violated and freedom is denied, then the potential for conflict inevitably grows between nations, and the delicate process of building confidence, cooperation and security is undermined.

At conference on Helsinki human-rights accords,
Vienna, Nov. 5/Los Angeles Times, 11-6:(I)6.

Ike Skelton
United States Representative,
D-Missouri

2

[Approving a bill that would overhaul the armed forces' chain of command in an effort to curtail inter-service rivalry]: Our collective work can be summed up in one sentence: It will encourage the four services to think jointly and, should the time come to go into action, to fight jointly. We are attempting to change a military mind-set. It is far more important to the successful military defense of our nation than the production of a thousand MX missiles.

Washington, Sept. 17/
Los Angeles Times, 9-18:(I)4.

Oleg M. Sokolov
Deputy Chief,
Soviet Embassy, Washington

3

[Criticizing the U.S. intention of abandoning the provisions of the SALT II arms treaty]: Should the current arms-control regime be allowed to disintegrate, a chaotic arms competi-

tion might ensue. The Soviet Union would not be able to remain a passive onlooker. When the United States breaks out of those agreements, all the limitations provided for in them will become invalid . . . The actual abandonment and actual technical and physical withdrawal of the United States from SALT II would affect the situation in the most serious, negative way. What we have to do is preserve the existing foundations for the arms-control regime rather than destroy them.

To reporters, Washington, June 13/
Los Angeles Times, 6-14:(I)14.

Larry Speakes
Principal Deputy Press Secretary
to the President of the United States

4

[On President Reagan's decision not to be bound in the future by the limits of the SALT II treaty]: The President's decision on May 27 means that the SALT treaty limits no longer exist. If we take future actions in the area of arms control, it would be for reasons other than the SALT agreement. Our strong preference is to enter into a regime of mutual restraint and reduction with the Soviet Union. The President has made it clear that he will take into account Soviet actions. Any decision based on how to compensate for Soviet actions will be based on what the Soviets do and not on the SALT agreements.

White House briefing, Washington,
June 12/The New York Times, 6-13:4.

Jeremy Stone
Director, Federation of
American Scientists

5

It would be unreasonable to hold arms control hostage to Soviet agreement to permit Jewish emigration. If one holds arms control hostage to general Soviet behavior on human rights, one would never get arms control because the Soviet Union, like many other countries in the world, does not have a good human-rights record.

Jan. 6/The New York Times, 1-7:4.

William H. Taft IV
Deputy Secretary of Defense
of the United States

1

[On the U.S. military-industrial complex]: It's defending our freedom. It's what brings us peace. It's what keeps the Soviets interested in arms reduction and protects our interests. What could be more valuable?

The Washington Post, 1-17:(A)8.

Edward Teller
Nuclear physicist;
Senior research fellow,
Hoover Institution, Stanford University

2

[On calls for the U.S. to institute a moratorium on nuclear testing to match a similar moratorium by the Soviets]: Before we accept this new moratorium, let us see old treaties [which the Soviets violate], like the Helsinki Accords, enforced. Let us see old wars [waged by the Soviets], like Afghanistan, ended.

USA Today, 3-24:(A)10.

Reginald Turnill
Editor, "Jane's Spaceflight Directory"

3

[On the proposed U.S. space defense system]: The super space powers [the U.S. and Soviet Union] may in the end conclude that a joint space defense system would threaten neither, and protect both East and West against the growing likelihood of irresponsible random nuclear attack from temporarily hostile smaller nations. Today's car-bomb terrorist will be operating in 10 years' time with nuclear-tipped missiles. The Soviets and the West will need "Star Wars" [the space defense system] for such an occasion where it is necessary to deal with irresponsible nations, such as Libya, or terrorism. Despite their protests [against the U.S. space defense system], the Soviets, too, have their own well-advanced "Star Wars" program. The fact is that "Star Wars" is a phony controversy . . . Space has always been militarized, the process having begun before *Sputnik I* [in 1957], with the devel-

opment of ICBMs and the spy satellites which quickly replaced their warheads.

Interview, London/
Los Angeles Times, 6-17:(I)6.

Malcolm Wallop
United States Senator, R-Wyoming

4

[Saying U.S. military policy is weak in protecting U.S. forces and threatening Soviet forces]: I do not mean to say to you that the 50 MX missiles that this [Reagan] Administration has programmed, or the 100 B-1 bombers, or the 600-ship Navy, or the sea-launched cruise missiles and perhaps a Stealth bomber fleet are nothing. In absolute terms they are impressive, though not so impressive as their cost. But in the real world, weapons must be judged in relation to their tasks—and to the enemy's weapons and strategy. And, in these terms, I fear that our costly buildup amounts only to more expensive things . . . for the Soviets to kill.

Interview, Washington/
The Christian Science Monitor, 3-21:19.

Paul C. Warnke
Former Director,
Arms Control and Disarmament
Agency of the United States

5

[On the late President Dwight Eisenhower's warning about the military-industrial complex]: It has become more complicated since President Eisenhower issued his warning. If you look at it today, the most rational people are in uniform. They recognize, as military commanders, that there's no sensible way to use nuclear weapons.

The Washington Post, 1-17:(A)8.

6

[Criticizing the Reagan Administration's planned future disregard for the limitations of the SALT II treaty because of alleged violations of the treaty by the Soviet Union]: I don't think there is any plausible argument that the Soviet Union has violated the core elements of SALT II . . . What we are talking about now is the gutting by the

(PAUL C. WARNKE)

United States of the central provisions of SALT II—the numerical limitations. The latest Joint Chiefs' posture statement set forth what they know to be the Soviet force structure, and it indicates that the Soviets are abiding by those limits. There are legitimate questions about some of the more tangential aspects of the SALT II agreement, for example with regard to the SS-25 [missiles]. The Soviet Union maintains that this single-warhead mobile ICBM is not a new missile but rather an improvement, a modernization of the SS-13. This is a debatable point . . . The other legitimate compliance question related to SALT II is whether there is excessive encryption of telemetry, which unfortunately is not a terribly clear provision in the treaty . . . But as far as the central elements of SALT II, the numerical limits, are concerned, these limits are very much in the security interests of the United States, and there is absolutely no question that the Soviets have complied with these core provisions.

Press briefing, May 29/
The Washington Post, 7-30:(A)22.

Caspar W. Weinberger
Secretary of Defense of the United States

1

The struggle of the [defense] budget is a serious problem, because that budget speaks volumes to the world about what kind of a people we are, what kind of a nation we will be, how strongly we will stand as protectors of freedom, and whether we will be able to negotiate successfully with the Soviet Union.

At luncheon sponsored by Carnegie
Endowment for International Peace,
Washington, Jan. 9/Los Angeles Times, 1-10:(I)5.

2

I was asked the other day, "When are you going to finish this, when is enough [deterrent] enough, when are you going to say you don't need any more?" And I said: "The day the Soviets, in a totally verifiable way, disarm and let us know they can be deterred at much lower levels of armaments"—which is what I want.

Newsweek, 2-3:16.

3

[Saying estimates of Defense Department budgets are partly guesswork]: There's only one continuing, never-changing factor about outlay estimates: They are always wrong.

Before Senate Budget Committee,
Washington, Feb. 6/The New York Times, 2-7:9.

4

The problem with deterrence is that it is an extremely dynamic equation. But it is an extremely important fact to bear in mind about deterrence that if we don't do enough, we will never know it until it is too late to do anything about it.

Debate before Harvard University alumni,
Washington, March 14/The New York Times, 3-15:8.

5

The Soviet Union has about 100,000 troops whose sole duty is chemical warfare. They have violated their treaty agreements not to use chemical weapons at least twice . . . If they've done it twice, they're very apt to do it again. So it's absolutely vital that we modernize our chemical weapons.

Brussels/The Christian
Science Monitor, 5-27:13.

6

Some advocates of deep defense [budget] cuts seem to view defense as just another government program. These critics see defense merely as something "nice to have," if we can afford it. To them, the defense budget is just a "wish list." Reasonable people can differ as to threats, defense needs and how best to fulfill those needs. But when defense decisions are determined on the basis of a tidy balance sheet, we are missing the essence of the issue. Defense needs must determine defense dollars.

Before American Legion, Cincinnati,
Sept. 2/The New York Times, 9-3:11.

7

If the Soviets want the kind of [arms-control] agreement that I think is essential to have, I think we can get one . . . What we want is to have zero [medium-range missiles] on both sides, so that none of our Asian friends is threat-

WHAT THEY SAID IN 1986

ened. [And verification is necessary,] the ability to go on each other's soil . . . to look in factories and look at gun sites . . . to do what bank examiners do.

Broadcast interview/
"Meet the Press," NBC-TV, 9-28.

1

Wishful thinking is equally as effective for arms control as it is for birth control.

Fairbanks, Alaska/USA Today, 10-6:(A)4.

Jim Wright
United States Representative, D-Texas

2

Democrats have supported a strong defense and always will . . . [But] we do have some very fundamental differences [with the Reagan Administration] over spending priorities and the amount of debt we are willing to place upon the backs of our children. We think the deficits themselves pose a danger to our national security. We know that it adds to the debt to double military spending and cut taxes at the same time. We believe that even the Pentagon should be held to strict standards of accountability in spending taxpayers' money. And we believe that true national security depends on a lot of things in addition to military weapons.

Broadcast address to the nation, Washington,
Feb. 26/The New York Times, 2-27:14.

3

[Criticizing the Reagan Administration's surpassing the SALT II limits by deploying the 131st nuclear-capable B-52 bomber]: It is embarrassing that our country now can be portrayed as the recalcitrant one in the search for peace and as the cause of the renewal of the nuclear arms race.

Nov. 29/Los Angeles Times, 11-30:(I)10.

The Economy • Labor

Richard Armey
United States Representative, R-Texas
1

The [labor-] union movement, like business and every other area of the economy, learns its worst habits from the government.

USA Today, 9-2:(A)4.

James A. Baker III
Secretary of the Treasury
of the United States
2

[On the proposed tax-reform plan]: A top individual rate of 28 per cent will be one of the lasting legacies of Ronald Reagan's Presidency. During his time in office, he has brought the top individual rate down from 70 per cent. That is an extraordinary achievement.

Time, 8-25:12.

M. Wendell Belew, Jr.
Former Chief Counsel,
House Budget Committee
3

One problem with the [Federal] budget process is that it is very, very difficult to predict with any certainty what the outcomes of policy are going to be and what the outcomes of matters beyond the control of policy, such as the economy, interest rates and unemployment, are going to be. Another problem that we've had is that even if you can get widespread agreement on goals, widespread agreement on the dangers of inaction, that doesn't necessarily mean that you can get agreement on the set of policies that would actually produce the goals or attend to the need to take positive action. In addition, nothing bad happens if you don't have a budget in place. Except for 1982, there has been no such point of crisis where something very, very bad happens if the problems aren't solved.

Interview, Washington/
The New York Times, 1-9:10.

Lou Bert
Director, labor studies department,
Wayne State University
4

Blacks have worked in the auto industry for a long time. Of course, they got the lousy, dirty jobs. They got pushed into the foundries, things like that. But today they're the majority of the UAW in the Detroit area—they're a dominant part of the industrial unions now. The only trouble is, our industrial base is collapsing and those jobs are shrinking by the millions.

The Christian Science Monitor, 11-19:20.

Kenneth E. Boulding
Professor emeritus of economics,
University of Colorado; Former
president, American Economic Association
5

[Saying there are "ominous" similarities between 1928, just before the stock-market crash, and 1986]: [Today's] stock-market boom, the debt situation, the erosion of profit by interest, the increasing burden of interest on the society, the unmanageable budget deficit, the cowardice of Congress as reflected by Gramm-Rudman [the budget-balancing plan], the Pollyanna charm of the President, the overly successful and rather puzzling control of price inflation, the big shift which now seems to be taking place in relative prices, in oil, for instance . . . One possible source of hope is that we do know more than we did in 1929. But in some ways we know less. Economics has retreated into a naive monetarism, into the absurdly simplistic theory of rational expectations, into a blind mathematization and model building, losing sight of the real world.

The New York Times, 7-16:26.

Beau Boulter
United States Representative, R-Texas
6

[On the Gramm-Rudman balanced-budget plan]: This is a five-year balanced-budget plan;

WHAT THEY SAID IN 1986

but the people still expect us to make the choices about how we're going to balance the budget, and what kind of government we're going to have. I don't want my people to think I'm so stupid as to turn over that responsibility to a computer . . . We [were hired] to determine what kind of government we [have] and we do that [by making] hard choices.

The Christian Science Monitor, 2-4:5.

Bill Bradley
United States Senator,
D-New Jersey

1

How can we expect only some Americans to pay for our national security, our schools, our health care for the elderly, our programs for the poor and our roads, subways and our ports? The answer is clear: We can't. It's time for us to look at the special interests and say get on board, be part of the community, be a part of America— pay some tax. It's time to remove the web of suspicion and inequity that covers our tax system.

Before the Senate, Washington,
June 4/The New York Times, 6-5:38.

William E. Brock
Secretary of Labor of the United States

2

This country is in a remarkably good position to continue to create a lot of jobs. We are going to have more jobs than there are people in the next 13, 14 years, until the turn of the century. The problem is, are we going to take those steps to allow everybody to have those jobs? Are we going to shape up our educational system so that our kids can have decent jobs? Are we going to continue to wipe out the last vestiges of discrimination so that equality will be available to all? Are we going to have more opportunity for child care, for day care, for flexible working hours, things that allow the man and the wife to work, or the single parent to work, and still have some sense of security about the well-being of their

children. These are the issues that we have got to deal with, and they are pretty basic.

Interview, Washington, Aug. 31/
The New York Times, 9-1:8.

Jack Brooks
United States Representative, D-Texas

3

[Revenue-sharing] violates the cardinal principle of accountability—the simple but vital idea that those officials who spend money on government programs should be responsible for raising the revenues to pay for those programs.

Interview/The Washington Post, 3-11:(A)8.

James McGill Buchanan
Professor, George Mason University;
Winner, 1986 Nobel Prize in economics

4

Once we have a basic tax structure, it ought to stay in being. Politicians ought not be allowed to dabble in changing taxes almost every year. Stability is as important as almost any other aspect of the tax structure.

U.S. News & World Report, 12-15:56.

Jimmy Carter
Former President of the United States

5

When I left office less than six years ago, we were the greatest creditor nation on earth. Now the United States is the greatest debtor nation on earth, which is a very rapid change. And the adverse consequences of this [change] are unpredictable. I think they are going to be much worse than anyone presently thinks.

Interview, Atlanta/The Christian
Science Monitor, 12-30:14.

Henry G. Cisneros
Mayor of San Antonio

6

[Criticizing the pending elimination of revenue-sharing]: In the absence of revenue-sharing, 25 per cent of the members [of the National League of

(HENRY G. CISNEROS)

Cities] will have to raise taxes. [That would be a] shifting of the tax burden from one level of government [Federal] to another [local]—the level least able to raise revenues.

At National League of Cities convention, Washington, March 10/The Washington Post, 3-11:(A)8.

Bill Clinton
Governor of Arkansas (D)

1

Over the last decade, we have been pulled into a world economy which we no longer dominate and for which we are still largely unprepared. While the percentage of our GNP directly tied to trade has grown to 13 per cent, the reconstructed economies of Japan and Europe have had higher productivity growth than ours. Newly emerging economies have captured many of our former markets by providing quality products at labor costs we can't hope to match. The long-term consequences are alarming.

At National Governors Association convention, Hilton Head, S.C., Aug. 26/ The New York Times, 8-27:11.

Allan Cohen
Professor of management, Babson College

2

We've had a culture in the last few years that glorifies the individual getting rich. Investment banking, Boesky [the stock-trading scandal], and the rest says to people that "I should be looking for mine." It's an attitude that has become more and more prevalent; whereas, we used to have "a penny saved is a penny earned." *The Christian Science Monitor, 12-29:14.*

Mario M. Cuomo
Governor of New York (D)

3

There is a dissonance in our national life as great as any in our history. We cannot watch the numbers of our poor grow, our middle class shrink, their

dreams wither, and think that the loss in productivity, the burden on our resources, the increased violence and disorientation will not threaten us all . . . There are farmers from Kansas, Nebraska, Georgia, the Dakotas and Missouri, factory workers from Pennsylvania, Ohio, New York, Illinois and Indiana—people with long traditions of hard work now reduced in dignity, now denied the chance to earn their own bread. [Under the Reagan Administration,] our prosperity has been purchased at the expense of the well-being, the hopes and expectations of a large part of the nation by the acceptance of such things as a level of unemployment that this nation would have considered a scandal only a decade ago.

At forum of newspaper publishers, San Francisco, April 22/The New York Times, 4-23:9.

John C. Danforth
United States Senator, R-Missouri

4

[Criticizing the proposed tax-reform bill]: Any time anybody punches the tax-bill button, you can be prepared for the spiel. Here I am, somehow with a spotlight on me relating to the tax bill, and what am I going to say? . . . Do we say to the American people, you know, "There's good news and bad news. The bad news is that we have a $2-trillion national debt. The good news is that [with this tax-reform bill] your responsibility for paying for this load is going to be reduced." Is that the message that always comes out of Washington? Eat, drink and be merry? Live for today? . . . I got companies in Missouri that are thrilled with this bill. Businesses that are delighted. But I think there is a strong underlying feeling on the part of the American people that this live-for-the-moment routine is wrong. I think there is a strong skepticism that the national debt is $2-trillion and their taxes are going to be reduced by five bucks a week . . . It's the politics of joy, to use [the late Senator Hubert] Humphrey's phrase. To me, that's a policy without a future, and someday we're going to have to face up to that—and I just want to help people face up to that.

Interview, Washington/ The Washington Post, 9-27:(C)2.

WHAT THEY SAID IN 1986

Roscoe L. Egger, Jr.
Commissioner, Internal Revenue
Service of the United States

1

[Arguing against a Federal tax amnesty which would permit people to pay back taxes without penalty]: [Such an amnesty] would further undermine taxpayer morale by sending a clear signal to the American public . . .: "Don't bother to pay now. We may forget you owe anything. Even if you have to pay tax, we won't charge interest." Amnesties can only reinforce the growing impression that the tax system is unfair and encourage taxpayer non-compliance.

Before House Ways and Means subcommittee,
Washington/Los Angeles Times, 3-5:(I)11.

Daniel Evans
United States Senator, R-Washington

2

Prohibition did not keep us from drinking; . . . a balanced-budget amendment will not keep us from spending. A drunk always has a way to get drunk, and a spender will always find a way to your wallet.

USA Today, 3-25:(A)8.

James J. Florio
United States Representative,
D-New Jersey

3

[On American companies moving their manufacturing operations to Mexico]: I think more and more people are thinking about Mexico as a place where jobs are going. I talk to auto workers on a regular basis, and they're very aware how much of the industry is moving to Mexico. You can't tell someone who has just lost his job, "Sorry, but you're a casualty to the higher purpose of allowing Mexico to pay off its debts to American banks." That approach just doesn't wash.

The New York Times, 12-29:1.

Mark S. Fowler
Chairman,
Federal Communications Commission

4

The marketplace is one important way people have to express what they want with their lives,

and in their lives. The market is not the alpha and omega of satisfaction. There are some things money cannot buy, to be sure. But a vigorous market, one that allows ease of entry and range of choice, is the start of the stuff of human happiness. And those who would over-regulate it would rob us of the flea market and leave us with the fleas.

Before Organization for Economic
Cooperation and Development, Paris/
The Wall Street Journal, 5-14:28.

Douglas A. Fraser
Former president, United
Automobile Workers of America

5

. . . this country has the most anti-union management of any democracy in the world. In no other will you find labor consultants whose only mission is to prevent the organization of unions or the destruction of unions once they're organized. This would be socially unacceptable in other countries. There, labor unions are accepted as a fact of life. Not here.

Interview, Wayne State University/
The Washington Post, 9-2:(D)3.

6

It's not economically sound to resist or even slow down the introduction of new technology [in the workplace]. New technology does not necessarily mean unemployment or loss of jobs. If you [have] the introduction of new technology and [an] expansion in the economy at the same, you won't have any unemployment.

Interview, Detroit/
The Christian Science Monitor, 10-28:16.

Lawrence Friedman
Professor of law, Stanford University

7

[On the trend toward states banning company mandatory-retirement rules and the increase in voluntary early retirement]: The two things, early retirement and the end of mandatory retirement, really go together. What is developing instead is a less-rigid view of what a career is,

(LAWRENCE FRIEDMAN)

replacing the idea that it's something that goes exactly until the 65th birthday.

The New York Times, 1-28:30.

John Kenneth Galbraith
Professor emeritus of economics, Harvard University

1

In earlier Administrations, when the President saw economists on his appointment schedule, he knew they were coming in to talk about something very agreeable [tax cuts, low interest rates, etc.]. After about 1970, he knew they were coming in to talk about higher taxes, lower spending and higher interest rates. And he postponed the appointment.

To reporters, Washington, Nov. 12/
The Washington Post, 11-13:(A)19.

Barry M. Goldwater
United States Senator, R-Arizona

2

[Freedom is] the sponsor of everything. You go to a town like Singapore—you've never seen such business! You [see it in] Arabian towns . . . I travel to a place like Taipei [Taiwan]; [it's growing so fast] they make our [U.S.] free-enterprise system look out of date . . . I think it's taking hold in Russia. I think [Soviet leader] Gorbachev's biggest worry is the economics of his country, and you can't have good economics when you have the government trying to run business . . . If this rebirth of free enterprise is as great as I think it is, we may not have to worry about the [Federal budget] deficit, because it could take care of itself. We've already had five reductions in interest rates in under a year and a half, and we have a normal inflation rate. No economist talks about this. [On the other hand,] if we don't do away with the deficit [within five years], then this country is in for real trouble. Because we'll have growth of interest rates, and we'll have growth of inflation, and we can't stand it.

Interview, Washington/
The Christian Science Monitor, 3-18:23.

3

[On the national debt and budget deficit]: I see it as the most serious problem we have in this country. Not right now, because right now we're in the middle of a hell of a good economy. In spite of what the economists say and the bankers and Wall Street, the economy is good and I think it's going to stay good—*but* if we continue deficit financing, if we continue to exceed the budget and constantly raise the borrowing we have to do, eventually, unless we correct it, inflation's going to hit us again, interest rates are going to go up again, and I think we can look forward to the bankruptcy of America. That's a violent thing to say, but I firmly believe it.

Interview, Washington/
The Washington Post, 11-4:(A)17.

Mikhail S. Gorbachev
General Secretary, Communist Party of the Soviet Union

4

The capitalism of the 1980s, the capitalism of the age of electronics and computer science, computers and robots, is leaving more millions of people, including young and educated people, without jobs. Wealth and power are being increasingly concentrated in the hands of a few.

At Soviet Communist Party Congress,
Moscow, Feb. 25/The New York Times, 2-27:4.

Phil Gramm
United States Senator, R-Texas

5

Those who argue for a tax increase are arguing that the deficit is the result of the working people of America not paying enough taxes. I believe the problem is that the Federal government spends too much money, by undertaking activities that do not enjoy popular support and that in many cases [could] be performed better by the private sector in a growing, dynamic economy or by a level of government closer to the people. My goal is cutting fat out of the Federal budget by setting priorities, rather than cutting the heart out of the family budget by raising taxes so government can go on with business as usual.

Interview/The Washington Post, 2-7:(A)13.

(PHIL GRAMM)

1

If government deficit spending was ever a stimulant to economic growth, that was during periods of depression. We have taken this drug of deficit spending in depressions, in inflations, in expansions and contractions, and we long ago became addicted to the drug. I believe deficit spending is a drag on the economy. It produces high interest rates. It makes our goods less competitive on the world market. It impedes over-all growth.

Interview/USA Today, 4-24:(A)11.

Charles E. Grassley
United States Senator, R-Iowa

2

The country would be better off if we would pass a one-sentence bill saying we're not going to change the tax law for five years. But the real world is that tax reform has taken on a life of its own. The Republican President is for it. The Democratic House passed it. The Republican Senate can't sit still, so we'll end up passing a bill.

The New York Times, 1-27:1.

William H. Gray III
United States Representative,
D-Pennsylvania

3

Last year we [in Congress] lowered the President's deficit. We did it by looking at every single Federal spending program, both domestic and in the Pentagon, and making cuts where they made sense. We didn't do it by taking education from our kids. We didn't do it by slashing science and research for our future growth. And we didn't do it by taking it from our elderly. We cared. We worked together and we solved the problem.

Broadcast address to the nation, Washington,
Feb. 4/The New York Times, 2-6:17.

Alan Greenspan
Former Chairman, Council of
Economic Advisers to the President
of the United States (Gerald R. Ford)

4

We have had all of the elements which . . . now should be affecting the American economy in a positive way. The fact that they are not raises some very serious questions about whether we are looking at the fundamental forces that are driving the economy. It's too early to say we're on the edge of a recession, but there is no question [that] the underlying framework is deteriorating.

Broadcast interview/
"Meet the Press," NBC-TV, 7-20.

John N. Gregg
Chairman, Fiber, Fabric
& Apparel Coalition for Trade

5

[Criticizing U.S. Special Trade Negotiator Clayton Yeutter's recent trade negotiations with South Korea]: Clayton Yeutter and his fly-by-night negotiating team has once again taken the back-alley route . . . excluding industry representatives from trade negotiations and [excluding] U.S. job-saving provisions from the agreement. Korea gets to export an additional 91 million square yards [of textiles], and the U.S. gets to export 9,000 American jobs to Korea over the next four years. Apparently, the [Reagan] Administration trade negotiators care more about South Africa and South Korea than South Dakota and South [New] Jersey.

Aug. 4/Los Angeles Times, 8-5:(I)13.

Alexander M. Haig, Jr.
Former Secretary of State
of the United States

6

I find myself rather embarrased as a Republican since over the last five years of Republican leadership we've managed to double the national debt from $1-trillion to $2-trillion. The consequences of this deficit are extremely significant in that they create imbalances in our economic structure. In the near term, the American economy is going to stay rather robust. I think that we have maybe four or five quarters to get this deficit under control.

Interview/USA Today, 12-2:(A)13.

David Halberstam
Author, Journalist

7

I think we're going to go into an era where we have to have diminished expectations. We've had

(DAVID HALBERSTAM)

this unusual era, this historical freak, where from 1945 to 1975, we were richer than anybody else on such a scale that the richness flowed to everybody. People whose parents never owned houses bought a house, bought a summer house, bought kitchen gear, car number one, car number two. We still expect to get so much, and that's going to have to end . . . We're living in good times, but are these good times? How much of that surge in Wall Street has been about companies that are well-run and done right and are profitable, and how much of it has been an attempt to use the market as a great casino?

Interview/USA Today, 10-28:(B)7.

Gary Hart
United States Senator, D-Colorado

1

You [President Reagan] may say that America is standing tall . . . but if you preside over the decline and collapse of the [American] steel industry in the 1980s, you cannot take pride in being a great, historic American leader. The chicken is coming home to roost on Ronald Reagan's doorstep some day. He may be back on his ranch, but I believe that history is just.

At Democratic Party national issues forum,
Buffalo, N.Y., July 28/The Washington Post, 7-29:(A)7.

Orrin G. Hatch
United States Senator, R-Utah

2

Congress, like the classic alcoholic, cannot stop deficit spending, and no one has found a way to hide the bottle.

USA Today, 3-25:(A)8.

Robert Heilbroner
Economist

3

It used to seem to me that the drift of all Western countries was toward something like socialism. But now, when I reflect on what is happening in the 1980s, it is not so clear. There is a sense of

a return to the market, because the task of planning in a modern economy is so complex.

Time, 7-28:39.

Robert Hormats
Economist; Vice president,
Goldman Sachs & Co.

4

The global return to market economics is very much inspired by events here [in the U.S.]. Perhaps the most lasting legacy of the Reagan years will be that they restored faith in the effectiveness of markets.

Time, 7-28:31.

Lee A. Iacocca
Chairman, Chrysler Corporation

5

My class, the class of '46, wasn't too worried about competing in the world. There was hardly anybody to compete with. But the class of '86 had better learn how to compete, because you're living in a very different world. Something else you'd better do better than we have: learn how to balance the books. We're leaving you with a $2-trillion national debt. Along with your own problems and your own bills, you're going to get the privilege of handling some of mine. I'll tell you one thing: Don't try to pay it off in cash. It would take the U.S. Mint 57 years, two months and two weeks just to print it. We've been using your credit card, and you didn't even know it.

At Duke University commencement/
Time, 6-9:62.

Carl C. Icahn
Financier; Chairman,
Trans World Airlines

6

I think that the [labor] unions are one of the very big areas that can be approached, especially in the low-tech companies, where the real problems are. And I'm convinced, beyond a shadow of a doubt, that you can work with the unions because the unions want to survive. If they are confronted simply with the question:

(CARL C. ICAHN)

Do you want this company to survive or do you want it to be broken up? They will listen. It's their livelihood.

Interview/Newsweek, 10-20:54.

Donald M. Kendall
Chairman, PepsiCo, Inc.

1

The biggest problem we've got in this country is the national debt. And Congress has refused to recognize this. These huge spending bills don't come out of the air; they're voted by Congress. Every year, that deficit keeps going up and up. The interest on that debt is becoming a big factor in our budget. And it's growing by leaps and bounds. We have to do something about it . . . You'll have to either get a balanced-budget amendment approved by getting the states to agree to a Constitutional convention—and I would hate to think that we'd have to go that far—or get Congress to pass a balanced-budget amendment. The President should have a line-by-line veto, the same as they have in many states around the country, because Congress has shown that it's totally irresponsible when it comes to spending. And that's why we have state tax increases. I'm against sending any more money to Washington, because the Congress will keep spending it.

Interview/USA Today,
4-21:(A)13.

Alfred H. Kingon
Cabinet Secretary to the President
of the United States

2

[On the way the government prepares the Federal budget]: Notwithstanding Democratic control of the Senate, there are very thoughtful people on both sides of the aisle, in both houses, as well as in the Executive Branch, who recognize that the [budget-preparing] system as it now exists is just not working. No business, no state, no foreign government operates this way. The system is badly in need of repair.

The New York Times, 11-14:1.

Arthur Laffer
Professor of economics,
Pepperdine University, Malibu

3

[On the new tax law which lowers tax rates]: By lowering rates, you reduce the attractiveness of tax shelters, accountants, lawyers, gimmicks and tricks. You'll see people investing their money more wisely, and you should get more employment and output and less tax evasion.

U.S. News & World Report, 11-24:56.

Richard L. Lesher
President, Chamber of Commerce
of the United States

4

The only legislative goal of public economic policy is to cause growth. You don't have to have recessions. Recessions are a terrible waste of our resources. The key is continued economic growth. We have said for a long time that the formula is to reduce Federal spending, reduce Federal regulation and reduce taxation. I'm glad to see that the message has finally come of age.

Nation's Business, May:8ORR.

John A. Makin
Senior economist,
American Enterprise Institute

5

[On proposed changes in the tax law that would reduce or eliminate many tax shelters for business]: The whole idea is that economic merits, not tax considerations, should determine business decisions. That won't preclude profitable investments from going forward; it will encourage it. [Movies like] Rambo IV and Rambo V will still get made. They will just be financed with real money rather than tax-shelter money.

Los Angeles Times, 6-4:(I)18.

Lynn M. Martin
United States Representative,
R-Illinois

6

[Saying she is voting in favor of the tax-reform bill, despite reservations]: The choice to-

(LYNN M. MARTIN)

day is not between this bill and a perfect bill; the choice is between this bill and the death of tax reform. If we do not seize this opportunity, we will insure the final and permanent victory of the special interests. The tax code will forever be their domain. And for my district and the nation, I cannot allow that to happen.

Washington, Sept. 25/
The New York Times, 9-26:35.

John Melcher
United States Senator, D-Montana

1

Rural America by and large depends upon the activities of agriculture, our most basic industry. Agriculture commodity prices have been in such a low and going-lower process over the past several years that producers on the land are losing money, many of them being liquidated. The cumulative effect is that they are going down the tube. All of us go home and talk to the people of rural America. When they ask us why we are not doing more, it has been fairly difficult to explain why the actions here in Washington have been sort of halfway, sort of lukewarm, but all in all insufficient to revive and revitalize and permit rural America to share in what has been described by the Reagan Administration as economic recovery.

Before the Senate, Washington,
June 2/The New York Times, 6-4:12.

Ruben F. Mettler
Chairman, TRW, Inc.

2

. . . the U.S. economy, as important as it is, is just part of something much bigger and more powerful: the world economy. Look at the signs of our declining competitiveness: lower world market share, lower profitability of our companies, the erosion of manufacturing, the enormous shift overseas of sources of investment capital. We must deal with those problems in a world-wide context. The alternative is to try and build a wall around ourselves and just keep dividing up what we already have.

Interview/USA Today, 4-28:(A)11.

James C. Miller III
Director, Federal Office
of Management and Budget

3

[On the U.S.' trillion-dollar budget]: It's a heady experience to think in those big numbers. People can relate to $1,000, or maybe $100,000. Some people relate well to a million dollars. It's kind of hard to talk about a billion. As [the late] Senator Everett Dirksen used to say, "A billion here and a billion there, and pretty soon it adds up to real money."

Interview/
USA Today, 12-31:(A)9.

Joseph Minarik
Chief tax analyst,
Urban Institute

4

[Supporting the proposed tax-reform program approved by Congressional negotiators]: The ideal tax system does not interfere with decisions in the marketplace. Our economy will be as prosperous as possible if people base their decisions on real business considerations rather than tax consequences. All the screaming you hear [against this tax-reform package] is just a measure of how far from that ideal the old tax system was.

Los Angeles Times, 8-21:(I)1.

Ralph Nader
Lawyer; Consumer advocate

5

The reason why I've stayed in the [consumer] movement, even though it's not considered heavyweight political stuff, is because the ultimate yardstick for our economy should be not GNP or production figures—but the extent to which the production side serves the health, safety and economic well-being of consumers.

USA Today, 7-31:(B)4.

Daniel Oliver
Chairman,
Federal Trade Commission

1

There is something at least seemingly anomalous about the existence of the FTC here in America. The FTC, after all, along with the Antitrust Division of the Justice Department, is engaged in prosecuting "economic crimes." Now, the joke around here is: If a producer sets his price lower than the competition, that's predatory pricing. If he raises it, that's monopolistic. And if he keeps it the same, that's collusion. One has to ask: Where's the American Civil Liberties Union when we need it? We tend not to think of economic crimes as an American activity. When I swore a few moments ago to support and defend the Constitution from enemies foreign and domestic, the domestic enemies I had in mind—as I'm sure you did—were the likes of Alger Hiss and Al Capone, not People Express [Airlines] and Crown Books. Indeed, I suspect, we think of economic crimes as manifestations of individuality and entrepreneurship occurring in the Communist countries. Blades of grass pushing their way up through cracks in the concrete. But economic crimes in a free society? What gives?

At his swearing-in ceremony, Washington,
May 5/The Wall Street Journal, 7-21:14.

Norman J. Ornstein
Resident scholar,
American Enterprise Institute

2

Everybody anticipates that a tax increase is coming, even if they don't know when, where or how. The key question then becomes: Who's going to be stuck with the bill, or, even worse from a political point of view, who's going to get the blame?

Los Angeles Times, 1-26:(I)1.

Robert Ortner
Chief Economist, Department of
Commerce of the United States

3

Economics is an empirical science, basically. One should use theories that work. Almost every theory has worked at one time or another. All of them are useful. I'm very happy to draw upon monetarist and supply-side theories and even, I hesitate to say, Keynesian theories. It's important to be flexible. One has to be careful that one makes recommendations that have a good chance to work.

Interview, Washington/
Los Angeles Times, 6-16:(IV)5.

Robert W. Packwood
United States Senator, R-Oregon

4

[On the tax-reform bill he is pushing through Congress]: For all those people who said, "Close those tax shelters; why isn't General Electric and General Dynamics paying?"—they're going to pay. "Why are millionaires escaping taxation?"—they're going to pay. It's all here . . . I'll be surprised if no less than two-thirds or three-quarters, generically, of American business interests does not support this bill. You're going to have some specific groups, highly leveraged, tax-sheltered commercial real estate, which are not going to like it. Are they powerful enough to overcome the Business Round Table and Chamber of Commerce and the AFL-CIO, and National Women's Political Caucus? I don't think so.

Interview, Washington, May 7/
The Washington Post, 5-8:(C)8.

5

[On his tax-reform bill that was approved by the Senate Finance Committee]: Both liberals and conservatives like it. The liberals like it because it closes loopholes, which they've wanted closed for years. The conservatives like it because they want lower rates, which they've wanted for years. So this is a happy marriage of both philosophies . . . [But] every interest group will want to put its loophole back in. The hurdle they will face is how they're going to pay for it. Who are they going to tax? Whose taxes are they going to raise to do it? Because, with few exceptions, most deductions are taken by upper-middle or upper-income taxpayers. Sixty per cent of the people don't itemize at all; they don't take any de-

(ROBERT W. PACKWOOD)

ductions. So anything that you put back in, in essence you're saying we're going to tax everybody, including the poor, to put back in deductions for upper-income groups.

Interview/USA Today, 5-19:(A)13.

John E. Porter
United States Representative,
R-Illinois

1

[On the just-passed Federal deficit-reduction legislation]: This is Washington at its worst—you get yours, I get mine, and the kids get the bill.

U.S. News & World Report, 10-6:74.

Leland Prussia
Chairman, BankAmerica Corporation

2

People tend to think that bankers abhor inflation more than anyone else. But inflation bails out a lot of problems. Disinflation or deflation are much more difficult. Debt service in many cases just disappears. But the same firms in the same industries under inflationary circumstances sail right along.

Interview, San Francisco/The Christian
Science Monitor, 4-7:21.

Joseph L. Rauh, Jr.
Civil-rights lawyer

3

Nothing could better illustrate [the] trend toward plutocracy and the dangers inherent in its effect on our lives than the story of the just-enacted tax-reform bill. Obviously, with budget deficits threatening our future and with a multitude of social needs unmet, the right answer on tax reform was the removal of the loopholes while leaving tax rates where they were. But this was not feasible with Congress awash in a flood of money from those who benefited from the loopholes. Bribery of the rich with drastically reduced tax rates was the only way to get rid of the loop-

holes, and that, of course, is exactly what happened.

Upon receiving Eugene V. Debs
Foundation Award, Terre Haute, Ind.,
Nov. 8/The Washington Post, 11-12:(A)18.

Ronald Reagan
President of the United States

4

Last year's [Federal budget] deficit amounted to nearly $1,000 for every man, woman and child in the United States. To eliminate the deficit solely by increasing taxes would mean imposing an extra $2,400 burden on each American household. But taxes are already higher relative to GNP than they were during the 1960s and early 1970s, before inflation pushed them to levels that proved insupportable. The American people have made it clear they will not tolerate a higher tax burden. Spending is the problem, not taxes, and spending must be cut. The program of spending cuts and other reforms contained in my budget will lead to a balanced budget at the end of five years and will thus remove a serious impediment to the continuation of our economic expansion. As this budget shows, such reforms can be accomplished in an orderly manner, without resorting to desperate measures.

Budget message to Congress, Washington,
Feb. 5*/The New York Times, 2-6:12.

5

The economic expansion we are now enjoying is one of the most vigorous in 35 years. Family income is at an all-time high; production and productivity are increasing; employment gains have been extraordinary; and inflation, which raged at double-digit rates when I took office, has been reduced dramatically . . . This dramatic improvement in the performance of our economy was no accident. We have put in place policies that reflect our commitment to reduce Federal government intrusion in the private sector and have eliminated many barriers to the process of capital formation and growth. We continue to maintain a steadfast adherence to the four fundamental principles of the economic program I presented in February, 1981: reducing the growth of

87

WHAT THEY SAID IN 1986

(RONALD REAGAN)

Federal spending; limiting tax burdens; relieving the economy of excessive regulation; and supporting a sound and stable monetary policy.

Budget message to Congress, Washington, Feb. 5*/The New York Times, 2-6:12.

1

The bad old days of runaway inflation, economic decline and national despair are long gone, but the crowd of big spenders and big taxers who created the mess are still lurking in the wings. They held out the dream that big government could solve every problem, that Federal money was free money, that the American economy was a horn of plenty which could be taken for granted. Usually, when people grow up, they quit believing in the tooth fairy.

At Republican fund-raising event, St. Louis, Feb. 12/ The New York Times, 2-13:15.

2

Again we hear that constant refrain coming out of Washington—"Raise taxes." It is time for Congress to take a responsible approach to spending decisions and, when it comes to taxes, let's get into the spirit of the times. I've said it before and I'll say it as often as it takes: I'll veto any tax hike that comes across my desk. Not only will we not raise taxes before I leave office, I plan to make sure we have a balanced-budget amendment that puts a permanent lid on taxes and doesn't let the government grow any faster than the economy.

News conference, Washington, June 11/ The New York Times, 6-12:10.

3

May I offer some advice from a fellow who deals with the liberals every day in Washington. When it comes to "tax and tax, spend and spend," some of them mean well, but they're just like Oscar Wilde—they can resist everything but temptation.

At Republican gathering, Dallas, July 23/ The New York Times, 7-24:8.

4

. . . how ironic it is that some continue to espouse such ideas as a "new international economic order" based on state control when the world is learning, as never before, that the freedom of the individual, not the power of the state, is the key to economic dynamism and growth. Nations have turned away from centralized management and government controls and toward the incentives and rewards of the free market. They have invited their citizens to develop their talents and abilities to the fullest and, in the process, to provide jobs, to create wealth, to build social stability and foster faith in the future for all.

At United Nations, New York, Sept. 22/ The Washington Post, 9-23:(A)16.

Alice M. Rivlin
Director of economic studies, Brookings Institution; Former Director, Congressional Budget Office

5

[On the Gramm-Rudman Federal budget-balancing plan]: Gramm-Rudman is analogous to a family who doesn't have a balanced budget, sitting down and saying, since we can't agree on what to do, let's cut everything we're spending money for by 20 per cent. You quickly find out that you can't do that. You have to pay the mortgage, the light bill. So you exempt some bills; they have done that in Gramm-Rudman. Then the percentage by which you have to cut the rest of your bills goes up. It's a way of saying: Let's not even think about what's most important; let's cut everything across the board because we can't agree what's most important. That's pretty foolish.

Interview/USA Today, 2-11:(A)9.

6

When a government is borrowing large amounts of money and living beyond its means, that is a misuse of the nation's savings. We're not a high-savings country; we need those savings to invest in modernizing our industries and improving our standard of living in the future. To use a large part of our savings simply to run the government is quite wasteful. We've been able to do that because the rest of the world has been lending us money—

(ALICE M. RIVLIN)

lending us their savings. That's a risky thing to do; when you borrow from the rest of the world, you eventually have to pay it back.

Interview/USA Today, 2-11:(A)9.

Charles S. Robb
Chairman, Democratic (Party) Leadership Council; Former Governor of Virginia (D)

1

What our government needs desperately is discipline. If defense spending has to be reduced, then let's reduce it. If domestic spending has to be cut, then let's cut it. If tax breaks have to be stopped, then let's stop them. It's going to take all of these steps, and all of us know it. These decisions aren't going to be easy or politically popular, but we've been making them in the states where 34 of the 50 Governors and two-thirds of the state legislatures are Democratic. The bottom line is this: America will never fulfill its destiny until it puts its own financial house in order.

Broadcast address to the nation, Washington, Feb. 4/The New York Times, 2-6:17.

Paul Craig Roberts
Former Assistant Secretary of the Treasury of the United States

2

The [Federal] debt buildup is proving to be a problem because the expected inflation has not materialized. Indeed, the large budget deficit has been mistakenly viewed as a source of inflationary fiscal stimulus to the economy when, in fact, it is a direct consequence of unexpected disinflation.

The New York Times, 9-5:30.

Georges F. Rocourt
Chief economist, Mercantile Safe Deposit and Trust Company, Baltimore

3

[On the proposed tax-reform proposals in Congress]: All the risks are on the downside. We're knocking big holes in 10 to 15 per cent of the economy, and we are bound to suffer in the

short term. I don't want to argue that the economy won't be better off in the long run because of lower marginal tax rates. I favor lower marginal tax rates, but as the old saw from Maynard Keynes goes, in the long run we could all be dead. There is going to be more severe dislocation over the next three years than anybody has realized, and the political and industrial consequences may end up easing the Republican Party out of power.

The New York Times, 7-28:23.

Dan Rostenkowski
United States Representative, D-Illinois

4

[On the jockeying among Congressional Democrats, Republicans and President Reagan to take credit for the current tax-reform bills]: The politics of the game have been played from the beginning. I don't think the President thought the House could pass a bill, but we did, and we fashioned a pretty good Democratic piece of legislation. The winners are going to be the taxpayers. I'd like to bask in some of the sun and have my party enjoy the warmth as well. But for a conservative President to have accepted this challenge, for Democrats not to take advantage of it would have been ridiculous. In the long run, we're helping our constituency as long as we take care of the middle-income people. The President will probably get the lion's share of the credit, but there's enough for all of us.

Interview/USA Today, 7-14:(A)9.

5

[On the recently passed tax-reform bill]: It was not the hope of tax cuts that stirred a doubting and often cynical nation. It was the sense that the family down the street or the corporation down the block will finally pay their share.

The Washington Post, 9-29:(A)12.

Warren Rudman
United States Senator, R-New Hampshire

6

[On the Gramm-Rudman-Hollings deficit-reduction act]: I have found it very interesting

(WARREN RUDMAN)

reading some of the columnists in the last several months, who have said that this bill is not working because we're missing the target. It's a little like telling a team that was a 50-point favorite on Sunday that they're lousy because they won only by 42. The fact of the matter is that we are going to have a gross reduction of the [Federal] deficit this year of somewhere between $40-billion and $60-billion. The increase in Federal spending has been at the lowest rate since the third year of the first term of the Eisenhower Administration. Gramm-Rudman-Hollings was looked at by too many people who had the minds of accountants rather than philosophers. This bill has set the agenda.

Interview/USA Today, 12-11:(A)11.

John Rutledge
Head, Claremont (Calif.)
Economics Institute

1

The cost of inflation is not what it does to people on fixed incomes. It's not what it does to the production economy. The cost is what it does to the capital base of the country. It destroys the financial markets, it creates phony net worth and it suckers people into destroying their real net worth. The cost of getting inflation out again is very heavy. So the moral of the story is that we should make sure we purge inflation all the way down to zero, and then make sure we never have to do this again.

Interview/U.S. News & World Report, 3-31:47.

Stephen I. Schlossberg
Deputy Under Secretary for
Labor-Management Relations, Department
of Labor of the United States

2

I don't believe in the tooth fairy. I don't believe we have all the answers to becoming competitive by labor-management cooperation. But it's a tremendous part of becoming competitive—

to motivate people better and increase the quality of work, and tailor machines to people, instead of people to machines.

Interview, Washington/
The Washington Post, 3-17:(A)9.

Bruce R. Scott
Professor of business administration,
Harvard University

3

Our foreign debts are now bigger than our foreign assets. The Reagan Administration has been essentially pumping up our standard of living by borrowing . . . I'm not expecting the trade deficit to correct itself.

The Christian Science Monitor,
7-24:19.

George P. Shultz
Secretary of State of the United States

4

The United States firmly believes that our own development experience is a useful guide to productive economic policies. What is the most fundamental lesson of that experience? That the talents of individual human beings are the greatest resource a society can bring to the tasks of national development. America has seen this truth at work in its agricultural era, in its industrial phase, and in its post-industrial development. And we have seen our dedication to that truth translated throughout our society into better opportunities for succeeding generations.

At United Nations, New York, May 28/
The New York Times, 5-28:5.

Paul Simon
United States Senator, D-Illinois

5

Many people now view unemployment as something like the weather—there's nothing you can do about it.

USA Today, 12-5:(A)4.

William E. Simon
*Co-chairman, Lay Commission on Catholic
Social Teaching and the U.S.
Economy; Former Secretary of the
Treasury of the United States*

1

[Criticizing a U.S. Catholic bishops' pastoral letter which chastised the U.S. economy for permitting poverty and unemployment and called for more government involvement in the economy]: Private economic initiative, and not the state, is the source of wealth in our country. In a world in which poverty is the rule and prosperity the exception, our bishops would do well to study the causes of *prosperity*.

The New York Times, 11-14:13.

Vincent Sirabella
*Organizing director, Hotel Employees and
Restaurant Employees International Union*

2

The labor movement permitted a generation of time to elapse, approximately 1955-1980, without preparing—by education and training—for this current generation of organizers. Labor must make organizing its principal priority for the balance of this century and well into the next century.

*At School of Industrial and Labor Relations,
Cornell University/Los Angeles Times, 4-7:(I)14.*

Rodney G. Smith
*Deputy Executive Director, President's
Commission on Organized Crime*

3

We are suggesting to every employer in the nation that he should consider the suitability of drug-testing [of employees]. What we are saying is that being drug-free ought to be a condition of employment.

*Press briefing, Washington, March 3/
The Christian Science Monitor, 3-4:3.*

Larry Speakes
*Principal Deputy Press Secretary to
the President of the United States*

4

The President [Reagan] thinks that if it's going to be called "the President's budget," it

should become more of the President's budget. But from the moment it leaves the White House in early February and arrives at Capitol Hill, it is no longer the President's budget; he has very little to do with it except his powers of persuasion.

*Washington, Jan. 10/
The New York Times, 1-11:8.*

Fortney H. Stark
*United States Representative,
D-California*

5

[Supporting the proposed tax-reform program approved by Congressional negotiators]: Most of those who are complaining now are upset simply because we won't let them escape paying their fair share of taxes any more. For everybody else, we may not make it any more fun to pay taxes, but at least they won't feel like chumps.

Los Angeles Times, 8-21:(I)1.

Don Starnes
*Mayor of Yuma, Colorado;
President, Farmers State Bank of Yuma*

6

[On the financial plight of farmers]: It's probably hard for people somewhere else to realize what's going on, because the economy's going strong for them. But the economy in rural America is not good. Fact is, it's about as bad as it's been since the Depression . . . It's very—well, very . . . unpleasant. It's unpleasant and hard, real hard, when you have to go to a farmer you've known for years and you have to foreclose, take away that fellow's home and his livelihood. Fact is, though, we're loaning other people's money—it's the depositors' money. And you have [to] protect that money, or there's no bank.

*Interview, Yuma, Colo./
The Washington Post, 6-3:(A)11.*

David A. Stockman
*Former Director, Federal Office
of Management and Budget*

7

[Republican members of Congress] get away with making speeches about how [Federal]

(DAVID A. STOCKMAN)

spending's out of control, but when it comes to their own turf, they say: "Don't cut you, don't cut me, cut the fellow behind the tree."

Interview/The New York Times, 2-5:24.

1

After four years, I am convinced that a large share of the [Federal budget deficit] problem is us. By that, I mean Republicans.

Interview/Newsweek, 2-17:13.

Margaret Thatcher
Prime Minister of the United Kingdom

2

You cannot go on trying to convince people they can get something for nothing and do not need people to create wealth. Socialist governments assume someone else created the wealth and it is there for them to distribute. Very soon the distribution runs out, the deficit is enormous, they get into the hands of the IMF and they come down to sound policies. They duck the fundamental questions as long as they can— as ours did. But sooner or later you have to run things soundly. That's why you'll find even socialist governments practicing these policies. Look at Spain—getting their borrowing down, their inflation down, putting emphasis on the efficiency of their industries.

Interview/Forbes, 7-28:93.

Alvin Toffler
Futurist

3

It's a myth to think the United States is not going to be a great manufacturing power. We will still build products. We just aren't going to use many people to do it with. The issue facing the United States is not the loss of our manufacturing base, but the transformation to modern, advanced technology. That raises tremendous social and economic problems.

Interview/USA Today, 3-11:(B)4.

Paul A. Volcker
Chairman, Federal Reserve Board

4

Economic history is replete with examples of countries that in attempting to correct overvaluation of their currencies . . . lapsed into a debilitating and self-defeating cycle of external depreciation and internal inflation at the expense of an eroding loss of confidence, higher interest rates and impaired growth.

*Before House Banking Committee, Washington,
Feb. 19/Los Angeles Times, 2-20:(IV)1.*

5

Should I have all the power I do? Ideally, I would say no . . . But if you're going to replace it with a system or a rule, you've got to have some conviction that the rule is better.

Newsweek, 2-24:53.

6

Huge and rising trade deficits in the United States and counterpart surpluses abroad [prevent the U.S. from building] a lasting foundation for sustained growth. Nor can we count on satisfying indefinitely so much of our own needs for capital by drawing so heavily on the savings generated elsewhere in the world—savings that have been so freely available in part only because internal growth in Europe and Japan has been relatively low.

*Before Senate Banking Committee, Washington,
July 23/The New York Times, 7-24:25.*

7

[On the U.S. trade deficit]: So much of the malaise, if I may use that word, in the industrial side of the economy is related to the trade position. I don't think you are going to see a dramatic change in that side of the economy without some prospect and actuality of improvement on trade . . . I don't want you to have the impression that there is some answer to all these problems by reducing the discount rate or easing policy . . . Our domestic demand, which is what presumably you affect most directly by monetary policy and discount rate changes, has been quite strong already. That is not the weak area in the economy. Consumption has been doing quite

(PAUL A. VOLCKER)

well. Housing is having one of its largest years on record. You can presumably pump up that part of the economy for a little while longer and a little more strongly. [But] that does not deal with the underlying imbalance, which sooner or later you have to deal with.

Before Senate Banking Committee, Washington,
July 23/The Washington Post, 7-24:(E)2.

Robert S. Walker
United States Representative,
R-Pennsylvania

1

We [in Congress] tend to forget that we pledged ourselves just a few months ago to a balanced-budget law called the Gramm-Rudman bill. That law was supposed to be met by doing several things. It was supposed to be met, for instance, by our having our budget in place by April 15 and beginning to work from there. Then by June 10 we were supposed to have passed all the appropriation bills relative to that budget. By the end of June we were supposed to have completed the whole budget process or not take a recess in July. Fat chance . . . We are forgetting the pledge we made to the American people that we are going to try to end deficits and move toward a balanced budget. We do not care. When it comes to spending money, Congress simply does not care. It does not obey the laws it puts in place. Every day we prove more and more that we are an outlaw Congress. We could care less about the law we pledged ourselves to for a balanced budget. I think it is high time that the American people begin to hold this body responsible for its irresponsibilities.

Before the House, Washington,
June 9/The New York Times, 6-13:10.

Alfred J. Watkins
Senior economist, Roosevelt
Center for American Policy Studies

2

[On the Gramm-Rudman Federal budget-balancing measure]: Gramm-Rudman will provide many members [of Congress] with new incentives to dig in their heels and refuse all compromise. Perversely, it could make stalemate the most palatable—the most politically feasible—game in town.

Los Angeles Times, 2-6:(I)14.

Marina Whitman
Vice president of public affairs,
General Motors Corporation

3

It's getting harder and harder to tell what's an American car or a Japanese radio. It may be made by Motorola, [but] part of it was put together in Singapore and another part in Mexico, and it was finally assembled in the United States. [But] there is still a very strong sense in people of nationalism, of a need for community. Nobody can quite deal with the global village as a community.

Interview, Detroit/
The Christian Science Monitor, 12-23:15.

George F. Will
Political columnist;
Commentator, ABC News

4

It's a mystery to me why so many conservative American businessmen complain about American [labor] unions. The principal effect of American unions has been to increase the purchasing power of American men and women. They buy what conservative American businessmen are selling.

TV Guide, 1-25:8.

Education

Mortimer Adler
Educator; Director, Institute
for Philosophical Research

1

Our educational system is absolutely inadequate—not relatively [but] *absolutely* inadequate—for the purposes of democracy. That's the Number 1 agenda item. If we don't solve the educational problem—if we have [only] the kind of citizens we have now—forget it.

Interview, Aspen, Colo./
The Christian Science Monitor, 9-23:16.

Lamar Alexander
Governor of Tennessee (R)

2

If America's greatest challenge is to compete in the world market, and if skilled people are essential to better jobs, then better schools shoot to the top of everyone's priority list. States and local government are charged with schools, not Washington. So what's going on, community by community and state by state to improve the schools, is essential to the U.S.'s ability to compete in the world.

Interview/USA Today, 2-20:(A)9.

3

What has suddenly riveted everyone's attention on our education system is that our standard of living is threatened. We're not going to have the jobs and the good incomes in America if we don't have the good skills.

Interview, Nashville/The Christian
Science Monitor, 2-21:6.

4

It may sound ridiculous to say it, but the quality of our teachers in the '90s will decide the future of America. It's that crucial. The whole problem boils down to whether the teachers' largest union [the National Education Association], and the teachers themselves, can accept our

finding ways to pay some teachers more than others [according to merit].

Broadcast interview/
"Meet the Press," NBC-TV, 5-18.

Walter Allen
Professor of sociology,
University of Michigan

5

[On whether black students are better off attending black colleges or white colleges]: Black students face a trade-off. They must decide whether they want psychological well-being or more-favorable physical circumstances. Blacks who choose white campuses purchase richly endowed physical surroundings and bureaucratic efficiency at the cost of less-favorable interpersonal relations and peace of mind.

USA Today, 5-20:(D)1.

Gregory Anrig
President,
Educational Testing Service

6

The country has reached a 95 per cent level of literacy. No other country has achieved that. There is still a problem for the remaining 5 per cent . . . But the real need is to work with the much larger proportion of the population that already can read but doesn't read well enough to cope with this technological society . . . We've shot for the minimum [in U.S. schools], and we're achieving that. Now let's move it up.

Sept. 24/The Washington Post, 9-25:(A)3.

James Ash
Provost, University of Miami

7

[On his university's decision, several years ago, to cut undergraduate enrollment in response to the decreasing size of the available student pool]: We made the decision to sacrifice size for

(JAMES ASH)

quality because we thought that, given the demographics, it was in our long-term interests. As it turned out, we didn't have to get as small as we thought we would. Raising standards had the effect of increasing demand. People who pay high tuition want to come to quality institutions with standards.

The New York Times, 3-10:13.

Gary Bauer
Under Secretary of Education
of the United States

1

[On the responsibility of schools to teach values]: I think schools have been very remiss, particularly for children from families and neighborhoods under a lot of pressure. We have had the worst of all possible circumstances. Just as there were cultural changes in the '60s and '70s, the schools began to give up on the idea that they could transmit values in the classroom that we can all agree on in a pluralistic society. They have to remind young people what makes good citizens.

Interview/U.S. News & World Report, 9-1:66.

Terrel H. Bell
Professor of education, University
of Utah; Former Secretary of
Education of the United States

2

[On the failure of the high-school class of 1986 to improve on its predecessors' Scholastic Aptitude Test scores]: [It's] the worst news we've had in education in a long time. The entire nation ought to feel bad about it. What's wrong with us? If you see how far down we've gone, we ought to be jumping up now.

Los Angeles Times, 9-24:(I)2.

3

Too many people still believe that you can have a successful life and make it in our society with a high-school education. [But today's world] calls for well-educated, disciplined minds.

It calls for us to become a nation of learners. We need perceptive and productive people, and we need millions of them. The masses need to be educated like they've never been before . . . Very few people will be able to cope, and succeed, and produce with the amount of education you get from high school. Higher education must be for the masses, not for the intellectually elite.

Speech/USA Today, 11-18:(A)8.

Ernst Benjamin
General Secretary, American
Association of University Professors

4

If you view [university presidents] as academics, they may seem over-paid. But if you view them as corporate heads of a very complex job, they're not.

USA Today, 10-7:(A)2.

William J. Bennett
Secretary of Education of the United States

5

[Criticizing strikes and complaints by teacher-union leaders]: [They have given teachers an image of being] hang-dog, down-in-the-mouth complainers who don't like children, strike at the drop of the hat, who are always screaming for more money and who are generally put upon and willing to tell you so every time you talk to them. Teachers are frankly better and more sensible human beings than the impression you would get from listening to some of their union leaders. [Most teachers] generally like life and are content with the state of the universe. A lot of these people who say they speak for them simply do not.

Interview/Los Angeles Times, 1-13:(I)4.

6

I do not think that the Department of Education is necessary to the education of the nation's children . . . I would not be disturbed if the Department disappeared. But I would be disturbed if the programs disappeared. In any case, the notion of abolishing the Department is moot politically.

Before Council of 100, Howard University,
Jan. 17/The New York Times, 1-18:9.

WHAT THEY SAID IN 1986

(WILLIAM J. BENNETT)

1

[Educational] institutions are defrauding students, and in many cases they are ripping off the American public, when they admit individuals who are manifestly unprepared for the work that will be required of them, or when they graduate students who cannot satisfy minimum standards in their field of study . . . Given the importance and growing cost of post-secondary education, it is only reasonable that students, parents, government officials and others should look for, and expect to find, evidence that they are getting their money's worth.

Before Senate Subcommittee on Education,
Arts and Humanities, Washington, Jan. 28/
Los Angeles Times, 1-29:(I)16.

2

Birth-control clinics in school may prevent some births—that I won't deny. The question is: What does it teach, what lessons does it teach, what attitudes does it encourage, what behaviors does it foster? . . . This is obviously a local [community] decision. But I would say this to any locality considering it—you had better be sure, really sure, that you have consulted fully and thoroughly with parents. Otherwise, you may find that you have created a full-enrollment policy for private schools.

Before Education Writers Association, Washington,
April 11/The Washington Post, 4-12:(A)3.

3

Instead of promoting tolerance, freedom of inquiry and the acquisition of knowledge, campus radicals nowadays tend to see the university as a kind of fortress at war with society, an arsenal whose principal task is to raise revolutionary consciousness, frustrate the government, discredit authority and promote a radical transformation of society. Just as a fortress under siege does not invite enemy spokesmen to address the troops, so too have campus radicals prevented [former U.S. UN Ambassador] Jeane Kirkpatrick, [U.S. Defense Secretary] Caspar Weinberger and other Administration spokesmen from presenting their point of view to the student body. What we have seen in recent years is the rise of a significant body of opinion on the campus which more or less openly rejects the democratic ethic.

Before American Jewish Committee, Washington,
May 15/The New York Times, 5-15:1.

4

[Supporting the IRS' confiscation of tax refunds from those who did not repay Federal student loans]: In this vast sea of Federal programs, some people might have thought that "If I don't pay, nobody will care." Well, we care . . . Our success is good news for all those young Americans who, sometime in the future, will find that they, too, wish to seek [a Federal student loan] . . . This collection is also something of a vindication for those nine out of 10 students . . . who do repay their loans on time, in full.

June 4/Los Angeles Times, 6-5:(I)17.

5

Every college president should write to his students this summer and tell them this: "Welcome back for your studies in September. But no drugs on campus. None. Period. This policy will be enforced—by deans and administrators and advisers and faculty—strictly but fairly." Such a policy could in fact be enforced. It should be enforced. And no parent or taxpayer would object if such a policy were announced and carried out. It would be good for our youth, good for our society and good for our institutions of higher learning. But putting in place such a straightforward policy would require a kind of reinvigoration of our institutions, a resumption of their basic responsibilities. Such a reinvigoration of our institutions and a resumption of responsibilities has, I believe, begun in America.

Before Heritage Foundation, Washington,
July 8/The New York Times, 7-11:24.

6

No school system—public or private—can accommodate the particular values of each family. What you look for is some broader consensus. Otherwise, you'd have to teach so many things that you wouldn't be able to teach anything. You have to courageously present your curriculum to your students, with community input, but that doesn't mean you're going to satisfy everybody.

(WILLIAM J. BENNETT)

If there is somebody who believes that two plus two equals five, and wants the public school to teach that, at some point the school says no.

Interview/USA Today, 9-22:(A)15.

1

The rhetoric of contemporary American higher education, the terms in which its practitioners and advocates speak of it, is often exceedingly pious, self-congratulatory, and suffused with the aura of moral superiority. The spokesmen for higher education tend to invoke the mission of the university as if they were Nicene Creed: one holy, universal and apostolic church . . . I have tried to criticize American higher education by the one yardstick that matters—namely, the relative success or failure of our colleges and universities at discharging the educational responsibilities that they bear. From the reaction, you would think I had hurled a rock through the stained-glass window of a cathedral. The response to my criticism was not "Prove it," or "You're wrong for the following reasons"; it was more like, "How dare you?" "Who do you think you are?"

At Harvard University, Oct. 10/
The Washington Post, 10-14:(A)14.

2

Most Americans want their schools to help form the character of their children . . . We should "teach values" the same way we teach other things—one step at a time. We do not argue against teaching physics because laser physics is difficult. Every field has its complexities and controversies. And every field has its basics. So the moral basics should be taught in school first. The tough issues can, if teachers and parents wish, be taken up later. And, I would add, a person who is morally literate will be immeasurably better equipped than a morally illiterate person to reach a reasoned and ethically defensible position on tough issues.

At Manhattan Institute, New York,
Oct. 30/The New York Times, 10-31:14.

3

Some of our colleges and universities charge [for tuition] what the market will bear. And

lately they have found that it will bear quite a lot indeed. The heart of the matter is that colleges raise costs because they can. And a very important factor in that ability to raise costs has been the availability of Federal student aid in the current form . . . More loan money does not make it easier for families to meet college costs. Rather, in the end, more loan money makes it easier for colleges to raise college costs.

At Catholic University, Nov. 19/
The New York Times, 11-20:13.

Richard Berendzen
President, American University,
Washington

4

A university in 1986 is in many respects a business. It's got a product; the product may be education, but nonetheless, in a very business-like sense, it is a product. Marketing seems very strange in higher education and yet, increasingly, universities are doing it, including the most prestigious in the country, for the simple reason that we're all competing for the same shrinking pool of people . . . and for the same dollars. We now have the bizarre competition between public institutions and private because many of the publics are now going out and fund-raising, and they're going to the same corporations, foundations and individuals that the rest of us [private institutions] are.

Interview, Los Angeles/
Los Angeles Times, 3-21:(V)4.

Derek C. Bok
President, Harvard University

5

[On what is the biggest lesson he has learned in his 15 years as Harvard president]: I suppose patience. Getting things done in academic life is necessarily a patient exercise . . . Bearing in mind nothing important in the university can ever be done without the assent—not only the assent, the active support—of a substantial number of people, that's a patient enterprise.

Interview, Cambridge, Mass./
Los Angeles Times, 9-3:(I)16.

WHAT THEY SAID IN 1986

(DEREK C. BOK)

1

In a world where scholars have to specialize so heavily and rely so much on external sources of recognition and support, loyalties are already divided between the university, the profession and the agencies that supply them with much needed funds.

At closing convocation, Harvard University, Sept. 6/The New York Times, 9-8:13.

Leon Botstein
President, Bard College

2

[On his school's new scholarship program that would reduce student costs to those at public colleges]: What we're doing is not "Crazy Eddie, we will not be undersold." We're saying make it a fair competition [between public and private institutions] of where the student really belongs and wishes to go, especially the best students. Shouldn't the best students in America have their pick and choice of the education most appropriate to their needs and aspirations?

The New York Times, 1-23:48.

Ernest L. Boyer
President, Carnegie Foundation for the Advancement of Teaching

3

This is our central dilemma: Historically, Americans have wanted local control of education but national results. Americans like the idea of localism. But how do they know their schools are doing a good job unless they have a national yardstick to measure them against? The problem is, we've never been able to devise a system that allows the excitement and flexibility of local control as well as the accountability of national results. In the end, we do the worst of all things: We not only mandate rigid standards but also hand out to the nation an annual report card based on SAT scores—yardsticks that were devised precisely to be school-proof, to measure aptitude rather than learning. And the media use these test averages to pass on to Americans the one bit of information the tests can't

reliably tell us: whether our schools are getting better or worse.

Panel discussion/Harper's, February:42.

4

Students don't have the foggiest idea why they're in school. We asked hundreds of students what they were doing in school. The most frequent response was, "I *have* to be here." They know it's the law. Or, "If I finish this, I have a better chance at a job." The "this" remains a blank. Or, "I need this in order to go to college." Or, "This is where I meet my friends." Not once in all our conversations did students mention what they were learning or why they should learn it. In general, we found among students a feeling of passivity and non-engagement, a sense that they don't fit, that they are not really being asked to become responsible adults. The schools have become institutions of passivity and are viewed by most students as adult places where rules are imposed and they must conform. If 40 million children do not see their schools as places for learning that somehow touch what they worry about every day, the prospects of making school a vital place are not good.

Panel discussion/Harper's, February:43.

5

[On the quality of college instruction today]: Technical knowledge, yes, that's fine. But what about the ability to integrate and apply knowledge wisely? That's the mark of an educated person. That's the urgent imperative of our time. But it's something most colleges aren't teaching.

Interview, Washington/ The Christian Science Monitor, 11-3:1.

6

[On college presidents]: It's almost impossible to make a separation between the president as institutional leader and the president as a private person with conscience and convictions. In the best of all worlds, a college president—just as anyone in an institutional position—should be able to speak freely and act individually. But the realities are that the president comes the closest of anyone to being the personification of his institution . . . Any public utterances he makes or

(ERNEST L. BOYER)

any stands he takes therefore carry enormous impact, and how those are received will reflect on how the institution is judged.

The Christian Science Monitor, 11-21:3.

Ronald Calgaard
President, Trinity University

1

I don't see anything wrong with academic elitism at all . . . We buy faculty.

Time, 4-28:56.

Hugh L. Carey
Former Governor of New York (D)

2

[Criticizing proposed Federal cutbacks in student aid]: Such losses are unacceptable to a nation committed for the last 30 years to making higher education available to every young person who has the ability and desire to pursue it. Such losses are unconscionable for a nation committed to racial equality and equal opportunity.

At Colgate University commencement,
May 25/The New York Times, 5-26:11.

Prince Charles
Prince of Wales

3

Perhaps . . . as parents you may be wondering, as I do on frequent occasions, whether the educational system you are confronted with is the right one to produce the kind of balanced, tolerant, civilized citizens we all hope our children will become . . . We may have forgotten that when all is said and done, a good man, as the Greeks would say, is a nobler work than a good technologist. We should never lose sight of the fact that to avert disaster we have not only to teach men to make things, but also to produce people who have complete moral control over the things they make.

At celebration of 350th anniversary
of Harvard University, Cambridge, Mass.,
Sept. 4/Los Angeles Times, 9-5:(I)24.

Lynne V. Cheney
Chairman, National Endowment for
the Humanities of the United States

4

I talk with young people a lot and make to them the case of how important liberal education is in a very practical sense. I talk about the personal rewards that come from a study of the humanities. The humanities need this kind of talk right now. From 1973 to 1983, the number of people majoring in the humanities in colleges was down by half.

Interview/USA Today, 11-10:(A)13.

Peter W. Cookson, Jr.
Senior research associate, department
of sociology, New York University

5

[On boarding schools]: The schools look like something out of the last century, with beautiful lawns and chapels, but in fact kids are placed under incredible stress. The schools ask the youngsters to give their all—to do well academically, be moral and develop service ideals. The parents expect them to get into the right college, marry the right person, have the right job. Then there is the student culture, which is extremely powerful—probably the biggest influence in their lives. It's in the dormitories that these kids learn the real rules of life . . . You find them saying things like: "Boarding school has made me more cynical. I've had to grow up faster." In the questionnaires they filled out for us, many students talked about seeing the dark side of life—going through the attempted suicide of a friend, or rooming with a friend whose parents were getting a divorce. Sometimes the youngsters almost become substitute parents for one another because they are so close. You have alcoholism, drug use, attempted suicide and all the rest. Many end up kind of burned out.

Interview/U.S. News & World Report, 1-27:73.

Norman Corwin
Visiting professor, School of Journalism,
University of Southern California;
Former radio dramatist

6

[Education is] the last, best hope. But it can be debased, perverted, misapplied. We're giving

WHAT THEY SAID IN 1986

scholarships to athletes who spend four years at a university and then cannot write a letter. Who are we kidding? That is what I call a trivialization.

Interview/USA Today, 8-18:(A)9.

Bill Cosby
Entertainer

1

As a parent, I know that four years of college bring nothing more than a learned person in terms of books, tests, notes. But that maturity, that ability to read other human beings, that maturity to make a decision based on what is needed as opposed to what you want—there's no degree for that.

At University of South Carolina commencement/Time, 6-9:62.

Jacques-Yves Cousteau
Explorer, Environmentalist

2

We lose our common sense progressively under the effects of the wrong education. That means that we are confusing education and instruction. Education should only be devoted to exercising judgment. And instruction is stuffing the brain with background. That's the only thing that they do with so-called education today—just stuff the brains of the kids with data. We are losing ground with common sense progressively.

Interview/USA Today, 6-5:(A)11.

Mario M. Cuomo
Governor of New York (D)

3

When you have kids in elementary school and you don't teach anything about values, I suspect the message you're sending is that there are no values. What's happened in the last 20 years is that we've said, "No values—we'll teach no values." It's all produced a vacuum. I don't think we're teaching any moral structure in any formal way.

Aug. 28/The New York Times, 8-29:1.

Bill Curry
Football coach,
Georgia Institute of Technology

4

I think of a coach as an educator if he's doing it right. The wonderful thing about a coach is that he has a youngster in the most intense moments, when he's fatigued, when he's at the height of his self-esteem, after a touchdown, after a devastating loss. He will remember things that happen in that crucible, in those moments, more vividly than almost anything else in his life, and what you say to him right then can have a major impact.

Interview/The Christian Science Monitor, 9-26:20.

Wilhelmina Delco
Texas State Representative;
Chair, Texas House Higher
Education Committee

5

We're embarking on another wave of school reform. In the first wave, despite the best of intentions, a lot of kids fell through the cracks. Now we not only have to pull kids out of the cracks but provide the people to do the pulling, the motivating, the exciting of those kids. It will take people who are comfortable and capable to reach out to the under-motivated, the under-educated, the under-excited, and bring them into the mainstream.

Interview, Austin, Texas/ USA Today, 5-19:(A)12.

A. Graham Down
Executive director,
Council for Basic Education

6

To make people more functionally competent and employable is only the implicit purpose of education. Surely its abiding, all-encompassing purpose must be to equip people with the taste for lifelong learning.

Panel discussion/ Harper's, February:42.

Thomas F. Eagleton
United States Senator,
D-Missouri

1

The quality of public education in this country has not been enhanced. And we are paying and will continue to pay some horrible, horrible penalties for it . . . [Supreme Court Justice] Thurgood Marshall felt, and as [civil-rights leader] Roy Wilkins felt, back in 1954 when *Brown v. Board of Education* came down, that, with deliberate speed and in due time, education would do the job. And it hasn't. I'm deeply saddened.

Interview, Washington/
The Washington Post, 10-31:(A)25.

Maurice Elias
Associate professor of psychology,
Rutgers University

2

Most children have trouble when they move from elementary school to middle school. The convergence of the child's developmental changes and the radical differences between a big, departmentalized middle school and a friendly, warm elementary school creates special stresses. We have worked with fourth and fifth graders to give them some of these problem-solving skills so they would have a strategy to turn to when they encountered serious pressures. Children who entered middle school with the ability to size up problems and plan in a detailed way how to cope with them had less severe difficulties.

Interview/U.S. News &
World Report, 4-21:64.

Chester A. Finn
Assistant Secretary of Education
of the United States

3

We should help the truly illiterate, but we must open our eyes to the much larger, if somewhat less poignant, problem of the many people who go through our schools and come out not literate enough.

Sept. 24/The Washington Post, 9-25:(A)3.

Norman L. Francis
President, Xavier University,
New Orleans; Former president,
United Negro College Fund

4

Black colleges do more than their share to educate black students, especially those with modest high-school grades and borderline college entry-test scores . . . Our [black] colleges accomplish the impossible with our students although we suffer in funding. State legislatures send out negative signals by discouraging the financing of public black colleges. Donors often are less than generous to our private schools. Yet everyone demands first-class performance. And we provide that! . . . High-school graduates are missing a great opportunity to turn their lives around when they neglect to check out black colleges . . . We offer quality study at affordable cost when compared to the expenses of a mainstream university, even state schools. Our UNCF campuses offer quality study, leadership opportunities and network potential to students often isolated on most campuses.

Interview/The Christian Science Monitor, 9-5:7.

Mary H. Futrell
President,
National Education Association

5

Responsibility for education is shifting more and more to the states. People talk about local responsibility. But when the states pay more, they make more decisions. The states are assuming more and more funding and leadership. But we believe the Federal government must remain involved to ensure there is equity.

News conference, April 23/
The Washington Post, 4-24:(A)1.

6

We've had dozens of reports telling us you need to upgrade the quality of education from kindergarten all the way through graduate school. What we've said all along is that that is going to cost money, big money, big bucks, and we can't bring about the level of change that you want without the money we need to do so . . . The revenue

WHAT THEY SAID IN 1986

increases we have experienced over recent years have, in reality, done little more than keep schools even with inflation.

News conference, Washington, April 23/
The New York Times, 4-24:15.

1

We know that only 23 to 25 per cent of parents ever visit [their children's] school. They don't go to the PTA meetings or parent-teacher conferences. They may go to a football game, but they don't go to the school and actually talk to the teacher. That's a national disgrace . . . I know that a lot of parents work and that there are a lot of single-parent families, but I won't accept that as an excuse. I'm from a single-parent family, and my mother knew my teachers. We didn't have a car and sometimes she had to change buses several times in order to get to the school. But she knew the teachers and all my teachers knew her.

Interview/USA Today, 8-26:(D)4.

David Gardner
President, University of California

2

We should . . . expect to see a career ladder [for elementary and secondary-school teachers] develop. As it is now, a teacher is a teacher is a teacher, regardless of competence or years of service. At least in higher education, you have assistant professors, associate professors and full professors. Schools should develop a cadre of master teachers—superior teachers who will serve as role models for junior members of their profession.

Interview/U.S. News & World Report, 5-5:64.

Robert M. Gates
Deputy Director for Intelligence,
Central Intelligence Agency
of the United States

3

Recent events here have again sparked broad discussion of both the propriety and wisdom of university scholars cooperating in any way with American intelligence. On December 3 of last year, *The Boston Globe* stated, "The scholar who works for a government intelligence agency ceases to be an independent spirit, a true scholar." These are strong words. In my view they are absolutely wrong. My remarks tonight center on two simple propositions: First, preserving the liberty of this nation is fundamental to and prerequisite for the preservation of academic freedom; the university community cannot prosper and protect freedom of inquiry oblivious to the fortunes of the nation. Second, in defending the nation and our liberties, the Federal government needs to have recourse to the best minds in the country, including those in the academic community. Tensions inevitably accompany the relationship between defense, intelligence and academe, but mutual need and benefit require reconciliation or elimination of such tensions.

At John F. Kennedy School
of Government, Harvard University,
Feb. 13/The New York Times, 2-14:26.

A. Bartlett Giamatti
President, Yale University

4

The health of educational institutions rests on the need to be mindful of the crucial distinction between education and indoctrination. There are many who lust for the simple answers of doctrine or decree. They are on the left and right. They are not confined to a single part of society. They are the terrorists of the mind. [But] if freedom does not first reside in the mind, it cannot finally reside anywhere.

At Yale University
commencement/Time, 6-9:62.

A. Bartlett Giamatti
President-designate,
National (baseball) League;
Former president, Yale University

5

Intercollegiate athletics are absolutely relevant to professional athletics. If people think drugs start at the pro level, they're wrong. And if people think the mania for sports in this country isn't fed

(A. BARTLETT GIAMATTI)

by the programs in the colleges, they're wrong. Talk about a cultural problem, that's a major one. What it's doing to those young people, particularly minority young people—black males in particular—who are simply used up for four years of eligibility. Then they're sent out into a world where they haven't been given the dignity and the chance to educate themselves. I think it's a sin.

Interview/USA Today, 7-29:(A)9.

Charles E. Glassick
President, Gettysburg College

1

[On his college's plan to reduce enrollment in response to the decreasing size of the available student pool]: The demographic facts of life are real. So far, we've kept enrollment up by more aggressive marketing and recruiting. Now we have to choose between size and quality and, in the long run, that's not a choice. If you don't sustain the quality, you eventually lose the numbers anyway.

The New York Times, 3-10:13.

Hanna Gray
President, University of Chicago

2

We've seen a shift from private universities to public universities, and we see fewer private universities. [It suggests that the nation lacks] a national sense of purpose and value about a pluralistic university system. Why is it, then, that all universities shouldn't be public? [In other countries,] systems of higher education that are monolithic and that are state-run ultimately become politicized—ultimately become instruments rather than critics of and contributors to the society. [The result is that they] ultimately can descend to mediocrity, ultimately lack the competitive edge that makes it possible for different ways, different approaches, creative ideas, the taking of risks, to happen.

Interview, Chicago/
The Christian Science Monitor, 11-25:20.

Ellen Greenberger
Professor of social ecology,
University of California, Irvine

3

[On the effect of teen-age employment on schoolwork]: One major study has found that kids who work long hours beginning at an early point in their high-school careers are at greater risk for dropping out. Research also suggests that working has contributed to a diminution in the quality of high-school education. When teachers look into a classroom and see tired faces and know that everybody has been at work the night before and is going back that afternoon, they often cut back on their expectations because it's hopeless to do otherwise. By the same token, students use a variety of corner-cutting strategies, including taking less-demanding courses, to make their work schedules compatible with the demands of the school. The investment of teen-agers in long hours of work is one of the contributing factors in the decline of quality education. Evidence also suggests that working long hours has a small but significant negative effect on grades. I know of no study showing that working is good for youngsters' grade-point averages.

Interview/U.S. News &
World Report, 11-10:93.

Theodore M. Hesburgh
President, University of Notre Dame

4

I think the fundamental concern [of a college president] is for the university itself and its growth and development, and to provide all your colleagues and co-workers with a vision. There are two jobs at hand. The first is to have a great university, a great faculty, great facilities, a certain panache, or esprit. After that, if you want it to be a Catholic university, you have to take that whole institution and somehow suffuse it with a faith. It's a place where the intellectual is the highest part of the endeavor, but the moral part of the endeavor is also important.

Interview, South Bend, Ind./
Los Angeles Times,
11-23:(I)22.

103

WHAT THEY SAID IN 1986

Ernest F. Hollings
United States Senator,
D-South Carolina

1

Claiming to support a strong education has become the latest fad. Unfortunately, as with most fads, such support appears to be all flash and little substance. The current [Reagan] Administration has done nothing to combat this threat and, in fact, has exacerbated the problem by refusing to commit to excellence in education. Since the release of "A Nation at Risk," 10 other reports which censure our nation's education system have been released. While all these reports set forth different ways in which to reform the educational system, they all agree that the system is in dire need of such reform. Incredibly enough, the response of the current Administration to this plethora of demands to reform and strengthen the educational system has been to decrease the amount of available funding. Federal funding for education has increased in dollar amount but, when adjusted for inflation, it has declined as a percentage of the total national expenditure for education. Federal expenditures now represent 7 per cent, or less, of the total spent on education. More to the point, education has dropped from 2.3 per cent of the Federal budget in 1980 to only 1.6 per cent in 1986.

Before the Senate,
Washington, April 23/
The New York Times, 4-30:14.

Bill Honig
California State Superintendent
of Public Instruction

2

[On the teaching of values in the schools]: The pendulum is swinging back from the romantic idea of the '60s that all societal values are oppressive and that the only thing that counts is the individual. Educators went along with all this craziness, so we've ended up with students who are ethically illiterate.

The New York Times,
9-15:11.

James B. Hunt, Jr.
Chairman, national board to establish
and certify teacher qualifications,
sponsored by Carnegie Forum
on Education and the Economy

3

We in America must commit ourselves nationally to getting and keeping the best people in education. We shouldn't resign ourselves to having the best go into law, medicine and business. We should be out there actively and aggressively competing to get the best into the classroom, and the best are attracted to professions with high standards that are accurately measured.

News conference, Washington,
Sept. 5/The New York Times, 9-6:11.

Auzville Jackson, Jr.
Director of intellectual property,
California Institute of Technology

4

The role of the university is, first, education. But it's become much more important to our society. The university is one of the most significant forces we have in economic development.

The Washington Post, 10-22:(A)15.

Barbara Jordan
Professor of public values and ethics,
University of Texas, Austin; Former
United States Representative, D-Texas

5

It makes a difference in this country if you have a college degree. People are more willing to listen to what you have to say and are more likely to believe you. A college education stretches your mind and opens you to perceive and take in the inner reality of others without judgment. An educated person is tolerant of the views of others and welcomes them into the marketplace of ideas. He does not feel that all wisdom begins and ends with him, but that there are others who may espouse different views of equivalent merit. It is a badge of being ill-informed to believe that you have the sole answer and none other will suffice.

At University of Arkansas commencement/
USA Today, 5-29:(A)11.

Walter Karp
Contributing editor,
"Harper's" magazine

1

Americans do not go to school in order to increase the social efficiency or economic prosperity of the country, but to become informed, critical citizens. A citizen is not a worker. The Soviet Union has workers, the American republic has citizens. A citizen is a political being; he has private powers and a public role. As Jefferson wrote, the education of a citizen must "enable every man to judge for himself what will secure or endanger his freedom." In practice, that goal is persistently betrayed. It is essential that citizens be able to judge for themselves and have the courage and confidence to think for themselves. Yet America's high schools characteristically breed conformity and mental passivity. They do this through large, impersonal classes, a focus on order as the first priority, and an emphasis on standardized, short-answer tests, among other things. Our schools do not attempt to make citizens; they attempt to break citizens.

Panel discussion/
Harper's, February:43.

Bobby Knight
Basketball coach,
University of Indiana

2

My thought has always been a very simple one—college isn't for everyone. College isn't for you if you aren't a pretty good reader and a pretty good writer. In athletics, we really haven't understood that, over the years. We have tried to take people who really are not bona fide college students and make college students out of them. They never become bona fide college students. Finally, we are putting together some rules and restrictions that are going to force high schools to pay more attention to academics. We are going to force high schools to do a better job of teachings kids. You can't believe the number of kids who come to college and can't put a full sentence together.

Before Downtown Athletic Club, Orlando,
Fla./Los Angeles Times,
4-20:(III)4.

Jonathan Knight
Associate secretary, American
Association of University Professors

3

[Criticizing the increasing incidence of censorship of school textbooks]: In any instance of censorship, the most corrosive effect is not that you don't learn about a specific subject. It undermines your belief that the way to deal with controversial ideas is not to suppress them, but to discuss them.

Oct. 9/The Washington Post, 10-10:(A)12.

Leslie Koltai
Chancellor, Los Angeles
Community College District

4

[Saying he emphasizes quality courses and libraries]: Some people [in community colleges] think we just need to expose students to college. Let them drive up . . . and drive away again, without ever getting near a library. They are happy if a student signs up for an auto-mechanics course and drops out after he learns to repair the carburetor. They say we [in the community colleges] have fulfilled a need.

Interview/Los Angeles Times, 2-5:(I)19.

Jonathan Kozol
Author

5

[On illiteracy in the U.S.]: It's a myth that we don't know what to do. The major obstacle to literacy is the parsimony of the Federal government. Illiteracy is one of the few problems in America that you can solve by throwing money at it.

Interview/The New York Times, 7-22:20.

Eugene M. Lang
Chairman, Swarthmore College

6

Politicians share the responsibility for our inadequate schools. The school system represents the interaction of institutional interests, the bureaucracy, the unions, political agencies. Each

(EUGENE M. LANG)

one of these institutions has its own interest to peddle. Education is a foil for their own political purposes. I don't like it. None of them puts the children first.

Interview/USA Today, 12-18:(A)15.

Norman Mailer
Author

1

. . . more people are going to college, but the education they get is the equivalent of what a good high-school education was in 1900. In 1900, a kid got out of high school and knew Latin. Now he knows domestic engineering, which is how to work your Cuisinart [home food processor].

Interview/Esquire, June:243.

Shirley Malcolm
Director, office of opportunity,
American Association for the
Advancement of Science

2

Education received by minority children is inappropriate for the high-technology era. The level of reading is [11 to 18 per cent] below white achievements. Although more young people are graduating from high school, dropout rates are increasing among minority students. Fewer black students are attending college than 10 years ago. A program directed toward moving the education of minority children out of the Dark Ages is needed . . . in most black communities through-out the nation.

At "Computers, Technology and Issues
of Equity" conference, Boston/
The Christian Science Monitor, 1-14:5.

Floretta D. McKenzie
Superintendent of Schools of
the District of Columbia

3

The word you hear [in education] everywhere today is *excellence;* everyone is concerned with

the quality of graduates, not the quantity. I worry that by wrapping ourselves in this cloak of "excellence" we'll be satisfied if the percentage of Americans graduating from high school continues to hover around 75 per cent when other nations are graduating 90 per cent. Excellence is important, sure; but we have to confront the simple fact that a high-school dropout is likely to become part of a permanent underclass with very little hope of decent employment.

Panel discussion/Harper's, February:41.

Norman Mintz
Executive vice president for
academic affairs, Columbia University

4

[On college football]: What we want is for football to be part of an educational process—not an end in itself. There's something about football that is an integral part of the American college experience—for the kids who play it and for the kids who watch it. A competitive program would make the school a lot more fun in a lot of ways.

The New York Times, 9-15:33.

Yasuhiro Nakasone
Prime Minister of Japan

5

So high is the level of education in our country that Japan's is an intelligent society. Our average score is much higher than those of countries like the U.S. There are many blacks, Puerto Ricans and Mexicans in America. In consequence, the average score over there is exceedingly low.

At meeting of Japan's Liberal
Democratic Party/Time, 10-6:66.

Eleanor Holmes Norton
Professor of law, Georgetown University;
Former Chairman, Federal Equal
Employment Opportunity Commission

6

It is no accident that the student activism of the 1960s and 1970s was played out against an expanding economy. I wonder if the students of

(ELEANOR HOLMES NORTON)

my generation would have been as open to their multiple causes if they had had the college debt burden that is characteristic even of many middle-income students. I wonder if the activist students would have been as active if the economy of those times had been as problematic as that which greets you today.

At Haverford College commencement, May 18/
The Christian Science Monitor, 6-13:24.

Benjamin F. Payton
President, Tuskegee University

1

You've 800,000 to 1 million youngsters effectively being pushed out of school as functional illiterates. So education is not just a pre-adult matter. It's a lifelong thing, and those who didn't get the right training in high school, often for no reasons of their own, must be able to still get it, through what I call recurrent education. Only then can they participate in a rapidly technologizing society.

Interview/USA Today, 4-28:(A)11.

Peter R. Pouncey
President, Amherst (Mass.) College

2

I believe with some passion that there is no institution on earth more pledged to renew itself every year and every day, than a college or university.

At Amherst College commencement, May 25/
The New York Times, 5-26:11.

Nathan Quinones
Chancellor, New York City Schools

3

If we are to take credit for improving academic achievement without considering the drop-out rate, then we are undermining that achievement. And if we don't do something, we are going to sap the strength of this country.

U.S. News & World Report,
3-3:77.

George Raveling
Basketball coach, University
of Southern California

4

[On the effects of college athletics on students' education]: Student-athletes should graduate. It's incumbent upon us to give them real direction. It's dangerous how much influence coaches have on them. We can put substance in their lives, or we don't have to care at all, or we can go about it half-heartedly.

Interview/Los Angeles Times, 5-5:(III)14.

Robert M. Rosenzweig
President, Association of
American Universities

5

[Criticizing Education Secretary William Bennett for saying radicals on campus are preventing democratic values from prevailing]: Those of us who spent the 1960s and 1970s on university campuses and fought the battles that occurred during those years on behalf of free speech and free inquiry are entitled to say that what Secretary Bennett has done is to exaggerate for his own purposes the behavior and views of a tiny minority of students and faculty in American universities.

The New York Times, 5-15:13.

Dorothy Rubin
Professor of education,
Trenton (N.J.) State College

6

Much of what goes on in school is at the literal comprehension level. Teachers usually ask questions that require literal responses, and children who answer these types of questions are generally looked upon as being excellent students. Teachers need to learn how to construct questions that call for higher levels of thinking.

Interview/USA Today, 12-22:(A)15.

George Rupp
President, Rice University

7

[On a Rice University plan to require students to take in-depth courses outside their major sub-

(GEORGE RUPP)

ject interest]: It is true the [curriculum] revision is a move toward constraining absolute free choice. But today there is a pressing social need for people whose center of interest is in the arts or humanities, for example, to have an informed knowledge of the world of science. A passing acquaintance at the level of abstraction is no longer enough.

The Christian Science Monitor, 12-12:8.

Benno C. Schmidt, Jr.
President-designate, Yale University

1

[On college athletics]: I believe deeply in athletics, in the fun and the value of athletics. But I regard the win-at-all-costs professionalism that one sees at so many major universities as a national scandal. I think the idea that athletics should displace—shunt aside—academic values is a disgrace. I think the idea that college athletes should go through on a different academic track is a fundamental denial of their best interests.

Interview/USA Today, 3-4:(A)9.

Jean-Jacques Servan-Schreiber
Author; Former Member,
French National Assembly

2

Today the U.S. faces a crisis in education. The level of primary and secondary education is well below the world-wide average. Young Americans entering college can hardly write a decent one-page text. They take little time and no pleasure in reading. They also ignore that there is a world of human beings outside the borders of the U.S., and they are confident that the U.S. remains No. 1 and unchallengeable.

Interview/Time, 6-16:53.

Donna E. Shalala
President, Hunter College

3

I have a dream where the Secretary of Education is testifying before Congress, asking for

more funding. On the right is the Secretary of State and on the left is the Defense Secretary. To the side is the U.S. Treasurer. All four argue that the survival of the nation depends on the willingness to support education. That's the kind of clout education needs.

Interview, New York/
The Christian Science Monitor, 9-30:7.

Albert Shanker
President, American
Federation of Teachers

4

The message out of the state capitals is: We think you [school] superintendents and principals and teachers are a bunch of idiots, so we're going to *tell* you to spend this number of minutes on this subject, and we'll provide a standard set of materials and standardized examination to make sure you follow orders. At a time when the [Reagan] Administration in Washington is claiming that our biggest sin has been to stifle initiative by over-regulation, we have entered the greatest era of educational regulation in history.

Panel discussion/Harper's, February:42.

5

If we're to avert a staffing disaster in the schools, we need to devote just as much attention to why we're losing so many teachers as we do to getting new ones. After all, we wouldn't need so many new ones if we weren't losing so many.

The New York Times, 4-22:15.

6

The revolution in teaching is getting away from thinking of teaching as lecturing. Imparting information can be done more easily through a book, videotape or computer. But motivating and coaching students to express themselves, organize their thoughts and think critically can only be done by a teacher . . . What's happening to teaching in many states is the opposite of professionalism. Legislation has been adopted telling teachers what textbooks or exams to use and how many minutes to teach each course. Teachers are now being treated more like hired hands who are told what to do and not as professionals who exercise

(ALBERT SHANKER)

judgment. If we continue to do that, we're not going to attract people of high caliber into teaching.

Interview/U.S. News & World Report, 5-26:57.

1

Even if we [teachers] were to get better salaries and some improvement in working conditions, intelligent, well-educated people . . . who have other options will not work for long in a traditional type of factory—and that's what the public schools of this country are. They will not work in a place where they are not trusted, where they are time-clocked, where they're supervised, where they're observed, where they are treated as people to be pushed around and instructed and regulated.

Los Angeles Times, 8-31:(I)26.

James M. Shuart
President, Hofstra University

2

The [Reagan] Administration in Washington talks about cutting education [funds] so that it can add to expenditures for defense. It is time that this nation understands that education is its first line of defense.

*At Hofstra University commencement,
May 18/The New York Times, 5-19:16.*

Benjamin Spock
Physician; Child-care specialist

3

Our emphasis on fierce competition and getting ahead minimizes the importance of cooperation, helpfulness, kindness, lovingness. These latter qualities are the things that we need much more than competitiveness. I'm bothered, for instance, at the way we coach young children in athletics and, even more ludicrous, the interest we focus on superkids. It hasn't gone very far, but there are parents who, when they hear that other children are learning to read at the age of 2, think, "My God, we should be providing reading instruction, too," without ever asking the most significant question: "Does it make the child a better reader or is there any other advantage to

learning to read at 2 rather than waiting until age 6?" It imposes strains on children. It teaches them that winning is the important thing. We've gone much too far in stressing winning.

Interview/U.S. News & World Report, 10-27:64.

John Thompson
*Basketball coach,
Georgetown University*

4

[Saying college athletics have become a scapegoat for education's problems]: I certainly wish intercollegiate athletics could clean up all its problems so that the intellectuals would have to deal with the real problem—education. Maybe that would give the academicians a chance to look at the tremendous educational problem in this country. It wasn't a coach who passed these kids from grades one through six when [they weren't] able to read. We're just giving educators something to blame for all their problems.

Interview/The Washington Post, 2-17:(D)8.

Jackson Toby
*Professor of sociology,
Rutgers University*

5

[Saying at some point disruptive students should be removed from school]: There comes a time when one has to temporarily give up [on those students]. School is not just a building to house warm bodies. If learning isn't taking place, there have got to be some trade-offs.

The Christian Science Monitor, 12-17:4.

Stephen Trachtenberg
President, University of Hartford

6

[On the increased dependency of public, as well as private, colleges on private funds and philanthropies]: You now have more of us trying to press toward the trough. The bad part is that many potential benefactors have a limited number of dollars to share. The positive side is that, as more and more publics go after private money,

(STEPHEN TRACHTENBERG)

the case for more public dollars for us [private institutions] becomes more compelling.

The New York Times, 7-29:1.

Marc S. Tucker
Executive director, Carnegie Task
Force on Teaching as a Profession

1

[On teaching]: Why would anyone want to go through all the effort and expense of becoming board-certified only to work in a school where salaries are low, the atmosphere is authoritarian and teachers lack the autonomy and responsibility that goes with other jobs requiring similar levels of training? . . . Just as law firms are run by lawyers, so schools should be run by teachers.

The New York Times, 5-16:9.

Hassler Whitney
Mathematician, Institute for
Advanced Study, Princeton, N.J.

2

[Learning mathematics should mean] finding one's way through problems of new sorts, and taking responsibility for the results. This has been completely forgotten [in most schools]. The pressure is now to pass standardized tests. This means simply to remember the rules for a certain number of standard exercises at the moment of the test and thus "show achievement." This is the lowest form of learning, of no use in the outside world.

The New York Times, 6-10:15.

Jim Wright
United States Representative,
D-Texas

3

Three years ago, the President's Commission on Education reported on what it called "A Nation at Risk." It said, "If an unfriendly foreign power had attempted to impose on America the mediocre education performance that exists today, we might well have viewed it as an act of war." And yet, three years later, the President's budget asks that we zero out the GI Bill for our Vietnam veterans and that we cut student loans and work-study grants, which make it possible for young Americans of modest means to get an education. We think that is a misplaced priority.

Broadcast address to the nation, Washington,
Feb. 26/The New York Times, 2-27:14.

The Environment • Energy

Lamar Alexander
Governor of Tennessee (R);
Chairman, President's Commission
on Americans Outdoors

1

[On the cost of protecting the environment]: America is a rich country, and a country with a value of outdoors. We are not so worried about the money . . . We want to present compelling ideas about the conservation movement in America, and let Americans know what needs to be done if they want to have an outdoors experience 10 or 15 years from now. I am convinced that if we do that well, the money will follow easily.

The Christian Science Monitor, 7-1:5.

James K. Asselstine
Commissioner, Nuclear Regulatory
Commission of the United States

2

[On the safety of nuclear power plants]: The question of how safe is safe enough is the most fundamental safety issue before the industry and the Commission today. Answering that question should have the highest priority of the Commission and the industry. In my own analysis of this question, I reach the following conclusion: The risk to the public posed by severe accidents at the existing plants is not acceptable for the full remaining operating lives of those plants. I would simply acknowledge the obvious: that the public and the Congress will not tolerate, and the industry and the NRC cannot allow, another severe accident as serious as the Three Mile Island accident [in 1979], or worse.

Before reactor safety panel of American
Nuclear Society/The New York Times, 4-17:12.

3

This Commission [the NRC] believes its job is to protect the [nuclear-power] industry and not the public. There's a willingness to accommodate industry wishes and a reluctance to take a strong and aggressive role to regulation. There's a misplaced sense of optimism even to the point of ignoring the [safety] messages we're getting from the operating experiences of the [nuclear] plants.

Interview/The Washington Post, 5-6:(A)17.

4

[On nuclear power plants]: Management is the fundamental aspect of safety. There is a wise diversity in management performance among the plants and we don't regulate management very well.

At Congressional hearing on nuclear safety,
Washington, May 22/The New York Times, 5-23:8.

5

[On the Chernobyl nuclear-plant accident in the Soviet Union earlier in the year]: The Chernobyl accident demonstrates vividly that nuclear safety is truly a global issue. We would be remiss if we ignored some of the accident's broader issues that transcend the design differences [in plants around the world]. In a very real sense, we are all hostage to each other's performance.

The New York Times, 10-27:1.

Ralph Bailey
Chairman, Conoco Corporation

6

I believe we [in the oil industry] should rely primarily on market forces rather than government intervention to adjust to current market conditions. The other side of the coin is that state and Federal governments should not erect barriers that prevent the domestic petroleum industry from operating economically and efficiently. In particular, they should resist the urge to target the petroleum industry whenever they need to supplement their revenues. When our taxes go up, the funds available for exploration and development inevitably have to go down.

Interview/The Wall Street Journal,
9-23:34.

WHAT THEY SAID IN 1986

Hans Blix
Director General, International
Atomic Energy Agency

1

[On the recent nuclear power-plant accident at Chernobyl in the Soviet Union]: I do not think one can really say that this changes [nuclear experts'] views about the need and justification for nuclear power. The probability analysis that has been made about the risks of accident [in Western-style reactors] indicates very low likelihood of nuclear accident. The experts, of course, will ask themselves what is the real scope of the [Chernobyl] accident, and how does it compare with other major industrial accidents in the world? And what are your alternatives to nuclear power? If you are saying no to further nuclear [expansion], it means more coal. And even with the current means of purifying emissions, you will have a great deal of sulphur dioxide and nitrogen oxide and carbon dioxide contributing to [dying forests], to acid lakes, decayed cities, [disease]. No one energy is without risks; we'll have to weigh them against each other.

Interview, Bonn, West Germany/
The Christian Science Monitor, 6-19:12.

George Bush
Vice President of the United States

2

[On the recent plummet in oil prices]:. . . the interest in the United States is bound to be cheap energy if we possibly can. But from our interest, there is some point where the national-security interests of the United States say, "Hey, we must have a strong, viable domestic [oil] industry."

Before American Businessmen's Group, Riyadh,
Saudi Arabia, April 6/The New York Times, 4-7:1.

3

The fall in oil prices has cut two ways in this country: It has been an enormous benefit to consumers and to the economy generally, but it is devastating in the Southwestern [oil-producing and processing] states. The oil business, unlike some other parts of our economy, is not sustained by government subsidy. Many drillers or oil producers have gone out of business. Many

metropolitan areas as well as rural areas are being hurt. It is important to our national security to have a viable, strong domestic oil industry. The danger is that output will get down to a level where production dries up and can't be brought on stream again. Then you have hurt the energy base of the United States.

Interview/U.S. News & World Report, 4-14:27.

Jimmy Carter
Former President of the United States

4

There are many environmentalists who, [while they] are quite enlightened and quite level-headed and responsible, look on the business community as surfeited with selfishness. I think that an inevitable relationship is going to develop [between these two sides], either through enlightened planning or through the reaction to crises.

Interview, Atlanta/The Christian
Science Monitor, 12-30:14.

Alston Chase
Chairman, Yellowstone Library
and Museum Association

5

The [U.S.] Park Service perceives its mission not to be the preservation of resources but, rather, the attraction of visitors to our parks. The Park Service has become the U.S.'s tourist agency, not its natural preservation agency. That's what's fundamentally wrong.

Interview/USA Today, 5-28:(A)11.

Jacques-Yves Cousteau
Explorer, Environmentalist

6

We are emphasizing the increasing relationship between the quality of water systems and the quality of life of the people who depend upon the water system, around the world . . . Scientists who are working around the world have found that the water system is deteriorating every year a little more—in the quality and quantity of the water. Now there are huge areas where there is not enough water for people, and in other countries

(JACQUES-YVES COUSTEAU)

water is wasted. We have a tendency to pass off the ocean as a vast system, but it's very small. The amount of water on the earth is very small.

Interview/USA Today, 6-5:(A)11.

1

I have found that governments can do very little [to improve the environment], I am afraid. The economic facts are there; the technical facts are there; but the wheels keep running, crushing this and that . . . It's frightening when a new, aware government comes in, and still nothing is done. The only way is to put pressure on public opinion. The public can change things, if they are well educated. That's what I am trying to do . . .

Interview, off Baja California, Mexico/
The Christian Science Monitor, 7-24:16.

Charles J. DiBona
President, American Petroleum Institute

2

[Saying he is concerned about declining U.S. oil production]: We're falling into the same trap of vulnerability. The less oil we produce, the more we'll have to import, and the less control we'll have over both supply and price.

The New York Times, 12-11:33.

Jack Doyle
Director, agriculture resources project,
Environmental Policy Institute

3

I think the writing is on the wall for the chemical and pharmaceutical people. They see that eventually pesticides will be moved out of the marketplace. But I think that having the chemical and pharmaceutical industries presiding over the transition means that we will see a lengthening of the pesticide era, rather than a rapid diminishing of it. Eventually, the Dows and Eli Lillys will be producing crops that are disease- and insect-resistant genetically. But getting there may take 25 to 30 years.

Interview/USA Today,
5-7:(A)9.

Werner Fornos
President, The Population Institute

4

[On the population of the world just passing the 5 billion mark]: Never before have so many people shared space on this planet . . . While the numbers are staggering, the consequences of such startling growth are even more so. The 5 billionth child was probably born in the Third World, where nine of every 10 babies are born today and where poverty, disease, hunger, illiteracy and unemployment make life a daily struggle for survival.

The Christian Science Monitor, 7-8:5.

Mikhail S. Gorbachev
General Secretary, Communist
Party of the Soviet Union

5

[On the recent nuclear-plant accident at Chernobyl in the U.S.S.R.]: The indisputable lesson of Chernobyl to us is that in conditions of the further development of the scientific and technical revolution, the questions of reliability and safety of equipment, the questions of discipline, order and organization assume priority importance. Further, we deem it necessary to declare for a serious deepening of cooperation in the framework of the International Atomic Energy Agency. What steps could be considered in this Atomic Energy Agency . . . Creating an international regime of safe development of nuclear power on the basis of close cooperation of all nations dealing with nuclear-power engineering. A system of prompt warning and supply of information in the event of accidents and faults at nuclear-power stations, specifically when this is accompanied by the escape of radioactivity, should be established in the framework of this regime. Likewise, it is necessary to adjust an international mechanism, both on a bilateral and multilateral basis, for the speediest rendering of mutual assistance when dangerous situations emerge.

Broadcast address to the nation, Moscow,
May 14/The New York Times,
5-15:8.

WHAT THEY SAID IN 1986

Robert Graham
Governor of Florida (D)

1

[On his proposal to save the Everglades]: In our enthusiasm to build a rich and powerful state, we nearly destroyed the heart of Florida, the Everglades, which continually replenish the richness of the land and which define its character . . . Success in this [rescue] endeavor means turning back the clock 100 years. By the year 2000, the Everglades will look and function more like they did at the turn of the century than they do today.

Marco, Fla./The New York Times, 1-20:13.

Harold Heinze
President, Arco-Alaska, Inc.

2

[Calling for more oil exploration in the wilderness areas of Alaska, despite environmentalists' concerns about the impact on that wilderness]: Backpackers are not representative of the U.S. population. This concept that Alaska needs to be preserved as wilderness for visitors is a crock. Most visitors want to have some reasonable access . . . [But] Alaskans have a better understanding of wilderness. We know that you can go over a hill and be away from the presence of man. I don't have to go 200 miles away from people to be in wilderness. It's okay for me to go two miles and not see them.

Interview/Los Angeles Times,
12-7:(I)2.

Joseph M. Hendrie
Former Chairman, Nuclear Regulatory Commission of the United States

3

[On the recent Soviet nuclear-plant accident at Chernobyl]: This is the hypothetical accident, the ancient accident of all the American studies. They [the Soviets] have dumped the full inventory of volatile fission products from a large power reactor directly into the environment. You can't do any worse than that.

The New York Times, 5-9:6.

John S. Herrington
Secretary of Energy of the United States

4

[Criticizing Saudi Arabia for over-production of oil, which is driving down oil prices in the U.S. and thus harming U.S. producers]: It's got to be apparent to the Saudis and the rest of the Arabs that their production is causing some problems in our producer industries. There is a point where forcing prices or increasing production has political implications. The Saudis have a lot of friends in the world, and forcing prices down by excess production has ramifications among their allies.

To reporters, Washington, March 31/
The Washington Post,
4-1:(A)1.

5

[On the decision to complete a new major storage facility for the Strategic Petroleum Reserve, even though there is no oil-supply crisis in the U.S. at the present time]: The Strategic Petroleum Reserve is this nation's first line of defense against the threat of a future oil-supply disruption. The Department has been reviewing policies about the reserve and, in light of the current world oil market, we have decided that a prudent course of action is to have in place the long-range flexibility to resume fill of the reserve, if necessary.

April 11/The Washington Post,
4-12:(A)10.

6

[Criticizing the Soviet Union for refusing to pay for damages caused to other countries by this year's nuclear plant accident at Chernobyl, in the U.S.S.R.]: [The Soviet Union needs to] appreciate that their nuclear program, although cloaked in secrecy, has had a profound impact beyond their borders. Radioactive releases from Chernobyl . . . have cost other countries hundreds of millions of dollars, yet there has been no serious talk of restitution. Whatever happened to the concept of right and wrong?

At special session of International Atomic
Energy Commission, Vienna, September/
Los Angeles Times, 10-6:(1)12.

Donald Hodel
Secretary of the Interior
of the United States

1

[Former President] Jimmy Carter's Interior Secretary was viewed as being 100 per cent preservationist, although it was not true. President Reagan's first Secretary of the Interior [James Watt] was destined to be accused of being a developmentalist, since environmental organizations supported Carter. Jim Watt moved the Department back to a proper course. He was accused of being totally pro-development—also not true. I have made clearly preservationist decisions and decisions that are clearly pro-development. Instead of being considered a moderate, I'm labeled as someone who flip-flops. You can't win in this business.

Interview/Christianity Today,
4-4:37.

Jesse L. Jackson
Civil-rights leader

2

[On the recent nuclear power plant accident at Chernobyl in the U.S.S.R. and the accident at the Three Mile Island nuclear plant in the U.S. some years ago]: The fact that both countries, the U.S. and the U.S.S.R., with about the same level of experience in nuclear power but with very different ways of managing it, have now had a disastrous accident tells us that the dangers of nuclear power are not derived from the quality of management, but are built into the technology itself. It tells us that the nuclear power industry is a dangerous and unnecessary way to produce electricity. It tells us that there are far better, much less dangerous, ways to produce our energy. We can produce the power we need from renewable solar sources, such as alcohol, which, produced on family farms, would help restore their economic stability as well. The Soviet accident tells us that the time has come to phase out nuclear power.

At New Directions conference, Washington,
May 2/The New York Times,
5-6:10.

Edward J. Markey
United States Representative,
D-Massachusetts

3

[On the Soviet nuclear-plant accident at Chernobyl and its implications for the U.S. nuclear-power industry]: The outcry over nuclear waste, the recurrent problems with nuclear safety, the precarious financial plight of many nuclear utilities all indicate that the industry's problems are coming home to roost . . . Wall Street has long been skeptical, the public has long been skeptical, and this accident confirms their fears.

The Washington Post,
4-29:(A)14.

Robert McClements, Jr.
President, Sun Oil Company

4

[On the decrease in oil prices and the general unpredictability of energy costs]: We were wrong about economic growth, we were wrong about the elasticity of demand, we were wrong about estimates of OPEC production. We've never been here before. What we're living with now doesn't have a prototype. We can't forecast the future. If someone asks me what's going to happen to oil prices, I tell him to go take a cold shower.

Los Angeles Times,
2-3:(IV)1.

J. Michael McCloskey
Chairman, Sierra Club

5

The Federal government has committed millions of acres in the Greater Yellowstone [Park] area to oil and gas development without either examining or understanding the consequences. We believe that the Forest Service, the Bureau of Land Management and the National Park Service should immediately begin to develop a comprehensive plan to limit the damage which will otherwise be caused by uncontrolled oil and gas development in this beautiful area.

The Christian Science Monitor,
7-18:4.

William P. Mott, Jr.
Director, National Park
Service of the United States

1

Parks are the only stable thing in the whole United States. Every city will be rebuilt in the next 100 years, but Yellowstone and Grand Canyon and all the other parks will still be here.

USA Today, 5-8:(A)10.

Brian Mulroney
Prime Minister of Canada

2

[The resolution of the acid-rain issue] is in the national interests of the United States and Canada. It is a trans-boundary issue and cannot be solved by one nation . . . If we don't deal with it on an urgent basis, then you will have left a legacy of a poisoned atmosphere and devastated links and a diminished environment. We have to deal with it.

Interview, Montreal/
The Christian Science Monitor, 3-18:1.

3

[On his discussions in the U.S. about acid rain, which he says crosses the border into Canada]: This is a front-burner issue. This is not going to go away until it is solved . . . Long after it is no longer fashionable to discuss Nicaragua in Washington, we will be discussing the environment. You can be certain of that.

To reporters, Washington, March 19/
The Washington Post, 3-20:(A)14.

Peter C. Myers
Assistant Secretary for Natural
Resources and Environment, Department
of Agriculture of the United States

4

[On Federal plans for stemming the phenomenon of farm soil erosion]: The government is through financing soil erosion. We're saying, "If you [the farmer] want to abuse your soil, do it on your own." I think the worst of our land will go into [a] reserve. Most of our erosive land can be brought into compliance by changing our way of farming . . . The biggest thing is that farmers

will have to change their attitude. Part of the problem is economics, but more of it is attitude. They all think that erosion is bad, but they don't think the problem is on their land.

The Washington Post, 2-18:(A)11.

Bruce C. Netschert
Vice president, National
Economic Research Associates

5

Of all the OPEC members, Saudi Arabia has the most to lose by a repetition of the experience it has just suffered through. Thus, although the price hawks in OPEC may argue for and even attempt the unbridled use of OPEC power, the Saudis will prevent it by doing just what they are doing now [keeping a cap on oil prices]. Above all, the Saudis want market stability. Once market firmness is re-established, they will permit only very slow growth in the real price of oil. The result, as I see it, will be an oil price in [the year] 2000 no higher than $25, in 1985 dollars, and probably somewhat less.

House committee testimony, March 6/
The Wall Street Journal, 4-29:28.

David Packard
Co-founder, Hewlett-Packard
Company; Former Deputy Secretary
of Defense of the United States

6

The most important question we have to deal with is a combination of population control and the control of our environment—how to utilize the world in as effective a way as we can for the future of mankind. Any time you look at the long-range situation, you come to the conclusion that, unless we can limit the population, the other problems are eventually going to become unmanageable.

Interview, New York/
The Christian Science Monitor, 11-21:22.

Cynthia Pollock
Researcher, Worldwatch Institute

7

Nearly four decades and 400 power plants into the nuclear age, the question of how to safely and economically dispose of nuclear reactors and their

(CYNTHIA POLLOCK)

wastes is still largely unanswered . . . Nuclear engineers have been attracted to the exciting challenge of developing and improving a new technology, not to figuring out how to manage its rubbish.

Before House subcommittee, July 30/
Los Angeles Times, 12-18:(I)28.

Peter H. Raven
Director, Missouri Botanic
Garden, St. Louis

1

[Lamenting the decline in the world's rain forests]: Within the next 30 years, all of the [tropical] forests will have been eliminated, with the exception of a few remnants on places too steep or too wet to cultivate. The major priority is the problem of extinction. The reduction of biological diversity is world-wide. Our boat is sinking, and we don't even act like we know it . . . Cutting tropical forests, like cutting all forests, contributes to carbon dioxide in the atmosphere. And the increasing carbon dioxide, most of which is due to burning fossil fuels, is certainly warming global temperatures, which does have world-wide impact. And although we don't know what the long-range global aspects of that are, we can be sure that since the climate . . . operates as one integrated system, deforesting huge areas is having an effect on the over-all system, and certainly will have [an effect] on us in due course . . . This is not the kind of an effort that you either win or lose. [But] what we do right now will have a real, definite and lasting effect on the shape of the world for many hundreds of years to come, precisely because we're in the time of [the] most explosive population growth, [the] greatest environmental damage, [and the] greatest extent of poverty that the world will ever see.

Interview, St. Louis/
The Christian Science Monitor, 8-7:1,4.

F. Sherwood Rowland
Professor of chemistry,
University of California

2

Prudent caution toward atmospheric change should have indicated regulation of chlorofluoro-

carbon emissions, even with some scientific uncertainty, because the upper range of possible ozone losses represented an intolerable risk. The governments of the world, instead, adopted prudent caution toward the chlorofluorocarbon industry and have avoided stringent regulation. With the exception of the bans in North America and Scandinavia of the chlorofluorocarbons as propellants in aerosol sprays, no effective regulations exist, and their world-wide usage is again expanding.

Before Senate subcommittee,
Washington/USA Today, 6-19:(A)8.

Nikolai I. Ryzhkov
Prime Minister of the Soviet Union

3

Satisfying the need for electric power depends to a greater degree on the growth of atomic energy. The correctness of such a course is confirmed in world and domestic practice . . . The determination of a technical policy that insures high reliability is of greater importance in nuclear-power generation than in any other sector. The [recent] accident at the Chernobyl nuclear-power station [in the Soviet Union] has shown the exceptional importance of the observance of such requirements.

Moscow, June 18/The New York Times, 6-19:7.

Abdus Salam
Director, International Center
for Theoretical Physics (Italy)

4

People do not take [the rain forests] as a global asset. People take it [the depletion of those forests] as a problem of Brazil, a problem of Malaysia. How many governments are willing to spend money on that sort of thing? None. Zero. [The problem is the lack of] the scientific infrastructure to look at the global problem. Everybody seems to be for himself. There is no global vision at all.

Interview, Trieste, Italy/
The Christian Science Monitor, 12-9:29.

David Schaenen
Oil-industry spokesman

5

[On criticism that oil and gas development harms environmentally sensitive areas]: The oil

WHAT THEY SAID IN 1986

(DAVID SCHAENEN)

industry didn't place the oil and gas where it's located. Mother Nature did that. Therefore we have to look for it where we can find it . . . Since the Federal government owns at least one third of all the mineral interests in the U.S., it is important that the oil industry have access to these lands.

The Christian Science Monitor, 7-18:4.

James R. Schlesinger
Former Secretary of
Energy of the United States

1

The United States and the West alternate between panic and complacency [in oil supplies]. If we are a barrel short world-wide, we talk about a shortage; if we are a barrel over, we talk about glut.

The Washington Post, 2-13:(A)16.

2

[Saying today's lower oil prices will result in a fall in U.S. oil production and more dependence on imports]: The United States is now in the process of creating a substantially increased oil dependency for the 1990s. We are sowing the seeds of the next oil crisis.

The New York Times,
3-13:1.

John F. Seiberling
United States Representative, D-Ohio

3

The cases of conflict between oil and other resources in the public lands is going to be increasing in the future. Just as the value of oil and gas has increased enormously in the last 30 years, so the value of other resources of the public lands has also increased enormously. As our population has . . . become more urban, the value of open spaces, wilderness, clean air and water, wildlife habitat, and recreation opportunities has increased, while the supply has diminished.

The Christian Science Monitor,
7-18:4.

S. Fred Singer
Professor of environmental sciences,
University of Virginia

4

[On the recent decline in oil prices]: The thing that may hurt us a great deal is volatility in prices. A downswing in price can force the premature abandonment of productive [U.S.] wells and thereby destroy some of our oil reserves. Oil companies will cut back on investments needed to produce future oil. If consumers start to believe that happy days are here again, and abandon conservation efforts, it will further raise our need for imported oil.

Interview/U.S. News & World Report, 4-7:51.

Weston Stacey, Jr.
Director, Fusion Research Center,
Georgia Institute of Technology

5

[On the recent accident at the nuclear power plant at Chernobyl, in the Soviet Union]: It's going to be a major setback for nuclear power in terms of building and using nuclear reactors. Clearly, we've had a case where a nuclear reactor has had a major accident. The people who run nuclear power plants all over the world are going to have to ask, "How did that accident happen? Are there any lessons there that we should learn?" That is clearly the responsibility of every organization in the world that is related to nuclear power—to ask those questions and assess them. In perspective, while it's a tragic accident, the magnitude of damage to human beings is small in comparison with many other industrial accidents. The [chemical] accident in Bhopal, India, killed and injured thousands, but no one has suggested closing down the chemical industry.

Interview/USA Today, 7-15:(A)11.

Robert T. Stafford
United States Senator, R-Vermont

6

The case against air pollution generally, and acid rain in particular, is becoming clear everywhere in the world. Lakes and forests are dying,

(ROBERT T. STAFFORD)

buildings are being destroyed and human health is at stake.

Sports Illustrated, 3-31:11.

Robert Stone
Author

1

For me, the bottom of the sea is the closest we can come to the mystic essence at the bottom of things. I mean, it seems as if you were looking at things as they are. Far more than taking drugs, or anything else. This is very dangerous and frightening—but it's also charged with joy. At the same time, I'm filled with a great fear. Because I know the uncontrollability, the unforgiving nature of the ocean. I feel that when you're looking at a coral reef you're seeing something very basic, essential: It's like the bones of the earth.

Interview/Newsweek, 3-17:73.

Arpad von Lazar
Energy consultant, Fletcher
School of Law and Diplomacy

2

[Saying Saudi Arabia is trying to take control of the world oil market]: The Saudis know exactly what they are doing. They are controlling the market to their advantage, squeezing out marginal producers [by keeping oil prices low], while the U.S. becomes more dependent on imports. In three to four years they will sock it to us, kicking the price back up to the mid-$20s [per barrel].

The Christian Science Monitor, 7-25:7.

Richard von Weizsacker
President of West Germany

3

We have been brought up, and our ancestors even more, to understand that nature is serving mankind. [But in the future,] we will have to realize, in our daily decisions and forms of behavior, that finally we are nothing but a little part in

the history of nature. And either we learn to preserve nature—or, if you wish, to preserve creation—or we will not survive.

Interview, Bonn/The Christian
Science Monitor, 12-12:26.

Walter Wallman
Minister for the Environment
and Nuclear Safety of West Germany

4

[On a nation's liability for damage to other countries caused by accidents at its nuclear plants]: The "polluter pays" principle must apply with regard to compensation for damage. An effective global system of liability for nuclear damage is indispensable.

At special session of International
Atomic Energy Agency, Vienna, September/
Los Angeles Times, 10-6:(I)12.

Mark White
Governor of Texas (D)

5

We cannot continue to shuttle back and forth in the Middle East on bended knee asking for some Middle Eastern oil power to set domestic [U.S.] energy policy.

USA Today, 4-8:(A)6.

Ahmed Zaki Yamani
Minister of Petroleum of Saudi Arabia

6

[Expressing concern that the current plummet in oil prices will cause a price and production crisis in the 1990s]: You are putting the whole world into a situation where you will have an energy crisis not invoked by a political crisis, like 1973 and 1979, but by a serious shortage in the supply of energy . . . What disturbs me is that some [production] cuts will be forever. Once you shut down stripper wells, you are not going to reopen them again unless the price of oil goes to $50 or more.

To reporters, Geneva, March 24/
The New York Times,
3-25:27.

119

Foreign Affairs

David Aaron
Former Deputy Assistant to the
President of the United States
(Jimmy Carter) for National Security Affairs

1

[Criticizing the Reagan Administration for involving the National Security Council in covert assistance to Nicaraguan rebels]: What they have done goes far beyond what anyone else has done with the NSC. Using the NSC in this kind of operational way is extremely dangerous. The National Security Council is the one place in government that is really beyond the purview of the Congress. The National Security Adviser and his staff are not subject to Senate confirmation. This is a little oasis, and if the President abuses it, he'll lose it.

The New York Times, 11-11:6.

Elliott Abrams
Assistant Secretary
for Inter-American Affairs,
Department of State of the United States

2

[On the Reagan Administration's use of covert activities in its foreign policy without advising Congressional committees]: How the hell do you conduct diplomacy when they [the committees] leak like sieves? The last two times I testified in the House in secret hearings, I had a leak the same day. That is what promotes efforts to use more-securer means of conducting government. But is it a great idea? No, it is not a great idea.

U.S. News & World Report, 12-15:31.

Corazon C. Aquino
President of the Philippines

3

In this year, when in so many parts of the world we see so many people struggling to achieve human rights, one must be frank to be relevant. I see this occasion as a chance to share with oppressed people everywhere my experience of how change is brought about. To be free, you can, as a people, appeal to the international standards of human rights set by others, such as the United Nations. But in the end, to vindicate those rights and achieve freedom, you are on your own.

At United Nations, New York, Sept. 22/
The New York Times, 9-23:8.

George W. Ball
Former Under Secretary
of State of the United States

4

[Arguing against the U.S. working to overthrow the governments of countries involved in international terrorism]: We're beyond the stage of civilization where international conflict is settled by the assassination of rulers, and we have no business messing around trying to overthrow governments just because we don't like them. History shows that almost always when we've done that we've something worse in its place. So-called reprisals are just a response to terror with terror, which only perpetuates an escalating cycle of terror . . . American credibility is on the line only when the President of the United States spends a week yammering about it and making threats he's not going to carry out. All this excitement about terrorism has become obsessive. Let me say that when I make that remark I'm trying to put this in some kind of perspective. We should understand that terrorism springs from certain causes and we ought to deal with the causes.

Interview/U.S. News & World Report, 1-20:79.

Roelof F. Botha
Foreign Minister of South Africa

5

[On U.S. foreign policy]: It is a pity. You [the U.S.] are the most powerful nation in the world. You should have had the most efficient foreign-policy instrument. And, at the moment, you have the worst . . . Not only we, but no govern-

(ROELOF F. BOTHA)

ment in Africa or elsewhere, can really rely on the consistency of the United States foreign policy. From Moscow, right through Africa to the Far East—including us—I think there is a consensus on this one.

Interview, Pretoria/The Christian Science Monitor, 12-9:1,51.

Willy Brandt
Chairman, Social Democratic Party of West Germany; Former Chancellor of West Germany

1

When the Americans and the Soviets had their tanks set up facing each other at Friedrichstrasse [in Berlin in the 1950s and early '60s], one could look into the barrels 100 yards away. It was demonstrated before our eyes, and before the eyes of the world, how terribly dangerous it is to let tensions reach the point where the hand touches the trigger.

On 25th anniversary of Berlin Wall, West Berlin, Aug. 13/ The Washington Post, 8-14:(A)15.

Zbigniew Brzezinski
Professor of government, Columbia University; Former Assistant to the President of the United States (Jimmy Carter) for National Security Affairs

2

[On longtime Soviet Ambassador to the U.S. Anatoly Dobrynin being recalled to become a Communist Party Secretary in Moscow]: Dobrynin understands the United States very well. And I strongly suspect that [Soviet leader Mikhail] Gorbachev may have gotten the feeling by now that over the last year his foreign policy has kind of floundered. He's been advised essentially by propagandists, and Gorbachev has gone for the grandstand ploys, the big grandstand play, but without any lasting effect. There's been no strategy, just antics. And I wouldn't be surprised that Dobrynin's coming to the Secretariat is part of an effort to strengthen the Soviet han-

dling of the American relationship, to exploit more fully and more intelligently our weaknesses, while at the same time promoting perhaps some degree of accommodation—but limited accommodation—with us.

Interview/The New York Times, 3-7:10.

3

. . . too many people in the U.S. government on this critically important, central relationship— the U.S.-Soviet relationship—are really operating on an ad hoc basis, without any larger view of the nature of the contest, and without any longer-range strategic design guiding their daily decisions. Policy-making is much more effective if it is driven by strategic concept.

Interview, Washington/ The New York Times, 6-17:5.

4

[Saying the U.S. is acting weakly in face of the Soviet's arrest of American journalist Nicholas Daniloff as a spy]: The Soviet Union has been reassured that it has a license to conduct spying with impunity in the United States [the U.S. recently arrested a Soviet diplomat in New York as a spy, after which Daniloff was arrested]. If a Soviet spy is taken in the future, another American will be grabbed, and the next time it is unlikely that the Soviets will repeat the mistake of taking a journalist hostage. It will be a businessman or a teacher or a tourist. This was the first genuine direct confrontation between this [Reagan] Administration and the Soviets. It was the U.S.A. that blinked. And maybe even more than blinked; in effect, it shut its eyes . . . The KGB chiefs in Dzerzhinsky Square must have been drinking Georgian champagne Friday afternoon . . . What is the point of [the U.S.] trying to catch so many [Soviet] spies if, once they're caught, we release them because we don't have the gumption to stand up to the Soviets' hostage-taking technique.

Interview/Newsweek, 9-22:24,25.

5

[On the current scandal involving secret U.S.-Iran arms deals and the covert diversion of funds from those deals to contra rebels fighting the Nicaraguan government]: We are witnessing a crisis of the President's [Reagan] foreign policy [caused by] the fragmentation of decision-making, disarray among the people involved and perhaps not a sufficient degree of direct Presidential involvement . . . An admission [by Reagan] that he did not know what was going on [in the Nicaraguan connection] is pretty damning. It boggles the mind.

Nov. 25/The Washington Post, 11-26:(A)14.

Patrick J. Buchanan
Director of Communications
for the President of the United States

1

Our problem is that we have a government and a country that is profoundly divided over what America's objectives in foreign policy should be, and even over what regimes are the real enemies of what we believe in. That's just a fact of life that didn't exist in the 1950s, and it complicates everything we do.

U.S. News & World Report, 12-15:27.

Warren E. Burger
Chief Justice of the United States

2

Our pride and confidence in our constitutional system have led Americans to cooperate with other countries that sought to develop a system patterned after our Constitution. In this respect we are markedly unlike the Soviet Union. For generations, the U.S.S.R. has sought to fix its system on other people without their consent, sometimes by guile and sometimes by force of arms.

Before American Bar Association, Baltimore,
Feb. 9/The Christian Science Monitor, 2-10:3.

Jimmy Carter
Former President of the United States

3

[At the UN], the Third World nations and their representatives almost always numerically

are in the majority. And they use this [majority power] as an irresponsible means by which to attack the developed nations of the world.

Interview, Atlanta/
The Christian Science Monitor, 12-30:15.

George A. Carver
Former Deputy Director,
Central Intelligence Agency
of the United States

4

[On the arrest of U.S. journalist Nicholas Daniloff by the Soviets for spying, which some say is in retaliation for the arrest in the U.S. of a Soviet accused of spying]: If they hold onto Daniloff and we go through with the [proposed U.S.-Soviet summit meeting], we look pretty wimpish. But if we get starchy and call off the summit [to protest Daniloff's arrest], [U.S. President] Reagan will be blamed for escalating superpower tensions. They [the Soviets] achieve a number of things and lose relatively little . . . The FBI and other agencies have been a lot more effective in their counter-intelligence efforts lately, and there are a lot of Soviet spies at work. They [the Soviets] want to send us a message: "Lay off our spies because, when you get one, we will pull someone [an American] off the street."

Los Angeles Times, 9-10:(I)18.

William J. Casey
Director of Central
Intelligence of the United States

5

International terrorism is the ultimate abuse of human rights. We should be prepared to direct a proportional military response against bona fide military targets of those states which direct terrorist attacks against us. And we need not insist on absolute evidence that the targets were used solely to support terrorism. Nor should we need to prove beyond all reasonable doubt that a particular element or individual in that state is responsible for specific terrorist acts. We must demonstrate our will to meet a terrorist's challenge with measured force, ap-

(WILLIAM J. CASEY)

plied quickly, whenever the evidence warrants. We cannot permit terrorists and their sponsoring states to feel that we are inhibited from responding or that our response is going to be bogged down in interminable consultations or debates; that we, in fact, do not really have a deterrent.

At Fletcher School of Law and Diplomacy,
Tufts University/The New York Times, 1-24:6.

1

[Too often,] Congressional oversight of the intelligence community is conducted off the cuff through the news media and involves the repeated compromise of sensitive intelligence sources and methods.

Time, 3-3:18.

2

[The Soviet Union requires] bridgeheads in Cuba and Vietnam, in South Yemen and Ethiopia, in Angola and Nicaragua, in Afghanistan and elsewhere. And these bridgeheads are being linked in a growing logistical and support network, supported by a standing Soviet naval and air power. And we have a new Soviet leader, Mr. [Mikhail] Gorbachev. And already a hallmark of his regime is an intensified attempt to nail down and cement these bridgeheads, make them permanent.

Before American-Israel Public Affairs Committee,
Washington, April 6/Los Angeles Times, 4-7:(I)1.

3

There was a day, not too long ago, when Soviet-style collectivism was widely seen as the panacea for all the problems afflicting the Third World. No one, not even the Soviets and their friends, believes this today. This is a tremendous reversal that could turn out to be one of the great historical turning points of our lifetime. But it will only work out this way if the indigenous Third World forces resisting Marxism-Leninism, together with the U.S. and the West, can act to take advantage of this open window of opportunity to advance democracy.

At national-security conference sponsored by
Center for the Study of the Presidency, Atlanta,
Nov. 8/The Christian Science Monitor, 11-10:8.

Lord Chalfont
British authority on terrorism

4

The whole time that I have been involved in [anti-] terrorist operations, which now goes back to 30 years, my enemy has always been a man who is very worried about his own skin. You can no longer count on that, because the terrorist [today] is not just *prepared* to get killed, he *wants* to get killed. Therefore, the whole planning, tactical doctrine [and] thinking [behind anti-terrorism measures] is fundamentally undermined.

The Christian Science Monitor, 5-15:19.

Jacques Chirac
Premier of France

5

[On international terrorism]: The international community, unless it chooses to delude itself, should recognize that it has not always shown the necessary lucidity toward this scourge which some would like us to think is the sole means of expression of the oppressed. The odious methods it uses, the slaughter of innocent people perpetrated in free societies, the ongoing blackmail over the lives of hostages rule out our confusing, even in some small way, those actions with genuine resistance.

At United Nations, New York, Sept. 24/
The New York Times, 9-25:6.

Clark M. Clifford
Former Secretary of
Defense of the United States

6

[On the current scandal involving Reagan Administration dealings with Iran and subsequent diversion of funds to Nicaraguan rebels]: We're going through a kind of ancient, barbaric war-dance now—it's almost an ultimate in absurdity. The President does not need to call in his aides; he knows what they did . . . In three Administrations, I have seen that people do not do things without the President knowing it.

The Christian Science Monitor, 12-9:1,8.

WHAT THEY SAID IN 1986

William E. Colby
Former Director of Central
Intelligence of the United States

1

[On spying on allies]: With hostile countries, like the United States and the Soviet Union, the impact of exposure [of espionage] is small; everyone knows we both do it. But with Canada, for example, we'd be out of our minds to run an operation there . . . We'd expect to get [the information just by asking for it], or, if it were too much a family secret, we'd be refused and just forget the whole thing.

Interview/Los Angeles Times, 6-23:(I)13.

Roger Conner
Executive director, Federation
for American Immigration Reform

2

We must find ways to insulate the process of immigration from political pressures . . . There should be a single standard [for asylum requests]: a well-founded fear of persecution. Churches shouldn't decide who gets in. Neither should Congress nor the Attorney General.

The Christian Science Monitor, 6-5:30.

Alan Cranston
United States Senator, D-California

3

[Criticizing President Reagan for making foreign arms-sales agreements without approval of Congress]: We specifically have a law that gives us [Congress] the power to veto an arms sale. It creates a misunderstanding elsewhere if we say that once a President makes a promise that it's as far as America goes. That's not the way America works.

The Washington Post, 8-7:(A)26.

Chester A. Crocker
Assistant Secretary for African Affairs,
Department of State of the United States

4

Diplomacy requires, to be effective, a degree of pressures that drive the parties toward a political compromise.

To reporters/
Los Angeles Times, 1-31:(I)18.

Nicholas S. Daniloff
Correspondent,
"U.S. News & World Report"

5

[On his being arrested in the Soviet Union on spy charges, which he denies, and his just being released]: I think it is obvious to everybody what has happened over this past month. I was arrested without an arrest warrant, a case was fabricated against me with a narrow political purpose of giving the Soviet Union some political leverage over the case of Genadi Zakharov [a Soviet arrested for spying in the U.S.]. The KGB did not punish me. The KGB punished itself.

Frankfurt, West Germany, Sept. 29/
The New York Times, 9-30:4.

Alexandre de Marenches
Former Chief of French Intelligence

6

. . . we're in dire danger from a colonial mammoth that I call the Soviet empire. The greatest weakness of the American system is that you always say, "Let's be friends." In world strategy, there are no such things as permanent friends, there are only permanent interests.

Interview/U.S. News
& World Report, 12-1:33.

Jeremiah Denton
United States Senator, R-Alabama

7

I wish to be deliberative, as a Senator, in foreign-policy matters because, in my respectful opinion, the main defects in the conduct of foreign affairs under Presidents Nixon, Ford, Carter and Reagan have not derived from the quality of the initiatives of the Presidents but from the tendency of Congress, led by liberal, all-too-powerful media, to seize the initiative in an untimely manner or to "devise and dissent" rather than advise and consent. I dream of more respect for the separation of powers, respect for Constitutionally mandated authority, and bipartisanship in foreign affairs and other matters of vital interest.

The New York Times,
3-1:10.

David Durenberger
United States Senator, R-Minnesota

1

[On the current scandal involving secret U.S.-Iran arms deals and the covert transfer of the payments to contra rebels fighting in Nicaragua]: This particular event is a deliberate effort on the part of a handful of people, including the President of the United States [Reagan], to avoid—deliberately avoid—Congressional oversight. The contrivance failed. Now the President is being held to account for it.

Washington, Dec. 16/
Los Angeles Times, 12-17:(I)18.

Lawrence S. Eagleburger
Former Under Secretary
of State of the United States

2

The essence of diplomacy is how you manage the day-to-day business, the confidence you build, the atmosphere you create, so that when the tough times come you can do business.

The New York Times, 6-23:5.

Carlos Fuentes
Mexican author-diplomat

3

What the U.S. does best is to understand itself. What it does worst is understand others.

Interview/Time, 6-16:52.

4

If there is not the understanding that cultures are different and that people have different ways of responding to the basic realities of life and economics and politics and love and eating and a million other things because of what their cultures have been, then we can't understand each other. [The U.S.] may think that the solution for the United States, the culture of the United States, is the universal culture and should benefit everyone. Well, no, no, no! I will not change a wonderful *mole* from Oaxaca [in Mexico] for a hamburger—I will not. And my politics will respond to the *mole*. This has to be understood by the United States, which has a democratic cul-

ture. I don't expect Moscow to understand that the Czechs have their own culture.

Interview, London/
The Christian Science Monitor, 11-28:29.

J. William Fulbright
Former United States Senator,
D-Arkansas

5

The [U.S.] arms buildup and our intervention everywhere has its origin in our lack of understanding of our relations to the world. This idea that we have been given a mandate by the Lord to be in everybody's business just isn't true—and it's not a very popular point of view.

Dec. 10/USA Today, 12-11:(A)2.

Alan Garcia
President of Peru

6

Someone ought to tell those powerful beings [in the U.S.], with their nuclear bombs and fortresses of dollars, that they are mortal. Others prefer to remain silent; we prefer to speak up. The U.S. is a formidable technological power. I am an admirer of that country. But the powerful reality is that the U.S. will have to develop an attitude that is more humane toward other nations, particularly toward Latin America. [Former U.S.] President [Jimmy] Carter signified an attitude that was encouraging. Today we are slipping backward.

Interview/
World Press Review, August:27.

Richard Gardner
Professor of law,
Columbia University

7

[On the U.S. order that the Soviets reduce the number of personnel at their UN missions because of their alleged spying activities in the U.S.]: This is an area where the law is not very clear, but to set arbitrary numerical limits strikes me both as bad law and as bad policy for the United States. How would the U.S. feel if the

WHAT THEY SAID IN 1986

(RICHARD GARDNER)

Swiss told us how large a staff we could have at the Geneva arms talks?

Interview/The New York Times, 3-11:6.

Robert M. Gates
Deputy Director for Intelligence,
Central Intelligence Agency
of the United States

1

[Saying covert action is an appropriate foreign-policy tool]: The experience of the last 10 years suggests that in many cases diplomacy alone is not an effective institution. That experience also would show that overt military action by the United States is either not appropriate or would not be supported by the American people or Congress. At that point, the United States has two options: develop other instruments to carry out its policies [such as covert action], or turn and walk away.

At hearing on his confirmation
as CIA Deputy Director, Washington,
April 10/The New York Times, 4-11:5.

Richard A. Gephardt
United States Representative,
D-Missouri

2

[Criticizing Reagan Administration covert operations in foreign affairs]: I think Congress has really got to begin asking, "Do we want foreign policy run out of the White House?" Congress shares a responsibility for foreign policy with the White House, with the President. And if we don't even know what they're doing and we can't even find out today, then I think we have to look at the laws and see if we don't need changes.

Broadcast interview/
"Meet the Press," NBC-TV, 11-9.

John Glenn
United States Senator, D-Ohio

3

[On the current scandal involving secret U.S.-Iran arms deals and the covert diversion of funds from those deals to contra rebels fighting the Nicaraguan government]: . . . it is a sad commentary on the President of the United States [Reagan]. If he knew about [the Nicaraguan funds diversion], then he has willfully broken the law; if he didn't know about it, then he is failing to do his job. After all, we expect the President to know about the foreign-policy activities being run directly out of the White House.

Nov. 25/The Washington Post, 11-26:(A)14.

Felipe Gonzalez
Prime Minister of Spain

4

I believe the way to fight [international] terror is to coordinate intelligence services and adopt a code of international conduct that won't allow any country to serve as a base or a shelter for terrorists. A few years ago, the U.S. didn't share the idea of coordination. Today, the U.S. is the main push. But we must avoid measures that may be popular domestically but are actually ineffective. In my opinion, force can cause more violence. I believe the Libyan raid [by the U.S. in retaliation for that country's involvement in terrorism] was a mistake of focus. You have to isolate any state that helps terrorism, but military action won't stop terrorists.

Interview, Madrid/
U.S. News & World Report, 7-7:38.

Mikhail S. Gorbachev
General Secretary, Communist
Party of the Soviet Union

5

I would say that never in the decades since the war has the situation in the world been so explosive, and consequently complex and uncongenial, as in the first half of the 1980s. The right-wing group that came to power in the U.S.A., and its main NATO fellow travelers, made a steep turn from the detente to a policy of military force . . . The drastic frosting of the international climate in the first half of the 1980s was a further reminder that nothing comes of itself: Peace

(MIKHAIL S. GORBACHEV)

has to be fought for, and this has to be a persevering and meaningful fight.

At Soviet Communist Party Congress, Moscow,
Feb. 25/The New York Times, 2-26:4.

1

[On international terrorism]: Undeclared wars, the export of counter-revolution in all forms, political assassinations, the taking of hostages, the hijacking of aircraft and bomb explosions in streets, airports and railway stations—such is the hideous face of terrorism, which its instigators try to mask with all sorts of cynical inventions.

At Soviet Communist Party Congress, Moscow,
Feb. 25/The New York Times, 12-19:6.

2

[Criticizing the U.S. for not responding more favorably to Soviet initiatives on arms reduction and detente]: It looks as though some people are simply afraid of the possibility . . . of a serious and long-term thaw in Soviet-American relations . . . The militaristic and aggressive forces would, of course, prefer to freeze and perpetuate the confrontation. But what should we do, comrades, slam the door? We do not intend to play into the hands of those who would like to force mankind to get used to the nuclear threat and the arms race.

At Soviet Communist Party Congress, Moscow,
March 6/Los Angeles Times, 3-7:(I)26.

3

If it were not for American interference in the affairs of other states, regional conflicts would be on the wane and be solved in far simpler and more just ways.

Interview/The Washington Post, 4-3:(A)23.

4

[On the prospects for another U.S.-Soviet summit meeting after the recent one in Geneva]: To make the matter absolutely clear, I will repeat anew: I stand for holding such a meeting. We make no preconditions for it. But we want it to pass in accordance with what the [U.S.] President [Reagan] and I agreed on, namely, it should mark

a step forward, that is, produce practical results toward ending the arms race. One more thing: It can take place if the atmosphere of Geneva is preserved or, it would be more correct to say, revived.

Speech, Togliatti, U.S.S.R., April 8/
The New York Times, 4-9:6.

5

[Criticizing the recent U.S. attack on Libya in retaliation for that country's involvement in international terrorism]: [The fight against terrorism] does not give the American Administration any right at all to behave as an international judge, to punish other countries arbitrarily and to replace the principle of international cooperation with the laws of the jungle . . . When one sees these things in an international context, then the crime against Libya, and also the persistence in nuclear tests and the threats against Nicaragua, cannot be seen in isolation. The American Administration must be aware that Soviet-American relations cannot be developed independently of how the U.S. behaves in the international arena.

At East German Communist Party Congress,
East Berlin, April 18/
The Washington Post, 4-19:(A)21.

6

[If the Americans] continue to act as they do today, if they continue to make the international situation explosive and to drive away the spirit of Geneva, then I think a shadow will be thrown over all plans for a future [U.S.-Soviet] summit [meeting]. That should be thought over in Washington. If a new summit is to be organized, then there must be an atmosphere in international relations that allows for real hopes that the summit will be a step forward. From our side, we are ready for a new series of steps.

To journalists, Potsdam, East Germany,
April 20/The Washington Post, 4-21:(A)1.

7

[Accusing Western nations of using the recent Chernobyl nuclear-plant accident in the Soviet Union for political purposes]: One involuntarily gets the impression that the leaders of the capitalist powers who gathered in Tokyo [for an economic summit conference] wanted to use Cher-

(MIKHAIL S. GORBACHEV)

nobyl as a pretext for distracting the attention of the world public from all those problems that make them uncomfortable. The accident at the Chernobyl station and the reaction to it have become a kind of a test of political morality. Once again two different approaches, two different lines of conduct were revealed for everyone to see.

Broadcast address to the nation, Moscow,
May 14/The Washington Post, 5-15:(A)32.

1

[On a proposed summit between him and U.S. President Reagan]: The President is always saying he wants a meeting. We put the question thus: To meet to shake hands with each other, to chat—this may also be meaningful. We did this in Geneva; we met, exchanged opinions, got to know each other. We had substantial discussions. However, it's necessary not only to talk, but to agree.

Stavropol, U.S.S.R., Sept. 19/
The New York Times, 9-20:4.

2

[Criticizing the American positions at his recent meeting with U.S. President Reagan in Reykjavik, Iceland]: We [Soviets] are realists. We clearly understand that questions that for many years, even decades, have not found their solution can hardly be resolved at a single sitting. We have sufficient experience in doing business with the United States. We know how changeable its political climate is, how strong and influential the opponents of peace are. That we are not losing heart and shutting the door—although there are more than enough grounds for that—is only because we are sincerely convinced about the need for fresh efforts in building normal interstate relations in the nuclear age . . . We did all we could [at the Reykjavik meeting]. Our [U.S.] partners lacked the breadth of approach, an understanding of the unique character of the moment, and, ultimately, the courage, responsibility and political determination that are so necessary for resolving vital and complicated world problems. They stuck

to their old time-eroded positions that contradict present-day realities.

Broadcast address to the nation, Moscow,
Oct. 14/The New York Times, 10-15:1.

Robert Graham
Governor of Florida (D)

3

America must regain control of its borders. Today, the problem is illegal drugs and immigrants. Tomorrow, it could be terrorists and bombs. We have the capability to secure our borders, but we have lacked the will to do so.

The Christian Science Monitor, 9-15:6.

Alexander M. Haig, Jr.
Former Secretary of State
of the United States

4

[The U.S. has] been guilty of a number of misjudgments in handling [international] terrorism. One, we are frequently more concerned about how our potential reaction will be received by the electorate at home than how it would be viewed by the perpetrator of the terrorist crime. We have to reverse that priority. Secondly, we have tended to camouflage the known involvement of terrorist governments for fear that labeling them would make them less than cooperative in achieving other objectives we have, such as the peace progress in the Middle East. Thirdly, we've tended to forget Teddy Roosevelt's advice: Speak softly and carry a big stick. We've tended to speak too threateningly while we carried a feather.

Interview/USA Today, 12-2:(A)13.

Gary Hart
United States Senator, D-Colorado

5

I don't think those of us [Democrats] who came into politics in the 1970s have quite articulated or worked out our foreign policy. About all I was able to articulate in 1984 was that we shouldn't go to war in the Persian Gulf for someone else's oil when we didn't need to, and we

(GARY HART)

shouldn't go to war in Central America over the Sandinista government [of Nicaragua]—a whole bunch of shouldn'ts.

Interview, Kittredge, Colo., Jan. 4/
The Washington Post, 1-6:(A)8.

1

The strictly bipolar world is gone. In its place is a world where secondary powers can defy superpowers, as we discovered in Vietnam and the Soviet Union is discovering in Afghanistan.

The Christian Science Monitor, 6-12:3.

2

. . . we are moving beyond the post-World War II era of the superpowers. The central change is the diffusion of power—the world around us has gotten more complex and more of a political and economic challenge. The doctrine of containment of the Soviets is becoming less and less relevant to the real problems of many nations. Yet, the foreign policy of both political parties [Republican and Democratic] seems frozen in time. The Reagan Administration's focus is constantly on the Soviet Union, or what I call the "credit-the-Russians-first" mentality. We've become preoccupied with heating up the confrontation or cooling off the cold war. It is backward-looking to narrow the world down to the U.S.-Soviet competition. It neglects what I think will be the principal issues of the 1980s and 1990s—Latin American debt, the emergence of nationalism in Africa, increasing our trading power through productivity, and so forth.

Interview/U.S. News &
World Report, 6-23:23.

Richard M. Helms
Former Director of Central
Intelligence of the United States

3

In any organization which runs intelligence operations, you want to keep high morale and you want your people sometimes to take chances. One of the ways to keep that kind of morale and to keep people wanting to work is to make it very

clear that if they get into trouble the organization is going to do everything it possibly can for them.

The Christian Science Monitor, 9-19:4.

Robert Hunter
Director of European studies,
Center for Strategic and International
Studies, Georgetown University

4

Americans don't want to fight. After Vietnam, [U.S. foreign-policy] goals have to be clear, and the methods have to be straightforward, relatively easy and quick.

The Christian Science Monitor, 5-27:44.

5

[On criticism of covert action by the National Security Council]: We want the [Arab-terrorist-held U.S.] hostages out, but we don't want to pay ransom; we don't want a Communist government in Nicaragua, but we don't want Americans to die. Running covert action out of the NSC is one way to get out of the dilemma.

The Christian Science Monitor, 12-8:48.

Hussein I
King of Jordan

6

Countries we have never heard of before threaten world prosperity and peace on a daily basis. Whether we realize it, or whether we like it, the world has become one. And regardless of the passport he carries, every person is a citizen of that world. No nation can ever again be an island unto itself.

At Westover School commencement, Middlebury,
Conn., June 6/The New York Times, 6-7:11.

Daniel K. Inouye
United States Senator, D-Hawaii

7

[Advocating more U.S. foreign aid to Third World countries]: [The] choice is not between farmers in the Third World and farmers in the United States. [Americans'] security, their well-being, is inextricably bound to the economic and

WHAT THEY SAID IN 1986

(DANIEL K. INOUYE)

social development of the Third World. We find there a cauldron of seething discontent which will spill over into the lives of all Americans if we do not address the needs of the [world's] poor.

At conference of development groups, Washington, Sept. 11/The Washington Post, 9-12:(A)11.

Brian Jenkins
Director, research program on subnational conflict and political violence, Rand Corporation

1

I can't think of any way you are going to eradicate international terrorism. It's a condition, not a specific disease, and you can treat the condition, but you can't cure it . . . I know this seems like a bleak and unpromising picture. But it's what's there, it's what there is.

Newsweek, 1-6:60.

2

[International] terrorism isn't going to go away because it serves a purpose. It has been demonstrated repeatedly that by using terrorist tactics, small groups with a limited capacity for violence can achieve disproportionate effects. They attract world-wide attention to themselves and their causes. They occasionally win concessions. And they oblige us to devote vast resources to protect against their attacks. Also, a handful of nations has sponsored terrorism as a cheap means of waging war—a substitute for diplomacy. State-sponsored terrorism is much more difficult to get at. As to the effects of increased security, terrorists retain one major advantage: Governments cannot protect everything, everywhere, all the time.

Interview/Newsweek, 9-15:27.

David Jordan
United States Ambassador to Peru

3

[On the lower profile forced on U.S. embassies by international terrorism]: The essence of diplomacy is to be with society, to feel its rich-

ness and texture. When you're so concerned about safety, it makes it more difficult to feel the pulse of the people, to know what it's really like for an ordinary person when the price of bread goes up. It makes you more dependent on the reports of other people's perceptions. That puts us one step removed from where we'd like to be.

The Christian Science Monitor, 1-29:15.

Bernard Kalb
Assistant Secretary for Public Affairs, Department of State of the United States

4

[On the U.S. order to expel 25 members of the Soviet UN delegation because of their involvement in espionage]: The Soviet missions to the United Nations have grown to the point where their size is unreasonable by any standard, an abuse of the right of representation, in flagrant disregard of the Soviets' responsibility. Under such circumstances, international law permits the United States, as host country, to take reasonable corrective measures.

Washington, Sept. 17/ Los Angeles Times, 9-18:(I)16.

5

[Saying he is resigning because of misinformation about U.S. Libyan policy disseminated by the U.S. government]: Faith in the word of America is the pulsebeat of our democracy. Anything that hurts America's credibility hurts America . . . You face a choice—as an American, as a spokesman, as a journalist—whether to [be] absorbed in the ranks of silence, whether to vanish into unopposed acquiescence, or to enter a modest dissent.

The New York Times, 10-23:7.

Jack Kemp
United States Representative, R-New York

6

I always intuitively believed that freedom led to prosperity. The freer people were, the freer markets were, the more prosperity would ultimately ensue. I recall believing that about—they

(JACK KEMP)

didn't call it the Third World then—about Mexico, about Asia, about Africa. I didn't see the world from an elitist standpoint, that democracy could work only in the West. I really did believe that freedom was both an Old Testament and a New Testament obligation.

Interview/Esquire, January:67.

1

Forty years of seeking agreements to ease Soviet anxieties and to enhance Soviet confidence, 40 years of ignoring Soviet violations of agreements reached, have not left the world safer nor the world more secure.

At Heritage Foundation,
Washington/Newsweek, 10-20:28.

Raymond E. Kendall
Chief of Interpol police network

2

[On international terrorists]: Their "fanaticism" is extremely overrated . . . They prepare their operations very carefully. If I were a professional criminal going to rob a bank, I would behave in the same way. It is a criminal approach.

Interview, Paris/
Los Angeles Times, 4-13:(I)2.

Edward M. Kennedy
United States Senator,
D-Massachusetts

3

We would be a lesser nation in a more dangerous world if we did not recognize it is as important for America to have a Peace Corps as it is to have a Marine Corps.

At luncheon celebrating 25th anniversary
of Peace Corps/USA Today, 9-23:(A)4.

Jeane J. Kirkpatrick
Former United States Ambassador/
Permanent Representative to the United Nations

4

Promoting democracy is a position with which everyone feels very comfortable . . . but it sets out

a task for American foreign policy that is very, very difficult. We've always been attracted to the idea of not only making the world safe for democracy, but also making the world a democratic Garden of Eden . . . I think it's just not practical as an operational goal.

Los Angeles Times, 3-6:(I)29.

5

The [former U.S.] Carter Administration . . . wanted to bring about moderate and democratic regimes in Iran and Nicaragua. And they had followed certain policies in the effort to bring about more-moderate and democratic regimes. But what they produced were the more-repressive, hostile regimes of the Ayatollah Khomeini and the Ortega brothers. The assumptions on which those policies were based were mistaken, and, in any event, they are markedly different from the theories and practices of the Reagan Administration. The present policy is to encourage democracy everywhere. Support for anti-Communist freedom fighters is an important dimension of the policy . . . I believe that in all aspects of our foreign policy we should be very careful that we do not pursue a policy that will lead to the exchange of a lesser evil for a greater one, which I think we did in Nicaragua and Iran.

Interview/U.S. News &
World Report, 3-10:36.

6

The United Nations' acceptance of so-called "national liberation movements" as legitimate is a good indicator of the moral confusion that has come to surround this view of violence as the preferred method of political action. Since the 1970s, the UN General Assembly has passed numerous resolutions asserting its support for the right of "national liberation movements" to "struggle by all means . . . to achieve power." It has consistently condemned countries for attempting to defend themselves against terrorist violence. The distinction between legitimate and illegitimate use of force has not so much been blurred as stood on its head.

At conference on terrorism,
Washington/Time, 4-14:50.

WHAT THEY SAID IN 1986

(JEANE J. KIRKPATRICK)

1

The most difficult thing about being an Ambassador is the fact that you are always bringing up positions set down by others for you to convey. Sometimes you don't agree with that position, and naturally, if it's a moral issue, you would have to leave the job.

USA Today, 11-3:(D)2.

Henry A. Kissinger
*Former Secretary of State
of the United States*

2

[Criticizing Secretary of State George Shultz for not supporting President Reagan during the current U.S.-Iran-Nicaragua controversy]: It is the duty of the Secretary of State to get along with the President, not of the President to get along with the Secretary of State. I am struck by the fact that in the middle of a crisis the President is all alone on the parapet and almost none of his close associates are supporting not only the tactics . . . but not even the general philosophy of what he has attempted to do.

Nov. 23/The Washington Post, 11-24:(A)26.

Edward I. Koch
Mayor of New York

3

[Addressing a visiting group of Soviet and American children]: I cannot let this occasion go forward without making some comment about the Soviet Union, which I believe, not the children in the Soviet Union, not the people in the Soviet Union, but the government is the pits . . . I don't want the people to think that because I issued a proclamation commenting on peace that somehow or other I'm at peace with the Soviet government. I am not . . . [There] is a lot of baloney that somehow or other when you come to City Hall this is a sanctuary and people don't speak the truth. I think we ought to use every single occasion to speak out against the offensive government that exists in the Soviet Union.

*New York, Sept. 15/
The New York Times, 9-16:13.*

Helmut Kohl
Chancellor of West Germany

4

[On his refusal to apply economic sanctions, as requested by the U.S., against Libya, which is alleged to have been involved in recent international terrorist attacks]: I can well understand the reaction of the Americans, but I ask them to understand that we have 1,500 Germans there [working in Libya]. When I became Chancellor I took an oath swearing to defend the interests of the German people. It is obvious that I must put German interests first and, when I do, it can produce a difference of opinion [with the U.S.].

*News conference, Bonn, Jan. 9/
The New York Times, 1-10:4.*

5

[On those in Europe who criticize the U.S. for its recent attack on Libya in retaliation for that country's involvement in international terrorism]: The Americans felt, as they tell us again and again, that they had been left alone in the fight against international terrorism . . . It is easy to criticize the United States for resorting to measures we would not have chosen. If we Europeans do not want to follow the Americans for reasons of our own, we must develop political initiatives. We will not eliminate international terrorism simply by wailing and lamenting [when the victims strike back].

*Before West German Parliament, Bonn,
April 16/The Washington Post, 4-17:(A)22.*

Robert H. Kupperman
*Senior adviser, Center for
Strategic and International Studies,
Georgetown University*

6

Our policy toward terrorism should be one where we understand that this is a covert business, that we will lose hostages and not be able to save everybody and that there must be plausible deniability [in attempts to rescue hostages]. That's a cardinal rule, and that is whatever you do, you distance the White House and the Presidency, and if something goes wrong you look for

(ROBERT H. KUPPERMAN)

the lowest level schnook. Don't get the President involved—that should be the rule . . .

The New York Times, 11-10:6.

Richard D. Lamm
Governor of Colorado (D)

1

[On the need for immigration reform]: Miami used to be the southernmost American city; now it's the northernmost Latin American city.

USA Today, 6-30:(A)4.

Patrick J. Leahy
United States Senator, D-Vermont

2

The new reliance [by the U.S.] on covert paramilitary action as a normal instrument of foreign policy—even as a substitute for foreign policy—has strained the current [Congressional] oversight process to the breaking point . . . The more fundamental cause of the current strained relationship between the Intelligence Committee and parts of the intelligence community is growing disagreement over the [Reagan] Administration's clear determination to make ever greater use of covert military operations . . . It involves a most basic question which can only be resolved in open debate, with the full awareness of the American people. That question is: Can a democracy like the United States engage in large-scale, so-called covert paramilitary operations, using our intelligence agencies as instruments in waging proxy wars against the Soviet Union or its clients?

Washington, April 21/
The New York Times, 4-22:4.

3

[Approving President Reagan's negotiating an agreement involving the exchange of an accused Soviet spy arrested in the U.S. for Nicholas Daniloff, an American journalist arrested as a spy by the Soviets and proclaimed innocent by Reagan]: The President did the right thing. In an absolutely perfect world, Nick Daniloff comes

home and the Soviets get nothing. But it's not a perfect world.

Washington, Sept. 30/
Los Angeles Times, 10-1:(I)7.

4

[Criticizing the Reagan Administration for not advising the appropriate Congressional committees about the recently revealed U.S.-Iran negotiations and arms deals]: Even after six years, this Administration doesn't understand the [Congressional] oversight process . . . The truth is that members of Congress want the President to succeed. They don't want him making bad, bad decisions. I've supported a lot of covert decisions in my time on the [Senate Intelligence] Committee. Most of them have been supported unanimously, knowing that some of them may go belly up.

Interview, Dec. 24/
The Washington Post, 12-25:(A)6.

Thomas E. Mann
Executive director, American
Political Science Association

5

Because of [U.S. President] Reagan's long-standing tough anti-Soviet position, he is bound to get the attention of the Soviets on those occasions when he does accommodate. You don't improve your position by being accommodating all the time. This kind of posture increases the likelihood of substantive agreement. It's a plausible, a reasonable, position to take. And Reagan uses it to his advantage.

The New York Times, 7-2:10.

John Martin
Chief of Internal Security, Department
of Justice of the United States

6

[On Soviet spying in the U.S.]: They run a vacuum-cleaner operation, sucking up everything. They want to know about the latest aircraft, Stealth technology, the space shuttle. They can't survive without stealing our trade, military, scientific and technological secrets . . .

133

WHAT THEY SAID IN 1986

(JOHN MARTIN)

An optimist would say we catch 50 per cent [of their spies], a pessimist, 2 per cent. The answer is probably in-between. But whatever it is, it's a pretty dismal picture.

U.S. News &
World Report, 9-29:26.

Lawrence Martin
Professor,
College of Communication,
Boston University

1

[On the U.S. use of disinformation when it wants to influence the policy of a particular foreign country, such as recently used to dissuade Libya from launching terrorist attacks]: The press is the messenger [of the disinformation]. However, if we use our own press against another country, at the same time we are deceiving not only the opponent, but ourselves . . . We are actually intervening into our spontaneous democratic process, and that is potentially dangerous because that could be a step toward authoritarianism.

Interview, Boston University/
The Christian Science Monitor, 12-4:12.

Charles McC. Mathias, Jr.
United States Senator,
R-Maryland

2

Foreign policy has got to be a coordinate decision of the Congress and the President. If it isn't, it isn't going to work . . . I must say I think that has been decreasing through the Carter years as well as through the Reagan years. It may have something to do with the fact that neither Carter nor Reagan were in the Congress. Now, in the Nixon period, in the Ford period and the Johnson period, there was a lot more interaction. I don't know if it ended up with more positive results, but at least there was a constant effort made on both sides to come together.

Interview, Washington/
The Washington Post, 12-11:(A)21.

Matthias A. Mathiesen
President, North Atlantic Council

3

[On international terrorism]: Western nations are faced with a multitude of cowardly acts to which they cannot respond in kind because they will be—and should be—judged by stricter moral standards than their adversaries.

At NATO foreign ministers meeting, Halifax,
Canada, May 29/Los Angeles Times, 5-30:(I)22.

Charles William Maynes
Editor, "Foreign Policy" magazine

4

[Criticizing the Reagan Administration's foreign policy]: The President is now like an athlete who has been training for four years and built up strength but won't enter any race. The Administration is basically practicing negative diplomacy. They have not used the power they have accumulated for positive purposes.

The Christian Science Monitor, 1-6:16.

Robert C. McFarlane
Former Assistant to the President
of the United States (Ronald Reagan)
for National Security Affairs

5

[Terrorists] are self-appointed minorities bent on violence against innocent people, [and it is necessary] to put aside the notion that there is any legitimate goal . . . [Terrorism] deserves no sympathy whatsoever. This is nihilism.

At conference on terrorism, Universal City,
Calif., April 6/Los Angeles Times, 4-9:(V)8.

6

This [Reagan] Administration has concluded, I think correctly, that the main competition with the Soviet Union over the next 15 years will occur in developing countries. People in Africa and Latin America are judging whether the Americans or the Soviets seem better able to deal with problems of development. We have a clear advantage over the Soviets—our ideas work better—but we must be able to deal with problems of Soviet-inspired violence. It is cen-

(ROBERT C. McFARLANE)

tral to the East-West geo-strategic balance in the next generation that we win one. We won't do that by spreading ourselves too thin in distant places at the beginning of this campaign. We must define the problem, focus on one area we can most easily defend as an important U.S. interest—which ought to be in this hemisphere—and win with whatever it takes to do it. Then, by dint of making it work in Nicaragua, you will stand a better chance of garnering support in other geo-strategic locations. Winning one first is very important.

Interview/U.S. News & World Report, 4-7:28.

Robert S. McNamara
Former Secretary of Defense of the United States; Former President, International Bank for Reconstruction and Development (World Bank)

1

In 50 to 100 years from now, we [in the U.S.] will find that it's in our interest to transfer from national sovereignty to international institutions certain of the powers that we exercise now as a nation-state. The longer we delay in addressing some of these issues—the East-West tensions, the institutional forms appropriate for an increasingly interdependent world, the return to our national traditions—the greater difficulty we're going to face in the 21st century.

*Interview, New York/
The Christian Science Monitor, 12-16:20.*

Peter McPherson
Administrator, Agency for International Development of the United States

2

[On his Agency's future]: Obviously, we have to continue to be very careful with our money and set priorities with the greatest care. But I think the public case will be made—and broadly accepted in Congress—that a fairly reasonable aid program is critical to U.S. foreign-policy interests. When you look at our security interests in the Middle East, the Horn of Africa, Central

America and so forth, it is clear that aid as a key part of our foreign policy will have to be maintained and supported. There is a compelling case for our involvement in places like the Philippines. As a country, we can't afford to walk away.

Interview/U.S. News & World Report, 11-17:40.

Daniel Moynihan
United States Senator, D-New York

3

[International] terrorism denies the distinction between state and society, public and private, government and individual, the distinction that lies at the heart of humane belief. For the terrorist, as for the totalitarian state, there are no innocent bystanders, no private citizens. Terrorism denies that there is any private sphere, that individuals have any rights or any autonomy separate from or beyond politics. There are thus no standards according to which the individual citizen, or the threatened society, can attempt to come to terms with the totalitarian terrorist. There is no way to satisfy his demands.

At conference on terrorism, Washington/Time, 4-14:50.

Brian Mulroney
Prime Minister of Canada

4

Nationalism . . . if left unchecked, can become very ugly, unattractive, and dangerous for any country. What you need is a healthy self-respect, a healthy sense of pride in your country . . . You need a sense of tolerance, a capacity to absorb new ideas, an understanding of how new wealth comes with new trade, of how open doors mean open minds and open minds mean a healthy society. I don't substitute national pride and strength for insolence, for arrogance which enables people to sarcastically attack their neighbors and their friends from time to time to make themselves feel stronger or better, less insecure.

*Interview, Montreal/
The Christian Science Monitor, 3-18:44.*

WHAT THEY SAID IN 1986

Benjamin Netanyahu
Israeli Ambassador/Permanent
Representative to the United Nations

1

[Saying terrorists are like kindergarten bullies]: The only thing you can do against bullies is say, "Stop, and I'll fight you if you don't" . . . very, very rarely are terrorists prepared to die. They're bullies. They think they can get away with it.

At conference on terrorism, Universal City,
Calif., April 6/Los Angeles Times, 4-9:(V)8.

David Newsom
Director, Institute for the Study of
Diplomacy, Georgetown University

2

This [Reagan] Administration has adopted a policy of unilateralism greater than that of any previous Administration. If we can claim some action is in our interest, we do it—regardless of international law.

The Christian Science Monitor, 4-4:16.

Richard M. Nixon
Former President of the United States

3

In terms of the long struggle . . . in terms of "We [the U.S.] have all the answers" and "American democracy is the best; it's best for Haiti, it'll work in Liberia, it'll work in Zaire or the Philippines or what have you," get all that nonsense out of your head, because it won't work.

Interview, Saddle River,
N.J./Newsweek, 5-19:33.

4

[On the current scandal involving the Reagan Administration's dealings with Iran and the Nicaraguan contra connection]: Defend the President for trying to seek his goals. Don't, don't weaken the man . . . And don't let Republicans go on with their favorite sport of cannibalism. Let's not weaken the man for his last two years in dealing with the big subject. It's a great big circus. Rather than look at the sideshows, let's

look at the main ring. That is Soviet-American relations.

Speech, Parsippany, N.J., Dec. 9/
Los Angeles Times, 12-10:(I)25.

Michael Novak
United States delegate to
"Helsinki process" human-rights
talks in Bern, Switzerland

5

[On why the U.S. vetoed a compromise human-rights document at the Bern talks]: We in America deeply cherish the Helsinki process. These are noble documents that gain nobility from performance. As our people review the record of performance [of the Soviet Union and Eastern bloc countries], there is concern that words without compliance would only undermine the whole Helsinki process. Thus, given the record, we imagine that a document would have to be of sufficient weight to offset the performance. We regret, after careful review, that we could not consent to this compromise.

News conference, Bern, May 26/
Los Angeles Times, 5-27:(I)1.

Sam Nunn
United States Senator, D-Georgia

6

[On secret U.S.-Iran negotiations involving arms deals, hostages and Nicaraguan contras]: The Reagan Administration has to understand that they cannot abuse the laws of democracy [at home] to foster democracy abroad.

Time, 12-8:20.

7

When a President, obviously as President Reagan is, looks at the broad picture and does not concern himself, particularly on foreign policy, with many important details, including arms-control details, it seems to me that he has to have top advisers . . . and he has to carefully delegate responsibility . . . That's a question for the future, and it's a very important question for our nation.

Broadcast interview/
"Meet the Press," NBC-TV, 12-22.

Joseph S. Nye, Jr.
Professor of international
affairs, Harvard University

1

The President can have a State Department-oriented foreign policy or a White House-oriented foreign policy. But if it's run from the White House, you need a President who is up to speed on these matters. The evidence is that this President [Reagan] is not.

Los Angeles Times, 11-28:(I)19.

Robert B. Oakley
Director, Office of Counterterrorism,
Department of State of the United States

2

[On terrorist attacks against Americans abroad]: I think that we cannot allow the terrorists to force us into a Fortress America. We have too many things to do abroad. We also have business abroad. We shouldn't be scared off by the terrorists. We shouldn't lock ourselves in a rose garden and then say we're not going to leave the United States until there is an end to terrorism abroad.

Broadcast interview/
"Face the Nation," CBS-TV, 4-6.

Andreas Papandreou
Prime Minister of Greece

3

We condemn [international] terrorism as a non-political and uncivilized action. [But] of course, we always make a difference between terrorism and the struggle of liberation movements. It is a very important difference, and it would be useful if every one in the world made that difference, because each country has the right and duty to struggle for its own independence.

At dinner in his honor, Belgrade, Yugoslavia,
Jan. 15/The New York Times, 1-17:3.

4

[On international terrorism]: We cannot accept the principle that terrorism is directly related to states characterized as terrorist because, if we had sufficient time, I could read a list of countries either in the West or the East, North

or South, that should be included in that category . . . We also do not accept the settlement of terrorist problems by the military intervention of one country against another, because this upsets the international legal order and nominates the strong powers as policemen of our planet.

At dinner honoring visiting Syrian
President Hafez al-Assad, Athens, May 28/
The New York Times, 5-29:4.

Samuel R. Pierce, Jr.
Secretary of Housing and Urban
Development of the United States

5

[Saying illegal aliens should not be entitled to housing aid in the U.S.]: I feel sorry for American citizens who are poor and who need the space [illegal aliens] are taking up in our housing. [The government] shouldn't house illegal aliens. They sneak into our country. They must realize when they do this that they are putting their own safety, health and future in jeopardy.

The Washington Post, 4-1:(A)17.

John M. Poindexter
Assistant to the President
of the United States for
National Security Affairs

6

[On the National Security Council]: The character of the NSC really hasn't changed over the years. In fact, a few weeks ago one of the news magazines ran an article that said the NSC staff was irrelevant. And now all the writing is about how we are so all-powerful, and going off and doing all these things on our own. Both points are exaggerations. As I define the role of the NSC staff, it is a matter of advising the President as the Chairman of the statutory National Security Council. We aren't policy-makers. It's a matter of presenting the options to the President and letting him decide.

Interview/USA Today, 11-19:(A)9.

Muammar el-Qaddafi
Chief of State of Libya

7

[On the non-aligned nations movement, of which Libya is a member]: What is the validity

(MUAMMAR el-QADDAFI)

of a movement that cannot defend a member country if it is attacked [such as Libya was recently by the U.S.]. I want to say goodbye, farewell to this funny movement, farewell to this utter falsehood. I am totally aligned against America, totally aligned against Israel, totally aligned against NATO. The dream of neutrality is over. There is no place for non-alignment any more.

At Summit Conference of the Non-aligned, Harare, Zimbabwe, Sept. 2/Time, 9-15:37.

1

I will . . . do my best to divide this world into two camps only—the liberation camp and the imperialist camp, as in actual fact there is nothing in the world other than these two camps.

At Summit Conference of the Non-aligned, Harare, Zimbabwe, Sept. 2/The Washington Post, 9-3:(A)13.

Ronald Reagan
President of the United States

2

I don't have to tell any of you about far left ideology and the power that it once wielded here [in Washington]. An ideology that automatically identified anyone wearing fatigues, carrying a rifle and spouting Marxist slogans as a liberator of his nation, an ideology that permitted many liberals to practice selective indignation, to hold to a double standard for certain dictators, to judge these dictators, no matter how repressive or cruel, less harshly because they called themselves socialists, Marxists or Communists. But, as I say, I think all of this is fading now and realism is returning. . . . What we're seeing is the end of the post-Vietnam syndrome, the return of realism about the Communist danger.

To conservative supporters, Washington, March 10/The New York Times, 3-11:8.

3

For more than two generations the United States has pursued a global foreign policy. Both the causes and consequences of World War II

made clear to all Americans that our participation in world affairs, for the rest of the century and beyond, would have to go beyond just the protection of our national territory against direct invasion. We had learned the painful lessons of the 1930s, that there could be no safety in isolation from the rest of the world. Our nation has responsibilities and security interests beyond our borders—in the rest of this hemisphere, in Europe, in the Pacific, in the Middle East and in other regions—that require strong, confident and consistent American leadership.

Message to Congress, March 14/ The New York Times, 3-15:4.*

4

. . . in recent years Congresses have tended to try to curb and take away from the Presidency some of the prerogatives that belong there—the handling of foreign policy and so forth—and placed restrictions on the office that in effect would have foreign policy determined by a committee of 535.

Interview/Time, 4-7:27.

5

[On the U.S. air attack on Libya in retaliation for that country's involvement in international terrorism]: Yesterday, the United States won but a single engagement in a long battle against terrorism. We will not end that struggle until the free and decent people of this planet unite to eradicate the scourge of terror from the modern world. Terrorism is the preferred weapon of weak and evil men and, as Edmund Burke reminded us, in order for evil to succeed, it's only necessary that good men do nothing. Yesterday, we demonstrated once again that doing nothing is not America's policy, it's not America's way.

Before American Business Conference, Washington, April 15/The New York Times, 4-16:14.

6

[On international terrorism]: These vicious, cowardly acts will, if we let them, erect a wall of fear around nations and neighborhoods. It will dampen the joy of travel, the flow of trade, the exchange of ideas. In short, terrorism, undeterred, will deflect the winds of freedom. And

(RONALD REAGAN)

let no one mistake this for a conflict between the Western democracies and the Arab world. Those who condone making war by cowardly attacks on unarmed third parties, including women and children, are but a tiny minority. Arab nations themselves have been forced to endure savage terrorist attacks from this minority. We hope and pray the Arab world will join us to eliminate this scourge of civilization.

Before International Forum of U.S.
Chamber of Commerce, Washington,
April 23/The New York Times, 4-24:8.

1

[The winds of freedom] are blowing in Latin America, where in recent years we have witnessed one of the greatest expansions of democracy in history. Today, 90 per cent of the population of this hemisphere lives in democratic countries, or countries in transition to democracy. In Europe, the new vigorous democracies in Spain and Portugal, and the revitalized democratic process in Turkey, have proven the pessimists wrong. The democratic workers movement in Poland, Solidarity, though suffering repression, still persists. In Nicaragua, Angola, Afghanistan and Cambodia, freedom fighters, struggling for liberty and independence, inspire the West with their courage in the face of a powerful enemy. In future years I think we may look back on the period we are going through as the vernal equinox of the human spirit—that moment in history when the light finally exceeded the darkness.

Before International Forum of U.S.
Chamber of Commerce, Washington,
April 23/The New York Times, 4-24:8.

2

[On international terrorism and the just-concluded Tokyo summit meeting of Western nations]: What we have agreed upon is that terrorism is a threat to all of us. It is an attack upon the world, the determination of terrorists who murder and maim innocent people in pursuit of some political goal, and that the way to deal with it is not individually or unilaterally, but to deal with it together. And this was the sense of the

agreement that we arrived at: that we are going to act together with regard to opposing terrorism, to isolate those states that provide support for terrorism—to isolate them and make them pariahs on the world scene and even, if possible, to isolate them from their own people.

News conference, Tokyo, May 7/
The New York Times, 5-8:10.

3

[On U.S.-Soviet relations]: I think they're on a more solid footing than they've been for a long time. For one thing because I think we've made it plain to the Soviet Union that we are realistic. We see them and what their goals are, and we're not deluding ourselves in any way. And I think in the past there has been a tendency to see them in a mirror kind of image and think, well, if we just are nice, they'll want to be nice in return.

Interview, June 23/
Los Angeles Times, 6-24:(I)18.

4

[Defending his approval of subsidies for U.S. wheat sales to the Soviet Union]: For some, this has been difficult to understand—after all, the Soviets are our adversaries and I've never been accused of being naive about that. The truth is, I didn't make this decision for them [the Soviets]; I made it for the American farmer. If that grain isn't sold to the Soviets, most of it will be stockpiled, costing the taxpayers and depressing grain prices here at home. So the grain would be sold at the same price the Soviets would pay to buy it from one of our foreign competitors.

News conference, Chicago, Aug. 12/
The Washington Post, 8-13:(A)15.

5

[On the arrest by Soviet authorities of U.S. journalist Nicholas Daniloff on spy charges]: The continuing Soviet detention of an innocent American is an outrage. Whatever the Soviet motive, whether it is to intimidate enterprising journalists or to trade him for one of their spies that we have caught red-handed, this action violates the standards of civilized international behavior. Through several channels we have made our position clear. The Soviet Union is aware of

WHAT THEY SAID IN 1986

(RONALD REAGAN)

how serious the consequences will be for our relations if Nick Daniloff is not set free. I call upon the Soviet authorities to act responsibly and quickly so that our two countries can make progress on the many other issues on our agenda—solving existing problems instead of creating new ones. Otherwise, there will be no way to prevent this incident from becoming a major obstacle in our relations.

At Republican fund-raising luncheon,
Denver, Sept. 8/The New York Times, 9-9:4.

1

[Defending his negotiating an agreement involving the exchange of an accused Soviet spy arrested in the U.S. for Nicholas Daniloff, an American journalist arrested as a spy by the Soviets and declared innocent by Reagan]: There was no connection between these two releases. There were other arrangements with regard to [the accused Soviet spy] that resulted in his being freed [such as the Soviet agreement to release an imprisoned dissident] . . . There have been several instances over the recent years in which we have arrested a spy, convicted a spy here in this country, and in each instance we ended up—rather than giving them board and room here—we ended up exchanging them for dissidents and people who wanted exit from the Soviet Union.

To reporters, Washington, Sept. 30/
Los Angeles Times, 10-1:(I)6.

2

It will be a cold day in Hades when I go soft on Communism. I was a long time ago in that battle, and I have never changed my view of it. On the other hand, as I said to [Soviet leader Mikhail Gorbachev] in our meeting in Geneva, he and I are uniquely in a position today where we could bring about World War III, or we're also in a position where we could bring about peace in the world. And I made it plain then that we don't like their system and we know they don't like ours, but we have to live in the world together. We're both going to be better off in a world of peace. So, I'm not going to give away

the store [in the forthcoming summit meetings] just to get an agreement on paper.

White House briefing, Washington,
Oct. 2/Los Angeles Times, 10-3:(I)6.

3

Things have really changed around the world. You know, America used to wear a "kick me" sign around its neck. Well, we threw that sign away; now it reads, "Don't tread on me." Today, every nickel-and-dime dictator around the world knows that if he tangles with the United States of America, he will have to pay a price.

At Republican fund-raising reception,
Columbus, Ga., Oct. 28/
The New York Times, 10-29:14.

4

[On the current scandal involving secret U.S.-Iran arms deals and the covert diversion of funds from those deals to rebels fighting the Nicaraguan government]: I've never seen the [scandal] sharks circling like they are now with blood in the water. What is driving me up the wall is that this wasn't a failure until the press got a tip from that rag in Beirut and began to play it up. I told them that publicity could destroy this, that it could get people killed. They went right on . . . This is a Beltway [the highway circling Washington] bloodletting. Frankly, I believe that as the truth comes out, people will see what we were trying to do was right. I'm not going to back off; I'm not going to crawl in a hole. I'm going to go forward. I have a lot of things to do in this job.

Interview/
The Washington Post, 12-1:(A)1.

Charles E. Redman
Spokesman for the Department
of State of the United States

5

On the general principle of who should be responsible for acting against international terrorism, we believe that those are actions that are best undertaken by the international community on a broad basis. If they are going to be effective, then they are going to have to be implemented

(CHARLES E. REDMAN)

forcefully by the international community and not just by one nation or a handful of nations.

Washington, Jan. 2/
The New York Times, 1-3:4.

Oliver Revell
Assistant Director, Federal
Bureau of Investigation

1

[Saying international terrorism must be viewed in perspective]: Don't panic. Don't let the notoriety reach a state of hysteria. [Terrorism] is an important phenomenon, but it is not threatening the American way of life or the Western democracies. And it won't as long as we don't let it. But if we let it, it causes us to develop a siege mentality and almost unilaterally curtails our own freedom.

The Christian Science Monitor, 5-21:17.

Rozanne Ridgway
Assistant Secretary for European
and Canadian Affairs, Department
of State of the United States

2

[On what the State Department should be looking for in its personnel]: So often one hears [that] this year they're looking for Soviet specialists, the next year they're looking for people who can go out and assist our embassies to catch up with the 20th century in systems management, or they're looking for a set of languages, or for skills in arms control. However, I think what State really needs . . . is a group of people broadly educated. I would say [the Foreign Service needs people grounded in] history, economics, and Shakespeare, individuals who have a sense of integrity and principle which is unshakable.

Interview, Washington/
The Christian Science Monitor, 11-6:6.

Charles S. Robb
Chairman, Democratic (Party) Leadership
Council; Former Governor of Virginia (D)

3

[Criticizing what he says is a new strain of neo-isolationism in the Democratic Party]: [It's]

bad policy because neo-isolationism in the United States emboldens our adversaries and enervates our allies. Bad politics because the public won't stand behind a party that won't stand up for American values and interests abroad. We need to apply all our strengths, not just military aid but also economic assistance or pressure, the backing of powerful allies and tough, persistent diplomacy, to win victories for democracy.

Before Coalition for a Democratic
Majority, Washington, May 6/
The New York Times, 5-7:13.

A. M. Rosenthal
Executive editor, "The New York Times"

4

[On the arrest by the KGB of American journalist Nicholas Daniloff as a spy, soon after the arrest of a Soviet in the U.S. as a spy]: I believe that the framing and arrest of Nick Daniloff was not a message from Moscow to Americans, but to Russians and primarily to the KGB itself. By holding Daniloff hostage, the Russians were telling the KGB network around the world that, come what might, Moscow would do its best to protect its members, even if the price was endangering the [forthcoming U.S.-Soviet] summit. Moscow made that point and once again showed that, to every man who rules the Soviet Union, nothing is more important than the KGB, because it is through the KGB that he rules. I am delighted Mr. Daniloff is out [following which the Soviet accused spy was released by the U.S.] and I think Secretary of State [George] Shultz did a fine job [in negotiations]; but it would have been far healthier to drop the double talk about this not having been a trade and to have told the American people honestly that we traded because we could not shake the power of the KGB in Moscow, a point worth remembering.

The New York Times, 10-2:5.

William V. Roth, Jr.
United States Senator, R-Delaware

5

I believe . . . that if we want our allies to share burdens, as we say we do, we need to de-

(WILLIAM V. ROTH, JR.)

velop stronger habits of meaningful consultations and complementary policy arrangements.

Speech/The Christian
Science Monitor, 10-24:14.

Oscar Schachter
Professor of law, Columbia University

1

[On the U.S. order that the Soviets reduce the number of personnel at their UN missions because of their alleged spying in the U.S.]: There is no unilateral right on the part of any government to send as many people as it wants [to their UN missions]. The United States has the right to claim that any mission is excessive in size and contrary to the aims and purposes of the agreement [between the UN and the host country], just as the United Nations has the right to challenge that claim.

Interview/The New York Times, 3-11:6.

Helmut Schmidt
Member of West German Parliament;
Former Chancellor of West Germany

2

. . . there hasn't been a continuous American policy vis-a-vis the Soviet Union over the last eight or 10 years. It has not been the one and same policy. On the other hand, changes in the Kremlin—four different leaders of that huge superpower within less than four years—also have led to an enormous amount of discontinuity. It seems to me [Soviet leader] Gorbachev is more flexible—at least he can behave in a much more flexible way—than his predecessors. So there are opportunities now. But the breakthrough has to come in the minds of Mr. Gorbachev and [U.S.] President Reagan.

Interview/U.S. News & World Report, 1-13:34.

Helmut Schmidt
Publisher, "Die Zeit" (West Germany);
Former Chancellor of West Germany

3

Governments should not organize [summit]

meetings in cities with so many hotels. They ought to go to Yalta, Casablanca, Guadeloupe, or Camp David, as they sometimes have done in the past. If during the Israeli-Egyptian peace talks [Israeli Prime Minister] Menachem Begin, [U.S. President] Jimmy Carter and [Egyptian President] Anwar Sadat had been at Washington's Watergate Hotel surrounded by TV cameras, instead of at Camp David, I doubt that they would have reached a settlement. Each participant would have been giving interviews constantly to his public. That would have made compromise difficult.

Interview/World Press Review, April:59.

Eduard A. Shevardnadze
Foreign Minister of the Soviet Union

4

[On the recent release by the Soviets of American journalist Nicholas Daniloff, who was arrested by the KGB as a spy, and the subsequent release by the U.S. of an accused Soviet spy]: There is speculation as to who [the U.S. or the Soviets] blinked first, and who outsmarted the other [in the negotiations to release the two accused people]. And who put the other side against a tree. I will say frankly, I will say directly, that you cannot get America on its knees. And the Russian people, the Soviet people, are not the kind of people who you can get on their knees. Some would like to engage us in a debate on prestige [who gained it and who lost it]. Points are argued, sounding as if this were a baseball game, or maybe a soccer match, a game more popular in the Soviet Union. But we have a different idea of prestige. The crucial test for our countries is to find solutions to problems that concern mankind. This is the essential task.

New York, Sept. 30/
The New York Times, 10-1:6.

5

Having proclaimed that peace is the supreme value of socialism, the Soviet Union rejects armed force as a method of asserting ideas and concepts. Any dispute about the advantages or disadvantages of any particular system of government can and must be resolved through

(EDUARD A. SHEVARDNADZE)

peaceful competition between socio-political and economic systems. We are not seeking to convert anybody to our credo. But we have been defending, and will continue to defend, the ideas that we hold dear. Over one and a half billion people in the countries that have chosen a socialist road of development have the right to demand that no one should impose from outside his concept of the basic values of existence.

At Conference on Security and
Cooperation in Europe, Vienna,
Nov. 5/The New York Times, 11-6:8.

1

Only by joining our efforts can we succeed in ridding Europe of terrorism, the plague of the 20th century. Those who unleash street warfare in European cities and shed the blood of innocent people are our common enemies. But in our collective wisdom, we should not identify the criminal actions of immoral, irresponsible assassins with entire countries.

At Conference on Security and
Cooperation in Europe, Vienna,
Nov. 5/The New York Times, 11-6:10.

Arkady N. Shevchenko
Former Soviet diplomat
(defected to the United States)

2

On the one hand, the Soviet leadership doesn't want any major confrontation with the West and the U.S.A. in the near future because of their preoccupation with domestic dilemmas. They want to improve the economy and to eliminate the growing gap in high technology between the West and the Soviet Union. But in the long range, you have to understand that the final objectives and goals of the Soviet leadership never change. It is the same thing—that they will win in the historical competition with capitalism, if not in this century, then in the next . . . It's a fantasy to think that the Soviet leadership really has a specific timetable and kind of a master plan of how to dominate the world. It's rather a philosophical concept in which they be-

lieve that capitalism contains elements of self-destruction.

Interview/USA Today, 2-19:(A)9.

R. Sargent Shriver
Former Director,
United States Peace Corps

3

I'm guessing that the people who volunteer [for the Peace Corps] today are even more aware of the difficulties and the challenges and the need for them to be skillful than the original volunteers may have been. Does that make them more idealistic? I guess you could make a pretty good argument that it does. The original ones had the opposite challenge. Nobody knew what it would be like. It takes a lot of spunk to zoom off into the center of Africa not knowing very much about what you would be doing, who you'd be doing it with, whether it would be dangerous. The spirit of those who volunteered in the beginning, in some respects, was just as great, but different.

Interview, Washington/
The New York Times, 9-20:6.

Martin Shugrue
Vice chairman,
Pan American World Airways

4

[On the decrease in overseas travel from the U.S. due to international terrorism]: People are trying to paint this as a problem just for U.S. [air] carriers. It's not. It's a world-wide problem that we as civilized nations of the world have to deal with. It wasn't a plane from a U.S. carrier on the ground in Malta where Egyptian commandos assaulted it. Nor was it a U.S. plane that was blown up over the North Atlantic, killing more than 300 people. I don't think Americans ought to let anybody intimidate them into not exercising their right to travel unencumbered in a free world. We shouldn't allow a bunch of lunatics to take that right away from us.

Interview/
USA Today, 5-22:(A)9.

WHAT THEY SAID IN 1986

George P. Shultz
Secretary of State of the United States

1

[On criticism of the State Department for not granting visas to persons with certain political stands]: This Administration is committed—and I am personally committed—to protecting free expression of all political ideas . . . No denial [of a visa] is ever based on a person's abstract beliefs. I want to make it clear, however, that we will deny personal access to people who aim to undermine our system through their actions, who are likely to engage in proscribed intelligence activities, or who raise funds or otherwise assist our enemies.

At International PEN Congress, New York,
Jan. 12/Los Angeles Times, 1-15:(V)3.

2

[On international terrorism]: Some have suggested that even to contemplate using force against terrorism is to lower ourselves to the barbaric level of the terrorists. I want to take this issue head-on. It is absurd to argue that international law prohibits us from capturing terrorists in international waters or airspace, from attacking them on the soil of other nations even for the purpose of rescuing hostages, or from using force against states that support, train and harbor terrorists or guerrillas. International law requires no such result. A nation attacked by terrorists is permitted to use force to prevent or pre-empt future attacks, to seize terrorists or to rescue its citizens when no other means is available. We are right to be reluctant to unsheath our sword. But we cannot let the ambiguities of the terrorist threat reduce us to total impotence. A policy filled with so many qualifications and conditions that they all could never be met would amount to a policy of paralysis. It would amount to an admission that, with all our weaponry and power, we are helpless to defend our citizens, our interests and our values. This I simply do not accept . . . We should use our military power only if the stakes justify it, if other means are not available, and then only in a manner appropriate to a clear objective. But we cannot opt out of every contest. We cannot wait for absolute certainty and clarity. If we do, the world's future will be determined by others—most likely by those who are the most brutal, the most unscrupulous and the most hostile to everything we believe in.

At National Defense University, Washington,
Jan. 15/The New York Times, 1-16:4.

3

This is the essence of statesmanship: to see a danger when it is not self-evident, to educate our people to the stakes involved, and then to fashion a sensible response and rally support. We must avoid no-win situations, but we must also have the stomach to confront the harder-to-win situations that call for prudent involvement, even when the results are slow in coming.

At National Defense University, Washington,
Jan. 15/The Washington Post, 1-16:(A)28.

4

President Reagan has never felt unable to use power in response to [international] terrorism. What I have said in this area has been with the full support and knowledge of him. I don't make speeches that differ from his policies. I have attempted to underscore the need for the U.S. to have an array of options—a toolbox, if you will—that can be used as circumstances demand. When we feel use of military force is appropriate, I'm sure the President will use it . . . I'm not frustrated by this issue, but I am very desirous that we do everything we can to deal effectively with terrorism.

Interview/U.S. News & World Report, 2-3:36.

5

[Saying security at U.S. embassies abroad must be strengthened]: [American diplomats and their families are] on the front lines, they are being shot at, they get killed, and we owe them. I remember the atmosphere when our embassy [in Lebanon] was bombed [in 1984], and coming here and people telling me that we have to do, the sooner the better, all the things that are necessary to make our embassies more secure, no ifs and buts about it. This has to be priority. We have to keep faith with the people on the firing line.

At Congressional hearing, Washington,
Feb. 5/The New York Times, 2-6:3.

6

[Criticizing recent public statements by Soviet leader Mikhail Gorbachev regarding arms

(GEORGE P. SHULTZ)

control, summit meetings and other possible U.S.-Soviet negotiations]: If we're going to get into genuinely serious discussions of the many difficult and important issues involved, we're going to have to sit down opposite Soviet leaders and talk carefully, thoughtfully and quietly about them so that you have a real interchange. To make a proposal for a major meeting between the President of the United States and the General Secretary of the Soviet Union, to make it over television, with no pre-warning or anything, is to simply put it in the public domain and not have it explored carefully.

Washington, March 31/
The New York Times, 4-1:10.

1

History shows us that nations which are economically successful are best equipped to resolve their differences with their neighbors. History also teaches that nations in deep economic distress are more vulnerable to political instability, to the simplistic appeals of demagogues who preach the siren songs of war and confrontation as a diversion from home.

At luncheon for visiting
Israeli Prime Minister Shimon Peres,
Washington, April 1/
The New York Times, 4-3:7.

2

A purely passive defense does not provide enough of a deterrent to [international] terrorism and the states that sponsor it. It is time to think long, hard and seriously about more active means of defense—defense through preventive or pre-emptive actions against terrorist groups *before* they strike . . . Experience has taught us that one of the best deterrents to terrorism is the certainty that swift and sure measures will be taken against those who engage in it. Clearly, there are complicated moral issues here. But there should be no doubt of the democracies' moral right, indeed duty, to defend themselves.

At conference on terrorism,
Washington/
Time, 4-14:50.

3

[On the U.S. response to international terrorism, such as the recent U.S. attack on Libya for alleged Libyan terrorist involvement]: . . . it has been shown that the United States will use military power in this fight against terrorism . . . we regard terrorism in general as a very important problem and, when the terrorists have the support and connivance of a state, it's particularly ominous. So you have to focus on that, and the President [Reagan] has set that out in clear and stark terms.

Interview/"Worldnet" TV service, 4-24.

4

[Saying covert measures are appropriate in fighting international terrorism]: We have to get over the idea that "covert" is a dirty word. Free nations accustomed to open debate are naturally uneasy about covert measures, just as they are uneasy about the ambiguous circumstances that require us to act in secret. Yet we must remember that intelligence breakthroughs and secret operations had a decisive influence on our victories in two world wars. Today, in our shadow war against terrorism, the use of these instruments is just as imperative . . . [We] will use such measures legally, properly and with the due involvement of designated legislative committees.

Before American Jewish Committee, Washington,
May 15/The Washington Post, 5-16:(A)1,27.

5

[Criticizing the decision to subsidize U.S. wheat sales to the Soviet Union]: The Soviet Union must be chortling at having sales to them subsidized and scratching their heads about a [U.S.] system that says we're going to fix it up so that American taxpayers make it possible for a Soviet housewife to buy American-produced food at a price lower than an American housewife. So I think there are a lot of problems with this, but obviously there must be a lot of pluses or it wouldn't have been decided. I can't think of any pluses myself.

Interview/USA Today, 8-5:(A)7.

6

[On the arrest by the Soviets on spying charges of American journalist Nicholas Daniloff

(GEORGE P. SHULTZ)

shortly after the U.S. arrested a Soviet UN delegate as a spy]: The cynical arrest of an innocent American journalist reminds us of what we already know: Our traditions of free inquiry and openness are spurned by the Soviets, showing the dark side of a society prepared to resort to hostage-taking as an instrument of policy. Let there be no talk of a trade for Daniloff. We and Nick have ruled that out. The Soviet leadership must find the wisdom to settle this case quickly in accordance with the dictates of simple human decency and of civilized national behavior.

At Harvard University 350th anniversary convocation, Sept. 5/ The New York Times, 9-6:7.

1

It's a mistake for government to get into the business of trading something of genuine importance for hostages [held by terrorists]. Why? Not because you don't want to get the hostages back. And, I suppose, not really because you care that much about a little dough-re-me. But [it's] because if you do that, all you do is encouraging the taking of more hostages and you put more Americans at risk. So that's the theory. I think it's a perfectly good theory, and it's a good practice, and we intend to stick to it.

Chicago, Nov. 17/ The New York Times, 11-19:7.

2

Only a few years ago, the democracies of the world were believed to be an embattled, shrinking handful of nations. Today, people struggling under oppressive regimes of the right and the left can see democracy as a vital force for the future. Vital but non-violent movements toward more open societies have succeeded. The failure of closed, command economies is more evident every day. A new wind of change is blowing. People who are ready to stand up for freedom and have no choice but to fight for their rights now know that Communism's march is not inevitable.

Before House Foreign Affairs Committee, Washington, Dec. 8/ The New York Times, 12-9:6.

3

[On the current scandal involving alleged covert operations by the National Security Council regarding Iran and Nicaragua]: If there is a lesson out of all this, insofar as how things operate are concerned, I think that the lesson is that operational activities, and the staff for conducting operational activities out of the National Security Council staff, is very questionable and shouldn't be done except in very rare circumstances. The example is given of [then-Secretary of State] Henry Kissinger's diplomacy with China. And, of course, that was spectacular— everybody refers to it—and it was a wonderful thing. On the other hand, to the extent that it causes other people to aspire to be Henry Kissingers, it can get you into trouble. There's only one. They broke the mold when they made him.

Before House Foreign Affairs Committee, Washington, Dec. 8/ The New York Times, 12-9:8.

Alan K. Simpson
United States Senator, R-Wyoming

4

[Criticizing the House for voting down a bill to control illegal immigration]: We have defaulted, we have deferred, we have relegated our legislative power away to a tough, tough bunch of guys [U.S. fruit growers who want cheap foreign labor] who really didn't give a crap about immigration reform, whose sole interest is that the people be in the fields on the date when the figs are ready, the peaches, the grapes—and everything else is just lip service.

Washington, Sept. 26/Los Angeles Times, The Washington Post, 9-27:(I)21.

Larry Speakes
Principal Deputy Press Secretary to the President of the United States

5

[On the arrest in the Soviet Union of U.S. journalist Nicholas Daniloff on spy charges]: Daniloff is innocent. We want his immediate release and we do regard it as very, very serious . . . What we [the U.S.] did [recently] is,

(LARRY SPEAKES)

we caught somebody—a Soviet diplomat in the United States, a person attached to the UN— spying. We arrested him. We will proceed under U.S. law. And then a few days later a newsman [Daniloff], who was going about his business as a newsman, was arrested on trumped-up charges.

Sept. 7/The New York Times, 9-8:1.

Ronald I. Spiers
Under Secretary for Management,
Department of State of the United States

1

A disturbing trend is the use of Foreign Service positions for political patronage. I believe this will have a corrosive effect on the career Service. . . . it is wasteful and demoralizing for well-qualified people to climb a 30-year career ladder only to be pre-empted at the top rung by someone with substantially lesser qualifications . . . An Ambassador's effectiveness depends on his professionalism, experience, familiarity with the country, knowledge of history, cultural sensitivity, managerial ability, coolness in a crisis and precise understanding of U.S. policy goals and objectives. These qualities are not monopolies of a career service; but, on the other hand, simply being "an early political supporter" of the President—a qualification often cited as the main reason for selecting a political Ambassador—or success in business do not guarantee the attributes essential for an Ambassador.

Before National Academy of Public
Administration/The New York Times, 11-21:12.

Milan Svec
Former Czech diplomat;
Now associated with the Carnegie
Endowment for International Peace

2

[On the forthcoming summit meetings between U.S. President Reagan and Soviet leader Mikhail Gorbachev]: One of these summits will have to have results. Otherwise, they will both look like two old ladies chatting in a coffee shop.

U.S. News & World Report, 10-13:17.

Margaret Thatcher
Prime Minister
of the United Kingdom

3

[Saying she does not approve of retaliatory strikes in fighting international terrorism]: I must warn you that I do not believe in retaliatory strikes that are against international law . . . We suffer from terrorism in this country and in Northern Ireland. Please, may I remind you that we have suffered over 2,000 deaths at the hands of terrorists, so are well aware of the problems, and at no stage has anyone in this country suggested that we make retaliatory strikes or go in hot pursuit or anything like that . . . Once you start to go across borders, then I do not see an end to it. And I uphold international law very firmly.

News conference, London, Jan. 10/
The New York Times, 1-11:1.

4

[On international terrorism]: I don't think sanctions [against the offending country] work. They only work if you go to the United Nations and get full agreement, and even then there are problems . . . They only work if they are adopted 100 per cent, and I don't know of any case where they have been adopted 100 per cent. I wish we could all get together against nations which have terrorist camps and which practice terrorism and supply armaments to terrorists, but at the moment I see no such possibility of that.

News conference, London, Jan. 10/
Los Angeles Times, 1-11:(I)1,12.

Malcolm Toon
Former United States
Ambassador to the Soviet Union

5

[On Soviet Ambassador to the U.S. Anatoly Dobrynin, who is leaving his post to return to a new assignment in the Soviet Union]: I'm delighted to see him leave. He has managed to snooker everyone in Washington—from Congressmen to Secretaries of State.

U.S. News &
World Report, 4-21:10.

WHAT THEY SAID IN 1986

Stansfield Turner
Former Director of Central
Intelligence of the United States

1

[On friendly countries spying on each other]: Of course it goes on. But there is a big difference. When you spy on an enemy, you risk having your agents captured and jailed, or killed. When you spy on a friend, you risk considerable embarrassment and impact on your foreign policy.

The Christian Science Monitor, 6-6:3.

Brian Urquhart
Former Undersecretary General
of the United Nations for
Special Political Affairs

2

The United Nations was born of a colossal tragedy [World War II], and sired by leaders who knew the nature of that tragedy intimately. Unless we have some excellent alternative, it is not wise to set aside their experience or to let wither the institutions they set up just because the world has become so complex and so difficult.

At International Institute
of Strategic Studies, London, March/
The Washington Post, 4-10:(A)21.

Cyrus R. Vance
Former Secretary of
State of the United States

3

[On when the Secretary of State disagrees with his President's policies]: Every Secretary of State has to make his own decision on something like this. I believe that when core values are at issue, then a Secretary of State must speak his piece frankly and strongly to the President; if a President overrules that, then I think he should resign. And then, if he wishes to challenge the President, to do that from the outside. I don't see how you can challenge the President when you're still acting as his Secretary of State.

Broadcast interview/
"This Week With David Brinkley,"
ABC-TV,11-30.

William von Raab
Commissioner,
United States Customs Service

4

There are too many people in the State Department who regard every issue as a knot in a finely woven tapestry, every knot of which, if it were to come undone, the whole tapestry would come undone. If you take that approach to life, that every issue is related to every other, you'll never do anything.

Interview, Washington, June 2/
Los Angeles Times, 6-3:(I)11.

Terry Waite
Personal envoy of the
Archbishop of Canterbury for
negotiating with hostage-holding terrorists

5

Terrorism is a blanket term. I first meet a terrorist as a person instead of under a stereotype. One has to recognize what stimulates or motivates them into acts of hostage-taking or terrorism.

Interview, London/The Christian
Science Monitor, 10-30:10.

Malcolm Wallop
United States Senator, R-Wyoming

6

[Saying Soviet defectors to the U.S. should be given a more public profile]: Defectors have much to offer and their experiences should be shared in the classroom, on the speech circuit. They should serve as useful beacons for future defectors.

U.S. News & World Report, 2-3:6.

7

[Criticizing President Reagan, saying he negotiated an exchange of an accused Soviet spy arrested in the U.S. for Nicholas Daniloff, an American journalist arrested as a spy by the Soviets and declared innocent by Reagan]: The President, having said that ransom is unacceptable, has proceeded to pay ransom. It has diminished our standing in relation to the [forthcoming U.S.-Soviet] summit.

Washington, Sept. 30/
Los Angeles Times, 10-1:(I)7.

Vernon A. Walters
United States Ambassador/Permanent
Representative to the United Nations

1

What's the difference between the diplomat and the military man? The answer is . . . they both do nothing, but the military get up very early in the morning to do it with great discipline, while the diplomats do it late in the afternoon, in utter confusion.

Newsweek, 3-3:13.

2

There is a widespread view in Europe that Americans are ingenuous and naive and simply do not have the historical background and understanding of the world that Europeans have. I can only note that when the U.S. had very little to do with running the world, like between the two world wars, there were 21 years of peace. Since the ingenuous, stupid Americans have had some part in it, we've had 41 years of peace . . . I live in a world where the Soviet Union every day . . . calls us bandits, pirates, criminals, thugs, imperialists and all sorts of things. When we say something harsh about that, everybody raises their hands in great cries. Now, the American people have committed 300,000 soldiers for the last 40 years to defend Europe. We feel, quite frankly, that in the light of that commitment, when we have asked our allies to do things we consider quite small, to be of assistance to us . . . we've had very little support. And I think there is a considerable feeling of resentment in the United States that we have had so little support.

Broadcast interview/"Nightline," ABC-TV, 4-15.

3

[Comparing authoritarian regimes, such as in Chile, with totalitarian regimes, such as in Cuba]: Cuba and Chile both have populations of 10 million. Two million have fled from Cuba, which is much harder to do. Only 15-25,000 have fled Chile, where they can simply walk across the border into Argentina, Bolivia and Peru. And don't denigrate right-wing dictatorships [such as Chile]: They almost always lead to democracy—Portugal, Spain, Greece, Argentina, Brazil . . . But with Communist dictator-ships, they've never become representative in this century. With a Communist dictatorship, there's little in the past to offer future hope. The [U.S.] Reagan Administration is as committed to human rights as anyone else. In my own personal trouble-shooting, I've told many a right-wing dictatorship to move toward democracy. But my own feeling is that we don't press left-wing dictatorships in the same way. The accusation that we favor right-wing dictatorships is absolutely false. We do business with [Communist] Romania and Hungary, and nobody accuses us of propping them up [as critics say the U.S. does for right-wing dictatorships].

Interview, United Nations,
New York/The Christian
Science Monitor, 4-18:12.

4

How can we discuss [United Nations] fiscal and budgetary restraint and then find that an official UN mission is visiting Bulgaria to explore the role of non-governmental organizations? There are *no* NGOs in Bulgaria. Even the lady who hands out towels in the toilet is a government employee.

Interview, United Nations, New York/
The Christian Science Monitor, 4-18:12.

5

[On how to deal with international terrorism]: I'm a participant in the doctrine of constructive ambiguity. I don't think we should tell them [terrorists] what we're going to do in advance. Let them think. Worry. Wonder. Uncertainty is the most chilling thing of all.

Interview, United Nations, New York/
The Christian Science Monitor, 4-18:12.

6

The United Nations is facing a crisis of confidence. Member states remain committed to the ideals of the United Nations—but member states no longer have confidence in the United Nations as an institution for effectively serving those ideals.

Before UN General Assembly,
New York, April 30/
Los Angeles Times, 5-1:(I)20.

WHAT THEY SAID IN 1986

Gary Waugh
Acting Director of
Strategic Investigations,
United States Customs Service

1

[On Soviet theft of U.S. high technology and the American businessmen who help them]: This is a free country. We can't restrict people from doing business. We try to carry out the mandate [to stop the theft] without restricting legitimate trade. There are very few people more sophisticated than international businessmen. You're not dealing with some schmuck on the street with half a lid of grass. You're talking about multi-multi-millionaires. It's like trying to stop narcotics: You can make a dent, but you can't stop it.

The Washington Post, 2-5:(A)17.

Caspar W. Weinberger
Secretary of Defense of the United States

2

[Saying the U.S. must be careful in responding to international terrorism]: I think that there are a lot of people who would get instant gratification from some kind of a bombing attack [to retaliate against terrorists] somewhere without being too worried about the details . . . We have a good idea as to where some terrorist bases are. [But we must have] a clear idea [before attacking them that they] are indeed bases that have spawned terrorism that is directed against us. A discriminate response, an appropriate response, is difficult. But it is important that we have that kind of response and we are quite capable of delivering that kind of response very quickly and very effectively. We have to have the appropriateness of the response carefully thought out, and we have to have the basic question of whether what we are doing will discourage and diminish terrorism in the future.

News conference, Washington, Jan. 16/
Los Angeles Times, 1-17:(I)12.

3

Embassies are used as terrorist arsenals and planning centers, and so-called "diplomats" actually plan and orchestrate murders and bombings in the nations hosting them. Yet, under the prevailing law of diplomatic immunity, the embassy is a sanctuary; there is no recourse against the so-called "diplomat" except expulsion . . . I think we should examine, very carefully, the whole idea of diplomatic privilege extending to support of terrorism. [Diplomatic immunity can be preserved] without cloaking terrorists in those privileges . . . I submit there are limits to the doctrine of diplomatic immunity. The task remains for our diplomats with the assistance of the legal profession to define those limits. Diplomatic title must not confer a license to murder.

At American Bar Association Conference
on Law in Relationship to Terrorism, Washington,
June 5/Los Angeles Times, 6-6:(I)23.

Elie Wiesel
Author; Chairman, United States
Holocaust Memorial Council

4

[Applauding the U. S. Senate for its approval of a UN convention against genocide]: I know that a law on genocide will not stop future attempts to commit genocide. But at least we, as a moral nation, whose memories are alive, have made this statement: We are against genocide, and we cannot tolerate a world in which genocide is being perpetrated.

Feb. 19/The New York Times, 2-20:4.

Paul Wilkinson
Professor, University
of Aberdeen (Scotland)

5

[On international terrorists]: They believe in [their] total rectitude. Intolerance, dogmaticism, authoritarianism, and a ruthless treatment of their own people who deviate from their own view are common to their mentality.

The Christian Science Monitor, 5-15:19.

Anthony Williams
British delegate to
"Helsinki process" human-rights
talks in Bern, Switzerland

6

[On those who criticize the U.S. veto of a compromise human-rights document at the Bern

(ANTHONY WILLIAMS)

talks]: In our eyes, the real problem is not the United States or its scruples. The problem is that, only too clearly, some countries in Eastern Europe continue to be so reluctant to turn their professions and commitments regarding humanitarian matters into anything worthwhile in the real world. Words without action make a mockery of human tragedy.

Bern, Switzerland, May 27/
Los Angeles Times,
5-28:(I)16.

151

Government

Mortimer Adler
Educator; Director, Institute
for Philosophical Research

1

I'm a firm believer [that] democracy is the only perfectly just form of government in terms of what human beings are. [But to make it work,] we have to make [the citizens] recognize their moral and intellectual responsibilities. I've often said that if this [recognition] is impossible, then we ought to give [democracy] up . . . If you take democracy seriously, [you find that] the citizens are the ruling class. The guys in Washington are their servants. We, the people, are the government.

Interview, Aspen, Colo./
The Christian Science Monitor, 9-23:16.

Lamar Alexander
Governor of Tennessee (R)

2

The Federal government ought to concentrate on what it now spends 85 per cent of its money on,which is war, welfare, Social Security and debt. There are a few other clearly national responsibilities that it must be involved in—the national park system, the interstate highway system. Some environmental issues cross state lines. But the Federal government ought to leave to the state and local government education, as much of roads as possible, prisons, clean water, initiatives for healthy children, and economic development. Now, that's a view not all of the Governors will agree with. Let me emphasize that that's my view.

Interview/USA Today, 2-20:(A)9.

3

Twenty years ago when I went . . . to Washington, the Senate had all the hype. Governors were considered custodians of remote provinces and could barely get their calls returned . . . [Now] it's completely reversed. The best job in government, except for the Presidency, is the Governorship.

Newsweek, 3-24:32.

Bruce Babbitt
Governor of Arizona (D)

4

Voters have begun to demand problem-solving abilities and administrative competence on the part of their [state] Governors. Partisan politics just isn't as important any more, which is why you have the unlikely pattern of popular Democrats in the West and a popular Republican in a state like New Jersey.

Newsweek, 3-24:31.

5

Washington is a place where no one has the moral courage to talk about priorities. There cannot be social progress in the absence of priorities.

Interview/The New York Times, 10-1:12.

Robert Bellah
Professor of sociology,
University of California, Berkeley

6

You don't get less government by ignoring it, or saying it is bad. An active, conscious citizenry asks the hard questions and demands answers.

Interview, Berkeley, Calif./
The Christian Science Monitor, 7-28:22.

Bill Bradley
United States Senator, D-New Jersey

7

For a member of Congress, the question is this: Do you believe your role is to represent the general interest, or is it your job to represent narrower interests—this one, that one—and put together a quilt of service? I believe a legislator's job is to represent the general interest.

Interview, Washington, May 8/
The New York Times, 5-9:32.

William J. Brennan, Jr.
Associate Justice, Supreme
Court of the United States

8

. . . we have given governments more power over our lives than ever before. The danger lies

(WILLIAM J. BRENNAN, JR.)

in that we seem not more concerned but more indifferent to the consequences of this surrender. We seem to have forgotten Justice Brandeis' admonition, "Experience should teach us to be most on our guard to protect liberty when the government's purposes are beneficent" . . . While the Founders wanted a stable government, they were also wary of it. They knew from history that too much power goes to the head of anybody, particularly rulers. They knew that in the name of liberty and governmental security, individual liberty had been periodically destroyed in the past . . . Rulers always have and always will find it dangerous to their security to permit people to think, believe, talk, write, assemble, and particularly to criticize, the government as they please.

At Brandeis University commencement, May 18/
The New York Times, 5-19:16; USA Today, 5-19:(A)4.

Patrick J. Buchanan
Director of Communications for
the President of the United States

1

Leaks [of classified government information] are like prostitution and gambling: You can control them and contain them a bit, but you're not going to eliminate them.

Los Angeles Times, 6-9:(I)6.

2

In the Nixon Administration, the White House staff was really all-powerful. The President went through his White House aides—Kissinger, Haldeman, Ehrlichman, etc.—and the Cabinet members virtually reported through the White House aides to the President. Orders came down from the President to White House aides, so when I picked up a phone and called a Cabinet officer, he knew that the instructions were coming from the top . . . This [Reagan] White House really is Cabinet government. We have very strong Cabinet Secretaries, all of whom have parcels of the Reagan franchise, and each implements it in his own area. Cabinet government lends itself to many more pub-

lic collisions between Cabinet officers, or collisions that eventually go public.

Interview/USA Today, 7-18:(A)9.

James MacGregor Burns
Historian

3

In the United States, in this century particularly, we have worked out the most marvelous and dubious method of evading and delaying compromises implicit in the Constitution of checks and balances . . . What we have done is to dump power into the Presidency, not so much because he has wanted it but because we have wanted him to have it . . . Practically nobody seems to question a President who takes war-like actions, whether it's a few days ago [the U.S. attack against Libya], or over the last 10 or 20 years, except when things go wrong.

At Douglas Adair Symposia, Pomona
(Calif.) College/Los Angeles Times, 4-30:(V)3.

George Bush
Vice President of the United States

4

[On what he has learned about the Presidency]: Take a few central themes that you believe strongly in and stay with them, and not get down on people who are criticizing you and just stay with what you think is the right course of action and manage through that. Don't be afraid to pass out assignments to others, to delegate, but lead through adherence to certain principles, and I've learned a lot on that.

Interview, Washington, June 6/
The Christian Science Monitor, 6-10:10.

Hodding Carter III
Journalist; Former spokesman,
Department of State of the United States

5

[Saying TV coverage of Senate proceedings won't change the way Senators operate]: Major figures in the Senate are already blow-drying their hair. They live in a television world right now, rushing out to talk to the cameras right af-

(HODDING CARTER III)

ter a vote. Almost all Senators have already become television human beings; so televising Senate proceedings won't change anything. Oh, there may be one or two Congressmen who will start talking in shorter verse, but there are only a handful of Senators left who treat the Senate as a place for extended debate, anyway. Certainly the television coverage of the House has not affected the procedural rules, and I don't think it is going to affect very much in the Senate either.

Interview, New York/
The Christian Science Monitor, 5-5:36.

1

The filibuster is not going to die as long as there are minorities in the Senate who feel it is the one way they can get hold of, obstruct, or alter the course of legislation. Besides, a filibuster is an invaluable asset to a politician with his own constituency. He doesn't care if he looks silly to the people who oppose it. If he looks good to the people he is representing and he does that in a filibuster, then he'll go at it forever.

Interview, New York/
The Christian Science Monitor, 5-5:36.

Albert V. Casey
Postmaster General of the United States

2

The smartest thing I really did—and I did it by accident, but it turned out to be brilliant—was to announce my resignation before I announced my acceptance of the job. Immediately everybody said, "Hell, you're nothing but a lame duck; you won't be able to do anything in Washington." Well, I view that everybody in Washington is a lame duck.

Interview/The Washington Post, 6-13:(A)17.

Dick Cheney
United States Representative,
R-Wyoming

3

What's happened in Washington, I think, in the era after Watergate, is that public officials now

have to avoid even the appearance of impropriety. It is not enough to be legally and technically clean. You must meet a higher standard in which you avoid situations which may be technically in compliance with the law but which could cause somebody to raise questions about your conduct.

To reporters, Washington/
The Christian Science Monitor, 5-20:17.

Clark M. Clifford
Former Secretary of
Defense of the United States

4

I have a theory about government service. Ordinarily, I believe that a four-year term fulfills a man's obligation and finds him at his most productive best. As I've watched careers, I have the feeling that, except in very unusual instances, there appears to be a period of less productivity after four or five years. If the man is in a policy-making position, he will have developed a host of opponents who have at some point resented decisions he's made, and it ultimately builds up until it adds to the natural resistance that is present in every important policy decision.

Interview/The Washington Post, 9-2:(A)17.

Henry Steele Commager
Historian

5

Without enlightenment about politics and information about government, democracy simply would not work.

USA Today, 4-11:(A)10.

Charles Cooper
Assistant Attorney General,
Office of Legal Counsel, Department
of Justice of the United States

6

There is virtually no area of public-policy concern in which the states can regulate, or otherwise make public policy, without fear of contradiction or oversight or overruling by the Federal government.

News conference, Washington, Nov. 10/
The Washington Post, 11-11:(A)4.

Walter Cronkite
Special correspondent, and
former anchorman, CBS News

1

It's very dangerous to suggest that the government should be prosecuting the press for revealing secrets that are clearly leaked to them, provided by members of our government. I can certainly see why the government would be concerned about leaks, and that's something that the government ought to be doing something about. But to attempt to punish the press in a free society for printing leaks that are all over the streets of Washington, that's something different. If there's any bit of information that's available to the meanest little embassy in Washington, I want the American public to share in it.

Interview/USA Today, 6-6:(A)13.

Mario M. Cuomo
Governor of New York (D)

2

[On his style of governing]: If a lot of intelligent people tell me not to do something, I think about it and take their advice. But the popular opinion of intelligent people can be off. When you have a powerful instinct, you ought to go with it.

Interview, Albany, N.Y./
The New York Times, 1-23:13.

3

[There is an] enormous gap between the poetry of politics and the prose of governance. When politicians govern—as distinguished from when they campaign—they come to understand the difference between a speech and a statute. And it's here—in the actual governance, in the palpable, sweaty, real world—that we're forced to come to grips with complexity, that we're required to look beyond labels and grapple with hard choices.

Interview/Los Angeles Times, 2-28:(I)25.

4

I'm not comfortable reading anything that isn't in my words entirely, so there are no major speeches where that happens. But to say I go off in a room and design a speech, sweat through it, change it and then waft it on the airwaves and say "It's mine, all mine," that's not how it happens. You can't write by committee, but I use everybody I can get my hands on, mostly for reaction.

Interview, Albany, N.Y./
The New York Times, 6-3:16.

Michael K. Deaver
Former Deputy Chief of Staff
to the President of the United States
(Ronald Reagan)

5

[On charges that he has used his White House contacts to further his current career as a lobbyist for foreign and domestic clients]: I wonder what people thought I was going to do when I left the White House: Be a brain surgeon? That [lobbying] was my business. That was the business I went back to . . . I'm very careful because I knew when I left the White House that I would be the target of interest for a lot of people, both in the media and outside the media. So I hired me a very fine law firm here in Washington, D.C., and I said I want to do everything within the law. So I never make an appointment with anybody connected anywhere near the White House without checking first with my own counsel to be sure it's appropriate.

Broadcast interview/
"MacNeil-Lehrer News Hour," PBS-TV, 4-4.

6

[On charges that he used his relationship with President Reagan to his advantage as a lobbyist after he left government]: I take very seriously the charges that have been leveled against me personally, against my firm, against my profession and, by inference, against the President and the tradition of public service to which many of us have dedicated our lives. . . . both in government and in my private business, my actions have been within the law at all times, [and I] have consistently sought to maintain a high standard of integrity. I only ask not to be judged on the basis of anonymous leaks.

Before House Subcommittee on
Oversight and Investigations, Washington,
May 16/The New York Times, 5-17:10.

WHAT THEY SAID IN 1986

John D. Dingell
United States Representative, D-Michigan

1

[On charges that former White House Deputy Chief of Staff Michael Deaver used his relationship with President Reagan to his advantage as a lobbyist after he left government]: The key issue here involves the ethical and moral standards required of those who serve in government. Those standards should, without question, be the highest possible, and the tone of any Administration should be set by the person who heads it. There are serious doubts about that tone in the current situation.

Washington, May 16/
The New York Times, 5-17:10.

Robert J. Dole
United States Senator, R-Kansas

2

I don't know how many people from Kansas have said, "I was in the [Senate] gallery and I didn't see you on the floor." As far as they're concerned, that's your office, the Senate floor; you ought to be there every minute. They don't know about your other office. There is a general misunderstanding. They don't know what a conference report is, probably, or a quorum call, or all these things that we sort of take for granted. Or why you can't get things through: They don't understand that it takes just one Senator to stop something.

Interview/USA Today, 1-21:(A)9.

Thomas J. Downey
United States Representative,
D-New York

3

[On Congressmen, such as himself, who make commitments to both sides in voting for controversial measures]: Yeah, I'm a lot like [actor] Zero Mostel in [the film] *The Producers*. Remember, [that's] where he sold shares of the program *Springtime for Hitler*. He sold about a hundred shares of 50 per cent [each] in the show. He wound up going to jail. Fortunately, we don't go to jail for over-extending our commitments.

Broadcast interview, "Frontline," PBS-TV/
The Wall Street Journal, 6-6:22.

Robert F. Drinan
Professor of law,
Georgetown University; Former United
States Representative, D-Massachusetts

4

Congress is responsive to public outrage. Going through history you look at the civil-rights movement, the abolitionist movement, and realize that it wasn't the politicians, it was the people. The environmentalist movement is a classic example.

The New York Times, 6-11:14.

Thomas F. Eagleton
United States Senator, D-Missouri

5

This country's had single-issue politics before. Slavery was single-issue politics; prohibition was single-issue policies. But today we have the most unlimited proliferation of single-issue politics, and the filibuster gives the single-issue politician his powerful voice . . . So the single-issue politician can hold up the HEW appropriation bill by amendments on abortion, amendments on [school] busing, amendments on [school] prayer.

Interview, Washington/
The Washington Post, 10-31:(A)25.

Marian Wright Edelman
President, Children's Defense Fund

6

As you leave Rutgers, I hope you will care deeply about the choices those who represent you [in government] make for America . . . I hope you will be tough and understand what is needed to solve problems and to change attitudes and policies. You can make a difference, but it requires hard, sustained work. Democracy is not a spectator sport.

At Rutgers University commencement,
May 22/The New York Times, 5-23:13.

Dianne Feinstein
Mayor of San Francisco

7

A woman in public office does best if she doesn't wear her sex or her race like a badge on

(DIANNE FEINSTEIN)

her sleeve. What you have to do to succeed is show the electorate you can do what they expect of you—carry out their dream.

U.S. News & World Report, 4-7:31.

Geraldine Ferraro
Former United States Representative,
D-New York; 1984 Democratic
Vice Presidential nominee

1

Women's voices are essential to good government. Instead of engaging in confrontation, women are more apt to negotiate. Instead of looking at short-term solutions, women think in terms of generations to come. Instead of thinking in win-lose terms, women are more apt to see the gray area in-between.

At women's conference aboard
"Mississippi Queen" steamboat/
USA Today, 4-23:(A)11.

Gerald R. Ford
Former President of the United States

2

We don't want an imperial President, nor do we want an imperiled Congress. And I don't want an impotent Congress, or an over-reaching Congress. Somewhere in the middle is where we want that relationship between the White House and the Congress to be.

Interview/USA Today, 7-28:(A)9.

Douglas A. Fraser
Former president, United
Automobile Workers of America

3

If our Founding Fathers looked at us now . . . and [saw] our inability to manage the [national] debt, [they might think that] we should have [gone] to the parliamentary system. Maybe we imposed so many checks and balances in the system [that] we immobilized ourselves.

Interview, Detroit/
The Christian Science Monitor, 10-28:17.

Alan Garcia
President of Peru

4

A government of the people is a government where the people produce their own history.

Rally, Casa Grande, Peru/Time, 1-27:28.

Leonard Garment
Lawyer; Former Adviser to the
President of the United States
(Richard M. Nixon)

5

[On Washington lobbyists]: I don't think this city could work without lobbyists. Nor could the Constitution actually be a live enterprise without lobbies, because that's the way one petitions for the redress of grievances. This is a country that is so large that the Federal notion of representative government saturates our life, and that's very much the case with lobbying . . . The general impression is that unless you have somebody representing you, you're in trouble. It's clumsy but roughly correct that [lobby-users] are like a lot of blind people groping in a closet. They know they should have somebody to explain the jargon, to read the hieroglyphics of this mysterious pre-Mayan culture called Washington. And they're told that there are this whole group of special guys that you find at the headwaters of the Potomac, and if you say the right words they'll put you in a canoe and take you up there and help you find your way into the mysterious culture.

Interview, Washington/
The Washington Post, 4-28:(A)10.

Jake Garn
United States Senator, R-Utah

6

. . . government and passing laws and appropriating money are not the answer to human problems. What good does it do to go down and be a Senator of either party and make a great speech about how you're concerned about your fellow human beings, and pass laws and go home and lead an elitist personal life, and you don't know what it is to be poor or hurt or sad? I see

(JAKE GARN)

too much of that in politics. Too much rhetoric. I realize, even more, government isn't the answer.

Interview/
The Washington Post, 11-13:(B)2.

David R. Gergen
Editor, "U.S. News & World Report";
Former Director of Communications for
the President of the United States
(Ronald Reagan)

1

To be sure, there is a long history of Administrations saying that they had a right to lie, stretching back a lot farther than Arthur Sylvester, the Assistant Secretary of Defense for Public Affairs in Lyndon B. Johnson's Administration. Even [former Presidential Press Secretary] Jody Powell, an honorable man, was trying to make that argument in the Carter Administration. The temptation is especially great in today's public life when what counts most is the appearance of things—not the underlying reality. That's the lesson one sees in a Congress that lies without compunction about its budget cuts. That's the lesson insiders on Wall Street have been teaching each other, too. But if there is any lesson we should have learned from the past, especially Vietnam and Watergate, it should be simple: governments lie only at their peril. Moreover, governments do not have a right to lie. They have a right to remain silent; they have a right not to answer sensitive national-security questions. But, once and forever, let a President make it plain: The government has no right to lie. And it won't.

Frank E. Gannett lecture sponsored
by Washington Journalism Center,
Nov. 25/Los Angeles Times, 11-27:(II)7.

John Glenn
United States Senator, D-Ohio

2

[On the advent of TV coverage of Senate proceedings]: You see so much posturing going on over here now that it has changed the nature of

the Senate. I'm not sure we could have the Last Supper in the U.S. Senate anymore. It would have to be the "Last Lunch," because we have to make the 6 o'clock news.

Washington/
USA Today, 7-28:(A)4.

Barry M. Goldwater
United States Senator, R-Arizona

3

I think the Congress today, the members, have a higher average of education than they did when I came here, but it's not the same kind of people. People then had practical knowledge, they had political knowledge and they put their country before their district or their state. If there's a big difference in the Congress of today, and 30, 35 years ago when I came here, it's in the fact that the average member of Congress today puts more importance on his district or his state than he does on his country.

Interview, Washington/
The Washington Post, 11-4:(A)17.

4

We've got Senators here with over 100 staff members, and they don't have anything to do, so they sit down and write amendments and bills. My God, the number of bills on the calendar every year is unbelievable. [Senators] have the feeling that, if they aren't re-elected, the country's going to hell. We've had over 1,500 Senators in the history of the country, and it's hard for me to remember the names of any of them.

Time, 11-10:25.

Albert Gore, Jr.
United States Senator, D-Tennessee

5

[Supporting the televising of Senate proceedings]: A lot of people around here give the American people too little credit for catching on. Let it [the Senate] be seen, and if that results in pressure for change, then so be it.

The Washington Post,
3-3:(A)4.

Alexander M. Haig, Jr.
Former Secretary of State
of the United States

1

[The Reagan] Administration has only vetoed 33 bills in five years. The average for a five-year Presidency would have been 200 to 300 vetoes. But Congress has learned to interlace pork barrel with major pieces of legislation that are needed to keep the government running. That's why the President has asked for and should have a line-item veto. What he's been confronted with is bringing the government to a shuddering halt or getting rolled by the Congress. I think he has to be far more vigorous in vetoing.

Interview/USA Today, 12-2:(A)13.

Jeffrey Henig
Associate professor of political science,
George Washington University

2

People's attention has turned to the fiscal side of governing. The executive rather than the legislator is coming into style.

U.S. News & World Report, 4-7:31.

Ed Herschler
Governor of Wyoming (D)

3

[After visiting Washington]: I would rather stick straw under my fingernails and light it than spend time in Washington, D.C.

U.S. News & World Report, 5-26:69.

William P. Hobby
Lieutenant Governor of Texas (D)

4

State government is a rather pedestrian operation concerned with schools, highways and hospitals. We don't get to decide about "Star Wars" [missile defense system], we don't get to decide who wins the war in Nicaragua, who should win that war, we don't get to decide what to do about the Russians in Afghanistan. All we do is worry about schools, highways, prisons and hospitals.

That's what the state budget is all about. And those are the services we need to protect.

Before San Antonio Chamber of
Commerce/The Washington Post, 8-7:(A)7.

Constance Horner
Director, Federal Office of
Personnel Management

5

Over the years, the Civil Service system has accreted a body of rules that runs 6,000 single-spaced pages long. That has caused a situation in which personnel offices, not managers, run the agencies. It has been very hard to get work done efficiently, timely and well. Now it's time to end the harassment of line managers and let them get on with the job.

Washington, April 30/
The New York Times, 5-1:15.

Harry Hughes
Governor of Maryland (D)

6

Every Governor has his own style, and mine has always been to respect the legislature, to seek the counsel of your leaders, and then to hold my own counsel . . . Some say I should have twisted more arms to get my way. Well, I'm not a wrestler—I was a pitcher. Some say I shunned the spotlight too much, wasn't visible enough on the 11 o'clock news to bring public focus to issues. Well, I was in the Navy as a young man, but not once did I ever have the desire to be an anchorman. I've always believed, and still believe, that a Governor's job is not to play to the crowd but to do the hard work away from the glare, to do it honestly and objectively, with sensitivity and caring, and then, and only then, stand before the cameras and take the heat.

Before Maryland Legislature, Annapolis,
Jan. 15/The Washington Post, 1-16:(A)15.

Lee A. Iacocca
Chairman, Chrysler Corporation

7

[On whether he would like to be President of the U.S.]: I'd enjoy it. I sure as hell could do it. But

159

(LEE A. IACOCCA)

it's a fantasy. I have no stomach for it. I haven't got the temperament either. I'd be a lousy politician. I'd last three days. I can make speeches, glad-hand, fix up the economy. But my way would be to shove everyone into a room and knock heads. You can't do that if you're President.

Interview/Ladies' Home Journal, March:205.

J. Bennett Johnston
United States Senator, D-Louisiana

1

[On televising Senate proceedings]: Unlimited debate . . . is not a pretty thing to watch on television. It is a messy, untidy spectacle to watch, but I think vital to the nation.

Senate debate, Washington, Feb. 27/
The Washington Post, 2-28:(A)6.

Thomas H. Kean
Governor of New Jersey (R)

2

Women have broken through in every other career, [but] the story is radically different in politics . . . The absence of women from our elective bodies skews our decisions. Our most important deliberative bodies are being deprived of half the nation's energy, creativity and talent.

At Barnard College commencement,
May 14/The New York Times, 5-15:16.

Jack Kemp
United States Representative,
D-New York; Former football
quarterback, San Diego "Chargers"
and Buffalo "Bills"

3

When I was a quarterback, I can remember saying that quarterbacking was not listening to people in the stands—or even coaches. It was getting a play called and telling people in the huddle to be quiet, and taking them down the field—doing what you thought best, and either succeeding or failing. But political leadership is different. It is listening and it is trying to take

people where they want to go, as opposed to where you think they ought to go. Presidential leadership is the ultimate test, in trying to find out where a country wants to go and advancing the ideas that will get it there. That's a lot different than being a quarterback of a football team or the architect of a bold new political idea.

The Washington Post, 9-2:(A)8.

Jeane J. Kirkpatrick
Former United States Ambassador/
Permanent Representative to
the United Nations

4

If one is a Cabinet officer . . . one ought to rally round [the President in times of controversy], or get out.

U.S. News &
World Report, 12-22:7.

Henry A. Kissinger
Former Secretary of State
of the United States

5

[On the controversy surrounding secret U.S.-Iran negotiations involving arms deals, hostages and Nicaraguan contras]: I think one iron rule in situations like this is, whatever must happen ultimately should happen immediately. Anybody who eventually has to go should be fired now. Any fact that needs to be disclosed should be put out now, or as quickly as possible, because otherwise . . . the bleeding will not end.

Time, 12-8:27.

Ray Kline
President, National Academy
of Public Administration

6

Laws and regulations like the Ethics in Government Act can only go so far. You ultimately come down to questions of discretion and good judgment, and that depends on the quality of people whom a President appoints.

Los Angeles Times,
8-18:(I)15.

Edward I. Koch
Mayor of New York

1

[On recent revelations of corruption involving high New York City officials]: I still believe that public service is the noblest of professions . . . Most people are honest and competent in government . . . I believe you have to accept people as honest, unless you have a cause to believe they're dishonest. You cannot work in or out of government with the supposition that everyone who comes in is . . . a crook.

Interview, New York/USA Today, 4-8:(A)2.

Patrick J. Leahy
United States Senator, D-Vermont

2

I wouldn't be a Senator if I couldn't come home. I find that no matter how tough it gets in Washington, I come back here [to Vermont] and get an entirely different perspective. Problems that seem insurmountable in Washington evaporate up here . . . One of the big problems in the Senate is that, more and more, we're getting Senators who don't even have a home in their home state. They're spending the holidays in Washington. There's a built-in incentive to spend time in Washington, where you succumb to the pressure to do what's politically popular in Washington—what's going to guarantee you a White House dinner . . . We're supposed to be citizen-legislators. I think people want to see you in your home state. You have to listen to what's on people's minds if you're going to represent them.

Interview, Middlesex, Vt./
The New York Times, 12-24:12.

Russell B. Long
United States Senator, D-Louisiana

3

[Arguing against the televising of Senate sessions, saying it would encourage grandstanding and prolonged debates]: Statesmanship is too scarce a commodity as it is now. It will be more scarce on TV.

USA Today,
2-28:(A)4.

4

I have found, in serving in this body [the Senate], that it is easy enough to vote for what the people in one state want. I believe that sometimes you can get away with voting contrary to what they want, if you convince them that you thought it was right, even though they did not. But what it is difficult to convince your people about is that you did it not because of what you thought was right, but what somebody else [such as the President] thought was right, contrary to your judgment and contrary to the judgment of those you represent in this body.

Before the Senate, Washington,
April 14/The New York Times, 4-19:9.

Dan Lungren
United States Representative,
R-California

5

[Saying members of Congress deserve a raise in pay and that $100,000 is a reasonable salary for them]: You want a mix in Congress, not just those who already had it made or those who could never do any better. Members of Congress are the 535 members of the board of the largest corporation in the world. We have to have the guts to say to people openly, "Would you trust your assets and your future to folks you weren't willing to pay for that responsibility?" I'm willing to stand up and say that we do a job worth a significant amount of money. If I'm defeated as a result of saying that, then the person who defeats me is going to get paid what he or she is worth.

The New York Times, 5-29:8.

David H. Martin
Director, Federal Office
of Government Ethics

6

[On conflict-of-interest cases in which former high government employees unfairly use their government contacts to further their careers in private business]: There has been a lot of notoriety about some cases—such as a retired General going to work for a defense contractor with whom he had done business. But there have been no studies

(DAVID H. MARTIN)

showing that the present laws do not adequately protect the integrity of the decision-making process in government, especially in the procurement area. These present laws prohibit representational activity by a former government employee with his old agency for a year, or with any agency for two years, or even a lifetime in some cases . . . Some people want the revolving door shut down even tighter—barring people from working for a company with whom they had any dealings while they were in government. I don't think that would solve the problem these sensational news stories focus on, and there could be serious Constitutional questions about prohibiting freedom of association.

Interview/U.S. News
& World Report, 4-28:32.

Charles McC. Mathias, Jr.
United States Senator,
R-Maryland

1

[Criticizing a proposed bill that would restrict lobbying by former Federal employees who might use their government connections in their lobbying careers]: How difficult do we want to make it for bright and mature people to come into the Federal government with the concept that they'll be there for a period of time and then return to private life? This bill would be another bar to having a bright, able lawyer willing to accept a Federal job, because he knows that his ability to earn a living thereafter is going to be circumscribed.

The New York Times,
9-16:12.

2

We [in the Senate] are trying to do more things than we have ever done before. It is a serious, serious problem to get 100 people in the Senate so organized that they can really pay attention to these subjects. We are writing legislation instead of dealing with principles and policies. We are worried about the commas.

Time, 11-10:25.

David McCullough
Historian

3

We appear to have a never-ending supply of patriots who know nothing of the history of the country, nor are they interested. We have not had a President with a sense of history since John Kennedy—not since most of you were born. It ought to be mandatory for the office. As we have a language requirement for the foreign service, so we should have a history requirement for the White House.

At Middlebury (Vt.) College
commencement/Time, 6-9:63.

Robert S. McNamara
Former Secretary of Defense
of the United States

4

[On the length of term for people in high Federal government office]: Wisdom is in part a function of experience, which in turn is a function of time in office, and I would recommend a minimum term of four years and preferably longer . . . I think that short tenure, rapid turnover in the senior positions of government carries with it a very heavy penalty, particularly in our system . . . where you can bring a person in from Ford Motor Company to be Secretary of Defense. If the turnover occurs every two years or less, as is frequently the case in some senior positions in government, one brings very severe limitations into these senior posts.

Interview/
The Washington Post, 9-2:(A)17.

Edwin Meese III
Attorney General of the United States

5

The toughest political problems deserve to have full and open debate. Whether the issue is abortion, pornography or aid to parochial schools, there is no Constitutionally explicit reason why people within the several states may not deliberate over them and reach a consensual judgment. What this means, to put it bluntly, is that Federalism would allow states the freedom to make choices

(EDWIN MEESE III)

which we as conservatives may very well disagree with. For example, Federalism properly understood means that states or localities may ban handguns. Also, they may ban pornography, as Minneapolis recently tried to do. Or they may enact liberal abortion laws that even go beyond Roe versus Wade [the Supreme Court decision that legalized abortion] . . . The objective is not simply less government over-all, although that may happen, but less government at the national level. The happy result will be better government at the state and local levels, levels where the government is closer to the people.

Before Conservative Political
Action Conference, Washington,
Jan. 30/The New York Times, 1-31:14.

1

This idea that somehow, on the Federal level, we can set a standard that everyone must adhere to simply is not consistent with the original principles of Federalism. Once you get something embedded in the Federal government, you have institutionalized special interests that keep it there.

Interview/Esquire, July:85.

2

I think every member of the Administration owes it to the President to stand shoulder-to-shoulder with him and support the policies that he has . . . My position is clearly that I think anyone who is a member of the President's Cabinet has an obligation either to support the policy decisions of the President or to get out.

To reporters, Washington, Nov. 25/
The Washington Post, 11-26:(A)6.

Barbara Mikulski
United States Senator-elect,
D-Maryland

3

I define public service as not only to be a help but to be an advocate. I plan to use the good mind, the good mouth, the good heart God gave me.

Time, 11-17:40.

Walter F. Mondale
Former Vice President
of the United States

4

[On the revelation of secret U.S.-Iran negotiations, arms sales and diversion of Iran arms payments to Nicaraguan contra rebels]: It's the same old story. Something bizarre, disastrous, possibly illegal happened, but nobody [in the U.S.] in a position of responsibility did it. That is not credible. I know the White House, and I can tell you there is not the slightest chance that this was carried out by one or two people without approval. We are faced here with the profoundest issue that ever occurs in America: the accountability of elected leaders before the law. Without that, we have nothing. The issue here is what happens to the country, and we have to behave in keeping with that. If people think our [Democratic] Party is quite happy to hurt the country for its own advantage, the country will turn against us, and it should turn against us.

The New York Times, 11-27:6.

Ernest Morial
Mayor of New Orleans

5

[Criticizing proposals to end the Federal revenue-sharing program]: A Federal program should be allowed to pass out of existence if it doesn't do any good, or if it doesn't do what it was created to do, or if the need for the program has disappeared, or if a better program has come along to replace it, or if the costs of the program exceed the benefits. As Mayors, we would dispense with programs that fit any of these descriptions. As citizens, we want the U.S. Congress to do the same. But revenue-sharing doesn't fit these descriptions at all. General Revenue Sharing works—it works very well—and it has worked very well for a long time.

At United States Conference of Mayors,
Washington, Jan. 23/ The New York Times, 2-12:32.

Daniel Moynihan
United States Senator, D-New York

6

[On revelations of government corruption in New York City]: In New York City, money cor-

WHAT THEY SAID IN 1986

(DANIEL MOYNIHAN)

ruption has once again appeared—at a time when we might have thought it was something the polity had grown out of. And indeed the polity *has,* and so all the more is the disgrace that it appears *we* have not. The more, then, our responsibility . . . I choose now to send a message, and I do not doubt it will be received: Show no mercy. [The late] Senator Jack Javits and I did not spend a year of our lives getting the Federal government to guarantee $1.65-billion in New York City loans—an event without precedent in the history of the republic—in order for it to be turned into "loot." Let the grifters and the boodlers and those who were merely playing piano downstairs hear this: Pray God you do not appear before one of the judges I have chosen for the Federal bench, for almost the first of their convictions is that public corruption is more than crime, it is betrayal and is contemptible and unforgivable. I expect this view to be shared by others.

Before New York State Democratic
Committee/USA Today, 4-9:(A)6.

Thomas P. O'Neill, Jr.
United States Representative,
D-Massachusetts

1

Today, there is a new conventional wisdom. Very often, you hear successful people talk about the "good old days." Their message is always the same: how good things were generations ago, when there was less government responsibility and fewer programs, when people were left to take care of themselves . . . This massive improvement in American life [today] did not come about by accident. It happened because the American people made a *national* decision to develop energy, housing, transportation and every other sector of the economy. Most of all, we invested in the most vital of all national resources, the individual human mind . . . I believe it is wrong for the people who have made it up the ladder to pull the ladder up behind them. If the success stories of this country needed a helping hand up the ladder, why should we not

164

give the same help to those young people trying to get ahead today? If government could offer opportunities to young people back in the 1950s and 1960s, why should we deny that same help to young people in the 1980s? Like most simple ideas, the new conventional wisdom has a great deal of appeal. It promises a life that is less complicated, where there is less government, less red tape and hardly any taxes whatever. But like most simple ideas, it ignores not only reality but our own national history.

Speech, Independence, Mo./
The New York Times, 5-16:27.

Norman J. Ornstein
Resident scholar,
American Enterprise Institute

2

[Supporting the televising of Senate proceedings]: The excess of informality that has characterized the Senate, the extreme bending over backwards to satisfy 100 prima donnas while losing control of the Senate in the process, will come to a stop.

The Washington Post,
3-3:(A)4.

3

What you've got is a Congress that is more and more following its instincts and disengaging itself from the White House in the policy-making process. It's not that Congress is blocking the President's ideas. It's a case of the President [Reagan] making his views known, but in many instances not following up and Congress moving into the vacuum.

U.S. News & World Report, 3-31:17.

4

What we know from studying previous Presidents is that when you get a two-term President after a big election win, a combination of fatigue and arrogance sets in [that could lead to lapses in good judgment]. A smashing [election] mandate gives an inflated sense of where you are.

Los Angeles Times, 12-8:(I)19.

Robert W. Packwood
United States Senator,
R-Oregon

1

What you discover, and I learned this from [Senator] Russell Long years ago, is that [in government] there are no permanent friends, no permanent enemies—just temporary alliances . . . It just doesn't do you any good to bear grudges in this business. The person who may be against you this week, you're going to need next week.

Interview, Washington, May 7/
The Washington Post, 5-8:(C)1.

Kevin Phillips
Republican Party political analyst

2

[On the recent national elections which saw the Democratic Party regain control of the Senate while retaining control of the House]: What you're seeing now is the start of a new fight for the center. The whole sense of a Calvin Coolidge restoration—limited government, tax cuts for the sake of limiting government—is over. The new interest is in a more activist government. That doesn't mean a government that responds to the wishes of the interest groups of the 1960s and 1970s. But people this year clearly expressed their support for a more prosaic kind of government activism—dams, harbors, trade, the energy industry.

Newsweek, 11-17:29.

Samuel R. Pierce, Jr.
Secretary of Housing and Urban
Development of the United States

3

I'm not a yes-man. A President who has a bunch of yes-men has nothing. I sometimes disagree with [President] Reagan. However, when he makes his final decision, I accept it. When I can't support him, I'll tell him so, turn my back, and leave the Cabinet.

Interview, Washington/
The Christian Science Monitor, 1-27:7.

Robert Pitofsky
Dean, Georgetown University Law Center;
Former Commissioner,
Federal Trade Commission

4

[On the conflict-of-interest controversy involving former White House Deputy Chief of Staff Michael Deaver, who is now a lobbyist representing foreign interests]: Most people I know take the position that in close-call questions, you don't do it. Mr. Deaver was the classic case of going the other way. He had the attitude that, "If it's questionable, I have a defense and I can go ahead and do it."

The New York Times, 6-11:14.

Roger B. Porter
Former Director, White House
Office of Policy Development

5

[President Reagan] likes to hear directly from the people who have a stake in an issue . . . Some Presidents have been uncomfortable with individuals in their Administration arguing strongly and vigorously in front of them. Ronald Reagan is not uncomfortable with that. He has a high tolerance for hearing competing views argued very intensely. At the same time, understandably, he is interested in officials in his Administration supporting fully the decision he reaches at the end of the day.

Interview/The New York Times, 1-20:12.

Jody Powell
Former Press Secretary to the
President of the United States
(Jimmy Carter)

6

[On Washington scandals, such as the current one involving the Reagan Administration's dealings with Iran and the Nicaraguan contra connection]: . . . if you're on the inside [of the White House], you wake up every morning and you hate to read the newspapers. If you're on the outside, you wake up every morning and you can't wait to read the newspapers. The adrenaline flows no matter which side you're on. Hav-

165

(JODY POWELL)

ing been on the receiving end, I can't help but have a little sympathy [for President Reagan and his aides]. The town certainly goes into a frenzy. You never realize what a company town it is until something like this happens. The garbage-men are talking about it, the people at other tables at restaurants are talking about it, stewardesses are asking you about it when you get on a plane. It dominates conversation in a way that has no parallel anywhere else.

Los Angeles Times, 12-10:(V)1.

William Proxmire
United States Senator, D-Wisconsin

1

The myth of the day is that honoraria—speaking fees [paid to members of Congress], in plain English—are paid by disinterested groups. The myth goes that these groups are willing to pay up to $2,000 solely to hear a Senator discuss a vital issue of the day. Oh, what a tangled web we have woven. Listen to a list of those paying the most honoraria: the Tobacco Institute, the Securities Industry Association, the American Bankers Association, the National Cable Television Association, the Chicago Board of Trade. What do those paying these speaking fees have in common? The answer is simple: They are all vitally interested in legislation. In fact, most could not exist without some type of legislative charter. And if you look on the list of those invited to speak, one fact stands out: They often serve on the committee with jurisdiction over that legislative charter. We have an obligation to be both careful and open when dealing with the rules governing the acceptance of honoraria. We have not met this standard.

Before the Senate, Washington/
The New York Times, 6-26:24.

Carl D. Pursell
United States Representative,
R-Michigan

2

[Arguing against a pay increase for members of Congress]: The idea that officials can't live on

incomes already five times greater than that of the average American worker is absurd.

USA Today, 12-17:(A)10.

Charles B. Rangel
United States Representative,
D-New York

3

A [House-Senate legislation] conference brings out the greatest fears in lobbyists. It's unbelievable. You come out of the conference room and they're all there in the hallway and they all think they have to make eye contact or say something to you, even if they shout something like, "Remember when we talked?" . . . I feel embarrassed for them.

USA Today, 7-17:(A)2.

Ronald Reagan
President of the United States

4

The government should not compete with the private sector. Traditionally, governments supply the type of needed services that would not be provided by the private marketplace. Over the years, however, the Federal government has acquired many commercial-type operations. In many cases, it would be better for the government to get out of the business and stop competing with the private sector, and in this [Federal] budget I propose that we begin that process. Examples of such "privatization" initiatives in this budget include sale of the power marketing administrations and the naval petroleum reserves; and implementation of housing and education voucher programs. I am also proposing the sale of unneeded assets, such as loan portfolios and surplus real estate, and contracting out appropriate Federal services. Many services can be provided better by state and local governments. Over the years, the Federal government has preempted many functions that properly ought to be operated at the state and local level. This budget contemplates an end to unwarranted Federal intrusion into the state and local sphere and restoration of a more balanced, Constitutionally

(RONALD REAGAN)

appropriate Federalism with more clearly delin-
eated roles for the various levels of government.

Budget message to Congress, Washington,
Feb. 5/The New York Times, 2-6:12.*

1

[Criticizing state-run lotteries]: I don't exactly like the idea of government engaging in
gambling . . . Call me a prude if you want to,
but I just think there's something a little bit un-
dignified in appealing to people's desire to gamble, [for a state] to raise its revenues.

At luncheon with editors
and broadcasters, Washington,
Feb. 10/Los Angeles Times, 2-11:(I)17.

2

Some people "become" President. I've never
thought of it that way. I think the Presidency is
an institution over which you have temporary
custody and it has to be treated that way . . .
Presidents that have come in and drastically
changed traditional things . . . I just have never
tried to do anything of that kind because I don't
think the Presidency belongs to the individual.

Interview/Time, 4-7:27.

3

I think the closest thing to the Presidency in
line of a job is being a [state] Governor. There
you sit at a desk in which the buck does stop
when it gets there, and there's a great similarity.
[So the Presidency] wasn't the great surprise that
it must be to some other people.

Interview, Washington,
July 2/USA Today, 7-3:(A)4.

4

[Saying he will cooperate with the Congressional investigation of the current scandal involving secret U.S.-Iran arms deals and the
covert diversion of funds from those deals to
contra rebels fighting the Nicaraguan govern-
ment]: We live in a country that requires we operate within rules and laws, all of us. Just cause
and deep concern and noble ends can never be
reason enough to justify improper actions or ex-

cessive means. In these past six years, we have
done much together to restore the faith and confidence and respect of our people and our country. We've done so not by avoiding challenges or
denying problems but, when confronted with
these problems, dealing with them directly and
honestly. We will continue to do so.

Broadcast address to the nation,
Camp David, Md., Dec. 6/
The Washington Post, 12-9:(A)12.

Charles E. Redman
Spokesman for the Department
of State of the United States

5

It is essential that the public be informed concerning the activities of its government. However, we must also recognize that the national
interest often requires that information concerning the national defense and foreign relations be
protected against unauthorized disclosure. Officials who leak [classified information] do not
serve the larger national interest by disclosing
information, but instead may well be undermining the process of making foreign policy and
protecting our national defense.

Washington, May 16/
The New York Times, 5-17:3.

Donald T. Regan
Chief of Staff to the
President of the United States

6

I think a lot of people are getting used to me
and my style and they recognize that I'm not
nine feet tall and 600 pounds. They are beginning to see that what I'm trying to do is merely
to carry out the President's program. When I
first came in, there were a lot of worries about
what was my agenda . . . and they recognized,
finally, I have no agenda of my own. I'm trying
to push the President's agenda as I see it . . .
This abrupt, punch 'em in the nose, damn the
torpedoes, full-speed-ahead type of thing is not
my 100 per cent style. I use that on occasion and
I veer on occasion and I think that, at times, I

WHAT THEY SAID IN 1986

(DONALD T. REGAN)

am compassionate and am mellow and I'm not always this just plunge-ahead type.

Interview, Washington/
Los Angeles, 2-23:(I)4.

1

[Comparing the power he had as chairman of the Merrill Lynch securities firm with that which he had when he became U.S. Secretary of the Treasury]: When I was chief executive and I said, "Jump," people asked, "How high?" As Secretary of the Treasury, when I said, "Jump," people said, "What do you mean by *jump?* What do you mean by *high?*"

U.S. News & World Report, 6-9:49.

Elliot L. Richardson
Former Secretary of
Defense of the United States

2

[On being in high Federal government office]: . . . there is enormous satisfaction in being in a position long enough to make a significant contribution to the public interest. It can be very rewarding to feel that your total energies and capacities are dedicated to trying to discern and further the public interest as best you can see it. In those dimensions, these are the best jobs there are.

Interview/The Washington Post, 9-2:(A)17.

Donald H. Rumsfeld
Former Secretary of
Defense of the United States

3

One of the problems in the [Federal] government is the rapid turnover in senior positions. If you think about it, we've had four National Security Advisers, three Deputy Secretaries of Defense, two ACDA Directors, two Secretaries of State—all within the last 5 ½ years. Companies, large institutions tend not to do that.

Interview/The Washington Post, 9-2:(A)17.

Antonin Scalia
Associate Justice-designate,
Supreme Court of the United States

4

If you have to put your finger on what makes our Constitution so enduring, I think it's the original document before the amendments were added, because the amendments by themselves don't do anything . . . The Russian Constitution probably has better or at least as good guarantees of personal freedom as our Constitution does. What makes it [the U.S. Constitution] work, what assures that those words are just not hollow promises, is the structure of government that the original Constitution established, the checks and balances among the three branches of government so no one of them is able to run roughshod over the liberties of the people.

At Senate Judiciary Committee hearing
on his confirmation, Washington,
Aug. 5/The New York Times, 8-6:11.

Arthur M. Schlesinger, Jr.
Historian

5

. . . the Vice Presidency does not seem to me a very useful office. It's an office which generally has the effect not of preparing people for the Presidency, but of reducing their capacity to be President . . . I think the experience of being a Vice President means you can't be your own man, you begin to lose a sense of your own identity. It seems to me we'd be better off if we used a system that the French, for example, use—that is, if a President dies, hold a new election.

Interview/USA Today, 11-25:(A)11.

Benno C. Schmidt, Jr.
President, Yale University

6

Privacy is absolutely essential to maintaining a free society. The idea that is at the foundation of the notion of privacy is that the citizen is not the tool or the instrument of government—but the reverse . . . I don't think one can have a society that rests on essentially democratic assumptions—that citizens control their govern-

(BENNO C. SCHMIDT, JR.)

ment, that citizens have the obligation of civic participation and [of] determining their own destiny—unless one has at the core a notion of what it means to be a free human being . . . [and that] there are limits to the power of society to make intrusions on the autonomy of the individual.

Interview, Yale University/
The Christian Science Monitor, 12-5:24.

Martha Seger
Governor, Federal Reserve Board

1

I've never worked for another government agency. But I've worked in corporate America, and there people will sit down and discuss things. They'll have what I'd describe as bull sessions, where you have an open exchange of views and it's not brought to a vote. Here, at least *I'm* not part of any discussions before these matters occur. You are handed an agenda a couple of days in advance. Memos are delivered to our desks; the rule of thumb is that we're supposed to get the material 48 hours before the meeting. Sometimes that deadline is met, sometimes it isn't. You go in and—bang, you have to vote . . . We Governors have very little input into what I call the formulation stage—which I'm not accustomed to. In corporate America there is input all along the lines. In an auto company, the president of the company isn't exposed to the new models the day he goes down to the auto show.

Interview/The Wall
Street Journal, 2-11:34.

George P. Shultz
Secretary of State of the United States

2

[Criticizing leaks to the press of classified government information]: Our basic problem is that we've lost all sense of discipline—all sense of discipline. It didn't used to be that way . . . There used to be a lot more restraint on the part of the press in what they would print. And as far

as our government's concerned, it's a gusher. It's disgusting, the way the stuff leaks out. We've got to find the people who are doing it and fire them.

Before Overseas Press Club, Washington,
May 14/The Washington Post, 5-15:(A)19.

3

Nothing ever gets settled in this town [Washington]. It's not like running a company or even a university. It's a seething debating society in which the debate never stops, in which people never give up, including me, and that's the atmosphere in which you administer.

Before House Foreign Affairs
Committee, Washington, Dec. 8/
The New York Times, 12-9:1.

Paul Simon
United States Senator, D-Illinois

4

[Supporting an increase in pay for members of Congress]: The weakest player on the Chicago *Bulls* basketball team, who spends most of his time on the bench, is paid substantially more than the person who makes our laws.

USA Today, 12-17:(A)10.

Howard Simons
Curator, Nieman Foundation,
Harvard University; Former editor,
"The Washington Post"

5

Many [government] secrecy labels are put on documents not to protect a true secret, but to avoid a true embarrassment or to cover up a cost overrun, or an abuse of power, or to stifle criticism, or to avoid public scrutiny, or out of habit.

USA Today, 4-11:(A)10.

Alan K. Simpson
United States Senator, R-Wyoming

6

[Approving of the televising of Senate sessions]: [TV] would let the American people find out how we really do our business, or, more im-

WHAT THEY SAID IN 1986

(ALAN K. SIMPSON)

portantly, how we don't do our business . . . They would begin to write: "I saw you. What were you doing?"

Los Angeles Times, 2:28:(I)6.

1

[On those in the Reagan Administration who were responsible for the current scandal involving secret U.S.-Iran arms deals and the covert diversion of those funds to contra rebels fighting the Nicaraguan government]: I've seen those guys. Their ears twitch. Their eyes are beady . . . They're young, and they go around talking about how they're going to change the world. They tell you, "We won [the Presidential election], and now we're going to stick it to 'em." That's what I think led to a lot of this.

The Washington Post, 12-12:(A)23.

Michael I. Sovern
President, Columbia University

2

Enormous [political] campaign contributions by those who seek to do business with the city are nearly as poisonous as bribes. Party leaders who profit from city contracts are shameful. Yet both are permitted by present laws . . . Let us not be lulled into the belief that corruption comes and goes with each scandal, each commission, each reform. It has never been eliminated. The attention of the public, of the investigators and of the press is sporadic and cyclical.

At Columbia University commencement,
May 14/The New York Times, 5-15:16.

David A. Stockman
Former Director, Federal
Office of Management and Budget

3

In this game [Wall Street] you can cover up errors for about five minutes. In that game [Washington] it seems you can cover up errors for several years.

Interview,
New York/Newsweek, 4-21:59.

Helen Thomas
White House correspondent,
United Press International

4

Secrecy seems to go with the [Presidential] turf. For all their good intentions, . . . a few days after Presidents assume office, they don't let the sunshine in any more.

Accepting William Allen White Foundation
Award/U.S. News & World Report, 2-24:74.

Strom Thurmond
United States Senator, R-South Carolina

5

I don't think it's right for people who have been in positions of government, and gained inside knowledge, to go right out of government and lobby the government [as a private lobbyist]. Nor is it right for them to represent foreign countries, using knowledge they've gained in government to help those foreign countries—against our own country, maybe. It's wrong for people in high positions—like a Secretary of State or Defense—to ever represent foreign countries, because they have gained information that could be of help to a foreign country for years and years in the future. That is why I've introduced legislation to address those problems. Beyond that, we need to give the right perception that people in government are honorable and are not going into government just to gain knowledge and contacts so they can later enrich themselves.

Interview/U.S. News
& World Report, 5-12:29.

Paul S. Trible, Jr.
United States Senator, R-Virginia

6

[On the televising of Senate proceedings]: There's a real tension there and it's hard to reconcile—the instant demands of television and the deliberate nature of the Senate. The Senate is not intended to operate as the House does but as a counterweight . . . I worry about maintaining the deliberate nature of this place.

The Washington Post, 3-3:(A)4.

Barbara Tuchman
Author, Historian

1

Everybody who gets into government wants to exert power and hold onto it. When they see things happening which are clearly signs of failure, they don't ring a bell . . . because they're afraid of losing their position. They don't want to tell their boss—whether it's [former Chinese leader] Chiang Kai-shek or [U.S. President] Reagan or [former U.S. President Richard] Nixon, or whoever it is—what he doesn't want to hear.

Interview, Cos Cob, Conn./
The Christian Science Monitor, 10-7:18.

Stansfield Turner
Former Director of Central
Intelligence of the United States

2

[On the current scandal involving secret U.S. arms deals with Iran and the covert transfer of the payments to contra rebels fighting in Nicaragua]: The management style of this President [Reagan] is such that he could have encouraged people [under him] to feel that he didn't want to know [the specifics of their activities]. Not necessarily because he wanted to be able to deny it, but because that was not a level of detail that he normally wanted to get into.

To reporters, Washington, Dec. 16/
The Christian Science Monitor, 12-17:32.

Jack Valenti
President, Motion Picture
Association of America

3

[On Washington scandals, such as the current one involving the Reagan Administration's dealing with Iran and the Nicaraguan contra connection]: No question this has become lunchtime, dinnertime and cocktail-party conversation. It reminds me of people who go to see [dare-devil] Evil Knievel jump the Snake River Canyon. You go because you think he might fall in. It's the in-

trigue, the mesmerizing fascination of watching two trains collide.

Los Angeles Times, 12-10:(V)1.

William von Raab
Commissioner, United
States Customs Service

4

[On the Customs Service]: We're important enough to be noticed, but not important enough to be cared about. That cuts both ways. When we centralized Customs functions, if we had been HUD, it never would have gone anywhere because the entire attention would have been on it. We were allowed to do it by Congress, the [Treasury] Department, the system, because we are small. But when it comes to other issues, maybe where we need more care, we're those three zeros that get dropped from the issues.

Interview/The Washington Post, 8-26:(A)6.

Fred Wertheimer
President, Common Cause

5

It used to be that, in order for influence-peddling [in government] to be successful, people had to do it secretly because it was considered wrong. Today, the key to success is to act very blatantly, to be public, to get credit for it . . . There are a lot of talented people in this country willing to serve their government honestly and ethically. Look at how demoralizing it is to people who are doing their jobs and playing by the rules in government and who see others come walking through and making a fortune by abusing their former positions. That's unfair to the taxpayer and unfair to the people who are playing it honestly.

Interview/U.S. News & World Report, 4-28:32.

Jamie L. Whitten
United States Representative,
D-Mississippi

6

[On Congress' seniority system]: Seniority doesn't necessarily mean anything. But experience means a lot.

USA Today, 10-21:(A)4.

Law • The Judiciary

Joseph R. Biden, Jr.
United States Senator, D-Delaware

1

[On future Reagan Administration Federal judgeship nominees, now that Biden will be new Chairman of the Senate Judiciary Committee]: They [the Administration] can send up a conservative, a scholar, an intellectually competent person. But they can't run these bimbos through any more.

USA Today, 11-14:(A)4.

Rose Elizabeth Bird
Chief Justice, Supreme Court of California

2

In California, the citizens in their wisdom have decided that they think judges should stand for election. I think then the issue becomes not the wisdom of the election, but what is important in the election. How do you decide how you are going to vote? What do you want in terms of a judge? In the legislative and executive branches, the bottom line is, "I vote for this because I like it or I don't like it." The Governor signs something or advocates it because it's popular or unpopular. In the judiciary, we uphold an awful lot of statutes that are very unwise. But if they've been passed by the legislature and signed by the Governor, and they comport with the Constitution, they're the law of the land. So you can't judge a judge by that kind of bottom line . . . We respect the rules. We follow them. We don't break them simply because we decide at the moment it would be useful to do that. I think people in the long run respect that. If you have a baseball or football game, you don't judge the umpire by what the score is. You don't want the umpire rooting for one side or the other and making decisions because he'd like to see a particular side win; you want an umpire who will follow the rules.

Interview/USA Today, 2-13:(A)9.

3

A judge, unlike a legislator or a Governor, is not given the prerogative of making decisions based on whether they like or dislike a law—you don't vote it up or down. If you judge a judge by the bottom line [of his or her rulings], you really are mistaken, because very often the judge's personal views may be very different than the ultimate decision that comes out.

Broadcast interview/
Los Angeles Times, 2-13:(I)35.

4

It takes enormous maturity on the part of society to understand the role of a judge. You have to believe in a set of rules. You have to believe in a process and you have to believe in a government that will be fair to everybody, including those who are the pariahs within the society and those who do terrible things. Nobody wants to make a hard job for the police catching criminals. That's not the role of the court. And that's not the role of the Bill of Rights. But it's very hard [for voters] to understand that when you [a judge] say to a police officer, "You should have gotten a warrant."

Interview, Los Angeles/
Los Angeles Times, 3-16:(V)1.

5

In a sense, the courts and the press both review each other's work. The court oversees the press' claims of First Amendment protection, and the press summarizes and critiques the court's decisions for the general public . . . The press and the judiciary must recognize their mutual interests in ensuring the preservation of a strong third branch of government.

Before California Broadcasters Association,
Monterey, Calif., July 28/
Los Angeles Times, 7-29:(I)3.

6

One of our greatest strengths is a court system with the courage to protect our form of government. We can worship freely, speak our minds and read uncensored newspapers. That's not true in places like the Soviet Union and

(ROSE ELIZABETH BIRD)

South Africa. Why are we so blessed? Because the words of our Constitution mean something, and our judges aren't afraid to say so.

Re-election campaign broadcast/
The Washington Post, 9-12:(A)3.

1

If we judges and lawyers are not to be popular, let it be because we are standing on the forefront of protecting people's rights during a time of transition. Let it be because we have the courage to represent unsympathetic individuals and make difficult rulings in order to give life and breath to our Constitutional guarantees. Should the bar see its role as merely pleasing the legislature, for example, or improving its public relations; should the judiciary see itself as a purveyor of popular views, as a mimic of the majority of the moment—then both institutions will have lost something fundamental to their heritage and essential to their preservation.

Before California State Bar, Monterey,
Calif., Sept. 14/Los Angeles Times, 9-15:(I)3.

Harry A. Blackmun
Associate Justice, Supreme
Court of the United States

2

The divisiveness of the [Supreme] Court has grown, as we [justices] are getting older. When one gets [cases about] abortion and sodomy in the home, the patience gets thin indeed. I think the center held generally this year, but it bled a lot. It needs more troops; where it's going to get them I don't know.

At 8th Circuit judicial conference, Minneapolis,
July 25/The Washington Post, 7-26:(A)2.

3

[On the nomination of Associate Justice William Rehnquist to be the new Chief Justice of the United States]: What I'm most interested in, and I think the other members of the Court are, is the exercise of the assignment power. As lawyers know, the Chief Justice, when he is in the majority, assigns opinions for cases out for opinion

writing, and when he is not in the majority that power passes to the Associate Justice who is in the majority. How Bill Rehnquist will exercise that, I don't know. Will he be fair? Will he be punitive? I think that power is a great power in the way the Court does its business. And that the public is not aware of this.

At 8th Circuit judicial conference, Minneapolis,
July 25/Los Angeles Times, 8-6:(II)5.

4

If [a Supreme Court Associate Justice is] in the doghouse with the Chief [Justice], he gets the crud. He gets the tax cases, and some of the Indian cases which I like, but I've had a lot of them. You know, there are cases that are fun to write. And there are cases that are not.

To group judges/
The New York Times, 12-22:12.

Vincent Blasi
Professor, Columbia
University Law School

5

[On new U.S. Chief Justice William Rehnquist]: Don't forget, Rehnquist is a radical. Nobody since the 1930s has been so niggardly in interpreting the Bill of Rights, so blatant in simply ignoring years and years of precedent.

Time, 6-30:28.

Bill Bradley
United States Senator, D-New Jersey

6

[Arguing against confirmation of U.S. Chief Justice-designate William Rehnquist]: His confirmation as Chief Justice will signal . . . that a dark cloud has descended over the Court. [Rehnquist's] positions on civil liberties and racial justice betray his pinched view of the Constitution and his disdain for minorities and individual rights . . . If we confirm a Chief Justice whose commitment to civil rights is in doubt, we betray our past, our future and ourselves.

At Senate debate on the confirmation, Washington,
Sept. 12/The Washington Post,
9-13:(A)3.

WHAT THEY SAID IN 1986

William J. Brennan, Jr.
Associate Justice, Supreme
Court of the United States

1

The [Supreme] Court can't go out and look for issues. It has to deal with issues that are brought to it. I agonize over every one of them, and in that respect I'm not at all different from all of my colleagues. One reason is the cases that get here that we agree to review can be answered not one way, not two ways, but sometimes several ways, and the considerations that go into the choice before you decide how you want to vote also are multiple.

Interview, Washington/
The New York Times, 6-24:10.

2

I personally have faith that freedom will survive and that the 14th Amendment's great principles will flourish. But they will successfully resist impending onslaught only as lawyers have the courage to understand and acknowledge their meaning.

Before American Bar Association, New York,
Aug. 8/The New York Times, 8-9:7.

Warren E. Burger
Chief Justice of the United States

3

[Saying Congress should restore the Social Security payroll exemption for senior Federal judges]: The experience and wisdom our senior judges provide is of even greater value than their substantial quantitative contribution. If we lose their services, we lose a priceless asset . . . Their [senior judges who continue to work] devotion to duty and concern for the public interest cannot be taxed forever.

Letter to the Vice President and
Speaker of the House, Jan. 21*/
Los Angeles Times, 1-22:(I)17.

4

[The Supreme Court] has not become more sharply divided. If you go back and read the opinions over 35, 40 years, you'd find there just isn't any substance to that. The reason there are

nine people up there—and there are days when I'd like there to be just one—the reason you have nine is to have this interchange and interplay. It goes on all the time. In the 17 years I have been there presiding over the conferences, never once, never once, has a voice been raised in any discussions. They're vigorous discussions, as they should be—always will be, I hope. We have cordial and good relations. We can disagree in a civilized way, and we do.

News conference, Washington,
June 17/The New York Times, 6-18:12.

5

We've gone from Chief Justice [Earl] Warren's first year with 65 signed opinions and we've been running over 150 for the last four or five years. We've gone from 1,400 and some filings back in Earl Warren's day to nearly 5,000—nearly 100 a week. The [Supreme] Court's got to have some relief somewhere. I'm astonished that we haven't had some judges fall over with coronary thrombosis or some other illness of exhaustion and overwork.

News conference, Washington,
June 17/The New York Times, 6-18:12.

6

[On the Supreme Court's changing previous Courts' rulings]: It is the business of judges, a new man who's coming on, to try to make the machine work the way it is, and in that process, you sometimes find that something needs to be changed. We've modified the Miranda rule a little bit; we've modified other rules to fit new situations that hadn't been encountered before. We've modified the exclusionary rule some, and, of course, a lot of the stories are that I was trying to overrule those things. I wasn't trying to overrule them; I was trying to make the system work. And that's what my colleagues tried to do. But when these changes occur, you read a lot of silly things.

Interview/USA Today, 6-26:(A)9.

7

Congress can review us [the Supreme Court] and change us when we decide a statutory question . . . But when we decide a Constitutional

(WARREN E. BURGER)

issue . . . that's it, until we change it or the people change it . . . The people made it, and the people can change it. The people could abolish the Supreme Court entirely.

Broadcast interview/
"The Burger Years," CBS-TV, 7-9.

1

[Defending Chief Justice-designate William Rehnquist against criticism that he wrote memos opposing school desegregation when he was a Supreme Court law clerk in 1952-1953]: There's nothing unusual about a justice telling one clerk, "Look, you give me memos on one side of this thing and be the devil's advocate." I've done it. If we were all held to what we said when we were college students . . . we'd all be in a lot of trouble.

Interview, Charlottesville, Va.,
July 23/USA Today, 7-24:(A)1.

2

What people think of the legal profession—the bench and the bar—is very important to us, and it is important to the country. During the last dozen years or so, many of us have had growing concern whether our profession was turning away from traditional values and standards and becoming more and more like a common trade in the marketplace . . . One need only look at the yellow pages of some of the telephone directories and the television advertising by some lawyers to see that those advertising lawyers have lost sight of the traditional values of our profession . . . Some of the advertising would make a used-car dealer blush with shame.

Before American Bar Association, New York,
Aug. 11/The New York Times, 8-12:12.

3

[Criticizing the practice of contingent fees by lawyers in many cases]: Every person in this room knows that in certain kinds of multiple disaster cases there is likely to be little question of liability. In such cases, there is no place for contingent fees of the kind now widely practiced.

Before American Bar Association, New York,
Aug. 11/The Washington Post, 8-12:(A)7.

Alan Cranston
United States Senator,
D-California

4

[On the nomination and confirmation of Federal judges]: [A judge who is an ideological extremist from either side of the political spectrum] can create a doctrinal conflict of interest fully as inappropriate as a financial conflict of interest . . . A Senator may want to seek a nominee's views to determine whether they are within a range of reasonableness, whether the nominee is willing to follow controlling law and seems fair-minded and sufficiently sensitive to the temper of the times.

Before the Senate, Washington,
July 21/Los Angeles Times, 7-22:(I)4.

Mario M. Cuomo
Governor of New York (D)

5

[On Presidential appointments of U.S. Supreme Court Justices]: It is not unusual for a President to try to bend the Court to fit his own ideological, social or political beliefs. Indeed, I would guess most observers expect that to be the case, and many approve . . . But, conceding it is legal, that it has been done before, and that the nation has survived the experience, I respectfully submit to you that this is not the only practical way to select judges—and it is certainly not the best way. An insistence on selecting those who are philosophically or politically in lock step with the President at the very least reduces the chance of finding the best judicial talent available . . . The use of ideology as a norm raises an issue even more fundamental than that of finding the best judicial talent available. To use ideology or political or social philosophy as a standard of selection is, I think, to confuse the basic nature of the judiciary . . . If this country wanted its Supreme Court to reflect the immediate social or political wishes of the nation's people, it would provide for the election of the Court. And if the Founding Fathers had wanted it that way, they could have said so—or at least hinted at it. They did just the opposite: They designed a system that tried to immunize the Court

WHAT THEY SAID IN 1986

(MARIO M. CUOMO)

from the changing moods and passions of the people. It comes down to this: Under our system, cases should be decided in the courthouse. They should not be decided in the Oval Office [of the President] or the Senate chamber.

Before American Bar Association, New York,
Aug. 11/The New York Times, 8-12:12.

Walter Dellinger
Professor of law, Duke University

1

[On retiring U.S. Supreme Court Chief Justice Warren Burger]: The Burger Court reaffirmed many of the basic decisions of the [Earl] Warren Court—for example, school desegregation and school prayer—and did not overrule decisions on [defendants' rights and police powers] but merely limited them. Burger was more conservative than the rest of his colleagues, and the Court would have taken a more conservative bent if his opinions had commanded a majority. But he was not a particularly strong intellectual on the Court, and his influence turned out to be more moderate.

June 17/Los Angeles Times, 6-18:(I)20.

2

[On Senate confirmation proceedings for Supreme Court nominees]: In the past, the Senate was willing to be much more candid about the role of philosophy in rejecting nominees. [But recently, they have felt compelled] to comb the record for some possible ethical violation. [This has led to] a raking over of some pretty old coals [in the current confirmation proceedings on Chief Justice nominee William Rehnquist]. It would make more sense for the Senate to openly acknowledge that just as the President may consider the philosophy of judges, so may the Senate.

The Washington Post, 9-9:(A)4.

Grant DuBois
Chairman, National Coalition
for Litigation Cost Containment

3

[Criticizing lawyers' contingency fees]: Con-

tingency fees, which can amount to 40 per cent or more of the money awarded to plaintiffs, are principally responsible for the explosion of huge verdicts and the logjam in our courts. The principle of strict liability allows lawyers to collect hundreds of thousands of dollars for what often amounts to very little work. We run the risk of creating an insuranceless society because the threat of liability suits has caused insurers either to drop coverage or charge sky-high rates.

Interview/U.S. News
& World Report, 1-27:43.

William W. Falsgraf
President, American Bar Association

4

[Criticizing proposed cuts in Federal funding for the Legal Services Corporation, which provides legal aid for the poor]: You've got to have some structure through which the cases can be funneled, and that's what the Legal Services Corporation is doing. They are currently funded at a level of $305-million. That is so miniscule as to hardly be worth consideration. You're not going to balance the [Federal] budget, and shouldn't, on the backs of the poor who require these services. I'm talking about 30-plus-million people in this country. You're saying to them, "You have to live under our system of justice. But you're priced out of it, and there's nothing we can do for you." That's the stuff of which revolutions are made.

Interview/USA Today, 2-6:(A)7.

5

[Defending the ABA's dealings with the Association of Soviet Lawyers]: [The ASL] is the only game in town. If you wish to have meaningful dialogue with the leading lawyers and the leading government officials of the Soviet Union, you deal with the ASL or you don't deal at all.

At American Bar Association forum, New York,
Aug. 9/The Washington Post, 8-12:(A)6.

Marc A. Franklin
Professor of law, Stanford University

6

The time has come to think seriously about developing a system of compensation that does

(MARC A. FRANKLIN)

not require . . . transfer of one-third of all damage awards and settlements to lawyers as fees.

USA Today, 1-30:(A)10.

Ira Glasser
Executive director,
American Civil Liberties Union

1

[Criticizing U.S. Attorney General Edwin Meese for suggesting that Supreme Court decisions are not necessarily binding on all government operations]: This latest speech by Mr. Meese continues his campaign against the rule of law. And it reinforces Mr. Meese's growing reputation as the most radical and dangerous Attorney General in this century . . . The trouble with this issue is if you look at it as an intellectual and academic exercise, it's pretty complicated. If you look at it in a political context, it's pretty clear what Meese is doing. This is a call to defiance and to undermining the legitimacy of abiding by decisions that you disagree with.

Interview, Oct. 23/
The New York Times, 10-24:14.

Harry L. Hupp
Judge, United States District Court
for the Central District of California

2

[On the judicial appointments by President Reagan]: Maybe you can say that [judges] appointed by Reagan tend less to be judicial activists, but you don't have that posed too often as a trial judge. We're all judges here. We don't run our courtrooms any differently. A judge is a judge. The rules of evidence are the same for all of us.

Interview/Los Angeles Times, 2-21:(I)30.

Edward M. Kennedy
United States Senator, D-Massachusetts

3

The confirmation of a Chief Justice of the United States is a more important responsibility for the Senate than our action on any other nomination to any other Federal office. It is historical nonsense to suggest that all the Senate has to do is check the nominee's IQ, be sure that he or she has a law degree and no arrests, and rubber-stamp the President's choice . . . It is no accident that the Constitution speaks not of the "Chief Justice of the Supreme Court," but of the "Chief Justice of the United States." As the language of the Constitution emphasizes, the Chief Justice symbolizes the rule of law in our society; he speaks for the aspirations and beliefs of America as a nation. In this sense, the Chief Justice is the ultimate trustee of American liberty; when Congresses and Presidents go wrong under the Constitution, it is the responsibility of the Supreme Court to set them right. And it is the Chief Justice's responsibility to ensure that the Court faithfully meets this awesome responsibility. Presidents and Congresses come and go, but Chief Justices are for life. In the 200 years of our history, there have been only 15 Chief Justices. The best of them, the greatest of them, have been those who applied the fundamental values of the Constitution fairly and generously to the changing spirit of their times.

At Senate Judiciary Committee hearing on
the nomination of William Rehnquist as Chief Justice,
Washington, July 29/Los Angeles Times, 7-30:(II)5.

4

[Criticizing the nomination of Associate Justice William Rehnquist to be Chief Justice of the U.S.]: Mainstream or too extreme, that is the question. By his own record of massive isolated dissent, Justice Rehnquist answers that question— he is too extreme on race, too extreme on women's rights, too extreme on freedom of speech, too extreme on separation of church and state, too extreme to be Chief Justice.

At Senate Judiciary Committee hearing
on Rehnquist's confirmation, Washington,
July 29/The Washington Post, 7-30:(A)1.

Gail J. Koff
Founding partner,
Jacoby & Meyers, attorneys

5

Historically, lawyers held themselves aloof. They had a monopoly, considered themselves

(GAIL J. KOFF)

above it all. It's only since 1977, when lawyers were allowed to advertise, that this has changed. Our firm was the first to advertise on television and, little by little, it is having a large impact on our profession. There's much more competition, and legal fees have been lowered . . . [The Federal Trade Commission] concluded that legal fees have decreased since lawyer advertising, with no impact on the quality of services. Lawyer advertising has had a very positive impact. It's given consumers more of a feeling that they have options, that they can ask lawyers questions. The younger generation is more used to thinking of the profession as a service business, and that means you're going to have even more demands placed on lawyers, which I think is positive.

Interview/USA Today, 7-2:(A)9.

Richard D. Lamm
Governor of Colorado (D)

1

Lawyering is a national scandal in the United States. We have two-thirds of all the lawyers in the world practicing [here] . . . A nation of lawyers is not going to beat a nation of engineers [such as the Japanese] in creating wealth.

*Interview, Denver/The Christian
Science Monitor, 8-18:21,22.*

Barry Mahoney
*Institute for Court Management,
National Center for State Courts*

2

I think that developing the courts' capacity to manage their caseloads can contribute significantly to improving the quality of justice in this society. Lawyers may have to give up a certain amount of flexibility. But what they get in exchange is a greater degree of certainty and predictability.

The New York Times, 1-3:6.

Edwin Meese III
Attorney General of the United States

3

[On the criteria for the appointment of U.S. Supreme Court Justices]: One is intellectual and

lawyerly capability. Secondly, integrity. And thirdly, a commitment to the interpretation of the law rather than being a law-maker.

USA Today, 6-23:(A)8.

4

[The U.S. Supreme] Court is the only branch of our government that routinely, day in and day out, is charged with the awesome task of addressing the most basic, the most enduring political questions: What *is* due process of law? How *does* the idea of separation of powers affect the Congress in certain circumstances? And so forth. The answers the Court gives are very important to the stability of the law so necessary for good government. But as Constitutional historian Charles Warren once noted, what's most important to remember is that "however the Court may interpret the provisions of the Constitution, it is still the Constitution which is the law, not the decisions of the Court." By this, of course, Charles Warren did not mean that a Constitutional decision by the Supreme Court lacks the character of law. Obviously it does have binding quality: It binds the parties in a case and also the Executive Branch for whatever enforcement is necessary. But such a decision does not establish a "supreme Law of the Land" that is binding on all persons and parts of government, henceforth and forevermore. This point should seem so obvious as not to need elaboration. Consider its necessity in particular reference to the Court's own work. The Supreme Court would face quite a dilemma if its own Constitutional decisions really were "the supreme Law of the Land," binding on all persons and governmental entities, including the Court itself, for then the Court would not be able to change its mind. It could not overrule itself in a Constitutional case. Yet we know that the Court has done so on numerous occasions.

*At Tulane University, Oct. 21/
The Washington Post, 10-29:(A)18.*

Burt Neubourne
*Legal director, American
Civil Liberties Union*

5

[On the U.S. Supreme Court's just-concluded term]: Perhaps the most striking aspect of the

(BURT NEUBOURNE)

term was the Court's consistent rejection of the extreme legal positions advanced by the [Reagan] Administration . . . But a shift of a vote or two turns the Administration from a loser to a winner. Whether it is successful in the long run depends on any new people who join the Court.

Los Angeles Times, 7-12:(I)19.

Peter Perlman
President, Association
of Trial Lawyers of America

1

[Supporting lawyers' contingency fees]: The contingency fee is the victim's key to the courthouse. It allows the person suffering from a tragedy to get a lawyer with the same abilities as the well-paid attorneys who represent the wrongdoer—often a rich and powerful corporation or special-interest group. Some cases require much expense and preparation. When you consider the chance of losing, in which case the lawyer gets nothing, the one-third contingency fee is most reasonable.

Interview/U.S. News
& World Report, 1-27:43.

Daniel J. Popeo
General counsel,
Washington Legal Foundation

2

[Approving the nomination of Antonin Scalia to the U.S. Supreme Court]: [The nomination signals] a new era that we are entering into in the Supreme Court. They're going to interpret law, not make it. The door is slowly closing for . . . those who use the courts to accomplish a social agenda.

The Christian Science Monitor, 6-19:3.

Lewis F. Powell, Jr.
Associate Justice, Supreme
Court of the United States

3

It is clear from the history of the [Supreme] Court, and certainly that of both the Warren and

Burger Courts, that Presidents frequently are disappointed in the performance of their appointees. The long-term stability of our legal system is based on the doctrine of *stare decisis* [following judicial precedent]. Commentators who expect radical changes on the Court seem to overlook our fidelity to this doctrine.

Before American Bar Association, New York,
Aug. 12/The Christian Science Monitor, 8-13:4.

Ronald Reagan
President of the United States

4

The Supreme Court of the United States is the final arbiter of our Constitution and the meaning of our laws. The Chief Justice and the eight Associate Justices of the Court must not only be just jurists of the highest competence, they must also be attentive to the rights specifically guaranteed in our Constitution and the proper role of the courts in our democratic system.

News conference, Washington,
June 17/The New York Times, 6-18:12.

5

I have never given a [political] litmus test to anyone that I have appointed to the bench . . . I feel very strongly about those social issues, but I also place my confidence in the fact that the one thing that I do seek are judges that will interpret the law and not write the law. We've had too many examples in recent years of courts and judges legislating. They're not interpreting what the law says and whether someone was violated or not. In too many instances they have been actually legislating by legal decree what they think the law should be. And that I don't go for.

Interview, June 23/
Los Angeles Times, 6-24:(I)18.

William H. Rehnquist
Associate Justice, Supreme
Court of the United States

6

The judges of any court of last resort, such as the Supreme Court of the United States, work in an insulated atmosphere in their courthouse

WHAT THEY SAID IN 1986

(WILLIAM H. REHNQUIST)

where they sit on the bench hearing oral arguments or sit in their chambers writing opinions. But these same judges go home at night and read the newspapers or watch the evening news on television; they talk to their family and friends about current events. Somewhere "out there," beyond the walls of the courthouse, run currents and tides of public opinion which lap at the courthouse door. Just as the 19th-century European astronomers discovered that the presence of the then-unknown planet Neptune had an effect on the orbit of Uranus, if these tides of public opinion are sufficiently great and sufficiently sustained, they will likely have an effect upon the decision of some of the cases decided within the courthouse. This is not a case of judges "knuckling under" to public opinion and cravenly abandoning their oaths of office. Judges, so long as they are relatively normal human beings, can no more escape being influenced by public opinion in the long run than can people working at other jobs. And if a judge, on coming to the bench, were to decide to hermetically seal himself off from all manifestations of public opinion, he would accomplish very little; he would not be influenced by current public opinion, but instead by the state of public opinion at the time he came to the bench.

At Suffolk University School of Law,
April 10/The New York Times, 4-17:12.

William H. Rehnquist
Associate Justice, and
Chief Justice-designate,
Supreme Court of the United States

1

I think that the Chief Justice can exercise a certain amount of leadership on the [U.S. Supreme] Court, but I don't think it's apt to be in a philosophical direction . . . I think the Chief Justice does have a couple of prerogatives . . . The power, the authority to lead the conference discussion and the authority to assign cases. And I think both of these, properly exercised, can lead to a smoothly functioning Court. But the idea that the power to lead the conference

discussion, to start off and be the first one to discuss, means that the Chief Justice can pull the wool over other people's [Justices] eyes by his discussion and make them think that green is blue—my 15 years on the Court convince me that is not the case.

At Senate Judiciary Committee hearing
on his nomination, Washington,
July 30/The New York Times, 7-31:8.

2

[On the Senate confirmation process of Chief Justice nominees]: What is this confirmation process all about? The President obviously has a role in it, but surely the Senate has its role too. And the President is a sole individual. He alone nominates, whereas a hundred Senators end up voting whether or not to confirm. And I suppose the question is, how is the Senate's power to be exercised? And I know a lot of people have spoken on it and written on it. I think you probably have to say that a Senator should not simply say "This is not the person [nominee] I would have appointed . . . Therefore, since this nominee does not share my views, I'm going to vote against his confirmation." And yet, obviously, the Senate certainly I don't think is limited to any particular qualifications. I think, again, putting myself in your [Senators'] place, which is very, very difficult: Have I fairly construed the Constitution in my 15 years as an Associate Justice?

At Senate Judiciary Committee hearing
on his confirmation, Washington,
July 31/The New York Times, 8-1:8.

3

The practice of law has always been a subtle blend between a "calling," such as the ministry, where compensation is all but disregarded, and the selling of a product, where compensation is all-important. The move over the last 25 years has been to increase the emphasis on compensation—to make the practice of law more like a business.

Speech, Sept. 12/
The Washington Post, 9-15:(A)10.

4

[Calling for a pay raise for Federal judges of at least $50,000]: The relevant [salary] compari-

(WILLIAM H. REHNQUIST)

son is not with salaries and wages throughout the economy but with the income of other lawyers. In 1985, the medium income of a 50-year-old partner in a law firm was $164,000. We must be able to attract this kind of person, among others, to the Federal judiciary if we are to maintain its tradition of excellence. We will always have men and women available to fill vacancies in the Federal judiciary, but if salaries are not made comparable to the average in private practice, fewer of these candidates will possess the first-rate talent which has always been a hallmark of the Federal bench.

Year-end statement on the Federal court system, Dec. 31*/The New York Times, 1-1('87):8.

Terrance Sandalow
Dean, University of
Michigan Law School
1

[There were] a lot of very idealistic young people in the '60s and into the '70s who saw the possibility of using law [broadly]. It's undoubtedly true that people have a greater rights consciousness, a sense that if there is a grievance, that there must be a recourse to law. We have, as a generation, come to believe that if something bad happens to a person, the legal system must offer some sort of redress. [Americans now see law] as a tool of social change rather than the tool of social stability it once was.

The Washington Post, 5-8:(C)5.

Benno C. Schmidt, Jr.
President-designate,
Yale University; Former dean,
Columbia University Law School
2

I believe that nothing is more socially important than law. Ours is the most just society in the history of the world—a society that respects human rights to the greatest extent, a society that offers to the greatest extent opportunities for individual dignity. That's because of the work of lawyers . . . [But] I believe that the practice of

law becomes slanted for its selfishness rather than for public service when making money is the primary end of the lawyer. I think there are too many lawyers whose motivation appears to be maximizing their income rather than being of service.

Interview/USA Today, 3-4:(A)9.

Marianna S. Smith
Executive director, Association
of Trial Lawyers of America
3

Trial lawyering is a bit like story-telling. Trial lawyers often learn their skills from each other. A lot of young lawyers sit in the back [of] the courtroom to watch the masters.

Washington/The New York Times, 6-25:10.

Mark Stevens
Author
4

Ten years ago there was really no such thing as giant [law] firms. Now there are these enormous firms that dwarf all the others. You have a profession today where a lot of midsize and smaller firms are struggling for business and profitability, and the giants have twice as much work as they can possibly handle. They have really cornered the market on corporate law . . . The whole thing is built on a house of cards. It assumes the need for legal practice is going to continue to accelerate as it has. They're all building enormous superstructures; their partners are used to making incredible salaries. If there's a slowdown at all, it could be a bust.

The Washington Post, 9-15:(A)1,11.

James Stewart
Director, National Institute of
Justice of the United States
5

[On community conciliation centers designed to handle minor civil and criminal cases and thus reduce the burden on courts]: The greatest benefit these centers have afforded us are not in easing system stress but in ameliorating sources of po-

WHAT THEY SAID IN 1986

(JAMES STEWART)

tentially damaging conflicts and personal retribution. Unresolved family violence, landlord-tenant disputes or contract problems can create enormous emotional conflict and destroy a person's sense of living in a just world. If people with conflicts can gain easy access to an impartial judge, hearing officer, arbitrator or mediation professional, the chances are that the parties will be satisfied in a high percentage of the cases.

Dec. 28/The New York Times, 12-29:11.

Geoffrey Stone
Professor of law,
University of Chicago

1

[Criticizing U.S. Attorney General Edwin Meese's recently stated opinion that a Supreme Court ruling is not necessarily and does not necessarily bind all government agencies]: Meese seems to be saying that no government official not bound by a particular ruling is Constitutionally obligated to abide by Supreme Court decisions. As a practical matter, it would produce anarchy. It would promote enormous amounts of litigation. Every single police officer, every single government official would have to be sued every time they act. If that's what he means, we might as well scrap the system of Constitutional law.

The Washington Post, 10-24:(A)12.

Laurence Tribe
Professor of Constitutional law,
Harvard University

2

[On the appointment of U.S. Supreme Court Justices]: I don't think it would be proper to reject any nominee on the theory that the extreme character of his views would make it difficult for him to play a cooperative or leadership role. It is the quality of intellect and character that determines that more so than ideology. It would be a mistake to think that there would be a managerial problem in the Court's being led by someone not in its middle.

Interview/USA Today, 6-19:(A)9.

Stephen S. Trott
Associate Attorney General
of the United States

3

The function of the prosecutor is to protect the decent elements of society against elements that are not decent. You simply try to do what's right for the right reasons. It was almost a luxury, a real comforting way to practice law, only trying to do what's right. I don't have to stand up knowing that my client is guilty of a rape and try to get him off . . . I represent the victims of crime . . . But if you have a question about the guilt—or you come to the professional conclusion you can't prove it—you do a disservice to people to throw bad cases into the system, just because you're afraid you're going to get lousy publicity if you decline . . . If you've got the horsepower, you indict someone, and if not, you shut up.

Interview/The Washington Post, 10-20:(A)11.

William Van Alstyne
Professor of law, Duke University

4

[Saying there are clashes of opinion among Federal judges appointed by President Reagan and former President Jimmy Carter]: [There is] a deep professional schizophrenia [within the 12 circuits]. We have a contrary matched set of judges. So it's only natural that you find among them much wider ranges of disagreement, much less consensus in common areas of the Federal law. We're getting diverse outcomes depending on who's sitting on the case.

Newsweek, 6-30:19.

Peter J. Wallison
Counsel to the President
of the United States

5

A government lawyer's role is an extremely delicate one because the client has no choice as to lawyers. The government lawyer carries a howitzer around with him. When he or she says no, it's no. Should the question ever be asked later, "What did your lawyer say?" it is impos-

(PETER J. WALLISON)

sible for a government official to say, "My lawyer said no, but I did it anyway."

Interview/The New York Times, 6-23:10.

Byron R. White
*Associate Justice, Supreme
Court of the United States*

1

The Constitution doesn't require a Supreme Court Justice to be a lawyer. All of them have been—of one kind or another. Nor does it require that a Justice have any prior judicial experience. And I hope that Presidents will not abandon the notion that from time to time a lawyer should be appointed from the bar who has no judicial experience. Such lawyers are closer to the public, they are closer to reality, and they bring a very different point of view and attitude to the Court than a circuit-court judge does. Judges tend, when they have been on the bench for a while, to become set in their ways. That goes for me, too. It was a wonderful thing to put Lewis Powell on the Court, and I hope that Presidents don't forget to appoint some Justices straight from the practice. It will make the Court more responsive, for the Court must remember that its decisions aren't going to last if they won't stand the test of time.

*At Ninth Judicial Circuit conference,
Sun Valley, Idaho/The New York Times, 11-24:10.*

Politics

Alexander W. Astin
Director, Higher Education
Research Institute, University
of California, Los Angeles

1

What the pundits have told us about the conservative tendencies of [today's college] students is simply not true. Materialism in the job market may have been mistaken for conservatism in the political arena. But conservatism in politics is not a characteristic of most American college students today any more than it has been in the past. In some areas, they are even more liberal today.

News conference, Oct. 30/
Los Angeles Times, 10-31:(I)1.

Ross K. Baker
Professor of political science,
Rutgers University

2

[Supporting the Constitution's requirement that members of the House of Representatives run for re-election every two years]: If you're looking at the genius of the Constitutional design, this is one good example. The two-year term assures that Representatives are not remote or distant figures. They're forced to be in touch.

The New York Times, 11-10:14.

James David Barber
Historian, Duke University

3

[On former President Richard Nixon, who resigned in the wake of the Watergate affair]: What you had with Nixon was a subversive in the Oval Office . . . What I'm resisting is the reduction of all Nixon's shenanigans to Watergate, and the reduction of Watergate to one break-in [at Democratic Party offices], and the reduction of all that—as he would dearly love us to think—to a few tapes, a little indiscretion.

Newsweek, 5-19:27.

William J. Bennett
Secretary of Education
of the United States

4

[On whether he will run for public office when his term as Education Secretary expires]: I won't be first violinist for the New York Philharmonic. I will not, to my chagrin, be defensive back for the Chicago *Bears*. And I will not work for a public-relations firm. Are the odds of my going into politics better than those three? Yeah.

Newsweek, 3-17:67.

Joseph R. Biden, Jr.
United States Senator, D-Delaware

5

We [Democrats] reached a point in the mid-'70s and early '80s when we forgot we had to constantly move on. And after 50 years of success, we stepped back and gazed with a paralyzing self-satisfaction at our handiwork . . . We said, "Don't change anything. If you attempt to alter housing programs, you are not a true liberal. If you attempt to alter the progress of civil rights, you are questionable. If you doubt the wisdom of anything we have done, you are not a true Democrat." And the cost to us was more than victory. It was our vitality. The Democratic Party became a fossilized shadow of its former self.

The Washington Post, 3-3:(A)3.

Paul Bograd
Associate director, Institute of
Politics, Harvard University

6

Let's face it. If you're an incumbent [running for re-election], you're addressing constituents at the PTA. As a candidate [challenging the incumbent], you're annoying strangers at the supermarket.

U.S. News & World Report,
10-27:28.

David Brinkley
Commentator, ABC News

1

[On debates between candidates before an election]: I don't think there should be debates at all. For one thing, the debate is just a hybrid of a press conference. And all it seems to do is test a candidate's ability to manipulate his personal mental Rolodex.

USA Today, 10-16:(A)8.

Zbigniew Brzezinski
Professor of government,
Columbia University; Former Assistant
to the President of the United States
(Jimmy Carter) for National Security Affairs

2

I have felt that the study of politics cannot be just an abstract exercise. It has to involve some genuine involvement in the process itself. It is in some ways like medicine or law or business, not a matter just of abstractions but of deriving insights from a combination of practice and practical experience, and then systematic analysis. Therefore, I have always been very impatient with highly jargon-driven, esoteric, abstract concepts, words which convey very little meaning to people.

Interview, Washington/
The New York Times, 6-17:5.

Patrick J. Buchanan
Director of Communications for
the President of the United States

3

[President] Reagan has given the conservative movement a touch of class, a touch of majesty, and never again will [critics of conservatism] be able to say the things they say about conservatives— because of Reagan, because of his policies, because of the manner in which he carried himself. Reagan is a class act, and everyone knows it.

Interview, Washington/
The New York Times, 3-25:10.

4

The future belongs to conservatives. They are younger, they are more energetic, they dominate the party caucuses, they dominate the nominating process. They are committed to ideas, not simply personal aggrandizement or title . . . They are in constant communication with one another and they believe themselves to be part of a movement.

Interview, Washington/
The Christian Science Monitor, 6-30:35.

5

Political capital is not something that is dissipated. It is a renewable resource. The more that you invest in it, the greater the return. [For example,] the idea that the President [Reagan] gave up political capital on the [Nicaraguan] contras is ridiculous. He put all his chips on the table up there [on Capitol Hill], and he won, and it's redoubled. It's the other side up on the Hill now, it's the liberals who are demoralized on the issue of contras, who are up there talking about vindictiveness and reprisals against their own. It's not us [in the White House]. The investment of political capital is something, when invested wisely, doubles and redoubles itself.

Interview/USA Today, 7-18:(A)9.

James MacGregor Burns
Historian

6

[A major reason that voters are turned off is the] absence of what I think is perhaps the most crucial value in the mechanics of democracy . . . and that is responsibility or accountability, the capacity of people to put their finger on who should get the credit or discredit for what's happening in the country.

At Douglas Adair Symposia, Pomona (Calif.)
College/Los Angeles Times, 4-30:(V)3.

George Bush
Vice President of the United States

7

If we're [the Republican Party] to be a majority party, we must make a home for people from all groups and all regions. I believe we must reach out. We must include, not exclude.

At Lincoln Day dinner sponsored by
New York County Republican Committee,
Feb. 12/The Washington Post, 2-13:(A)17.

(GEORGE BUSH)

1

[On his decision not to become politically visible in preparation for running for the Presidency in 1988]: People keep wanting me to change that. My view is, look, the best thing for me to do is to support this President [Reagan], which I can do enthusiastically from a philosophical standpoint and do it from my assessment in my view as to how one ought to act in this job. And the President ought not to have to worry about the Vice President out there taking some high-profile position to feather his own nest . . . So you pay a price for approaching your job the way I've paid it. And sometimes it's not very pleasant personally, because you get attacked by people for refusing to do that which everyone craves to know—where do you differ from Reagan? What're you going to do different? . . . If that doesn't keep people happy in the journalistic profession or in the political profession . . . and that costs me, so be it. I can't do it differently, and so there it is.

Interview, Washington, June 6/
The Christian Science Monitor, 6-9:48.

Robert C. Byrd
United States Senator,
D-West Virginia

2

[On why voters should elect more Democrats in the forthcoming national elections]: People want a Congress up here that can balance off what at times has been a very arrogant and partisan [Reagan] White House—a White House that has not attended to the problems of mainstream America. They're going to go into that voting booth and they're going to vote for the local candidate. They want someone who's going to be watching the store at this [Capitol Hill] end of Pennsylvania Avenue. So it doesn't all go off in one direction. [President] Reagan has been saying, "It's one more time to vote for me" [by voting for Republicans]. Why, hell, we're not voting for him. Voters want to know, "Who's going to vote for *me*?" It's not, "Who's going to be on Mr. Reagan's side?"

Interview/USA Today, 11-4:(A)11.

3

[Criticizing the financing of election campaigns which requires Senators to spend much time fund-raising]: Senators are always coming to me and saying, "I've got to go here [to raise money], I've got to go there." It's become impossible to schedule the work of the Senate. Too much money was spent in the last election, and everybody knows it. Raising that kind of money is demeaning, and it's time-consuming.

The New York Times, 11-19:10.

Jimmy Carter
Former President of the United States

4

[On President Reagan's ability to shake off criticism of his Administration, while Carter seemed to attract more than his share of criticism for his mistakes]: I never quite understood this phenomenon myself. In the first place, we have a different political philosophy. I am more in tune with [the late President] Harry Truman; I had that sign on my desk, "The buck stops here." It was my government; I took responsibility for it. President Reagan has a different philosophy. He avoids responsibility, successfully, for anything unpleasant or unpopular or disappointing or embarrassing or a failure. It's never his fault. It's always the fault of his Cabinet members, of Congress, his predecessor in the White House, or some foreigner. Never his fault. And third, I would say that he's just a better politician—than I am, or was.

Interview/USA Today, 5-12:(A)11.

5

I predict the Democrats are going to do very well in the elections this year and two years from now. I represented a Democratic Party philosophy of resolving international disputes with diplomacy and negotiation instead of belligerency, emphasizing human rights abroad and civil rights here, negotiating in good faith on nuclear-arms controls and a commitment to environmental quality. At the same time, I was quite conservative on trying to balance the budget, hold down the deficits and deregulate the private-enterprise system. I think that's the basic

(JIMMY CARTER)

philosophy that the Democratic party is moving toward now.

Interview/U.S. News &
World Report, 7-21:19.

Tony Coelho
United States Representative,
D-California

1

The Republicans have always had the fat cats. But now they have found a way to keep the fat cats while at the same time raising money from a lot of little cats.

The New York Times,
3-5:12.

2

There is a group of folks out there who are no longer loyal Democrats. They're intrigued with [Republican President] Reagan, and they voted for him, but they're not so intrigued with the Republican Party. We have to remind them—here's why you were a Democrat—and tell them why they should be with us.

The New York Times,
6-3:10.

Alan Cranston
United States Senator, D-California

3

[Saying his re-election campaign is concentrating on TV spots rather than in-person campaigning]: Door-to-door work is harder to do when you are interrupting people watching their favorite television show. Rallies take a lot of staff work, a lot of time. They're a risk. If you get a small crowd, you get a very negative story instead of a positive one. It's hard to get people away from their TV sets to come out to rallies . . . Unfortunately, campaigns have come down pretty much to a candidate raising money and translating that money into television commercials.

Los Angeles Times,
10-16:(I)22.

Walter Cronkite
Special correspondent, and
former anchorman,
CBS News

4

[On President Reagan]: I'm amazed at this Teflon Presidency. This Administration has had scandals, rumors of major influence-peddling and the like, yet it has no effect on the popularity of the President. Reagan is even more popular than [Franklin] Roosevelt, and I never thought I'd ever see anyone that well-liked. Roosevelt, you'll remember, had his major critics, major figures who actually disliked him. Nobody hates Reagan. It's amazing.

USA Today, 5-12:(D)2.

5

In these days of instant communication and the requirement for fairly instant decision-making, it is important that our President be able to communicate with the people. There are those who find that highly distasteful, who don't like the idea of our candidates being elected on the basis of their popular appeal through television. I don't find that offensive. I have felt all along that television has a certain X-ray quality, that it does reveal the person behind the one-dimensional facade.

Interview/
USA Today, 6-6:(A)13.

Mario M. Cuomo
Governor of New York (D)

6

[Saying he does not intend to run for President in 1988, but he will not unconditionally rule it out]: It's not good for the state [to rule out a Presidential bid]. It's not good for me. So why do it? . . . What do you gain by saying I'm going to pretend to be God, foresee all the future and tell you—even if you strike me from my horse by lightning and say, "You used to be Mario and now you're Matthew, go forward and run"—"No, the answer is no, I ruled that out." How does that make any sense?

News conference, New York,
May 19/The New York Times, 5-20:15.

WHAT THEY SAID IN 1986

(MARIO M. CUOMO)

1

[On whether he will run for President in 1988]: I have decided to run for [re-election as] Governor. I have no plans to run for the Presidency . . . [But] I don't want to lock the door against eventualities that I don't even understand or imagine. I'm not God. If you have a crystal ball, if you can tell me what's going to happen, fine. But I can't.

News conference, Albany, N.Y./Time, 6-2:28.

William E. Dannemeyer
United States Representative,
R-California

2

[On his decision not to continue his campaign for the Senate]: A person [running for the Senate] must have several million dollars available to, in effect, sell soap. It has little to do with the candidate's qualifications, his position on the issues, his or her voting record or aspirations for the future. You have to be able to buy those 30- and 60-second [TV] spots that say nothing about issues or the candidates but that in some cases make a silk purse out of a sow's ear.

News conference, Santa Ana, Calif.,
Feb. 10/Los Angeles Times, 2-11:(I)3.

Robert J. Dole
United States Senator, R-Kansas

3

[On "negative" political campaign advertising, which seeks to attack opponents, rather than extol oneself by campaigning on issues]: It's unfortunate we have to rely on negative ads. On the other hand, you do have to point out someone's record—though some may have gone over the line. But I don't think voters want ads with the little fishing scene with the children or the candidate walking through the park—all the fluff. There's got to be a mix . . . The problem is too much money in campaigns, but I have yet to figure out a way to reduce it. Candidates in effect become collectors for TV stations. There may be a better way to do it.

Interview/USA Today, 11-4:(A)11.

Michael S. Dukakis
Governor of Massachusetts (D)

4

Notwithstanding the current [Reagan] Administration in Washington, I think the people of this country want political leaders who are activists, who see challenges and go at them, who are deeply involved in building economic opportunity, good schools, quality environment, affordable housing, all of those things that most of us Democratic Governors are deeply involved in. Instinctively and philosophically, Democrats tend to be people who are doers, and believe that one of the reasons we are elected is to deal with problems, to deal with challenges, and to do so effectively.

Interview/The Christian
Science Monitor, 9-18:19.

Thomas F. Eagleton
United States Senator, D-Missouri

5

[Election] campaign spending has gotten to the level of being dangerous and obscene and odious . . . I said to one journalist yesterday . . . there's the stench of money around this [Senate office] building. And there is. If I were running for re-election, I might not have had time for this interview. Because I could put my time maybe to better use by being on the phone, talking to fat cats that I don't even know; imploring them to send me X dollars, because somebody gave me a list of names and said these are rich people that might give you something. And that's the way it's become around here. An inordinate amount of a Senator's time is spent preparing for fund-raising, and fund-raising itself. And we all know that when somebody gives you five thousand or 10—you know, five in the primary and 10 in the general—you're not getting that money out of the Red Cross or the Little Sisters of the Poor. They expect something for that money. And when you receive the money, you know that those folks have that expectation. You're not blind.

Interview, Washington/
The Washington Post, 10-31:(A)25.

(THOMAS F. EAGLETON)

1

I used to say the worst thing about politics was the enormous scandalous sums of money candidates had to raise. Now I am not so sure. After watching the 1986 Congressional races, I'm beginning to think an even worse thing is the way that money is spent. Not in my experience, maybe not in our history, has there been anything quite like it. Many campaigns around the nation came to be dominated by gimmicks, by trivia and by crude, vilifying personal attacks on an opponent's character. Demagoguery and slanderous attacks have sometimes been a regrettable part of the American political process, but 1986 was different from any campaign I have known. Negative, personal attacks saturated the airwaves and the campaign rhetoric in too many states. The whole process was taken over by the mass marketers. It was anything goes provided only you could fit it into a 30-second TV spot. Anything, that is, but a serious discussion of issues.

*Before National Democratic Institute
for International Affairs, Nov. 7/
The Washington Post, 11-11:(A)20.*

Don Edwards
*United States Representative,
D-California*

2

[On the Reagan Administration]: We've been witnessing a day-to-day, hour-by-hour flouting not only of laws, but also regulations and customs. They're all out of the entrepreneur, dog-eat-dog American business community. They have different rules, and don't seem to have a great respect for the way men and women have to behave.

The New York Times, 11-28:12.

Linda Ellerbee
Broadcast journalist, NBC-TV

3

[Saying politicians hate news reporters]: Most of them do. Their interests are different from ours. A politician's first duty is to get re-

elected. That's not our first duty: to get them re-elected. That makes their interests different from ours. It makes it a natural adversarial position. I don't believe that the only way to look at a politician is down. But I do think sideways is a good idea.

Interview/USA Today, 6-2:(A)11.

Jane Eskind
*Chairman, Tennessee Public Service
Commission; Candidate for 1986 Tennessee
Democratic gubernatorial nomination*

4

[On being a woman running for Governor]: The presumption was that I was not going to win. That presumption came from the traditional political gray heads who tend to talk to one another. They tend to think a woman can't win. I find voters are much more willing to accept a woman candidate than the politicians. I think the distinction is not so much in the gender of a candidate, but in how professional a campaign he or she runs.

The Washington Post, 8-7(A)10.

Geraldine Ferraro
*Former United States Representative,
D-New York; 1984 Democratic
Vice Presidential nominee*

5

When Walter Mondale chose me for his running mate, he did more for the cause of equal opportunity [for women] in one day than [President] Ronald Reagan did in four years. After the election, a poll found 27 per cent of the people surveyed said they would be more likely to vote for a woman than before the 1984 election; 7 per cent said less likely. But the huge majority—64 per cent—said it would make no difference. That is by far the best news of all—that the majority of voters sampled are ready to judge candidates not by their gender, but by their ideas and principles. It's about time.

*At business conference aboard "Mississippi
Queen" steamboat/USA Today, 4-23:(A)11.*

WHAT THEY SAID IN 1986

Mervin Field
Public-opinion analyst

1

[On people who split their votes among more than one party at election time]: . . . the public has a sense that is part cynicism and part playing it safe. Voters don't mind having a President of one party and a Congress of another, or a Senate delegation of one party and a Governor of another. It's somehow safer—a check on power.

The Christian Science Monitor, 7-16:4.

Orville Freeman
Former Governor of Minnesota (D)

2

[On why there are eight former Governors still living in Minnesota]: We elect 'em young and fire 'em quick.

USA Today, 5-28:(A)4.

Barry M. Goldwater
United States Senator, R-Arizona

3

I wouldn't trust [former President Richard] Nixon from here to that phone. He had a good foreign-policy head on him, but he was dishonest. Anybody that would lie to his wife and lie to his children and then to his country, I have no use for.

Interview/Newsweek, 9-29:27.

4

Let's look at some great [Presidential] leaders: [Franklin D.] Roosevelt. Roosevelt had the ability to bring people together. I think that's a basic of leadership. [Harry S.] Truman. I think he's going to be our greatest President this hundred years. He had the ability to be honest above *everything* else. You might disagree with him, you didn't like what he did, but by God you never had to go to bed at night wondering what the hell he was going to do. [Dwight D.] Eisenhower had the same qualities as Roosevelt. He could get through to the people and let them understand that the problem was theirs. Now, we haven't had, in my opinion, any great Presidential leaders since then. I think Jack Kennedy

would have been. Reagan has a great ability to speak, and people can sit all over this country and cuss at him, get mad at him but, once he stands up to speak, they forget all about it.

Interview, Washington/
The Washington Post, 11-4:(A)17.

5

I don't want to see three parties. Two parties are enough. And I don't believe in preaching party loyalty. But I think if you took a poll amongst people today, my guess would be that nearly 50 per cent of the people would say they're going to vote for the man or woman they like, not because he's a Republican or a Democrat.

Interview, Washington/
The Washington Post, 11-4:(A)17.

Gary Hart
United States Senator, D-Colorado

6

[On whether he is the "front-runner" for the 1988 Democratic Presidential nomination]: Front-runnership is conferred by the "Great Mentioner"—a group of people in Washington decide so-and-so is the front-runner. It's based on things like whether you've held or run for national office before, whether you've got money in the bank, your standing in the polls. The establishment thing is equally intangible. It's the [telephone] calls that establish that. You [call] the state chairs, the labor leaders, the key figures and ask what's going on. If they say, "Well, I'm for Hart," then you kind of assume the mantle.

Interview, Troublesome
Gulch, Colo./Newsweek, 1-13:33.

7

. . . I don't think my [Democratic] Party, which has won only one Presidential election in 20 years, is going to get back in power without ideas. [President] Reagan is where he is because of the power of his ideas. I think they are wrong, but he got there on ideas, not because he's a charming actor who reads scripts well. Our ideas must be better.

Interview/U.S. News &
World Report, 6-23:23.

Peter D. Hart
Democratic Party
public-opinion analyst

1

The interesting thing about women running [for political office] in 1986 is you don't have women aged 30 and 40. They're women aged 50 and 60. They're serious and professional candidates. They have their names at the top of the ticket because the party is looking for proven vote-getters.

The New York Times, 9-11:1.

Jesse Helms
United States Senator,
R-North Carolina

2

I was elected to stand as firmly as I can for what I believe in, and against what I don't. That fellow who came down from Sinai was a nay-sayer, too—although I don't put myself in his class.

Interview, August/U.S. News
& World Report, 8-18:9.

Charlton Heston
Actor

3

Never doubt that performance is an essential ingredient in political leadership. It even involves such things as props and wardrobe. These things are part of performance. People are irritated by this. They say it isn't real. Bull. It is real. President Reagan [a former actor] is one of the first people of whom it is true.

The Washington Post, 8-9:(A)3.

Don Hewitt
Executive producer,
"60 Minutes," CBS-TV

4

How did political conventions become the end-all and be-all of television reporting? Each network loads up God knows how many trucks and moves out to the convention city. Then we arrive and unload our trucks like Ringling Brothers unloads the circus. And we take over . . .

When I first went to political conventions, we were observers and reporters. Now we're participants. And there's something a lot wrong with that. In the old days, before the primaries took the steam out of political conventions, you could watch a good credentials fight or a good platform fight—even though a week later no one could remember what they were fighting about. Today, if you want to see a good fight at a political convention, if you want to see a real fight at a political convention, let CBS News' sign be an inch bigger than NBC's. Now you'll see a fight at a convention. All hell breaks loose. It's time we gave the politicians back their convention. Tell them it's nothing but a big commercial and that it's not [news anchormen Dan] Rather, [Tom] Brokaw or [Peter] Jennings' job to be the emcee of their commercial.

At National Press Foundation dinner,
Washington, Feb. 25/The New York Times, 2-28:14.

Jim Hightower
Commissioner of Agriculture of Texas

5

Fundamentally, populism addresses the problem that too few people have too much money and power, which is the same old struggle of the old populism. It doesn't seek a liberal solution, to give welfare to the farmer who's been forced off his land, or a conservative solution, which is to say, "I got mine, so long, sucker." The idea is to put the tools of self-help in people's hands, to free up their enterprise so that prosperity doesn't trickle down, it percolates up.

At conference on populism, Washington,
May 9/The Washington Post, 5-10:(A)5.

Donald Hodel
Secretary of the Interior
of the United States

6

The President [Reagan] is not unduly swayed by the politics of the day. At Cabinet meetings, we're not supposed to make political arguments. He wants to decide matters according to what's right. He encourages us to do the same.

Interview/Christianity Today, 4-4:37.

WHAT THEY SAID IN 1986

Thomas H. Kean
Governor of New Jersey (R)

1

The unifying themes for Republicans are opportunity, growth and equal opportunity, whether they are speaking in a black church, a union hall or a chamber-of-commerce meeting.

Newsweek, 3-24:31.

2

[On the black community's traditional overwhelming support of the Democratic Party]: This is a community that has given 90 per cent of its vote to one party, and what have they gotten in exchange? How many black Senators are there? How many black Congressmen are there? How many black state party chairmen, how many black county chairmen are there? You have one party [the Republicans] that says there's nothing they can do to get the black vote, so they ignore them. And the other party says there's nothing they can do to lose the black vote, so they take them for granted. So the black agenda doesn't advance.

Interview/Los Angeles Times,
10-27:(I)14.

Jack Kemp
United States Representative,
R-New York

3

[On the Republican Party]: We've got to be the party of labor. Economic growth doesn't mean anything if it leaves people out. If we trust our ideas, we have to take them into the ghetto, into the barrio and into the trade-union hiring hall. Franklin Roosevelt made his party the party of hope, and now we must do the same thing for the party of Lincoln.

At Waukesha County Republican Party's
Lincoln Day dinner, Oconomowoc, Wis./
The New York Times,
3-10:12.

4

[The new conservatism] trusts people and markets. It is more optimistic about the future. And it is activist. It isn't content with the status quo. The new conservatives . . . want to make change. It is a liberative idea.

Interview, Washington/
The Christian Science Monitor, 3-18:22.

Paul G. Kirk, Jr.
Chairman, Democratic
National Committee

5

The [Democratic] Party has to be in the position as a national party to embrace all of what's needed to win, and clearly, in my view, what's needed to win is some significant portion of the Southern region of the country. You know, the days are gone when a party chairman can name the ticket and why they are and where they're from. But if you looked at it today, I would say it would make sense to have a Southerner on the ticket.

To reporters, Washington, Jan. 13/
The New York Times, 1-14:9.

6

The public perception [of the Democratic Party] in 1984 was a proliferation of disparate groups rather than a party that broadens its core and speaks to a national base of people and their families. That's a perception we are gradually changing.

Interview/The Washington Post, 11-29:(A)4.

Jeane J. Kirkpatrick
Former United States Ambassador/
Permanent Representative
to the United Nations

7

[On whether she would consider running for President]: I can imagine myself doing the job. I can't imagine myself running for it. I don't mind the campaigning or schlepping around. I really like those people out there more than anyone realizes. Growing up in small towns means living in a microcosm of the whole societal universe. The result is I feel comfortable with all kinds of people. [But] I don't know. I am an inordinately proud woman. For me, the difficulty of running is the asking—and the risking.

Interview, Washington/
Ladies' Home Journal, May:179.

Henry A. Kissinger
Former Secretary of State
of the United States

1

Politics, relatively speaking, is the art of gaining and holding power. Statesmanship is the art of shaping power toward ends.

Interview/Penthouse, December:82.

Everett Ladd
Director, Roper Center
for Public Opinion Research

2

Democrats have the edge in the number of voters who identify themselves by party allegiance, but Republicans have the edge when people are asked which party does a better job handling the country's problems. It's as close to parity as you can get.

U.S. News & World Report, 2-24:73.

Richard D. Lamm
Governor of Colorado (D)

3

I am absolutely disgusted when I think about running another campaign [for political office]. I don't want to go back into that process where you have to go around to all the special interests and adjust your views. Very few Old Testament prophets also became kings. The best contribution I can make is saying, "This is how I see it," and not pulling any punches—and that means not running for office.

Interview/People, 1-20:49.

Paul Laxalt
United States Senator, R-Nevada

4

[On whether he will run for President in 1988]: If I don't have enough people in this country who have enough faith in me to invest a thousand dollars a pop to accumulate $8 million to $10 million [for an election campaign], I'm not going to take the trip . . . I'm not going to go out starry-eyed and run a Presidential campaign insufficiently funded and end up with a

campaign that isn't well-conducted, and if I lose, be in debt for the rest of my life. That unfortunately has been the legacy of many, many Presidential candidates in recent years. The landscape is littered with them, and I'm just not going to let that happen.

Interview, Reno, Nev./
Los Angeles Times, 11-9:(I)12.

Eugene Lee
Director, Institute of Governmental Studies,
University of California, Berkeley

5

[On the use of debates between opposing political candidates]: This public hankering for debates is a reflection of [a desire to] see the campaign in something other than the context of fund-raising and television spots. There's just not much spontaneous contact and communication between the voter and the candidate.

Los Angeles Times, 10-2:(I)1.

Ann Lewis
Director, Americans
for Democratic Action

6

The movement for a woman [Vice President] on the Democratic ticket in 1984 showed there were too few women in the pipeline. One thing that became clear is how few women we had available for that office . . . Young women are climbing what until now has been a male ladder. You are now seeing women, as well as men, who are getting into state legislatures early, finding they like politics and looking to see how to move up.

U.S. News & World Report, 2-24:23.

Norman Mailer
Author

7

I think the women have ruined the Democratic Party. The Democratic Party has had candidates throughout the last 12 years that are about as rousing as oatmeal. And one of the reasons is that no man can rise in the Democratic

193

(NORMAN MAILER)

Party now who doesn't say "Women first. The women are wonderful. Whatever the women want."

On "Open Mind,"
PBS-TV/Newsweek, 3-3:13.

Charles McC. Mathias, Jr.
United States Senator, R-Maryland

1

Under the current system, few [political] candidates relish the task of getting elected. There is increasing awareness that modern campaign technologies have fostered a remoteness from the voters. Nowhere is this more apparent than in the allocation of resources. The overwhelming percentage of campaign dollars now goes to television, neither an intimate medium of communication nor a very profound one. As a *Washington Post* headline described it, "In 30-second bursts, TV ads shape the campaign" . . . I continue to believe that the best means for remedying the ills in our system of campaign finance is to institute some form of public financing of Congressional elections. In the long term, no one is served by the stresses that tear at the current system of financing campaigns.

Speech/USA Today, 11-5:(A)14.

J. Michael McKeon
Public-opinion analyst

2

[On the recent Illinois primary successes of candidates backed by Lyndon LaRouche, considered by many to be an ultra-right extremist]: [LaRouche's campaign supporters] were getting insulted 10,000 times, but at 10,001, someone would listen. They taught themselves how to talk to Joe Six-Pack. They started tapping into the feelings that are out here in blue-collar America . . . There is a mood of frustration and anger settling in deeper and deeper. These people who have been left behind and can never catch up. They are vulnerable in all sorts of ways. Somebody gets mugged and the whole neighborhood gets so mad they can't see

straight. It's the kind of thing that dominates and dictates peoples' lives. And they are tough on crime and hate drug dealers. They'd like to see them all killed—Ramboed. This is what the LaRouche candidates have been saying, too. Maybe the national politicians haven't been listening. But voters out here have.

Interview, Joliet, Ill./
The Washington Post, 3-26:(A)8.

Edwin Meese III
Attorney General of the United States

3

[On his "unsympathetic" image]: Some of this is simple distortion. In many cases, the press just doesn't understand the complex issues I am talking about . . . And then you have in Washington some people who are constantly engaged in a power struggle, whether there is any need for one or not.

Interview/Esquire, July:81.

Richard Moe
Senior advisor to Democratic
Presidential nominee Walter
Mondale during 1984 campaign

4

[President] Reagan proved that ideas matter [in election campaigns]. His idea was we had to reduce government and cut taxes and everyone would be better off. I don't agree with that; but he put it in an appealing way, and it was this idea that underpins his Presidency.

Los Angeles Times, 9-8:(I)16.

Tom Murphy
Speaker of the Georgia House

5

[On the 1988 Southern "super-primary" election]: Us folks in the South are tired of being eaten over [by the primaries in the rest of the country]. We want to be recognized and we're going to be recognized . . . the Southern primary is going to elect the next President of the United States.

At Southern Legislative Conference, Fort Worth,
Texas, July 16/The Washington Post, 7-17:(A)4.

George H. Nash
Historian

1

This is the moment of conservative opportunity, the era when—for the first time in half a century—principled conservatives have gained access to executive power. No observer of this phenomenon can fail to detect a feeling of having arrived among those who once felt beleaguered and ignored. It is a feeling conveyed by [former U.S. UN Ambassador] Jeane Kirkpatrick's recent remark about the political opposition: "The Democrats are in a real bind. They won't get elected unless things get worse, and things won't get worse unless they get elected."

At Hillsdale College/
The Wall Street Journal, 5-5:20.

Irene Natividad
Chairman, National
Women's Political Caucus

2

Women are more experienced office-holders and savvy campaigners these days. It is no longer a sideshow to have them competing against men or even against each other.

U.S. News & World Report, 11-3:21.

Richard M. Nixon
Former President of the United States

3

[On the Watergate affair which drove him from office]: A lot was a self-inflicted wound. It was a very mishandled thing. Churchill said his study of history showed that great leaders more often stumble on little things than on big things. And this is not an excuse but it is to a certain extent a reason. [1972] was a busy year: my God, we went to China, we went to Russia, we were winding down the war in Vietnam. There was no way [George] McGovern was going to win the [Presidential] election. So we should have faced up to [Watergate] very early and said, "Look, who did this thing, and so forth and so on; we're sorry that it happened." When you try to compare the deed itself [the break-in at Democratic Party offices], rather than the cover-up of the deed—the deed itself was a nonsense thing. It didn't produce anything.

Interview, Saddle River,
N.J./Newsweek, 5-19:34.

Lyn Nofziger
Former Special Assistant to
President of the United States
Ronald Reagan for Political Affairs

4

[On doctrinal conservatives who have criticized President Reagan for not being far enough to the right in his policies]: The hundred-percenters would rather go down in flames than compromise on anything. The problem is they're not political. In this world, you take what you can get and you move ahead. The [purists] ought to see that Ronald Reagan has done more for conservatives than anybody in this century.

U.S. News & World Report, 12-29:27.

Thomas P. O'Neill, Jr.
United States Representative,
D-Massachusetts

5

[On his retirement from government service]: I suppose I'm the last of an old style. I'm a caricature of an old, fat, behind-the-scenes politician, which I probably have been.

U.S. News & World Report, 10-13:27.

6

That group that came in [to Congress] in '74, more of those people had never served in public life than any other group, I believe, in the history of Congress. The Party itself, the Democratic Party, it had changed. You didn't have the leadership across the nation; you didn't have the Party organizations. So when these people came in—they were highly educated, very, very sophisticated, many of them were junior executives well on the road to success—they had no loyalty to the Party whatsoever. And we ran into difficulty. They set up their own caucus and they were a factor. They had 54 and, if they left you, you were in trouble. The old boys were running the shop and they wanted to have a part of it.

WHAT THEY SAID IN 1986

(THOMAS P. O'NEILL, JR.)

And so you came in with the system of so many subcommittees. Too many now. The Party is dispersed in the hands of too many people. But the pendulum is swinging back.

Interview, Washington,
Oct. 22/The New York Times, 10-23:12.

Howard Phillips
President, Conservative Caucus

1

[Saying the Reagan Administration hasn't been conservative enough]: Conservatives have been out of power for the last six years. The problem is that most haven't realized it . . . There is a widespread perception that [former President] Jimmy Carter policies are being implemented behind the ruse of conservative imagery. Reagan may be a superb Chief of State, but he's been a lousy Chief Executive.

U.S. News & World Report, 12-29:27.

Kevin Phillips
Republican Party political analyst

2

[Saying President Reagan, despite being in his last term, is not a lame duck, but only because the Senate objected to many of his policies]: If the Administration had stuck to its 1985 programs across a broad sphere, they'd be in a disastrous circumstance right now, with the President down in the polls. Luckily for [the Administration], they have [Republicans] in the Senate who want to get re-elected and who have a sense of what the public wants. The Senate saved them from themselves. The attempt [by the Administration] in 1985 to turn back on the farmers, the attempt to slash government programs in agencies as the key to deficit reductions, the inattention to the trade issue—sort of laughing it off—the early 1985 White House view that the strong dollar was an expression of foreigners' faith in America, was a flawed blueprint that the Senate objected to. If [the Administration was] still pushing these, if they hadn't

backed away, Reagan would be very much of a lame duck today.

The New York Times, 8-28:10.

3

[On how the Democratic Party gains in the Senate in the just-concluded elections will affect the Presidential chances of Republican Vice President George Bush in 1988]: This has to give George Bush concern. This election suggests that the Federal tide is moving away from what Bush and [President] Reagan represent. It moves both parties into the post-Reagan era and into a spirited competition for the center of American politics.

The New York Times,
11-6:19.

Nancy Reagan
Wife of President of the
United States Ronald Reagan

4

[On President Reagan]: People may disagree with him politically, or whatever, but I don't think anybody can ever question his integrity, his honesty. And I think that's what the people feel—that he's not doing something for political gain but he honestly believes it. They have the feeling that he's sincere, honest, a good man.

Interview, Washington/
The Washington Post, 2-6:(C)4.

5

[On President Reagan]: What's always been true is that people have underestimated him, ever since he ran for Governor [of California]. They've underestimated him politically, intellectually, in every way. There was no way he was ever going to be a lame duck, no way. He's a very strong man with very strong ideas and principles he believes in and has believed in for a long time. When people get into trouble is when they don't have that well to draw from, they don't have that base. And he's had it all this time.

Interview, Tokyo/
The New York Times, 5-7:22.

Ronald Reagan
President of the United States

1

We [conservatives] must tell the American people that the progress we made thus far is not enough; that it will never be enough until the conservative agenda is enacted, and that means enterprise zones, prayer in the public schools and the protection of the unborn [from abortion] . . . [This year's Congressional elections] will decide whether the days of high taxes and higher spending, the days of economic stagflation and skyrocketing inflation, the days of national malaise and international humiliation, the days of "Blame America First" and "inordinate fear of Communism," will all come roaring back at us once again.

Before Conservative Political Action Conference, Washington, Jan. 30/ The New York Times, 1-31:14.

2

In [the elections of] 1980 and 1984, the American people have repudiated the Democratic Party's politics of envy at home and weakness abroad. But don't think for a moment that the [Democrats have] been chastened . . . Given half a chance, they would quickly begin to dismantle the strong and proud America that we've spent these 5 $1/_2$ years building. They'd gleefully take it down, piece by piece, all the while talking on and on about their so-called "fairness."

At Republican Congressional dinner, Washington, May 21/The Washington Post, 5-22:(A)7.

3

[On the upcoming fall Congressional and gubernatorial elections]: Believe me, the liberals in Washington know what's at stake in this election. They know this may well be their last chance to steer American politics way over to the left. They know that if we Republicans do well this November it's going to permanently alter the political landscape.

At Republican gathering, Dallas, July 23/ The New York Times, 7-24:8.

4

[On the Democratic Party gains in the Senate in the just concluded elections]: The truth is, the voters elected us [his Republican Administration] in 1984 to keep the [Reagan] revolution alive—not just for two years but for four. And believe me, if you'd been out on the campaign trail with me hearing all those chants of "four more years," you'd know just how much the country is with us.

To his senior staff members, Washington, Nov. 5/Los Angeles Times, 11-6:(I)18.

Joe Rothstein
Democratic political analyst

5

If the Republicans maintain control of the Senate [in the coming fall elections], and defeat the historic trend toward the opposition party in an off-year election, I'd say they begin the 1988 Presidential campaign with a very strong, positive outlook. But if the Republicans lose the Senate, you will stop seeing stories about the realignment of the parties. There will be a feeling that the Democratic Party is on the way back.

The New York Times, 6-9:10.

Larry J. Sabato
Professor of government, University of Virginia

6

[The Reagan] Administration is the most ideological in modern American history and, therefore, more zealots have been appointed to major positions than has been the case in other Administrations. We also never have had a President so disengaged from the details of government. So the zealots who were in place had more authority and more leeway than Presidential staffs have had in most Administrations.

Los Angeles Times, 12-8:(I)19.

Helmut Schmidt
Publisher, "Die Zeit" (West Germany); Former Chancellor of West Germany

7

Television has modified considerably the quality and structure of the democratic process. The public gets a more vivid, realistic view of

197

the people to whom they entrust their destiny. But the negative side is that, in the future, television actors will become politicians, and the best actor will have the best chance with the public.

Interview/World Press Review, April:59.

William Schneider
Resident fellow,
American Enterprise Institute

1

[The Democrats] have to recover their credibility on economic issues. Losing that credibility under [former President] Jimmy Carter, then having to face [President] Reagan's successes, has been utterly devastating to them. When voters are asked what they like about the Democratic Party, the answer is: It's for the average worker, not the rich. What do voters dislike about Democrats? The answer is too much government spending.

Interview/U.S. News &
World Report, 9-8:18.

Patricia Schroeder
United States Representative,
D-Colorado

2

[On women running for public office]: [Today's] Rambomania, the macho, feel-good, real-man, thumbs-up kind of mood, makes it really hard for a woman candidate. The electorate seems to be looking for representatives that are half-Marine, half-legislator. That's tough for a woman to pull off.

U.S. News & World Report, 11-3:22.

John Sears
Republican political analyst

3

[On the possibility of Vice President George Bush running for President in 1988]: If you're Vice President, what you ought to be doing is looking around the local premises for things that you can do that might make you look more Pres-

idential. Your real power . . . is that the closeness you have to the office gives you a better chance to look as though you ought to be President. And you ought to take advantage of that. The minute you step out and start doing the same things that other people do who want this office, you are giving up a section of your power. And you allow yourself to look just like the rest of them [candidates].

To reporters, Washington/
The Christian Science Monitor, 7-10:3.

Stuart M. Statler
Commissioner, Consumer Product
Safety Commission of the United States

4

It's not enough to be a Republican any more . . . Being a good Republican these days means you have to click your heels and subscribe . . . to a right-wing ideology.

Interview/The Washington Post, 3-31:(A)9.

David A. Stockman
Former Director, Federal Office
of Management and Budget

5

The Reagan Revolution . . . is really a radical, anti-welfare-state view of how society is best served. And, essentially, that view is not shared by elected Republican politicians. They adhere to the [Congressman] Tip O'Neill maxim: "All politics is local." And so, therefore, all policy is local. If you're from the wheat belt, you are for wheat subsidies. If you're from Detroit, you're for the Chrysler bailout.

Interview, New York/Newsweek, 4-21:58.

6

[On President Reagan]: There's no consistent, credible or serious intellectual content to Reaganism. After four years [on the job], I had to conclude that what comes out of the White House typewriter is all hot air. There is a startling disconnection between Reagan the campaigner, the scourge of big government, and Reagan the chief executive officer of the American government. He has proved to be very

(DAVID A. STOCKMAN)

pragmatic. Constituencies are given their due and, if they demonstrate, he's willing to call it a day. That's what he did on Social Security, on farm programs, even aid to education. [Reagan] plays to the ambivalence of the American public. There's a big element of self-deception.

Interview/Los Angeles Times, 8-23:(I)27.

Margaret Thatcher
Prime Minister of the United Kingdom

1

In politics, if you want anything said, ask a man. If you want anything done, ask a woman.

USA Today, 9-11:(A)2.

Richard L. Thornburgh
Governor of Pennsylvania (R)

2

When you look at the differences between the two parties, and the role of business and industry and economic development, the Republicans are much more tilted toward the free-enterprise system and away from centralized planning or industrial policies. When you look at fiscal responsibility, that's always been a creed of the Republican Party against taxing, spending and borrowing.

Interview/The Christian Science Monitor, 9-18:19.

George C. Wallace
Governor of Alabama (D)

3

[Announcing that he will not run again for Governor]: Although I am doing very good at the present time, as I grow older the effects of my problem [his wheelchair confinement as a result of an assassination attempt in 1972] may become more noticeable and I may not be able to give you the fullest measure you deserve from a Governor. I feel I must say I have climbed my last political mountain. There are still some personal hills I want to climb, but for now I must pass the rope and pick to another climber, and say, climb on to higher heights . . . While it

may be tempting to live in the past and what might have been, I must realize, as Peter the Great did, it is time to lay aside what will never return and pick up the future. My heart will always belong to Alabama.

To friends and supporters,
Montgomery, Alabama, April 2/
The Washington Post, 4-3:(A)1,6.

Lowell P. Weicker, Jr.
United States Senator, R-Connecticut

4

[Saying he has decided not to run for President in 1988]: Would I like to do it? I'd love to do it. When I see what's out there in terms of candidates and Presidents, I think I can do a better job. I think in terms of issues, debates and the act of being President, I'm probably the best thing the Republican Party has going for it. On the other hand, in terms of delegate votes, I probably have none. So, there's no point in engaging in an academic exercise. I would stand no chance whatsoever in a Republican convention for getting the nomination for President.

Broadcast interview, Greenwich, Conn.,
Dec. 24/The Washington Post, 12-26:(A)17.

Caspar W. Weinberger
Secretary of Defense
of the United States

5

The unorthodox opinions of the conscience of American conservatism have now taken root and they are embraced by all except the most unreconstructed liberal.

At Pentagon ceremony honoring
Senator Barry Goldwater, Dec. 10/
Los Angeles Times, 12-11:(I)28.

Fred Wertheimer
President, Common Cause

6

[On the Reagan Administration]: I have this image that I play around with of an Administration that rode in from the West to tame the evil government, and rode in with the fresh air of the

199

WHAT THEY SAID IN 1986

(FRED WERTHEIMER)

West to clean up this polluted air center; and now they're moving in, they're running around town like classic Washington insiders and they are feeding off the government.

Interview/The Washington Post, 4-28:(A)10.

Richard B. Wirthlin
Republican public-opinion analyst

1

For me, the critical election of the decade is 1986. We [Republicans] have to hold the Senate and see gains in the states and in [voter] registration figures, or the 1980-84 years will reflect only a move toward a personable and attractive President [Reagan]. But if we see young people staying the most Republican group in the electorate, if we see first voters registering Republican . . . then we'll have a good chance to win the Presidency again in 1988 and become the majority party of the 1990s.

The Washington Post,
1-2:(A)8.

Social Welfare

Mortimer Adler
*Educator; Director, Institute
for Philosophical Research*

1

Up until 1900, in every country in the world, you had privileged minorities and oppressed majorities. In the 20th century, in the United States, for the first time you had a privileged *majority*. Let's suppose we [now] have 15 million really destitute persons—illiterate, ill-kept, ill-nourished. That's a very small portion of the country—terrible, but it's a small portion of the population, considering the vast number of 235 million who are, on the whole, well off. We have given those 235 million, the vast majority, all the conditions of a good life.

*Interview, Aspen, Colo./
The Christian Science Monitor, 9-23:17.*

Bruce Babbitt
Governor of Arizona (D)

2

America will never solve its welfare problems without both the heroic efforts of responsible individuals and a helping hand from government . . . Self-sufficiency requires the poor to do the best they can, but their best will not be good enough unless we help them find the power to make it so.

The Christian Science Monitor, 12-5:8.

Marion Barry
Mayor of Washington, D.C.

3

I am the Mayor of all the people, but a lot of people can take care of themselves. People making $50,000, $60,000 a year can make it without government assistance. They need safe streets, the fire put out if their house catches fire, quality schools. But the poor, those who don't have power, they have to have government be their power.

*Interview, Washington/
The Christian Science Monitor, 9-18:7.*

Gary Bauer
*Under Secretary of Education
of the United States; Chairman,
White House task force studying the
effects of Federal programs on families*

4

In an ideal world, women who choose not to work would be able to maintain their families without that extra income. And we should do whatever we can—say, through stimulating economic growth—to make that possible. For women who want to work, there are limits to what the Federal government can do in requiring businesses to help them, such as offering maternity benefits. That creates an economic disincentive for the employer, making it less likely that a woman will get a job. We're still taking a close look at day care, but the tight budget makes that area difficult. Generally, our approach to working women is that government policy ought to be neutral.

Interview/U.S. News & World Report, 9-1:66.

Bill Benson
*Staff member, United States
Senate Special Committee on Aging*

5

There are some really good [nursing] homes, and I've been in some excellent ones. But for the bad ones, you could not fictionalize them, you could not write a horror story to match what goes on there.

Los Angeles Times, 9-29:(I)1.

Stuart Butler
Economist, Heritage Foundation

6

Just watching the welfare debate, conservatives have never been able to frame a model of where they ought to go. It had always been the Great Society versus the nit-pickers. There was a necessity to paint an entire model and not demonstrate to liberals that we're trying to get rid of

(STUART BUTLER)

everything. We [conservatives] need a blueprint, a backdrop to respond to issues all the time.

Interview, Washington/
· Los Angeles Times, 7-7:(IV)5.

Jimmy Carter
Former President of the United States

1

If a family with a starving child, or children, is faced with the question, "Do you want bread, or freedom?", it's not inevitable that they will say, "I prefer freedom."

Interview, Atlanta/
The Christian Science Monitor, 12-30:14.

Wilbur J. Cohen
Former Secretary of Health, Education
and Welfare of the United States

2

I think of Social Security in a much broader way than [President] Reagan or any of the ideologues who only look at it as a governmental intervention in the private market. I look at Social Security as a social invention we have created for you to go to work and lessen your anxiety for the future. This has always impressed me as something that is bigger than myself and bigger than life itself, because it supports life.

Interview, Washington/
The New York Times, 11-25:12.

Mario M. Cuomo
Governor of New York (D)

3

In Lincoln's time, one of every seven Americans was a slave. Today, for all our affluence and might, despite what every day is described as our continuing economic recovery, nearly one in every seven Americans lives in poverty, not in chains—because Lincoln saved us from that—but trapped in a cycle of despair that is its own enslavement.

Before Abraham Lincoln Association,
Springfield, Ill., Feb. 12/
The New York Times, 2-13:16.

Eric Frumin
Health director, Amalgamated
Clothing and Textile Workers Union

4

OSHA under [President] Reagan is a disaster. They have virtually abandoned the responsibility Congress gave them to set standards and then vigorously enforce them. The only time they do it is when a court orders it, when political pressure mounts, or when the bodies pile up at the door.

The Washington Post, 8-25:(A)13.

Richard A. Gephardt
United States Representative,
D-Missouri

5

[Criticizing the Reagan Administration's attitude toward welfare recipients]: I find the vast majority of people I've talked to hated being on welfare, wanted a job, wanted to be trained, wanted skills . . . The Administration, I think, feels there are a lot of people who love being on welfare.

To reporters, Washington, Dec. 22/
The Washington Post, 12-23:(A)4.

Newt Gingrich
United States Representative,
R-Georgia

6

[Proposing to replace Social Security with private retirement accounts]: The real dividing line in American politics for the next decade will be between those who maintain we can avoid fundamental change and those who believe we must totally rethink our welfare state.

USA Today, 11-7:(A)6.

Lou Glasse
President, Older Women's League

7

Far from retiring to a comfortable pension plan, older women are least likely to reap the benefits of a lifetime of work . . . [There is a] growing myth of an affluent elderly population

(LOU GLASSE)

that is using up government benefits that could better be used by the young.

Washington, May 7/
The New York Times, 5-8:16.

Judith Gueron
President, Manpower
Demonstration Research Corporation

1

[Approving "workfare" as an alternative to welfare]: Even the cheap, primitive [workfare] programs make a difference. I'm talking about results like an increase in employment rates of 5 to 8 percentage points, increased earnings of 10 to 30 per cent, and reductions in welfare grants of 5 to 10 points; and these results were consistent across very different environments, ranging from Arkansas to California to Maryland . . . You put some money in up front, and you get a return down the line. It's particularly cost-effective for the Federal government, and therefore there is a lot of logic for a Federal investment in this area, because the Federal government gets most of the savings [in food stamps and Medicaid] when people go off welfare. It's fine to give states a large role in designing the programs, but you need some national resources to run the programs.

Interview/The New York Times, 12-17:(A)27.

Randolph Hale
Vice president, industrial relations,
National Association of Manufacturers

2

[Arguing against legislation that would require companies to grant leaves of absences to mothers and fathers for the birth of a child]: Such leave is a good practice where companies can afford to offer it voluntarily and employees want it. But we oppose the legislation because it would also apply to companies that can't afford to give such leave. We have to ask: How would this affect the ability of the United States to compete with the rest of the world? . . . I think the key for any benefit is how much employees want it. If employees want a benefit, companies in an area will have to offer it to stay competitive in at-

tracting good people. But the point is that such benefits should be set by each company and by the marketplace, and not mandated for all companies whether large or small, whether in good economic health or poor.

Interview/U.S. News & World Report, 7-28:63.

Dorcas R. Hardy
Commissioner-designate,
Social Security Administration
of the United States

3

We must maintain the fiscal integrity of the Social Security programs . . . provide the best service across the country that we know how . . . use the best technology available to administer the Social Security programs . . . emphasize education of the public so that people understand what they can expect from the system.

At Senate Finance Committee hearing
on her confirmation, Washington, May 15/
The Washington Post, 5-16:(A)21.

Gary Hart
United States Senator, D-Colorado

4

When this [Reagan] Administration says there are no hungry people in America, I think it is a moral outrage. When they see 8 million able-bodied Americans out of work and call it full employment, that is a moral outrage . . . We need leaders who demand an end to hunger in our lifetime. We need leaders who challenge us to end illiteracy by the end of this century . . . It won't simply be enough to wait for prosperity to trickle down. We must build a ladder of opportunity that puts education, skills, jobs and business ownership within every American's reach.

At NAACP convention, Baltimore,
July 1/The New York Times, 7-2:9.

Benjamin L. Hooks
Executive director, National Association
for the Advancement of Colored People

5

Following the crowd into drugs and crime is not the way out of misery and lack [for blacks].

WHAT THEY SAID IN 1986

(BENJAMIN L. HOOKS)

Forming gangs and mugging old people and women is not the way out of the ghetto. Premature parenthood and welfare is not the life for a teen-ager. Yet, today, these are basic factors that create single-parent families headed by immature young people, unprepared to make a living, not yet ready to rear children.

The Christian Science Monitor, 11-20:35.

Jesse L. Jackson
Civil-rights leader

1

We cannot be blindly anti-government. The government has made significant interventions in many, many areas for the common good. Without public schools, most Americans would not be educated. Without land-grant colleges, the United States would not have the Number 1 agricultural system in the world. Without Federal transit programs, we would not have an interstate highway system. Without subsidized hospitals, most Americans could not afford decent medical care. And the government has played a significant role in providing a base for many American industries. The defense industries, for example, may be considered private, part of the market, but many of them are almost wholly supported by government contracts . . . But when we shift from the notion of subsidy as something that serves our national interest, to that of welfare, the attitudes suddenly shift from positive to negative. In this country there is a negative predisposition toward the poor. We must learn to see the development of people who are poor as in our national interest, as cost-efficient, as an investment that can bring an enormous return to every American. The government definitely has a big role to play.

Panel discussion,
New York/Harper's, April:36.

2

We must whiten the face of poverty. It's an *American* problem, not a black problem. But the face of poverty in this country is portrayed as a black face, and that reinforces certain attitudes.

I mean, [the late President] John Kennedy holds up a sick black baby in his arms and people say, "Gee, he's a nice guy." He holds up a sick white baby in West Virginia and people say, "We've got to *do* something about this," Of the 34 million people living in poverty in America, 23 million are white. The poor are mostly white and female and young. Most poor people work every day. They're not on welfare; they're changing beds in hospitals and hotels and mopping floors and driving cabs and raising other people's children. And there is no basis for taking a few people who cheat the system as examples, and using them to smear millions of people who by and large work very hard.

Panel discussion,
New York/Harper's, April:39.

John E. Jacob
President, National Urban League

3

America has been intimidated by the [Reagan] Administration to believe that the government need not act to eradicate the misery of the poor and handicapped. Self-help is praised as the remedy, but self-help is no panacea. Americans are accepting the idea that the victims are at fault.

Interview, San Francisco/
The Christian Science Monitor, 7-28:8.

Edward M. Kennedy
United States Senator,
D-Massachusetts

4

[Criticizing President Reagan's statement that those who are hungry in America are hungry because they lack the knowledge of where to go for food assistance]: The President announced today that hunger in this country is caused by ignorance. In a sense, the President is correct—hunger is caused by the ignorance of those who do not see the suffering of millions of Americans . . . This did not happen because millions of people suddenly became ignorant; it happened because they or their parents cannot find work and the safety net was cut away [by the Reagan Administration].

May 21/The Washington Post, 5-22:(A)1.

(EDWARD M. KENNEDY)

1

The failed economic policies and harsh budget cuts that hurt the poor mark this [Reagan] Administration as the most anti-family Administration in modern history.

USA Today, 11-21:(A)12.

Agnes Lattimer
*Medical director, Cook
County Hospital, Chicago*

2

People often refer to care for the poor as free care, but too often we exact the most significant coin of the realm from these patients, and that's their self-respect.

Interview/Ebony, September:48.

Glen C. Loury
*Professor of economics,
Harvard University*

3

Public assistance too often underwrites dependency . . . The new welfare will recognize the obligations of the client, will require a properly conceived workfare that compels welfare recipients to do meaningful work. It will have meaningful support.

*At symposium, Harvard University/
The Christian Science Monitor, 9-8:7.*

George L. Maddox
*Chairman, Council on Aging and
Human Development, Duke University*

4

[Criticizing early retirement]: We've got to rethink how we're going to use a lot of years. Anybody who comes to age 55 thinking "I'm getting out," had better ask the question, "What am I going to do with the next 25 or 35 years of my life?" We can delude ourselves into saying "early retirement" without realizing how long we're talking about. Some thought ought to be given to the implications of this. Not just personal thought—our society needs to do some rethinking about creating new options and teaching people. You find

people busily, desperately looking for something to do that's significant . . . Our public policy is encouraging people to think of aging as associated with decrepitude. The contrary evidence is startling. What we're seeing is more and more people living vigorously, certainly through their 60s, well into their 70s. But public policy is out of kilter with reality.

*Interview/The Christian
Science Monitor, 3-13:30.*

John May
*Roman Catholic Archbishop of
St. Louis; President-elect, National
Conference of Catholic Bishops*

5

[Free enterprise] has been the basis of much of the economic growth of our country. And we [Catholic Bishops] accept all that. But that doesn't mean things can't be better. Look at the failure in this country to provide for the poor people, and then say that the private sector ought to take care of that, and the government has no responsibility for any of that. They can talk about the social programs having failed, but the social programs also succeeded to a great extent. The government has a great responsibility, especially toward the weakest members of our society, who are the poor people.

Interview/USA Today, 11-17:(A)13.

Martha A. McSteen
*Acting Commissioner, Social Security
Administration of the United States*

6

Social Security is intended to provide for only the most basic income needs. It provides a floor or foundation onto which many beneficiaries may build by adding income from private sources, such as individual savings and private pensions.

Nation's Business, July:31.

George Miller
*United States Representative,
D-California*

7

[Saying the Reagan Administration is reappraising its cutbacks in social programs for

(GEORGE MILLER)

children]: There's a realization that the disinvestment in our children is getting to be very expensive, a realization that it is in the investment of resources in children and families at risk that the savings will occur. It is not in the withholding of those services. When we do it right and put in adequate resources, the benefits are overwhelming. The flip side is to pay for the failures. Because the children don't go away.

The Christian Science Monitor, 9-22:29.

Daniel Moynihan
United States Senator, D-New York

1

Poverty has in fact been transformed. In the mid-'60s, poverty was conspicuously a problem of the aged. In the mid-'70s, however, a great crossover took place. We became the first society in history in which the poorest group in the population were children. A solid 20.5 per cent of children under 18 in families. Under 3 years of age the rate was 23 per cent. The two great contemporary initiatives with respect to poverty were President [Richard] Nixon's Family Assistance Plan and President Reagan's recent tax-reform proposal which will take some 6 to 7 million persons out of poverty simply by ceasing to tax them into it. It happens I have been involved in each of these efforts and I remain much impressed by the clarity with which some Republicans at least perceive poverty as a condition of not having enough money. But something more will be needed. Something, frankly, spiritual. These are our children and we're not looking after them right.

At symposium, Harvard University,
Sept. 4/The New York Times, 9-5:14.

Charles Murray
Senior research fellow, Manhattan
Institute for Policy Research

2

Let me tell you why I truly throw my hands up in despair when it comes to employing kids

with real problems who have already reached late adolescence. It's not that job programs in the past failed because they were truncated after two years. Even if we have a sustained effort, here is my prediction: If you start with 100 of the hard-core problem kids, after about six months you will already have lost half of them; after nine months maybe another 15 to 30 per cent. The most depressing aspect of this to me is that I am driven more and more into the very brutal statement that there is nothing we can do for the generation there right now. They've got a lid on their future that we don't know how to lift.

Interview/U.S. News &
World Report, 3-3:22.

3

During the late 1960s and early 1970s, we began a major effort to bring people out of poverty, to educate the uneducated, to employ the unemployable. We have to confront the fact that the effort to help the poor did not have the desired effect. In terms of education, crime, family stability, the lives of poor people have gotten worse since the 1960s, and we have to explain why. During those years we, in effect, changed the rules of the game for poor people. Essentially we said, in a variety of ways: "It's not your fault. If you are not learning in school, it is because the educational system is biased; if you are committing crimes, it is because the environment is poor; if you have a baby that you can't care for, it's because your own upbringing was bad." Having absolved everybody of responsibility, we then said, "[With welfare,] you can get along without holding a job. You can get along if you have a baby but no husband and no income. You can survive without participating in society the way your parents had to." A lot of young people took the bait.

Panel discussion,
New York/Harper's, April:36.

Mary Rose Oakar
United States Representative,
D-Ohio

4

Two-thirds of the elderly poor happen to be

(MARY ROSE OAKAR)

women. To be 70 years old and female is to be alone and poor.

News conference, Washington, May 7/
The Washington Post, 5-8:(A)7.

Thomas P. O'Neill, Jr.
United States Representative,
D-Massachusetts

1

Through the years, our society has accepted a strong role in caring for those who cannot take care of themselves: the sick, the handicapped, the elderly. We have provided a safety net for those who need protection, who cannot, for whatever reason, fend for themselves. But such achievements are rarely recognized today. There are those who speak to our young people and preach the gospel of gloom and doom. They tell how great things were way back when and how bad things are today. They go on to say how much better we would be without government.

Speech, Independence, Mo./
The New York Times, 5-16:27.

Sally Orr
Director of public policy,
Association of Junior Leagues

2

The U.S. is the only industrialized nation that does not guarantee parents—primarily mothers in most countries—time off to be with their [newborn] children. Almost half of American women with children under 1 year old are now in the work force, and yet currently only about 40 per cent of Americans receive some type of benefit at childbirth. The legislation we support would require employers with 15 or more employees to provide both mothers and fathers alike with a job-guaranteed leave of up to 18 weeks over a two-year period in connection with the birth or adoption of a child if the worker wants it. Salary payments wouldn't be mandatory during such leave, but any health-insurance coverage would have to be continued . . . I would like to point out that this leave would be

available to all parents, married or single. Furthermore, all people, regardless of parenthood, should recognize that our children are our future. The children of today are going to pay the Social Security for the retirees of the next generation. If we want a strong, healthy nation, we must have strong, healthy families—and that includes taking care of our children.

Interview/U.S. News & World Report, 7-28:63.

William Proxmire
United States Senator, D-Wisconsin

3

My Myth of the Day is that the vast majority of our nation's nearly eight and one-half million unemployed workers are receiving unemployment-compensation benefits. Losing a job is a terrible blow to an individual and his or her family. Even under the most generous unemployment-compensation programs, only a portion of a worker's salary is replaced by unemployment benefits. Even with these benefits, the families of unemployed workers are often forced to postpone all but absolutely necessary spending and may have to go into debt. How much tougher the situation becomes if no unemployment-compensation benefits are available while a worker seeks a new job. This is why we should concern ourselves with the fact that there has been an astonishing decline in the percentage of those unemployed individuals who are collecting unemployment-insurance benefits. If we look at the most recent statistics, we see that only 3.2 million of the unemployed, or a mere 38 per cent, are currently receiving these benefits. Clearly, there are gaping holes in the unemployment-insurance system safety net, and these gaps appear to be growing frighteningly larger.

Before the Senate, Washington,
April 28/The New York Times, 5-1:14.

Ronald Reagan
President of the United States

4

I have never thought that Social Security plays a part in the [Federal] deficit. It doesn't,

207

WHAT THEY SAID IN 1986

(RONALD REAGAN)

because Social Security is supported by its own tax and that tax can't be used for anything else. So it's playing games to pretend that Social Security is a part of a budget and can affect the deficit. As a matter of fact, a previous President put it in the budget only because the bookkeeping in ink would look like the deficit was smaller if you could count as an asset the Social Security tax. Well, I think that's not playing fair with the people, so we've taken it out.

News conference, Washington,
Jan 7/The New York Times, 1-8:6.

1

[Where there is hunger in the U.S.,] you have to determine that that is probably because of a lack of knowledge on the part of the people as to what things are available. Not only is the government doing much in that line, but there has been about a three-times increase in private charity and aid in our country. We're unique in all the world—in 1984, American people voluntarily gave $74-billion to charitable causes in this country; 1985, they gave $79.8-billion. It continues to go up. Much of that is in providing shelters, in providing programs of food, in school lunch programs and so forth. And between those two sectors, I don't believe that there is anyone that is going hungry in America simply by reason of denial or lack of ability to feed them; it is by people not knowing where or how to get this help.

To high-school students, Washington,
May 21/The New York Times, 5-22:1.

Joseph Riley
Mayor of Charleston, S.C.

2

[On urban poverty]: These are national problems, not just because they occur throughout the nation but also because they go far beyond the ability of local governments to respond. We have a national problem that demands a national response, an appropriate and adequate national response . . . We are all seeing more people on the streets because there are not enough safe, de-

cent, affordable housing units to offer them. Our problems clearly go much deeper than a shortage of emergency shelter for "street people." Our problems now encompass working families who simply have no place to go.

News conference, Washington,
Dec. 18/The New York Times, 12-19:15.

Charles S. Robb
Chairman, Democratic (Party)
Leadership Council: Former
Governor of Virginia (D)

3

The real question in social policy is not whether we should spend more or less [on social programs for the poor]. It's whether our social programs clearly convey a sense of mutual and reciprocal obligation. I think we've become accustomed to treating welfare recipients as society's victims—as people who should be indemnified for past injuries but otherwise left alone. Instead, we should view welfare as a social contract that obligates both society and recipients. It's not enough to maintain a safety net. We need also to launch new and carefully targeted social initiatives designed to foster self-help and self-sufficiency. We need to credit recipients with having not just the desire but also the ability to fulfill their obligations as citizens. The benefits and requirements of any new social programs should be crafted in a way that clearly defines those obligations.

Before Federal City Council, Sept. 30/
The Washington Post, 10-1:(A)18.

Pat Robertson
Evangelist

4

Much of welfare is perpetuating, especially in the black community, a sense of dependency, a breakup of families. Something has got to be done to help bring these people to a sense of dignity and a sense of worth. The illiteracy rate in the black community is appalling, and the unemployment rate tracks the illiteracy rate, and over 50 per cent of the births in the black community are to unmarried women. And those things have got to be addressed. It is the churches that could

(PAT ROBERTSON)

take the lead. It is not something government can get involved in.

Interview, Washington/Time, 2-17:66.

John Rother
Director of legislation, American Association of Retired Persons

1

The private sector does some things a lot better than the government. But there are also some things that government does better, and social insurance [Social Security] is a very efficient thing that the government does.

Nation's Business, July:31.

Donna E. Shalala
President, Hunter College

2

There are 14 million children living in poverty in this country today . . . And, because of unjust Federal budget cuts and policies, they are more likely to suffer death and disease, hunger and cold, and abuse or neglect than they were four years ago . . . An article of faith that is at the very foundation of our nation, one that has guided us throughout the centuries and molded our vision of democracy, is in grave danger. I am referring to our faith in a better future . . . Presidents as differing in philosophy as Coolidge, Eisenhower, Nixon, Carter, Roosevelt and Johnson have had that kind of faith. And because they did, they initiated programs and introduced legislation that gave children futures that held promise . . . We can prove that investments in programs for poor children create long-term savings that more than offset short-term costs. The truth is that most of the public programs for children and youth have worked.

Before League of Women Voters Education Fund/The Washington Post, 5-27:(A)20.

David A. Stockman
Former Director, Federal Office of Management and Budget

3

I don't accept the proposition, which is pure liberal ideology, that every time you give someone a dollar in our society, you're helping him. When you give somebody money to milk cows and there's no demand for milk, you're not doing anybody a favor, except getting that guy stuck in a business which is counter-productive and wasteful.

Interview/ USA Today, 4-25:(A)13.

William Julius Wilson
Chairman, department of sociology, University of Chicago

4

Today's ghetto neighborhoods are populated almost exclusively by the most disadvantaged individuals and families, many of whom are dependent on welfare or various forms of illicit earnings. These communities are plagued by massive joblessness, open lawlessness, low-achieving schools. Residents of these areas—whether you're talking about welfare families or aggressive street criminals—have become increasingly isolated from mainstream behavior. In such communities, teachers become frustrated and do not teach; children do not learn. It becomes a vicious cycle. What feeds the cycle is not welfare but the loss of jobs from the inner city and chronic unemployment. You can go to any inner-city hospital ward and predict with near certainty how a baby is going to end up.

Interview/U.S. News & World Report, 3-3:21.

Edward Zigler
Director, Bush Center in Child Development and Social Policy, Yale University

5

Children are in the absolute worst status they have been in during my 30 years of monitoring child and family life in this country. Every day, more and more children are slipping into poverty, which immediately puts them at very high risk for optimal social development.

The Christian Science Monitor, 9-16:25.

Transportation

C. Edward Acker
Chairman, Pan American World Airways

1

Pan American, which has been a survivor and a leader in the past, will continue to be a survivor and a leader in the future. It will continue to carry the United States flag to a very wide part of the world, although not to all of the world as we have sought to do in the past. We believe we should do those things which we have total capability for, rather than trying to stretch ourselves too much.

Interview/USA Today, 2-11:(B)4.

Gerald L. Baliles
Governor of Virginia (D)

2

[On the ground traffic congestion at Washington National Airport]: National Airport has become a national disgrace. They used to sell you life insurance before you got on the plane; now they sell it to you when you get out of the car.

*At rally calling for privatization
of Washington's airports, Washington/
Nation's Business, Aug.:13.*

Morton Beyer
*President, Avmark, Inc., aviation
management and marketing service*

3

[The airline industry] has become an ugly jungle where the big and powerful carriers prey relentlessly on their weaker, smaller competitors. The confusion and uncertainty are overwhelming and the casualty rate from bankruptcies, mergers, acquisitions and outright collapse is appalling.

Los Angeles Times, 11-2:(I)9.

Frank Borman
Chairman, Eastern Airlines

4

Our Number 1 concern is a safe and reliable airline. The cheapest way to run an airline is to run it on time without cancellations, and that

means having excellent maintenance. The FAA, basically, doesn't set standards; it monitors the individual maintenance programs that the carriers develop. We try to make certain that the areas that are really critical are covered as frequently as we think they ought to be.

*Interview/U.S. News &
World Report, 3-31:72.*

Frank H. Cassell
*Professor of industrial relations,
Kellogg School of Business,
Northwestern University*

5

The minute [discount airline] People Express went down the drain [a pending sale of the carrier to Texas Air Corp.], that changed the ballgame. We're now in the fourth stage of deregulation and the [airline] industry is headed back toward an oligopoly. I knew the fares would rise. That's what we predicted all along.

The Christian Science Monitor, 10-3:19.

Donald Engen
*Administrator, Federal
Aviation Administration*

6

[Saying airlines should be honest with passengers about the cause of flight delays]: If the delay was for air traffic . . . [or] for weather, so be it. If the delay was for over-booking, call it an over-booking delay. If . . . luggage didn't show up on time, call it some kind of administrative delay. I do not need an air carrier out there calling over-booking . . . an "air-traffic delay." I know they do.

Interview/USA Today, 12-15:(A)3.

Gerald Greenwald
*Chairman, automotive division,
Chrysler Corporation*

7

By 1990, we will be within reach of the defect-free car. Five years from now, maybe

(GERALD GREENWALD)

eight years from now, we will have come close to having people think about their cars the way we think of television sets today [in terms of trouble-free operation].

The New York Times, 18-19:53.

Stephen D. Hayes
Spokesman for the Federal
Aviation Administration

1

[On airport take-off delays due to increased airline flight schedules]: Our primary responsibility is to insure that air traffic operations are handled safely. Scheduling and delays are obviously something we're concerned about, but they're secondary. We have encouraged airlines to voluntarily spread out their schedules. We continue to encourage them. But the responsibility rests with the airlines.

The New York Times, 9-24:13.

Alfred E. Kahn
Professor of political economy,
Cornell University; Former Chairman,
Civil Aeronautics Board
of the United States

2

Deregulation [of the airline industry] has done most of the things we expect it to do. There has been an enormous increase in the intensity of competition. It has resulted in dramatically reduced fares. It has aligned fares much more closely with costs. It has offered travelers a greater variety of price/quality choices than they had before. It has imposed enormous pressures on companies to increase efficiency, and it has put downward pressure on grossly inflated wages. Small towns have had, on average, an increase in weekly departures.

Interview/USA Today, 10-10:(B)5.

Julian Lapides
Maryland State Senator (D)

3

[Arguing against laws requiring the use of

automobile seat belts]: In a democracy, people have the right to be stupid, if they care to.

USA Today, 3-12:(A)8.

Herbert R. McClure
Deputy Director,
General Accounting Office
of the United States

4

[On the shortage of air-traffic controllers]: The FAA does not have as many fully qualified, experienced controllers at major air-traffic control centers as managers, supervisors and controllers believe are needed . . . Air-traffic activity has reached record levels and is at the point where . . . 70 per cent of the controllers who work radar believe they are handling more traffic during peak periods than they should be handling . . . The FAA faces some difficult obstacles in building toward its staffing goals. First, it takes time for a controller to qualify as an FPL [full performance level]. Second, training attrition is higher than expected. Third, many of the experienced FPLs and supervisors have retired or are approaching retirement.

To House Investigations and Oversight
Subcommittee, Washington, March/
Los Angeles Times, 12-29:(I)15.

Burt Rutan
Aircraft designer

5

When someone demonstrates what can be done [such as the just-completed first round-the-world non-stop flight without refueling accomplished in the experimental *Voyager* aircraft he designed], other people say, "Hey, that's the new level." I think we're going to see, by the turn of the century, cargo planes able to haul big loads half-way around the world without refueling, which is very expensive. And we're going to see reconnaissance drones able to stay at high altitudes for weeks. These planes are going to have 30% to 40% better performance. And they're going to look a lot like the *Voyager*.

Interview, Dec. 23/
Los Angeles Times, 12-24:(I)6.

Richard G. Rutan
Aircraft pilot

1

[On his and Jeana Yeager's just completing, in the experimental aircraft *Voyager,* the first round-the-world non-stop flight without refueling]: This was the last major event of atmospheric flight. That we did it as private citizens says a lot about freedom in America.

Edwards Air Force Base, Calif.,
Dec. 23/The New York Times, 12-24:1.

Martin Shugrue
Vice chairman,
Pan American World Airways

2

We've been in favor of deregulation [of airlines]. We'd like to be put into the same operating rules as every other U.S. business has—that's the freedom to succeed, and the freedom to fail, and the freedom to put your product where you want it, and the freedom to design it and the freedom to price it. We believe in that.

Interview/USA Today, 5-22:(A)9.

Roger B. Smith
Chairman,
General Motors Corporation

3

[On the increasing number of foreign manufacturers entering the U.S. automobile market]: With many new players now entering the game and building new production facilities on this continent, we're in a deadly game of musical chairs. When the music stops, one or more vehicle manufacturers could be left without a chair, and some of their employees without jobs.

The New York Times,
8-19:2.

Thomas Tripp
Spokesman, Air Transport Institute

4

To the extent that any airline flies in violation of safety regulations, they should have the book thrown at them. But from my perspective, I can almost say that whether the FAA inspects or not is irrelevant. As an airline executive, I am personally responsible, morally, legally, to maintain FAA standards . . . I can't deny that maintenance is one of the elements that comes under pressure [to cut costs]. But balanced against that is the pressure to have an extra reliable fleet of airplanes . . . The only way to make them reliable is to go the extra mile. In a competitive marketplace, you can't take shortcuts if you expect to stay in business.

The Christian Science Monitor,
6-4:24.

Urban Affairs

Henry G. Cisneros
Mayor of San Antonio;
President, National League of Cities

1

This year all of us together face a new problem that none of those who sat in these chairs has faced before. It is a disastrous dismantling of the Federal-local partnership. It is a meat-axe chopping of the domestic obligations of government . . . We must be determined to stand up for what is right in the face of what I can only call disrespect: a disrespect for our cities, disrespect for the people who govern them and disrespect for the people who live in them . . . How else can one account for the fact that since 1980, when urban programs were $69-billion in our nation's budget, today they are $17-billion—a dramatic cut? Yet over the same period of time, the [Federal] deficit has grown from $27-billion to $200-billion. Picture that for a minute: a deficit that has grown from $27- to $200-billion, our [city] programs have gone from $69-billion to $17-billion, and it is we who are blamed for the deficit. It is just not true, and don't you believe it!

At Congressional-City Conference,
Washington, March 10/
The Washington Post, 3-19:(A)18.

2

Three things have kept me politically solid. One is conveying the perception of fairness. I call them as I see them. And if a Hispanic [like himself] wins on a particular question, fine; if an Anglo wins, fine. People can understand that. Second, I have fallen into the role of a broker, arbiter and mediator among factions and forces. My job is to spend an awful lot of time negotiating, bargaining, informing, creating consensus. Third, there has to be a feeling that I'm always trying. I may not succeed on every project, but I'm always trying.

Interview/U.S. News &
World Report, 4-7:32.

W. Wilson Goode
Mayor of Philadelphia

3

As Mayor, I accept responsibility for all the actions of city government: the good which we work so very hard to accomplish, the bad when it touches us, and the tragic when it tears us apart. And when the bad and the tragic touch us and we lose momentum, I, too, must take responsibility to bring about recovery and renewal.

Broadcast address, Philadelphia,
March 9/The New York Times, 3-10:8.

4

I don't think the Reagan Administration has an urban program. The only urban program it has is to dismantle programs that assist urban areas. If there is a program, it's a negative program, not a positive one.

Interview/USA Today, 5-13:(A)11.

Jesse L. Jackson
Civil-rights leader

5

The problem of inner-city people is not innate or congenital. It's the result of social, government and corporate policy. We are divesting in the inner city and investing in the suburbs. Where there's investment, communities flourish. Where there's divestment, communities perish.

Interview/The Christian
Science Monitor, 11-20:33.

Richard D. Lamm
Governor of Colorado (D)

6

[Criticizing the Federal government's planned cuts in aid to cities and states as a budget-balancing measure]: The consequences of Federal mismanagement are being placed on state and local governments. This is buck-passing without the bucks.

Before Colorado Legislature, Denver,
Jan. 9/The Washington Post, 1-10:(A)10.

Ernest Morial
Mayor of New Orleans

1

[Criticizing the planned termination of the Federal government's revenue-sharing program with the cities and states]: Washington: Don't balance your budget on the backs of America's cities, counties, towns and villages. You'll break our backs and the essential services upon which all Americans depend.

At meeting of Mayors, New York,
Jan. 9/The Washington Post, 1-10:(A)11.

Cathy Reynolds
President-elect,
National League of Cities

2

[On the Federal government's attitude toward cities]: Some days, I'd say hostile, and other days I'd just say they kind of ignore us. There seems to be a reluctance on the part of a lot of the officials in Washington to recognize that U.S. cities are really the heart of the nation, and that their constituents live there. We [in the cities] produce 85 per cent of the wealth of the country. Without our economies, there is no national economy. What happens with Federal decisions on things like trade policies and investment policies drastically affects cities. We have been, unfortunately, largely unsuccessful in convincing the folks in Washington that that is the case, or in getting them to listen to those of us who are experts in the cities.

Interview/USA Today, 12-15:(A)13.

Kathy Whitmire
Mayor of Houston

3

People who manage cities don't spend money they don't have; they can balance a budget, and they know the real problems of personnel management to make the city work. That type of philosophy is going to serve us well in state or national government.

U.S. News & World Report,
4-7:31.

PART TWO

International Affairs

Africa

Adebayo Adedeji
Executive Secretary, United Nations
Economic Commission for Africa

1

Africa must demonstrate in every practical way its recognition of the need to bear the burden of its development. It must convince the skeptical and increasingly cynical world of its commitment and determination by tightening its belt and putting in place appropriate austerity measures, as well as by accepting the self-discipline required to achieve an economic turnaround.

The Christian Science Monitor, 5-28:14.

Bolaji Akinyemi
Minister of Foreign Affairs of Nigeria

2

We in Africa are fully aware that the task of [economic] structural transformation will require, on our part, a radical change in development priority. It is obvious that the widespread low level of productivity of the African economies is the fundamental cause of their continued under-development and persistent economic crisis.

At United Nations, New York, May 27/
The New York Times, 5-28:5.

Ibrahim Badamasi Babangida
President of Nigeria

3

I'm here to provide service to the nation. I look forward to the day that the armed forces and I will disengage and the whole system [of government] will be transferred into some kind of political arrangement—a people-oriented political system that everybody understands. We have said that there will be less government in the economic sector . . . What government should do is to create an environment for economic growth. We want to leave behind a legacy of political stability in the country. I want to see Nige-

ria, in the next 20 years, a better place than it was 25 years ago. We will continue to have an important role within the continent of Africa. We want to live in harmony with our neighbors.

Interview/Time, 2-17:45.

Herbert Beukes
South African Ambassador
to the United States

4

[Criticizing proposed U.S. economic sanctions against South Africa to protest that country's apartheid system]: The current American debate over policy toward South Africa can either influence events toward these goals of democracy and justice—or drive South Africa into the *laager* of self-reliance and self-defense in which American influence will be ended for years, if not decades. Sanctions are not the answer, for they are only a means, not an end. The paramount issue today is how to bring about negotiations among the government and all black leaders and organizations to produce a mutually acceptable political framework for democracy in South Africa. My government needs no pressure to enter these negotiations. It has time and time again called for them to begin, has invited all black leaders to come up to the negotiating table and, to evidence its seriousness and intent, has rejected apartheid as the basis for the country's future, and abolished apartheid foundations . . . [The U.S.] seeks to apply the pressure of sanctions against a government which has already stated its commitment to negotiations and political rights for blacks. And, tragically, it prolongs violence by giving no incentive . . . to those who refuse negotiation and to give up their strategy of violence to achieve political ends.

Aug. 1/The Washington Post, 8-20:(A)18.

5

[Saying that, despite progress his country is making in dismantling apartheid, the rest of the world still condemns South Africa and imposes

(HERBERT BEUKES)

economic sanctions]: Our perception, after two years of steady and, in our view, fundamental changes in our country's Constitutional setup and political process [is that], after all that, it has not gained us an ounce or an inch of credit [in the rest of the world]. Instead, we get a kick in the teeth . . . This is not a science laboratory that we're working with. It is not an experiment . . . [or] theoretical exercise. If after a while things don't work out the way that they intended, you can't just take that product and put it away into some kind of archive . . . It's survival stakes we're talking about . . . Democratic values [should be upheld, values] like the right to hold private property, the free-market system, the right to freedom of assembly, free press, freedom of religion and independent judiciary . . . My own feeling is that [continued white support for racial] restrictions that we have at the moment . . . will have less to do with the desire to maintain apartheid than the fear of that kind of black dictatorship that has become the trademark of Africa.

Interview, Washington/The Christian Science Monitor, 9-5:1,36.

Joseph R. Biden, Jr.
United States Senator, D-Delaware

1

[On U.S. policy toward South Africa and its apartheid system]: Damn it, we have favorites in South Africa. The favorites in South Africa are the people who are being repressed by that ugly white regime. We have favorites. Our loyalty is not to South Africa, it's to South Africans. And the South Africans are majority black, and they are being excoriated. It's not to some stupid puppet government over there. It is not to the Afrikaner regime. We have no loyalty to them. We have no loyalty to South Africa. It's to South Africans. And the fact of the matter is . . . it is the leaders of South Africa and their people, black and white, who have the majority responsibility. They must rise to it. Well, they are rising to it. They are rising to it with the only thing left available to deal with that repulsive, repugnant

regime of Afrikaners there. They have begged; they have borrowed; they have crawled; and now they're taking up arms.

At Senate Foreign Relations Committee hearing, Washington, July 23/ The Washington Post, 7-25:(A)17.

2

[Criticizing Reagan Administration policy on apartheid in South Africa, saying it is not tough enough]: I'm ashamed of this country that puts out a policy like this that says nothing, nothing! It says, "Continue the same." We put no timetable on it [for dismantling apartheid]. We make no specific demands. We don't set it down. I'm ashamed that's our policy. That's what I'm ashamed of. I'm ashamed of the lack of moral backbone to this policy. You may be ashamed.

Addressing U.S. Secretary of State George Shultz during Senate Foreign Relations Committee hearing, Washington/Time, 8-4:14.

Allan Boesak
South African anti-apartheid activist; President, World Alliance of Reformed Churches

3

If there is a situation in the world today which justifies armed rebellion by the people, it's [the apartheid system in] South Africa. But you will not hear me say that easily. In the midst of all this, someone's got to be sane enough to remind people of what violence really does. Someone's got to be sane enough to hold onto visions of the things that truly make for peace.

Interview, Washington/ The Washington Post, 6-9:(C)1.

4

[On the apartheid situation in South Africa]: For more than two years now, the South African government has been waging war. Our [black] townships are besieged, the women and the children of our communities terrorized, our people dying. Constantly, down the streets, we wade knee-deep in blood. Our churches have been desecrated, our church services have been disrupted by police and tear gas and dogs and guns.

(ALLAN BOESAK)

Our communities have been threatened and victimized. Many of our people have disappeared. Many of our community leaders have been systematically assassinated.

Interview/USA Today, 6-13:(A)11.

1

[Criticizing the U.S. and other countries for not supporting strong economic sanctions against South Africa to protest that country's apartheid system]: . . . South Africa still has the active support politically, economically, diplomatically, of countries like the United States, Great Britain and West Germany. Today they stand as sole supporters of a regime that has very clearly decided that white privilege and the maintenance of apartheid and oppression in South Africa is worth the price of the death of [black South African] children. If I were American, I would be too ashamed to live.

Before National Association
of Black Journalists, Dallas,
Aug. 14/The New York Times, 8-15:3.

Pieter W. Botha
President of South Africa

2

[On apartheid in South Africa]: We believe that human dignity, life, liberty and property of all must be protected, regardless of color, race, creed or religion. We believe that a democratic system of government, which must accommodate all legitimate political aspirations of all the South African communities, must be negotiated. All South Africans must be placed in a position where they can participate in government through their elected representatives.

Before South African Parliament, Cape Town,
Jan. 31/Los Angeles Times, 2-1:(I)1.

3

In a world where freedom is becoming increasingly rare, our country today is a symbol of the expansion of freedom, of the upholding of freedom of religion and free enterprise, sustained by equal rights before an independent

judiciary. The Republic of South Africa is therefore a powerful bastion against Communist domination and enslavement. Yet the campaign against the Republic of South Africa from abroad [protesting the country's apartheid system] has greatly intensified. Attempts are continually being made to belittle each step forward and to brand all government initiatives [toward ending apartheid] as merely cosmetic, while conditions more appalling than those ostensibly prevailing in South Africa are sanctimoniously tolerated elsewhere.

State of the Union address, Cape Town,
Jan. 31/The New York Times, 2-1:6.

4

We have outgrown the outdated colonial system of paternalism as well as the outdated concept of apartheid, [and] we accept one citizenship for all South Africans, implying equal treatment and opportunities.

State of the Union address, Cape Town,
Jan. 31/The Washington Post, 2-1:(A)1.

5

I do not want sovereignty for whites in South Africa, because that is not politically practical . . . But what I do say is the white's standard of living must be protected; he has a right to bring up a child as he chooses, not to bring his language under threat and his residential areas . . . If these things, if the riches he has collected for himself, if these are taken away from him, then I say we are looking for trouble.

Transcript of talk with leader of Progressive
Federal Party/The Washington Post, 2-20:(A)27.

6

[Defending South Africa's recent raids on African National Congress facilities in three neighboring countries]: The smugglers of terrorist arms into our country and the murderers of innocent people must be hunted down. We will not tolerate terrorists hiding in other countries with the intent to perpetrate crimes against the people in our country . . . I assure the country that we will do it again when the occasion demands . . . We will fight international terrorism in precisely the same way as other Western countries, despite the

WHAT THEY SAID IN 1986

(PIETER W. BOTHA)

sanctimonious protests of that guardian of international terrorist movements, the United Nations.

Before South African Parliament, Cape Town,
May 20/Los Angeles Times, 5-21:(I)1,10.

1

[On the apartheid system in South Africa]: Since 1948, we have changed the colonial system and have given more political, economic and citizenship rights to other population groups. We wanted to share in freedom. The white man is making sacrifices. He is contributing to the upliftment and freedom of other groups. I can't imagine for one moment that, if this process continues, white South Africans will find it necessary to take part in a racial war. But what about the black man? My belief is that most black South Africans, wherever they live, are law-abiding. Most are inclined to accept Christian religious principles. Most of them want work, proper education and training for their children, and better housing. Many have already succeeded in that direction. These people certainly prefer evolutionary processes to racial confrontation.

Interview, Cape Town/
U.S. News & World Report, 5-26:29.

2

[On foreign economic sanctions against his country to protest South Africa's apartheid system]: The world must take note and never forget that we are not a nation of weaklings. We do not desire and we do not seek it but, if we are forced to go it alone, then so be it . . . I do not underestimate the sacrifices and problems that sanctions will bring. I do not think that it will be in our interest, or in that of our neighboring states, or that of our trading partners. But South Africa will not crawl before anyone to prevent it.

Broadcast address to the nation, June 12/
The Washington Post, 6-13:(A)1,26.

3

[On foreign criticism of his government and the apartheid system in South Africa]: A carefully calculated propaganda game is unfolding against us internationally and even internally, es-

pecially with the assistance of some of the media. When "South Africa" and "apartheid" are mentioned, common sense disappears. Then hypocrisy, double standards and a twisted morality come to the fore.

At police parade, Pretoria,
June 20/The New York Times, 6-21:4.

4

[Criticizing other nations for not recognizing his government's progress toward the easing of apartheid]: It would only be reasonable to expect members of the international community, given their own experiences and those of others, to appreciate that we have committed ourselves to something [the elimination of racial discrimination] that has often proved impossible or that, at the very least, has taken centuries to achieve elsewhere. Yet, instead of encouragement and cooperation, we find that Western democracies and totalitarian states alike are neither prepared to acknowledge the sincerity of our efforts nor grant us the opportunity to achieve our goals.

News conference, Pretoria,
July 29/Los Angeles Times, 7-30:(I)6.

5

[Condemning foreign economic sanctions against South Africa to protest his country's apartheid system]: The international campaign against South Africa, especially from the ranks of certain leftist Western leaders and countries, is one of the most extreme forms of political fraud of the 20th century. We are probably no better, but certainly no worse, than the rest of the world . . . We do not desire sanctions, but if we have to suffer sanctions for the sake of maintaining freedom, justice and order, we will survive them. Not only will we survive them, we will emerge stronger on the other side . . . The historical hatred of the Third World and the historical guilt complex of the First World interface in the vendetta against South Africa. The blood of a sacrificial lamb is sought as penance for centuries of injustice. That sacrificial lamb is South Africa and, more specifically, white South Africans.

At National Party congress, Durban, South
Africa, Aug. 12/Los Angeles Times, 8-13:(I)12.

(PIETER W. BOTHA)

1

[South Africa will proceed with orderly reform of the apartheid system,] in contrast to the so-called liberation of violent revolutionaries. In Africa, we have repeatedly seen the consequences of premature liberation without proper preparation and planning. We as South Africans, unlike the former imperial powers, cannot flee from the chaos and misery that may result from so-called liberation.

At National Party congress, Durban, South Africa, Aug. 12/The Washington Post, 8-13:(A)18.

2

[On foreign criticism and economic sanctions against South Africa for its apartheid system]: The obstacles placed before us by the opportunistic and selfish considerations of international organizations and governments must inspire us to greater determination and a national will to overcome. It is ironic and disturbing that all this came about while we were in the very process of moving forward with our reform program and had registered significant further progress in our policies of development and upliftment of the under-developed population groups and areas of our country. Now, suddenly, it is "too little, too late" [according to the country's foreign critics]. The tragedy is that, while we in South Africa have taken strides ahead, compared with other African states, these negative actions by some foreign governments and their local fellow travelers served only to frustrate our attempts to reach our goals. The actions taken against us have been totally counter-productive.

Broadcast address to the nation, Dec. 31/Los Angeles Times, 1-1('87):(I)6.

Roelof F. Botha
Foreign Minister of South Africa

3

[On U.S. economic sanctions against South Africa to protest that country's apartheid system]: [The sanctions have shown to Africa that, in a crisis, the U.S.] for internal domestic political reasons will drop you. The U.S. is going to find out that the signal is going to cause far more damage and harm than they thought when they so gleefully introduced it. You are going to find that in the long run there will be a tendency not to be too closely associated with the West ever again in our history.

News conference, Cape Town, Feb. 6/The New York Times, 2-7:7.

4

As long as we can agree in a suitable way in the protection of minority rights without a racial sting, then it would possibly become unavoidable that in the future you might have a black President of this country. If blacks share in the power of this country, that to me becomes the inevitable result in the future, as long as the minorities feel safe.

News conference, Cape Town, Feb. 6/ Los Angeles Times, 2-7:(I)11.

5

[On apartheid in South Africa]: We have shown we are prepared to reform this country. We have desegregated sports with great success. The number of [racially] mixed trade unions is growing. We have removed the offensive racial provisions in our immigration laws. We have declared parity of education as an objective, and it will cost us billions and billions to improve black schools, improve the quality of teacher education and train teachers. We have removed the prohibition on mixed marriages. We are in the process of dismantling further forms of apartheid. We have declared our readiness to remove apartheid, to share power up to the highest level of government. We did not undertake these changes to please the outside world. We undertook these reform measures because we believed that we must extend democracy. It is one of the most tragic phenomena of history. At a time when this government is extending democracy and can demonstrate that we took steps in one year that the U.S. could not take in 20 years, not only do we get no credit for it, not only do you Americans have no perspective of history as far as this is concerned, not only have you forgotten your own trauma, hesitance and difficulties in persuading your people to accept a new order of civil rights, you punish us for doing what you

(ROELOF F. BOTHA)

did, but in less time than you took to do it.

Interview, Cape Town/Time, 6-9:38.

1

[On those foreign countries that propose economic sanctions as a way to end South Africa's apartheid system]: They made a fatal error. They see economic measures as a peaceful way to effect change, while we see it as a violent measure. How could the purposeful creation of unemployment be a peaceful measure?

June 12/Los Angeles Times, 6-13:(I)17.

2

[On U.S. President Reagan's recent speech in which he condemned both South Africa's apartheid system and the African National Congress, and in which he called for no foreign economic sanctions against South Africa]: The South African government welcomes President Reagan's stand that it is under no compulsion to negotiate the future of the country with an organization [the ANC] that proposes a Communist regime and that uses terrorism to bring this about. It is encouraging that President Reagan acknowledges the dramatic changes brought about under the leadership of [South African] President [Pieter] Botha. It is also encouraging that President Reagan underlines the fact that South Africa's problems are complex and that solutions should not be transplanted from outside.

July 22/Los Angeles Times, 7-23:(I)9.

3

[Criticizing the increasing foreign economic sanctions against South Africa to protest his country's apartheid system]: Our options are clear. Either we capitulate under pressure only to be confronted with more pressure until we are destroyed . . . or we say, "So far and no further." And this is what the South African government is saying. So, all right, do what you like . . . We are convinced our people are prepared to make the sacrifice. It does not matter whether it takes 10 years, 20 years, 30 years or more, but eventually it will be South Africans who decide around a conference table the consti-

tutional structures for this country. We are prepared to pay the price for our ideals . . . We are not going to take this lying down. There will be ways and means to circumvent some of the sanctions. But even if we cannot, we are prepared to accept a lowering in our standards of living. We are prepared to make a sacrifice for what we believe in . . . We are told this [sanctions] action was taken to force us to end, dismantle, remove apartheid. The South African government is committed to do that and has, in fact, over the past few months repealed or amended dozens of laws, proclamations and regulations discriminating on the basis of race.

News conference, Pretoria,
Aug. 5/Los Angeles Times, 8-6:(I)10.

4

[Saying he has advised several U.S. Senators that if they override U.S. President Reagan's veto of harsh economic sanctions against his country, South Africa will not buy American grain]: I informed them that, if the Senate should reverse President Reagan's veto and legalize the ban on the export of South African agricultural products [as a way to protest South Africa's apartheid system] . . . then South Africa would purchase no grain from the United States. [And] it would not only be South Africa that would not buy any grain from the United States. All its neighbors which are dependent on the South African transport system will also no longer be able to purchase grain from the United States . . . If South African farmers can no longer sell this product on the U.S. market, the South African government will have no choice but to prohibit the purchase of American grain.

Pretoria, Oct. 1/
Los Angeles Times, 10-2:(I)1.

5

[Criticizing the U.S. Senate for overriding U.S. President Reagan's veto of economic sanctions against South Africa to protest that country's apartheid system]: The decision of the Senate must make it clear to all South Africans that other countries cannot solve our problems. It remains our responsibility. It is also clear the decision was taken without considering our

(ROELOF F. BOTHA)

[apartheid] reform program and that no reason or argument could have stemmed this emotional tide. I hope from my side that they would now at least leave us alone so that South Africans, without outside intervention, could give attention to solving their problems.

News conference, Johannesburg,
Oct. 2/The New York Times, 10-3:6.

George Bush
Vice President of the United States

1

The President [Reagan] and I have repeatedly stated our abhorrence to apartheid in South Africa. On behalf of the American people here today . . . I call again for the end to apartheid. To the government of South Africa, I say here today, it's time to take bold, dramatic steps to demonstrate your own commitment to reform. The time for delay is past.

At ecumenical service for the late U.S.
civil-rights leader Martin Luther King, Jr.,
Atlanta, Jan. 20/Los Angeles Times, 1-21:(I)16.

2

[On why the U.S. Reagan Administration does not advocate economic sanctions against South Africa to protest that country's apartheid system]: Because we don't think sanctions are going to solve the problem of apartheid. We believe that if you disengage, and essentially that's what a lot of this is going to be about, you lose your ability to shape things. One of the things that troubles me is the allegation that if you're not for sanctions, that means you're for apartheid. That is absolutely unfair and ridiculous. We're dealing in a highly emotional climate about a subject that is very, very important to us, and that is the elimination of apartheid. But we just simply don't subscribe to the view that mandatory, across-the-board sanctions are the way to go about it . . . I happen to think, when you are engaged and you are talking, it's better. I don't think it is fair or correct to assign some kind of racist motive to a President [Reagan] because he disagrees with you on sanctions.

Interview/USA Today, 10-2:(A)9.

Gatsha Buthelezi
Chief Minister of KwaZulu
(black South African homeland);
Leader, South African Zulu people

3

The violence that is now inflicted on black people by other black people in South Africa has all the makings of a terrible social tragedy. It poses the immediate threat of a black civil war and, what is worse, it may preclude the establishment of a genuine, Western-style South African democracy in the foreseeable future . . . South Africa will be destroyed by black politicians unless they can gather together all of the positive forces for change without destroying the fabric of human decency. In the end, only those organizations that work to establish a civilized Western-style democracy with a market economy can save South Africa from both apartheid and the impending crisis. I emphasize a market economy and free enterprise because I do not see any other system devised by human beings that is such a potent force for development. In a country where more than half the population is 15 years old or younger, we desperately need the jobs that only free enterprise can create. Oliver Tambo, head of the ANC mission-in-exile, said in a recent interview that he is going to nationalize industries in South Africa [if his organization takes control of the country], and that we must all look forward to a socialist future. He wouldn't mind ruining the economy; he says that we will have to build on the ruins. The major obstacle to the liberation of South Africa is divisiveness among black peoples. And what the West must understand is that the current struggle must be directed not only at eradicating apartheid, but also at replacing it with a free and open society.

At Manhattan Institute for Policy Research,
New York/The Wall Street Journal, 1-28:28.

4

[Criticizing South African President Pieter Botha's stand on apartheid]: This man has got his head so deeply buried in the sand that you will have to recognize him by the shape of his toes.

Before KwaZulu Parliament, Ulundi,
April 7/The New York Times, 4-9:3.

223

WHAT THEY SAID IN 1986

(GATSHA BUTHELEZI)

1

[On the apartheid system in South Africa]: We must recognize that a solution to our problems, a political system for the future, must be based on compromise. We tell that to whites all the time. They cannot maintain their monopoly on political power and expect to live in peace, but blacks should be prepared to compromise, too. One-man, one-vote is not worth destroying ourselves and our country for when we can work out a compromise. I am not abandoning that ideal and all that it means, but I don't want to see our liberation postponed and the country torn apart to attain it. No, the time has come to talk, to negotiate, to compromise, to reconcile . . . For someone in whose veins courses the blood of warriors who fought the English and the Afrikaners, whose people staged the last armed struggle against white rule in this country, it is not easy to preach non-violence and negotiation. But I recognize that [South African President Pieter] Botha's defense forces cannot now be challenged . . . and that most of the casualties of an armed struggle today would be black . . . Besides . . . I am now at last convinced that there is a groundswell of white demand for the normalization of South Africa as a modern, Western-style industrial democracy. I do not fear my white compatriots. They are Africans, too, and have a God-given right to remain here.

Interview/
Los Angeles Times, 8-11:(I)1,10.

Fidel Castro
President of Cuba

2

Angola, whose sovereignty we have always respected and will continue to respect in absolute faith, may decide at any time if it needs our military there or not. What I have just expressed is simply our readiness to keep [Cuban] troops in Angola as long as apartheid exists in South Africa.

At meeting of non-aligned nations,
Harare, Zimbabwe, Sept. 2/
The Washington Post, 9-3:(A)13.

Alan Cranston
United States Senator,
D-California

3

[Calling for the withdrawal of all U.S. commercial interests in South Africa to protest that country's apartheid system]: In confronting the evil of apartheid, half-way measures are not acceptable. We wouldn't profit from Nazism; we shouldn't profit from racism.

The Washington Post, 8-16:(A)6.

Chester A. Crocker
Assistant Secretary for African Affairs,
Department of State of the United States

4

[Rejecting economic sanctions against South Africa to protest that nation's apartheid system]: We don't seek to wage economic war on South Africa and its people. We don't think reform can flourish in a climate of economic decline and deterioration . . .

News conference, Johannesburg, Jan. 14/
The Washington Post, 1-15:(A)7.

5

[Criticizing the state of emergency declared by South Africa because of anti-apartheid violence there]: We think that what the South African government has done in recent weeks is to shoot itself in both feet. [The emergency restrictions] simply get in the way of any dialogue and polarize the situation further. These measures of repression, which is all that they are, will not address the basic grievances and the basic problems. What they will do is to put a buffer between our eyes and what is going on in the black townships. It doesn't really fool anybody.

Broadcast interview/
"This Week with David Brinkley," ABC-TV, 6-22.

6

[On proposals for foreign economic sanctions against South Africa to protest that country's apartheid system]: We never said that pressures—some call them sanctions—are, ipso facto, to be ruled out. The question is what is the target, what are you trying to accomplish [with sanctions],

(CHESTER A. CROCKER)

what are the consequences of your action? . . . one could say there is a mood of siege politics [in South Africa today] which de-emphasizes the external factor and strikes at least the apparent posture of being ready to go it alone and suffer the consequences. Our influence is at the margins, but it is there and we are determined to use it.

At Overseas Writers Club, Washington,
July 10/The New York Times, 7-11:6.

Sam de Beer
Deputy Minister of
National Education of South Africa

1

I see it of the utmost importance that we succeed in educating our black people. We need them, and I think it is the only way of working out a peaceful future . . . We are working toward a situation where all population groups will receive the same education, and we are committed to this.

Cape Town, South Africa/
Los Angeles Times, 1-29:(I)18.

F. W. de Klerk
Minister of National
Education of South Africa

2

[On South Africa's apartheid system]: I am not against people getting to know each other. I am not against interaction by people, including youth, of various population groups . . . But the solution of South Africa's problems does not lie in integrated education.

Feb. 4/Los Angeles Times, 2-5:(I)6.

Dennis de la Cruz
Member of South African Parliament

3

[On South Africa's apartheid system]: Just what is the difference between the members of the [ruling] National Party, those racists in the Conservative Party and our supposed friends of the Progressive Federal Party? The answer, I

suppose, is that a black man is quite welcome as long as he doesn't move in next door.

Debate in House of Representatives,
Cape Town, Feb. 4/Los Angeles Times, 2-5:(I)7.

Samuel K. Doe
Chief of State of Liberia

4

I just cannot understand why so many African countries condemn the United States with one hand while reaching out for U.S. aid with the other.

At meeting of non-aligned nations, Harare,
Zimbabwe, Sept. 5/The New York Times, 9-6:3.

Colin Eglin
Leader, Progressive Federal
Party of South Africa

5

[Criticizing South Africa's recent raids on African National Congress facilities in three neighboring countries]: Any short-term advantage the government may have achieved in the security field will undoubtedly be offset by the damage it will have done to South Africa in the field of international relations. These raids, whatever they were intended to achieve, will take South Africa yet another step down the road of violence and counter-violence along which we have been moving at gathering speed. The government has stated it wants to get the process of [black-white] negotiation going in South Africa. Does it really think the raids will help? I fear they will not.

Before South African Parliament, Cape
Town, May 20/Los Angeles Times, 5-21:(I)10.

6

[Criticizing foreign sanctions against South Africa and the pull-out of U.S. companies which are being imposed to protest South Africa's apartheid system]: I don't believe that coercive pressure from outside is going to speed up the process of reform. Weakening the economic muscle that blacks have achieved and driving whites into the *laager* is not a recipe for positive change. The pass laws were not changed because

(COLIN EGLIN)

of Uncle Sam. Home ownership for blacks didn't happen because of [Britain's Foreign Secretary] Geoffrey Howe. These are the result of the urbanization of the black population. The thrust for change has been economic . . . The time has come for the West to spell out its alternatives to apartheid. It is no longer enough to say you are anti-apartheid. Marxists can be anti-apartheid. Fascists can be anti-apartheid. Power-seeking politicians can be anti-apartheid. Now it's time to give that opposition a positive form. And I would assume that America and Europe believe in participatory democracy, civil liberties, the rule of law.

Interview, New York, Nov. 11/
The New York Times, 11-12:11.

Elisio de Figueiredo
Angolan Ambassador to
the United Nations

1

[On Jonas Savimbi's rebels who are trying to overthrow the government of Angola]: Savimbi's UNITA consists of no more than a band of mercenaries. Savimbi himself is a traitor, a bandit, and South Africa's stooge, whose claims to represent the Angolan people are spurious.

Interview, United Nations, New York/
The Christian Science Monitor, 1-31:9.

Malcolm Fraser
Former Co-Chairman, Commonwealth
Eminent Persons Group on South Africa;
Former Prime Minister of Australia

2

[On South Africa's apartheid problem]: The choices before the West are very stark now. If the major Western nations do not take dramatic action against the South African government by the end of this year, I would tell businessmen that if they can get out even 20 cents on the dollar, they should get out. Because if they wait until the black government takes over in eight to 10 years, they won't get anything. If the black leadership doesn't receive very obvious and overt

support from Western governments, particularly Britain, the United States and West Germany, as South Africa's largest trading partners, they'll decide they have no choice but to fight for it, and that will mean hundreds, thousands, even millions killed.

Interview, Beaver Creek,
Colo./The New York Times, 6-23:4.

William H. Gray III
United States Representative,
D-Pennsylvania

3

[Calling for U.S. economic sanctions against South Africa to protest that country's apartheid system]: We leave [South Africa] with the commitment that financing racist policies with American dollars is wrong. Our country has walked through the fires of racism itself, and we must not allow American dollars to fuel racial conflict anywhere else in the world.

Johannesburg, Jan. 10/
Los Angeles Times, 1-11:(I)9.

4

[Criticizing U.S. President Reagan's speech in which he reconfirmed his objections to American economic sanctions against South Africa to protest that nation's apartheid system]: Today, President Reagan declared the United States and Great Britain [whose Prime Minister Margaret Thatcher also is against sanctions] co-guarantors of apartheid. By joining Mrs. Thatcher in opposing economic sanctions, the President protects Pretoria from the one weapon it fears most. The President failed to recognize what the American public, the Congress and the world community have known for a long time—the [Reagan] Administration's policies in South Africa have failed . . . Today the President sent a message to South Africa. To the racist [minority] regime of Pretoria he said, "We are your friends, don't cut our friendship off. We want your minerals. We want to work with you and continue our investments and loans." Then the President said to the 28 million [black] majority, whose rights have been denied, whose lives are

(WILLIAM H. GRAY III)

being lost and [to] whom justice is being denied, "Maintain your hope, but do nothing to end that oppression." Is this the message of America? Have we not learned from Nuremburg what will happen in Johannesburg? And why the Western democracies must raise the cost and totally disassociate from apartheid if we are to accomplish our goals?

Broadcast address to the nation,
Washington, July 22/
The New York Times, 7-23:7.

Denis Healey
Foreign-policy spokesman,
Labor Party of Britain

1

[Criticizing British Prime Minister Margaret Thatcher for opposing foreign economic sanctions against South Africa to protest that country's apartheid system]: Can you [Thatcher] not see that on South Africa, as on so many issues closer to home, your total incapacity to understand how the victims of society feel about their predicament makes you unfit for office?

In the House of Commons,
London, June 17/
The New York Times, 6-18:6.

Jesse Helms
United States Senator,
R-North Carolina

2

[Criticizing the U.S. Senate vote for economic sanctions against South Africa to protest that country's apartheid system]: Here we go again, kicking a friend in the teeth because they aren't acting like we want them to. This issue has nothing to do with Africa. It has to do with domestic politics in the United States. If and when Africa falls into the clutches of Communists—and I'm talking about the continent of Africa—I can tell my grandchildren, "Well, I tried" [by voting no on sanctions].

Washington, Aug. 1/
The Washington Post, 8-2:(A)15.

Geoffrey Howe
Foreign Secretary
of the United Kingdom

3

[Criticizing proposed foreign economic sanctions against South Africa to protest that country's apartheid system]: Britain remains opposed to comprehensive economic boycotts because they do not work. Our purpose must be to bring down apartheid and not the South African economy.

To journalists, Luxembourg/
The Christian Science Monitor, 6-18:9.

4

[On the clamor for South Africa to abandon its apartheid system]: After 25 years, the wind of change in Africa is shaking its southern part to its roots. The question is not whether, but how far and how fast will South Africa change. In peace—or in deepening violence . . . To discover as a conciliator that my mission [to South Africa] is viewed [by South African blacks] with mingled doubt, suspicion and even hostility does not discourage me. If it were not so, there would be no problems between those who want more change and those who resist it. All I can say, to every side, is that talking can solve many problems, however difficult, and violence very few.

Pretoria, South Africa,
July 23/Los Angeles
Times, 7-24:(I)15.

5

[On the apartheid situation in South Africa]: What is needed is that the South African government should agree to release [black leader] Nelson Mandela and other political prisoners, to un-ban the African National Congress and other political parties and to enter into peaceful dialogue—against a matching commitment from the ANC to call a halt to violence and to enter into peaceful dialogue as well. In short, each side needs to make an offer that the other can't refuse.

News conference,
Pretoria, July 29/
Los Angeles Times, 7-30:(I)1.

227

WHAT THEY SAID IN 1986

Leabua Jonathan
Prime Minister of Lesotho

1

[On South Africa's economic blockade of his country]: It is a full economic siege, a complete blockade, like the one that existed in Berlin. I am surprised that Britain and America, to whom I have spoken, have not come to my assistance because they did go to Berlin . . . They [South Africa] have infiltrated all the echelons of administration in this country—the chiefs, civil servants, security forces, people in the village—with the sole purpose of trying to get me out of power. Somebody in Pretoria does not like me.

News conference, Maseru, Lesotho,
Jan. 19/The New York Times, 1-20:6.

Kenneth D. Kaunda
President of Zambia

2

[Criticizing U.S. support for rebels fighting the government of Angola and its support for South Africa which has also been involved in fighting in Angola]: I think it is appalling that the great American people are led by their President [Reagan] to support a rebellion in a country that is fully independent and internationally recognized . . . The U.S. has now taken sides with a country [South Africa] that is destabilizing all of us in this region. It is joining in that destabilization.

Interview, Lusaka, Zambia/
The Washington Post, 3-14:(A)31.

3

[On South Africa's apartheid system]: When we had discussions with [South African] President [Pieter] Botha, my countrymen and I were called all sorts of names by radicals. Yet I saw sense in that meeting. At the time, I said to him: "Mr. President, you tell me you are called a moderate in your party. I can assure you that if you don't deal with [ANC leaders] Oliver Tambo and Nelson Mandela, they, too, will be called moderates very soon. While you are pushed by right-wingers, they have left-wingers pushing them, leftists who are saying enough is enough. So can't you find a way to release Mr. Mandela? If you release him, let Oliver Tambo come back, and [with him] form a nationalist movement for all

South Africans. You will carry the majority of the people in the middle. Those on the left will be hounding Nelson Mandela and Oliver Tambo, and those on the right will be hounding you. Can you find a way of creating this big movement? You will have many blacks following you, many whites following you, many colored people following you. Once you have that support from the middle, you will be home and dry. But the only way you can do that is by your government talking to the ANC without conditions."

Interview/The Wall Street Journal, 6-27:26.

4

[Calling on Britain to institute economic sanctions against South Africa to protest that country's apartheid system]: We call upon Britain to lead this war against Nazism in its new form in South Africa. [Failure to impose sanctions will result in a] holocaust which is unprecedented, and racial hatred that is going to generate in this part of the world is also unprecedented.

Lusaka, Zambia, July 9/
Los Angeles Times, 7-10:(I)12.

5

[Criticizing the apartheid system in South Africa as well as the U.S. and British stands against foreign economic sanctions to force South Africa to abandon apartheid]: I see the whole avalanche running down the hill. I am very pessimistic. We can no longer talk about peaceful resolution, just bloodshed . . . this is the problem with the [U.S.] Reagan and [British] Thatcher Administrations: they still believe the racists [in South Africa] will negotiate. They resist sanctions. The crunch is here. The political volcano is boiling hot. It is erupting now. Lava will cover the entire region, and hundreds of thousands will die.

Interview, Lusaka, Zambia/
The Christian Science Monitor, 7-28:9.

Edward M. Kennedy
United States Senator,
D-Massachusetts

6

[Calling for U.S. economic sanctions against South Africa to protest that country's apartheid

(EDWARD M. KENNEDY)

system]: I deeply regret that Congress did not act last year [to impose sanctions]. We cannot let another year go by. The [no-sanctions] policy of the [U.S. Regan] Administration is a disgrace and an embarrassment. The Congress must act now to put the United States back on the side of history . . . The United States of America has become the last best friend of apartheid.

At Senate subcommittee hearing, Washington,
July 15/The New York Times, 7-16:4.

Alan L. Keyes

Assistant Secretary for International
Organizations, Department of State
of the United States

1

[Arguing against foreign economic sanctions on South Africa to protest that country's apartheid system]: It is not enough that we seek to destroy apartheid, unless in the process we see and help to build the foundations for a South Africa that is just, democratic and free. Clearly, it is impossible if we allow the reality of apartheid to blind us to the complex reality that is South Africa itself. In South Africa the injustice is not simply racism. It is the arbitrary domination of one faction of the society, skillfully employing racism to keep all its other elements in check . . . Justice, therefore, is not simple majority rule. As an American, especially a black American, nothing is more evident to me than this oft-neglected truth.

Before National Urban League, San Francisco/
The Christian Science Monitor, 7-25:5.

Lane Kirkland

President, American Federation of Labor-
Congress of Industrial Organizations

2

[Calling for U.S. economic sanctions against South Africa to protest that country's apartheid system]: We have supported this legislation and will continue to do so until it is enacted. If anything, the need for U.S. action is greater than ever . . . I get quite fed up with the hypocrisy of

the notion that the issue is [black] hardship occasioned by sanctions. It ought to be clear that it is not sanctions that cause the hardship—it is apartheid that causes the hardship.

News conference, Johannesburg, July 20/
Los Angeles Times, 7-21:(I)1,9.

Jeane J. Kirkpatrick

Former United States Ambassador/
Permanent Representative to
the United Nations

3

[On Angolan UNITA rebel leader Jonas Savimbi]: Linguist, philosopher, poet, politician, warrior . . . Savimbi has admirers the world over, and I have long been one of them. [He is] one of the few authentic heroes of our time, [and the U.S. should give] real assistance [to Savimbi in his fight against the Angolan government]. Real assistance means real weapons. Real helicopters . . . real ground-to-air missiles . . . Whether that help is overt or covert is a bureaucratic detail.

At Conservative Political Action
Conference, Washington, Jan. 31/
The Washington Post, 2-3:(B)3.

Tom Lodge

Political scientist,
University of Witwatersrand
(South Africa)

4

[On the African National Congress' attacks in South Africa as part of its fight against that country's apartheid system]: Most of the ANC's armed actions are calculated primarily for psychological impact on both whites and blacks. Among blacks, the attacks are intended to enhance the ANC's standing as the organization that can bring them liberation, and they do seem to encourage even greater resistance, particularly among the youths in the townships. Among whites, the bomb explosions and other urban terrorism appear intended to spread the conflict out of the townships and into the cities . . . Such attacks as we have seen so far are not aimed at defeating the government militarily, though some

(TOM LODGE)

people here do mistake them for that and as a result conclude that the ANC's armed struggle can never succeed. Instead, they should be seen as part of a broader ANC strategy intended over some time to increase all-around pressure on the regime to the point where it can no longer hold on.

Los Angeles Times, 7-14:(I)8.

Richard G. Lugar
United States Senator, R-Indiana

1

[Calling on U.S. President Reagan not to veto legislation that would increase economic sanctions against South Africa to protest that country's apartheid system]: We really need to be on the right side of history on this issue. It's an opportunity that we really can't miss historically . . . If the bill is vetoed and [the veto] is sustained, the United States will be seen as an ally of the [South African President Pieter] Botha government, no matter how much we protest. We will be seen as the apologist of apartheid.

To reporters, Washington, Sept. 23/
Los Angeles Times, 9-24:(I)5.

Sadiq Mahdi
Prime Minister of Sudan

2

We [Sudan] support the continuation of good relations with Libya. At the same time, we believe the United States to be a superpower with which cooperation is a necessity. The important thing is that the interest of our country and our foreign policy should not have its headquarters in either Washington or Tripoli.

Interview/The Washington Post, 4-24:(A)35.

3

The tendency in America is to feel that anyone who does not play to the American tune must be dangerous. I have been telling them [U.S. officials] that no one governing Sudan with any credibility can sustain relations with America and not take into account his internal constituency.

Interview/The Washington Post, 12-2:(A)24.

Magnus Malan
Minister of Defense of South Africa

4

[Criticizing proposed foreign economic sanctions against South Africa to protest that country's apartheid system]: We're not cheap and we have no intention of surrendering. Those of Africa who chant loudest in the chorus for sanctions and condemnations should take note: We have not even started to use our muscle and capabilities . . . The Western world, with its demands about [jailed anti-apartheid activist Nelson] Mandela, about talks with the ANC and the unbanning of the ANC, should also note: We will not be manipulated by words which clothe the devil in the cloak of an angel.

At National Party convention,
Durban, South Africa, Aug. 13/
The Washington Post, 8-14:(A)16.

Winnie Mandela
South African anti-apartheid activist

5

[Calling on black South African gold and diamond miners to stop digging as a way to protest apartheid]: The moment you stop digging their [the government's] gold, their diamonds, that's the moment we shall be free. You dig the wealth—and you hold that golden key to our liberation . . . There may very well be a time when your [anti-apartheid] leaders will ask you for greater sacrifices than a one-day strike, because you are digging the wealth that lets the police sit on those Casspirs [armored police vehicles] and continue our oppression. The time for speeches that land on deaf ears in Pretoria has come to an end . . . The time for talking has gone.

Evander, South Africa/
Los Angeles Times, 9-25:(I)6.

Mengistu Haile Mariam
Chief of State of Ethiopia

6

[On U.S. antagonism toward his government]: Unfortunately, the United States government, out of its dislike of the social economic system we

(MENGISTU HAILE MARIAM)

have opted for ourselves to free ourselves from under-development, and also out of sheer arrogance, has taken this unfriendly stance against us.

News conference, Addis Ababa,
May 19/The New York Times, 5-22:8.

1

We are now on the threshold of the formation of the People's Democratic Republic of Ethiopia. The Constitution was drafted by representatives of the people themselves. It has been submitted to all Ethiopian citizens, including those living abroad, and it will be promulgated after it is put to a referendum. Such democratic participation is unparalleled in the history of Ethiopia. Once the Constitution assumes its final shape, Ethiopia will never again be ruled by the personal absolutism of any one individual or a handful of individuals. There will be no more discrimination according to sex, religion or ethnic origin, no more nepotism or exploitation.

Interview, Addis Ababa/Time, 8-4:34.

Robert S. McNamara
Former President, International Bank for
Reconstruction and Development (World Bank)

2

No set of statistics, however dramatic, can convey the level of human misery that exists and is increasing throughout the [African] continent. The most helpless victims are the children. It is they who reflect most quickly in physical terms the fact that tens of millions of human beings are living, literally, on the margins of life . . . The reality is that the average African, who depends critically on agriculture for a living, is poorer today than he was in 1970. If the problems of agriculture are not addressed more effectively, he will be poorer in 1990 than he was at the time his country became independent. And what is even more ominous, the disastrous famines that are currently restricted to years of drought and to only a few countries will become everyday occurrences affecting a majority of the sub-Saharan nations.

The New York Times, 5-27:4.

3

In sub-Saharan Africa as a whole, with the population of something on the order of 350 million people, food-production growth rates—on average, per capita—have been *negative* for 10 years. Now, 10 years ago malnutrition existed, and if you have had a negative per-capita food-production rate since that time, then there's less food per capita today than there was 10 years ago.

Interview, New York/
The Christian Science Monitor, 12-16:21.

Brian Mulroney
Prime Minister of Canada

4

[Supporting foreign economic sanctions against South Africa to protest that country's apartheid system]: The movement to end apartheid is irreversible. It's just a matter of when it takes place. The motives are just as irresistible as the motives that brought about American independence, and no less noble. Can you imagine if 4 million blacks controlled 25 million whites in Canada? What do you think the reaction will be? . . . So why should our reaction be any different simply because it's taking place a world away? . . . You can be absolutely certain that when the history of this day is written, what is going to count is that they achieved freedom and what countries assisted in the process. We can't forget the long sweep of history. I spent a weekend watching the United States celebrate [the Statue of] Liberty. Someday the people of South Africa are going to be organizing such a celebration. They will remember who helped them.

Interview, Ottawa,
Canada/Newsweek, 8-18:25.

Yoweri Museveni
President of Uganda

5

No regime has the right to kill any citizen of Uganda. No regime has got a right to beat a citizen of Uganda. As for the killing, this is absolutely out. You [soldiers] kill a citizen, we kill you. Any individual, any group of persons who

WHAT THEY SAID IN 1986

threaten the security of our people should be smashed without mercy. The people should die only from natural causes beyond our control, but not from fellow human beings.

Inaugural address, Kampala, Jan. 29/
The Washington Post, 1-30:(A)29.

1

[Criticizing African leaders for condemning apartheid in South Africa but keeping silent on black-on-black atrocities elsewhere in Africa]: Tyranny is color-blind and should be no less reprehensible when it is perpetrated by one of our own kind. The idea that one should not interfere in the internal affairs of others should not be used as a cloak to shield genocide.

Before Organization of African Unity,
Addis Ababa, Ethiopia, July 29/
The New York Times, 7-30:4.

Beyers Naude
General secretary, South
African Council of Churches

2

[Criticizing what he says are insufficient reforms in the apartheid system by the South African government]: From its point of view, the government has come an enormous way [in eliminating aspects of apartheid]. But power-sharing [with blacks], as the government understands it, means not upsetting the apple cart of Afrikaner political dominance.

The Christian Science Monitor, 6-12:17.

Babacar N'Diaye
President, African
Development Bank

3

Africa in the '80s is not taking account, as far as economics is concerned, of ideology. We are pragmatists. Countries that are on the moderate left, or even left-left, have recognized that too much centralization is a burden on the economy.

Interview, New York/
The New York Times, 6-3:30.

Louis Nel
Deputy Minister of
Information of South Africa

4

We have a state of emergency in South Africa for very good reason—we are experiencing a revolutionary onslaught [by those trying to overthrow the government as a means of ending apartheid]. This government is determined to bring this revolutionary onslaught to an end . . . In the process, certain limitations have been put on press reporting in and from South Africa.

To newspaper editors, Pretoria, June 25/
Los Angeles Times, 6-26:(I)5.

5

[On the banned African National Congress]: The ANC, supported by the South African Communist Party, is responsible for these horrendous deeds of terror, and yet the ANC is not condemned by the outside world. The most glaring example of double standards by the Western world is, on the one hand, to try to eradicate terrorism world-wide, and, on the other, aiding and abetting those responsible for blatantly brutal acts of terror in South Africa. The succor and the tacit support given to the perpetrators of these murders, friends of [U.S. Senator] Ted Kennedy, [Australian Prime Minister Bob] Hawkes and [U.S. Congressman] Bill Gray, again demonstrate the double standards applied to South Africa.

News conference, Pretoria, Aug. 18/
The New York Times, 8-19:4.

Carl F. Noffke
Director, American Studies Institute,
Rand Afrikaans University (South Africa)

6

[On U.S. President Reagan's recent speech in which he condemned South Africa's apartheid system but called for no foreign economic sanctions against that country]: Reagan has moved significantly closer to [South African President] P. W. Botha's position. This speech will help a lot in preventing the wholesale imposition of sanctions on us. That onslaught would probably drive us into such a defensive posture that the

(CARL F. NOFFKE)

[apartheid] reforms would inevitably be put aside. Reagan has not only bought us more time for reform but, at a considerable political risk to himself, has tried to end the siege mentality that has been building in South Africa. I would hope that we will have the confidence now to proceed with reforms and to take a more realistic approach to major Western countries that are concerned about developments here.

July 22/Los Angeles Times, 7-23:(I)9.

Alan Paton
South African author

1

[On U.S. economic sanctions against South Africa to protest that country's apartheid system]: I do think that self-righteous Americans are trying to over-simplify the issues, and they think, "Ah, well, if we don't buy gold and platinum and coal, and don't let South African Airways fly to Washington and New York, then those people in South Africa will have to improve the [racial] situation." I think that is very naive. Won't happen . . . I know the Afrikaner very well, the Afrikaner nationalist, and he wants to do better. I'm satisfied about that. But he doesn't want America to tell him what to do. The Afrikaner is a very devout believer and he knows that he's behaved very badly toward the other people of the country and he would like to make amends. But it's a very hard thing to make amends after he's behaved as he has for 38 years; it's a very hard thing to make amends when you're insecure. It's very easy to be good when you're secure; very hard to be good when you're insecure, and the Afrikaner is insecure.

Interview, New York/
The Washington Post, 11-25:(E)2.

Shimon Peres
Prime Minister of Israel

2

[Saying Israel is not going to take a lead in urging foreign economic sanctions against South Africa to protest that country's apartheid sys-

tem]: We don't feel that it is for us to be making world policy vis-a-vis South Africa. We are a party to world policy. We shall follow the resolutions, but I don't think that we have to take the lead in formulating a policy toward South Africa. That does not mean that we are indifferent. A Jewish person could never support apartheid.

To reporters, Yaounde, Cameroon,
Aug. 25/The New York Times, 8-26:6.

Edward J. Perkins
United States Ambassador-
designate to South Africa

3

[On U.S. economic sanctions against South Africa to protest that country's apartheid system]: It's not a question of whether I support the sanctions. I support the law. I am a Federal officer. The sanctions bill is the law of the land . . . The President [Reagan] himself has stated that the sanctions bill is now the law. He also has stated very clearly what our objectives are . . . The great debate has taken place. Now we are in the position where we can move beyond that. I will do everything that I can to impress on South African blacks and whites that America does care about ending apartheid and racial injustice.

At Senate Foreign Relations Committee
hearing on his confirmation, Washington,
Oct. 6/The Washington Post, 10-7:(A)6.

Ronald Reagan
President of the United States

4

Working as true partners, the African people and the international community, through both its public and private sectors, can lay the basis for a prosperous Africa in which the African people contribute fully to their own as well as their national well-being. It is the prayer of the American people that peace will come with prosperity so that the great continent of Africa can realize its vast potential.

Written statement,
Washington, May 27/
The New York Times, 5-28:5.

WHAT THEY SAID IN 1986

(RONALD REAGAN)

1

The root cause of South Africa's disorder is apartheid, that rigid system of racial segregation wherein black people have been treated as third-class citizens in a nation they helped to build. America's view of apartheid has been, and remains, clear: Apartheid is morally wrong and politically unacceptable. The United States cannot maintain cordial relations with a government whose power rests upon the denial of rights to a majority of its people, based on race . . . Many in [the U.S.] Congress, and some in Europe, are clamoring for sweeping [economic] sanctions against South Africa. The Prime Minister of Great Britain [Margaret Thatcher] has denounced punitive sanctions as immoral and utterly repugnant. Well, let me tell you why we believe Mrs. Thatcher is right. The primary victims of an economic boycott of South Africa would be the very people we seek to help. Most of the workers who would lose jobs because of sanctions would be black workers. We do not believe the way to help the people of South Africa is to cripple the economy upon which they and their families depend for survival . . . Our own experience teaches us that racial progress comes swiftest and easiest not during economic depression but in times of prosperity and growth. Our own history teaches us that capitalism is the natural enemy of such feudal institutions as apartheid . . . This Administration is not only against broad economic sanctions and against apartheid; we are for a new South Africa, a new nation where all that has been built up over generations is not destroyed; a new society where participation in the social, cultural and political life is open to all peoples; a new South Africa that comes home to the family of free nations where she belongs. To achieve that we need not a Western withdrawal, but deeper involvement by the Western business community as agents of change and progress and growth.

Before foreign-policy groups, Washington,
July 22/The New York Times, 7-23:6.

2

[On the anti-apartheid African National Congress, now exiled and banned from South Af-rica]: The African National Congress started out some years ago and there was no question about its being a solid organization. But in 1921 in South Africa the Communist Party formed, and some years later the Communist Party of South Africa joined with, and just moved into, the African National Congress . . . We've had enough experience in our own country with so-called Communist fronts to know that you can have an organization with some well-meaning and fine people, but you have an element in there that has its own agenda, and that is what's happened with the ANC. And right now, the ANC in exile, the ones we're hearing from and that are making the statements, are the members of that African Communist Party. [If] you could do business with, and separate out and get the solid citizens in the ANC to come forward on their own, that's just fine.

News conference, Chicago, Aug. 12/
The New York Times, 8-13:8.

3

[Saying he is vetoing a bill that would impose strong sanctions against South Africa to protest that country's apartheid system]: This Administration has no quarrel with the declared purpose of this measure. Indeed, we share that purpose: to send a clear signal to the South African government that the American people view with abhorrence its codified system of racial segregation. Apartheid is an affront to human rights and human dignity. Normal and friendly relations cannot exist between the United States and South Africa until it becomes a dead policy. Americans are of one mind and one heart on this issue. But while we vigorously support the purpose of this legislation, declaring economic warfare against the people of South Africa would be destructive not only of their efforts to peacefully end apartheid, but also of the opportunity to replace it with a free society. The sweeping and punitive sanctions adopted by the Congress are targeted directly at the labor-intensive industries upon which the victimized people of South Africa depend for their very survival. Black workers, the first victims of apartheid, would become the first victims of American sanctions.

Veto message, Washington, Sept. 26/
The New York Times, 9-27:4.

(RONALD REAGAN)

1

The system of apartheid and the state of emergency in South Africa are unconscionable and must be ended. The brutality and repression in Ethiopia, Angola, or any other repressive African regime, are of no less concern.

Human Rights Day address, Washington,
Dec. 10/Los Angeles Times, 12-11:(I)6.

Gavin Relly
Chairman, Anglo-American
Corporation (South Africa)

2

[On Zimbabwe]: Its philosophy currently teeters between, on the one hand, a pragmatic view of the efficiency of private enterprise as a wealth producer and, on the other—even in this day and age—the blandishments of an old-fashioned and tired Marxism. Tribal conflict between the ruling Shona peoples and the minority Matabele has—since independence—reached a pitch unknown in this century . . . A solution favored by Zimbabwe's very shrewd Prime Minister, Mr. Robert Mugabe, is the panacea of the one-party state, popular in Africa. This concept has the pleasing effect of removing conflict from the public eye of an open parliamentary forum to the backstage, where sharper weapons than those of debate can demonstrate their efficacy. But the limits of South Africa's democracy preclude any superior feelings.

Speech/The Wall Street Journal, 10-27:24.

Jonas Savimbi
Leader, National Union for the
Total Independence of Angola

3

[On criticism of his being allied with South Africa in his fight against the Angolan government]: I am not a Communist. I am a Christian. I am a Protestant. I don't approve of [South African] apartheid. How can I, as a black leader, approve of apartheid? . . . On one side I am branded as a Communist, on the other side I am a puppet of South Africa!

At Conservative Political Action
Conference, Washington, Jan. 31/
The Washington Post, 2-3:(B)3.

4

[On U.S. policy toward Angola]: If you lose Angola to Communism, you lose southern Africa. By losing southern Africa, you lose access to strategic minerals that are critical to your economy. Also, you lose the strategic [trade] lines of the South Atlantic and Indian Ocean.

The Christian Science Monitor, 2-11:6.

Eduard A. Shevardnadze
Foreign Minister of the Soviet Union

5

[On the apartheid system in South Africa]: It is our conviction that were it not for the racist regime of Pretoria, the black, white and colored people in South Africa would have long ago found a common language—a language of equality, concord and racial peace. The dividing line is drawn not by ethnic differences but by the cruel policy of apartheid, which is hostile to everyone, irrespective of the color of one's skin. To fail to see that is to encourage, willingly or unwillingly, genocide against the majority of South African people.

At United Nations, New York, Sept. 23/
The New York Times, 9-24:4.

Robert Shrire
Chairman, department of
political science, University
of Cape Town (South Africa)

6

[On the increased restrictions on certain aspects of South African life instituted by the government after foreign economic sanctions were imposed against his country to protest the apartheid system there]: Essentially the government is saying, to hell with the rest of the world. [President Pieter] Botha's intention now is to wrap himself and his government in the South African flag. The government believes that it cannot appease its international critics. No matter what it does it is damned, and there is no longer any point in restraint. And, domestically, it feels there are more votes in being tough than there are in punting reform.

The Washington Post, 12-15:(A)34.

WHAT THEY SAID IN 1986

George P. Shultz
Secretary of State of the United States

1

[Criticizing South Africa's raids against anti-apartheid rebels and their supporters in Botswana, Zambia and Zimbabwe]: We share an outrage at South Africa's raid on Botswana as well as other countries. It was totally without justification and is completely unacceptable. The situation in South Africa is a continuing tragedy, and this is the latest episode. It's as I said, intolerable, unacceptable; so what to do? I think the thing to do is to be clear in our minds about the nature of the problem, about the fact that it's fundamentally seated in apartheid, which is the basic condition that must be changed, and to keep working at it, to never give up trying to achieve a constructive result, discouraging though it may be.

To reporters, Washington, May 23/
The New York Times, 5-24:1.

2

We all agree that Africa needs resources, but those resources must be well used. In the United States, our own budgetary constraints dictate major cutbacks in domestic programs as well as in international commitments. If we expect to maintain current aid levels to Africa, the American people will insist that our assistance be well used.

To African leaders, United Nations, New York,
May 28/The Washington Post, 5-29:(A)29.

3

[Criticizing proposed U.S. economic sanctions against South Africa, including a pull-out by American firms, as a protest against South Africa's apartheid system]: The American private sector must remain involved. American companies in South Africa are the building blocks of our influence. That is why we oppose disinvestment. If American companies withdraw, we and the black majority of South Africa will be deprived of a major source of influence . . . Let us remember our goal: We seek the end of apartheid, racism and repression. Hence, our actions should target apartheid policies and institutions and disassociate ourselves from them. Our aim is not—I repeat not—to in-

flict random, indiscriminate damage on the South African people and their economy . . . Change is taking place in South Africa. It is occurring unevenly, slowly, sometimes reluctantly or by stealth, but it is simply inaccurate to view apartheid in South Africa as a static system . . . Our policy is based on the premise that South Africa is a society in transition . . . The question we face now is not whether apartheid will end, but how and when it will go, and what will replace it. Will it end in bloody, violent kind of confrontations, strung out over some years and totally destructive? Can we find a way to bring it to an end through a process of no doubt very difficult, tough negotiations and struggle? I don't know how probable it is, but I know it's possible. And as long as it's possible, we would be derelict in our duty if we didn't stay engaged and try to be constructive and try to bring something good out of the situation.

At conference of U.S. religious leaders,
Washington, June 2/Los Angeles Times,
6-3:(I)1, 10;The New York Times, 6-3:4.

4

[Arguing against foreign economic sanctions against South Africa to protest that country's apartheid system]: Those who feel the best way to bring about change in South Africa is to bring the South African economy down as much as they can, must realize that in doing so they bring down the economies of the neighboring states which depend on South Africa. In our own assessment of what is to take place, we will want to look at the [entire] southern Africa picture . . . We want to remain engaged [in South Africa]. I don't think there is any doubt of that from the [U.S. Reagan] Administration standpoint. And we want to engage in a constructive manner. So I have never really seen what the problem with those words is. Some have interpreted them as meaning we have not done anything [to hasten the end of apartheid]; but we have done a great deal, and we continue to try to engage ourselves. The counsel of disengagement is the wrong counsel; but just how to engage and just what is constructive—those are the questions.

To reporters en route from Asia to Washington,
June 30/The New York Times, 7-1:7.

(GEORGE P. SHULTZ)

1

[On the apartheid system in South Africa]: Our policies and those of our allies should ensure that expanded political liberties in a post-apartheid South Africa are accompanied by an expansion of economic opportunities for *all* South Africans. This will require an expanding economy that is strong enough to meet South Africa's pressing social and economic needs, healthy enough to raise black living standards rapidly toward those of whites, and open and vigorous enough to spur economic development region-wide. Only a South Africa which preserves Africa's strongest and most developed industrial economy can galvanize a dynamic and balanced regional economy, mobilize capital and labor, spread advanced technology and management, and strengthen trade and transport ties.

Before Senate Foreign Relations
Committee, Washington, July 23/
USA Today, 7-24:(A)6.

2

[Arguing against U.S. economic sanctions and business pull-outs from South Africa that protest that country's apartheid system]: Sanctions by themselves do not amount to an effective policy in southern Africa. The time ahead is one for diplomacy, guided by a long-term view of our interests and objectives . . . The attacks on American corporate involvement in South Africa are both ironic and unwarranted because American business has been a force for promoting interracial decency and equality . . . It is not enough to campaign against apartheid. South Africans must know what the West stands for as the country redefines itself politically. We believe that the leaders of southern Africa—whatever their rhetoric of the moment—want us to be there, lending a hand . . . It is the road of involvement—not disengagement—that will bring us closer to our goals.

Before International Management
and Development Institute,
Washington, Dec. 4/
Los Angeles Times, 12-5:(I)1,16.

Mathias Sinamenye
Foreign Minister of Burundi

3

[The] Namibian problem should not be seen through the deforming prism of competing ideological blocs. All the nations of the world should easily understand that one doesn't fight the supposed risk of Communist expansion in southern Africa through the installation of destructive and retrograde Fascist [regimes].

At United Nations, New York, Oct. 9/
The New York Times, 10-10:4.

Frederik van Zyl Slabbert
Leader, Progressive Federal
Party of South Africa

4

[Criticizing South African President Pieter Botha, saying Botha does not believe in fundamental reform of the apartheid system]: The state President still believes there must be communities predetermined by the government and that power must be shared on that basis and no other . . . I see no chance for peaceful change as long as we compel people to belong to racial and ethnic groups . . . That is not power-sharing, but a form of co-optive domination.

News conference, Cape Town,
Feb. 7/Los Angeles Times, 2-8:(I)4.

5

[Saying the South African government isn't doing enough to end apartheid]: It is not enough just trying to persuade the whites and foreign bankers that apartheid is being dismantled. What is much more important is to persuade the people who are the practical victims of apartheid—and that you are not going to do with newspaper advertisements and double-speak statements.

News conference, Cape Town, Feb. 7/
The Washington Post, 2-8:(A)12.

6

[Criticizing the South African government for not moving to end apartheid]: The ideological abandonment of apartheid that the government refers to when it speaks of reform is not the

(FREDERIK van ZYL SLABBERT)

same as the abdication of political control and white dominance. What we have in this so-called "reform process" of the government is a search for ways and means of accommodating black South Africans at the political center without the loss of white control . . . We can either work toward a non-racial society, that is a system where there will be no "group security" and thus no longer white control, and try to make the transition as painless as possible. Or, we can be dragged into it as painfully as we ourselves can make it. Everything the government is doing is meant to ensure continued white control when politics, history and, most of all, demography, are all against it.

Los Angeles Times, 8-25:(I)14.

David Steward
Director, Bureau of
Information of South Africa

1

[On U.S. criticism of apartheid in South Africa]: There is a philosophical law that the degree of morality involved in the solution to a problem is almost exactly equal to the distance from the problem. In the United States, there is a level of rhetoric and there is a level of reality. Everyone gives lip service to the predominant reality. But they [in the U.S.] live in segregated suburbs and send their children to segregated schools . . . The foreign media is catering to one of the most self-indulgent emotions we have: righteous indignation. Americans like to feel righteously indignant about distant problems which remind them of their own days in the '60s, when they had causes for which to fight. They like to feel that such and such is a baddie, and such and such is a goodie. It gives them a warm feeling in their breasts when they commute into New York from Connecticut. It gives them direction in life. It's very pleasant.

Interview, Pretoria/
The New York Times, 7-9:4.

2

[On new censorship steps taken by the South African government on the media's reporting of

anti-apartheid unrest, saying radicals use the media for their own ends]: They use the media as a means of mobilizing the population for the purposes of radical revolution. It is a struggle of propaganda and perceptions. These perceptions are being manipulated consciously and unconsciously by elements in the media . . . How are we supposed to restore law and order and the circumstances for further political reform when people are being conditioned in favor of the radical element?

Interview, Dec. 11/
Los Angeles Times, 12-12:(I)5.

Helen Suzman
Member, South African Parliament

3

[Criticizing proposed foreign economic sanctions against South Africa to protest that country's apartheid system]: I understand the moral abhorrence and the pleasure it gives you when you demonstrate [against apartheid]. But I don't see how wrecking the economy of the country will insure a more stable and just society . . . No doubt you've been told that the blacks [in South Africa] don't care [about the sanctions' effects on the economy], that they've suffered so much they don't worry about it. But they do care. Those who say they don't care are already unemployed or have sheltered employment or have nothing and want nothing and want the revolution to roll on.

At Hebrew Union College-Jewish Institute
of Religion commencement, New York,
June 1/The New York Times, 6-2:18.

4

[On the strife over apartheid in South Africa]: South Africa has become like El Salvador and Argentina, where thousands upon thousands of people go missing and the government won't acknowledge where they are or whether they are dead or alive.

Before Parliament, Cape Town, June 24/
Los Angeles Times, 6-25:(I)5.

5

[Criticizing U.S. economic sanctions against South Africa to protest that country's apartheid

(HELEN SUZMAN)

system]: . . . the aim to get rid of apartheid is not the issue, because that's common cause. It's the strategy that's being employed. And I believe that sanctions will not bring down the South African government, as some optimists hope . . . I know the Pretoria regime very well, having had an eyeball-to-eyeball confrontation with them over 30 years. If anything, it's going to make them more intransigent. It will put the reform program on the back burner, because they do not like to appear to be bowing down to international pressure . . . All the major changes that have come about in South Africa, so far, have been as a result of economic forces inside the country. I believe economic forces are the major cause of change, and this has got to be in an expanding economy, not in a stagnant economy.

Interview/USA Today, 12-17:(A)11.

Oliver Tambo
President, banned African
National Congress (South Africa)

1

[Saying his organization will step up its attacks in South Africa to overthrow that country's white minority government]: We have called for a rapid and extensive escalation of our military and political offensive . . . Even the most stubborn racist can now see that we are no longer prepared to live as slaves and are determined to liberate ourselves whatever the price we have to pay in human lives . . . Nearly four decades of illegal rule by the heirs of Hitler are coming to a close and with them centuries of colonial and racist white minority domination. There is nothing the Pretoria regime can do that can change this historic outcome of our struggle.

News conference, Lusaka, Zambia,
Jan. 9/Los Angeles Times, 1-10:(I)8.

2

We must continue to make South Africa ungovernable and apartheid unworkable. In the attack, we must aim to weaken the regime drastically, to sap its strength, to take away from it even the capacity to launch a limited counter-

offensive. We must build our forces into an ever-more-formidable united mass army of liberation, an army that must grow in strength continuously, able to deliver and actually delivering bigger blows at every stage . . . Nothing else has worked, absolutely nothing. When we were peaceful and non-violent, we got nowhere. Now that we have the initiative . . . people say, "Ah, but we must be non-violent, we must not launch our people's war, we must not make the Afrikaner [whites] angry." But we know that the Afrikaner understands only violence.

To reporters, Lusaka, Zambia/
Los Angeles Times, 1-13:(I)17.

3

[On South Africa, if the ANC takes over]: Our freedom charter recognizes that the white people are part of the South African nation, despite their different origins. We see them simply as people, fellow citizens who belong there with the rest of us [blacks] and we will join together in running and building our country. We have to get that idea across. If whites see themselves as a minority in a democratic South Africa it is only because they see themselves as separate. That is a product of apartheid. We have got to fight this concept of racism. We must destroy it.

Interview, Lusaka, Zambia/
The Washington Post,
3-7:(A)29.

4

There can be no solution of [South Africa's apartheid] problems without the ANC. As the crisis in the country grows, more and more whites realize this, as does the international community. The basic reason is very plain—that people accept the leadership of the ANC entrusted to articulate their demands . . . We have always hoped that the outside world, along with fair-minded white South Africans, would make it unnecessary for us to raise this conflict to the highly destructive, massively destructive level that would be required to end apartheid through armed struggle. That is why we appeal to the West to impose economic sanctions on South Africa, to match the internal pressure, and it is the reason we are trying now to reach the white

WHAT THEY SAID IN 1986

population of the country and form a united front with the forces for change in it.

Interview, Bonn,
West Germany/
Los Angeles Times, 4-11:(I)10.

1

[Expressing skepticism about trying to negotiate reforms in South Africa's apartheid system, saying the system must be abolished instead]: A cancer cannot be its own cure. The fanatical racists who have spent more than half a century drawing up the apartheid system . . . cannot at the same time be the agents for the abolition of that system . . . No amount of political maneuvering or killing of our [black] people will blunt or stop the offensive to destroy racism in our country.

Malaysia/
Los Angeles Times, 5-10:(I)24.

2

[Calling for foreign economic sanctions against South Africa as a way of ending the apartheid system there]: As far as sanctions are concerned, there is a point beyond which [South African President Pieter] Botha will not want to continue with the apartheid system. The point will be reached before the economy has been destroyed.

News conference,
Paris, June 18/
The New York Times, 6-19:6.

3

[On the ANC]: We are nobody's puppets. When we talk about the ANC, we are talking about a body that is not the Communist Party but which has always had CP members since the 1920s. They have always behaved as 100 per cent ANC men. The ANC is a national movement. We all—Communists and non-Communists alike—want a non-racial, democratic, united South Africa. We are too clear about where we are heading to be diverted from our goals.

Interview, Lusaka,
Zambia/Time, 10-27:56.

Eugene N. Terre'Blanche
Leader, Afrikaner Resistance
Movement (South Africa)

4

[Calling on white South Africans to mobilize and be ready to fight blacks in a coming confrontation over apartheid]: South Africa is at the beginning of the bloodiest revolution yet between black and white in Africa. The white man in Africa is now going through his biggest crisis ever . . . If I, as a white man and as an Afrikaner, want to continue to live in this country, I have no alternative but to continue with the Brandwag [his group's armed militia] and establish protection units whose job it will be to defend life and property when the police and defense force can't be there. They [anti-apartheid forces] call us terrorists, but do they know what would really happen if we were white terrorists? They should pray to God they never find out.

At Afrikaner Resistance Movement rally,
Krugersdorp, South Africa/
Los Angeles Times, 3-18:(I)11.

5

[Criticizing South African President Pieter Botha for his policy of reform of the apartheid system]: The Afrikaner Resistance Movement wants to avoid war and revolution. But we know that P. W. Botha is leading us there because the blacks will never agree to share power [with the white minority]. They will try to seize everything, and for the white man it then will be a fight to the death.

At rally, Potgietersrus,
South Africa, Oct. 16/
Los Angeles Times, 10-17:(I)5.

Margaret Thatcher
Prime Minister of the United Kingdom

6

[Arguing against foreign economic sanctions as a means of protesting apartheid in South Africa]: What is moral about sitting in this room, in a good conference center, with good jobs, returning to an expensive hotel, deciding who [in South Africa] will be put out of work because we say so? What is moral about deliberately and

(MARGARET THATCHER)

willfully depriving many black people—and whites and coloreds and Indians—of the living they are honestly gaining when most of the moderates [in South Africa] are not asking for that and hoping to goodness it will not come about?

Interview, London/
The New York Times, 7-10:4.

Desmond M. Tutu
Anglican Bishop of
Johannesburg (South Africa)

1

[Calling for foreign economic sanctions against South Africa to protest that country's apartheid system, despite critics who say sanctions will hurt black South Africans]: For goodness sake, let people not use us as an alibi for not doing the things they know they ought to do. We [blacks] are suffering now, and this kind of suffering seems to be going to go on and on and on. If additional suffering is going to put a terminus to our suffering, then we will accept it. When did white people suddenly become so altruistic and suddenly become so concerned about black suffering, when over a long period of time those who have invested have benefitted from cheap labor supplied by blacks?

News conference, New York,
Jan. 6/The New York Times, 1-7:6.

2

[On the apartheid system in South Africa]: I am a peace lover . . . [but] there comes a time when it is justifiable to overthrow an unjust system by violence . . . I am a peace lover and could get to a point where I would agree with the church's tradition that if you have two evils, a repressive system such as Nazism was and the possibility of overthrowing it, then I would say there comes a time when it is justifiable to overthrow an unjust system by violence.

Broadcast interview/
"Today," NBC-TV, 1-9.

3

[On the apartheid system in South Africa]: Our [black] people are peaceful to a fault. We

stand up and we keep saying: "We will use peaceful means" [to end apartheid]. And each time we say that, they [the government] use tear gas, dogs, bullets and whips. Our people are killed as if they are flies, you know, like they are swatting flies and it doesn't really matter.

At anti-apartheid conference,
Atlanta, Ga., Jan. 19/
Los Angeles Times, 1-20:(I)8.

4

[On the apartheid system in South Africa]: I have been saying we are looking forward to the day when we will have a truly non-racial and truly democratic and just society. We will have a government where all of the people will have decided on who will govern them. I am sure we will have a multiparty parliamentary democracy . . . Without a doubt, the ANC leader, [now-imprisoned] Nelson Mandela, is head and shoulders above any contenders for leadership, but you would still be surprised to find that some whites will be in his government, holding fairly high positions. In Zimbabwe, where [Prime Minister] Robert Mugabe did not really need white cabinet ministers, he still appointed two in his first government. Nelson would clearly be way up there, and most of the ANC hierarchy would hold fairly important positions. People of other persuasions will also find a place in our first national government.

Interview/USA Today, 1-20:(A)11.

5

[Calling for foreign economic sanctions against South Africa to protest that country's apartheid system]: We face catastrophe in this land, and only the action of the international community by applying pressure can save us. I have no hope of real change from this government unless they are forced . . . Our children are dying; our land is burning and bleeding, and so I call on the international community to apply punitive sanctions against this government to help us establish a new South Africa—non-racial, democratic, participatory and just. This is a non-violent strategy to help us do so . . . I hope that those who [claim economic sanctions will hurt black South Africans and thus should not be implemented] would just drop it quietly and stop being so hypocritical. It is amazing how everybody has become so solicitous for blacks and become such wonderful altruists. It is remarkable that, in South Africa, the most vehement in their concern for blacks [when economic sanctions are proposed] have been whites.

News conference, Johannesburg,
April 2/Los Angeles Times, 4-3:(I)1,20.

1

[Calling for foreign economic sanctions against South Africa to protest that country's apartheid system]: A clear message resounds in which more than 70 per cent of [South African] blacks supported sanctions against the government. Blacks are saying: "We are suffering already. To end it, we will support sanctions, even if we have to take on additional suffering." Our people have shown they mean business by their use of consumer boycotts. Last year, organizations representing more than 12 million South Africans called for sanctions and economic pressure. These are not insignificant actions or irresponsible bodies or individuals . . . You hear [some] people say sanctions don't work. That may be so. But if they don't work, why oppose them so vehemently? If they don't work, why did [British Prime Minister] Margaret Thatcher apply them to Argentina during the Falkland war? Why did the United States apply them to Poland and to Nicaragua? Why was [U.S.] President Reagan so annoyed that his European allies did not want to impose sanctions against Libya? If sanctions are so ineffective, why does the United States still maintain a blockade of Cuba? Yet we have all this wonderful sophistry [against sanctions] when it comes to South Africa.

At Hunter College commencement,
New York/The New York Times, 6-16:19.

2

[Criticizing U.S. President Reagan for not supporting tough economic sanctions against South Africa to protest that country's apartheid

system]: [The U.S. President] sits there like the great, big white chief of old. Your President is the pits as far as blacks are concerned . . . I am quite angry [at Reagan]. I think the West, for my part, can go to hell.

Interview, Johannesburg, July 22/
The New York Times, 7-23:6.

Desmond M. Tutu
Anglican Archbishop of
Cape Town (South Africa)

3

[On South Africa's apartheid system]: I am not sure the government wants real change, which would mean an entirely new dispensation with a new disposition of political power and a greater sharing of the good things so abundant in South Africa—the land, wealth and other resources. In this, they are not different from politicians everywhere, wanting to gain power and hold on to it for as long as possible. I am amazed that there are many white people who actually want this kind of change. If I were white, I would need considerable grace to oppose a system that provided me such substantial privileges.

At his enthronement as Archbishop, Cape Town,
Sept. 7/Los Angeles Times, 9-8:(I)6.

4

[Criticizing U.S. President Reagan's policies regarding the apartheid system in South Africa]: I don't think he understands black people. I don't think he accepts black people, well, as really human. I think he and people like [British Prime Minister Margaret] Thatcher and [West German] Chancellor [Helmut] Kohl think that blacks are expendable.

Interview, Houston, Dec. 10/
The New York Times, 12-11:6.

Anthony Ukpo
Minister of Information, and member of
Armed Forces Ruling Council, of Nigeria

5

[On the Nigerian government's policy of inviting the public to debate and discuss signifi-

(ANTHONY UKPO)

cant national issues]: When this Administration came into being, if you like, a quick study was done as to what was responsible for the constant collapse of various governments. I think we discovered that one of the principal things that was wrong was the fact that everybody in the country has always seen government as "them and us." There was that straight line that divided government from the people. So we thought that one of the ways we could stabilize the Administration was to make the people themselves take responsibility for what government does. And so we felt that for major issues there would be a need for us to hear what the people have to say. Funny enough, at the time nobody thought in terms of a tool to popularize government. We were thinking strictly in terms of how can we make the people and government be one rather than the way it was perceived before. But now, of course, it would seem that it has also helped to generate popular support for the government.

Interview, Lagos/
The New York Times, 1-20:7.

Stoffel van der Merwe
Deputy Director, Bureau of
Information of South Africa

1

[Saying the South African government will censor all news reports of political unrest resulting from anti-apartheid and Communist activity in the country]: The government's aim is not to establish a totalitarian system. It is to establish a democratic system . . . But in doing that we have to touch upon elements that are normally part of the free democratic process, but that in this context have become part of the revolutionary movement.

Before Foreign Correspondents Association,
Johannesburg, Dec. 10/
Los Angeles Times, 12-11:(I)29.

John T. Walker
Episcopal Bishop of Washington, D.C.

2

[Expressing reservations about U.S. companies pulling out of South Africa because of that

country's apartheid system]: There is a way, by isolating that government totally, we could bring it to its knees and cause a crash of major proportions. Are we going to do that to blacks in South Africa? To destroy the black infrastructure and then walk away? I say, no, we should not do that. If the alternative [for U.S. companies] is to simply pull out and turn over their operations to the South African government or someone who is not in concert with the notion of the destruction of apartheid, then I'd say I'd rather have them stay because we can work with [them].

Interview/
The Washington Post, 10-20:(A)20.

Frank Wisner
Under Secretary for African Affairs,
Department of State of the United States

3

We want to see a post-apartheid democratic order evolve [in South Africa] and evolve as quickly as possible. This is a year of testing, a year in which we all hope that South Africa will be able to evolve from its present unhappy circumstances into a time where black leaders and white leaders can negotiate this country's future.

To reporters, Johannesburg,
March 14/The New York Times, 3-15:5.

Goshu Wolde
Foreign Minister of Ethiopia

4

[Announcing his resignation and criticizing his country's dictatorship]: The government is surely out of touch with the genuine aspirations of, and insensitive to the plight of, the Ethiopian people, while increasingly determined to rule against their grain. All efforts to moderate its policies from within were to no avail . . . I have recently watched with helplessness as my country slipped further and further into totalitarianism and absolute dictatorship, with the inevitable consequences of intolerance and repression.

To reporters, United Nations, New York,
Oct. 27/Los Angeles Times,
10-28:(I)12.

243

WHAT THEY SAID IN 1986

Denis Worrall
South African Ambassador to the United Kingdom
1

[On the possibility of foreign economic sanctions against South Africa to protest that country's apartheid system]: [If sanctions are applied,] we are able to reciprocate with sanctions. We could cause chaos in southern Africa, something that is not sufficiently recognized. If there were sanctions [against South Africa] on the scale [recommended by a Commonwealth commission], then South Africa would consider not repaying its international loans. All Mexico and a few others need is a precedent, and it would bring down the whole Western financial system . . . The point is, if you place South Africa in an extremist situation, that kind of consideration might apply.

Before House of Commons Foreign Affairs
Committee, London/Los Angeles Times, 7-6:(I)1.

I. William Zartman
Director of Africa studies,
School of Advanced
International Studies,
Johns Hopkins University
2

[Criticizing U.S. President Reagan's opposition to foreign economic sanctions against South Africa as a way to protest that country's apartheid system]: There is an absolute block in the President's comprehension. He is an old man who has gotten some images in the formative point of his life, and he isn't going to change. The idea that the [black] majority [in South Africa] is anything but savages is something he can't come to understand.

Aug. 13/
Los Angeles Times,
8-14:(I)22.

The Americas

Elliott Abrams
Assistant Secretary for Inter-American
Affairs, Department of State
of the United States

1

[On Sandinista Nicaraguan President Daniel Ortega]: He's my greatest [anti-Sandinista] lobbyist in the U.S. Congress. He's not on salary but he really ought to be, because he has turned around Congressional opinion on Nicaragua . . . A couple of years ago, there were an awful lot of Congressmen who still had hopes for democracy in Nicaragua. Now that everyone has met Daniel Ortega and watched what he has done to the church, to the press, to the trade unions in Nicaragua, we have no reason to doubt him and I think I need to say a word of thanks to that.

Broadcast interview,
Washington, Jan. 17/
Los Angeles Times, 1-18:(I)17.

2

[On Contadora, the program of a group of Latin American countries working for peace in Central America]: Contadora's document of objectives includes pluralism, democracy, reconciliation. Those are among the most important of the Contadora objectives. How do you get the Sandinista Communists to agree to that? The answer seems to me clear, and it is pressure.

Interview/The New York Times, 1-18:5.

3

Efforts to reform Mexico's economy and turn it into a more efficient, competitive direction are critical to Mexico's long-run stability and to our own interest in a strong, prosperous and stable neighbor. The outcome will affect our trading interests, our banking system, the movement of Mexicans illegally into the United States, and even the economic incentives for Mexican farmers to produce illicit drug crops.

At Senate Foreign Relations
subcommittee hearing, Washington,
May 13/Los Angeles Times, 5-14:(I)12.

4

[On U.S. criticism of Mexico's drug trafficking]: We have told the Mexicans in no uncertain terms that we are deeply troubled by widespread drug-related corruption. [The Mexican government will be] angered by this kind of discussion in public . . . [But] our purpose is not to call names. It's to look forward to a better chance in the future. This is a very serious business . . . They have got to get organized to stop this before it gets too late. And it *can* get too late.

At Senate Foreign Relations
subcommittee hearing, Washington,
May 13/The Washington Post, 5-24:(A)19.

5

[On the Contadora talks aimed at a negotiated settlement of the U.S.-Nicaraguan confrontation]: Until now, many of the [Contadora] participants were interested in getting an agreement that would be unacceptable to the United States because it would give Nicaragua a blank check for subversion in the region or in using the negotiations as a way to defeat contra aid in [the U.S.] Congress. Now we're making clear that can't be done.. When it's recognized that the contra [rebels fighting the Nicaraguan government] pressure is going to be there until Nicaragua is willing to change its ways, we think that perhaps we might start to see a chance for negotiations that are meaningful.

Interview, Washington/
The Washington Post, 7-21:(A)13.

6

[On the arrest by Nicaragua of a private American citizen for helping supply arms to rebels in that country]: I am happy to reiterate here, once again, that the flight in which Mr. Hasenfus [the arrested American] took part was a private initiative. It was not organized, directed or financed by the U.S. government. Many private citizens have come forward to help in that struggle for freedom [against the Nicaraguan government]. I do not know who they all are, any more than I know the identify of the

(ELLIOTT ABRAMS)

Americans who are helping the Communist [government] in Nicaragua. Americans are free to support either side in Central America, and it is not a legitimate task of the U.S. government to track down who is contributing what to whom, so long as U.S. laws, including the neutrality acts, are obeyed.

Before House Subcommittee on
Western Hemisphere Affairs, Washington,
Oct. 15/The New York Times, 10-16:4.

Ricardo Alarcon
Deputy Foreign Minister of Cuba

1

[Saying many Latin American nations are re-establishing their diplomatic ties with Cuba]: [Cuba wants] to develop these relations, widen them, deepen them . . . It is clear that an objective of the [U.S.] Reagan Administration was to reinforce the isolation of Cuba. Despite that being the declared policy, they are now unable to impose it . . . With the United States there can be dialogue, communication, but the United States does not belong to this region . . . In practice, the counteraction of interests with relation to the United States is what unites Latin America.

Interview, Havana/
Los Angeles Times, 8-8:(I)10.

Raul Alfonsin
President of Argentina

2

If democracy does not flourish or affirm itself in all of Latin America, in all the South, the world will not be safe or stable for anyone.

Speech/Los Angeles Times, 6-15:(I)13.

3

The search for the true meaning of democracy must develop further in Latin America so that democracy does not remain solely a formality. We would be very wrong to suppose that because democracy is not complete we should look for other forms of government. We must begin with political democracy and advance toward so-cial democracy. Economic democracy is still 50 years away, at best. The problem of Latin America is that we are living through "Lebanonization." The flags of different countries fly—never one flag for the whole.

Interview, August/
World Press Review, October:47.

4

It is a bitter paradox that the advanced democracies, which encourage us [in Latin America] to consolidate our reborn democracies, also chastise us through trade discrimination, through the lowering of the price of our exports by subsidizing products that compete with ours, harshly demanding the payment of a debt that is bleeding us, undermining, in summary, the meager possibilities we have to alleviate a crisis that threatens the survival of the same democracy they encourage us to sustain.

Before Carter Institute of Emory University,
and Institute of the Americas, Nov. 17/
The Washington Post, 11-21:(A)26.

Bayardo Arce
Member, Sandinista national
directorate of Nicaragua

5

[Saying his government would not tolerate dissenters who support anti-Sandinista rebels or their U.S. backers]: We have tolerated things that no country in our situation, or even not in our situation, would tolerate. We have been permitting citizens to act openly as agents of a country that is at war with their own country . . . We are not going to permit people to say that giving $100-million to the counter-revolutionaries [as the U.S. is doing] is justified because they defend human rights. It can be said that we have been stupid, but we are not idiots.

To foreign correspondents, Managua,
July 1/The New York Times, 7-2:4.

Oscar Arias
President-elect of Costa Rica

6

[On Costa Rican-U.S. relations]: I value nothing more than friendship, friendship between

246

(OSCAR ARIAS)

people, friendship between nations. Friendship implies loyalty, but loyalty is not synonymous with servitude or unconditionality.

Speech/The Christian Science Monitor, 5-8:14.

Oscar Arias
President of Costa Rica

1

[Saying he will not allow the contras, U.S. backed rebels fighting the Sandinista government of Nicaragua, to use Costa Rica as a base]: I can guarantee that I will not permit any foreigners to act militarily from our territory. It is the desire of the Costa Rican people that their territory not be used to launch attacks against other regimes, and I want that desire to be respected . . . Friendship [with the U.S.] should not mean being servile. A friend who does everything you want is not a friend, but a slave . . . You can't overthrow the Sandinistas with $100-million [in U.S. aid for the contras], or even with two or four hundred million. The more you give the contras, the more [Nicaraguan President Daniel] Ortega gets from the Soviets. The aid to the contras was supposed to oblige Ortega to change, to become more tolerant and flexible. But what has actually happened is just the opposite.

Interview, San Jose, Costa Rica/ The New York Times, 9-10:3.

Nora Astorga
Nicaraguan Ambassador/Permanent Representative to the United Nations

2

[Denying that Nicaragua is exporting revolution to neighbor countries]: Revolutions are not exportable like Coca-Cola or paperbacks or something like that. You don't produce it internally and send it away. Revolutions are made in a country when the conditions in that particular country are for a process of change.

To reporters, United Nations, New York, March 11/The New York Times, 3-12:6.

3

[Criticizing the U.S. refusal to comply with a World Court ruling against U.S. support of the contras, rebels fighting the Sandanista government of Nicaragua]: [The U.S. veto of a UN resolution urging compliance is] a vote against the fundamental principles and norms of this organization, a vote against the International Court of Justice, a vote against a peaceful settlement of disputes, a vote against international peace and security, and a vote for war, intervention and the use of force in international relations.

At United Nations, New York, July 31/ The Washington Post, 8-1:(A)18.

Jose Azcona
President of Honduras

4

[Calling for continued U.S. aid to the contras, rebels fighting the Sandinista government of Nicaragua]: We believe that the contras should be fighting inside Nicaragua, and that they can do so only if they receive assistance. We are not to blame for the existence of the contras, nor are we to blame for the large number of Nicaraguans who leave Nicaragua every day because they do not like the way of life being imposed upon them . . . There can be no peace, even if the Nicaraguans throw all their artillery and their helicopter gunships into Lake Managua, if there is no democratic opening in Nicaragua. The Nicaraguan people, both inside and outside, will keep fighting for their freedom, and Honduras and Costa Rica will keep suffering the effects of their struggle.

At National Press Club, Washington, May 28/The New York Times, 5-29:6.

5

[On fighting within Honduras between Nicaraguan contra rebels and Nicaraguan Sandinista government forces]: We Hondurans are not to blame if one oppressive dictatorship [that of Anastasio Somoza] existed in Nicaragua for 40 years and now an even worse one [the Sandinistas] has come to power. We're just suffering the negative consequences.

To reporters, El Paraiso, Honduras/ The Washington Post, 11-11:(A)24.

Virgilio Barco
President of Colombia

1

I will create an organism directly under my Presidency that will direct and coordinate all the political, social and economic measures designed to rehabilitate the regions torn by violence and reincorporate those who chose the road of armed subversion . . . My authority will not serve as the guardian for shocking inequalities nor unjustifiable advantages that now exist. Those who now enjoy privileges will not save what they have by walling themselves off from their fellow citizens, or by obstructing changes and necessary reforms.

Inaugural address, Bogota, Aug. 7/
Los Angeles Times, 8-8:(I)8.

Marc Bazin
Former Minister of Finance of Haiti

2

[On the recent overthrow of Haitian President Jean-Claude Duvalier]: This is an ideal opportunity to reverse the course of the past 182 years. I believe that we should not miss the opportunity for real change. We have had an enormous potential in terms of human resources. We are very courageous, hard-working people, and an extremely disciplined population. We have a resource base that has not been tapped properly. A serious government should start working on that.

Washington, Feb. 7/
The New York Times, 2-8:4.

Belisario Betancur
President of Colombia

3

[Criticizing proposed U.S. military aid to the contras, rebels fighting the Sandinista government of Nicaragua]: I think that an initiative such as the request for $100-million taken by [U.S.] President Reagan is wrong. I know we can get more [results] through negotiations [with Nicaragua]. I know that the Reagan Administration is aware of the fact that Latin America has its own language and that language is expressed through Contadora [the group of Latin American countries aiming for negotiations with Nicaragua] . . . It consists in telling the guerrilla groups in Central America: Why not talk; why not search for diplomatic solutions, and negotiate?

Interview, Bogota, Colombia/
The Washington Post, 3-10:(A)17.

Bill Bradley
United States Senator,
D-New Jersey

4

[Supporting the proposed $100-million in U.S. aid for the contras, rebels fighting the Sandinista government of Nicaragua]: We face a genuine dilemma. The [U.S. Reagan] Administration's failed policies have alienated potential allies, facilitated consolidation of the Sandinista regime and may have precipitated the outbreak of a regional war. [But] I also believe the Nicaraguan people deserve a chance at democracy. That chance will be denied them if the Sandinistas are allowed to consolidate their totalitarian regime . . . In the final analysis, [President Reagan] has left us little choice but to back the contras.

Los Angeles Times, 4-13:(I)23.

Leonel Brizola
Governor of
Rio de Janeiro (Brazil)

5

Any government committed to transforming Brazil would obviously face difficulties. It would have to mature slowly to avoid frustrating the country. It could not rely on the backing of the armed forced or economic groups, but an unquestioning popular support. Above all, it would have to replace the present colonial economic system, which, as you know, has nothing to do with the sort of capitalism that exists in the United States. We would have a drastic regime of austerity, but the majority, instead of giving, would receive the basic means of survival.

Interview, Rio de Janeiro/
The New York Times, 12-30:4.

Patrick J. Buchanan
Director of Communications for
the President of the United States

1

[Calling for U.S. military aid to the contras, rebels fighting the Sandinista government of Nicaragua]: If we don't get that assistance to the contras, they'll be defeated. The Communists . . . will roll up Nicaragua and then we'll be left with two options: Basically, the United States can then step aside and watch the Warsaw Pact roll up Central America, or we send in the Marines.

Broadcast interview/
"CBS Morning News," CBS-TV, 3-4

2

[On the controversy in the U.S. between the Reagan Administration, which supports U.S. aid to rebels fighting the Sandinista government of Nicaragua, and those who are against such aid]: Nicaragua is an issue which engages the heart as well as the mind. It's an issue of Communism versus anti-Communism. It is perceived by both on our side and the other side as a moral issue, an issue of right and wrong, and on issues like this emotions run deep and passions run deep and strong. We recognize this, but we have no apologies . . . I look at it like this: We're like a group of doctors here. We're sitting down and looking at a patient we want to save. What we've been saying early on is, "Gentlemen, all the symptoms are there—this [the Sandinistas] is a cancer." And what the other side is saying is, "Look, this is a tumor, but it's not cancerous." And I think, as more and more of the evidence comes in, more and more Democrats and Republicans [in the U.S.] will come to believe that these people who told us it was cancer appear to be right.

Interview, Washington/
The New York Times, 3-25:10.

Dale Bumpers
United States Senator,
D-Arkansas

3

[Arguing against U.S. military aid to the contras, rebels fighting the Sandinista government

of Nicaragua]: Revolutions, like romance, rarely work when they're arranged by outsiders.

Before the Senate, Washington, March 27/
USA Today, 3-28:(A)4.

4

[Arguing against $100-million in U.S. aid to the contras, rebels fighting the Sandinista government of Nicaragua]: I don't believe $100-million will do the trick, and I don't know of anybody that does. That means that next year you will be back here asking for another $100-million or $200-million. And the year after that . . . Assume that the contras are losing and that the Sandinistas have solidly entrenched themselves—and there we sit. What do we do then? Do we send the Marines in?

Addressing U.S. Secretary of State
George Shultz at Senate hearing, Washington,
April 12/Los Angeles Times, 4-13:(I)23.

George Bush
Vice President of the United States

5

[On the contras, rebels fighting the Sandinista government of Nicaragua]: [Former U.S. Senator] George McGovern wrote [that the contras consist of] "the corrupt and brutal national guardsmen of the late and unlamented Anastasio Somoza." What planet is this man living on? Many of those fighting the Sandinistas fought against Somoza. The majority . . . were in their early teens, or younger, during Somoza's reign.

At Conservative Political
Action Conference, Washington/
The Christian Science Monitor, 2-3:44.

Albert Bustamante
United States Representative,
D-Texas

6

[On President Reagan's backing of the contras, rebels fighting the Sandinista government of Nicaragua]: We have no real Latin American policy. We have always been the big brother telling little brother what to do . . . Something must be done about the Sandinistas. [But] it's

(ALBERT BUSTAMANTE)

not as simple [as Reagan says]. The President got people wound up with an emotional pitch that the Commies are two days away from Texas . . . It's an insult to my intelligence to come in with simple slogans.

Washington, April 10/
USA Today, 4-11:(A)4.

Robert C. Byrd
United States Senator,
D-West Virginia

1

[Criticizing the U.S. Reagan Administration's policy in Central America]: The evidence has mounted that the Administration has no earthly idea how to address the region's many complex problems other than to escalate U.S. military involvement. The excessive military focus of the Administration's policies toward Central America has become even more obvious despite the fact that our allies in the region continue to indicate serious doubts about the wisdom of those policies.

The New York Times, 9-18:53.

2

[On how the new Democratic majority in the U.S. Senate will deal with the Sandinista government of Nicaragua]: The Democrats are going to emphasize the use of all the tools—diplomatic, economic, political as well as military—with diplomatic at the top and military as a last resort. Our objective is certainly not to see American boys fighting in Central America.

Broadcast interview/
"Meet the Press," NBC-TV, 11-9.

Omar Cabezas
Vice Minister of the
Interior of Nicaragua

3

[Saying the government will crack down on those in Nicaragua who support the U.S. backing of the contras, rebels fighting Nicaragua's Sandinista government]: From here on, for any-

one who supports [U.S.] President Reagan for sending $100-million [to the contras], the state-of-emergency law will be applied. *La Prensa* [the independent newspaper which was closed down by the Sandinistas recently] was closed by the U.S. Republicans. They closed it. If it weren't for the vote [in the U.S. House of Representatives to send the contra aid], it would be open tomorrow. We have been flexible to show that we wanted national unity. But the flexibility begins to end because the U.S. Congress approved war against us . . . We are not going to turn the other cheek.

Managua, June 26/
Los Angeles Times, 6-27:(I)15.

Adolfo Calero
President, national directorate,
Nicaraguan Democratic Force

4

[On his organization's struggle to topple the Sandinista government of Nicaragua]: We can do the job in Nicaragua, but the amount of money we get regulates the amount of time it takes. If we don't get what we need, we will be fighting a protracted war, which is what I've always been afraid of . . . A year ago, we said that with $50-million we could do the job, to bring the Sandinistas to their day of reckoning. But the ante has gone up. A year ago, the Sandinistas didn't have helicopters, didn't have as much armament, hadn't opened as many roads to the north where our troops used to be safe . . . For Nicaragua, we propose democracy, and that is Western-type democracy in keeping with Western values: religion, freedom, family and private property. The Sandinistas must either mend their way or go.

Interview, Washington, Jan. 2/
Los Angeles Times, 1-3:(I)13.

Dante Caputo
Foreign Minister of Argentina

5

[On the foreign-debt burden of many Latin American nations]: This debt is the epicenter in the fragility of our democratic systems.

Time, 3-10:64.

Juan Cariaga
Minister of Finance of Bolivia

1

[On the drug-trafficking problem in Bolivia]: If we don't destroy the money power of the cocaine traffickers now, they will take over the economy from legitimate businessmen and be able to elect the next President of Bolivia in 1989.

Los Angeles Times, 7-17:(I)14.

Jimmy Carter
*Former President
of the United States*

2

Perhaps the next major crisis for our country is going to be caused by Mexico, [because] we are wedded to Mexico in an unbreakable fashion. And I think there's an increasing awareness now—at least in the South and Southwestern [U.S.] states—that Mexico's problems are our problems.

*Interview, Atlanta/The Christian
Science Monitor, 12-30:15.*

Fidel Castro
President of Cuba

3

[Announcing the outlawing of free peasant markets in Cuba]: The peasant free market will pass without glory, leaving behind a great lesson, much damages and many millionaires . . . Before the activity of certain individuals who want to become rich at the expense of the sweat of others, we make clear that one thing is respect of initiative and quite another thing is tolerance of abuses and enrichment. The struggle against all kinds of exploitation and parasites is a struggle without truce, because such a deviation could damage the revolutionary cycle of the people. The free market became an obstacle to the development of the cooperative movement and was useful only for a group of intermediaries to get rich individually.

The New York Times, 5-20:6.

4

[Saying there are problems, economic and otherwise, in Cuba]: We have to wash the dirty linen.

I am convinced that what is suffocating us, infecting us, choking us is not washing the dirty linen for fear that the enemy in Miami [anti-Castro Cubans] might find out, or the imperialists, and use it to attack us. I am convinced that discussing all these problems out in the open within a socialist, revolutionary exchange of criticism . . . gives us tremendous strength . . . We have not taught the people that the first duty of a revolutionary and of socialism, and the first duty of the citizen, is to work hard and produce, with responsibility and discipline.

*Before Cuban Communist Party
Central Committee, Havana, July/
Los Angeles Times, 8-11:(I)1,6.*

Vinicio Cerezo
President of Guatemala

5

In our political life, violence has been a permanent substitute for negotiation and compromise. Some Guatemalans opted for the absurd and primitive language of physical damage and armed reprisal . . . Thousands of Guatemalan lives have fallen in this frightful vortex of fratricidal violence, hundreds of thousands of us have suffered in one form or another from the effects of this general climate of oppression.

*Inaugural address, Guatemala City,
January/Los Angeles Times, 2-9:(I)15.*

6

What people [in Guatemala] have to do is to go out and run the risks of democracy, create a serious opposition. And the government will protect them, not persecute them. I am really a true democrat. I believe that people have the right to disagree with me . . . I think that in five years time this will be a country where the conditions for the consolidation of a democratic system will be in place.

*Interview/The Christian
Science Monitor, 6-23:12.*

7

[On his country's recent return to democracy]: [Before democracy returned,] we breathed violence, we could feel it in the atmosphere, it conditioned our responses. Despite this, probably because of our magical and utopian culture, by virtue of our ancestral humanism, because of our religious formation, instead of this becoming a generalized form of life, it was a reason for our systematically and permanently rejecting authoritarian governments and violence as political instruments.

At United Nations, New York,
Sept. 29/The New York Times, 9-30:5.

Jaime Chamorro
Editor, "La Prensa" (Nicaragua)

1

Sandinista [government] strategy is to take Nicaragua to Communism and into the Soviet orbit. To do this, they have to be pragmatic, and they can't take away all our freedoms at once. The Sandinistas want to sell an image that they are running a democratic, pluralist revolution. This helps them get aid from Europe and also protects them by giving them popular support in many places. The level of freedom that exists today is a tactic of the moment. Any day, they can do away with *La Prensa* and the rest of the opposition.

The New York Times, 3-20:4.

Henry G. Cisneros
Mayor of San Antonio, Texas

2

[On the problem of illegal aliens crossing into the U.S. from Mexico]: Our fundamental problem is that we have one of the wealthiest nations in the world, with a 2,000-mile border with a country that is very poor and, one could say at the moment, an economy that is deteriorating . . . We don't have enough money in the Federal Treasury to put enough agents, arm-in-arm, on the border, which is what it would take to stop people from coming across the border . . . You're either going to get [Mexican] products [by lowering restrictions to their sale in the U.S.], or you're going to get their people. But you cannot seal the border and expect neither

products nor people, because there's seething unemployment and poverty [in Mexico] that cannot be addressed in any other way.

To reporters, Washington, March 11/
The Christian Science Monitor, 3-12:4.

Miguel de la Madrid
President of Mexico

3

Mexicans have made increasingly strenuous efforts in the last three years to cope with the country's severe economic crisis. My people have responded to this uncommon challenge with exemplary responsibility. However, the challenge is growing even greater because of adverse international factors, as shown by the dramatic instability of world raw-materials prices and the negative flow of foreign financing.

At meeting with U.S. President Reagan, Mexicali,
Mexico, Jan. 3/The New York Times, 1-4:3.

4

At present, 70 per cent of [Mexico's] deficit stems from interest payments. In spite of having increased revenue and reduced expenditures, the load of the interest on the debt has us traveling in a vicious circle. If we could reduce the debt-service burden, we would be strengthening the balance of payments and that would give us greater capacity to import—and most of our imports are from the U.S. In addition to being a real economic problem, the debt has become a very important psychological problem for the people of Mexico. A person or a country can work with greater enthusiasm if they can see a light at the end of the tunnel. But if they see that, however many efforts and sacrifices they make, there seems to be no way out, a problem of despondency arises.

Interview/Time, 3-24:46.

5

Inasmuch as Mexico is able to recover its economic activity and generate more employment, there will be a decrease in immigration flows toward the United States. We Mexicans think the immigration phenomenon is due to structural problems of both economies. The U.S. economy, be-

(MIGUEL de la MADRID)

cause of its dynamism, has required Mexican labor, and the Mexican economy has not been able to generate sufficient jobs at adequate pay levels.

Interview, Mexico City, Aug. 8/
The Washington Post, 8-11:(A)12.

1

[On U.S. criticism that his country is not doing enough to fight drug trafficking]: The country continues to do its part in this bitter struggle. Nevertheless, we have been subjected to a number of pressures from abroad. It has been said that the action we have been taking has not been sufficiently effective in combating this crime, without any recognition of the fact that the activities undertaken by the Mexican government are on the increase and are proportionately superior to those of other countries . . . In 1985 alone, 10 agents of the Federal Judicial Police were killed. The sacrifice of these fellow countrymen is an example of integrity and courage.

State of the Union address, Mexico City,
Sept. 1/The Washington Post, 9-2:(A)15.

Leslie Delatour
Minister of Finance of Haiti

2

[Saying many monopolies continue to exist in Haiti after the fall of dictator Jean-Claude Duvalier]: The guy who was married to the sister of the former President's wife had the monopoly on copper electrical cable. Another guy had the monopoly on mosquito deterrent devices . . . We've been eliminating these private monopolies that were protected by very high tariffs. But every now and then you bump into another one. Why do you think I'm one of the most unpopular guys in some quarters? The name of the game has changed.

Interview/The Washington Post, 12-22:(A)1.

Miguel d'Escoto
Foreign Minister of Nicaragua

3

[Criticizing U.S. support for the contras, rebels fighting the Sandinista government of

Nicaragua]: The great North American power, which says it struggles against terrorism, has its own army of terror, paid to murder, to destroy, to terrorize. We find ourselves confronted with an avoidable reality: the conversion of state terrorism into official policy and an imminent escalation of intervention by the United States in Central America . . . In the name of freedom and democracy, in the name of the sacred values of Christianity, or civilization, this great and powerful nation [the U.S.] has created mercenary bands, training, financing and directing them. In the name of God and democracy, they have slaughtered our women, our children.

At United Nations,
New York, July 1/
The New York Times, 7-2:4.

Christopher J. Dodd
United States Senator,
D-Connecticut

4

[On the contra rebels and the Sandinista government of Nicaragua they are fighting]: We've had the [U.S.] President and others calling the contras Jeffersonian democrats, and we've had others referring to the Sandinistas as some new order of Franciscan monks. Frankly, both observations are terribly simplistic, and I think it makes it more difficult to really trying to come up with intelligent solutions to this problem.

At Senate Foreign Relations
Committee hearing, Washington, Feb. 27/
The New York Times, 2-28:8.

Jose Napoleon Duarte
President of El Salvador

5

For me, the problem is that Nicaragua has created destabilization in the region as a sort of vanguard, because they have become the center of operations for the export of revolution which has threatened the national security of the United States.

Interview, Guatemala City,
Guatemala, Jan. 15/
Los Angeles Times, 1-16:(I)12.

WHAT THEY SAID IN 1986

(JOSE NAPOLEON DUARTE)

1

My government's first priority is to achieve peace [with the rebels fighting to overthrow the government]: We already have a negative response from the guerrillas. They say they aren't willing to give up their arms or the war, that they don't accept the Constitution or the government. Their proposal and my proposal are completely opposed. They say force can take them to power. I say dialogue can bring about democracy. At the same time, they are ready to talk. What happens when two opposite sectors confront each other and begin to talk? The tensions begin to relax. And this relaxation process can bring about agreements on those matters where key ideological points are not at stake.

Interview/Newsweek, 6-16:46.

2

[Saying that governing El Salvador has proved more difficult than he thought when he took office three years ago]: I found on examination that the disease here was far more grave than I thought. They gave me a patient who was dying. I can give morphine or I can offer a cure, but for this I have to pay a political price. The medicine is bitter, and the patient will complain.

Interview, San Salvador, Sept. 23/
The New York Times, 9-25:9.

Jean-Claude Duvalier
President of Haiti

3

[Announcing his resigning office and going into exile]: I take God as a witness that I have never wanted bloodshed. Unfortunately, during the recent past, we have had to deplore that there have been a certain number of victims. Today, I have not been able to detect, through a meticulous consideration of the situation, any sign which would encourage me that this nightmare of blood would be spared to my people. That is why, wanting to go down in history with my head held high with a clean conscience, I have decided tonight to trust the destiny of the nation and the power to the armed forces of Haiti, de-

siring that this decision will allow a peaceful and rapid solution to the present crisis.

Radio broadcast, Port-au-Prince,
Feb. 7/The Washington Post, 2-8:(A)17.

Daniel Evans
United States Senator,
R-Washington

4

[On the contras, rebels fighting the Sandinista government of Nicaragua]: I don't have a great deal of confidence that the current contra leadership, which the [U.S. Reagan Administration] tends to support most avidly, is doing the job; and if they come into power, I don't think they would be a very good influence in Nicaragua. For any revolutionary group to succeed, it must have the support of the people, but I don't detect that that has really happened.

The Christian Science Monitor, 4-11:32.

Harold Ezell
Western Regional Commissioner,
Immigration and Naturalization
Service of the United States

5

[On illegal immigration to the U.S. from Mexico]: The United States is on its way to becoming a Third World nation. There are 100 million people between the Rio Grande and Panama. We can't take them all in.

U.S. News &
World Report, 10-13:75.

Leon Febres Cordero
President of Ecuador

6

I don't think the [economic] failures we've seen in Latin America are due to the people, but to leaders who don't go through with policies. Ecuador is still an oasis in Latin America from an economic point of view—we have growth, even though we may be politically very unstable.

Interview, Quito, Ecuador/
The Christian Science Monitor, 6-30:11.

Thomas S. Foley
United States Representative,
D-Washington

1

[Arguing against U.S. military aid to the contras, rebels fighting the Sandinista government of Nicaragua]: [On] one issue the overwhelming majority of Americans are united: We will not permit the establishment in Nicaragua of Soviet or other hostile military bases or the introduction of offensive weapons that directly threaten other countries in Latin America or the United States. There is no question that any [U.S.] President would have full bipartisan support in action necessary to remove such a threat. But such a direct threat does not exist. Nevertheless, the [U.S. Reagan] Administration proposes expanding this proxy war in Nicaragua—a war fought with American money, American weapons and Nicaraguan lives in which, at best, only a bloody stalemate can be achieved . . . Is there another way? We believe there is. Four countries of Latin America—Mexico, Panama, Venezuela and Colombia—the so-called Contadora countries, with the support of other major Latin American nations, have urged a regional solution based on negotiations . . . Could such negotiations be successful? With the wholehearted support of the United States, we believe that they could.

Broadcast address to the nation,
Washington, March 15/
The Washington Post, 3-18:(A)18.

2

[Arguing against U.S. support for the contras, rebels fighting the Sandinista government of Nicaragua]: What will we do if, after hundreds of millions of dollars, years of support, training and equipment, and an incalculable investment of American political and diplomatic currency, the contras eventually face defeat? What if they face decimation or capture? Will we never send our own forces to help them, no matter how desperate their situation? Or will we leave them to their fate in a giant replay of the Bay of Pigs?

The Christian Science
Monitor, 4-18:15.

Alan Garcia
President of Peru

3

We [in Peru] must think of the immense masses at the bottom of the social pyramid who never got any attention from the state. The peasant communities, for example, which have more than 5 million Peruvians, remain at a subsistence level, with no government health or education services, no technology, no way to increase their production. Parallel to that, in the cities there is a huge mass of poverty resulting from migration from the rural communities in the Andes. These two sectors have never had the state pay attention to them. The state has been the patrimony of the owners of the means of production who run the economic system, or of the middle class, and administrators who live from this system or from the state itself. We believe that the state is not theirs. We believe that we must move toward a new division of property. If we are allowed to continue our efforts, in five years we will have achieved a redistribution in which the lowest classes benefit the most.

Interview/World Press Review, August:25.

Gary Hart
United States Senator,
D-Colorado

4

[On U.S. policy against the Sandinista government of Nicaragua]: Our current designs seem to allow the Nicaragua junta to choose only whether it wishes to be ousted peacefully or by force. They are unlikely to choose either course. Since [the U.S.-backed contra rebels] also appear to have little chance of [military] success [against the Sandinistas], we find ourselves at a dead end, applying just enough pressure to guarantee a close relationship between Managua and Moscow.

The Christian Science Monitor, 6-12:4.

5

We have a right to prevent a Soviet military base from being established, not only in Nicaragua but anywhere in the Hemisphere . . . We ought also to interdict arms supplies that may flow outside of

(GARY HART)

Nicaragua. But unless we are prepared to overthrow the Sandinista government [of Nicaragua] and use American troops to do so, we ought to be seeking some other solution to whatever problems we perceive the Sandinistas to represent.

Interview/U.S. News & World Report, 6-23:23.

Jesse Helms
United States Senator, R-North Carolina

1

[On U.S. policy toward Chile]: The policy of [U. S.] President Reagan is to promote the democratic transition on an orderly schedule. [But] the policy of [U.S.] Ambassador [to Chile Harry] Barnes is to disrupt the orderly transition, to promote the totalitarian left that Chile once threw off just in the nick of time, and to defame the government [of Chilean President Augusto Pinochet] that rescued Chile from the clutches of international socialism.

Before the Senate, Washington,
Aug. 7/The New York Times, 8-8:7.

Henry J. Hyde
United States Representative, R-Illinois

2

[Criticizing those Congressmen who are against U.S. military aid to the contras, rebels fighting the Marxist Sandinista government of Nicaragua]: Our friends on the left have never met an anti-Communist they liked. As the refugees stream north, history is going to assign you folks the role of pallbearers at the funeral of freedom in Central America.

Before the House, Washington/
The New York Times, 3-20:12.

Fred C. Ikle
Under Secretary for Policy,
Department of Defense
of the United States

3

I fear that if the United States continues to opt for inadequate aid to the Nicaraguan freedom fighters [the contra rebels fighting the Sandinista government], it would in effect be inviting [Soviet leader Mikhail] Gorbachev to build a second Cuba in Central America. How are boots and food supplies [for the contras] going to counter Soviet tanks and helicopter gunships? If our legislators did continue to tilt the odds in Nicaragua in favor of the Communists, the democratic resistance would be eliminated in a few years. Nicaragua would then be turned into an arsenal for Communist insurgencies, tightly controlled by a totalitarian Leninist regime . . . Leninism demands pushing forward with the bayonet until it hits steel. Either we openly choose appeasement of the Communists in Nicaragua . . . or we choose to support the side of freedom and democracy at a level sufficient so that it can prevail.

Before Inland Empire of Southern
California World Affairs Council,
San Bernardino, Calif., Jan. 30/
Los Angeles Times, 1-31:(I)18.

4

In light of today's disagreement about Nicaragua, it is worth recalling yesterday's disagreement about El Salvador. From 1981 to 1983, opponents of [U.S.] President Reagan's policy argued the Communist insurgents in El Salvador could not be defeated, that they were too strong, that they had popular support. And the government of El Salvador, they argued, was too weak, too flawed, not worthy of our assistance. With your indulgence, I'll quote from a speech I gave in 1983: . . . "What we seek to do is to open the doors to democracy and close the doors to violence. But we have to use military means against those who insist—till they have imposed their rule—on using violence. Let me make this clear to you: We do not seek a military defeat for our friends; we do not seek a military stalemate; we seek victory for the forces of democracy." For saying this, I was roundly criticized by many editorial writers . . . [But] most people would admit today that El Salvador has come a long way toward accomplishing that goal of democracy. While the democratically elected [President Jose Napoleon] Duarte government still has to ward off insurgent attacks, acts of terrorism, and cope

(FRED C. IKLE)

with massive economic problems, the military stalemate has been overcome. But now, President Reagan's policy in Nicaragua still faces opposition in the [U.S.] House of Representatives, as did his policy for El Salvador a few years ago.

Before Council on Foreign Relations,
May 29/The Wall Street Journal, 6-13:18.

Daniel K. Inouye
United States Senator, D-Hawaii

1

[Arguing against U.S. aid to the contras, rebels fighting the Sandinista government of Nicaragua]: People do not support [U.S. President Reagan in his backing of the contras] because the policy does not make sense. They do not believe a country [the U.S.] of 233 million people, and untold power, is threatened by a backward nation [Nicaragua] of three million people. They do not believe the contras will renounce the past and become champions of democracy.

Before the Senate, Washington,
Aug. 12/The New York Times, 8-13:4.

Nancy Kassebaum
United States Senator, R-Kansas

2

[Criticizing President Reagan for questioning the patriotism of those in Congress who oppose military aid to the contras, rebels fighting the Sandinista government of Nicaragua]: There is the argument that this is a matter of patriotism— those who love America will support the President and those who oppose want to abandon San Diego to the Sandinistas. I find this simplistic reasoning to be highly offensive.

March 6/Los Angeles Times, 3-7:(I)1.

Edward M. Kennedy
United States Senator,
D-Massachusetts

3

[Arguing against U.S. support for the contras, rebels fighting the Sandinista government

of Nicaragua]: The syndrome of the quagmire, slowly but surely sucking us deeper into an endless military conflict that we cannot escape, applies to Nicaragua as much as it did to Vietnam.

Washington, Aug. 12/
Los Angeles Times, 8-13:(I)9.

John F. Lehman, Jr.
Secretary of the Navy
of the United States

4

Today we have a very changed naval situation in the Caribbean—fundamentally changed over the last 10 years—in that the Soviets have steadily and methodically built up a major naval capability in Cuba. They have a well-trained navy now with modern equipment, both aircraft and ships. The Soviets deploy surface action groups to the Caribbean about twice a year for cruises.

Interview/USA Today, 3-19:(A)9.

Robert Leiken
Senior associate,
Carnegie Endowment for
International Peace

5

[On the contras, rebels fighting the Sandinista government of Nicaragua]: Despite their shortcomings, the contras are an authentic army of Nicaraguans, mainly peasants, fighting for their liberty against a repressive tyranny supported and maintained in power by the Soviet Union. The contras are many times larger than the Sandinistas ever were. If you put the major leftist insurgencies in Latin America together, they still wouldn't add up to as many as the contras . . . They're facing a military machine that, after the Cubans, is the most sophisticated and best trained in Latin America, far and away the biggest in Central America. You need people, but you've also got to have equipment. Another way of looking at it is that it's stunning that [the contras have] done as well as they have in the face of a very sophisticated state security system. There's a morale factor, too. They feel the other side has got a superpower [the Soviet

WHAT THEY SAID IN 1986

(ROBERT LEIKEN)

Union] committed to it, whereas the U.S. is ambivalent [about backing the contras].

Interview, Washington/Time, 4-21:49.

1

[On the Nicaraguan Democratic Force, or contras, who are fighting the Sandinista government of Nicaragua]: The problem is that the leaders of the Nicaraguan Democratic Force seem to have a very narrow political and ideological perception of what happened in Nicaragua. They are concerned with recovering the land and property they lost [in the Sandinista revolution]. The politics they practice is the style of [deposed Nicaraguan President Anastasio] Somoza—relying on cliques rather than institutions.

The New York Times, 5-23:6.

Dave McCurdy
United States Representative,
D-Oklahoma

2

[Criticizing recently revealed secret U.S.-Iran arms sales, with the proceeds going to the contra rebels in Nicaragua]: I cannot see further [U.S. aid to the contras]. The contras are on their own. The power of the [U.S.] President [Reagan], the personality of the President, is not going to carry the day for them again.

Washington, Nov. 26/
The New York Times, 11-27:8.

Robert C. McFarlane
Former Assistant to the President
of the United States (Ronald Reagan)
for National Security Affairs

3

[On the war between the ruling Sandinistas of Nicaragua and the contra rebels]: The greatest vulnerability of the Sandinistas is their reliance on foreign support. The contras have to cut that off. It isn't all that hard. You don't have to win battles on the battlefield; you do what is easy for guerrillas to do. You close down the ports. You

take out all those helicopters, which you can do without losing a man, with mortars miles off. There's no better than a 30 per cent probability the contras can do that. They are well-meaning people with no sense of warfare. They are Coca-Cola bottlers and clerks and nice people— political folks who just haven't thought a lot about Russian strategy and how to counter Marxist revolution. If they are going to show they can win, it has got to be quick because they can see the U.S. ability to support them is drying up. The moment of truth is going to be played out in the next year.

Interview/U.S. News &
World Report, 12-22:24.

Robert S. McNamara
Former Secretary of Defense
of the United States; Former President,
International Bank for Reconstruction
and Development (World Bank)

4

The Mexicans want to live in Mexico, but the operative word is *live*. And if they can't live *there*, they're going to live *here* [in the U.S., through illegal immigration]. [The U.S.-Mexican border] cannot be protected no matter how much we expand the Immigration Service. I think we must recognize as a fact that for many purposes we are one market . . . We have no choice but to take either their men or their goods.

Interview, New York/
The Christian Science Monitor, 12-16:20.

James Mills
Author; Authority on
narcotics trafficking

5

[On Mexico's involvement in drug trafficking]: Mexico is probably the most corrupt nation on earth. There are DEA agents who have been investigating Mexican corruption for a long, long time. Some of them have been investigating it very intensely since a DEA agent was tortured to death in Mexico. I was speaking to one of these agents not long ago, and he referred to Mexico as a "thugocracy." He said it is a country that is governed by thugs. I believe it is. The

(JAMES MILLS)

government of Mexico is in the control of narcotics traffickers.

Interview/USA Today, 7-8:(A)9.

Langhorne A. Motley
*Former Assistant Secretary for
Inter-American Affairs, Department of
State of the United States*

1

[On U.S. criticism of Chile's dictatorship under President Augusto Pinochet]: [At a meeting with Pinochet in 1985,] he put his finger under my nose and said, "We're not a colony of the United States, relations have not been very good between us for a long time, we almost went to war in the last century, and I don't take advice." I told him I was not there to lecture but that I wanted to tell him what the reaction was outside, in Europe and the United States. I told him that if he were writing the script for the Communists, he couldn't write it better than he was doing then. He responded with a long lecture about how he was the Number 1 Communist target in the world. I said I agreed, but that he was helping the leftists in places like Washington and Paris and that he ought to do something to let the air out of the balloon.

*Interview, Washington/
The New York Times, 5-16:4.*

Brian Mulroney
Prime Minister of Canada

2

We don't need people who are contemptuous of their friends and allies at any time. Canada is a loyal friend and ally. And . . . you give your friend the benefit of the doubt. There is a growing sense of maturity and awareness in Canada.

*Interview, Montreal/
The Christian Science Monitor, 3-18:44.*

Henri Namphy
*President, National Council
of Government of Haiti*

3

[On his new government, which took over after the overthrow of President Jean-Claude Duvalier]: We are going to work for the blooming of real and functional democracy founded on absolute respect for human rights, press freedom, the existence of free labor unions and the functioning of structured political parties. We are aware that the country aspires to the elaboration of a liberal constitution, to the rebuilding of a legislative power that is the product of free elections and to Presidential elections with direct, universal suffrage. Such is the program of this provisional government, eager to hand over power to a democratically elected government, which is an indispensible condition for the social stability and harmonious development of our country.

*At installation of new Cabinet, Port-au-Prince,
Feb. 10/The Washington Post, 2-11:(A)1.*

4

We have to give the people an education so they may consciously vote for their leader, not as they did in the past. When we have freedom of speech, freedom of the press, free unions and a real civil service, we will hold elections, starting with sheriff. If the base is not solid, you cannot build on it.

Interview/Time, 5-26:37.

5

[On the problems in Haiti since the overthrow of dictator Jean-Claude Duvalier]: Acts of terrorism, including arson, the isolation of our provincial cities by stupid roadblocks, killings, which are like the prelude to a civil war. In short, under the incitement of groups trained in the game of destabilization, the country finds itself on the edge of anarchy. Haitian people, it was not to create such a situation that you broke the yoke of a long and cruel dictatorship.

*Broadcast address to the nation,
June 5/Los Angeles Times, 6-6:(I)13.*

6

If Haiti fails to turn to a policy of total effort to promote exports, our economy will continue to stagnate, bringing as a probable consequence extreme political and social tension . . . Haiti is ready to transform the basic structure of its economy to break the bonds of poverty forever.

(HENRI NAMPHY)

[Private foreign investment must] help us infuse a new dynamism into the industrial sector, whose accelerated expansion is viewed as essential in today's economy, if the tendency toward stagnation is to be reversed.

At Miami Conference on the Caribbean,
Nov. 19/Los Angeles Times, 11-20:(I)12.

Richard M. Nixon
Former President of the United States

1

[On the contras, rebels fighting the Sandinista government of Nicaragua]: Support for the anti-Communist contras is in the interest of the Nicaraguan people, who suffer under a repressive Communist dictatorship which denies them any chance to bring about peaceful change. It serves the interest of the United States. Nicaragua is more important to the United States strategically than the Philippines; it would provide the first Soviet base on the Latin-American mainland. But even more dangerous strategically is the threat an avowedly expansionist Nicaragua would pose to its Central American neighbors . . . What happens in Nicaragua will have world-wide implications. If the contras, with our aid, can succeed, it would be the first time that a Soviet-sponsored government was forced to abandon its repressive and expansionist policies because of the success of a people's counter-revolution.

Before American Newspaper
Publishers Association, San Francisco,
April 21/ USA Today, 4-22:(A)11.

2

[Supporting U.S. backing of the contras, rebels fighting the Sandinista government of Nicaragua]: . . . we should support anti-Communist rebels fighting against tyranny in Nicaragua. To deny help to our friends fighting for freedom, while accepting the fact that the Soviets are assisting their comrades [the Sandinistas] fighting for tyranny, is strategically stupid and morally indefensible.

Before American Newspaper
Publishers Association, San Francisco,
April 21/The Washington Post, 4-22:(A)12.

3

[On the Sandinista government of Nicaragua and U.S. backing of the contra rebels fighting that government]: Some of the hawks [in the U.S.] are saying, "Let's go in and knock off the Sandinistas [with U.S. troops]." Well, we could do that, but . . . what are you going to do with it when you conquer it? That's the problem with Nicaragua: Who's going to run the damned place? Therefore, the military option is not one that is very useful. That's why you have to have it done by Nicaraguans [the contras].

Interview, Saddle River, N.J./
Newsweek, 5-19:34.

Manuel Antonio Noriega
Commander, National
Defense Force of Panama

4

[On U.S. criticism of the ousting of Panama's President Nicolas Ardito Barletta last September by military officers led by Noriega]: There have been opinions and criticisms, and often there is an excessive readiness to accept the complaints of the opposition. The United States and Panama need each other. The United States cannot change its policy to suit the ego of certain functionaries, and Panama cannot get into a fight with the United States in response to their complaints. The United States has certain strategic priorities in this region, and Panama is a part of that.

The New York Times, 2-17:6.

5

The role of the defense force in this country is different from any other armed forces. Here the President of the republic, who rules and makes decisions, is a friend of ours. We are his subaltern and his support. We've learned to walk together.

Interview, Panama, June 17/
The New York Times, 6-18:3.

Miguel Cardinal Obando y Bravo
Roman Catholic Primate of Nicaragua

6

[Criticizing Nicaragua's Sandinista government for persecuting the church]: I have told our

(MIGUEL CARDINAL OBANDO y BRAVO)

people that some priests have been called to legal proceedings where their fingerprints are taken, and that is no lie. I have said that our social promotion office was taken over at 8:45 on the morning of October 15, before the emergency laws had been announced or taken effect, and this is no lie. I have said there are shortages and that some of our people are hungry, and this is no lie. I said the Catholic radio station has been kept silent since January 1, and you are witnesses that the station is closed. They attack us, they slander us, they say our hands are drenched in blood. But fortunately, we have an intelligent, mature people that knows how to interpret this. If you bombard the people with information that deforms their morality, sows the seeds of division and creates a desire for vengeance, you are eliminating the possibility of salvation.

At mass, Managua, March 27/
The New York Times, 3-28:3.

David R. Obey
United States Representative,
D-Wisconsin

1

[Arguing against U.S. military aid to the contras, rebels fighting the Sandinista government of Nicaragua]: We view the aid package not as a way to avoid American involvement, but as a means that will put us on the slippery slope to involvement. [In the Philippines, where dictator Ferdinand Marcos was overthrown recently,] we let the people there do it. If we learned one lesson from the Philippines, it is, "don't give $100-million to the contras [in Nicaragua]."

At House Appropriations Subcommittee
hearing, Washington, March 4/
The Washington Post, 3-5:(A)25.

Thomas P. O'Neill, Jr.
United States Representative,
D-Massachusetts

2

This [Western] Hemisphere is moving toward democracy today not because of American fire-

power, but because the people themselves believe in democracy. It is also because our country has tried to foster democracy in Latin America—through the Good Neighbor policy, through Point Four, through President [John] Kennedy's Alliance for Progress and through [former President] Jimmy Carter's strong commitment to human rights. President [Raul] Alfonsin of Argentina has said publicly that his country would never have restored democracy without the relentless campaign President Carter waged for the principle of human rights, not only in the Soviet Union but among the nations of this Hemisphere.

Accepting Harry S. Truman
Good Neighbor Award, Kansas City,
May 8/The Wall Street Journal, 5-20:30.

Daniel Ortega
President of Nicaragua

3

[Rejecting U.S. Reagan Administration proposals for the Nicaraguan government to negotiate with the contras, rebels fighting Nicaragua's Sandinista government]: Why does the Reagan Administration want dialogue with the counter-revolutionaries—to achieve peace in Nicaragua? They want dialogue in order to destroy the revolution, and those Nicaraguans who repeat these words are either stupid or, more likely, are being paid by the CIA.

Before Nicaraguan Parliament, Managua,
Feb. 21/The New York Times, 2-22:4.

4

[On U.S. charges that Nicaraguan troops crossed into Honduras to attack contras, rebels fighting the Sandinista government of Nicaragua]: This combat has taken place in the Nicaragua-Honduras border territory. It is a very tense territory, which has been turned over to the United States and the counter-revolutionary forces. From Honduras, mercenary forces set out to strike against our territory. What Nicaragua has done is to defend itself against attacks by the counter-revolution, which is based in Honduras. This is a legitimate right which Nicaragua will continue to exercise . . . We are not violating any princi-

WHAT THEY SAID IN 1986

(DANIEL ORTEGA)

ples. The one that violates the principles of territorial integrity and national sovereignty is the United States, which has placed the mercenaries in Honduras so they can invade Nicaragua and violate Nicaragua's border.

News conference, Managua, March 28/
The New York Times, 3-29:4.

1

We will never negotiate with the contras [rebels fighting his government]. We are prepared to negotiate and discuss with the chief of the contras, [U.S. President] Ronald Reagan, and his functionaries. If the U.S. feels that Nicaragua is a threat to its interests in the region, we will look for mechanisms of security so the U.S. feels secure. Nicaragua's internal situation cannot be negotiated . . . I would invite [Reagan] to normalize relations with Nicaragua, to have a friendly policy. I would invite him to convert himself into a factor for peace in Latin America and the world. If he says he is a Christian, that he believes in God, he could have a more Christian policy. He could be more humble. He could try a new type of relationship with a revolutionary government, a government that is not a threat to the United States.

Interview,
Managua/Time, 3-31:17.

2

[On whether Nicaragua's Sandinista revolution will spread to other countries]: We need the right of self-determination to be respected and for us to be allowed to solve our own problems. We're not the ones to decide what the future of Central America will be; the people will decide that. People all over the region are demanding solutions—economically, politically, socially. The demand is so overwhelming that almost every Latin American leader has incorporated a social program in his platform. This issue is whether you respond from above by promoting income distribution or whether people seize it themselves from below.

Interview, Managua/U.S. News
& World Report, 6-2:27.

3

[Criticizing the U.S. House of Representative's approval of $100-million in military aid to the contras, rebels fighting the Sandinista government of Nicaragua]: [The House vote is] nothing more than the ratification of the warlike and criminal policy of the United States against Nicaragua. This policy does not frighten or intimidate us, nor does the possibility that American troops may intervene in our country. We are going to continue defending the revolution.

To reporters, Managua, June 25/
The New York Times, 6-27:5.

4

[Saying his government is cracking down on those in Nicaragua who support the U.S. in its aid to the contras, rebels fighting the Nicaraguan Sandinista government]: [The government cannot continue to] permit traitors to function brazenly and with impunity in their shameless functions as agents of the American government, justifying the aggression . . . and giving "civic" cover to the counter-revolutionary plans.

Broadcast address to the nation,
Managua, June 26/
Los Angeles Times, 6-27:(I)15.

5

[Defending his government's closing of the opposition newspaper *La Prensa*]: We are at war [against the U.S.-supported contra rebels] . . . The owners of the *La Prensa* newspaper have been in Washington lobbying for United States aid for the contras. We don't intend to do with them what the United States did with the Japanese [the internment of Japanese-Americans in World War II]. We stand by the right to publish anything of any ideology. But when a media organ begins to defend anyone making war against our own people, that is something else.

At Park Slope Methodist Church,
Brooklyn, N.Y., July 27/
The New York Times, 7-28:5.

6

[On Soviet-Nicaraguan relations]: Politically, we have relations of mutual respect and independence. The Soviet Union knows we have a gov-

(DANIEL ORTEGA)

ernment of political pluralism, a mixed economy and a stand of non-alignment. There has never been any insinuation that we should change our policies or make changes more along the lines of the Cuban or socialist model. Militarily, we are but one more country that is supplied by the Soviet Union. It is not that we have any particular fondness for Soviet weapons. There is no Soviet military base in Nicaragua. There are no Soviet troops. We don't have military maneuvers with the Soviets, and we are willing to put all of those facts in a treaty with the U.S. Economically, the Soviet contribution is substantive. But socialist cooperation and European cooperation pretty much balance.

Interview, New York/Time, 8-11:27.

1

[Defending Nicaraguan troops' pursuit of contra rebels into Honduras]: As long as the contras' camps continue in Honduras, they will be an extension of our border, because we are not going to give up our right, our obligation to defend our sovereignty . . . We have not invaded Honduras. We have no problem with Honduras. But Honduras has created the problem by yielding to pressure by the United States to hand territory over to mercenary camps. We are fighting against those mercenary forces that are present in Honduran territory [and that are fighting the Nicaraguan government] . . . The United States is trying to provoke a war between Honduras and Nicaragua. It is looking for any pretext for intervention by North American troops.

Broadcast address to the nation,
Managua, Dec. 10/
Los Angeles Times, 12-11:(I)11.

2

[On his decision to release captured U.S. gunrunner Eugene Hasenfus, who was convicted of aiding the contra rebels fighting Nicaragua's Sandinista government]: Let this contribute to reflection by the American government. Let [U.S.] President Reagan and his advisers, who call themselves Christian, not commit the insane terrorist act of launching an invasion, a direct in-

tervention against our country that would mean more deaths for the youth of the United States and Nicaragua.

News conference, Managua, Dec. 17/
The New York Times, 12-18:10.

Eden Pastora
Anti-Sandinista
Nicaraguan rebel leader

3

[Saying he is giving up his armed fight against Nicaragua's Sandinista government]: We don't want to be soldiers of the United States in a war of pressure. We want to be soldiers of the Nicaraguan people in a war of ours, the Nicaraguans, to overthrow the extreme left [Sandinistas]. We are withdrawing from the armed struggle because we believe there is no possibility of a military victory, because of the incapacity imposed by the North American sectors that want to negotiate.

Costa Rica, May 16/
Los Angeles Times, 5-17:(I)1.

Victor Paz Estenssoro
President of Bolivia

4

[On drug-traffickers in Bolivia]: If we do not address this problem decisively, to eliminate it, the day could come when the economic power they wield could result in their governing the country.

USA Today, 7-21:(A)10.

Gustavo Petricioli
Minister of Finance of Mexico

5

[Asking foreign banks for new loans to Mexico]: For 19 months, we have punctually paid interest [on Mexico's existing foreign loans] without receiving any credit, either in cash or public opinion. Through devastating earthquakes and just as devastating drop in oil prices, we have been willing to take the necessary adjustment measures and continue to honor our commitments. Any realistic analysis would con-

263

WHAT THEY SAID IN 1986

(GUSTAVO PETRICIOLI)

clude that Mexico cannot continue to do so without the appropriate external support.

To world bankers, New York, July 23/
The Washington Post, 7-24:(E)1.

Augusto Pinochet
President of Chile

1

The people will decide if the work of this government is extended. The people will responsibly decide whether they return to chaos . . . or if they want to continue living . . . under the leadership of a democratic government with authority.

Newsweek, 8-4:20.

2

[On the recent assassination attempt against him]: People don't realize the danger we are confronting. We are in a war between democracy and chaos. Either we accept the chaos that the degenerate politicians are pushing, or we support the government, seeking democracy as the logical solution.

Santiago, Sept. 8/
Los Angeles Times, 9-9:(I)10.

3

[On the recent guerrilla attack on his motorcade]: We are going to get tough. Those people talking about human rights and all those things must be expelled from the country or locked up. The war against Marxism is on. The war is going to start from our side.

Time, 9-22:43.

Mario Rappaccioli
Leader, Conservative Party
of Nicaragua

4

[On the contras, rebels fighting the Sandinista government of Nicaragua]: The contras exist because the Sandinistas didn't keep their commitments. As civilians, we don't like to see Nicaraguans killing each other. But since the

Sandinistas don't allow the opposition to do real political work, there are always other alternatives, including the alternative that the Sandinistas themselves used to come to power [guerrilla warfare].

Interview, Managua/
The New York Times, 6-25:6.

Ronald Reagan
President of the United States

5

This [Western] hemisphere is truly the cradle of democracy. Communism is an unwanted, foreign ideology. The Soviets realize that it will never be established by choice in this hemisphere, so they resort to subversion and support for terrorism. Their malevolent activities in this hemisphere affect our bilateral relations with them . . . And the link between the governments of such Soviet allies as Cuba and Nicaragua, and international trafficking and terrorism, is becoming increasingly clear. These twin evils, narcotics trafficking and terrorism, represent the most insidious and dangerous threats to the hemisphere today.

Interview*/The Washington Post, 1-3:(A)9.

6

[Cuban President Fidel] Castro has turned a once-thriving economy into a basket case . . . Castro's tyranny still weighs heavy on the shoulders of his people and threatens the peace and freedom of the hemisphere.

At ceremony celebrating the 1983 overthrow of
Grenada's Communist government, St. George's,
Grenada, Feb. 20/USA Today, 2-21:(A)4.

7

. . . let us not forget that there are still those who will do everything in their power to impose Communist dictatorship on the rest of us. [Cuban President Fidel] Castro's tyranny still weighs heavily on the peace and freedom of the hemisphere. Doing the bidding of his faraway masters, he has shipped Cuba's young men by the thousands to fight and die in faraway lands. When one recalls the tons of military equipment captured [when the U.S. and others invaded

(RONALD REAGAN)

Grenada to throw out the Communist government in 1983], we can thank God things were changed before young Grenadians, too, were sent off to fight and die for an alien ideology.

At ceremony celebrating the 1983 overthrow of
Grenada's Communist government, St. George's,
Grenada, Feb. 20/The Washington Post, 2-21:(A)14.

1

[Calling for U.S. military aid to the contras, rebels fighting the Sandinista government of Nicaragua]: I see several parallels to the Philippine situation [in which a dictator, Ferdinand Marcos, was recently deposed]. We stood for democracy in the Philippines. We have to stand for democracy in Nicaragua and throughout Central America and in our own hemisphere. We can ignore the fraudulent elections [Nicaraguan President Daniel] Ortega held. We can ignore the repression and we can ignore the subversion, terrorism and drug-trafficking. But if we ignore it in Nicaragua and don't deal with it now, when will we deal with it? I maintain we have to deal with it now.

To Congressional leaders,
Washington, Feb. 27/
Los Angeles Times, 2-28:(I)5.

2

[Calling for U.S. military aid to the contras, rebels fighting the Sandinista government of Nicaragua]: If we don't help the freedom fighters [contras] now, a Communist Nicaragua will over the next few years attempt to destabilize its neighbors in Central America, cause untold violence and pain for the people there and create what Communism always creates—a huge refugee machine.

To reporters, Washington, Feb. 28/
Los Angeles Times, 3-1:(I)6.

3

[Calling for U.S. military aid to the contras, rebels fighting the Sandinista government of Nicaragua]: [If the Sandinistas are victorious over the contras,] I think it would place in jeopardy the survival of each of those small and frag-

ile democracies now in Central America, open up the possibility of Soviet military bases on America's doorstep, could threaten the security of the Panama Canal [and] inaugurate a vast migration northward to the United States of hundreds of thousands of refugees. And those who would invite this strategic disaster [those in the U.S. Congress who vote against U.S. military aid to the contras] . . . will be held fully accountable by history.

To reporters at White House meeting with
contra leaders, Washington, March 3/
The Washington Post, 3-4:(A)21.

4

[On his support of the contras, rebels fighting the Sandinista government of Nicaragua]: On my trip to Grenada, nine heads of state of the Caribbean island nations brought up the subject. All of them in total agreement leaned on me and said please don't stop what you are doing down there because Nicaragua under the Sandinista government represents the greatest threat to our democracies that we have ever experienced. So I know where they stand.

To reporters, Washington, March 5/
The Christian Science Monitor, 3-6:32.

5

[Criticizing those members of Congress who oppose U.S. military aid to the contras, rebels fighting the Sandinista government of Nicaragua]: It's what the choice comes down to, whether it is knowingly or not. And I've had enough experience with Communist subversion back in my former profession [acting] to know that a great many people are deceived and not aware that what they're doing is inimical to the United States.

To House Republicans/
Los Angeles Times, 3-7:(I)33.

6

[Calling for U.S. military aid to the contras, rebels fighting the Sandinista government of Nicaragua]: The way I see it, [the late Nicaraguan dictator Anastasio] Somoza's been gone a long time, the revolution that toppled him then became a Communist coup, and so the contras,

(RONALD REAGAN)

so-called, are against it, and so I guess in a way they are counter-revolutionaries and God bless them for being that way. I guess that makes them contras, and so it makes me a contra, too.

To state and local officials, Washington,
March 14/Los Angeles Times, 3-16:(I)13.

1

[Criticizing the House vote against his proposal to give military aid to the contras, rebels fighting the Sandinista government of Nicaragua]: Today's vote in the House of Representatives was a dark day for freedom. This vote must be reversed. The Soviet Union cannot be permitted to enjoy the luxury of knowing that, once captured, a country will be relegated forever to the Communist camp. We declare our unwavering support for freedom and for peace-loving people struggling to overcome Communist tyranny. Those Democrats and Republicans who stood with the forces of freedom have the nation's profound gratitude and my own. But you have more. You have my solemn determination to come back again and again until this battle is won—until freedom is given the chance it deserves in Nicaragua.

Washington, March 20*/
Los Angeles Times, 3-21:(I)25.

2

[Addressing members of the contras, rebels fighting the Sandinista government of Nicaragua]: We're in this together. The future of Central America is not with Communism. The future of Central America is with democracy and all those who are fighting for freedom. You are the future of Central America. Today, I give you my solemn pledge: I will not rest until freedom is given a fighting chance in Nicaragua. We'll spare no effort and give no ground in supporting the democratic resistance in Nicaragua.

Washington, March 21/
Los Angeles Times, 3-22:(I)1.

3

[Criticizing those who are against U.S. military aid to the contras, rebels fighting the San-

dinista government of Nicaragua]: At the same time our opponents claim to support negotiations, they move to eliminate any incentive for the Communists [Sandinistas] to negotiate. Will serious talks be more likely once the democratic resistence has been stripped of its leverage? Does anyone really believe that the ruling clique that runs Nicaragua will enter into a serious dialogue simply to prove they are good guys?

At Republican luncheon, New Orleans,
March 27/The New York Times, 3-28:3.

4

[On his support of the contras, rebels fighting the Sandinista government of Nicaragua]: All of this talk that I am nursing an ambition to send in the [U.S.] troops—no. To send in [American] troops would lose us every friend in Latin America. They want us to help the contras, but not with troops. The only thing I've uttered is a warning that if this revolutionary, this Sandinista, group is allowed to solidify their base, they intend to spread that revolution to other countries . . . We've made 10 attempts to negotiate with them. But when have we ever seen a Communist totalitarian government voluntarily give up their power and say, "Well, okay, we want to have democracy?" We haven't. Diplomacy must have behind it strength. The Sandinistas are not going to agree to all the things that Contadora [a Latin American peace group] has been asking of them unless they feel the pressure of the contras.

Interview, Washington/
Time, 3-31:16.

5

That picture making the rounds showing [Nicaraguan President] Daniel Ortega standing with [Libyan leader] Muammar Qaddafi and raising his fist in a gesture of solidarity is very much to the point. I hope every member of the [U.S.] Congress will reflect on the fact that the [ruling Nicaraguan] Sandinistas have been training, supporting and directing as well as sheltering terrorists. And in this sense they are trying to build a Libya on our doorstep.

Before Heritage Foundation, Washington,
April 22/The New York Times, 4-23:6.

(RONALD REAGAN)

1

In recent years, we've witnessed in the Americas the greatest expansion of democracy in this century. We cannot stand by and permit [in Nicaragua] a Soviet beachhead, which will be used to undermine this process, to be consolidated on the mainland of the Western Hemisphere. The zeal of the Communist regime in Managua for internal repression is matched only by its commitment to subvert neighboring democracies and to spread terror and chaos, far and near . . . Deserting the Nicaraguan [anti-government] freedom fighters would be a national security disaster for the United States.

To Republican candidates and elected officials, Washington, June 6/The New York Times, 6-7:4.

2

[Calling for Congress to approve U.S. military aid for the contras, rebels fighting the Sandinista government of Nicaragua]: Delay is deadly and plays right along with the Communist game-plan because while we may have tied our own hands, the Soviets, Cubans and Libyans haven't tied theirs. With over a billion dollars of support and some of the most fearsome weapons in the Soviet arsenal, the Communist strategy is simple: hold off American aid as long as possible in the hope they can destroy all opposition before help arrives. It's time for an up-and-down vote on freedom in Nicaragua, an up-and-down vote on whether the United States is going to stop Soviet expansionism on the American mainland, while the price is still not too high and the risks are still not too great. We must act now in a bipartisan way to do the right thing, to rescue freedom in Nicaragua and protect the national security of the United States.

News conference, June 11/ The New York Times, 6-12:10.

3

Too often in the past, the United States failed to identify with the aspirations of the people of Central America for freedom and a better life. Too often our government appeared indifferent when democratic values were at risk. So we took the path of least resistance—and did nothing.

Today, however, with American support, the tide is turning in Central America. In El Salvador, Honduras, Costa Rica—and now in Guatemala—freely elected governments offer their people the chance for a better future—a future the United States must support. But there is one tragic, glaring exception to that democratic tide—the Communist Sandinista government in Nicaragua . . . From the very first day, a small clique of Communists worked steadily to consolidate power and squeeze out their democratic allies.

Broadcast address to the nation, Washington, June 24/The New York Times, 6-25:7.

4

The Soviets take the long view, but their strategy is clear—to dominate the strategic sea lanes and vital chokepoints around the world . . . The Soviet Union already uses Cuba as an air and submarine base in the Caribbean. It hopes to turn Nicaragua into the first Soviet base on the mainland of North America. If you doubt it, ask yourself: Why have the last four Soviet leaders—with a mounting economic crisis at home—already invested over a billion dollars and dispatched thousands of Soviet-bloc advisers into a tiny country in Central America? I know that no one in [the U.S.] Congress wants to see Nicaragua become a Soviet military base. My friends, I must tell you in all seriousness: Nicaragua is becoming a Soviet base every day that we debate and debate and debate—and do nothing.

Broadcast address to the nation, Washington, June 24/The New York Times, 6-25:7.

5

[On U.S. support of the contras, rebels fighting the Sandinista government of Nicaragua]: What our attempt has always been in these nine meetings with [the Sandinistas] is to persuade them to sit down and negotiate the democratization of Nicaragua. And in every instance, the freedom fighters [contras] had agreed with us they would lay down their arms to come to the table and have a peaceful political solution to the problem. And nine times there was failure on the part of the Nicaraguans—the Sandinista government—they refused. We believe that it's going to take the pressure off the freedom fight-

267

(RONALD REAGAN)

ers. And what we really think will be the best goal is if they have the strength to impose leverage—exert leverage on the Sandinista government; then we could still have a peaceful political settlement.

Interview/The New York Times, 8-20:2.

1

[Criticizing those Democrats in the U.S. Congress who oppose U.S. military aid to the contras, rebels fighting the Sandinista government of Nicaragua]: Imagine if that great Missourian [the late Democratic President] Harry Truman were here today, what he'd think. This was the man who battled back Communist aggression in Korea and whose timely aid saved Greece and possibly much of Europe from Communist enslavement. What would he say about a party who sees the Soviets building another fortress Cuba on the American mainland and won't even lift a finger to stop it? You can bet whatever he had to say, it would be unprintable.

At Republican Party rally,
Kansas City, Sept. 29/
The New York Times, 9-30:10.

Charles E. Redman
Spokesman for the Department
of State of the United States

2

The [recent Central American] summit demonstrated that there are real and profound differences between the democracies and the Nicaraguan government. The summit made clear the view of the democracies that democratization is fundamental to peace in Central America. Commitments on security issues alone are not sufficient to bring peace. There is more and more firmness in being willing to take on the [Nicaraguan] Sandinistas on those questions. This seems to be a new phenomenon, this kind of unity among the democracies.

Washington, May 27/
Los Angeles Times, 5-28:(I)1.

Charles S. Robb
Chairman, Democratic (Party)
Leadership Council (U.S.);
Former Governor of Virginia (D)

3

We've got to face two realities [about Nicaragua]. First, the [ruling] Sandinistas will continue their attempts to subvert their democratic neighbors because that's what they believe in. They are dedicated Marxists and we shouldn't have any illusions about their intentions in Central America. Second, a consolidated Communist regime in Managua, allied solidly with the Soviet Union, will pose a long-term threat to America's strategic interests.

Before Coalition for a Democratic Majority,
Washington, May 6/The New York Times, 5-7:13.

Alfonso Robelo
Leader, United Nicaraguan Opposition
(contra rebels fighting the Sandinista
government of Nicaragua)

4

[Criticizing the U.S. Congress for not being firm in supporting the contras, and for more readily giving humanitarian aid rather than military aid]: People keep telling us military pressure [against the Sandinistas] hasn't produced results. I'm telling you there hasn't been military pressure. [The Sandinistas] see us as losers. Why? Because of the yo-yo policy of the Congress . . . Humanitarian aid is not humanitarian aid at all. That only gives us food, medicine and clothes to keep on killing and being killed, with no possibility to put the needed pressure on Nicaragua. On that basis, I prefer to say let's have no aid.

Interview, Washington/
The Christian Science Monitor, 3-12:5.

5

[Saying he is happy that the U.S. House of Representatives has approved $100-million in military aid to his rebels]: We will now be more effective in our political struggle [against Nicaragua's Sandinista government]. We can anticipate popular insurrection, massive defections from the Sandinistas, massive enrollment [in the

(ALFONSO ROBELO)

contra rebel army] and rebellions from the regional armies of the Sandinistas . . . This is a message—to us, the contras inside Nicaragua—that the United States, the leader of the free world, is not abandoning us in our struggle for freedom and democracy. This is a challenge, and we are going to take it, and we are going to show results.

News conference,
Washington, June 26/
The Washington Post, 6-27:(I)15.

Dean Rusk
Former Secretary of State
of the United States

1

[On the U.S. criticism of the Sandinista government of Nicaragua and American support for the contras, rebels fighting the Sandinistas]: The U.S. should be putting the Nicaraguan issue before the OAS with insistence and conviction. If the OAS council were meeting regularly, more facts would come to light about Nicaragua's activities, and the U.S. hand might be strengthened. It's a problem for the whole hemisphere, and we're letting it become a unilateral issue.

The Christian Science Monitor, 4-4:17.

Julio Maria Sanguinetti
President of Uruguay

2

[Calling for increased foreign trade with Uruguay]: If there is anything I want to be eloquent about, anything about which I really want to convince the developed countries, it's over the magnitude of this theme. It's very difficult, after 12 years of dictatorship [in Uruguay] to reestablish a democracy, to consider the natural demands of the people, who think democracy, besides bringing liberty, also comes with bread under the arm, and to pay the foreign debt; all this while also confronting the protectionist measures of the developed countries.

Interview, Montevideo/
The New York Times, 6-16:8.

Jose Sarney
President of Brazil

3

[On the success of his anti-inflation plan]: It has achieved its objective. Brazil has changed . . . The notion is over that we are a country which only attracts the curiosity of the world for the picturesque character of our soccer and carnival, for the suffering of the Indians, and for the death squads.

Broadcast address to the nation, April/
The Washington Post, 5-9:(A)21.

Jim Sasser
United States Senator,
D-Tennessee

4

[On the contras, rebels fighting the Sandinista government of Nicaragua]: There is a general sense [in Central America] that the contras do not constitute a reasonable alternative to the Sandinistas. They are simply a force that can bring pressure. They do not have the military capability to overthrow the Sandinistas and, in the unlikely event that that occurred, they don't have the political capability to run the country.

Interview, Key West, Fla./
The New York Times, 3-3:2.

5

I think the [U.S. Reagan] Administration and the President are overstating the danger Nicaragua represents. They are using excessive rhetoric to alarm Americans and to denounce those who don't agree with them . . . I believe the [ruling] Sandinistas are Marxist-Leninists. They are seeking to build Nicaragua on the Cuban model. But Nicaragua is a small country—it's about the same size as Tennessee, and it has about 2 million people. They are just not going to constitute the peril to the U.S.A., to a nation of 260 million, that [U.S. President Reagan] suggests.

Interview/USA Today, 3-10:(A)7.

6

We have called for fair and open elections in Nicaragua, and the [ruling] Sandinistas refused

(JIM SASSER)

to go along. Some of the democratic leaders in Central America think if there were free elections in Nicaragua today the Sandinistas would be voted out. This is in contrast to the situation three or four years ago, when there was general consensus that they would have won. But their economy has declined, they have taken repressive measures against political opposition and the Catholic Church—they've made people unhappy.

Interview/USA Today, 3-10:(A)7.

1

[Arguing against U.S. President Reagan's request for $100-million in aid for the contras, rebels fighting the Sandinista government of Nicaragua]: We in the Congress agree with the President about what our goals should be in Central America. We agree that the Sandinista government has betrayed the promise of its own revolution, has suppressed the freedom of its own people, and supported subversion against its neighbor, El Salvador. We agree that Nicaragua must never become a base for Soviet military adventurism in this hemisphere. Never . . . [But] at a time of belt-tightening at home, when tens of thousands of [U.S.] family farms are failing and hundreds of thousands of young Americans are seeing their student loans eliminated, the President seeks an additional $100-million to expand the undeclared war being fought in Nicaragua. Our concern is that the President is seizing military options before he has exhausted the hope of a peaceful solution. We believe the United States should grasp the initiative, seeking peace through negotiations before taking a fateful step which would lead to war in Central America.

Broadcast address to the nation, Washington,
March 16/USA Today, 3-17:(A)11.

2

[Arguing against the U.S. giving $100-million in aid to the contras, rebels fighting the Sandinista government of Nicaragua]: We are at a watershed in American foreign policy. People understand that we're not simply talking about

$100-million for the funding of a military operation in a distant land. We are talking about the first step toward war, one in which the young people of this country will be directly involved. If we fund the contras, the last precious chance to avoid war may be lost forever.

Before the Senate, Washington,
Aug. 12/The New York Times, 8-13:4.

Richard Schifter
Assistant Secretary for Human Rights,
Department of State of the United States

3

There is a democratically elected government in El Salvador pledged to reaching the goals of democracy. [But] Nicaragua, in our view, is led by a group of Leninists who have a different view . . . We do not believe in ideologies that view repression as effective means of governing . . . What stands out in the Western Hemisphere is how, in the last five years, country after country has moved to democracy. In 1980 and '81, we would not have predicted that such progress would be made.

News conference,
Washington, Feb. 13/
The Washington Post, 2-14:(A)31.

James R. Schlesinger
Former Secretary of Defense
of the United States

4

[Arguing against U.S. military aid to the contras, rebels fighting the Sandinista government of Nicaragua]: In Central America, there is a mismatch between the [U.S. Reagan] Administration's objective and the instruments available, reminiscent of our ill-fated adventure in Lebanon. Mere dislike of the Sandinistas is not an adequate basis for policy. To define the American interest as that of the contras is to identify with a losing cause. To suggest that money for—and victory of—the contras is the only way to avoid introducing American troops is to come close to committing us to the introduction of our forces.

Interview/Time, 3-17:23.

William Schonfeld
Dean of social sciences,
University of California, Irvine

1

[On the current government of Haiti, which came to power after the ouster of dictator Jean-Claude Duvalier]: The government is offering a sort of abstract schedule for the democratic process, and the people don't understand the democratic process. They have lived in only one kind of political system, and that is the exploiter and the exploited.

Port-au-Prince,
Haiti, June/
Los Angeles Times, 6-19:(I)5.

Angel Roberto Seifart
Member, ruling Colorado
Party of Paraguay

2

[Saying Paraguayan President Alfredo Stroessner should begin to allow democratization of the country]: When the President took office [in 1954] after so many years of chaos, some sort of authoritarianism was necessary. He was the man circumstances demanded, and he achieved the goal of growth and stability. Now we need to recover the democratic ideals of the [Colorado] Party and change the image of government. There is nothing that requires such strict authority to assure a peaceful national life.

Los Angeles Times, 4-25:(I)16.

3

[Saying Paraguayan President Alfredo Stroessner should not run in the 1988 national elections]: The formula of authoritarian populism, with the Colorados supporting a military leader [Stroessner], enabled Paraguay to emerge from anarchy. But the country is now ready for a more solid democratic system. We're not conspiring, we're not trying to overthrow Stroessner. We want to keep the Constitutional timetable, but without Stroessner seeking re-election.

Interview,
Asuncion, Paraguay/
The New York Times, 5-22:3.

George P. Shultz
Secretary of State
of the United States

4

[Calling for U.S. military aid to the contras, rebels fighting the Sandinista government of Nicaragua]: [A Sandinista victory over the rebels] would severely damage our credibility with adversaries who would test our mettle and with those around the world who rely on us for support in their battles against tyranny. If democratic aspiration is snuffed out in Nicaragua, then where can we claim to nurture or protect it? If an armed aggressor on our own doorstep is allowed to have its way . . . then how can our reputation for deterring aggression be credible in places farther removed?

Before Veterans of Foreign Wars, Washington,
March 2/Los Angeles Times, 3-3(I)11.

5

[On U.S. opposition to the Sandinista government of Nicaragua]: Our goals are limited and reasonable. We want the Nicaraguan regime to reverse its military buildup, to send its foreign advisers home, and to stop oppressing its citizens and subverting its neighbors. We want it to keep the promises of the coalition government that followed [dictator Anastasio] Somoza's fall: democratic pluralism at home and peaceful relations abroad.

Before Veterans of Foreign Wars, Washington,
March 2/The New York Times, 3-3:2.

6

Foreign intervention in the form of alien ideologies and foreign cadres—from Cuba, the Soviet Union, East Germany, North Korea, even Vietnam and Libya—is at this moment promoting instability and violence in Central America. The only road to peace and stability is to eliminate that alien threat . . . Does anyone really think the United States wants to turn Central America into a vortex of East-West turmoil? The United States provided aid to help Nicaragua rebuild after the fall of [former dictator Anastasio] Somoza in 1979, but what did the Nicaraguan Communists do? They sought arms from the Soviet bloc and used them to deny the Nicaraguan

WHAT THEY SAID IN 1986

(GEORGE P. SHULTZ)

people their right of self-determination. It is impossible to imagine peace and stability returning to the region until this massive growth in [Nicaraguan] armaments is constrained and, ultimately, eliminated. Failure to confront this threat will only guarantee that the region will be increasingly drawn into great-power rivalries.

Before Organization of American States,
Guatemala City, Nov. 11/
Los Angeles Times, 11-12:(I)6.

1

[On private American citizens aiding the contras, rebels fighting the Sandinista government of Nicaragua]: It was clear that—from private sources, presumably—some aid was flowing to the [contras] fighting for freedom and independence in Nicaragua. And, personally, I applaud that. There's a lot of [private] aid flowing from America to the Nicaraguan [Sandinista] Communists, quite a few Americans [helping the government] down there. That's their right to be. And it shouldn't be surprising that there are Americans who want to help the people [contras] fighting for freedom.

Before House Foreign Affairs Committee,
Washington, Dec. 8/
The New York Times, 12-9:6.

Rafael Solis Cerda
Secretary of the National
Assembly of Nicaragua

2

There are restrictions on political rights and some civil rights [in Nicaragua]. Outdoor political meetings are not permitted and more material is censored than should be. [But these] steps the government has to take to protect itself from an armed movement [the contra rebels fighting Nicaragua's Sandinista government]. It is not part of the Sandinista program to restrict public liberty. There should always be political life and political dissent, as long as it does not become advocacy of armed rebellion.

The New York Times, 3-20:4.

Allan R. Taylor
President, Royal Bank of Canada

3

[Calling for a free-trade agreement between Canada and the U.S.]: As you do that and build a bigger pie, it's not the same size pie that gets divided up in a different way. I'm saying that the pie is larger because of what we can do together through a freer trade arrangement. And that's what creates jobs. That's why Canadians will have a greater opportunity.

Interview, Toronto/
The New York Times, 5-19:30.

Alvin Toffler
Futurist

4

The Mexican government has no money. The drop in oil prices has destroyed their Federal budget, because it was based 50 per cent on oil. So it has a $97-billion debt, with people hungry, with earthquakes and corruption. We're [the U.S.] living with a volcano next door. If that volcano starts spreading lava, it could easily spread over to Texas, Arizona and California. It already is, in the form of immigration.

Interview/USA Today, 3-11:(B)4.

Carlos Tunnermann
Nicaraguan Ambassador
to the United States

5

[Saying his government will not negotiate with the contras, rebels fighting the Sandinista government of Nicaragua and who are backed by the U.S.]: Any self-respecting government would refuse to negotiate with a group armed by a foreign power. We will not negotiate with the contras, either directly or indirectly. We are going to carry out national reconciliation through the Contadora peace process. Why should a legitimate government negotiate with opponents armed by a foreign power just because [U.S. President] Reagan doesn't like us.

Interview, Washington, March 24/
Los Angeles Times, 3-25:(I)1,15.

Gabriel Valdes
President, Christian
Democratic Party of Chile

1

[Applauding the recent U.S. support for the overthrow of dictators in Haiti and the Philippines]: We have seen the re-sprouting of the spirit of Jefferson and Lincoln. After Haiti, after the Philippines, the conscience of the world has turned toward Chile. It is Chile's time, the time of the final choice between dictatorship and democracy. [But] the dictatorship will not fall like objects fall because of the laws of physics. It will not fall through the work of third parties. No one can do our work for us.

At Christian Democratic Party rally/
Los Angeles Times, 3-15:(I)8.

Tim Valentine, Jr.
United States Representative,
D-North Carolina

2

[Arguing against U.S. military aid to the contras, rebels fighting the Sandinista government of Nicaragua]: It would just be pumping money down a sinkhole. I try to find ways to support my President [Reagan, who supports the aid]. But I don't like giving away money to a bunch of illiterate farmers and cutthroats in Nicaragua when we can't find money to pay for rural electrification or to help the struggling textile industry in the United States.

Interview, Washington/
The New York Times, 3-20:12.

Armando Vargas
Director of Communications for
the President of Costa Rica

3

[Saying Costa Rica is swinging to the right politically]: All of Latin America is going through a period of political polarization. It is being felt strongly in Central America, especially Costa Rica, because we have always been politically conservative. The political pendulum in the United States has swung to the right, and

we're feeling the effects of that. If the President of the U.S. talks about Nicaragua, we listen.

Interview, San Jose, Costa Rica/
The Christian Science Monitor, 1-14:9.

Pablo Antonio Vega
Exiled Nicaraguan
Roman Catholic Bishop

4

The only public opinion in Nicaragua is silence. He who breathes a bit of freedom loses his ration card, loses his rights.

Newsweek, 8-4:48.

5

[Criticizing the Sandinista government of Nicaragua]: What we have down there is an international operation supported by international Communism and, if we don't realize that, we're acting like children . . . My return [from exile to Nicaragua] must not be negotiated in the context of a blackmail that would attempt to silence the church. There has been a practice of the government of putting people in jail and then freeing them to say it was due to the magnanimity of the government. Human rights are not a gift from the government, but something human beings are endowed with . . . [The 1979 Nicaraguan revolution has turned into an] oppressive, militaristic enterprise that suppresses the rights of people.

News conference, New York, Oct. 1/
The New York Times, 10-2:2.

Carlos Eugenio Vides Casanova
Minister of Defense of El Salvador

6

[Saying that his government's armed forces are winning the war they are fighting against Communist rebels]: [Cuban President] Fidel Castro once said he was going to breakfast in Nicaragua, lunch in El Salvador and dine in Guatemala. I think he is on a good diet, because he is never going to lunch in El Salvador.

Sesori, El Salvador/
Los Angeles Times, 9-22:(I)5.

273

WHAT THEY SAID IN 1986

William von Raab
Commissioner,
United States Customs Service

1

[On Mexican involvement in drug smuggling into the U.S.]: It is a modern-day horror story. Smugglers have been building new landing strips in Mexico less than 100 miles south of our border. They are building warehouses to store vast amounts of drugs . . . The Mexicans are, in effect, the freight forwarders and security services for Colombian drug smuggling groups. If [Mexican] law enforcement can be so easily bought by drug smugglers, it can just as easily be bought by terrorists. This is a terrorist threat by every definition, and if we ever hope to combat this threat to our nation, there must be a significant change in attitude from our southern neighbors.

Before House Select Committee on
Narcotics Abuse and Control, Washington,
March 18/The Washington Post, 3-19:(A)7.

2

Until I'm shown that an individual [in the Mexican government] is not corrupt . . . my presumption is that he is.

Before Senate subcommittee,
Washington/Newsweek, 5-26:17.

Vernon A. Walters
United States Ambassador/Permanent
Representative to the United Nations

3

[There is] a large and continuing effort of the [Nicaraguan ruling] Sandinistas to materially support Marxist insurgents in neighboring countries. As they have put into practice their policy of "revolutionary internationalism," they have flouted international law and violated their pledge to the international community not to export their revolution. The evidence is massive and undeniable that the Sandinistas have provided a wide range of support . . . They have facilitated the use of Nicaragua as a rear-area sanctuary for the rebels [In El Salvador] and a headquarters for their political arm.

At United Nations, New York, Oct. 22/
The Washington Post, 11-13:(A)20.

Caspar W. Weinberger
Secretary of Defense of the United States

4

The Nicaraguan leadership now makes it clear that they are guided by Communist principles. There is really no debate about this. We should not, therefore, be amazed when they act like the Communists we have already known, when their rhetoric is utopian, and their actions brutal.

At conference sponsored by Georgetown University's
Center for Strategic and International Studies,
Washington, June 9/The New York Times, 6-10:3.

Jim Wright
United States Representative, D-Texas

5

We [the U.S.] worry about Communism, but we don't seem to worry about the conditions that breed Communism. Oh, surely, we are big enough and powerful enough that we could physically overthrow the government in Managua [Nicaragua], or the one in Havana [Cuba], if that should be necessary. It would cost a lot more than $100-million and a precious lot of bloodshed, but we could do it. Yes, but what then? The problems of Latin America would still be with us— problems of illiteracy and malnutrition and disease, the problems of joblessness and a bondage of debt that amounts almost to servitude and a growing sense of hopeless disillusionment with society. In the last century, patriots like Bolivar and San Martin patterned their popular people's movements after us. We were the inspiration and the example, and we have a residue of good-will if we'll build upon it. If we would reap the respect of our neighbors to the south, we'll have to cultivate a sustained interest in them and their very real problems, not just that of a fire engine which rushes in to put out a fire and departs as swiftly to ignore the cumbustibles that lie everywhere upon the tattered landscape of a civilization cruelly battered by a history of neglect. They have a saying south of the border: "El manero a tener amigo es ser amigo"—the way to have a friend is to be a friend. In seeking a policy for Latin America, that may be the best place to start.

Broadcast address to the nation, Washington,
Feb. 26/The New York Times, 2-27:14.

Asia and the Pacific

Abdul Kadir Sheikh Fadzir
Deputy Foreign Minister of Malaysia
1

[Saying the U.S. should pay more attention to the island nations of the Pacific]: The U.S. has got to stop waiting until the last minute. When the situation is too late, you suddenly see Americans. If the Americans acted now, they could nip these tendencies [to move toward increased Soviet influence in the area]. Just $10-million spread around the area would make some very beautiful people very happy.

Interview, Kuala Lumpur, Malaysia/
The New York Times, 5-19:4.

Corazon C. Aquino
Candidate for the Presidency
of the Philippines
2

I would be the last person in the world to be a Communist. I have never been a Communist, and I do not intend to be a Communist. [But] so long as the Communists renounce all forms of violence, we [would] welcome them into the government. Certainly, we need everybody's help. All Filipinos who sincerely desire to help the government and the country are very welcome in the government.

News conference,
Baguio, Philippines, Jan. 2/
The New York Times, 1-3:3.

3

[Criticizing Philippine President Ferdinand Marcos]: I am generally disgusted with the way he is conducting his [election] campaign, because, without batting an eye, he tells the most brazen lies. What do we do with this overgrown child? . . . This man is desperate. He will stoop to anything. Can we allow an inveterate liar to represent us in the family of nations? . . . He succeeded in ripping out the heart and soul of our old democratic system. The Marcos Consti-

tution today, instead of protecting us from dictatorship, institutionalizes dictatorship.

Before Manila Rotary Club, Jan. 23/
Los Angeles Times, 1-24:(I)14.

4

[When Philippine President Ferdinand Marcos was elected in 1965,] there were 165 [anti-government] insurgents. Today there are more than 16,000 of them getting closer to the palace doors. Today, 20 years after he became President, 13 years after he imposed martial law and suspended the privilege of the writ of habeas corpus, nine years after he acquired the power under Amendment 6, the problem of insurgency is worse than in 1965, worse than in 1972, worse than in 1976. To his question, therefore, "What does Cory Aquino know about insurgency?", my first answer is that, with his dismal record, he should be ashamed to ask the question at all: It is beyond debate that Mr. Marcos is the most successful recruiter for the insurgency. He is leaving to us as one of his shameful legacies the difficult task of reversing the drift toward a Communist take-over.

Before Manila Rotary Club, Jan. 23/
The Washington Post, 1-24:(A)24.

5

When [President Ferdinand] Marcos began his rule in 1965, our country was touted as the economic miracle of Asia, next only to Japan. Today, we have earned the unflattering title of the basket case of Southeast Asia. In 20 years, Mr. Marcos has stripped legitimate entrepreneurs of their ability to compete and has rewarded his friends with fiefdoms which have enabled them, like vampires, to suck the lifeblood of a once-vigorous economy.

Before American, European and Filipino
Chambers of Commerce, Manila, Feb. 3/
Los Angeles Times, 2-4:(I)15.

6

[On whether, if she is elected President, she would renew the current agreement with the

(CORAZON C. AQUINO)

U.S. to maintain American military bases in the Philippines after 1991]: I must state with candor that no sovereign nation should consent that a portion of its territory be a perpetual possession of a foreign power.

Before American, European and Filipino Chambers of Commerce, Manila, Feb. 3/ The New York Times, 2-4:6.

1

[Claiming victory in the just-concluded Philippine Presidential election and calling on President Ferdinand Marcos to resign]: Our power has been the people and their spirit. His has been guns. We hope we do not have to mobilize this nation. We hope that Mr. Marcos will find it in himself to concede now so that I can begin the process of reconciliation in a climate of amity, unity and peace. It is not just in the interest of the Filipino people but our allies abroad that the transition takes place now.

News conference, Manila, Feb. 11/ The New York Times, 2-12:8.

Corazon C. Aquino
President of the Philippines

2

[On her assumption of the Presidency following the overthrow of Ferdinand Marcos]: Last night, the people celebrated their victory. The celebration had no particular venue. It took place everywhere any number of Filipinos congregated and congratulated each other for a job well done in the liberation of their country . . . All the world wondered as they witnessed, in the space of two months, a people lift themselves from humiliation to the greatest pride. The challenges and difficulties that I and our people face are daunting. But I am fortunate to be the President of a people who have demonstrated the courage, the tenacity, the idealism and the self-sacrifice to meet any goal and overcome any obstacle.

News conference, Manila, Feb. 26/ The New York Times, 2-27:6.

3

[On her new government]: I remind you that we owe our mandate to our people and that they must be served. Should organized people-power take issue with any of us in government, listen to what they want to say, answer their questions, dialogue with the people. If we are at fault, let us correct ourselves, lest the people once again correct it for us, as they have shown in the past week they are capable of doing [when they overthrew President Ferdinand Marcos] . . . I will be uncompromising about corruption, graft, nepotism, usurpation and abuse of power and authority. Also against extravagance, incompetence, abuse of human rights, and the guarantee of the basic freedoms of speech, assembly, thought and non-violent action.

At rally, Manila, March 2/The New York Times, 3-3:6.

4

[On the Communist insurgency in the Philippines]: Under the [recently deposed] Marcos regime, the balance was in the Communists' favor. The people distanced themselves from a government they feared and despised. They gave it neither cooperation in its spurious programs nor intelligence about the movements of the insurgents . . . I have no illusions that peace will come easy. For the Communist true believer, the road to victory bristles with arms and resounds with combat.

At University of the Philippines commencement, Manila, April 20/The Washington Post, 4-21:(A)15.

5

I shall honor our lease agreements [for the U.S. military bases in the Philippines] until they expire in 1991. As for what happens afterward, I keep all my options open. No other country has had closer ties to the Philippines than the U.S. The fact that a million and a half Filipinos live in the U.S. contributes a great deal to this special relationship. But my main concern will be to act in the interests of the Filipino people, not of the Americans.

Interview/World Press Review, May:34.

6

[On U.S. relations with her new government]: I am a little disappointed, to tell you the

(CORAZON C. AQUINO)

truth. My feeling is that I am still being watched and examined. What is America waiting for? Do they believe my government is not a popular government? I don't think so. Do they believe I am anti-American? I should hope not. Certainly I have not said anything that would indicate that. I wish that somebody would explain to the American people what Filipinos are all about. Since 1983, great change has come about in this country. If I were not convinced myself of how many sincere Filipinos there are, I would have given up long ago. But I really believe that we have enough dedicated people to see this through. I have already explained what our needs are. I don't like to nag. It's just a question of are we friends or aren't we?

Interview, Manila/Time, 5-26:34.

1

[Saying the member nations of ASEAN have become too dependent on foreign aid from rich nations that have not always acted in ASEAN's best interests]: Charity begins at home. My own country is learning the hard way that strength must be built first from within . . . We're established for economic cooperation and progress. What we have accomplished in these respects is more kindly left unmentioned. I think the time is well past for talking . . . It is not malevolence that moves the developed economies to act in derogation of our interests, but their own survival. The seeming indifference of the rich countries to our economic situation should have been motivation enough for ASEAN countries to take the initiative in looking into the potential of the region for alternative paths to sustained progress.

At ASEAN meeting, Manila, June 23/
Los Angeles Times, 6-24:(I)8.

2

[On a recent failed armed rebellion against her Presidency]: Certain people have trifled too long with the dignity and stability of the present government. I am compelled by reasons of national interest and unity to require a pledge of loyalty to the Constitution from the leaders in

that illegal act of defiance . . . You are within your rights to criticize the policies of this government or flay its members on their performances. There will be elections soon where you can test the continuing mandate of this government. But nowhere in the fundamental law is there a right to undermine the Constitutional basis of the new democracy our people struggled so long and hard to establish.

News conference, Manila, July 9/
Los Angeles Times, 7-10:(I)6,7.

3

[Addressing Filipino and foreign businessmen and criticizing them for not increasing their investment in the Philippines]: When I agreed to stand as candidate for the Presidency, I did so with the assurance that I could count on all of you for your support. That support has not been forthcoming. Let us get one thing clear: The support is not for me, but for your country, for yourselves and your posterity—unless you all want to be immigrants . . . I remember your wild applause when I vowed to remove the obstacles that prevented you from being the engine of our economy. I have removed the obstacles, but where is the engine? Five months ago, the excuse was [then-President Ferdinand] Marcos. You gave me the impression that you did not want to put out your best silver because he might steal it, as he had done with everything else. Well, he's gone. So where is it?

Manila, July 21/
Los Angeles Times, 7-22:(I)1,11.

4

My only claim is that I have always been honest. I have always been sincere. And, most important, you must realize that, when I am convinced of something, no one can dissuade me.

To Philippines rebel leader Nur Misuari,
Sulu, Philippines, Sept. 5/
Los Angeles Times, 9-15:(I)1.

5

My predecessor [deposed Philippine President Ferdinand Marcos] set aside democracy to save it from a Communist insurgency that numbered less than 500. Unhampered by respect for human rights, he went at it with hammer and tongs. By the time he fled, that insurgency had grown to more than 16,000. I think there is a lesson to be learned about trying to stifle a thing with the means by which it grows.

Before joint session of U.S. Congress,
Washington, Sept. 18/
The New York Times, 9-19:6.

1

Of late, my circumspection has been viewed as weakness, and my sincere attempts at reconciliation as indecision. This cannot continue. It is clear that the extreme left has no interest in the peace I have continually offered. I have, therefore, given the government negotiating panel until the end of the month to produce a cease-fire [with the Communist insurgents] or terminate all further negotiation. This morning I summoned the Cabinet to a special meeting. I directed all Cabinet members to give me their resignations . . . I hereby give notice to all those who may be inclined to exploit the present situation that the sternest measures will be taken against them if they try. I have appealed again and again to all sectors of our country to unite in the protection of our democracy and in the reconstruction of our country. In the same spirit in which we won our liberation, let us work as one for the preservation of our freedoms and the progress of our nation.

Broadcast address to the nation, Manila,
Nov. 23/The New York Times, 11-24:6.

Benazir Bhutto
A leader of opposition
to Pakistani government

2

[On her recent greeting by hundreds of thousands of supporters in Lahore]: The crowd in Lahore could have burnt down the assemblies, it could have burnt down the [military] cantonment, it could have burnt down the homes of [government] ministers. But my party will never

permit such a change to come over because my party does not want to stand for violence.

News conference, Lahore,
Pakistan, April 11/
The Washington Post, 4-12:(A)19.

Stephen Bosworth
United States Ambassador
to the Philippines

3

Last year at this time [when Ferdinand Marcos was President of the Philippines], we seemed to be dealing in an atmosphere of certainty. Things were bad, and it seemed certain that they were going to get worse. Now [after Marcos was overthrown and replaced by President Corazon Aquino] we are dealing in an atmosphere of uncertainty. Things are still not good, but they are getting somewhat better, and there is the prospect that they are going to get better still.

Los Angeles Times, 12-31:(I)16.

Chiang Ching-kuo
President of Taiwan

4

There are certain changes taking place [in China]. But they are cosmetic. The essence of Communism remains the same. They may change their outfits from Mao suits to Western suits, but the essence remains the same. Just think of a tree. [Chinese leader] Deng Xiaoping has been trimming the branches, but the root stays the same . . . Unless they forsake Communism and return to Chinese traditions, there will be no real change.

Interview, Taipei, Oct. 7/
The Washington Post, 10-8:(A)18.

Chun Doo Hwan
President of South Korea

5

I am prepared to meet [North Korean leader] Kim Il Sung whenever and wherever he responds in kind. But the fact is that for 40 years the Koreas have been at odds. The key to successful dialogue is a modicum of mutual confidence, not

(CHUN DOO HWAN)

blind trust. We are prepared to build that [confidence]. [But] Kim Il Sung's son has said that South-North talks are tactical steps to a new goal, a strategy for revolution in South Korea and union with the North. They feel these talks can help [achieve] this goal.

Interview, Seoul/Newsweek, 2-10:52.

1

Those who say I regard [domestic] opposition members as enemies have less than perfect understanding of the political picture. I believe the existence of a healthy majority depends on the existence of a healthy minority. Opposition members in the halls of the National Assembly act very freely. I can assure you that they speak out and act of their own free will.

Interview, Seoul/Newsweek, 2-10:52.

William Crowe

Admiral and Chief of Operations,
United States Navy; Chairman,
Joint Chiefs of Staff

2

The Soviets are in real trouble in the Pacific. They haven't been able to make much headway ideologically or politically. They have acquired some shabby allies—North Korea, Vietnam— whose economies are either stagnant or declining. At the same time, we are enjoying a better relationship with China than many people anticipated we would. The whole Far East—not just Japan—is becoming the most active, most prosperous market in the world, and the Soviets can't even penetrate it . . . I have visited leaders all over East Asia, and they constantly stress one theme: A big reason for their prosperity and political health is the American military shield that we threw over that area a long time ago. They want us to remain strong and maintain our forward-deployed forces in the Pacific. Every year that peace continues in the Pacific, our friends and allies are winning there—and the Soviets are losing.

Interview/U.S. News &
World Report, 8-4:38.

F. Rawdon Dalrymple

Australian Ambassador
to the United States

3

[Saying Japan should open up its home market to more imports]: Now is the time for a self-satisfied Japan-as-Number-one generation to an area where the Soviet Union, Cuba and others of that stripe can find fertile ground for anti-U.S. propaganda, then continue with a policy of indifference to what the French are doing there.

The Christian Science Monitor, 6-4:7.

John C. Danforth

United States Senator, R-Missouri

4

[Saying Japan should open up its home market to more imports]: Now is the time for a self-satisfied Japan-as-Number-one generation to learn that there's more to leadership than flooding the world with Walkmen [radios] and VCRs. No other nation contributes so little to the open-trading system of the world, in proportion to what it gains [from its exports] . . . Japan is a great country. It should begin to act like one . . . Japan imports only what it cannot produce itself . . . The world trading system cannot long function when its second-largest economy abdicates its responsibilities. Because of its size, a Japanese economy that formally or informally remains closed threatens the openness of the system itself.

Before Foreign Correspondents Club
of Japan, Tokyo, Jan. 13/
The Washington Post, 1-14:(D)6,10.

Deng Xiaoping

Vice Chairman,
Communist Party of China

5

If we say there are . . . obstacles between China and the Soviet Union, there is also an obstacle between China and the United States—that is the Taiwan issue, which means the reunification of China. I believe the United States, especially President Reagan, can do something on this issue.

American broadcast interview/
"60 Minutes," CBS-TV, 9-7.

WHAT THEY SAID IN 1986

Juan Ponce Enrile
Minister of Defense
of the Philippines

1

The more we depend on our foreign friends, the more influence they will exert on our national life . . . We would give them the avenue to influence us over the course of our national life and our future. That is what we want to avoid. At that point in time, to us it will be a matter of survival; to them it will be simply a matter of foreign policy.

Los Angeles Times, 10-24:(I)12.

2

In the final stages of the revolution [which recently ousted President Ferdinand Marcos], we [the military] had complete control almost of the levers of power in the land. We decided not to accept that power and wield it, but instead we handed it to a civilian government headed by [current President Corazon] Aquino . . . And so, therefore, no one can tell us that they handed to us [the military] an appointment of a position, because we were holding those positions before any one of them had their positions.

At nurses' convention, Oct. 29/
The Washington Post, 10-30:(A)29.

Rajiv Gandhi
Prime Minister of India

3

We talk of the high principles and lofty ideals needed to build a strong and prosperous India. But we obey no discipline, no rule, follow no principle of public morality, display no sense of social awareness, show no concern for the public weal. Corruption is not only tolerated but even regarded as the hallmark of our leadership.

At 100th anniversary celebration of
Congress Party, Bombay/
The New York Times, 1-9:8.

4

[Criticizing violence caused by India's Sikh separatist extremists]: They kill and loot in the name of religion. Violence of any kind is bad, but violence in the name of religion is reprehensible.

Independence Day address, New Delhi,
Aug. 15/Los Angeles Times, 8-16:(I)14.

Barry M. Goldwater
United States Senator, R-Arizona

5

[Criticizing U.S. plans to sell sophisticated military radar and computers to China for its air force]: Red China is an uncertain and unproven military partner whose government leaders and policies can change erratically . . . [And] should the United States allow the Republic of China on Taiwan to be neutralized or fall under the control of Peking, it would foreclose the use of facilities on Taiwan to the United States and to the non-Communist coalition of free nations in the region.

Before the Senate, Washington, April 8/
Los Angeles Times, 4-9:(I)1,10.

Mikhail S. Gorbachev
General Secretary, Communist
Party of the Soviet Union

6

[On Soviet military intervention in Afghanistan]: Counter-revolution and imperialism have turned Afghanistan into a bleeding wound. The U.S.S.R. supports that country's efforts to defend its sovereignty. We should like, in the nearest future, to withdraw the Soviet troops stationed in Afghanistan at the request of its government. Moreover, we have agreed with the Afghan side on the schedule for their phased withdrawal as soon as a political settlement is reached that insures an actual cessation and dependably guarantees the non-resumption of foreign interference in the internal affairs of the Democratic Republic of Afghanistan.

At Soviet Communist Party Congress, Moscow,
Feb. 25/The New York Times, 2-26:4.

7

[Saying that improved Soviet-Chinese ties could pave the way for improvement in the situation in Cambodia, where both Soviet-backed

(MIKHAIL S. GORBACHEV)

Vietnamese and Chinese-backed forces contend]: It looks as though the moment is good. The whole of Asia needs that. Through its suffering, Cambodia has earned the right to choose its own friends and allies. It's impermissable to try to pull it back into the tragic past, to decide Cambodia's future in distant capitals or even at the United Nations. And with other Southeast Asian problems, much depends on normalization of Sino-Vietnamese relations.

Broadcast address, Vladivostok, U.S.S.R.,
July 28/The Christian Science Monitor, 8-7:9.

1

[Saying his country will recall six regiments of its troops from Afghanistan by the end of the year]: In taking so serious a step, the Soviet Union is striving to speed up a political settlement [in the war with Afghan rebels], to give it another impetus. The Soviet Union also proceeds from the view that those who have been organizing and implementing armed intervention against the Democratic Republic of Afghanistan will correctly understand and duly appreciate this unilateral step of ours. It must be answered by the curtailment of outside interference.

Broadcast address, Vladivostok, U.S.S.R.,
July 28/The New York Times, 7-29:4.

2

What we [the Soviets] are doing in improving relations with China will not weaken our relations with India. Those steps never will be detrimental to India. I hope that the better our relations are with all countries in the region . . . the better the atmosphere [for all] in the region.

News conference, New Delhi, Nov. 28/
The Washington Post, 11-29:(A)19.

Oliver Greeves
Managing director,
Chase Manhattan Asia

3

In the ongoing struggle [in the capital markets] between the two cousins, Hong Kong and Singapore, the game appears to be moving rapidly in Hong Kong's advantage. For those of you who play tennis, from a score of 15-all in early 1984 when everything in Hong Kong seemed to be going wrong, the score is now 40-15 in Hong Kong's favor. Undoubtedly, the stabilization of the Hong Kong political situation and the economic boom there has helped, but of greater importance is the flexibility of the place. Not only does it have low taxes and few regulations but also a very industrious people who are traders by nature and a government with a hands-off approach to the march.

Speech, Jakarta, Indonesia/
The Wall Street Journal, 8-4:14.

I. K. Gujral
Former Indian Ambassador
to the Soviet Union

4

The proclivity of the Indian mind is pro-American. This is where American policies fail. They don't know how to take advantage of it.

The New York Times, 11-25:3.

Bhabani Sen Gupta
Political analyst, Center of
Policy Research (India)

5

The Prime Minister [of India, Rajiv Gandhi] completes his two-year term without making a political impact on India. In fact, you'll find him on the defensive across the board on almost all of his key policy goals—a government that works faster, good relations with neighbors, a conciliatory approach in domestic politics, and economic centralization.

The Christian Science Monitor, 10-31:14.

Selig S. Harrison
Senior associate,
Carnegie Endowment for
International Peace

6

[On the Soviet military involvement in Afghanistan]: The Soviets are not anxious to get

WHAT THEY SAID IN 1986

out in the sense that they're ready to admit defeat [to the rebels fighting the Soviet-backed government]. They want what they consider to be a compromise. They want to get their combat forces out—but only if they can keep a political infrastructure [in Afghanistan] that protects them against the risk of a hostile regime.

The Christian Science Monitor, 2-26:4.

Bill Hayden
Foreign Minister of Australia

1

[Criticizing the U.S. subsidy for its wheat sales to the Soviet Union, saying the subsidy hurts Australian farmers]: Great damage is being done to the interests not only of Australia but potentially to the stability of our region by the actions of countries which are massively subsidizing their agricultural export. I have to inform you of the genuine outrage felt through all sections of the Australian community at the recent actions . . . Is this the way the Congress of the United States treats old and firm allies? Does the Congress realize that the tidal wave of protectionism it has unleashed has consequences for regional stability in which both Australia and the United States have vital interests?

At ANZUS treaty meeting,
San Francisco, Aug. 11/
The Washington Post, 8-12:(A)14.

He Dongchang
Senior Vice Minister,
State Education Commission of China

2

[On recent student demonstrations for democracy in China]: They believe they know a lot, but in fact they know little . . . They are the sons and daughters of new China. We take great care of them. God allows young people to make mistakes. When we were young, we basically did the same thing.

Los Angeles Times,
12-31:(I)17.

Hu Yaobang
General Secretary,
Communist Party of China

3

[On young people in China who have lost faith in the Communist Party]: I think it's not only in China but also a world-wide phenomenon. For years, the image of socialism has not been very good. I think this is a fact. The image is not too good because . . . first, economic development has not been very fast. Second, there have been problems, politically speaking, in the field of democracy and in the field of human rights.

Interview, Peking, Sept. 23/
The Washington Post, 9-24:(A)18.

John Paul II
Pope

4

[India] is the world's largest republic, where the principles of democracy are strictly observed. It would be tempting to resolve India's problems with a dictatorial system. Instead, they prefer the other principle, the principle that man is free and that one must let man have his due liberty even in the political field. And this is a great lesson that many Europeans could learn from.

On plane enroute to Rome, Feb. 10/
The New York Times, 2-12:6.

Stanley Karnow
American journalist and historian

5

[On new Philippine President Corazon Aquino, who came to power after the overthrow of Ferdinand Marcos]: Her task is to turn a movement into an administration, and many Filipinos tend to see it as our [the U.S.'] task, too. Campaigning is poetry, and we know she's good at that; but governing is prose, and we have no evidence about her skills in that area.

The New York Times,
2-26:9.

Edward M. Kennedy
United States Senator,
D-Massachusetts
                                    1

[Approving U.S. President Reagan's role in the transition of power from overthrown Philippine President Ferdinand Marcos to new President Corazon Aquino]: It is a day whose peaceful dawn could not have come without the leadership of President Ronald Reagan. He reversed a failing policy [of U.S. support for Marcos]. He discarded his own preconceptions. And he acted on the basis of reality, not right-wing assumptions.

Feb. 25/Los Angeles Times, 2-26:(I)7.

Sahabzada Yaqub Khan
Foreign Minister of Pakistan
                                    2

[Criticizing the Soviet invasion of Afghanistan]: Inside Afghanistan, a sinister design is being pursued through genocide and large-scale uprooting of population. A million Afghans are estimated to have laid down their lives.

At United Nations, New York, Sept. 29/
The New York Times, 9-30:5.

Kim Dae Jung
A leader of opposition to
government of South Korea
                                    3

[On the recent overthrow of Philippine dictator Ferdinand Marcos]: The Philippine situation will greatly influence [South] Korea by demonstrating that people-power is a basic element in politics.

The Christian Science Monitor, 3-4:13.

                                    4

[Saying the South Korean government persecutes him]: One hundred government plainclothesmen surround this house from every angle, three cars follow me when I leave, visitors are watched, my phone is tapped. You will see agents in alleys and windows as you go . . . I can't speak to the public, but I am happy. I can stay with my people and I can do something for them, push them toward democracy, moderate violent attitudes. My presence bolsters the cause . . . our people are highly educated and will continue to demand the restoration of democracy until they get it. We have demonstrated our ability to modernize economically and our past, steeped in Confucianism, guarantees high political awareness and activity.

Interview, Seoul/
The Christian Science Monitor, 7-25:9,10.

Kim Young Sam
Adviser, New Korea Democratic
Party (South Korea)
                                    5

[On the possible return to democracy in South Korea and the possibility of his party's being elected to run the country in 1988]: I sense on the part of the public a desire for some kind of retribution against those who have discriminated against and exploited us. But I think we have to be generous enough to cross this chapter of history. Otherwise, our party and government may not last longer than half a year, even if we have a chance to take power . . . There is no question that the military constitute a very important class in the dynamics of politics in South Korea. But they appear to be aware of the fact that there is a limit to military involvement in politics. I see a growing consensus on their part that should allow, by 1988, a traditional civilian government . . . If the other side agrees to the direct Presidential election system, everything else will be a blank piece of paper on which we can negotiate . . . and make concessions.

Interview, Seoul, June 10/
Los Angeles Times, 6-11:(I)11.

Henry A. Kissinger
Former Secretary of State
of the United States
                                    6

[The Vietnam war] was quite a moral war in the sense that America wanted nothing for itself except the independence of these [South Vietnamese] people who were truly menaced by an aggressive neighbor [North Vietnam].

Interview/Penthouse, December:80.

283

WHAT THEY SAID IN 1986

Mochtar Kusumaatmadja
Foreign Minister of Indonesia

1

We are not against press freedom. On the other hand, we don't have to like it.

U.S. News & World Report, 5-12:8.

David Lange
Prime Minister of New Zealand

2

[On the U.S. decision to revoke its security guarantee to defend New Zealand as a result of New Zealand's policy of not allowing U.S. nuclear warships into its ports]: People of New Zealand are not afraid, because they do not see a nuclear-weapons defense of New Zealand as a security assurance. They, in fact, do not see being defended by nuclear weapons as any sort of assurance . . . It does not mean that New Zealand is not discharging its responsibilities. It has bilateral cooperation with Australia. We are meeting our defense obligations to our neighbors. We are increasing our defensive exercises with the small Pacific island states near it. That is what New Zealand does best and that is what New Zealand should do. We will not have nuclear weapons in New Zealand.

News conference, Manila, Philippines,
June 27/Los Angeles Times, 6-28:(I)1,11.

3

[On the U.S.' formal suspension of its AN-ZUS treaty obligations to New Zealand because of that country's decision not to allow U.S. nuclear ships into its ports]: New Zealand voted overwhelmingly against having nuclear weapons. This government has honored that commitment. We will not have nuclear weapons in New Zealand. If the price is suspension from the operational activities of ANZUS, we are the better for it . . . New Zealand's main contribution in support of Western security interests is the substantial security and economic role it plays in the South Pacific. That will continue. Perhaps the Americans will one day come to recognize its value.

Wellington, New Zealand, Aug. 12/
The Christian Science Monitor, 8-13:12.

Salvador H. Laurel
Vice President and Foreign Minister of the Philippines

4

[On U.S. President Reagan's recent conversation with deposed Philippine President Ferdinand Marcos]: What was said, as it was explained to me, was that Mr. Reagan made it very clear to Mr. Marcos that the United States government recognizes the new government in Manila and that Mr. Marcos should give up trying to destabilize or hoping to make a comeback like [World War II's Douglas] MacArthur. That to me was a very important message, because the Aquino government is already beset with so many problems. We have our hands full with the Communists, we have our hands full with the Muslims, separatists. And then there is Marcos' loyalist group trying to make a comeback.

Interview, Denpasar, Indonesia, April 30/
The New York Times, 5-1:3.

5

[On the new government of the Philippines following the recent overthrow of President Ferdinand Marcos]: We are a country in need right now. We are a two-month-old government, a child government which is faced with the task of feeding, clothing, housing and protecting 54 million people . . . The child government needs all the help it can get from friends.

Interview, Manila, May 9/
The Washington Post, 5-10:(A)13.

Jim Leach
United States Representative, R-Iowa

6

[Criticizing Taiwan for jailing human-rights activists there]: It is an embarrassment in our age that any government anywhere finds the advocacy of human rights and democracy a challenge to its legitimacy. Although Taiwan properly prides itself on its strong anti-Communist stance and its alliance with the free world, the government's commitment to democratic values and principles is unimpressive. The continued incarceration of democratic oppositionists . . .

(JIM LEACH)

is an embarrasssment to friends of Taiwan and a stumbling block to internal reconciliation . . . To the degree that a government finds it necessary or convenient to imprison individuals for defending democratic rights, it cannot help but find its reputation tarnished and its friendship valued less highly.

The Washington Post, 5-28:(A)20.

Lee Kuan Yew
Prime Minister of Singapore

1

[Chinese leader] Deng Xiaoping wants to make up for more than 20 years China has lost. Deng knows what a free market has done in Japan, Korea, Taiwan, Hong Kong and the ASEAN countries. He wants to use the free market to boost China's growth. But I do not think they want to dismantle the control the Communist Party has over political life . . . If China continues to concentrate on economic constructions, then her relations with the countries of the Pacific, especially Southeast Asia, will be constructive.

Interview,
Singapore, Dec. 16/*
The New York Times, 12-22:7.

Lee Yong Ho
Former Minister of
Sports of South Korea

2

[On South Korea being the venue for the next Asian Games and the 1988 Olympics]: After we stage the Asian Games and the Olympics, a lot more people around the world are going to know where we are and have a more positive feeling about our country . . . We are becoming [a significant] nation—economically, culturally and militarily. The Olympics won't alter those facts, but it will change the images many countries hold about us, including the Soviet Union and China.

Los Angeles Times,
9-20:(I)6.

Winston Lord
United States Ambassador to China

3

[On U.S.-Chinese relations]: We are friends. This does not mean that we are allies or that we don't have differences. Neither country is looking for a treaty relationship. But the improvement in our relations over the last 15 years is one of the most positive developments on the international scene. For us, good relations mean we don't have to target a lot of our resources on China, as was the case two decades ago. Eliminating or at least reducing tensions between our two countries has removed some of the causes of instability in Asia. There are many areas where we actively cooperate—such as Afghanistan and Cambodia—and others where we may have different perspectives but share common objectives—such as maintaining peace on the Korean peninsula. For the first time in a century, the U.S., China and Japan have a mutually cooperative relationship.

Interview/U.S. News &
World Report, 9-8:33.

Richard G. Lugar
United States Senator,
R-Indiana

4

[Criticizing the U.S. decision to sell subsidized wheat to the Soviet Union despite complaints from Australia that the subsidization will undercut their sales efforts]: Our relationship with Australia has gone unbelievably sour in a course of a week of time. [The Australians believe they have been betrayed by] their closest friend, literally, for a very small price . . . What has not surfaced as much as it ought to is that Australia has really been very, very helpful in thinking through with us all of the problems of various islands in the Pacific that are receiving overtures from the Soviets. For a small amount of cash, the Soviets are buying up fishing rights but also buying up some foreign-policy chits.

To reporters,
Washington, Aug. 5/
Los Angeles Times, 8-6:(I)4.

WHAT THEY SAID IN 1986

Antonio Lukban
General, and head of logistics,
Armed Forces of the Philippines

1

[The recently toppled Administration of President Ferdinand Marcos was] so concerned with their own security and the security of their cronies that they never really worried about the security of their nation. And it shows how the Communist Party of the Philippines and the New People's Army were able to grow so fast in the rural areas . . . First and foremost in our country, the best weapons against insurgency are the people themselves—the soldiers. If they know what they are fighting for, they don't need that much equipment. If you see the enemy, you know they are ill-equipped but have been winning because they know what they are fighting for. The key is in the leadership. Under the Marcos regime, our soldiers saw their leaders enjoying a comfortable, luxurious life in the city when they were fighting it out in the mud and saying, "What the hell are we fighting for?"

Los Angeles Times, 4-7:(I)1,10.

James A. Lyons, Jr.
Admiral and Commander-in-Chief of
the Pacific Fleet, United States Navy

2

[Criticizing New Zealand's decision not to allow U.S. nuclear ships into its ports]: America has fewer allies in the Pacific than in the European theatre. New Zealand's denial of port privileges, not only to nuclear-powered warships, but also to nuclear-capable ships, leaves a gap in our deterrence structure. Not being able to rely on New Zealand's armed forces means I have six fewer frigates and destroyers to patrol the South Pacific . . . We've never asked New Zealand to join our strategic nuclear policy. All we want is for it to live up to its responsibilities as a member of ANZUS and provide facilities where we can make repairs and rest our crews. Without these port visits, we can't maintain a presence in the region. The door always is open to New Zealand, but I find it very difficult to order my men and women to go out and sacrifice their

lives for a country that will not welcome us into its ports.

Interview/Los Angeles Times
Magazine, 8-10:17.

Mike Mansfield
United States
Ambassador to Japan

3

In response to the Japanese government's call [to buy more foreign products], many Japanese firms have issued press releases professing good intentions, and sent highly publicized buying missions to the U.S. Speaking frankly, so far results have been disappointing. Despite the government's campaign, in 1985 Japanese imports of American manufactured goods rose by less than 2 per cent. It reminds me of an old Asian expression: "Much thunder and little rain." By contrast, in 1985 Japan's manufactured-goods exports to the U.S. increased by over 30 per cent. Japan must do better than this to cope with the tremendous and growing protectionist pressures [in the U.S.]

Before Japan Foreign Trade Council,
Tokyo/The Wall Street Journal, 9-18:26.

Ferdinand E. Marcos
President of the Philippines

4

[Criticizing his election opponent, Corazon Aquino, who said she may allow Communists into her government if she is elected President]: Danger! Danger! Beware of what the opposition is saying. They said they would allow the Communists to come in. If the Communists were allowed into the government, there would be fighting all over the country. You and I—who have no guns—we would be the first to suffer. Many will die. It will be a bloody civil war.

At campaign rally, Manila, Jan. 21/
Los Angeles Times, 1-22:(I)9.

5

[On his Presidential re-election campaign against his major opponent, Corazon Aquino]: How can I wage political battle against a widow

(FERDINAND E. MARCOS)

who does not mean anyone any harm, except only the President himself? She means no harm to Communists with whom she will dialogue if they promise to be good boys and put down their arms. My opponent grossly simplifies when she reduces the complex world of politics into a Manichean battle between good and evil. If she truly believes the caricature she has made of me, then she is dangerously naive.

Presidential Campaign address, Manila,
Jan. 30/The New York Times, 1-31:7.

1

So many crimes have been attributed to this Administration [by Marcos' critics] that if they were true at all, the country would need exorcism instead of free elections.

Presidential campaign address, Manila,
Jan. 30/The New York Times, 1-31:7.

2

[On accusations against him of fraud and violence in the recent Presidential election]: I'm still the President of the Republic of the Philippines, whatever anybody may say. I intend to convince everybody that the fraud or violence was committed by the opposition more than by the government. This vote, as far as I am concerned, reflects the will of the Filipino people. We are beating a dead horse by talking about whether the people are supporting me or not. To me, it's over. The moment they [the opposition and other critics] can prove to me that I'm an unwanted—what they call a dictator—then I'll get out. I am the President. They are not going to drive me out, because the people are behind me.

News conference, Manila, Feb. 16/
The Washington Post, 2-17:(A)32.

3

When I first became President, I realized that most of our people were bogged down in resignation to ignorance and poverty, which they had been taught under the Spanish regime as their destiny from heaven. They were resigned to spiritual hopelessness. In short, what the church was supposed to have done—which was to strengthen the spirit and morality of our people— has failed in creating a people who could be called a united and dynamic race. So it became my vision—the linchpin of the entire program— to bring about spiritual regeneration, not just the theoretical morality and spiritual change that people like to talk about, but which is never manifested in the freedom of the soul, the strength of the spirit, its resurgence, its effort to be above all things material. And from there . . . the people . . . would be proud of their past, of their culture, of their race. This is usually brought about by such material manifestations like self-reliance—men and women and children who are able to stand up on their feet. This requires a spiritual regeneration to begin with. To us, we have begun this effort. We have probably partially succeeded. It is my hope that we can contaminate the younger generation with the same flame that burns in our hearts for our people. To me, that is the principal objective.

Interview, Manila/
The Christian Science Monitor, 2-18:10.

4

[On foreign criticism of the recent elections in the Philippines, in which Marcos was accused of fraud in claiming victory]: There are those in foreign lands who for their own reasons have . . . impugned the integrity of our recent Presidential elections, and have even called for foreign intervention in our national affairs. We deplore . . . the acts of ungracious electoral losers and of modern-day imperialists that evidently think that a nation like the Philippines would willingly submit to their dictates and wishes. I would like to remind them that Filipinos have many times before paid with their blood, their lives and their honor to preserve their freedom and national integrity, and so will they again.

Press release, Feb. 21/*
The Washington Post, 2-22:(A)16.

Ferdinand E. Marcos
Exiled former President
of the Philippines

5

I have no political intentions. My only purpose is to see to it that the Philippines does not come under totalitarian regime . . . To me, that is the greatest danger. The question of who will rule, who is the President, and the like, these are now almost irrelevant, because . . . the way things are moving, either the military or the Communists [will] take over.

Interview, Honolulu, Hawaii, May 12/
The Christian Science Monitor, 5-13:9.

1

I'm irrelevant. An exile is always irrelevant.

Interview, Honolulu/Newsweek, 9-22:46.

Yasuhiro Nakasone
Prime Minister of Japan

2

[On Japan's large surplus in its trade with the U.S.]: I believe there is an awareness that we Japanese must make greater efforts in that regard [to redress the imbalance] . . . [But] there is another feeling that, why can't our trade partner understand the serious efforts made by the Japanese? Our American friends are too impatient. Given the fact that we are living in the free world, economic problems cannot be resolved overnight by simply using a gimmick or magic.

Interview, Tokyo/Newsweek, 2-3:31.

Saturnino Ocampo
Negotiator, Communist Party
of the Philippines

3

[On the Communist guerrilla war against the government of Philippines President Corazon Aquino]: The prospects of a peaceful political settlement are getting narrower. The President has been drawn to rely on the military for support, and it seems the liberals in her government are losing by default. Such a drift does not work in favor of the prospects of achieving a comprehensive political settlement . . . Mrs. Aquino herself has said the cause of the insurgency is the mass impoverishment of the people and the unjust social structures, and that to solve the in-

surgency problems we should address these problems. She should research into these questions rather than trying to address the problem from a very, shall we say, shallow perception that with the removal of [deposed President] Marcos there is no longer any valid reason for us to be struggling.

Interview/
The New York Times, 9-26:6.

Geoffrey Palmer
Deputy Prime Minister
of New Zealand

4

We [New Zealand] used to be European in our vision. Then we went through a period when Southeast Asia was important to our strategic thinking. Now we are fixed in the South Pacific. We realize that is how it should be. That recognition is a step forward in maturity and realism in this country.

The Christian Science Monitor, 4-17:9.

Mosese Qionibarawi
Deputy Prime Minister of Fiji

5

[Criticizing France for conducting nuclear-weapons tests in the South Pacific]: How much longer can a country which professes to be a leader in its respect for international law and obligations continue to act so arrogantly? If, as France maintains, nuclear testing is so vital to the security of the Western Alliance, perhaps the United States might consider allowing France to use the Nevada test site. On the other hand, if the tests are as safe as claimed, then there is good reason to move testing to the Mediterranean island of Corsica, or to mainland France itself.

The New York Times, 10-7:4.

Burhanuddin Rabbani
A leader of Afghan resistance fighting
Soviet intervention in Afghanistan

6

[Criticizing the current UN-sponsored peace talks to end the Soviet military intervention in

(BURHANUDDIN RABBANI)

Afghanistan]: These current negotiations are a part of the Soviet political strategy and propaganda. It is designed to fool the world into believing that the Soviets are reasonable men who seek a reasonable way out of the war. The Soviets will leave only if they pay a higher material and political price. Only when many more of their men are killed, or when more Soviet gunships are destroyed, when mothers complain about their sons who are killed or wounded, when the world cries out for justice in Afghanistan so loudly, will the Soviets consider withdrawing.

News conference, Washington, June 16/
The New York Times, 6-17:4.

1

Some of you American press are calling us "rebels," as if we were fighting a legal government. We are fighting against invaders. And this is why we are hurt, and sometimes it is more painful than the bullets fired by the enemy. Because this is not done by the enemy, but is being done by the free press. And a free press must call us by the name we really are. Mujahedeen: Freedom Fighters!

Interview, Washington, June 18/
The New York Times, 6-19:12.

Fidel V. Ramos
General and Commander,
armed forces of the Philippines

2

[On the rift within the Philippines government over how to handle the Communist insurgency in the country]: We [in the military] are the first ones to know, we are the first ones to feel and to believe that military action alone will not solve this problem, because the insurgency itself is just a symptom of the basic problems of poverty. We are in a championship bout with a very, very strong opponent. So we say, please don't make this a bout between the armed forces and the civilian government. This is a bout against the armed groups that are out there . . . and we are still in the earlier rounds.

Interview/Los Angeles Times, 10-25:(I)15.

Ronald Reagan
President of the United States

3

[On the forthcoming Presidential election in the Philippines]: If the will of the Filipino people is expressed in an election that Filipinos accept as credible—and if whoever is elected undertakes fundamental economic, political and military reforms—we should consider, in consultation with the Congress, a significantly larger program of economic and military assistance for the Philippines for the next five years. This would be over and above the current levels of assistance we are providing.

Washington, Jan. 30/
The New York Times, 1-31:1.

4

[On the recent Presidential election in the Philippines, in which election fraud by President Ferdinand Marcos has been alleged]: I think any of us would be concerned. But I think what we have to watch for is that, in spite of all these charges, there is at the same time the evidence of a strong two-party system now in the islands. And we certainly are accustomed to that. We want to help in any way we can, that once the election is over that the results of the election can go forward and that the two [candidates] can come together to make sure the government works, and that we can retain the historic relationship that we have had with the Philippine people and the Philippine islands. But actually, the election, that is for the people of the Philippines to decide, and not for us to interfere in.

At luncheon with editors and broadcasters,
Washington, Feb. 10/
The New York Times, 2-11:6.

5

[On the recent Presidential election in the Philippines]: First, it is a disturbing fact that the election has been flawed by reports of fraud, which we take seriously, and by violence. This concerns us because we cherish commitment to free and fair elections, and because we believe the government of the Philippines needs an authentic popular mandate in order effectively to counter a growing Communist insurgency and

(RONALD REAGAN)

restore health to its troubled economy. And second, the election itself—the obvious enthusiasm of Filipinos for the democratic process and the extraordinary vigor of the campaign—also tell us something. They tell us of the profound yearning of the Filipino people for democracy, and indeed of the vigor of the underlying forces of pluralism and democracy. Only the Communists boycotted the election. The political process in the Philippines continues. Further, it does not end with this election. Our task for the future is to help nurture the hopes and possibilities of democracy; to help the people of the Philippines overcome the grave problems their country faces, and to continue to work for essential reforms.

Washington, Feb. 11/USA Today, 2-12:(A)7.*

1

[On the recent election in the Philippines and the subsequent overthrow of President Ferdinand Marcos who was replaced by new President Corazon Aquino]: We've just seen a stirring demonstration of what men and women committed to democratic ideas can achieve. The remarkable people of those 7,000 islands joined together with faith in the same principles on which America was founded—that men and women have the right to freely choose their own destiny. Despite a flawed election, the Filipino people were understood. They carried their message peacefully, and they were heard across their country and across the world. We salute the remarkable restraint, shown by both sides, to prevent bloodshed during these last tense days. Our hearts and hands are with President Aquino and her new government as they set out to meet the challenges ahead. Today the Filipino people celebrate the triumph of democracy, and the world celebrates with them.

Broadcast address to the nation, Washington,
Feb. 26/The New York Times, 2-27:14.

Charles E. Redman
Spokesman for the Department
of State of the United States

2

We've made very clear to the highest levels of

the Pakistani government the serious consequences for our relationship should Pakistan fail to exercise restraint in the nuclear area. The Pakistanis understand that, under U.S. law, possession of a nuclear explosive device would preclude further U.S. assistance. Pakistan has strongly asserted that its nuclear program is for peaceful purposes only.

Nov. 4/The Washington Post, 11-5:(A)29.

George P. Shultz
Secretary of State
of the United States

3

[Saying the South Korean government is making efforts to bring democracy to the country]: The idea that somehow there isn't an effort to bring into play democratic institutions and have an orderly transition of power is all wrong. It is right there for everyone to see . . . There will be a transition of power in early 1988, which is not very far away. As that happens, it will be the first time that it has been possible to do that in an orderly way in Korea in 40 years. So it will be an achievement. I think that it deserves our support, and gets it.

To reporters, Seoul/
The Christian Science Monitor, 5-12:11.

4

I'm bullish on the Philippines. The manner in which the Filipino people and their new leaders [after the overthrow of President Ferdinand Marcos] have overcome nearly impossible odds to restore democracy in their country gives me good cause for optimism . . . It is still early in [new President Corazon Aquino's] tenure. But already she has dispelled many initial uncertainties. Her government is off and running hard and it is headed in the right direction.

Before Foreign Policy Association, New York,
June 4/Los Angeles Times, 6-5:(I)16.

5

[Criticizing New Zealand's policy of not allowing U.S. nuclear warships into its ports]: We don't have ships with nuclear weapons on them because we like it. We have them because the

(GEORGE P. SHULTZ)

United States has a responsibility to deter aggression, and that comes from the Soviet Union. The Soviet Union has very large nuclear stockpiles and, if we don't have nuclear weapons and have the capability to deter their aggression with them, then we subject everyone, including ourselves, to nuclear blackmail from the Soviet Union. So it would be a tragedy for freedom and Western values for the policy of New Zealand to spread.

News conference, Manila, Philippines,
June 27/The New York Times, 6-28:5.

Jaime Cardinal Sin
Roman Catholic Primate
of the Philippines

1

[On the recent overthrow of Philippine President Ferdinand Marcos]: We solved the political dilemma in just four days, but the other problems of the nation are just as serious, and I am afraid they cannot be solved in just four days. Twenty years of Marcosian misrule made us more materialistic. Money became the ruling yardstick, and we measured success only in terms of how much wealth a person accumulated. In our obsession to learn the price of everything, we forgot to appreciate the value of everything. Corruption became a way of life.

To businessmen, Manila, April 9/
Los Angeles Times, 4-10:(I)16.

Stephen J. Solarz
United States Representative,
D-New York

2

[Criticizing U.S. White House statements he says support Philippine President Ferdinand Marcos despite alleged vote fraud by Marcos in the recent Presidential election]: The suggestion that the [Philippine] opposition should accept with equanimity the fact that the election has been stolen constitutes prima facie evidence that they are smoking hashish in the White House. They appear to have lost touch with reality.

The New York Times, 2-11:6.

Robert G. Torricelli
United States Representative,
D-New Jersey

3

[On the U.S. granting sanctuary to deposed Philippine President Ferdinand Marcos]: I have a concern about the United States appearing as a haven for thieves and bandits. Political asylum in the United States was intended to protect the innocent and not to shield the guilty, to be a refuge for the oppressed, not a means of escape for those who are oppressors. That is a poor precedent and a poor signal to the world.

Interview/The New York Times, 3-4:7.

Caspar W. Weinberger
Secretary of State
of the United States

4

[On whether U.S. support of the South Korean government is in the best interests of democracy there]: I am satisfied that what we are doing is essential for the preservation of the government in the Republic of [South] Korea and for freedom and peace in the whole peninsula. The American commitment to doing that is complete and absolute.

News conference, Seoul, April 3/
Los Angeles Times, 4-4:(I)1.

Paul D. Wolfowitz
Assistant Secretary for East Asia
and Pacific Affairs, Department of
State of the United States

5

I see no contradiction between our interest in the two U.S. bases in the [Philippine] islands and our larger interest in promoting democratic development and finding effective means of fighting the Communists. Some who see a conflict believe the way to fight the Communists is somehow to cut off all U.S. assistance to the Philippines. They think our bases are an obstacle to that. Quite apart from its impact on our base agreement with Manila, that would be a terrible mistake. We believe that with any democratically elected government in the country,

WHAT THEY SAID IN 1986

arguments for the American bases are very strong and probably will prevail. If they don't, we'll make our adjustments and we'll go elsewhere. We are prepared.

Interview/U.S. News &
World Report, 2-10:34.

1

I believe the [Communist guerrillas in the Philippines] can be beaten and will be beaten. But if, in fact, they end up taking over that country—in that unlikely event—the consequences will be far more than just the possibility that the Russians may get themselves a base in the Philippines. It would mean 50 million more people under the kind of tyranny that has driven so many Asians into leaky boats to find safe haven in the free world.

Interview/U.S. News &
World Report, 2-10:35.

Woo Roh Tae
Chairman, ruling Democratic
Justice Party of South Korea

2

In the past, the government and the people have emphasized the need for strong, centralized leadership because of the acute [need for] security. But now that we are revising the Constitution, we must reflect the changes which have occurred in all sectors of society. Koreans now have a per capita income of $2,000 a year. The people's education has improved. Diverse and pluralized interests are being articulated in all sectors of society. With great power concentrated in one person, we cannot deal with all of the diverse demands put upon us. It is time to start democratization in the true sense of the word by introducing local autonomy, and autonomy in every social field as well—to allow decisions to be made by the people concerned.

Interview, Seoul, June 13/
Los Angeles Times, 6-14:(I)18.

Yim Churl Soon
Member, South Korean National
Assembly; Director, South Korean
Institute of National Policy

3

There are two main groups [in South Korea]: a group that wants hasty changes and reforms in every aspect of our society, and another group with a go-slow approach that expects gradual changes. What is the response of the government and ruling party to these different approaches? The focus has been on the majority that wants gradual changes. But it is also understood that a democratic administration cannot ignore the views of the minority. And, in that regard, the government is interested in compromise and dialogue, trying step by step to make additional changes and reforms . . .

Interview/Newsweek, 6-23:19.

Damaryn Yondon
First Deputy Foreign
Minister of Mongolia

4

Over the centuries, whenever China is strong, it has used that strength to dominate or conduct aggression against its neighbors. Today, China is a militarily strong power, a nuclear-weapons power, and a rapidly developing industrial power with military links to the U.S. and Japan. And by the Chinese Communist Party's 100th year anniversary in 2049, China intends to emerge as a world power.

Interview, Ulan Bator, Mongolia/
The Christian Science Monitor, 10-21:9.

Mohammed Zia ul-Haq
President of Pakistan

5

[On the insurgents fighting the Soviets in Afghanistan]: To expect that the greater the insurgency, the less the time the Soviets will spend in Afghanistan, is wrong. You've got to find a political solution to the problem. The insurgency is a tactic. It will help find a political solution [to

(MOHAMMED ZIA ul-HAQ)

the Soviet presence], but it will not bring about a solution. So if anybody's thinking that the greater the heat of the insurgency, the easier the solution, he is wrong. The freedom fighters must continue their effort at the present level . . . I don't call this a regional problem, I call this a global problem. Because if you accept in Afghanistan that might is right, that a superpower [the Soviet Union] can walk in and subjugate a country, then we are leaving very little for posterity, and the free world will have nothing to offer.

Interview, Islamabad, Pakistan/
Los Angeles Times, 3-23:(V)1,2.

Zhao Ziyang
Premier of China

1

Our country has a vast population, but not enough arable land and grassland. Consequently, for many years to come, the diet of our people cannot improve too quickly, and there can only be gradual increases in the consumption of meat, poultry and eggs. With respect to clothing, people should be encouraged to wear more garments made of cotton, synthetics and blends, while consumption of woolen fabrics and leather products can only be increased to a certain extent.

Before National People's Congress, Peking,
March 25/Los Angeles Times, 3-26:(I)19.

Europe

Morris B. Abram
Chairman, (U.S.) National
Commission on Soviet Jewry

1

[On the Soviet Union's allowing selected dissidents to emigrate to the West]: We must not be deceived that the dove has come from Noah's Ark with a green twig in his beak, because the Soviets have the capacity of releasing people in driblets and then creating new prisoners. They receive much publicity from the release of one person and then imprison others who receive no publicity. In this way they throw dust in our eyes.

The New York Times, 10-17:1.

Gerry Adams
Leader, Sinn Fein party
of Northern Ireland;
Member of British Parliament

2

The British like to think simplistically, like to say that what is wrong here [in Northern Ireland] is not a colonial situation, an unjust situation [of British occupation], but the work of one or two clever people who are able to orchestrate it all by terrorizing their own communities. But you can't intimidate 100,000 people to go out and vote for you.

Interview, Belfast, Northern Ireland/
The New York Times, 9-18:4.

Ulf Adelsohn
Leader, Conservative
Party of Sweden

3

[On the assassination of Swedish Prime Minister Olof Palme]: It is an almost unbelievable shock. It is a thing one cannot believe could happen in Sweden. It is a tragedy not only for Olof Palme's family but for the democratic ideal all Swedes support. Sweden will never be the same. The meaningless violence will always throw a shadow over our political life.

Feb. 28/The New York Times, 3-1:1.

Giulio Andreotti
Foreign Minister of Italy

4

. . . it [is] evident how Europe, a vulnerable peninsula on the edge of the Asian continent, would be at risk if its defense became dependent upon conventional [non-nuclear] forces alone.

At NATO foreign-ministers meeting, Brussels,
Dec. 11/Los Angeles Times, 12-12:(I)16.

Georgi A. Arbatov
Director, Soviet Institute of
U.S.A. and Canadian Affairs

5

[On criticism of the Soviet's handling of news from the recent Chernobyl nuclear plant accident in the U.S.S.R.]: . . . I'm not sure what was expected from us, from the first moment of the catastrophe. Really, you have to think about people—to save people there. You don't know dimensions. You don't know yet the causes. And the Americans don't know the causes, for instance, of catastrophe, calamity with *Challenger* [the recent explosion of the U.S. space shuttle] or some other things. So we said what we did know. And our first and major concern at this moment was not to think about how to please American government or some other government but how to deal with this extremely dangerous situation—and we did it. What we really got to know is the extent of hate against the Soviet Union, which was nourished in many world governments. It has grown a hate campaign immediately.

Broadcast interview, Moscow/
"It's Your World,"
British Broadcasting Corp., 5-4.

Edouard Balladur
Minister of Finance of France

6

[On France's policy toward international terrorism]: We have begun a vigorous internal anti-

294

(EDOUARD BALLADUR)

terrorist program which will protect order and security. But this doesn't mean that France supports any actions of another country in the fight against terrorism.

The Christian Science Monitor, 4-15:10.

Peter Barry
Foreign Minister of Ireland

1

[On the recently signed British-Irish agreement giving Ireland limited influence in the affairs of Northern Ireland]: The major aspect of this agreement is the new sense of confidence that it has given nationalists in Northern Ireland. For the first time, an Irish government has a permanent presence in Belfast and input into all policy matters affecting Ulster Catholics.

U.S. News & World Report, 11-17:38.

Yelena G. Bonner
Wife of Soviet dissident
Andrei D. Sakharov

2

[On her returning to the Soviet Union from the U.S. to be with her husband, who is being held in internal exile in the U.S.S.R. for political crimes]: I want to return to him, but it is extremely sad and extremely difficult for many reasons. I fear the isolation in which we have lived our last two years in Gorky. I fear life under constant supervision under the lenses of hidden cameras used everywhere.

News conference, Boston, May 24/
The New York Times, 5-26:4.

Irving Brown
Director of international relations,
American Federation of Labor-Congress
of Industrial Organizations

3

[On his fight against Communism in France]: We're defending democracy in France. Let's go back to [Thomas] Jefferson: "The price of liberty is eternal vigilance." France is not threat-

ened by the 10 per cent vote of the Communist Party. It is threatened by the Communist apparatus. Is it a clear and present danger? It is a clear and present danger if the present is thought of as 10 years from now.

Interview, Paris/
Los Angeles Times, 2-6:(I)25.

Zbigniew Brzezinski
Professor of government,
Columbia University; Former Assistant
to the President of the United States
(Jimmy Carter) for National Security Affairs

4

[The Soviet-U.S. conflict] is not just a freak, but a longterm historical competition between a great land power which aims at the domination of Eurasia, and a great transcontinental and transoceanic power like the United States, which has to make certain that the extremities of Eurasia are not dominated by the Soviet Union.

Interview, Washington/
The New York Times, 6-17:5.

5

[On the release from internal exile of Soviet dissident Andrei Sakharov]: I think we're on the eve of something very significant, perhaps even momentous, happening in the Soviet Union. I don't think it's cosmetic at all. I think it's very serious. The fact that [Sakharov] comes back in triumph is a source of enormous encouragement to every would-be dissenter in the Soviet Union. What is happening is that [Soviet leader Mikhail] Gorbachev is trying to renovate the system, to rejuvenate it, to make it more modern, without reforming it—and that's a very dangerous game . . . You set in motion forces which ultimately you cannot yourself control.

Broadcast interview, Washington/
"This Week with David Brinkley," 12-28.

Zbigniew Bujak
Former leader, Warsaw region,
now-banned Solidarity
(independent Polish trade union)

6

[On the recent release by the Polish government of virtually all political prisoners it was

(ZBIGNIEW BUJAK)

holding]: The decision to release political prisoners is an important fact and it creates a chance to change the social climate in the country. The step should be followed immediately by such measures that will break the deadlock between authorities and society. If this will not happen, then the results of this decision will be short-lived. The prisons will begin to fill up again and a dangerous further deterioration of the economy and ecology will follow.

News conference, Warsaw, Sept. 30/
The New York Times, 10-1:3.

Vladimir Bukovsky
Exiled Soviet dissident

1

Ask anybody who has lived in the Soviet Union and they will tell you that the least effective thing in the Soviet Union is to sit down and talk. If you have any leverage, use it. The Soviets are chess players. If you just sit and talk over the chessboard, how much will it advance your game? What counts are the moves you make.

Interview, Palo Alto, Calif./
The Christian Science Monitor, 11-4:14.

Lord Carrington
Secretary General, North
Atlantic Treaty Organization

2

It can plausibly be argued that Western Europe is now rich enough, and potentially strong enough, to provide a sufficient counterweight to Soviet military power on our continent. But what a go-it-alone strategy would require by way of a sustained transfer of resources to the military sector would have serious implications for the sort of society we are seeking to defend.

Speech, Edinburgh, Oct. 22/
The Christian Science Monitor, 10-23:9.

3

[Arguing against a "no first use" declaration by Western Europe regarding nuclear weapons]: The fact remains that uncertainty of what might

happen is in itself a very important deterrent. And this is one of the reasons why, for example, a pledge by the West, by NATO, of no first use of nuclear weapons would in itself lead to less deterrence . . . If the other guy attacks us, and he has the certainty that we are not going to use nuclear weapons, you are removing one of the factors in his mind as to whether or not it is possible to wage a successful conventional war.

Interview, Brussels/
The Christian Science Monitor, 12-2:13.

Geoffrey Chandler
Director, British Industry Year 1986

4

Britain is the only industrialized country in the world with an anti-industrial culture. You still hear parents tell their children that they are too good to go into industry.

Maclean's, 5-5:27.

Prince Charles
Prince of Wales

5

Well-worn cliches, I know, are inclined to abound when talking about the Anglo-American relationship—special or otherwise—but, when all is said and done, the mortar that holds all the bricks together is so often made up from warm personal relationships between individual human beings. Such friendships help to withstand the destructive nature of the appallingly simple generalizations by which nations tend to judge each other and through which so much harm can come to the fragile relationships between so many countries.

At celebration of 350th anniversary of
Harvard University, Cambridge, Mass., Sept. 4/
Los Angeles Times, 9-5:(I)24.

Jacques Chirac
Premier of France

6

For decades—some would even say centuries—the French temptation above all was for state direction. Whether it was a question of economy

(JACQUES CHIRAC)

or education, culture or research, new technologies or defense of the environment, the citizen has always turned to the state to ask for ideas and subsidies. [This temptation] destroys itself by its own obesity while it threatens to diminish individual liberty. It is time we turned our backs on closed ideologies, on systems constructed to substitute one or another collective undertaking for the individual . . . [The French] do not want it any more.

Before French National Assembly, Paris,
April 8/Los Angeles Times, 4-10:(I)4;
The New York Times, 4-10:9.

1

[On U.S.-French relations]: It is true that our view of the events which mark the world, as well as our interests which are linked to our respective geostrategic positions, do not necessarily coincide. This we have never tried to hide. However, such difficulties of analysis, far from calling into question our relations, on the contrary, enrich them.

At ceremony marking 100th anniversary of
the Statue of Liberty, Paris, June 23/
The New York Times, 6-24:6.

2

[On the outbreak of terrorist bombings in Paris]: One of the people placing these bombs will inevitably be caught and he will talk. And we will take draconian measures; we will be without pity for anybody, absolutely anybody found to be manipulating these terrorists. Terrorists should expect from the French government no clemency of any sort, direct or indirect, official or unofficial, secret or open.

Broadcast address to the nation, Paris,
Sept. 14/The New York Times, 9-15:2.

3

[On the current rash of terrorist bombings in Paris]: Following other friendly countries, France is now exposed to a severe test. The French will shoulder this burden with calm, courage and the determination to which I have to pay my tribute. This is the only attitude which

will permit us, all together, to overcome this test . . . [The action we must take] is clear. First of all, to undertake everything and work to protect us all, if this involves imposing certain constraints and certain discipline. Then in no way to yield to blackmail or threat of force. Finally, to do everything, and I mean everything, to punish pitilessly the assassins and those who are manipulating them. On the whole of the territory of France, the police are at work. The assassins, I assure you, will not escape us. Justice, thanks to the law which we have just adopted, will be meted out rapidly to them.

Broadcast address to the nation, Paris,
Sept. 18/The New York Times, 9-19:4.

Birgitta Dahl
Minister of Energy of Sweden

4

[On the current radiation accident at the Soviet nuclear power plant at Chernobyl and the Soviet government's failure to notify neighboring nations of the situation]: They should immediately have warned us . . . We must also demand that in such situations one alerts one's neighbors; and furthermore, we shall reiterate our demand that the whole Soviet civilian nuclear program be subject to international control . . . I hope that the Soviet Union learns from this incredibly brutal experience. It is a matter of the Soviet Union protecting its own people. It means that the Soviet Union must show concern for the neighboring countries and their good, neighborly relations. I assume that they will now take measures that should have been taken a long time ago.

USA Today, 4-30:(A)12.

Rauf Denktash
President, Turkish Republic
of Northern Cyprus

5

[Saying the U.S. and Britain should recognize the Turkish Cypriot people as equals in their dispute with the Greek Cypriots, who officially control the government of Cyprus]: [The U.S. and Britain are] pretending that devolution of

(RAUF DENKTASH)

powers by the "legitimate government" to a "rebellious people" would settle the Cyprus problem. They have been overlooking that the fundamental fact is the political equality of the two peoples. This is the formidable impediment over which the Greek Cypriots refuse to jump . . . We have to show the world that we are a proper side, an equal side in the conflict of Cyprus. It cannot be settled without us.

Interview, Cyprus, July 12/
The New York Times, 7-14:2.

Christopher J. Dodd
United States Senator,
D-Connecticut

1

[Arguing against U.S. Senate approval of a treaty which would permit the extradition from the U.S. to Britain of suspected Northern Irish terrorists]: The principle of political asylum . . . has protected people of every color and stripe. Once you start picking among groups and deciding who you like and who you don't like, you'll never get out of that morass.

USA Today, 5-21:(A)9.

Pete V. Domenici
United States Senator,
R-New Mexico

2

[Saying Western European countries are not supportive enough of U.S. foreign-policy initiatives, such as the recent U.S. retaliation attack against Libya]: It is inconceivable to me that our European allies should disagree with us 100 per cent of the time and still expect to be treated as allies.

U.S. News & World Report, 4-28:22.

Lawrence S. Eagleburger
Former Under Secretary of
State of the United States

3

Throughout much of the commentary from across the Atlantic there has often been a hint,

sometimes more than a hint, that Europeans are far more adept at the conduct of foreign policy than we [the U.S.]. It is hard to avoid remarking, in the face of this self-congratulation, that much of the travail of this century had its origins in European diplomacy and policy, which is not particularly good advertising for a claim of prescience. And yet, their argument is not without merit. Our European allies have, over the past four decades, had a profound influence on America's foreign policy, an influence that has, on the whole, proved beneficial to both sides of the Atlantic. We bring to the table a sense of a drive and purpose; our European allies often have a better sense of nuance and sophistication. And the result has been, on many occasions, a synthesis that has married the best of both worlds. But to achieve this result has required respect on all sides, as well as a compassionate understanding of the vital interests and emotional concerns of each of the parties.

At George Washington University School of
Public and International Affairs commencement,
May 4/The New York Times, 5-8:14.

James Eberle
Director, Royal Institute of
International Affairs (Britain)

4

[On the controversy and counter-claims surrounding the recent U.S.-Soviet arms-control summit in Reykjavik, Iceland]: Reykjavik was the last straw in showing the Europeans the penalties of over-dependence on American leadership. But there was some good news, too. Europeans now realize they must do more for themselves.

U.S. News & World Report, 12-29:52.

Garret FitzGerald
Prime Minister of Ireland

5

[On the British-Irish cooperation agreement for Northern Ireland]: I think there are difficult months ahead, but we always thought that the first year would be difficult. The two governments will keep on course with what we're do-

(GARRET FITZGERALD)

ing, steadily, unprovocatively, firmly improving security cooperation, making the changes necessary so the minority can identify in the future with the system, and trying to create conditions into which the unionists can come into the discussion of the future government of our land.

Interview, Dublin, March 5/
The New York Times, 3-6:4.

Felipe Gonzalez
Prime Minister of Spain

1

[On the just-held national referendum in which voters approved Spain's remaining in NATO]: The result is a success for the whole Spanish people. Aside from the outcome, I consider that every time we have a vote with full normality and a high turnout, it gives a strength to our system of free and peaceful coexistence. Spain's policy of peace and security has emerged strengthened and confirmed by a majority of our people. The result will enable us to continue to take part in European and Western security and make an active contribution to maintaining peace and the support of peaceful solutions on conflicts in the world. I am firmly convinced that this result strengthens and consolidates the path of peace, coexistence, democracy and progress which Spain set out on 10 years ago.

Broadcast address to the nation, Madrid,
March 12/Los Angeles Times, 3-13:(I)1.

2

There's a consciousness on both sides of the Atlantic that we need one another for security and peace. But we're also conscious that Europe is not conferred with enough [by the U.S.]. So it's imperative to strengthen the European pillar by giving it a greater sense of autonomy and involvement. Economically and politically, the U.S. is a superpower before which European countries seem greatly diminished. What is needed is more of an equal relationship. Frequently, one of the things we agree on is that we don't always understand one another. Right now, the immense majority of West Europeans want disarmament.

I don't think this is true of the American Administration. We Europeans feel East-West tensions by virtue of proximity. The U.S. is far away. There's a psychological problem of approach.

Interview, Madrid/
U.S. News & World Report, 7-7:38.

Mikhail S. Gorbachev
General Secretary, Communist
Party of the Soviet Union

3

Acceleration of the [Soviet Union's] socio-economic development is the key to all our problems: immediate and long-term, economic and social, political and ideological, internal and external. That is the only way a new qualitative condition of Soviet society can and must be achieved. By the end of this century we intend to increase the national income nearly two-fold while doubling the production potential and qualitatively transforming it. Labor productivity will go up by 2.3 to 2.5 times; energy consumption per ruble of national income will drop by 28.6 per cent; and metal consumption by nearly 50 per cent.

At Soviet Communist Party Congress, Moscow,
Feb. 25/The New York Times, 2-26:4.

4

[On the Soviet economy]: Prices must be made more flexible, and their level must be coordinated not just with production costs, but with consumer value of the goods, balance between supply and demand and correspondence of the product to the actual needs of the society as well. Prices must become an active instrument in economic and social policies. A planned, methodical reconstruction of the pricing system must be done, in the interests of setting up an efficient self-financing mechanism in our economy and in agreement with the task of increasing the real income of the population.

At Soviet Communist Party Congress, Moscow,
Feb. 25/Los Angeles Times, 2-27:(I)8.

5

It is fundamental for us to increase public openness. Sometimes, when it is a question of

299

WHAT THEY SAID IN 1986

(MIKHAIL S. GORBACHEV)

public openness, one hears calls for greater caution in talking about our shortcomings and deficiencies. There can be only one answer to this: Communists always need the truth.

At Soviet Communist Party Congress, Feb. 25/
The Christian Science Monitor, 5-5:13.

1

What is at stake today is the ability of the Soviet Union to enter the new millennium in a manner worthy of a great and prosperous power . . . Without the hard work and complete dedication of each and every one, it is not even possible to preserve what has been achieved.

U.S. News & World Report, 3-3:30.

2

Do not believe the mere figments of the imagination about the aggressiveness of the Soviet Union. Never and under no circumstances will our country start war against West Europe if we and our alliance partners are not the object of an assault by NATO. I repeat: Never!

At East German Communist Party Congress,
East Berlin, April 18/The New York Times, 4-19:3.

3

[On the recent nuclear-plant accident at Chernobyl in the U.S.S.R.]: It is impossible to leave without attention and political assessment the way the event at Chernobyl was met by the governments, political figures and the mass media in certain NATO countries, especially the U.S.A. They launched an unrestrained anti-Soviet campaign. It is difficult to imagine what was said and written these days—"thousands of casualties," "mass graves of the dead," "desolate Kiev," that "the entire land of the Ukraine has been poisoned," and so on and so forth. Generally speaking, we faced a veritable mountain of lies—most dishonest and malicious lies. It is unpleasant to recall all this, but it should be done. The international public should know what we had to face. This should be done to find the answer to the question: What, in actual fact, was behind that highly immoral campaign? Its organizers, to be sure, were not interested in ei-

ther true information about the accident or the fate of the people at Chernobyl, in the Ukraine, in Byelorussia, in any other place, in any other country . . . Bluntly speaking, certain Western politicians were after very definite aims—to blast the possibilities for balancing international relations, to sow new seeds of mistrust and suspicion toward the socialist countries.

Broadcast address to the nation, Moscow,
May 14/The New York Times, 5-15:8.

4

The [Soviet] economy is very disordered. We lag in all indices. In 1969 we had a problem in Stavropol—what to do with meat and milk. We were awash in butter. Today there is nothing. The relations between money and goods, income and goods have been lost. We have forgotten how to work. Not only that, we have forgotten how to work in democratic conditions. This is very difficult.

To Soviet writers, June 19/
The New York Times, 12-22:10.

5

[Saying the U.S. has too much influence on Western Europe]: In Greek mythology, there is the legend about the abduction of the goddess Europa. Now, as a geographical concept, Europe remains in place; but the impression is created that the independent policy of some Western European countries has been abducted and taken across the ocean.

At Polish Communist Party Congress,
Warsaw, June 30/The New York Times, 7-1:5.

6

[On the Solidarity independent trade-union movement in Poland]: The Polish crisis was not a protest of workers against socialism, but a show of disagreement with distortions of socialism that pained the working class. It was the adversaries of socialist Poland inside the country and outside who managed to take advantage of this disagreement. We know what is sought by those in the West who hypocritically describe themselves as friends of the Polish people. They are not in the least concerned about the destinies of the Polish nation. Their intention is to dis-

(MIKHAIL S. GORBACHEV)

mantle socialism, to liquidate socialist gains. Really, the worse it is in Poland, the better it is for them.

At Polish Communist Party Congress,
Warsaw, June 30/The New York Times, 7-2:6.

1

[On foreign criticism of human rights in the Soviet Union]: A nation without rights, as attempts are being made to this day to portray the Soviet people, would never have been able to amaze the world by transforming a backward country into a major power that is confidently following the road of progress. [The Soviet Union is prepared for] international cooperation on humanitarian problems, and these are not mere words.

At dinner for visiting French President
Francois Mitterrand, Moscow, July 7/
The New York Times, 7-8:4.

2

Everybody sees that Europeans are tired of nerve-racking confrontation and tension. They need the air of detente. Europe's economic and political potential is large enough for it to speak more definitely and confidently on its own behalf, to press for progress at all the ongoing talks. It is necessary to get rid of the political thinking that views Europe as a "theatre of operations" [for the U.S.]. Europe must set an example of coexistence among sovereign, different but peaceful countries, countries aware of their interdependence and building their relations on trust.

At dinner for visiting French President
Francois Mitterrand, Moscow, July 7/
The New York Times, 7-8:4.

Oleg A. Grinevsky
Soviet Ambassador to
Stockholm Conference on Security
and Confidence-Building Measures
and Disarmament in Europe

3

[On the just-concluded agreement that would allow mutual inspections of military maneuvers

in East and West Europe]: Of course I am satisfied, and I'm sure that everybody who took part in this very difficult negotiation is satisfied professionally, emotionally and as human beings. Of course, I'm sorry we could not manage to do more. But I think that in the present situation, this is the maximum of what was possible . . . I am very proud that my country has been a leader in concessions to common sense and peace.

News conference, Stockholm, Sept. 21/
Los Angeles Times, 9-22:(I)1.

Gary Hart
United States Senator,
D-Colorado

4

At some time in the 21st century, the United States might assume more of the air and sea defenses [of NATO], and Europe more of the burden of land defense . . . Any move to alter NATO doctrine and forces should be evolutionary . . . but we must also make it clear we are not the Romans. We do not intend to stay in Germany for 300 years, or until we are driven out.

At Georgetown School of Foreign Service,
Washington, June 11/
The Washington Post, 6-12:(A)9.

5

[On the Soviet government under its leader, Mikhail Gorbachev]: I sense a very different style of government. I believe this leadership is trying to make reforms and changes, particularly at home . . . It is more open in the sense of a willingness to listen, to debate and not just to lecture.

News conference, Moscow, Dec. 17/
Los Angeles Times, 12-18:(I)9.

Arthur A. Hartman
United States Ambassador
to the Soviet Union

6

[On the Soviet Union]: There is a highly developed, sophisticated part of this economy that can produce guidance systems to introduce weapons of war, but a society that has trouble

WHAT THEY SAID IN 1986

(ARTHUR A. HARTMAN)

keeping my street fixed out front . . . [The Soviet Union] is a lot more Russian than it is Communist. I see in looking around me, in the everyday way that Soviets behave, more of their Russianness, more of their deep formation via history than I really do of the Soviet influence that was imposed on this country since the revolution. Many of the policies pursued in this country are pursued as they would have been pursued in the 19th century, via Czars.

To Western reporters, Moscow, Dec. 19/
The Washington Post, 12-20:(A)15.

Denis Healey
Foreign-policy spokesman,
Labor Party of Britain

1

[On the Labor Party's plans for a non-nuclear British defense policy if they are elected]: The Labor Party believes that its defense policy, particularly if accompanied by similar decisions in other countries, will so strengthen NATO conventional forces in Europe as to rule out military aggression.

News conference, London, Dec. 10/
Los Angeles Times, 12-11:(I)9.

Michael Heseltine
Former Defense Secretary
of the United Kingdom

2

[On his resignation as Defense Secretary, saying Prime Minister Margaret Thatcher is too authoritarian in the decision-making process]: To serve as a member of a Tory Cabinet within the Constitutional understandings and practices of a system under which the Prime Minister is *primus inter pares* [first among equals] is a memory I will always treasure. But if the basis of trust between the Prime Minister and her Defense Secretary no longer exists, there is no place for me with honor in such a Cabinet.

News conference, London, Jan. 9/
The Washington Post, 1-10:(A)1.

3

[Britain's] Tory Party has got to widen its horizons and remember its past. The Tory Party has always believed in the wider national interest, and yet we see today large areas of unemployment, growing deprivation and dereliction in the inner cities and a concentration of financial wealth in the City of London. It adds up to a concern about the balance of policies.

Maclean's, 5-5:27.

Erich Honecker
First Secretary, Communist
Party of East Germany

4

[Praising the Berlin Wall, which his country put up 25 years ago]: Our measures of August 13 [1961] served peace. We can say with full justification that they opened the way from confrontation to detente . . . It was a historic deed that preserved the liberty of our people and laid the foundations for the sustained prosperity of our socialist state.

At ceremony marking 25th year of Berlin Wall,
East Berlin, Aug. 13/Los Angeles Times, 8-14:(I)8;
The New York Times, 8-14:1.

Arnold Horelick
Director, Rand-UCLA Center for the
Study of Soviet International Behavior

5

[On the current radiation accident at the Soviet nuclear power plant at Chernobyl and the Soviet government's refusal to supply adequate information about it to the world]: There will be a lot of people in the Soviet system, below the Politburo level, who will find it hard to understand that their own government found it impossible to share with them information important to their own health and well being . . . Leave aside the question of whether it was a poor design from the start. Here you have a national catastrophe of frightening if not fully known consequences, and for all his talk of new "openness," you have not a peep from [Soviet leader Mikhail] Gorbachev. He's handling it like [his predecessor Leonid] Brezhnev would. Soviet of-

(ARNOLD HORELICK)

ficials in and around the elite will be asking: "Have things really changed?"

Interview, April 30/
Los Angeles Times, 5-1:(I)4.

Geoffrey Howe
Foreign Secretary of
the United Kingdom

1

[Criticizing Soviet non-compliance with the 1975 Helsinki human-rights accords]: We have held meetings about human rights and human contacts which have sadly illuminated a bleak human landscape. Families remain divided. Individuals who do not conform are brought ruthlessly to heel. Religious believers are harassed. Would-be immigrants are denied fundamental rights. We salute those, like [Soviet dissident] Andrei Sakharov, who keep alight the flame of human spirit. And we remember those whose names are not well known but whose lot is one of daily harassment [by the Soviet government], labor camps, exile or prison. While these things are so, it will remain impossible to establish full confidence between our states.

At conference on the Helsinki accords, Vienna,
Nov. 4/Los Angeles Times, 11-5:(I)14.

Wojciech Jaruzelski
Prime Minister of Poland

2

[On the Solidarity independent trade-union movement in Poland]: Millions of people pinned their hope on this movement. [But] it also became a springboard and a plane of activity for the mob of anti-socialist players, leaders and fanatics of counter-revolution and various renegades from socialism, including the miraculously converted. [Today this opposition is] disintegrating and isolated. A great majority of former Solidarity members actively participate in public life.

At Polish Communist Party Congress, Warsaw,
June 29/The New York Times, 6-30:6.

[On Western economic sanctions against his country to protest Poland's human-rights situation]: It is high time that some capitalist states, especially the United States, relinquish various bizarre speculations that are insulting to us and rectify their views on the essence and character of our policy. Poland is not interested in special relations but in normal relations. This normalization lies not only in our interest but equally in the interest of our Western creditors. A withdrawal of restrictions and development of economic relations is, objectively, one of the conditions of repaying the debt.

At Polish Communist Party meeting,
Zielona Gora, Poland, Sept. 16/
The Washington Post, 9-19:(A)18.

Roy Jenkins
British politician; Former Chancellor
of the Exchequer of the United Kingdom

4

. . . on Constitutional and international matters, this country [Britain] got peculiarly stuck in the form of government peculiar to the end of the last century. Our constitutional thinking is very much founded on the view most clearly and most seminally promulgated by [English jurist Albert] Dicey in the '70s and '80s of the last century in which he promulgated and took pride in the absolute sovereignty of Parliament. This belief in the absolute sovereignty of the British Parliament fits extremely uncomfortably with our subscribing to any international human-rights conventions, be it the UN or the Council of Europe expressing itself through the Strasbourg Court.

Interview, London/
The Christian Science Monitor, 12-17:18.

Janos Kadar
First Secretary,
Communist Party of Hungary

5

An indication of [Hungary's] over-all [economic] success is, that since 1960, industrial production has increased more than $3 \frac{1}{2}$ times,

WHAT THEY SAID IN 1986

(JANOS KADAR)

agricultural production has nearly doubled and national income has nearly trebled. That we have held ground, particularly in the past five years, is, I think, of no less significance. In the past few years we have stood the test of unfavorable international economic conditions, halted the process of accumulating debt, preserved the country's solvency, and even slightly improved upon our achievements. It proves that the political and economic foundations of our society are firm. When accounting for these results, I should like to lay particular emphasis on the fact that our people feel this country belongs to them. To sum up, let me say that in the past four decades we have built a new country here along the Danube and Tisza rivers, namely, socialist Hungary, whose people are incomparably better off both materially and culturally than ever before and enjoy more extensive rights and greater freedom and democracy than at any other time during their long history.

Interview, Budapest/Time, 8-11:30.

Tom King
British Secretary of State
for Northern Ireland

1

[On the Protestant-Catholic strife in Northern Ireland]: It's a tough job [being the Secretary of State]. It's a very challenging job . . . Contrary to the television pictures, there are marvelous people here. Unfortunately, on both edges of the political extreme, there are some extremely nasty people as well. And those are the people in any society you have to fight against.

Interview, Belfast/
The Christian Science Monitor, 6-12:8.

Neil Kinnock
Leader, Labor Party of Britain

2

There are millions of reasons for ridding Britain of this Tory government. You see the reasons in the unemployment queues, in the hospital and housing waiting lists . . . amongst the

families in poverty and the pensioners in need . . . in the communities flattened by the closure of industries and isolated by the withdrawal of transport . . . amongst the children and young people hit by education cuts.

At Trades Union Congress, Brighton, England,
Sept. 2/The Washington Post, 9-3:(A)16.

Helmut Kohl
Chancellor of West Germany

3

[Criticizing the Berlin Wall, put up by East Germany 25 years ago]: We demand humanity and peace at the border through the middle of Germany. Walls, barbed wire and orders to shoot to kill [those from the East who try to escape] must all go . . . We must not and will not come to terms with this monument to inhumanity, which tears families apart and prevents human contact . . . [The Berlin Wall is] perhaps the most visible expression of the moral gulf between moral democracy and totalitarian dictatorship.

At ceremony marking 25th year of
Berlin Wall, West Berlin, Aug. 13/
Los Angeles Times, 8-14:(I)8.

4

The [Atlantic] Alliance is as united as it has rarely been before. The most important governments in Europe are in agreement as far as this issue is concerned. Think of what the situation was like at the end of the [U.S. President] Carter Administration and in 1983. The Soviets felt they could storm the country [West Germany]. If you had told the Soviets that we are going to deploy [Euromissiles], that we are going to extend the draft and that we will win the elections, they wouldn't have believed it. Nor would anybody have believed it in the United States. Another element is the development of the Soviet Union. [Soviet leader Mikhail] Gorbachev took on a very difficult legacy: In military terms, they are a world power, but in economic terms they are not. They have to do something about this. Time is working in our favor.

Interview,
Bonn/Newsweek, 10-27:25.

(HELMUT KOHL)

1

[On Soviet leader Mikhail Gorbachev]: He is a modern Communist leader who understands public relations. Goebbels, who was one of those responsible for the crimes of the Hitler era, was an expert in public relations, too.

Interview/Newsweek, 11-17:58.

Hans Mast
Executive vice president,
Credit Suisse (Switzerland)

2

Unemployment in Europe has many demographic, structural and social causes that cannot be redressed simply . . . Ultimately, Europe cannot prosper unless the rest of the world is prospering.

At "Time" magazine's European Board of
Economists meeting, Madrid/Time, 1-27:36.

Francois Mitterrand
President of France

3

[Addressing U.S. President Reagan on France's recent refusal to allow U.S. planes to fly over French territory on their way to attack Libya]: There has been a difficult situation between your country and ours. There has been a divergence, but we have to place that in the context of 200 years of history. We did not set out 200 years ago to agree on everything, but we have succeeded in agreeing on the most important issues . . . Our friendship is our mainstay. We do not wish to settle into a crisis situation with the United States.

Tokyo, May 6/
The Washington Post, 5-7:(A)25.

4

[Soviet leader Mikhail] Gorbachev appears to me a man of his time. He sees things as they are in 1986 . . . I believe that the Soviet Union really feels the need to marshal all its energies in order to master [its] economic crisis.

News conference, Moscow, July 10/
The Christian Science Monitor, 7-11:36.

Yuri Orlov
Exiled Soviet dissident

5

It's very important to note here something that Westerners simply don't understand. Living in the Soviet Union is like living in a large, underground labor camp. You are deformed as a person. This process of deforming a personality begins in kindergarten, and it doesn't end even if a man becomes a scholar and academician. The process continues.

Interview, New York/
U.S. News & World Report, 10-20:23.

Olof Palme
Prime Minister of Sweden

6

Social democracy is the third way, the only viable way. It provides a society with full employment, with general welfare, and with political freedom. In Sweden, it is alive and kicking, and my ambition is to improve it, if anything.

Interview, Stockholm/
The Christian Science Monitor, 2-27:11.

Andreas Papandreou
Prime Minister of Greece

7

It would take two things to repair Greek-Turkish relations. The first is to end Turkey's occupation of 37 per cent of Cyprus, which belongs to neither Turkey nor Greece. We will remove our last soldier when the Turks remove the last of theirs. Second, Turkey must accept the legal status of the Aegean as defined by existing laws and international treaties. But Turkey prefers another approach, which it calls "equity." It wants to split the Aegean down the middle of the continental shelf. The eastern islands of the Aegean—since ancient days, Greek—would become Turkish. How can any Greek enter discussions from which the only possible result is that we give part of our sovereignty to another?

Interview/
U.S. News & World Report, 2-24:45.

8

The deployment of our country's armed forces is aimed at the defense of Greece's territory

(ANDREAS PAPANDREOU)

against the existent and important Turkish threat. It is clearly not aimed at the north [Bulgaria, Yugoslavia and Albania], where our relations are truly excellent and follow a genuine upward course.

Before Greek Socialist Party central committee/
The New York Times, 9-4:8.

Ronald Reagan
President of the United States

1

It is important to begin by distinguishing between the peoples inside the Soviet Union and the government that rules them. Certainly, we have no quarrel with the peoples—far from it. Yet we must remember that the peoples in the Soviet Union have virtually no influence on the government. We must remember that the Soviet government is based upon and drawn from the Soviet Communist Party—an organization that remains formally pledged to subjecting the world to Communist domination. This is not the time to delve deeply into history, but you should know that the emergence of the Soviet Union is in many respects an expression of the terrible enchantment with the power of the state that became so prominent in the first half of our century. In his widely acclaimed book, *Modern Times,* Paul Johnson has argued just this point— that modern ideologies had exalted the state above the individual.

Before graduating class of Glassboro
(N.J.) High School, June 19/
The New York Times, 6-20:6.

2

The Soviet government, despite a few gestures this year, gestures that reflect posturing more than flexibility, continues its systematic violation of human rights. The new Soviet emigration law, for example, purports to ease restrictions. Yet, for far too many, the opposite is true. The restriction of emigration, the suppression of dissent, the lengthy separation of families and spouses, the continued imprisonment of

religious activists in the Ukraine and throughout the Soviet Union are the orders of the day.

Human Rights Day address, Washington,
Dec. 10/Los Angeles Times, 12-11:(I)6.

Donald T. Regan
Chief of Staff to the
President of the United States

3

[Criticizing the Soviet Union for the way it handled news from the recent Chernobyl nuclear plant accident in the U.S.S.R.]: Frankly, the way they've handled it is an outrage . . . We think that, with over a third of the world's population directly affected by this accident, they have a moral obligation to tell the world what's going on; and to try to stonewall it, to keep the information [to] themselves and let the rest of the world try to figure out whether they're in danger or not, is beyond what civilized nations should do.

Broadcast interview/
"Meet the Press," NBC-TV, 5-4.

Bernard W. Rogers
General, United States Army;
Supreme Allied Commander/Europe

4

The great irony is that, if . . . the nuclear threat [in Europe] were completely neutralized, we would be right back with the very problem that the Supreme Headquarters Allied Powers-Europe has been wrestling with for years. That problem was and is Soviet-Warsaw Pact conventional non-nuclear military superiority. The key issue facing NATO is to improve its conventional forces. . . . it's always the conventional that has holes. What we're working on is *not* the closing of the gap between NATO's capabilities and those of the Warsaw Pact. We're trying to keep that gap from getting too big—and that task is not yet beyond NATO's means. But down the road, if the trends continue and that gap gets wider, Western Europe will end up dancing to the tune of the Soviet piper.

Interview/
U.S. News & World Report, 1-20:29.

(BERNARD W. ROGERS)

1

[Saying the Soviet Union has large stockpiles of conventional war materiel for offensive operations against Western Europe and are much better equipped to fight conventionally than the NATO nations]: I don't think the Soviets want a war and intend to attack. They'll try to achieve their objective without firing a shot, through intimidation and coercion. But if they were to attack conventionally today, I have no option under my guidance from political authorities but to request the release of nuclear weapons . . . If there is a major confrontation between superpowers in Western Europe, it would go global, and we would face two options fairly quickly in NATO: One would be to suffer defeat and the other would be to escalate to nuclear weapons.

Interview, Los Angeles, March 13/
Los Angeles Times, 3-14:(I)31.

2

[Criticizing the British Labor Party's stated policy of removing all nuclear weapons from Britain if it wins the next election]: Should plans such as those in the Labor Party ever be realized, America would decide: Good, that does it, we will no longer expose our soldiers to the risk of the kind of thinking which shifts responsibility for defense onto others . . . How should we ever be able to drive the attacker from our soil without so-called offensive weapons? The effectiveness of a defense depends mainly on the counter-attack.

Interview/Los Angeles Times, 12-5:(I)6.

Andrei D. Sakharov
Soviet dissident

3

[Saying there is greater public candor in Soviet life now than before Soviet leader Mikhail Gorbachev took office]: The sort of articles that are now appearing [in the newspapers] read like some of the declarations from dissidents that were issued in the 1970s and for which many of my friends were jailed. There was practically no *glasnost* [openness] before, and this change is a very important move forward which promises a great deal. It is necessary for any healthy society. And it is an essential condition for other changes. I welcome it with all my heart. It is to the great personal credit of [Gorbachev] that we have it now, even though it was in fact an historic necessity for our country . . . I know that some [dissidents] have been released, others have won conditional release, and still others have been allowed to go abroad. That is all very good. But many people remain in terrible, inhuman conditions in camps and prisons.

Interview after being released from internal exile,
Moscow, Dec. 24/Los Angeles Times, 12-25:(I)1;
The New York Times, 12-25:1.

Anatoly Shcharansky
Exiled Soviet dissident

4

[On whether his recent release from prison camp by the Soviet government may signal a change in Soviet policy toward Jewish emigration]: Well, I think that [Soviet leader Mikhail] Gorbachev does try to demonstrate to the Western world that he is ready to make some changes in his policy and wants to encourage the West to meet his aims in other branches—economic, military and political. But, unfortunately, there is a set tradition that almost always, when the Soviet Union makes such signs, it immediately takes some steps in its inner policy in order to discourage those who could be encouraged by those gains.

Broadcast interview, Tel Aviv, Israel/
"Meet the Press," NBC-TV, 2-16.

5

No public relations, no cosmetic changes can hide the face of tyranny [in the Soviet Union], that tries to deprive a nation of its freedom. The call of solidarity breaks all the fences which Soviet leadership tries to build. The word solidarity is heard in the cities and the camps of the Soviet Union. It echoes in the dark corridors. The Soviet leaders today are trying to separate, to remove Jews from the bonds of their nation. Four hundred thousand Soviet Jews are kept as prisoners in the Soviet Union. New attacks are made against our Hebrew culture and lan-

WHAT THEY SAID IN 1986

guage . . . The Soviet leaders must be brought to understand they will never be able to destroy our solidarity.

At rally, New York, May 11/
Los Angeles Times, 5-12:(I)1.

1

[On his recent release from a Soviet prison]: They let me go not because they became more human, but because they understood that without solving this problem there will be no progress in the direction they're interested in. At the same time, it was like an attempt to make some cosmetic improvement without solving the problem as a whole—the problem of emigration . . . Of course, a lot of people would leave [the country if they could] . . . But there are many people who would never like to leave. Nevertheless, the very fact that there would be free choice for every citizen, whether to leave or not, makes such a big influence on the minds of the people and undermines . . . the foundation of the system that it's a real danger [to the Soviet system].

Interview, Washington, May 16/
The Washington Post, 5-17:(C)4.

George P. Shultz
Secretary of State of the United States

2

Nowhere does the problem of distrust and division between East and West have greater meaning than in the context of Europe. Since 1945, an artificial barrier has divided the Continent and its peoples. This barrier is not of Western construction. The members of the Atlantic Alliance and the various neutral and non-aligned nations of Europe have not forced the division of families nor denied our citizens the right of free movement. We have not sought to cut our societies off from competing ideas through press censorship, radio jamming or other means. We have not used threats or armed intervention to enforce bloc discipline upon individual countries.

At Conference on Security and Cooperation
in Europe, Vienna, Nov. 5/
The New York Times, 11-6:8.

Henry Siegman
Executive director,
American Jewish Congress

3

[On the recent election of Kurt Waldheim as President of Austria, following disclosures about his alleged involvement in Nazi war crimes]: Given his diplomatic immunity, Waldheim can probably not be barred from this country [the U.S.]. But we and the other democracies can make it clear to him and his countrymen who elected him that he is unwelcome. Should he venture outside the borders of Austria, he should expect the kind of reception reserved for countries that elect former Nazis as their President.

June 8/The New York Times, 6-9:6.

Dmitri Simes
Senior associate,
Carnegie Endowment for
International Peace

4

[On the current radiation accident at the Soviet nuclear power plant at Chernobyl and the Soviet government's refusal to supply adequate information about it to the world]: The whole thing reminds us that the Soviet Union is really a Third World nation when it comes to the safety of their people and security. They still see no need to share information unless forced to, despite all of the talk that [Soviet leader Mikhail] Gorbachev has brought a new "openness" to the Kremlin. They just don't know how to release unpleasant news intelligently. It is just like the [1983 Korean Air Lines] incident. [The Soviets] shot down the plane, and then tried to cover it up, then gave inconsistent explanations.

Interview, April 30/
Los Angeles Times, 5-1:(I)4.

Bruce Smart
Under Secretary for International Trade,
Department of Commerce
of the United States

5

Europe is still a large number of states, with language barriers, ancient hostilities, no com-

(BRUCE SMART)

mon government or currencies. They have a stagnant population, stagnant employment and a built-in rigidity against change. While they are very close to us culturally, militarily and many other ways, it is not as dynamic a segment as the Pacific Rim. Or as the United States.

Interview/USA Today, 1-30:(B)9.

Stephen J. Solarz
United States Representative, D-New York

1

[Saying that, with the Polish government's recent release of political prisoners, the U.S. should now cancel its economic sanctions against that country]: Let us move quickly to lift the last remaining sanctions—the denial of most-favored-nation status and the prohibition of government-guaranteed credits—that were imposed upon Poland. A failure to respond positively to Warsaw's initiative would forfeit our best chance of exerting influence on the course of events in Poland. It would push Poland into a still greater dependence on the Soviet bloc. It would enable the [Polish] regime to shift the blame for Poland's dreary economic situation from the government's own ideology and incompetence—where it rightly belongs—to American sanctions.

News conference, Washington, Sept. 26/
The New York Times, 9-27:6.

Helmut Sonnenfeldt
Former Member, National Security
Council of the United States

2

[On the Soviet Union's current "peace offensive"]: Whether you call it a "peace offensive" or something else, this Kremlin is interested in a period of relative calm to tackle its massive and pervasive problems. You just have to watch [Soviet leader Mikhail] Gorbachev on Soviet television trying to exhort people to work harder, stop lining up for vodka, produce better goods, to appreciate the enormous inertia of the people there and the size of the mobilizing effort he's taken on himself.

Los Angeles Times, 9-24:(I)11.

Romuald Spasowski
Former Polish Ambassador
to the United States

3

[On his 1981 defection to the U.S.]: I will be always stateless. I can never be a citizen of another country. Yet my Poland does not exist any more. . . . their Warsaw is not my Warsaw. All Poland is now a political prison and the people are the prisoners.

At book party for his autobiography, Washington,
April 2/ The Washington Post, 4-3:(B)6.

Elan Steinberg
Executive director,
World Jewish Congress

4

[Criticizing the possibility that Kurt Waldheim, accused of pro-Nazi ties during World War II, will be elected President of Austria]: In a perfect world, he would stand trial. In an imperfect world, he would go away. In this *most* imperfect world, he may become President of Austria.

Newsweek, 6-9:30.

Margaret Thatcher
Prime Minister of the United Kingdom

5

I have always regarded part of my job as—and please do not think of it in an arrogant way—killing socialism in Britain.

Maclean's, 5-5:28.

6

[Criticizing the U.S. Senate for not yet approving a treaty which would permit the extradition from the U.S. to Britain of suspected Northern Irish terrorists]: What is the point of the United States taking a foremost part against terrorism [in the world] and then not being as strict as they can against Irish terrorism, which afflicts one of their allies?

USA Today, 5-21:(A)9.

7

Everyone went to America, not for a subsidy—there were not any—but to be free to pioneer,

309

(MARGARET THATCHER)

free to be self-reliant, free to make and create their own future. I envy tremendously when I hear [U.S.] President Reagan say: "Do you know these enterprising people created 9 million jobs in the last 3 $1/2$ years!" Do you know what mine say? "This unemployment. What is the government going to do about it?" What do I say? We can only create the conditions. Do not expect me to ask bureaucrats to turn out from Whitehall, bowlers and brollies in hand, to go set up a dozen small businesses in every hamlet in the country. They would not know how to do it. It is not their job. Ours is to get the conditions right. There is no way we shall get prosperity unless the people respond.

Interview/Forbes, 7-28:93.

1

[Criticizing the Labor Party's stance against nuclear weapons in Britain]: Labor would remove Britain altogether from the protection of America's nuclear umbrella, leaving us totally unable to deter a nuclear attack. [Britain would be] exposed to the threat of nuclear blackmail [from the Soviet Union]. There would be no option but surrender.

At Conservative Party conference,
Bournemouth, England, Oct. 10/
The Washington Post, 10-11:(A)23.

Philip Tirard
Cultural editor, "Le Vif"
newsmagazine (Belgium)

2

[On the dichotomy in Belgium between the French- and Dutch-speaking populations]: People like [the late Nobel Prize-winning Belgian poet and playwright] Maurice Maeterlinck wrote in French. But they wrote with a special baroque, coarse, down-to-earth spirit that was Flemish [Belgian-Dutch]. They were not French writers full of airy ideas and reason. I think that is the essence of Belgian culture—expressing a Flemish spirit in the French language. But that is not a very popular idea these days. If I were to state this idea on television, a moderator would

say, "Thank you very much," and quickly pass on to something else.

Los Angeles Times, 12-29:(I)10.

Richard von Weizsacker
President of West Germany

3

In the long run, it is not a question of the reunification of Germany. It is a question of overcoming the division of Europe. That is, our task is not to change the borders but to minimize the dividing character of those borders. To that end, I prefer taking small concrete steps rather than insisting on grand principles . . . On the one hand, we have the strong will to belong to the West, to be a member of the Western Alliance. But at the same time, we want to search for agreement with the East. This is an uncomfortable situation for many Germans, and also for our allies.

Interview/Los Angeles Times, 8-19:(I)13.

Franz Vranitzky
Chancellor of Austria

4

Socialist parties in Europe are becoming more pragmatic than dogmatic. This means seeking a more pragmatic approach to the welfare state, and making it more efficient. In Austria, the shelter that the state has given to almost everyone—employee as well as entrepreneur—has led to a situation in which a lot of people think not what they can do to solve a problem but what the state can do. This is particularly true in international competition. This needs to change. Once people have sniffed the fresh air of self-initiative, it will change.

Interview, Vienna/
The Washington Post, 9-2:(A)12.

Kurt Waldheim
Candidate for the
Presidency of Austria

5

[On calls for his dropping out of the race for the Presidency because of his alleged involve-

(KURT WALDHEIM)

ment in Nazi war atrocities]: I see no reason why I should follow the suggestion of my political opponents, who are of course not happy that I have a good chance to win. If I had the slightest feeling that I had done anything wrong, I would certainly do it [drop out of the race]—but I haven't. What I am accused of are lies.

Interview, Vienna, April 16/
The New York Times, 4-17:4.

Kurt Waldheim
President-elect of Austria

1

[On criticism of his alleged Nazi activities in World War II]: The fact that the accusations brought against me during the last weeks have been taken up by so many media can probably be explained only by the immense suffering that National Socialism [Nazism] brought to the world and, in particular, to our Jewish compatriots. Even today, more than 40 years later, we stand deeply shaken before the horror of this period and its inhumanity . . . I will fight anti-Semitism wherever it appears, not for opportunistic reasons but as my own inner convictions. I shall make particular efforts to open up the dialogue, especially with our Jewish citizens, and shall make every attempt to counteract all forms of religious, racial and ethnic discrimination.

News conference, Vienna, June 11/
The New York Times, 6-12:3;
Los Angeles Times, 6-12:(I)7.

Lech Walesa
Former chairman, now-banned Solidarity
(independent Polish trade union);
Winner, 1983 Nobel Peace Prize

2

[On the Polish government's announcement that it will release all political prisoners]: Obvi-

ously, I received the news about the release of prisoners with great pleasure. The last six years of our national history have proved in a convincing way that there is a need for deep changes if we are to find a solution to our problems. All Poles want to have a chance to work for their country, while at the same time hold their own views. In other words, only the road of social pluralism can lead to a situation in which prisons will not be refilled very soon again with political prisoners.

Gdansk, Poland, Sept. 11/
The New York Times, 9-12:16.

Des Wilson
President, Liberal Party of Britain;
Chairman, Campaign for
Freedom of Information

3

When it comes to the real information people need for democracy to really operate as it should, the situation [in Britain] is appalling and getting steadily worse. For instance, very little background information on government decision-making is available [to the public].

The Christian Science Monitor, 12-17:18.

Vidoje Zarkovic
First Secretary, Communist
Party of Yugoslavia

4

We are face to face with stagnation in development, with weakening unity in the Yugoslav community and in the League of Communists of Yugoslavia, with greater distortions and departures from proclaimed aims and with violations of some of the social norms and values which we asserted in the revolution.

At Yugoslav Communist Party Congress,
Belgrade, June 25/
The New York Times, 6-26:6.

The Middle East

Abdel Halim Abu Ghazala
Minister of Defense of Egypt

1

There is no way to predict the course of the Iran-Iraq war. Most of the fixed elements of the old formula become variables. The old variables become more variable. The risk the war will broaden to threaten nearby states is growing. The old hopes of peace and cease-fire are diminishing. The possibilities of escalation are greater. We have to prepare ourselves for "the worst case" outcome of the new phase of this war. The prospects in the long term are simply a human tragedy. There will be the memories of blood, suffering and more hatred. There will be a severe impact on the policies of the region, the trade, the oil production, a new arms race. All your Western policies and Western interests, and ours, will be living in a threatening environment.

Interview,
Cairo, Dec. 25*/
The New York Times, 12-27:3.

Jack Anderson
American journalist

2

[On Libyan leader Muammar el-Qaddafi, who is accused by many of being involved in international terrorism]: He certainly talks rationally. [But] he's a hard man to understand. His face is sort of divided against itself. The top half of his face is dominated by this fierce, blazing Bedouin scowl, but the bottom half of his face is rather gentle and disarming. And the words that come out are soft-spoken. You don't realize until you've written them down how harsh they really are. He spent a lot of time asking me about the CIA and worrying audibly about the Egyptians on his border. I had an impression that he is haunted by the same fears that he seeks to generate.

Interview/
USA Today, 1-8:(A)9.

Yasir Arafat
Chairman, Palestine
Liberation Organization

3

We believe the [U.S.] Reagan Administration is not willing to achieve peace [between the Arabs and Israel]. The Israeli Cabinet in this shape hasn't the ability to accept any kind of peace. They are only maneuvering. We are still waiting for the American approval of self-determination for 5 million Palestinians. The latest American proposals continue to exclude that. I don't know why. We are insisting not to be red Indians. We are human beings.

Interview/
Newsweek, 2-10:56.

Qadi Abdul Karim Arashi
Vice President of North Yemen

4

[Addressing U.S. Vice President George Bush]: We implore you to put an end to the Israeli violations of human rights, the rights of the Palestinian people who are being subjected to mass annihilation inside occupied [lands] and outside. We are looking forward to the role that the United States can play in support of the right of self-determination for the Palestinian people so that they may have their own independent state . . . under the leadership of the Palestine Liberation Organization, which is the only legal representative of the Palestinian people.

At dinner for Bush, Sanaa, North Yemen/
The Washington Post, 4-11:(A)21.

Abdulkarim Musavi Ardabili
Supreme Justice of Iran

5

[Saying the recently revealed U.S.-Iran arms deals were a victory for Iran]: The Islamic Republic [of Iran] must be proud of this victory, because the pride in victory does not only involve the military. Sometimes political victory is

(ABDULKARIM MUSAVI ARDABILI)

a hundred times more valuable than military victories.

Sermon, Teheran University, Nov. 21/
The Washington Post, 11-22:(A)18.

Hafez al-Assad
President of Syria

1

Syria has no connection with terror. We challenge [Western] intelligence services to prove that Syria was behind a single terrorist operation anywhere. No terrorist acts are carried out from Syria, by Syrians or others. We do advocate struggle against Israel, by all means, to expel the Israelis from our occupied land. But our struggle is here, on Arab land, not in Europe or the United States.

Interview, Damascus/Time, 10-20:56.

2

To make the American taxpayer know who the aggressor is [in the Arab-Israeli conflict], it is enough to publish maps of Palestine in 1940, 1948, 1956, 1967 and now, to see how Israel expanded. He will conclude that the Arabs, not Israel, need weapons and money to defend themselves.

Interview, Damascus/Time, 10-20:57.

Haider abu Bakr Attas
Acting Head of State
of South Yemen

3

We welcome good relations with all countries that respect our national sovereignty and don't interfere in our internal affairs. However, the United States does not respect our national sovereignty, interferes in our domestic affairs and stands against the interests of the Arab nations and our central just cause, the Palestinian issue.

Interview, Aden, South Yemen, Jan. 31/
Los Angeles Times, 2-1:(I)4.

Tariq Aziz
Foreign Minister of Iraq

4

[On his country's war with Iran]: Since the very beginning of this conflict, Iraq has expressed its readiness to settle the dispute by peaceful means according to the rules of international law and on the basis of respect for the sovereignty of each people. The Iranian regime has rejected all this, and insisted on continuing the war while declaring its intention to overthrow the government of Iraq.

At United Nations,
New York, Sept. 25/
The New York Times, 9-26:4.

Raymond Baker
Middle East specialist,
Williams College

5

[On the current military confrontation between the U.S. and Libya in the Gulf of Sidra]: On narrow legal grounds [the issue of international waters], America is fully within its rights. But what seems just shockingly absent is a sense of the political repercussions. This is an area of the world where we [the U.S.] have substantial stakes we can't protect by military means. To narrow concerns to a legal issue which we try to defend militarily is a dangerous illusion when, in fact, we're jeopardizing our larger political interests.

The Christian Science Monitor, 3-26:32.

George W. Ball
Former Under Secretary of State
of the United States

6

We [the U.S.] are subject to . . . attacks by the extremist Arabs because we've taken a totally one-sided role in the Mideast. We've shown absolutely no sympathy for the plight of the Palestinians, who have enormous frustrations. U.S. Mideast policy is largely made in Jerusalem [Israel], and the net result is to escalate violence and bring discredit to our role.

Interview/
U.S. News & World Report, 1-20:79.

313

WHAT THEY SAID IN 1986

Abolhassan Bani-Sadr
Exiled former President of Iran

1

[On reports of a U.S. arms deal with Iran in return for Iran's help in freeing U.S. hostages currently held by Arab terrorists]: [Ronald] Reagan is now President of the United States in part because of the [U.S. hostages held by Iran in 1979]. [Iranian leader the Ayatollah] Khomeini is a fanatic, and Reagan is also a fanatic. Reagan is a fanatic in politics, and Khomeini is a fanatic in religion. The hostages encouraged the two in their fanaticism. Perhaps Mr. Reagan does not like the hostage crisis, but he profits from it. Perhaps he does not like to furnish arms to the [Iranian] regime, but he has done so.

Interview, Versailles, France/
USA Today, 11-12:(A)9.

William S. Broomfield
United States Representative,
R-Michigan

2

[On the current scandal involving secret U.S. negotiations and arms deals with Iran, the release of Arab-held U.S. hostages and the diversion of funds to Nicaraguan contra rebels]: The Iran initiative apparently began with a good idea; namely, that the U.S. should make an effort to try to improve relations with some moderate elements in Iran. I think that was a worthy objective, which we could have supported. But some of the means used in the efforts to achieve that objective, such as arms transfer, were extremely ill-advised and mistaken. I remain gravely concerned that officials were—who thought that they saw a promise of quick success—endangered long-term objectives of U.S. foreign policy. I think the greatest disappointment with this whole matter stems from the transfer to the Nicaraguan resistance of funds generated by arms sales to Iran in a [manner] the Committee has yet to ascertain.

At House Foreign Affairs Committee hearing,
Washington, Dec. 8/
The New York Times, 12-9:6.

George Bush
Vice President of the United States

3

[Saying Libyan leader Muammar Qaddafi supported the recent terrorist attacks at Rome and Athens airports]: We know that he's a liar when he says he had nothing to do with the slaughter. We know that Qaddafi has the blood of an 11-year-old girl on his hands, a pretty little American girl with a bright future who died in her father's arms in Rome, riddled by bullets that Qaddafi bought and paid for.

Before New York Conservative Party,
Jan. 23/Los Angeles Times, 1-24:(I)1.

4

[On the current scandal involving secret U.S.-Iran arms deals and the subsequent release of Arab-held U.S. hostages]: What we in this Administration have tried to do is reach out to moderate elements in Iran. Now, the dilemma we're in is that in the hearts of the American people is a hatred and a detestation of everything that [Iranian spiritual leader] Ayatollah [Ruhollah] Khomeini stands for. I feel that way myself. So in making any contact with Iran, there has been—and perhaps for a long time to come will be—a risk that the American people wouldn't understand. You have to know [U.S. President Reagan] to know how strongly he feels about the release of hostages. The problem on all this, of course, is the perception that arms were traded for hostages. The President is absolutely, totally convinced in his mind that that isn't what happened. I know him; I know what his feeling is on this. I have heard what he said, and I accept it.

Interview, Maine, Nov. 28/
The Washington Post, 12-2:(A)10.

5

[On the scandal involving U.S. arms deals with Iran and the subsequent release of Arab-held U.S. hostages]: We may not like the current Iranian regime, and I've said we don't. But it would be irresponsible to ignore its geopolitical and strategic importance. [Iran's leader, Ayatollah Ruhollah] Khomeini, will pass from the scene. A successor regime will take power. And we must be positioned to serve America's inter-

(GEORGE BUSH)

ests, and indeed, the interests of the entire free world. Apart from the strategic reasons, humanitarian concern about American hostages in Lebanon provided another reason to open a channel to Iran The Iranians themselves are not holding our hostages. But we believe that they have influence over those who do hold some of our hostages . . . I can tell you that the President [Reagan] is absolutely convinced that he did not swap arms for hostages. And still the question remains of how the Administration could violate its own policy of not selling arms to Iran. Simple human hope explains it perhaps better than anything else. The President hoped that we could open a channel that would serve the interests of the United States and of our allies in a variety of ways.

Before American Enterprise Institute,
Washington, Dec. 3/
The Washington Post, 12-4:(A)50.

Jimmy Carter
Former President of
the United States

1

[Criticizing the recent U.S. air attack on Libya in retaliation for that country's involvement in international terrorism]: It's fairly obvious that terrorist leaders like [Libya's Muammar] Qaddafi want publicity. They want stature. They want to be placed on an equal basis with the leaders of major nations. They want to be famous. And they want to intimidate their enemies by making it uncomfortable or impossible for American tourists to travel and difficult for U.S. business to compete abroad. And I think that mounting a bombing attack [on Libya] in response to terrorist acts gives the terrorist leaders most of those goals: fame, publicity, stature, importance, popularity. And it has intimidated American citizens.

Interview/USA Today, 5-12:(A)11.

2

[Criticizing the U.S. Reagan Administration for not taking a more active role in the Middle

East peace process]: I think my approach was proper. Every leader in the region knew that they would get a fair hearing from me and from the Secretary of State in the peace process if they came to us. And every leader also knew, if they had an initiative to put forward, they would have an eager ally in the White House and the State Department. And that's what's been missing for the last 5 ½ years—a constant American presence that we will be your partner on a confidential basis, or otherwise, if you want to take a step toward peace. . . . our commitment to Israel is deep and binding and the Soviets have a similar commitment—not as deep—to Syria and some of the others. And both Syria and Israel, we know from experience, are practically uncontrollable. And although we are obligated to Israel, we don't have control over what they do.

Interview, Atlanta, Sept. 9/
Los Angeles Times, 9-11:(I)5.

3

[Criticizing U.S. dealings with Iran, which involved arms deals and the release of U.S. hostages held by Arab terrorists]: We've paid ransom in effect to the kidnappers of our hostages, and whether we did it indirectly through Israel or indirectly through Danish ships is insignificant. The fact is that every terrorist in the world who reads a newspaper or listens to the radio knows that [when] they've taken American hostages, we've paid them to get the hostages back. This is a very serious mistake in how to handle a kidnapping or hostage-taking.

Broadcast interview/
"Today" show, NBC-TV, 11-18.

William J. Casey
Director of Central Intelligence
of the United States

4

[In South Yemen early this year, the government] had begun to open up to the West. [But] hard-line pro-Soviet exiles returned from Moscow and initiated a coup against the South Yemen President [Ali Nasser Hasani]. This coup soon escalated into a bloody civil war between military and tribal elements loyal to the Presi-

(WILLIAM J. CASEY)

dent and those of the hard-line Soviet camp there. After the Soviets watched the blood flow for a few days, planes flown by Soviet pilots began pounding pro-government forces, and Soviet weapons began to be flown into the country to rebel forces.

Before American Israel Public
Affairs Committee, Washington, April 6/
Los Angeles Times, 4-7:(I)10.

1

Libya, Syria and Iran use terrorism as an instrument of foreign policy. They hire and support established terrorist organizations . . . These countries make their officials, their embassies, their diplomatic pouches, their communications channels and their territory as safe havens for these criminals to plan, direct and execute bombings, assassinations, kidnappings and other terrorist operations.

Before American Jewish Committee, May/
The Washington Post, 5-22:(A)22.

Farouk Charaa
Foreign Minister of Syria

2

The Israelis are trying to run away from their guilt over driving out the Arabs and Palestinians from their land, so they have been very keen on giving a nasty image to Arabs about terrorism. Who is a terrorist and who is not? The world has seen Israeli tanks destroy towns and villages in Lebanon and terrorized Arabs off land their families owned for generations. But to change this image, the Israelis put out the view that only Arabs are terrorists and they are men of peace.

Interview, United Nations, New York,
Sept. 29/The Washington Post, 9-30:(A)18.

Jacques Chirac
Premier of France

3

[Criticizing the recent U.S. attack on Libya in retaliation for that country's involvement in international terrorism]: The intolerable and inad-

missible escalation of terrorism has led to an action of reprisals that itself revives the chain of violence.

U.S. News & World Report, 4-28:25.

4

[Defending France's continued good relations with Syria—despite reports of that country's involvement in international terrorism—saying Syria is an opponent of anti-Western Islamic fundamentalism]: The biggest fish of all is to prevent this religious, anti-Western fanaticism from engulfing the entire region. And that, let me reiterate, is far more important than severing relations with Syria over some incident in London or some bomb that goes off down the street.

Interview/
The Christian Science Monitor, 11-12:14.

Clark M. Clifford
Former Secretary of Defense
of the United States

5

[Criticizing the U.S. for its recent military confrontation with Libya in the Gulf of Sidra]: It is unwise, dangerous and irresponsible to go test that boundary [the extent of Libya's claim to more than the 12-mile limit for territorial waters] when it does not mean anything, practically, to us. You don't ordinarily choose to provoke disputes about boundary lines that are in dispute . . . It is the wrong policy to go about engaging in provocative acts—whether mining Nicaraguan waters, sailing into Soviet waters, or steaming into Sidra.

The Christian Science Monitor, 4-4:17.

Ray S. Cline
Former Deputy Director,
Central Intelligence Agency
of the United States

6

[On the recent U.S. attack on Libya in retaliation for that country's involvement in international terrorism]: [U.S. President Reagan has] finally done what he's been getting ready to do for months and months: strike at the infrastruc-

(RAY S. CLINE)

ture of terrorist activities. I think the Administration has been building up to this . . . It was mostly a question of when the right case would come along. We don't know how [Libyan leader Muammar] Qaddafi will react. But it was perhaps more a symbolic action than a specifically successful tactic. If the Administration didn't act, they would lose their credibility and terrorists would feel they had a free ticket.

April 14/Los Angeles Times, 4-15:(I)4.

Bettino Craxi
Prime Minister of Italy

1

[Criticizing the U.S. role in the current military confrontation between the U.S. and Libya in Gulf of Sidra]: The repeated military exercises by the government of the United States in the Gulf of Sidra, in an area already shaken by serious tension, did not seem appropriate to the goal of re-establishing respect for the principle of international law [in international waters]. We consider it inadmissable that a controversy of this nature, concerning the international or internal character of the waters of the Gulf of Sidra, should be dealt with by military means.

Before Italian Parliament, Rome,
March 25/The New York Times, 3-26:5.

2

Libya is not a military power. The Libyans have many arms, but they do not know how to use them. Libya cannot threaten anyone.

Broadcast interview, Rome, March 26/
The New York Times, 3-27:8.

George Crist
General, United States Marine Corps;
Commander-in-Chief,
U.S. Central Command

3

We have two overriding interests in the [Persian] Gulf. One is keeping the Soviets out, off the backs of the small countries there. The other is guaranteeing access to the oil resources of the region. The Gulf's importance is obscured by the

present petroleum glut, but all the experts predict that, by the mid-1990s, we will again be very dependent on that region for oil—as our allies in Japan and Korea are now. What concerns me is that we may be lulled into a false sense of security and ignore the dangers that are developing.

Interview/U.S. News & World Report, 4-21:34.

Alexandre de Marenches
Former Chief of French Intelligence

4

[On dealing with international terrorism sponsored by Syria and Libya]: Syria is not a very strong country. The whole setup is run by a small band of Alawites who are a small percentage of the population. They get arms from the Soviets, sweet talk from the West and money from conservative Arab states. We should cut terrorists' finances before we cut their heads. What should we have done with Libya? All you have to do is destroy Libya's oil wells or pipelines and, within a few months, [Libyan leader] Colonel Qaddafi is broke and finished.

Interview/
U.S. News & World Report, 12-1:32.

Lawrence S. Eagleburger
Former Under Secretary of State
of the United States

5

[On reports that the U.S. Reagan Administration made a deal with Iran to supply arms materiel in return for help in freeing American hostages held by Arab groups]: An Administration which says, "We will not negotiate with terrorists," if it is, in fact, negotiating . . . is contradicting everything they said. I also happen to think it is very bad policy.

Los Angeles Times, 11-7:(I)28.

Abba Eban
Member of Israeli Knesset (Parliament);
Former Foreign Minister of Israel

6

[On criticism of Israel's recent forcing down of a Libyan airliner suspected of carrying a Palestin-

WHAT THEY SAID IN 1986

(ABBA EBAN)

ian terrorist, and then later letting the plane go when the terrorist wasn't found]: There is nothing that stands in more contradiction to the law than terrorism. But terrorism hides behind the wings of the law. What determines the international reaction is the success or lack of success. If that person were on the plane, the free world would hail our action. Since the effort failed, I assume there will be criticism on the grounds of the need to respect the law. It is easier for me to describe that paradox than to solve it.

Feb. 4/The New York Times, 2-5:7.

1

[On the drop in oil prices and its effect on Arab oil countries]: We [Israel] have probably benefited more than any other country by what has happened to OPEC . . . A decade ago, countries were taking their political stands almost entirely on the basis of oil. There was a kind of swagger to the Arab gait as they went about the world. It was in this atmosphere that in 1975 the United Nations passed the resolution equating Zionism with racism. It was in this atmosphere that the Palestine Liberation Organization really legitimized itself, and that [PLO leader] Yasir Arafat was invited to the United Nations.

The New York Times, 3-24:1,7.

2

There may be a real dichotomy between American rhetoric and interests. But the fact is that in each of the contractual agreements between ourselves and the Arabs since 1973, the United States has involved itself at very high levels of responsibility. Without that active involvement, any real progress is very unlikely.

Interview/The Washington Post, 8-23:(A)17.

3

[On Israeli arms dealing with Iran]: If an Iranian regime is friendly, we let them have arms to celebrate the friendship. But if it is hostile, we let them have arms to mitigate the hostility. We end up in a situation where the selling of arms is the only constant.

The Washington Post, 12-12:(A)14.

Elias Freij
Mayor of Bethlehem,
Israeli-occupied West Bank

4

I fear that the whole world, including the Arabs, are getting fed up with the Palestine issue. It is 40 years now, and there is nothing new in it. We just keep repeating the same old slogans. Nobody is thinking about the future. And since the *Achille Lauro* [terrorist incident], a new chapter has been opened. The world's biggest superpower, the United States, has cursed us with the stamp of "terrorists." So now they are not just bored with us, they are openly hostile.

The New York Times, 7-9:5.

Amin Gemayel
President of Lebanon

5

I am not the problem [in Lebanon]. I am trying to solve the problem. It was here before I took office . . . It is not a piece of cake, the Presidency at this stage. I am convinced that my presence here is a duty and necessary for the sake and future of the nation. For that I am still here, and I will remain in office.

To journalists, Beirut, Feb. 5/
The Washington Post, 2-7:(A)39.

Gennadi Gerasimov
Chief spokesman for the Foreign
Ministry of the Soviet Union

6

[Criticizing the recent U.S. attack on Libya in retaliation for that country's involvement in international terrorism]: The Soviet Union has always stood and stands now against international terrorism. [But] we are against the method of hiding behind the words of international terrorism and attempts to subjugate an independent country [Libya]. We consider that the policy of the United States cannot be justified by anything. The American government has turned the Libyan government into a scapegoat. They are trying to represent it as a terrorist state. Libya is a victim of aggression on the part of the U.S.

Press briefing, Moscow, Aug. 28/
The Washington Post, 8-29:(A)18.

Ehud Gol
Deputy Spokesman, Foreign
Ministry of Israel

1

[On his watching weekly American football games being broadcast by a TV station in Lebanon]: A few weeks ago I was waiting for the game to start and there was no picture. Finally, I checked with their office in Jerusalem, and they told me that some Shiites had bombed their station in South Lebanon. Imagine, trying to watch a football game and having the Shiites bomb your station! That's the Middle East.

Jerusalem/The New York Times, 1-11:6.

Barry M. Goldwater
United States Senator, R-Arizona

2

[Criticizing the recently revealed secret U.S. negotiations with Iran, which involved arms sales to Iran and the release of American hostages held by Arab terrorists]: [Sending arms to Iran is] one of the major mistakes the United States has ever made in foreign policy. [It may have been legal,] but it's not moral . . . to give anything to get a hostage. [President] Reagan has gotten his butt in a crack.

Time, 11-24:20.

Mikhail S. Gorbachev
General Secretary, Communist
Party of the Soviet Union

3

[Criticizing the U.S. for the recent U.S.-Libyan military confrontation in the Gulf of Sidra]: This policy is provoking regional conflicts and jeopardizing international peace and security. It is directed against all independent peoples and contravenes the interests of the American people as well. We resolutely denounce the aggressive anti-Libyan actions of the U.S.A. The Soviet Union is in solidarity with the Libyan people, standing up for their sacred right to freedom and independence from imperialist encroachments.

At dinner for visiting Algerian President
Chadli Bendjedid, Moscow, April 26/
Los Angeles Times, 3-27:(I)34.

Slade Gorton
United States Senator,
R-Washington

4

[Arguing against U.S. President Reagan's proposed arms sale to Saudi Arabia]: A whole bunch of us are sick and tired of hearing about people who are supposed to be our allies. The State Department says they [the Saudis] use back channels to help us, but of course they have to denounce us publicly. A lot of Senators have run out of patience with the Saudis. If they want to be treated like allies, they should act like allies.

The New York Times, 5-19:12.

Hassan II
King of Morocco

5

[On his recent meeting with Israeli Prime Minister Shimon Peres]: I said, "You have to talk to the PLO," and Peres said no. He said, "I don't recognize it." I asked, "What do you say about the [Israeli-] occupied [Arab] lands? You have to free them." He said, "I am not going to withdraw." I told him, "If that is how things are, then good night." Everybody will go his own way.

Broadcast address to the nation, Morocco,
July 23/Los Angeles Times, 7-24:(I)1.

Mark O. Hatfield
United States Senator, R-Oregon

6

[Criticizing the U.S. for the current U.S.-Libyan military confrontation in the Gulf of Sidra]: We are engaging in child-like games of dare and double-dare with a sick and dangerous clown [Libyan leader Muammar Qaddafi]. The geopolitical stakes will be serious indeed should the repercussions of this fall upon our moderate allies in the Arab world.

Washington, March 24/
Los Angeles Times, 3-25:(I)13.

Loutof Haydar
Syrian Ambassador to the
United Kingdom

7

[On British charges that he and his government were involved in a plot to blow up an Is-

(LOUTOF HAYDAR)

raeli airliner departing from London]: I don't believe there is any country in the world . . . that would get their Ambassador personally involved in any illegal activity. Because after all, the Ambassador, any Ambassador, is the personal representative of the head of state—the King, the Queen, the President, whoever. And no President, King or Queen, would like to get himself personally involved in illegal activity in any country in the world. It's inconceivable that my government would get me involved in this, even if it were true.

Broadcast interview, London, Oct. 24/
The Washington Post, 10-25:(A)19.

Richard M. Helms
Former Director of Central Intelligence
of the United States; Former United
States Ambassador to Iran

1

If we lose Iran to the Russians, the world gets cut in half. It would be a grievous setback for the United States.

Newsweek, 11-17:53.

Salim Hoss
Minister of Education of Lebanon

2

[On the continuing strife and violence in Lebanon]: We chased away businessmen, teachers, diplomats and foreign journalists. We had no mercy on anyone, and in the end we had no mercy even on ourselves.

To reporters/
Los Angeles Times, 4-23:(I)12.

Hussein I
King of Jordan

3

I and the government of the Kingdom of Jordan hereby announce that we are unable to continue to coordinate politically with the PLO leadership until such time as their word becomes their bond, characterized by commit-

ment, credibility and constancy . . . To you, our Palestinian brethren in the [Israeli-] occupied territories, I renew my pledge that here in Jordan we will remain as we have been: brothers committed to your cause and supporters in all you have to face. We will continue to support you, by every available means.

Broadcast address, Amman, Feb. 19/
The New York Times, 2-20:1,4.

Henry J. Hyde
United States Representative,
R-Illinois

4

[Saying Israel has much influence in the U.S. Congress]: The perception that Israel and its supporters are against something is all that's necessary now. The sensitivity of Congress to perceived interests of Israel is phenomenal.

U.S. News & World Report, 5-26:17.

Abu Iyad
Second-in-command,
Palestine Liberation Organization

5

[On whether Arab governments want an independent Palestinian state in the Middle East]: Frankly, no. Syria and Jordan are most opposed. If there were a Palestinian state, there would be no logical reason for Jordan to exist. As far as Syria is concerned, she wants a Greater Syria. There isn't an Arab [leader] who will declare publicly that he is against a Palestinian state. But because it would be democratic with a highly educated population, it would be a dangerous model for them. Certain Arab regimes are as much our enemy as Israel.

Interview, Tunis, Tunisia/
U.S. News & World Report, 12-15:38.

Abdel-Salam Jalloud
Libyan political leader

6

[On the recent U.S. attack on Libya in retaliation for that country's involvement in interna-

(ABDEL-SALAM JALLOUD)

tional terrorism]: We have not declared war, and we do not want to make war on America. However, America is making war on our houses, hospitals and schools. We are fighting in defense. To be at war or not depends on America . . . [U.S. Secretary of State George] Shultz has declared that he wants to see a *coup d'etat* take place in Libya and that Libyans are not happy. There is no possibility of a coup in Libya because the people are in power . . . We shall continue to support world liberation movements and we shall continue to fight capitalists and imperialist forces . . . As revolutionaries, we can never be intimidated by power.

News conference, Tripoli, April 18/
Los Angeles Times, 4-19:(I)1,20.

Brian Jenkins
Director, research project on
subnational conflict and political
violence, Rand Corporation

1

[On Libyan leader Muammar Qaddafi's involvement in international terrorism]: Quite clearly, Qaddafi has played a major role in terrorism, but he by no means exercises control over the myriad Middle East groups who target the U.S. and the West for a variety of reasons. Qaddafi may have a "go" switch for some terrorist groups, but not a "stop" switch.

Time, 4-28:27.

2

[Libyan leader Muammar] Qaddafi's terrorism is hot; [Syrian President Hafez] Assad's terrorism is cold. For Qaddafi, terrorism is like a banner; for Assad, it's as quick and silent as an assassin's bullet.

U.S. News & World Report, 11-10:30.

Walid Jumblatt
Leader of Lebanese Druze

3

[Saying Syria should be the only channel for the Arab struggle against Israel]: We will say it

quite frankly, we are not ready any more to become an appendage to the Palestinian resistance movement as we were in the past. To have the poor Lebanese people pay the price for this so-called confrontation is no longer acceptable. The road to Palestine passes through Damascus and through Moscow.

Oct. 29/The Washington Post, 10-30:(A)53.

Bernard Kalb
Assistant Secretary for Public Affairs,
Department of State of the United States

4

There have been several published offers to mediate between the United States and Libya. The United States has not responded because there has been no need for mediation or go-betweens. If the [Libyan leader Muammar] Qaddafi regime wants to improve its international acceptability, it knows precisely what it must do. It must cease its unacceptable policies and actions and show it is prepared to become a member of the civilized community. It must cease its support for terrorism. It is a lack of action—a lack of terrorist action—that is important.

Washington, April 2/
Los Angeles Times, 4-3:(I)1.

Mohammed Kamal
Jordanian Ambassador
to the United States

5

[Criticizing the reported U.S. arms deal with Iran in return for Iran's help in arranging release of U.S. hostages held by Arab terrorists]: [The U.S.] has always declared openly that it would not negotiate with terrorists. Now it has lost credibility.

Interview, Washington, Nov. 9/
Los Angeles Times, 11-10:(I)1.

Geoffrey Kemp
Specialist on Middle Eastern affairs;
Former aide to National Security
Council of the United States

6

[Criticizing a reported U.S. arms deal with Iran in return for Iran's help in arranging release

(GEOFFREY KEMP)

of U.S. hostages held by Arab terrorists]: Whether or not it makes matters worse by encouraging more hostage-taking, I don't know. It makes not only our policy toward Iran look hypocritical but makes our policy about not negotiating with the PLO a little shallow after this deception. To me, the most *prima facie* flaw has been to mix the strategic goal of having a dialogue with dissident groups inside and outside Iran, with the more tactical and humane and I would imagine political concerns of dealing with the hostages. Two separate types of programs got muddled up. What makes it so depressing is the arms factor. Had there been no arms involved, I don't think the opposition by [U.S. Secretary of State George] Shultz and [U.S. Defense Secretary Caspar] Weinberger would have been so strong and I don't think our allies and moderate Arabs would have felt as profoundly compromised. With moderate Arabs, this must be seen as a betrayal.

Interview/The New York Times, 11-10:6.

Edward M. Kennedy
United States Senator,
D-Massachusetts

1

[Urging European countries to join with the U.S. in isolating Libya because of that country's involvement in international terrorism]: [The Europeans] have to become involved. And I would hope that the [U.S. Reagan] Administration would take a very tough position on it. I would expect that they would. Every one of the European countries ought to prohibit Libyan planes from landing or any domestic flights from flying to Libya. There ought to be an economic embargo for any Libyan products, and there has to be a dramatic escalation in economic sanctions. And the United States clearly ought to lead the way, and this ought to be the top priority . . . [And] I would hope that any kind of future naval maneuvers in the [Gulf of] Sidra would have a European contingent.

Interview, Washington, April 8/
Los Angeles Times, 4-9:(I)14.

Ali Khameini
President of Iran

2

As long as the U.S. has this spirit of aggression and hegemonism, its present attitude toward Moslem, Palestinian and Arab nations, and this support for the Zionist regime [Israel], I declare there will be no reconciliation [by Iran] with America.

At prayer meeting, Teheran, Nov. 14/
The Washington Post, 11-15:(A)28.

Ruhollah Khomeini
Spiritual leader of Iran

3

[On Western speculation as to what will happen in Iran when he dies]: Our enemies must understand that the Islamic Republic [of Iran] . . . has been stabilized and is not dependent on any person, but on the people and the armed forces . . . Every day there are rumors that this and that has happened, that so-and-so has had a heart attack, that so-and-so is on his death bed. So let it be. Of course, death comes to everyone, and to me, too. They [Iran's enemies] should not rejoice. This is something that happens and you will see that, God willing, the Islamic Republic will remain, whether or not I stay.

To military personnel, Jamaran, Iran,
Nov. 9/The Washington Post, 11-10:(A)25.

4

[Criticizing those in the Iranian government who have been secretly negotiating with the U.S. in an effort to improve relations and obtain arms]: I never expected such things from these people. This is a time when they should be screaming at America. But they are shouting at themselves . . . Why should we be so Western-oriented or Satan-oriented? You mustn't break our people's hearts. Don't create hard-liners and moderates. These are against Islam, against religion, against grace . . . One thing I congratulate everyone on is the great explosion [of criticism by Americans of U.S. President Reagan's decision to negotiate with those Iranians] which has occurred in Washington's Black

(RUHOLLAH KHOMEINI)

House [the White House] and the very important scandal which has gripped leaders of America.

Teheran, Nov. 20/
The New York Times, 11-21:6.

Henry A. Kissinger
Former Secretary of State
of the United States

1

[Criticizing a reported U.S. arms deal with Iran in return for Iran's help in arranging release of U.S. hostages held by Arab terrorists]: To negotiate for hostages makes it more likely that other hostages are going to be taken. To trade arms—in a [Iran-Iraq] war in which a victory of Iran is against our national interest—is unwise. Above all, I'm deeply concerned about announcing one policy [the U.S. policy of not making deals with terrorists for hostages] in public, pressuring other countries to follow it, and then, in private, carrying out another policy.

Broadcast interview/
"This Week With David Brinkley,"
ABC-TV, 11-9.

Philip Klutznick
Former president, World Jewish Congress;
Former Secretary of Commerce
of the United States

2

Many people who talk about [the Arab-Israeli conflict] know one side and have never closely examined the other. I suffer from the fact that I have been to the Arab countries and know some of the people. I have also been to Israel and I know my people . . . I suffer from the fact that I try to be fair. I see there's a certain amount of justice on both sides. It's not black and white.

The Washington Post, 8-8:(A)31.

Helmut Kohl
Chancellor of West Germany

3

[On the U.S. air attack against Libya in retaliation for that country's involvement in international terrorism]: Those who practice and preach violence like [Libyan leader Muammar] Qaddafi

must consider that those threatened will protect themselves. I have understanding for the growing exasperation of the American people [toward terrorism against them]. On the other hand, we have always said a violent solution will not be successful and is not very promising.

Bonn, West Germany, April 15/
Los Angeles Times, 4-16:(I)5.

Robert H. Kupperman
Senior adviser, Center for
Strategic and International Studies,
Georgetown University

4

[On the recent U.S. attack on Libya in retaliation for that country's involvement in international terrorism]: It's a great mistake to equate the cathartic victory we achieved in Libya with comparative safety with attacking Syria and Iran [if they are shown to also engage in terrorism] . . . In the case of Libya, the Russians feel only a marginal commitment to [Libyan leader Muammar] Qaddafi. They use him opportunistically. Syria is another matter. Syria's their real entrance to the Middle East, their only stronghold. Syria's a genuine Soviet client state. If we were to start bombing Syria, we would risk Soviet military intervention.

The Christian Science Monitor, 4-28:3,8.

5

[On the recent U.S. attack on Libya in retaliation for its involvement in international terrorism]: If we genuinely believe that [Libyan leader Muammar] Qaddafi is more than just a booking agent for terrorism, then covert means of getting rid of him should be considered. We seem to be dealing in niceties. We think we can use the larger instruments of warfare to bring about his elimination, but that we shouldn't use the smaller ones, such as a pistol.

Time, 4-28:20.

Patrick J. Leahy
United States Senator, D-Vermont

6

[Charging that Libyan leader Muammar Qaddafi permits Palestinian terrorist training camps

WHAT THEY SAID IN 1986

in his country]: There are terrorist training camps in Libya. The suggestion that there aren't is about as incredible as Qaddafi's statement that the terrorists' actions were considered the holiest actions throughout the world. Qaddafi knows they're there. I believe, in some instances, he encourages having them there. And certainly they exist only with his willingness and acquiescence.

Interview, Washington, Jan. 5/
The New York Times, 1-6:1.

Moshe Levy
Lieutenant General and
Chief of Staff, Israeli Army

1

All the time, and for years, [Syrian President Hafez al-Assad] has been preparing for war with Israel. He never stops. You can ask, "How are these preparations manifested?" Each time differently. One time he deploys missiles along the [Israeli-Lebanese] border. Another time he digs positions in the southern Bekaa Valley. Another time he holds preparatory maneuvers. The basic ideology of Syria is to all the time make preparations. We respond with our own deployments constantly, depending on what is happening in the field. And these have an effect on the situation.

To reporters, May 20/
The New York Times, 5-21:4.

Samuel W. Lewis
Former United States Ambassador to Israel

2

The Arab world is as divided and as confused as it has been in a long time. It is having to face up to its weakness and its inability to have an impact on anybody's policy. [U.S.-Arab] relations may be as bad as they have been since the [1973 Arab-Israeli war], but they are not as bad as they have been at some earlier times. This is all quite cyclical.

Los Angeles Times, 5-19:(I)6.

3

[On U.S.-Israeli relations]: I think there is a widespread conviction among Israelis of all po-

litical stripes . . . that we [the U.S.] are a long way away, that we have a political system that produces rather wide swings in foreign policy, and that we have a lot of other fish to fry in the region and in Europe.

Interview/Los Angeles Times, 8-9:(I)16.

Richard G. Lugar
United States Senator, R-Indiana

4

[On U.S. President Reagan's support for a $354-million arms sale to Saudi Arabia]: It is important for those who are strongly pro-Israel to come to the aid of the President in this situation. Because if he is hobbled [by the U.S. Congress which recently voted down the sale] . . . Israel is going to suffer . . . For the President to deal effectively in the Middle East he has to be able to work with the moderate [Arab] states.

To reporters, Washington/
The Christian Science Monitor, 5-15:8.

5

[Criticizing a recent Reagan Administration disinformation campaign in the U.S. press aimed at keeping Libyan leader Muammar Qaddafi off balance in his plans for international terrorism]: It was just simply stupid to be involved in this type of thing at this point. I think Qaddafi is a menace. I think terrorism is a menace. The American people want to see this connection exposed and then suppressed. But I think our greatest strength is still that we tell the truth as a government, and there's credibility in what we say. And to the extent that we undermine that, we lose a very big foreign-policy initiative.

Broadcast interview/
"This Week With David Brinkley,"
ABC-TV, 10-5.

Edward C. Luttwak
Senior fellow, Center for
Strategic and International Studies,
Georgetown University

6

[On the recent military confrontation between the U.S. and Libya in the Gulf of Sidra]: The

(EDWARD C. LUTTWAK)

state of the American opinion allows only small bites. The Grenada situation can be totally dealt with in one small bite. The Libyan situation cannot be. So we end up wounding Libya. It's like wounding a wild beast; you don't prevent him from doing a lot of harm.

The Christian Science Monitor, 3-28:1.

Robert J. Magomarsino
United States Representative,
R-California

1

[Supporting a proposed U.S. arms sale to Saudi Arabia]: [Rejection of the sale] will signal that the United States cannot distinguish between radical Arab states that practice terror and moderate Arab states that seek protection.

The Washington Post, 5-8:(A)13.

M.T. Mahdi
President, American-Arab
Relations Committee

2

[On U.S. President Reagan's verbal attacks on Libyan leader Muammar Qaddafi, who is allegedly involved in international terrorism]: President Reagan's orders and measures [for economic sanctions against Libya] will not hurt Qaddafi economically. Rather, they will increase his popularity from Jakarta to Casablanca among one billion human beings. The speech reflects Reagan's personal grudge against Qaddafi, calling the Libyan leader "barbarian" and "flaky." The President is over-reacting to Qaddafi as [movie hero] Rambo did. This is to the distress of Arab-Americans and all thoughtful people in America, Europe, and throughout the world.

New York, Jan. 7/
The New York Times, 1-9:6.

Moshe Maoz
Syria specialist,
Hebrew University, Jerusalem

3

[Syrian President Hafez al-] Assad is truly ideologically committed to the struggle against Is-

rael. He wants to build enough military strength to defend Syria, to deter an Israeli attack, and eventually to attack Israel . . . He believes deeply that Israel is a danger to the rest of the Arab world.

The Christian Science Monitor, 6-3:9.

Robert C. McFarlane
Former Assistant to the President
of the United States (Ronald Reagan)
for National Security Affairs

4

[On Libyan leader Muammar Qaddafi's alleged involvement in recent terrorist attacks at the Rome and Vienna airports]: By his own statements publicly and his endorsement originally of these attacks that his association with them, his support for them, the fact that his graduates are spreading violence from the Philippines to the IRA, the man's culpability is clear. For this specific act, whether he directed it, I rather doubt it, but I think his association with this attack and others like it is irrefutable.

Broadcast interview/
"This Week with David Brinkley,"
ABC-TV, 1-5.

5

[On his involvement in recently revealed secret negotiations between the U.S. and Iranian officials which have been strongly criticized in the U.S. because they included arms sales to Iran]: However well-meaning and defensible our purposes were, to the extent that the introduction of arms transfers into the process led to understandable turmoil that can have a very damaging effect on the ability of our country to lead, it was a mistake. As a senior adviser to the President, I should have anticipated this potential outcome. The failure to do so represents a serious error in judgment for which I accepted full responsibility.

Nov. 20/The New York Times, 11-21:6.

6

[On the current scandal involving secret U.S. arms deals with Iran and the subsequent release of Arab-held U.S. hostages]: I want to stress that

WHAT THEY SAID IN 1986

(ROBERT C. McFARLANE)

throughout, from the outset last July in 1985 to the time I left government in December of 1985, it was very clear that the President of the United States [Reagan] was motivated by two concerns. And that was the imperative of trying, if it were possible, to establish contact with those [in Iran] oriented toward changing Iranian policy and, secondly, toward the recovery of Americans and other nationals held hostage. The President was profoundly concerned for the welfare of these human beings. At no time, in my experience, nor since leaving government, can I imagine that the President would ever countenance nor endorse any departure from law nor of policies in promotion of U.S. interests against terrorism.

Before House Foreign Affairs Committee,
Washington, Dec. 8/
The New York Times, 12-9:7.

1

The economic dimension has to be oriented toward Egypt and the West Bank. The way you show Middle Easterners that peace works is that Egypt gets well. Concurrent with a peace initiative, a major economic renewal in Egypt should be launched—a multi-billion-dollar investment. On the West Bank it wouldn't take a great program—up to $300-million—to show the benefits of peace to the next generation. Japan [as well as the U.S.] should be a participant and pay her way—not only in fostering economic development in Southeast Asia but by subscribing to global development that includes the Middle East. Germany should contribute, and Saudi Arabia. If that happens, you can bet that Morocco, Sudan, Tunisia and the rest of the Middle East will conclude: "Look what happened to Egypt in the wake of peace."

Interview/U.S. News & World Report, 12-22:24.

Ariel Merari
Head of terrorism study project,
Center for Strategic Studies,
Tel Aviv University

2

Paradoxically, although Israel is seen as an example of successful retaliation against terror-

ists, most [Israeli] retaliatory activity in the past was ineffective in deterring states from sponsoring terrorism. The [recent U.S. retaliatory] raid [on Libya] was different; first of all, because it was considerably greater in scope than any Israeli retaliatory raid and secondly, because the United States made it amply clear that it is going to repeat the action, in greater dose, if state sponsorship of terrorism by Libya or other countries continues. And the most important aspect of deterrence is the perception [by terrorists] of the future: What will happen if we go on doing what we do? How large a punishment will we sustain? Can we sustain this kind of punishment?

Interview/
Los Angeles Times, 6-26:(I)15.

Karmenu Mifsud Bonnici
Prime Minister of Malta

3

[Saying Malta notified Libya in advance of the impending U.S. air attack in April, which was in retaliation for Libyan involvement in international terrorism]: We've committed ourselves to exchange information with all friendly countries, north and south. Any information that might be beneficial to our allies we pass on to them. We do that regularly and systematically and will continue to do so. The provision of such information should never be construed as a threat. It is the withholding of information that is dangerous. If we know that any nation is planning an attack on Libya, we will pass it on, just as we would to Italy, or to the United States.

Interview, Valletta, Malta, Aug. 5/
The New York Times, 8-6:1.

Yitzhak Modai
Minister of Justice of Israel

4

[On the recent revelation of Israeli spying in the U.S. and allegations that it is widespread]: Not only are they [the allegations] lies, they are completely unfounded. If you . . . intimate this is the tip of the iceberg, where is the iceberg? If you intimate that there are other cases, where are the other cases? If you suggest that Israeli au-

(YITZHAK MODAI)

thorities knew about it, where is the proof? . . . I wish and pray that current events . . . complete their course and get out of the way of the important type of relationship that we have developed between our two countries, not only for the benefit of the two countries, but also for the benefit of the free world.

News conference, Washington, June 17/ Los Angeles Times, 6-18:(I)17.

Salim Saleh Mohammed
Secretary, Central Committee, Socialist Party of South Yemen

1

We have learned not to centralize the power in one hand. In the Third World, when power is in one hand it leads to catastrophe. In our country there should not be a strong man or a weak man. We really believe in collective leadership.

Interview, Aden, South Yemen, Jan. 31/ The New York Times, 2-1:3.

Walter F. Mondale
Former Vice President of the United States

2

[On Libyan leader Muammar Qaddafi's alleged involvement in international terrorism, which led to the recent U.S. air attack on Libya]: It bothers me deeply that a character like Qaddafi, head of a government, can just go out and assault the basic underlying principles of civilized society and kill people at random, in great numbers, and there's no risk to it . . . When the evidence came in that the Libyan government had deliberately decided to kill Americans, then we really had no choice but to respond with some kind of force, especially in light of the fact that we were unable to get European cooperation, economic sanctions or something that would have stung.

Interview, Washington, April 25/ The Washington Post, 4-26:(A)19.

Benjamin Netanyahu
Israeli Ambassador/ Permanent Representative to the United Nations

3

The first armed, forceful, international action by a leading Western country against terrorism was [the U.S.] bombing of Libya [earlier this year in retaliation for Libya's involvement in international terrorism]. If we take more such actions, we can cork this genie back into the bottle. If we don't, it'll get worse and it could reach catastrophic proportions when terrorists and the states that sponsor them could possess the means of mass destruction . . . [Israel has] always responded with force. The act of doing this puts the terrorists at risk. We have always punished the terrorists and pre-empted their activities by going to their concentrations and punishing the regimes that support them . . . We haven't had an Israeli airplane, let alone El Al [the Israeli airline] itself, hijacked for over 10 years. That's not because [PLO leader] Yasir Arafat has become a Zionist, or [Libyan leader Muammar] Qaddafi and [Arab terrorist] Abu Nidal lovers of Israel. It's because they know, and the people that they send know, that they are very likely to die. Unless the West adopts this attitude, it will not be able to stop terrorism.

Interview/USA Today, 9-29:(A)13.

Richard M. Nixon
Former President of the United States

4

[On the recent U.S. attack against Libya in retaliation for that country's involvement in international terrorism]: As far as what we call the bombing option is concerned, that cannot be used again unless it is massive. We learned in Vietnam, one of the lessons of the many we had to learn, is that gradual escalation does not bring down a fanatic. With [Libyan leader Muammar] Qaddafi I think we did the right thing at that time, but from now on we've got to think in bigger terms. If [U.S.] bombing [of Libya] is resorted to again it must be a knockout blow. The only problem with that . . . is whether or not public opinion, not just in Europe but in this

(RICHARD M. NIXON)

country, would take it . . . And I would add one other thing. Remember when [U.S. President] Reagan said, "If [Syria and Iran] do it [engage in terrorism] we'll bomb them, too," or words to that effect, and then the State Department said, "No, we're not considering that." A great mistake. Always, always—never talk about what you're going to do, but [also] don't tell them what you're *not* going to do.

Interview,
Saddle River, N.J./
Newsweek, 5-19:34.

Sam Nunn
United States Senator,
D-Georgia

1

[Criticizing recently revealed secret U.S. negotiations with Iranian officials that involved U.S. arms sales to Iran]: You have to understand that there are other countries that are on the verge and have been wanting to send shipments of weapons to Iran for a good many months—even years—[but have refrained due to U.S pressure], because of profit more than anything else, and we may have [by the U.S. sales] given the green light for very large arms shipments by other countries . . . You have to understand that there is a psychological balance as well as a military balance [in the Persian Gulf], and I think that we already have begun to shift that psychological balance, and I think it's adverse to our interests in the Middle East.

Nov. 20/Los Angeles Times, 11-21:(I)28.

2

[Criticizing U.S. President Reagan for not advising Congress of his secret dealings with Iran, which involved covert arms sales]: It goes to the fundamental question of Congressional oversight of covert activities. Timely notice on the Iranian deal was not forthcoming; 18 months or 12 months was fundamentally a violation of the spirit if not the letter of the law.

The Christian Science Monitor, 11-21:3.

John Cardinal O'Connor
Roman Catholic Archbishop
of New York

3

Any honest observer who asks questions out there [in the Middle East] always comes back to a fundamental question that in my judgment we continue to ignore. And that is the Palestinian question. Somehow, a homeland has to be provided for the Palestinian peoples. Somehow. It's not for me to talk about statehood or protocol or official recognition or whatever. All that is for the people in public office. But from a moral perspective, those people have to be given a homeland. Otherwise, everything spills over into every area, and that has to result in a very volatile situation. So I think it's imperative.

Interview, Rome, June 18/
The New York Times, 6-19:4.

Thomas P. O'Neill, Jr.
United States Representative,
D-Massachusetts

4

[On the current U.S.-Libyan military confrontation in the Gulf of Sidra]: [The U.S. Reagan] Administration's handling of this matter is on the right course. Its actions in protecting America's armed forces in international waters are justified. Based upon the briefing given me at the White House, the American planes attacked by Libya today were on a peaceful mission in international waters. Libya had no right to shoot at our planes.

Washington, March 24/
The New York Times, 3-25:1.

Andreas Papandreou
Prime Minister of Greece

5

[Criticizing the recent U.S. attack on Libya in retaliation for that country's involvement in international terrorism]: [The U.S. action] sets dynamite to peace and destroys the independence of a nation in the name of imposing a hegemonistic United States presence in the area.

April 15/The New York Times, 4-16:12.

Richard B. Parker
Former United States Ambassador
to Morocco, Algeria and Lebanon

1

[On the recent U.S. raid on Libya in retaliation for that country's alleged involvement in international terrorism]: The raid puts most of our friends [in the Arab world] in an awkward position. As Arabs, they're going to have to show solidarity with Libya, even though most of them would be happy to see [Libyan leader Muammar] Qaddafi disappear tomorrow. Whatever their feelings about him, there is a nationalist commitment to opposing intervention by outside powers in the Middle East.

April 16/The Christian
Science Monitor, 4-16:32.

2

[Saying the U.S. Congress' vote to block an arms sale to Saudi Arabia is not in the U.S.' best interests, even if President Reagan vetoes the block]: Whether or not the veto is overridden, the vote is symptomatic of attitudes in the Congress, and the public at large, about the Arabs . . . We are guilty of a deep-seated prejudice against Arabs. We think of them as ragheads that you can insult with impunity . . . The Congressional vote should make the Saudis sit up and take notice, but I'm not sure that the full significance has sunk in yet. When things happen, they analyze them from their own perspective and usually come up with the wrong answers.

Los Angeles Times, 5-19:(I)1,6.

Shimon Peres
Prime Minister of Israel

3

[On recent terrorist attacks against civilians at Israeli airline airport ticket counters in Rome and Vienna]: There are some who propose a military operation against Libya [a nation which allegedly supports and encourages such terrorism]. However, before one speaks of military operations, some simple questions have to be asked: "Why is Libya treated with a measure of forgiveness and a closing of eyes [by other nations]?" [Libyan leader Muammar] Qaddafi is

accorded receptions. His country is exempt from political, legal or economic punitive measures, as though diplomatic rules are honored toward that country while it does not honor them with respect to others . . . Israel will neither rest until it catches up with those who harass us, nor will it desist from calling on the world to launch a proper international effort in order to free the world of this terrible and unnecessary danger.

Before Israeli Knesset (Parliament),
Jerusalem, Jan. 1/The New York Times, 1-2:6.

4

[On Israel's stand against terrorism directed against it]: I don't want to declare war against anybody, against any country. I don't think it is necessary. We are not talking about war or war declarations. On the other hand, I say clearly that we are not going to guarantee the security of any terrorist, no matter where he is . . . I distinguish between state and terroristic organizations.

Broadcast interview/
"This Week with David Brinkley,"
ABC-TV, 1-5.

5

[Supporting the U.S. in its recent military confrontation with Libya in the Gulf of Sidra]: [Although this incident met with vocal criticism of the U.S. by some world leaders,] I'm sure that before they made their anti-American speeches, they went to the churches and the mosques to thank heaven that the United States did something that they have needed—though they didn't admit they need it . . . Libya and [its leader Muammar] Qaddafi became a real danger for peace of many countries and for the security of many innocent people. Contrary to other countries that whenever they meet a problem or a danger they are becoming reluctant and hesitant and neutralistic, it is the United States which keeps character, hope and strength to every person and every country who wants really to be free and maintain freedom all over the world. I think it was a great move, and nobody should be impressed by the rhetoric of the countries that stood up, so to speak, against it.

Washington, April 1/
The New York Times, 4-2:6.

(SHIMON PERES)

1

[Supporting the recent U.S. attack on Libya in retaliation for that country's involvement in international terrorism]: If the Libyan government issues orders to murder American soldiers in Beirut in cold blood, in the middle of the night, what do you expect the United States to do? Sing Hallelujah? Or take action in her defense?

Nazareth, April 15/
The New York Times, 4-16:11.

2

[On charges of Israeli spying in the U.S.]: U.S.-Israeli relations are marked by closeness, and it is inconceivable that attempts to foul the atmosphere between them should succeed . . . Israel reiterates that no espionage activities are conducted against the United States on its behalf.

Written statement, June 8/
The New York Times, 6-9:10.

3

[On Soviet-Israeli relations]: We want cultural ties, economic ties, commercial ties. The Russians also want to participate in an international conference [on Middle East problems], which will open if the negotiations between us and the Arabs get under way. We do not oppose their [the Soviets'] participation . . . on the condition that they establish full diplomatic relations with us, and with the hope that they will stop taking one-sided stands in the Middle East.

Interview, Jerusalem, Aug. 5/
The Washington Post, 8-6:(A)23.

4

[Saying that, although his country wants to have relations restored with the Soviet Union, Israel would not be silent on the plight of Soviet Jews]: It's very hard to analyze what makes Soviet diplomacy move or stop. But if the Russians really want to partake in political developments in the Middle East as far as Israel is concerned, they have to renew their diplomatic relations with Israel . . . [But] Israel is not just a state;

we are a people. And for us, the fate of Russian Jewry will remain a central consideration in our feelings, in our deeds, in our positions. Nothing will change this historic fact.

To reporters, Netanya, Israel/
The Washington Post, 8-20:(A)25.

5

[On the "rotation" aspect of Israel's current two-party Prime Ministership, in which he and current Foreign Minister Yitzhak Shamir will trade places shortly]: It is basically a government made of two large parties. I am head of one of the two and, unless there will be a common effort in an agreed direction, there won't be a common government. We are changing jobs, we are not changing direction, and we are not changing the nature of the government. If there will be a change [in the nature of the government], the government will not be able to exist.

Interview, Jerusalem/
The Christian Science Monitor, 9-2:10.

6

[On whether the Soviet Union will reestablish diplomatic relations with Israel as a prerequisite to Soviet participation in a Middle East peace conference]: Whether the Russians will accept it or not nobody really knows. You have a smile on the Russian face, you have a warm Russian hand. [But] the Russian policy reminds me so much of a British bathroom where you have cold water and hot water, but you can't mix them together to wash your face.

At forum sponsored by Washington Institute
for Near East Policy, Washington, Sept. 16/
The New York Times, 9-17:6.

7

[On the Israeli Likud Party's criticism of his summit meeting with Egyptian President Hosni Mubarak]: I don't give a damn what the Likud ministers say. I said I was going to do A, B, C, D and E when I got into office, and I did it. Did the Likud get Israel out of Lebanon or repair the economy? All the gentlemen who are now criticizing the idea of an international peace conference were against the Camp David peace treaty

(SHIMON PERES)

with Egypt. What credibility do they have to provide advice to a nation?

*Interview/The Christian
Science Monitor, 10-9:10.*

Shimon Peres
*Foreign Minister, and former
Prime Minister, of Israel*

1

[On reports that Israel aided the U.S. in its purported arms deal with Iran that was designed to get Iran to arrange release of U.S. hostages held by Arab terrorists]: Israel, when it comes to saving the life of any individual, whether Israeli or American, considers it part of a democratic way of life to respect human life and human freedom. As I would expect the United States to help us in saving the life of an individual, I would expect my own country to do likewise toward an American citizen—and this is without giving up at all the determined way to confront terrorism, to fight it, on all occasions and on all fronts. While not submitting to terror, one should never ignore the value or safety of the life of a single person no matter what his citizenship is. I believe that a good and strong democracy in our days should act on two bases: to fight terror without any hesitation and to respect human life without any reservation.

*Interview, Jerusalem/
The New York Times, 11-10:1.*

2

[On Israel's involvement in secret U.S.-Iran dealings which involved U.S. arms sales to Iran and the diversion of Iran's payments for those arms to the contra rebels in Nicaragua]: It was not an Israeli operation. It was an American affair. Israel was asked to help and did so . . . We have no part in the contra issue and we have not received any financial or other gains. Our intention was in all seriousness and innocence to help a state. We, arms dealers? We did not make a penny. What kind of dealers are we?

*Before the Knesset (Parliament), Jerusalem,
Nov. 26/The New York Times, 11-27:9.*

Daniel Pipes
*Director, Foreign Policy
Research Institute*

3

Of the four major sponsors of [international] terrorism—the PLO, Libya, Iran and Syria—the first two get all the attention. But it's the other two we should be watching, and particularly Syria. It is quiet and deadly in its effectiveness, and until this slipup [being implicated in an attempted bombing of an Israeli airliner in London], it has always managed to stay in the shadows.

U.S. News & World Report, 11-10:29.

John M. Poindexter
*Assistant to the President
of the United States for
National Security Affairs*

4

[On whether he is sorry he and the Reagan Administration got involved in dealings with Iran, that involved U.S. arms and the freeing of U.S. hostages held by Arab terrorists]: Not at all. I think we've made some very significant progress. We've gotten three hostages out, we have the Iranian Ambassador to the United Nations making statements that in relative terms are much more positive than Iranian officials have said about the United States in a long time, and even one of the Iranian newspapers is talking about a relationship with the United States. Now, these changes aren't going to consolidate or wrap up overnight, because there are still some significant disagreements and differences in our policies, and what Iran defines in its interest at this point. The other thing is that I think we have made some progress in convincing Iran that the war with Iraq is not one that they can win. That's an important step forward.

Interview/USA Today, 11-19:(A)9.

Muammar el-Qaddafi
Chief of State of Libya

5

[Warning the U.S. and Israel not to retaliate against Libya for the recent terrorist attacks at

WHAT THEY SAID IN 1986

(MUAMMAR el-QADDAFI)

the Rome and Vienna airports]: If Israel acts against this action there will be strong and furious counter actions by the Palestinians. Tit for tat. If you come back, we come back. If the Israelis want to take action in this place, then they are welcome. This is what the Palestinians want because the Israelis cannot keep up with this race. We hope that America and the Israelis make a mistake and mount an invasion . . . We have the right to follow American citizens in their own streets and we have the right to follow Jews in occupied Palestine [if they retaliate]. If there is an aggression on Libya . . . then there is goodbye to peace in the Mediterranean zone. There will be no peace in the Mediteranean, no trade, no American planes, military or non-military. Aggression on Libya means war. Libya will not act in a limited fashion. Libya will declare war in the Middle East and in the Mediterranean zone.

To reporters, Tripoli, Jan. 1/
The Washington Post, 1-2:(A)17.

1

[Warning the U.S. not to retaliate against Libya for recent terrorist attacks at the Rome and Vienna airports]: If America can hit any place—these aircraft carriers and strategic bombers—then we can reach any place, not through aircraft carriers or bombers but through suicide groups. We would act inside American streets, but I think it is a dangerous turn—madness.

News conference, Wadi el Khair, Libya,
Jan. 5/Los Angeles Times, 1-6:(I)8.

2

[Denying there are Palestinian terrorist training camps in his country]: If they were here, they would then be my responsibility. But they are not here. They have their camps in Lebanon and in other parties near occupied Palestine. They have no need to be trained in Libya, this place which is far, far, far away from their field of battle, Palestine.

News conference,
Wadi el Khair, Libya,Jan. 5/
The New York Times, 1-6:6.

3

[On current U.S. naval exercises in the Mediterranean Sea off Libya]: Libya stood firm and declared before the world that Parallel 32.30, which marks the beginning of the Gulf of Sidra, is the Line of Death and, despite all air and naval attempts during two months, the U.S. was unable to come near this line, for it knows that it is the Line of Death.

At convention of underground and revolutionary
organizations, Tripoli, March 15/
The New York Times, 3-27:8.

4

[On the recent conflict in the Gulf of Sidra between U.S. and Libyan naval and air forces, in which the U.S. claims none of its planes were shot down]: The Americans are lying. They can't believe a small country could shoot down three planes. We shot down three planes, and the six fliers are being eaten by the fish in the Gulf of Sidra. America has gone mad in the past few days. They shot a fishing boat and claimed it was a warship . . . We will impose our sovereignty in the Gulf of Sidra with our blood. If they fight us, we will fight back.

At rally, Tripoli, March 28/
The New York Times, 3-29:3.

5

[On indications that the U.S. may attack Libya in retaliation for Libyan involvement in international terrorism]: We have just finished military preparations in response to the latest American threats against us. It is axiomatic that America will be defeated militarily. It is axiomatic that, if aggression is staged against us, we shall escalate the violence against American targets, civilian and non-civilian, all over the world.

News conference, Tripoli, April 9/
Los Angeles Times, 4-10:(I)23.

6

[On the possibility that the U.S. will attack Libya in response to Libya's alleged involvement in international terrorism]: It is axiomatic that the Americans will be defeated militarily. It is axiomatic that if aggression is being staged against us, we shall escalate the violence against

(MUAMMAR el-QADDAFI)

American targets, civilian and non-civilian, all over the world. It should be clear from now on that the [U.S.] Reagan Administration is responsible, and not us, if American security is threatened in American cities.
News conference, Tripoli, April 9/
The New York Times, 4-10:10.

1

[On the U.S. air attack on his country in retaliation for Libya's involvement in international terrorism]: We are ready to die and we are ready to carry on fighting and defending our country. [U.S. President Reagan is] guilty of issuing orders to regular forces to murder children and attack houses. We have not issued any orders for murdering anybody, but we are inciting revolution. Inciting revolution and establishing popular revolution everywhere in the world is one of our aims. We will never abandon the uniting of the Arab nation, and the [U.S.] raids will not make us abandon this call, which concerns only us and does not concern the Americans or anybody else in the world. It is a great thing that a small country like Libya can confront Britain and the United States. It was as if they were launching a third world war, coming 4,000 kilometers and refueling so many times. We know that airplanes came from Britain, and we know that France did not allow overflights. We thank France for that . . . If the United States hits us with nuclear bombs, we will stand up to it because Allah is stronger than the United States. We are ready to die. It is very clear we did not carry our fight to the United States. They came here.
Broadcast address to the nation,
April 16/The New York Times, 4-17:8.

2

[On his reaction to the recent U.S. air attack on Libya in retaliation for Libya's role in international terrorism]: We don't have long-distance missiles, but we have other things. We must be prepared to die. We are not afraid of the American terrorists. We are not afraid of nuclear bombs. We must fight and dance at the same time. We do not want to live under constant terror. We are ready to make an alliance with the Soviet Union and the Socialist Bloc. The non-aligned movement is not enough.
Broadcast address to the nation, Tripoli,
June 11/The Washington Post, 6-12:(A)38.

3

[On charges that he supports international terrorism]: If supporting the struggle of people for liberation is terrorism, then we're responsible for such acts. [Libya] has trained fighters in Zimbabwe and the fighters of SWAPO, and we train the fighters of the Palestinian people, the Palestine Liberation Organization.
Broadcast interview, Sirt, Libya/
"Good Morning America," ABC-TV,10-16.

4

The mad dog [U.S. President] Reagan and the whore [British Prime Minister Margaret] Thatcher are leading a fanatic crusade against the Arab world . . . [Reagan and Thatcher are] the two Hitlers [who are] responsible for criminal terrorism in the Arab world. The fish in the sea are waiting for them.
Interview, Tripoli/Newsweek, 11-10:42.

5

[On charges that he supports international terrorism]: What you [Americans] view as terrorism is the Palestinian struggle for liberation against the Israelis. And whatever [U.S. President] Reagan is calling terrorism is actually a struggle of the people's liberation movement against terrorism. What the Americans are doing is a terrorist act, and what the Israelis are doing is a terrorist act. What the Palestinians, Nicaraguans, the Lebanese are doing—this is a liberation movement.
Interview, Tripoli, October/
U.S. News & World Report, 11-10:31.

6

We don't hate the Jews, because some Libyans are Jews and some Arabs are Jews and Judaism is a religion. We don't hate religion. We are against Zionism. More clearly, we are against colonialism. We would consider Palestine as oc-

333

cupied by these people—whatever name you give them—even if they were Moslems. They [the Israelis] are occupying Palestine, and they have to be resisted.

Interview, Tripoli, October/
U.S. News & World Report, 11-10:32.

William B. Quandt
Former staff specialist on the
Middle East, National Security
Council of the United States

1

We are seeing some of the consequences of the perception that oil is no longer as strategically important to us as it was. [Among other indications is] the unwillingness of the United States to take the extra step in the Middle East peace process. This reflects the precept that no vital interest is at stake. People have a hard time convincing themselves why we ought to bother.

The Washington Post, 2-13:(A)16.

Yitzhak Rabin
Minister of Defense, and
former Prime Minister, of Israel

2

[Criticizing those in Israel who call for Palestinian self-determination]: Whoever brings up now the question of self-determination is an idiot. The main rift between Jordan and the [Yasir] Arafat-led PLO was over this issue. Arafat's interpretation of self-determination is the creation of a totally independent Palestinian state in the West Bank, East Jerusalem and the Gaza Strip. Jordan's interpretation . . . is to have . . . some Palestinian entity that will come under Jordanian sovereignty. For an Israeli to bring it up now is a double idiocy. It means making Arafat alive again. Therefore, I totally oppose it . . . It's something that will undermine Israel's security and political posture.

Interview/The Christian
Science Monitor, 7-31:8.

3

[On Israel's alleged involvement in U.S. arms deals with Iran and the diversion of funds from those deals to contra rebels fighting the government of Nicaragua]: [Israel] does not maintain contacts or ties with the rebels in Nicaragua, nor does it supply arms from here to them. Israel did not grant permission to any Israeli to assist, supply know-how or sell weapons from Israel to the rebels in Nicaragua. As to the rumors concerning the transfer of money to rebels fighting the regime of Nicaragua as a result of Israeli aid to the United States in the transfer of American weapons to Iran, I can do no more than repeat what was declared by the Israeli government: We did not know and we did not do it.

Before Israeli Knesset (Parliament),
Dec. 2/The Washington Post, 12-3:(A)33.

Hashemi Rafsanjani
Speaker of the Iranian Parliament

4

We have an appointment with Israel after we finish off with the Iraqi regime [in the current Iran-Iraq war]. The day will surely come when we face Israel to destroy it, and we shall then get by force $700-million they owe us since the reign of the entombed Shah [of Iran].

During weekly prayers, Teheran, Nov. 28/
The Washington Post, 11-29:(A)11.

Ronald Reagan
President of the United States

5

We have urged repeatedly that the world community act decisively and in concert to exact from [Libyan leader Muammar] Qaddafi a high price for his support and encouragement of [international] terrorism. The United States has already taken a series of steps to curtail most direct trade between our two countries, while encouraging our friends to do likewise. Terrorists, and those who harbor them, must be denied sympathy, safe haven and support . . . Civilized nations cannot continue to tolerate, in the name of material gain and self-interest, the murder of innocents. Qaddafi deserves to be treated as a

(RONALD REAGAN)

pariah in the world community. We call on our friends in Western Europe and elsewhere to join with us in isolating him.

News conference, Washington, Jan. 7/
The New York Times, 1-8:6.

1

[On the recent U.S. air attack on Libya in retaliation for that country's involvement in international terror]: Sometimes it is said that by opposing sanctions against [Libyan leader Muammar] Qaddafi, or by striking at his terrorist installations, we only magnify the man's importance; that the proper way to deal with him is to ignore him. I do not agree. Long before I came into this office, Colonel Qaddafi had engaged in acts of international terror, acts that put him outside the company of civilized men. For years, however, he suffered no economic or political or military sanction. And the atrocities mounted in number as did the innocent dead and wounded. And for us to ignore, by inaction, the slaughter of American civilians and American soldiers, whether in nightclubs or airline terminals, is simply not in the American tradition. When our citizens are abused or attacked anywhere in the world on the direct orders of a hostile regime, we will respond so long as I'm in this Oval Office. Self-defense is not only our right, it is our duty.

News conference, Washington,
April 14/USA Today, 4-15:(A)9.

2

[On the U.S. air attack against Libya in retaliation for that country's involvement in international terrorism]: The United States won but a single engagement in the long battle against terrorism. We will not end that struggle until the free and decent people of this planet unite to eradicate the scourge of terror from the modern world . . . We would prefer not to have to repeat the events of last night. What is required is for Libya to end its pursuit of terror for political goals. The choice is theirs.

To business leaders, Washington,
April 15/Los Angeles Times, 4-16:(I)1.

[Defending the recent U.S. attack on Libya in retaliation for that country's involvement in international terrorism]: It's something you regret any time children or innocent people are wounded or killed [such as during the U.S. attack] . . . On the other hand, I was equally sorry about a little baby that was blown out of the side of an airplane and fell 15,000 feet to its death along with her mother and grandmother. I also feel badly about an 11-year-old girl that was shot down in cold blood for simply standing in the airport in Rome. I think that was one of the deeds that [Libyan leader Muammar] Qaddafi referred to as a noble deed . . . Terrorism hasn't succeeded. Terrorism will have succeeded when we decide that we shouldn't take any action against it.

Interview, Washington, April 21/
The Washington Post, 4-22:(A)10.

4

[On the recent U.S. air attack on Libya in retaliation for that country's involvement in international terrorism]: America will never watch passively as our innocent citizens are murdered by those who would do our country harm. We are slow to wrath and hesitant to use the military power available to us. By nature, we prefer to solve problems peacefully. But as we proved last week, no one can kill Americans and brag about it. No one. We bear the people of Libya no ill will, but if their government continues its campaign of terror against Americans, we will act again.

Before International Forum of U.S.
Chamber of Commerce, Washington, April 23/
The New York Times, 4-24:8.

5

[Backing a U.S. arms-sales package for Saudi Arabia]: It is not just a favor to our friends in Saudi Arabia. Moreover, it is not being done at anyone's expense . . . This sale will not endanger Israel's defenses—a fact that is underscored by Israel's decision not to oppose the sale . . . In a region living in the shadow of the gruesome Iran-Iraq war and threatened by religious fanaticism at its worst, we cannot afford to take stability for granted . . . Several times in recent

WHAT THEY SAID IN 1986

(RONALD REAGAN)

months, [the Saudis] have been helpful in offsetting unjust criticism of the United States and preventing radical states from taking joint action against our country.

Message on his veto of Senate legislation
barring the sale, Washington, May 21/*
Los Angeles Times, 5-22:(I)18.

1

[Calling on the Senate to approve an arms sale to Saudi Arabia]: American influence in the region is absolutely vital to world peace. And to exercise this influence, we must retain the trust of moderate Arab nations for the sake of our own national interest and of security in this vital region—indeed, for the sake of world peace itself, I ask you to permit this arms sale to go forward.

At White House breakfast with 75 Senators,
Washington, June 5/
Los Angeles Times, 6-6:(I)15.

2

[On criticism that he has sold out to terrorism by making an arms deal with Iran in return for Iran's help in freeing U.S. hostages held by Arab terrorists]: The charge has been made that the United States has shipped weapons to Iran as ransom payment for the release of American hostages in Lebanon, that the United States undercut its allies and secretly violated American policy against trafficking with terrorists. Those charges are utterly false. The United States has not made concessions to those who hold our people captive in Lebanon. And we will not. The United States has not swapped boatloads or planeloads of American weapons for the return of American hostages. And we will not . . . During the course of [secret U.S.-Iranian] discussions, I authorized the transfer of small amounts of defensive weapons and spare parts for defensive systems to Iran. My purpose was to convince Teheran that our negotiators were acting with my authority, to send a signal that the United States was prepared to replace the animosity between us with a new relationship . . . But why, you might ask, is any relationship with

Iran important to the United States? Iran encompasses some of the most critical geography in the world. It lies between the Soviet Union and access to the warm waters of the Indian ocean. Geography explains why the Soviet Union has sent an army into Afghanistan to dominate that country and, if they could, Iran and Pakistan. Iran's geography gives it a critical position from which adversaries could interfere with oil flows from the Arab states that border the Persian Gulf. Apart from geography, Iran's oil deposits are important to the long-term health of the world economy. For these reasons, it is in our national interest to watch for changes within Iran that might offer hope for an improved relationship . . . It's because of Iran's strategic importance and its influence in the Islamic world that we chose to probe for a better relationship between our countries . . . We have not, nor will we, capitulate to terrorists. We will, however, get on with advancing the vital interests of our great nation, in spite of terrorists and radicals who seek to sabotage our efforts and immobilize the United States.

Broadcast address to the nation,
Washington, Nov. 13/
The New York Times, 11-14:6.

3

[On the recently revealed secret U.S.-Iran negotiations which involved arms sales to Iran and the release of American hostages held by Arab terrorists]: Eighteen months ago . . . this Administration began a secret initiative to the Islamic Republic of Iran. Our purposes were fourfold: to replace a relationship of total hostility with something better; to bring a negotiated end to the Iran-Iraq war; and to bring an end to terrorism; and to effect the release of our hostages. We knew this undertaking involved great risks, especially for our people and for the Iranian officials with whom we dealt. That's why the information was restricted to appropriate Cabinet officers and those officials with an absolute need to know. This undertaking was a matter of considerable debate within Administration circles. Our policy objectives were never in dispute; there were differences on how best to proceed. The principal issue in contention was whether

(RONALD REAGAN)

we should make isolated and limited exceptions to our arms embargo, as a signal of our serious intent. Several top advisers opposed the sale of even a modest shipment of defensive weapons and spare parts to Iran. Others felt no progress could be made without this sale. I weighed their views, I considered the risks of failure and the rewards of success, and I decided to proceed and the responsibility for the decision and the operation is mine, and mine alone. As [Abraham] Lincoln said of another Presidential decision: If it turns out right, the criticism will not matter. If it turns out wrong, 10 angels swearing I was right will make no difference.

News conference, Washington, 11-20:8.

1

[On the investigation into secret U.S.-Iran negotiations involving arms sales to Iran, release of U.S. hostages held by Arab terrorists and diversion of funds to Nicaraguan rebels]: You will have the full cooperation of all agencies of the Executive Branch and the White House staff in carrying out your assignment. And I want to assure you and the American people that I want all the facts to come out—about learning of a possible transfer of funds from the sale of arms to Iran, to those fighting the [Nicaraguan] Sandinista government. We acted to learn the facts. And we'll continue to share the actions we take and the information we obtain with the American people and the Congress. The appointment of this [investigative] board and the stature of its membership are a demonstration of a commitment to learn how this happened and how it can be prevented in the future.

To panel reviewing the National Security Council, Washington, Dec. 1/ The New York Times, 12-2:4.

2

[On the controversy surrounding secret U.S.-Iran negotiations which involved arms sales to Iran, the freeing of U.S. hostages held by Arab terrorists and the diversion of Iran's arms payments to contra rebels in Nicaragua]: Since the outset of the controversy over our policy relating

to Iran, I've done everything in my power to make all the facts concerning this matter known to the American people. I can appreciate why some of these things are difficult to comprehend, and you're entitled to have your questions answered. And that's why I've pledged to get to the bottom of this matter, and I've said earlier that I would welcome the appointment of an independent counsel to look into allegations of illegality in the sale of arms to Iran and the use of funds from these sales to assist the forces opposing the Sandinista government in Nicaragua . . .
If the investigative processes now set in motion are given an opportunity to work, all the facts concerning Iran and the transfer of funds to assist the anti-Sandinista forces will shortly be made public. Then the American people, you, will be the final arbiter of this controversy. You will have all the facts and will be able to judge for . . . yourselves.

Broadcast address to the nation, Washington, Dec. 2/ The New York Times, 12-3:8.

3

[On the controversy surrounding secret U.S.-Iran negotiations involving arms deals, hostages and Nicaraguan contras]: I have to say that there is bitter bile in my throat these days [about the press' handling of the controversy]. I've never seen the sharks circling like they now are with blood in the water. What is driving me up the wall is that this wasn't a failure until the press got a tip from that rag in Beirut and began to play it up. I told them that publicity could destroy this, that it could get people killed. They then went right on . . . This whole thing boils down to a great irresponsibility on the part of the press. I told them when this broke that there were a whole lot of questions I couldn't answer. I said to them, "Please don't ruin this." [David] Jacobsen, the hostage who had just been released, asked them not to pursue it.

Interview, Washington/Time, 12-8:18.

4

[On the secret U.S.-Iran negotiations involving arms deals and hostage releases]: The Iranians came to us at first. They wanted to talk about

(RONALD REAGAN)

a better relationship. I would not do that with them being a sponsor of terrorism. They said they were trying to do something about terrorism. We said that if they were really sincere, then they could show us by getting the [Arab-held U.S.] hostages released. That was an easy way to prove their sincerity. We got three people back . . . I think we took the only action we could have in Iran. I am not going to disavow it. I do not think it was a mistake. No, it has not worked out the way we hoped [because of the publicity surrounding the revelation of the negotiations]. But I don't see anything I would have done differently.

Interview, Washington/Time, 12-8:18.

Charles E. Redman
Spokesman for the Department of
State of the United States

1

[On the Iran-Iraq war]: We seek the earliest possible end to the war, without victor or vanquished, and with the sovereignty and territorial integrity of both Iran and Iraq intact. To that end, we welcome constructive diplomatic efforts for a settlement. We don't sell arms to either side, nor do we allow transfers by others of U.S.-sourced or licensed arms to either side. We actively discourage shipments of arms from any source to Iran, which remains the intransigent party in the war. Iraq, on the other hand, has indicated its willingness to cooperate with various efforts to bring the war to a negotiated or mediated end.

Dec. 15/The New York Times, 12-16:1.

Donald T. Regan
Chief of Staff to the
President of the United States

2

[On criticism of President Reagan's secret negotiations with Iran, which involved Iran arms purchases and the release of U.S. hostages held by Arab terrorists]: I ask you, what's a human life worth? . . . We're being scorned for this.

[But] if you were taken [hostage], or one of your relatives taken, what would you have us do? Sit as the head of the government in the United States and say, "Look, we won't even talk to you about those hostages"? The President is a man of compassion . . . You have all the families saying, "Please, you've got to do something." We're being branded as calloused, [that] we don't give a darn about these hostages . . . But when you try to do something to get the hostages out, immediately "You're swapping human flesh; you're indulging in some nefarious practice." I ask you, think it through. What would you have us do if you were in our position?

To reporters,
Washington, Nov. 14/
The Washington Post, 11-15:(A)26.

3

[On the recently revealed U.S. secret negotiations with Iran which involved arms sales to Iran and the release of American hostages held by Arab terrorists]: We had tried many, many channels to get the hostages back, and they all failed. So we tried this one. [The Iranians] wanted us to send some defensive weapons as evidence of our good faith. We demanded they stop terrorism and show us evidence of their good faith. And we got three [hostages] back.

To reporters, Washington,
Nov. 14/Time, 11-24:20.

Zaid Rifai
Prime Minister of Jordan

4

[Criticizing the recently revealed secret sale of arms by the U.S. to Iran]: [The shipment was] the exact opposite of the declared American policy. It was certainly against our joint efforts with the United States to contact all our friends and others to prevent arms from reaching Iran . . . It was a very shocking development and a regrettable one. The explanations that are given are not convincing and did a lot of damage to American credibility in the area.

Interview, Amman, Nov. 19/
The New York Times, 11-20:9.

G. Henry M. Schuler
Authority on Libya, Center for
Strategic and International Studies,
Georgetown University

1

[Criticizing the U.S. for the military confrontation with Libya in the Gulf of Sidra]: [Libya leader Muammar] Qaddafi is a zealot and a revolutionary, and Lenin said a revolutionary probes with a sword until he encounters steel. Qaddafi has been probing now for 17 years and has never encountered steel . . . I have been a longtime advocate of getting tough with Qaddafi, but my preferred vehicle for that was economic sanctions, tough sanctions to isolate him politically and economically because, without the oil exports and the revenues, [he can't] stir up terrorism around the world or suppress the domestic discontent . . . [But U.S. President Reagan] gives the orders and [U.S. Defense Secretary] Cap Weinberger says, "Aye, aye, sir!" And off they go [with the U.S. Navy to the Gulf of Sidra]. With sanctions you've got to get all those bureaucrats in the State Department . . . and all the vested commercial interests to work together, so it's just easier to use the military . . . and I think that's a damn shame!

Interview, Washington/
The Washington Post, 3-27:(D)8.

Talcott Seelye
Former United States
Ambassador to Syria

2

[Saying the U.S. pays too much attention to Libyan leader Muammar Qaddafi as an instigator of international terrorism]: This reflects a juvenile and ridiculous obsession with this small dictator, who is only a pinprick in our side and no threat to our national security. Anytime we get involved in trying to overthrow the head of a government, we will be shown up sooner or later and we stigmatize the people we're trying to support and the subsequent regime is weakened.

The Christian Science Monitor, 10-3:32.

Yitzhak Shamir
Foreign Minister of Israel

3

[On Israel's recent forcing down of a Libyan airliner suspected of carrying a Palestinian terrorist, and then later letting the plane go when the terrorist wasn't found]: It is known that Libya is a center of international terrorism, and the Libyan government assists the terrorist organizations to perpetrate terrorist acts against Israel, against Israelis and against Jews. And when reports come in about such a danger, Israel has the right to take measures in order to prevent acts of murder and sabotage.

Feb. 4/Los Angeles Times, 2-5:(I)14.

4

All the Arab leaders at the time of the Second World War were great admirers of [Adolf] Hitler, and they are still admirers of him. [Both radical and moderate Arab leaders admire Hitler for his] hatred of the Jews, his leadership, his success in exterminating so many hated Jews. They admire force and violence. It's not very pleasant to say, but it's a fact in the Arab world that democracy doesn't have any meaning.

Interview, United Nations,
New York, May 2/
The New York Times, 5-3:8.

Yitzhak Shamir
Foreign Minister, and
Prime Minister-designate, of Israel

5

Of course I will try to improve our contacts with all our [Arab] neighbors. I don't say that I will accept their positions. That's impossible. But we will try to discuss and find common ground. You don't have to be desperate. Never be desperate. That is my slogan. I am not afraid of taking risks. We have to take risks for peace. I admit there is a Palestinian problem. They are not happy to live under our rule. We have to find a solution without giving up our rights in the [occupied] territories. A very large majority of Israelis is against giving up our rights. And the Arab side is not yet ready for compromises. It's a fact. Therefore, we have to find a stable solution—not a permanent solution—a stable solution, a modus vivendi.

Interview, Jerusalem/
The New York Times, 10-21:4.

Yitzhak Shamir
Prime Minister of Israel

1

In general, we know that countries that manufacture arms must also export arms. Otherwise they are incapable of maintaining an arms industry. These countries publish virtually nothing about their arms exports. This is accepted procedure everywhere because there is competition . . . Israel, which also has to take part in this race, cannot be the exception. Therefore, we do not talk very much about this subject.

Broadcast interview/
The Washington Post, 12-12:(A)14.

Farouk al-Sharaa
Foreign Minister of Syria

2

[Saying the anti-terrorism campaign in the U.S. has turned into an anti-Arab campaign]: I cannot understand the unjustified campaign against the Arabs in the United States. It is not in the interests of peace in the region and in the world at large, and we believe this is a racist campaign against the Arabs which must be stopped.

Broadcast interview/
"Face the Nation," CBS-TV, 5-25.

3

[The Israelis] consider the Lebanese national resistance movement as terrorists, while we don't. We believe they are heroes defending the sovereignty of their country . . . We in Syria condemn terrorism in all its forms . . . [meaning] any act of violence directed against civilians, innocent people.

Interview, New York/Newsweek, 10-13:52.

Ariel Sharon
Minister for Industry and
Trade, and former Minister of
Defense, of Israel

4

[On the recent terrorist massacre of Jews at a synagogue in Turkey]: The terrible pogrom carried out against Jews during their prayer in a synagogue in Istanbul is the horrible and single answer of the Palestinians and their supporters to the pleas for peace and to the Israeli concessions. The concessions to the PLO, [Jordan's] King Hussein and [Morocco's] King Hassan, including the grave concessions on the Taba issue, were interpreted as Israeli weakness and invited the aggressiveness of the Palestinian terrorism, which is supported by Libya and Syria and also finds refuge until this day in Jordan. This endless running after unreliable peace plans, which have no foundation, while at the same time our enemies conduct an endless war against us, has contributed to a slackening of the Israeli defense, a decline in our preparedness and vigilance and to making Jews in Israel and all over the world even more vulnerable to Palestinian terror.

Message read to Israeli radio, Sept. 6/
The New York Times, 9-8:1,4.

Rashad Shawa
Former Mayor of
Israeli-occupied Gaza

5

[Saying the PLO should concentrate on negotiating the peaceful return of such Israeli-occupied territories as Gaza and the West Bank, rather than on trying to militarily overthrow Israel]: I don't think anybody can truly feel what is going on in the occupied territories other than those living there 24 hours a day. Outside, people talk about how awful the occupation is, then they go to work and forget about it. If there are those who want Haifa [Israel] back, let them go fight for it. If they cannot, they must save what is left.

Interview/The Christian
Science Monitor, 7-21:9.

George P. Shultz
*Secretary of State of
the United States*

1

[On the current military confrontation between the U.S. and Libya in the Gulf of Sidra]: The purpose is not to put [Libyan leader Muammar] Qaddafi in his box—but that is where he belongs. The purpose is to assert an international right that all countries recognize . . . the freedom of the seas [in international waters].

USA Today, 3-26:(A)10.

2

I think it is interesting what is happening in people's attitudes toward Libya. Nobody argues that there are any particular merits to Libya or [Libyan leader Muammar] Qaddafi anymore. Everyone seems to agree that Qaddafi is a problem. The only argument is what is the right tactic in handling him. I think people are moving in the direction of more action. We [the U.S.] are the most active. [It is impossible to] ignore it [Libyan policy such as support for international terrorism] and hope it will go away. You have to combat it. We are trying to persuade people of that.

*To reporters on flight en route to Washington,
March 30/Los Angeles Times, 3-31:(I)8.*

3

[Addressing Libyan leader Muammar Qaddafi, saying the Western nations are now united in their fight against terrorism as practiced by Qaddafi]: You've had it, pal. You are isolated. You are recognized as a terrorist. And, as far as terrorists are concerned, more and more the message is: No place to hide.

*News conference, Tokyo, May 5/
The New York Times, 5-7:12.*

4

[Supporting U.S. President Reagan's proposal for a $354-million arms sale to Saudi Arabia]: [If Iranian influence grows in that area,] America's strategic interests will be harmed and, needless to say, so will Israel's. There are many in the Arab world who want peace and stability and moderation—and who can be brought

to accept the permanent reality of the state of Israel. But if America cannot demonstrate that we are a constant, effective, strong and responsive presence in the Middle East, those with the best of inclinations inevitably will make their accommodations with those who bear the worst intentions toward us.

*Before American Jewish Committee,
Washington, May 15/
The New York Times, 5-16:6.*

5

[On the U.S. attack on Libya last April in retaliation for Libya's involvement in international terrorism]: I think our actions, not only the raid against Libya but our whole coordinated set of actions, have had a good effect and are helping us in the effort to win the war against terrorism. The war is far from over, but I think we've made important progress. There's no doubt that [U.S. President Reagan's] actions had an impact on Libya. Libya has been isolated, and we also got the attention of other states involved in terrorism as well. So I think it's been a very good Presidential action. I thought it looked very good in prospect, but I think as you look back on it and see what's happened since the strike, it's a better and better decision.

Interview/USA Today, 8-5:(A)7.

6

[On criticism by the U.S. press that the U.S. used misinformation, reported by the press, to confuse Libyan leader Muammar Qaddafi regarding U.S. military maneuvers and other actions so as to keep him off guard and discourage further Libyan involvement in international terrorism]: You people in the news business enjoy not allowing the U.S. to do anything in secret if you can help it. So if the fleet moves from one place to another, you are determined to report it even though we might want to have it operate secretly. It is very difficult for that to happen. So we can absolutely bank on the fact that if the fleet does something or other, you will scream. Qaddafi will hear it, and the fleet may, or may not, be getting ready to do something [against Qaddafi] . . . If I were a private citizen reading about it, and I read that my government was try-

WHAT THEY SAID IN 1986

(GEORGE P. SHULTZ)

ing to confuse somebody who was conducting terrorist acts and murdering Americans, I would say, "Gee, I hope it is true" . . . If there are ways we can make Qaddafi nervous, why shouldn't we? And I described one of them. That is not deceiving you [the press], but just using your predictable tendencies to report things that we try to keep secret. So we label it a big secret and you will find out about it and you will report it. You know that. The higher the classification, the quicker you will report it. So you are predictable in that sense.

News conference, United Nations, New York, Oct. 2/The New York Times, 10-3:4.

1

[On whether he thinks any further U.S. arms should be sent to Iran after the secret U.S.-Iran negotiations were recently revealed]: Under the circumstances of Iran's war with Iraq, its pursuit of terrorism, its association with those holding our hostages, I would certainly say, as far as I'm concerned, no.

Broadcast interview/ "Face the Nation," CBS-TV, 11-16.

2

[On the current scandal involving secret U.S. negotiations and arms deals with Iran]: I supported and continue to support . . . the idea of trying to see if we can't rearrange the furniture a little insofar as [U.S. relations with] Iran is concerned. And there are various ways to try to do that which I support, and which is the President's [Reagan] basic intent. So I support his policy. However, when it comes to the use of arms [sales], I have a different view. But I do believe it's a legitimate subject for debate as a policy matter. The President listened to views, pro and con, and he has said publicly that in the end he decided that he should send a signal—I think that was his word—to Iran to show our serious intent. And so he authorized some arms shipments to Iran for that purpose.

Before House Foreign Affairs Committee, Washington, Dec. 8/ The New York Times, 12-9:6.

Larry Speakes
Principal Deputy Press Secretary to the President of the United States

3

[On the current U.S.-Libyan military confrontation in the Gulf of Sidra]: [U.S. naval maneuvers in the Gulf was] not an act designed to provoke a response or to humiliate [Libyan leader Muammar] Qaddafi. The exercise was one among many in a global program in support of the traditional maritime rights—which, if we do not assert from time to time, tend to be eroded and encroached upon. We simply cannot allow other nations to dictate where we or anyone else cannot go if that place happens to be recognized international waters and airspace . . . We were there. We filed a notice. We indicated that we were going to operate in this zone in a peaceful manner. We did so. We were attacked. We were attacked by six missiles. And then, and only then, did we respond.

News conference, Washington, March 24/ Los Angeles Times, 3-25:(I)13.

4

[On the U.S. attack on Libya in retaliation for that country's involvement in international terrorism]: U.S. military forces this evening have executed a series of carefully planned air strikes against terrorist-related targets in Libya. These strikes have been completed and our aircraft are returning. Libya bears direct responsibility for the bombing in West Berlin on April 5 that resulted in the death of [U.S.] Army Sergeant Kenneth Ford and injury to a number of American servicemen and others. In light of this reprehensible act of violence and clear evidence that Libya is planning future attacks, the United States has chosen to exercise its right of self-defense. It is our hope this action will preempt and discourage Libyan attacks against innocent civilians in the future.

April 14/The Washington Post, 4-15:(A)21.

Margaret Thatcher
Prime Minister of the United Kingdom

5

[On the current military confrontation between the U.S. and Libya in the Gulf of Sidra]:

(MARGARET THATCHER)

The United States ships and aircraft were operating in international waters and airspace and they have every right to do so. It is important that international waters and airspace be kept open and we support their right to so operate.

London, March 25/The New York Times, 3-26:5.

1

[On her country's recent cooperation in allowing U.S. attack planes based in Britain to attack Libya in retaliation for Libya's involvement in international terrorism]: Terrorism is a scourge of the modern age. Libya has been behind much of it and was planning more. The United Kingdom itself has suffered from Libya's actions . . . The United States, after trying other means, has now sought by limited military action to induce the Libyan regime to desist from terrorism. That is in the British interest. It is why the government supports the U.S. action.

Before British House of Commons, London, April 15/The Washington Post, 4-16:(A)20.

2

[On the recent U.S. attack on Libya in response to Libya's alleged involvement in international terrorism]: Terrorism thrives on appeasement. The time had come for action. The United States took it. Their decision was justified. As friends and allies, we support them.

Before British House of Commons, London, April 16/Los Angeles Times, 4-17:(I)18.

3

We believe you [Israel] will only find the security you seek by recognizing the legitimate rights of the Palestinian people . . . A future in which two classes of people [Israelis and Palestinians living in Israeli-occupied West Bank and Gaza] have to coexist with different rights and different standards is surely not one which Israel can accept. [Israel should allow] the Palestinians to play a greater role in managing their own affairs [to encourage] the emergence of responsible political leaders ready for peace.

At dinner in her honor, Jerusalem, May 25/Los Angeles Times, 5-26:(I)8.

4

We support the right of self-determination for the Palestinian people. We believe that the present proposal of a federation with Jordan would be the one most likely to achieve success and the welcome of the states concerned and among the wider world. You try always when you are working on these matters to go for the situation which will achieve the widest acceptance, because there's no point in working toward anything that will raise other difficulties and other problems.

News conference, Jerusalem, May 27/The Washington Post, 5-28:(A)25.

Harry Wald
Israeli representative, U.S.-based Anti-Defamation League of B'nai B'rith

5

[On the increasing orthodox-secular strife in Israel]: What we're trying to say is that extremism, of whatever stripe, threatens the fabric of a democratic society . . . As American Jews, we don't feel we can afford to ignore this kind of malady and look forward to a society we can enjoy and identify with in the coming years. If we, the Diaspora Jewry, become alienated from Israel, it is going to become very difficult for us to do our work maintaining support for Israel in the United States.

Los Angeles Times, 6-17:(I)8.

Vernon A. Walters
United States Ambassador/Permanent Representative to the United Nations

6

[On the recent U.S. air attack on Libya in retaliation for that country's involvement in international terrorism]: Three days ago, the United States, joined by several other members of this [UN Security] Council, voted against [a] flawed document which unjustifiably condemned U.S. action in Libya. [Those voting for it] should know that my country is deeply indignant and will not forget this totally one-sided view of these recent events. I repeat, how many Americans must die before we will be recognized as having the right to take some action? . . . It has

(VERNON A. WALTERS)

been astonishing for me to hear my country denounced before this Council by some countries
which have sought and received active cooperation from the United States in dealing with their
own problems involving terrorism and have not
shrunk from using extreme force themselves to
deal with this problem.

At UN Security Council meeting, April/
The Washington Post, 5-22:(A)18.

1

[Defending the U.S. air attack against Libya in
retaliation for that country's involvement in international terrorism]: When quiet diplomacy, public
condemnation, economic sanctions and demonstrations of military force failed to dissuade
[Libyan leader Muammar] Qaddafi, this self-
defense action became necessary . . . [Qaddafi]
has made terrorism an integral element of his
foreign policy. Libyan attacks are not simply the
random use of violence, but concerted violence
directed against the values, interests and democratic institutions of all freedom-loving states. It
is a clear assault on international order.

At United Nations, New York, April 15/
Los Angeles Times, 4-16:(I)12.

Caspar W. Weinberger
Secretary of Defense of the United States

2

[Approving the recent U.S. attack on Libya in
retaliation for that country's involvement in international terrorism]: We shouldn't do any indiscriminate act or take action simply because
we're angry or tired or irritated. We had very
clear evidence of the ordering of the act [the recent terrorist bombing in Berlin], the reporting
of the act, the congratulations that passed back
and forth [between Libya and operatives in
Berlin], and so on . . . The other thing important to do is pinpoint your response to people
you know perpetrated [terrorism], and do it in a
way that minimizes collateral damage . . . The
question is what [else can] you do when you
have tried a great many things, including economic boycotts, allied persuasion, and attempts

to reason and all the rest, and actually advised
that future terrorist acts would bring this kind of
cost? What do you do when it continues? When
you have complete proof of connection to the
very terrible act of terrorism?

Interview, Boston/
The Christian Science Monitor, 4-18:6.

John C. Whitehead
Deputy Secretary of State of the United States

3

[Saying he hopes the U.S. will not have to use
military force to dissuade Libyan leader Muammar el-Qaddafi from further involvement in international terrorism]: I feel optimistic from what
I've seen that while this man may be pretty crazy,
he's also crazy like a fox, and he will do what he
needs to do to keep himself in power . . . The
answer lies not in our hands, but in Qaddafi's
hands, because if he continues to sponsor and
direct and conduct these atrocities around the
world, aimed at innocent people, murders of innocent people, we cannot stand idly by, neither
we nor our allies . . . I think sometimes that too
much is made of the details of Libyan involvement in particular incidents. And I just ask you
all a sort of rhetorical question: Can there be
any question that Qaddafi is generally involved
in widespread terrorist activity—widespread incidents where innocent people are murdered?

News conference, Washington, Jan. 27/
The New York Times, 1-28:5.

Elie Wiesel
Author; Winner, 1986 Nobel Peace Prize

4

[On the Israel-Palestinian conflict]: . . .
there are the Palestinians to whose plight I am
sensitive but whose methods [used against Is-
rael] I deplore. Violence and terrorism are not
the answer. Something must be done about their
suffering, and soon. I trust Israel, for I have
faith in the Jewish people. Let Israel be given a
chance, let hatred and danger be removed from
her horizons, and there will be peace in and
around the Holy Land.

Accepting Nobel Peace Prize, Oslo,
Dec. 10/The New York Times, 12-11:8.

War and Peace

Mortimer Adler
*Educator; Director, Institute
for Philosophical Research*

1

The agenda for the world, I think, puts world peace at the top, the prevention of nuclear devastation. [But] the world must understand peace as something other than a negative condition, which is the absence of fighting. Peace, as a positive condition, is that situation in which individuals and peoples can solve all their problems, all their conflicts, by law and by talk rather than by force. That has been said by the wisest men of all times. [But] how do you do that? You do it only through the operation of the machinery of government. Wherever you have peace positively, you have civil peace. And civil peace is the product of civil government—the use of law and authorized force to maintain peace.

*Interview, Aspen, Colo./
The Christian Science Monitor, 9-23:17.*

Sissela Bok
*Social philosopher;
Teacher in humanities and ethics,
Brandeis University*

2

I think that almost all approaches that try to move toward peace have something to be said for them. But one problem I guess I see . . . with many peace movements all over the world is that they are so focused on weapons. I certainly would say that we have to do something about weapons—we have to move toward disarmament, absolutely. But that is far from the only approach that we have to take. I think, if anything, it's more important to work at the political attitudes that nations have toward one another, and the various political actions that they choose to take.

*Interview,
Cambridge, Mass./
The Christian Science Monitor, 10-22:16.*

Mikhail S. Gorbachev
*General Secretary, Communist
Party of the Soviet Union*

3

In our efforts for peace, we should be guided by an awareness of the fact that today history has willed our two nations [the U.S. and the Soviet Union] to bear an enormous responsibility to the peoples of our two countries and, indeed, the peoples of all countries, for preserving life on earth. Our duty to all humankind is to offer it a safe prospect of peace, a prospect of entering the third millennium without fear. Let us commit ourselves to doing away with the threat hanging over humanity. Let us not shift that task onto our children's shoulders.

*Broadcast address to the U.S., Moscow,
Jan. 1/The New York Times, 1-2:4.*

John Paul II
Pope

4

Justice and peace cannot be separated. A peace which does not take justice into account would only be a mirage. An authentic peace must have deep roots founded on the dignity of man and his inalienable rights. There cannot exist true peace if there does not exist a serious commitment and resolution to the application of social justice.

*To diplomatic corps, Bogota, Colombia,
July 2/The New York Times, 7-3:3.*

Curtis LeMay
*General (ret.) and former Chief of Staff,
United States Air Force*

5

. . . I don't think much of war. I think that's a stupid way to solve all of your problems. But sometimes you can't make the decision, because somebody makes it for you, and you either have to fight or give up. Once you're in a war, or you've made the decision to use military force to

(CURTIS LeMAY)

solve your problem, then you ought to use it, and get the thing over with as quick as you can.

Interview/USA Today, 7-23:(A)9.

Colman McCarthy
Newspaper columnist; Adjunct professor, American University
1

[On the classes he teaches promoting pacifism and non-violence]: We masterfully educate our kids in the history of war: Caesar's wars, Napoleonic wars, civil wars, World Wars I and II, preparation for World War III. We romanticize the militarists: George Washington, Robert E. Lee, Davy Crockett, Patton. The kids are taught all about battles of Valley Forge, Gettysburg, Lexington and Concord. But they know little about Gandhi, King, Dorothy Day, Tolstoy, Jeanette Rankin, Jesus, St. Francis of Assisi, Jane Addams, Daniel Berrigan, or the triumphs of non-violence from the salt march in India to the successful resistance of the Danes to the Nazis. I begin by explaining that it is okay to believe in force as a way to solve a problem or a conflict—the force of justice, force of love, force of sharing wealth, and the force of organized non-violent resistance. Fighting with those kinds of effective forces is the essence of pacifism. The force of violence has failed.

Interview/USA Today, 1-28:(A)7.

Robert S. McNamara
Former Secretary of Defense of the United States; Former President, International Bank for Reconstruction and Development (World Bank)
2

I don't believe that any well-informed, coolly rational military or civilian leader on either side, East or West, would initiate the use of nuclear weapons. But it has been my experience—and I think it is a widely shared experience—that military and civilian leaders in times of crisis are neither well-informed nor coolly rational. And I, for one, am not prepared to accept the

risk that these [East-West] political rivalries will not, over a period of decades, upon occasion lead to military confrontation.

*Interview, New York/
The Christian Science Monitor, 12-16:20.*

Roger Mollander
President, Roosevelt Center for American Policy Studies
3

[On the proliferation of nuclear weapons]: The mindset to fight what I call "nuclear creep" can only come by seeing how bad it could become. There is no chance of talking countries out of the bomb if the U.S. and the Soviet Union keep building them. So the first thing you realize is, you've got to corral that competition and get it going in the other direction. Second, you slow down this diffusion of nuclear technology . . . The [human] species has survived for four billion years, partly from reasoning our way past difficult problems, although this one is the Everest of earthly problems. We could get better at resolving conflicts so they don't fester to the point where somebody says, "I'm going to build a bomb."

Interview/USA Today, 6-10:(A)9.

Richard M. Nixon
Former President of the United States
4

The world was technically at peace in the late 1970s and yet, during that time, 100 million people fell under the rule of Communist regimes or were otherwise lost to the West. That is an example of the Soviet Union's definition of peace at work. Real peace is the absence of war combined with the perpetuation and the extension of freedom. That is the definition of peace upon which the United States and its European allies agree.

Interview/USA Today, 12-24:(A)7.

Linus Pauling
Winner, 1954 Nobel Prize in chemistry; Winner, 1962 Nobel Peace Prize
5

[On nuclear weapons]: While it is surely great that we have them, I deplore the fact that

(LINUS PAULING)

they killed so many millions of people at Hiroshima and Nagasaki [in World War II]. Back in 1945, before the atomic bombs were exploded, I thought it would be impossible to avoid the third and the fourth world wars. War was such a part of the history of human beings that I couldn't see it being abolished. But with the nuclear deterrent, of course, we have abolished war between the United States and the Soviet Union.

Interview/USA Today, 3-11:(A)7.

Betty Williams Perkins
Co-winner, 1977 Nobel Peace Prize

1

[1986 was a] devastatingly bad year for peace, but a good year for peace workers . . . People are at the stage where they see the insanity of war.

Interview/USA Today, 12-22:(A)4.

Ronald Reagan
President of the United States

2

We want to make this a more peaceful world. We don't just want signing ceremonies and color photographs of leaders toasting each other with champagne. We want agreements that really work—with no cheating. We want an end to intimidation, threats and the constant quest for domination. We want real peace.

Broadcast address to the nation,
Washington, Feb. 26/
USA Today, 2-27:(A)9.

3

We owe a promise to look at the world with a steady gaze, and perhaps a resigned toughness, knowing that we have adversaries in the world and challenges, and that the only way to meet them and maintain the peace is by staying

strong . . . We must be strong enough to create peace where it does not exist, and be strong enough to protect it where it does.

Memorial Day address, Washington,
May 26/The Washington Post, 5-27:(A)12.

4

The United States believes that respect for the individual, for the dignity of the human person . . . does not belong in the realm of charity or "humanitarian" causes. Respect for human rights is not social work; it is not merely an act of compassion. It is the first obligation of government and the source of its legitimacy. It also is the foundation stone in any structure of world peace. All through history, it has been the dictatorships and the tyrannies that have surrendered first to the cult of militarism and the pursuit of war. Countries based on the consent of the governed, countries that recognize the inalienable rights of the individual, do not make war on each other. Peace is more than just the absence of war. True peace is justice; true peace is freedom. And true peace dictates the recognition of human rights.

At United Nations, New York, Sept. 22/
The Washington Post, 9-23:(A)16.

Richard von Weizsacker
President of West Germany

5

I believe it is not totally unthinkable that the kind of war which history has taught us [up through] the 20th century . . . is not the kind of power struggle [that will characterize] the next century. I don't think mankind, in its character, will change. And I don't think power struggles will be exterminated altogether. But it is possible that . . . [the] means to go ahead with this power struggle will not necessarily include war, a military [form of] war, as it did in history.

Interview, Bonn/
The Christian Science Monitor, 12-12:27.

PART THREE

General

The Arts

Heinz Berggruen
Art collector

1

[On today's prices paid for art at auctions]: It's insane. It's a hyped market, overplayed. There is a lot of people involved with fresh money who don't know what this is all about. I find it absolutely frightening and out of proportion, when a tiny Leonardo drawing goes for exactly the same price as a Jasper Johns painting. I think there's too much speculation. The market is over-extended, and there may be a rude awakening when people wake up and find they went too far.

The New York Times, 11-24:12.

John Brademas
President, New York University

2

Ronald Reagan is the first [U.S.] President of the last quarter-century to have mounted an assault on programs to support the arts . . . It is sheer nonsense to expect that state and local governments, corporations or foundations can fill the immense gap in funds for the arts that would be the consequence of [such] proposals.

At meeting of National Council of Grant Makers in the Arts, New York/ Los Angeles Times, 11-17:8.

Joseph Brodsky
Exiled Soviet poet

3

[Expressing skepticism that recent claimed liberalization in Soviet policy toward the arts will soon restore the country's cultural glory]: I do not think administrative changes are instrumental in the flowering of culture. Literature is the product of an individual's intuition. That can't be orchestrated.

U.S. News & World Report, 12-15:69.

Norman Corwin
Visiting professor, School of Journalism, University of Southern California; Former radio dramatist

4

In entertainment, and in literature, there is a deliberate aim taken at a particular audience. An audience whose tastes are not high, an audience that ranges from passive to voyeuristic, to one that is hungry for titillation. That explains the success of the formula novel, the success of many television programs, and films too.

Interview/USA Today, 8-18:(A)9.

Thor Eckert
Music critic, "The Christian Science Monitor"

5

It seems to me that, on the most obvious level, we remember in the course of history more about the artworks and the art masterworks of a civilization—be they plays, paintings, sculpture or whatever—than we remember about the day-to-day, nitty-gritty life-style of that particular civilization. So art is, in a sense, the enduring testament of a civilization about what it has been able to achieve. We look to the arts, perhaps, to connect to what is best in the history of mankind.

Interview, New York/ The Christian Science Monitor, 7-22:23.

Asher Edelman
Art collector

6

[Winning at art auctions] has become the substitute for a car with fins or a view in your apartment. I don't like going [to art auctions] any more, because it's like a hog pit. It's the place to exhibit your manlihood in its fullest fashion. It makes the auctions a less pleasant place to be. But it's patronage. It creates an environment in which more art, and more good art, is created.

351

WHAT THEY SAID IN 1986

(ASHER EDELMAN)

So I think one should not be so quick to criticize.

The New York Times, 11-24:12.

Frank Hodsoll
*Chairman, National Endowment
for the Arts of the United States*

1

[On the Endowment's support of large arts institutions]: It is important to say that for the best of the big boys, we will continue to support them with an important measure—it will never be a large measure—of their support. Probably our largest individual grants will still go to the banner institutions that set the standards of excellence for everybody else. While they have greater access to the power structure, they have greater needs. I guess I am speaking out of two sides of my mouth. While we are going to try to provide a special safety net for the smaller arts groups, we are also very mindful of our duty toward the best, who may be big.

*Washington, Feb. 5/
The New York Times, 2-6:11.*

Arata Isozaki
Architect

2

[On the boom in museum building]: In the past, religious buildings had a strong role in the society. Now art is coming to take over the position where the gods are no more. Making art is something like the religious act. Even the activity of raising funds and collecting art for the museum is like the religious activity of the past.

Interview/Los Angeles Times, 5-23:(I)1.

Yousuf Karsh
Portrait photographer

3

[On his portrait subjects]: I can tell you this: The men are more vain than the women. The one problem with actors is they often like to look like their professional roles. You must disarm them

of their public masks . . . For me, each photograph is a biography. I am interested in people who make their mark on this world, not only the great and famous but the unknown as well. But it is hard to find someone who has made a mark like Churchill.

*Interview, Washington/
USA Today, 1-21:(D)5.*

Richard Koshalek
*Director, Museum of
Contemporary Art, Los Angeles*

4

Museums have become a sexy subject. More people want to be involved. We already have 25,000 members, which is practically unheard of [for a new museum]. Everybody is excited, but also worried. Is there enough art and people and money to support all this? I'm worried about finding talented people to be curators and run the museums.

Interview/Los Angeles Times, 5-23:(I)22.

Nathan Leventhal
*President, Lincoln Center for
the Performing Arts, New York*

5

[Criticizing the proposed Federal tax-reform plan which would reduce incentives to contribute to arts organizations]: It seems a little inconsistent to me for the [Reagan] Administration to be continually emphasizing the importance of private voluntary support of the arts, while at the same time reducing tax incentives for that private support. Arts organizations will feel the pinch of this whipsaw action.

Interview/The New York Times, 6-17:12.

Samuel Lipman
*Member, National Council on the Arts;
Publisher, "The New Criterion"*

6

It is illusory to raise mone, for the arts by advertising the tax benefits that come to the giver. One is under the illusion that one is developing a class of patrons, but they are not really patrons

(SAMUEL LIPMAN)

because the gifts are relatively cost-free. It is not enough for a donor to give money. He should give part of his life, representing some commitment to the arts. The best patronage is motivated not by tax considerations, but by love and knowledge of art.

The New York Times, 6-17:12.

Alison Lurie
Pulitzer Prize-winning author

1

I think the problem, not only in literature but in all the arts, in the theatre and sports, is that there's a very great "what-have-you-done-for-me-lately?" view. If you haven't done something within the last 12 months, your reputation shrinks every day, and the temperature goes down until you do something else. I see this happening to all my friends who are writers. Their temperature goes up and down in this ridiculous way.

Interview/USA Today, 4-18:(A)13.

Robert Motherwell
Painter

2

One wonderful thing about creativity is that you're never wholly satisfied with what you're trying to do. There's always the anguish, the pleasurable challenge . . . I was startled at how many people asked, "Have you retired yet?" They explained that they thought so because I'd been well-known for so long. Then, the idea of age became very vivid to me. For me to retire from painting would be to retire from life.

Interview/The New York Times, 1-22:16.

Anne Gaynor Murphy
Director, American Arts Alliance

3

. . . the product I'm lobbying for [the arts] is so important to the future of society that I can think of nothing I'd rather do. Because without creativity, we're going to self-destruct. Society does not move forward without vision, and vi-

sion is inspired by creativity. The role of the arts in this country is to inspire creativity, to make people have a new way of looking at something. It may only happen twice in your lifetime, but if something helps you to look at something differently, you're a different person . . . And right now we're looking at a society that is being limited, and my role is to say, "I won't accept those limits" . . . A community doesn't choose whether it's going to support a fire department or a police department. We're not talking about either-or. If everything is gray and we have no outlets, we're not going to move forward.

Interview, Washington/
Los Angeles Times, 4-9:(VI)1,4.

John Pope-Hennessy
Art historian and critic

4

Art history, to me, is made up of a continuing succession of evaluations and re-evaluations; just because something has been said or written before does not mean it can stand as the last word. I have always been interested in results, in original conclusions which will then inevitably supersede old ones—not just in the writings of others, but very much in my own work as well. I will continue to try to strike a balance between the necessity for a "program"—an intellectual scheme applied to the work itself—and free invention. Both must coexist in order for art history and art criticism to be properly undertaken.

Interview/Publishers Weekly, 1-24:59.

Earl Powell
Director, Los Angeles
County Museum of Art

5

Museums used to be musty places for musing alone. Today we have a better-educated audience that wants something more than backpacking on the weekend. One study found the average museum-goer today—along with increasing numbers of school groups and senior citizens—is young, college-educated and upward mobile. The description tallies almost exactly with that of the yuppie. Museums are becoming

WHAT THEY SAID IN 1986

(EARL POWELL)

easy-way-to-learn formats for general education.

Interview/Los Angeles Times, 5-23:(I)22.

Lloyd Richards
Dean, School of Drama,
Yale University

1

The arts, for me, [have] always been something that brought perspective to events—that *illuminated*, not just *represented*, the moment . . . The arts must in some way retain a position of attempting to find perspective for man in all of this. [They must] define whatever [the] new society is that we're evolving—to find what are the values, and hopefully to try and find better methods of human exchange and interchange.

Interview, New Haven, Conn./
The Christian Science Monitor, 11-4:18,19.

Irving Sandler
Professor of art history,
State University of New York, Purchase

2

[Calling for legislation that would increase artists' rights to include resale royalties, protection against alteration of their work by others, etc.]: A work of art is not just a piece of property like a chair or a table. At least, it ought to possess the status of a dog or a cat. We have laws prohibiting cruelty to animals. We ought to have laws prohibiting cruelty to works of art.

At discussion of the proposed legislation,
New York, Nov. 18/The New York Times, 11-19:16.

Andres Segovia
Guitarist

3

Art renews the spirit. If you get tired of reading the same poem, or seeing the same painting, the fault isn't in the art. It's in yourself, when you fail to vibrate to beauty.

Interview, New York/
Los Angeles Times, 7-16:(VI)5.

Vitaly Suslov
Deputy curator,
Hermitage Museum,
Leningrad, U.S.S.R.

4

A museum is a storing place for the ideas of humans, from generation to generation . . . Experience shows us that each generation has more of an interest in the past than the preceding one.

Interview, Leningrad/
The Christian Science Monitor, 5-22:15.

Paul Taylor
Choreographer

5

Everyone asks how you do it, where it comes from. As far as I know, nobody's been able to say. I certainly haven't. But there are many people like me, who early in life were encouraged to think of themselves as being special and at the same time isolated. They were forced to entertain themselves with made-up games and imaginery playmates, and their imaginations flourished. Later, if they go into some artform, they tend to carry that childhood creativity with them . . . What we're all trying to do is create a little world—maybe not a real one, but you populate it with idealized, imaginery beings . . . Art is just a grown-up game!

Interview, New York/
The Christian Science Monitor, 4-28:30.

Gary Trudeau
Cartoonist

6

What's happening in fine arts right now is something that's anathema to me. When it comes to art, I am at heart a cultural conservative. I believe in anachronistic concepts like discipline and craft and draftsmanship. There's a kind of careerism at work, a repudiation of any sense of synthesizing and creating a body of work over a period of time. There's more of an emphasis on making it immediately than letting the work evolve.

Interview, New York/
The Washington Post, 11-12:(D)15.

Jon Vickers

Opera singer

1

The foundation on which I stand as an artist is that art must appeal to the intellect. When it passes through the senses to the intellect, then we're making a contribution to civilization and the uplifting of humanity. But if we choose to indulge ourselves and chase dollars and fame at the expense of artistic integrity, if we smear the line between what is entertainment and what is art, between what is art and what is artifice, between what is a service to the art performed and what one could get out of exploiting that art form, we're in trouble.

Interview, London/Opera News, 3-1:43.

Ted Weiss

United States Representative, D-New York

2

In spite of the efforts of cultural organizations to take on a larger part of the financial burden [in supporting the arts], their efforts are continually being undermined. The [Reagan] Administration's persistent efforts to eliminate postal subsidies for non-profit organizations have resulted in a 45 per cent increase in mailing costs since January 1 . . . Spiraling real estate costs are squeezing artists out of necessary rehearsal and performance space. Insurance costs have become prohibitive. Corporate mergers are eliminating corporate arts programs, and proposed changes in the tax code may limit charitable contributions. And with the prospect of Gramm-Rudman [the Federal budget-balancing act] taking huge amounts of money from state and local governments, their funding programs will focus more acutely on the needs of the hungry, the homeless and the unemployed.

At House Appropriations Interior
Subcommittee hearing, Washington, April 17/
Los Angeles Times, 4-19:(V)9.

Charles Z. Wick

Director, United States Information Agency

3

I would hope that American pop culture

would penetrate into other societies, acting as a pilot parachute for the rest of American values.

Time, 6-16:73.

Elie Wiesel

Author; Winner,
1986 Nobel Peace Prize

4

[On his winning the Nobel Prize]: I don't think that prizes validate work. They give stature, texture, the possibility to reach more people. There's a mystique about the Nobel. It gives you a better loudspeaker.

Time, 10-27:66.

Andrew Wyeth

Painter

5

I think any creative person, whether he is painting a tree, a model, a house or a hill, has to have a deep love for it, and that's the love you are trying to reach in the work. I think I put it well once . . . when I said that I go as far as my love goes. No, that doesn't mean sexual, of course. As a painter, you are trying to catch the warmth and spirit for something. That's what we have left in art—love . . . If you are painting an animal—I'm painting my hound—if I can capture my affection for that object, that's what is meant by love. Love, not "in love."

Interview, Cushing, Maine/
The Washington Post, 8-11:(C)10.

6

There are no rules in my work. I don't have studios. I wander around people's attics, out in fields, in cellars, any place I find that excites me. I dream a lot. I do more painting when I'm not painting. It's in the subconscious. I begin to see an emotion building up in my mind before I ever put it down on the panel. Sometimes when there is great tension, or lots taking place, I may get an idea or an emotion, and it hits me strong. It can be a tree, or the tone of a shadow of clouds on the ground, or light on the side of a hill, or light on a white surface. Sometimes I do my best work after the models have gone away, purely

WHAT THEY SAID IN 1986

(ANDREW WYETH)

from memory. And that's what makes me laugh when critics say I'm photographic. I'm not photographic at all. Nothing against the camera, but it doesn't work with me.

Interview/Time, 8-18:57.

Yevgeny Yevtushenko
Soviet poet

1

I absolutely believe in the power of the word, or picture. If we [artists] don't change the world, who will? It seems to me, sometimes, we are giving up very easily. We are saying to ourselves, "I am a little man. What can I do?" But a real artist mustn't give up. A real artist must believe in his creative role. He creates the present and is responsible for the present. And responsibility for today means responsibility for the future.

Interview, New York/
The Christian Science Monitor,
2-10:31.

Floyd Abrams
Lawyer specializing in
First Amendment issues

1

[On CIA Director William Casey's criticism of the news media for reporting certain intelligence information revealed during a recent espionage trial]: I really don't mind when he tries to persuade *The [Washington] Post* and other publications not to publish something. That is . . . his job. The difficulty is when urgings turn into warnings and the warnings are then expanded to cover the most routine of journalistic endeavors.

The Washington Post, 5-30:(A)12.

Oscar Arias
President-elect of Costa Rica

2

The democratic system demands that its citizens and journalists comment, debate and criticize the actions of its public figures. However, the democratic system suffers when its citizens and journalists guard silence [or] slant facts or words, thereby confusing public opinion.

The Christian Science Monitor, 8-18:12.

Ray Bradbury
Author

3

[Saying aspiring journalists should stay away from journalism schools]: That's fatal. You don't learn a goddamn thing. Journalism has nothing to do with writing. The great newspaper writers are not journalists, they are essay writers.

Interview, Beverly Hills, Calif./
Writer's Digest, February:28.

Ben Bradlee
Executive editor, "The Washington Post"

4

[On what he looks for in a journalist]: Sometimes I think it all boils down to energy. Energy is certainly something I look for, and curiosity. In-

telligence, obviously, and an ability to write. But I find the best reporters are the ones who work the hardest and who aren't impressed with their successes or the high positions of their friends.

Interview, Washington/
The Christian Science Monitor, 5-28:16.

5

[On the press coverage of the current scandal involving Reagan Administration dealings with Iran and fund diversion to Nicaraguan contras]: If you're the type of journalist who takes glee out of a good day's work with a lot of stories that boggle the mind, yeah, there is reason for glee. But there is no joy.

Los Angeles Times, 12-7:(I)18.

Ed Bradley
Correspondent,
"60 Minutes," CBS News

6

However people feel about the press, there's still two things that are paramount. One is that most people in this country trust the press. They might not like some of the things we do, or the way we do some things, but they trust the press. And most people in this country value a free press. They can see the difference in the kind of reporting that takes place in this country and the kind of reporting that takes place in the Soviet Union, for example.

Interview, New York/
The Christian Science Monitor, 10-16:18.

David Brinkley
Commentator, ABC News

7

Writing is what got me into journalism in the first place. I liked to write, I was good at it, and I still am. That's the only virtue I will claim. I do write well. In my opinion, the most valuable attribute for a journalist is the ability to write the English language. That's what did it for me. I

(DAVID BRINKLEY)

ain't good lookin'. I can't do many things any better than anybody else. But I am a very good writer. That's the only thing I'm really any good at. Anyone who wishes to be successful in broadcast news must write his own stuff. Otherwise he will never have any style, any individuality. No one will ever recognize him/her as anything more than some voice. If you don't want to write it yourself, you should go and sell insurance.

Interview, Washington/
Emmy Magazine, May-June:47.

Tom Brokaw
Anchorman, "Nightly News," NBC-TV

1

We [at the *Nightly News*] have to do better with the [ratings] numbers. We have to hit all the markers. That goes with the turf. It's risk and reward in this business. But no, I don't wake up in a cold sweat thinking about it in the middle of the night. I've never had a major failure—how do you face up to it? What might happen? I've thought about it. My family's thought about it. I'm always struck by the grace of people who emerge from difficulty.

Interview/Esquire, March:93.

2

The information cycle has become intense. You've got CNN; you've got longer local newscasts; you've got all-news radio. You've got national newspapers: *The New York Times* reaches parts of the country that it didn't. *USA Today* is out there, for better or worse. And *The Wall Street Journal*'s national now. The general level of awareness in the country, I think, is slowly going up all the time. So we have to figure out where we [TV network news] fit in that cycle.

TV Guide, 8-23:8.

Patrick J. Buchanan
Director of Communications for
the President of the United States

3

[Criticizing the appearance on ABC-TV of Radio Moscow commentator Vladimir Posner,

who rebutted a speech made by U.S. President Reagan]: We were rather astonished last night, following the President's address on the nation's security needs, and majority leader Jim Wright's response—to see ABC give eight minutes of rebuttal time on national television to a trained propagandist for the Soviet Union . . . Would you have felt it an expression of fair and balanced journalism if, in the 1930s, [British Prime Minister Winston] Churchill's calls for the rearmament of his country were immediately followed by the BBC's granting of an unrebutted commentary to some functionary of the Third Reich?

Letter to ABC News, Feb. 27/*
The New York Times, 2-28:9.

4

All newsmen should remember that they're Americans first and newsmen second. All who don't feel that should tell us so. We will know which stations not to watch and which newspapers not to buy.

At Cuban-American rally,
Miami, Dec. 8/
The New York Times, 12-10:8.

William J. Casey
Director of Central
Intelligence of the United States

5

[On his criticism of the news media for reporting certain intelligence information revealed during a recent espionage trial]: I think that certainly the press has been very hysterical about [the criticism], saying we're trying to tear up the First Amendment and scuttle the freedom of the press. We're not trying to do that . . . Every method we have of obtaining intelligence—our agents, our relationships with other intelligence services, our photographic, our electronic, our communications capabilities—have been damaged . . . This is costing the taxpayers billions and billions of dollars, and, more importantly, Americans and our national security are at risk. We can't permit this to continue.

Interview, May 29/
The Washington Post, 5-30:(A)12.

Joel Chaseman
President, Post-Newsweek Stations

1

I don't know of a single [local TV] station, independent or affiliate, that's willing or able to cover national or international news itself on a sustained, daily basis. We can focus for our viewers on a given story that might be of special interest to them. If there's a new Pope and we have a large Catholic population [in a local station's area], we might want to assign someone to that and go live. That's a wonderful capability to have . . . and, I have to admit, highly promotable. but we couldn't afford the people or technology or time—and we don't have the editorial expertise—to do that every day.

Los Angeles Times,
12-29:(I)17.

Ray S. Cline
Former Deputy Director,
Central Intelligence Agency
of the United States

2

The freedom we give the press . . . does assist the Soviet Union and other hostile nations in collecting information . . . The intelligence agencies accept that. It's the price you pay for living in an open society . . . But if you wrap everything together and put it on a silver platter on the front page of *The Washington Post,* you can be very sure that every aspect of that problem will be [discussed] in Moscow the next day.

TV Guide, 2-15:6.

William E. Colby
Former Director of Central
Intelligence of the United States

3

People in the national-security area have a responsibility to protect secrets. News guys have the responsibility to find them out. They're natural antagonists.

TV Guide, 2-15:8.

Norman Corwin
Visiting professor, School of Journalism,
University of Southern California;
Former radio dramatist

4

Journalism has responsibilities, second only, if second, to education because it is, in a sense, an ongoing educational course. I think the whole profession of journalism is, almost as much as medicine, in need of the observance of a kind of Hippocratic Oath on ethics. When you want to trivialize, you can do a very good job of trivializing a candidate you disapprove of.

Interview/USA Today, 8-18:(A)9.

Walter Cronkite
Special correspondent,
and former anchorman,
CBS News

5

I have always been a critic of personality in the news. I never liked the ratings battles and advertisements over who beat who this week. But it is the nature of the beast and there's nothing we can do about it. The good thing about it is that it creates competition, and competition benefits the people. If CBS wants to do better than NBC, then the public benefits.

USA Today, 5-12:(D)2.

6

What does one mean by the "best" anchor?—the most popular anchor?; the best-informed anchor?; the one who works hardest at producing the broadcast? This is one of the fallacies. The public can't really judge who is the best anchor. They can judge who they like the best, but no one knows the background that goes into it. This has always been the problem, separating the news ability from performance. Clearly, the anchorperson has to perform well. I think the problem that all of us have is when performance is judged to be more important than the news ability. That's a problem.

Interview,
Edgartown, Mass./
The Washington Post, 7-29:(C)4.

WHAT THEY SAID IN 1986

Mario M. Cuomo
Governor of New York (D)

1

[Addressing the press]: If you want to be protected against the regulation that I think would be an impediment to the free flow of information, you had better regulate yourselves—and what that means, if I may say so to the press, is don't be so thin-skinned. If every once in a while a politician goes crazy and says, "I think you're imperfect," I don't think the media should suddenly get up in arms and take this as a challenge to the First Amendment. Rather, what they should do is say, "I wonder if that story was inaccurate; I wonder if we could do it better."

Before members of Audit Bureau of
Circulations, New York, Nov. 13/
The New York Times, 11-14:13.

2

[Saying the press must be more careful today about what they say about people because of the increased incidence of libel cases]: We are approaching a time when shifts in our law may seriously dilute the protection of the press and thereby weaken the fabric of this society. [A press] regarded by the public as reckless invites the attention of the Supreme Court and tempts it to perform corrective judicial surgery.

Before New York City Press Club, Nov. 25/
The Washington Post, 11-26:(A)4.

3

The truth is that criticism of the press by their natural targets—by public officials, Governors, Presidents—however illustrious, is not necessarily good evidence of the press's imperfection. Indeed, it can be argued that it is the best evidence of the press's effectiveness.

Before New York Press Club, Nov. 25/
The New York Times, 11-26:18.

Sam Donaldson
White House correspondent,
ABC News

4

. . . I really think that the job of a reporter anywhere, certainly at the White House, is to try to scratch around at the programs, policies and personnel, and see if anything is wrong. If it's not wrong, terrific, I couldn't be happier . . . But there are people in this country who, for some reason, don't think the President ought to be questioned sharply. I don't understand that. I guess they want a king or a Pope. But the President's got to be questioned, and we get very few opportunities to do that. So if people want to say I'm a target for their wrath at the media, or their belief that [President] Ronald Reagan, poor man, is being mistreated, it's okay with me.

Interview/TV Guide, 1-4:30.

Richard Dreyfuss
Actor

5

I don't speak to the printed press any more. I'll talk to you on radio or television because the public can then hear my words and judge me accordingly. In the printed press, you get the reporter's view of me, and often the quotes are wrong or out of context with the meaning. Let people react to me as me, not as others perceive me.

USA Today, 2-17:(D)2.

Douglas Edwards
Anchorman, CBS News

6

. . . television is great for show business. It is a marvelous sales tool. But I think it is probably best in the coverage of news. However, having said that, we go back to the admission that it is show business, and a lot of people expect to be entertained. I don't find any quarrel with the effort to make news a bit more attractive, to put a little icing on the cake, so long as there is no diminution of the main theme, which is the hard news. It may come off once in a while as a little glitzy, but news audiences are still way up there, and I don't think the country is malserved by an occasional trip over into the entertainment field.

Interview/USA Today, 10-7:(A)9.

Linda Ellerbee
Broadcast journalist, NBC-TV

1

Most of the bad television news that you get comes because most of the people who put it together are absolutely certain they're smarter than the people who watch it—the "plumber-in-Albuquerque" theory. "We can't put this on; the plumber in Albuquerque won't understand it. The plumber in Albuquerque has no interest in the Third World. This is too complicated for the plumber in Albuquerque" . . . Can you imagine a [news] producer in New York City who's afraid to ride the subway—and too dumb to start a fire in the fireplace, except with a phony log, and too confused to file his own tax returns—looking down on the plumber in Albuquerque because the plumber watches television news? At least the plumber in Albuquerque has steady work. Which is more than you can say for most of us [in broadcast journalism]. Until we stop that attitude, we're not going to get much better than Dick-and-Jane newscasts. It is a dreadful attitude.

Interview/USA Today, 6-2:(A)11.

2

Not all [TV news] anchors are twinkies. A twinkie almost doesn't need definition, because anyone who's watched more than five minutes of television knows what a twinkie is. When you're watching someone telling you the news, and you're not certain that person has read it—much less written it—that's probably a twinkie. When you're watching someone tell you the news, and you're not certain that person hasn't blow-dried his or her brains along with their hair, that person is a twinkie. A twinkie is someone who acts the news.

Interview/USA Today, 6-2:(A)11.

Reuven Frank
Executive producer of documentaries,
and former president, NBC News

3

Part of journalism is editing. Unedited material has certain charms of its own, as with political conventions and football games. But serious journalism, serious information, requires editing. Professional news, regardless of the medium, means giving people something that they themselves, if present, would not have gotten. The reporter is more than bystander, and the editor is part of the process.

The New York Times, 4-28:16.

Fred W. Friendly
Professor emeritus of journalism,
Columbia University;
Former president, CBS News

4

[Network TV news today] is not what the news used to be. Locked in fierce ratings battles over a fraction of a [rating] point, the networks continue to doctor and meddle with their product to maintain the numbers. Substance is being sacrificed for the sensational tabloid snapshots in the constant search for brevity and pace . . . I am equally concerned, in fact, embarrassed, by the financial appetites of the anchor stars and their hustling agents who play one network against another. All this, while producers, correspondents and camera operators are being laid off or early-retired. [News stars Tom] Brokaw, [Dan] Rather, [Peter] Jennings, [Barbara] Walters, [Mike] Wallace and all the others are not quarterbacks or pitchers or centers with fragile knees and eight-year career risks. They have virtual lifetime tenure. [News stars should] volunteer a cut in pay to provide the salaries of able colleagues who are desperately needed to keep network news the national asset which their mandate requires.

Before Radio-Television News Directors
Association, Salt Lake City, Aug. 29/
Los Angeles Times, 9-1:(V)1,9.

Lawrence K. Grossman
President, NBC News

5

[On White House criticism of the appearance on ABC-TV of Radio Moscow commentator Vladimir Posner, who rebutted a speech made by U.S. President Reagan]: It's a free country with free speech, and the White House can say any-

WHAT THEY SAID IN 1986

thing it believes; it's fair game. But I disagree with the White House. It is appropriate, when the President is accusing the Soviet Union of aggressive behavior, to get a perspective from the people on the other side. We [at NBC] didn't do it ourselves, but I see nothing wrong with it. In fact, I think it was a good thing to do.

Feb. 27/The New York Times, 2-28:9.

Nat Hentoff
Writer

1

There is a tendency among journalists to go into a story like a prosecutor goes in, except the journalists are not bound, except by libel laws, by any kind of legal strictures, nor should they be. A prosecutor must be careful in making his case. But if you [as a journalist] go in with that kind of prosecutorial pre-set, you are in danger of deciding which facts don't fit your thesis and leaving them out. That's as bad as having wrong facts. The means and ends still have a lot of meaning to me. If your means are distorted, the ends are not going to work out. You can do a perfectly good muckraking job, exposing all kinds of skulduggery, by sticking to the rules of fairness. Not "objectivity," because I don't know what that is. But fairness, that's what you go after.

Interview, New York /
The Christian Science Monitor, 5-2:(B)8.

Don Hewitt
Executive producer,
"60 Minutes," CBS-TV

2

[Criticizing those who say TV news salaries are too high]: Journalism is not a public utility. [Print] journalism made some of the biggest fortunes in America. [Publishers] Hearst, Luce, Graham, Sulzberger, Neuharth, the Binghams of Louisville—a lot of people got very rich on [print] journalism. What's wrong with [TV] journalists getting rich on journalism? Is it all right for publishers to get filthy rich but no one

else should make any money from the product they got rich on?

Interview/USA Today, 3-7:(A)11.

Haynes Johnson
Pulitzer Prize-winning journalist

3

The experience of crossing the line into fiction and trying to tell a larger truth through fiction has made me even more appreciative of the confines of daily journalism and the real reasons there should be confines and limits upon us. We shouldn't try to pretend that we can read people's minds, hearts, souls, motivations, in a daily newspaper.

Interview/USA Today, 7-24:(A)7.

David Jones
National editor,
"The New York Times"

4

[On newspapers printing rumors]: [There is often] a difficult line between simply being a . . . transmission belt for irresponsible statements . . . and having to nail down the absolute, iron-clad authenticity of everything everybody says before you can put it in the paper. One of the roles the press has, I think, is to open public debate on issues.

Los Angeles Times, 9-2:(I)1.

Serge July
Editor, "Liberation" (Paris)

5

Reporting comes first. People here enjoy reporting most; no one wants to write editorials, columns or analysis. Those are considered inferior chores for people who do not know journalism. People come here because they want to investigate and write articles. Every member of the editorial staff, including management, is a reporter. Another of our ideas is a bit extreme, but it has borne a lot of fruit. It is that journalism is the true literature of today. The approach is similar to that taken by the "new journalism" in the U.S. We favor techniques—ways of begin-

(SERGE JULY)

ning an article, for example—that are literary. We also seek a style of writing—the main contribution of [co-founder and author] Jean-Paul Sartre—that is a combination of both spoken and written language. It does not include slang, but it is a style that starts from the way people talk on the street. I would add a fourth, ideological, element: We distrust everyone. When the President tells us something, we have to think that it may not necessarily be true. We believe that elements needed for verification are not always available. This attitude is obvious in our style— especially in headlines, which often are ironic.

Interview/World Press Review, June:58.

Ted Koppel
Anchorman, "Nightline," ABC-TV

1

[On the increase in network news anchormen doing their broadcasts from locations around the world]: We're living in a changing era in terms of TV news. In this era of satellites and portable earthstations, it's no longer unusual to have a station in Chicago to have someone reporting from the Middle East, or a station in Texas to have someone reporting from Mexico. The local newscasts are starting to look a great deal like the nightly network newscasts. So, the networks are starting to rethink what they do. It's what the critics have said—they're starting to go into the more important stories with greater depth.

Interview/The New York Times, 2-27:26.

2

[On U.S. news media coverage of international terrorist incidents]: [American TV is] particularly vulnerable to misuse. We are vulnerable to misuse by our own leaders. We are vulnerable to misuse by our international adversaries. And that obviously includes terrorists. That fact, that terrorism by definition tends to be dramatic, [and] the fact that by definition it tends to involve acts which are pictorial, makes us even more vulnerable. [But] don't make the mistake of jumping to the conclusion that the im-

mediate impact of that day's visual message is the final impact. The American media . . . operate under what ultimately is our basic assumption in this country, a Jeffersonian notion, that if you allow the public access to all the information, no matter how dramatic or devastating it may be at any given point, ultimately they will reach the proper conclusions.

Interview/
The Christian Science Monitor, 5-16:19.

Charles Kuralt
Correspondent, CBS News

3

I may be the only reporter people are sort of glad to see coming. I've had a really pleasant time of it, making a living. I was never perfectly suited to being a hard-news reporter. I was always afraid another newsman was sneaking around behind my back finding out something I didn't know. But since I started doing these simple little feature stories, I get to go anywhere I want to go and do anything I want to do, and CBS doesn't even know or much care where I am. Where could you ever find a better job than that?

Interview/U.S. News &
World Report, 1-20:77.

Bill Kurtis
News anchorman, WBBM-TV, Chicago;
Former anchorman,
"CBS Morning News"

4

[On the growing importance of networks covering local issues on their newscasts]: The networks are going to have to shift their priorities to cover the stories we [locals] want covered. You [a local affiliate station] just make a call to[the independent] Cable News Network and say, "Could we buy your service, because CBS isn't serving us" . . . Now, you multiply that by 250 affiliates—with everyone asking the same question—and that collective pressure is what brings these [network] guys to their knees.

TV Guide, 10-11:9.

WHAT THEY SAID IN 1986

David Lamb
News correspondent,
"Los Angeles Times"

1

I could give you six examples of *The New York Times*, *The Washington Post* and the *Los Angeles Times* sharing information [among correspondents] . . . With rare exceptions, you share everything with your colleagues . . . And why shouldn't you? The readers are better-served if we share information. Who are we supposed to serve anyway—our readers or our editors' egos?

Los Angeles Times, 7-8:(I)15.

George Lauder
Spokesman for the Central Intelligence
Agency of the United States

2

The press says that the public has a right to know everything. That's a load of garbage. The public has a need to know that it is being protected, but there is a constant tension between that need to know and what the press so often decides to report.

TV Guide, 2-15:5.

Patrick J. Leahy
United States Senator, D-Vermont

3

[On prosecuting the press for printing leaks of classified or sensitive government information]: I think when you go after press organizations, you're treating the symptoms rather than the problem. You should go after the persons doing the leaking. Going after the press raises some very serious First Amendment issues in my mind, and really won't get at the problem.

Washington, May 7/
The Washington Post, 5-8:(A)3.

S. Robert Lichter
Professor of political science,
George Washington University;
Fellow, American Enterprise Institute

4

The typical leading journalist is an urbane cosmopolitan, comes from an upper-status background, probably grew up on the East Coast in a big city, had professional or business parents. There aren't very many Horatio Alger stories. He or she tends to be liberal, particularly on social issues. Most of the journalists we interviewed, for example, are pro-choice on abortion, favor strong affirmative action, and favor gay rights. They are less liberal on economic issues, possibly because they are an upper-status group and do very well. They fit the mold of what's sometimes called the "yuppie liberal" . . . I don't believe that bias in the major media is a major problem in the sense of a conscious, unfair coverage, or a conscious effort to push people toward their own beliefs . . . The question is, rather, among a homogenous group of people, do you gradually get a news agenda that reflects their backgrounds without their realizing it or intending it?

Interview/
USA Today, 12-30:(A)9.

Peter Maas
Author; Journalist

5

When you're an investigative reporter, there's a certain ego in that. You think you're going to change the world, and at some point in your life you discover you're not changing the world. You're changing faces.

Interview, Washington/
The Washington Post, 5-3:(A)2.

Ferdinand E. Marcos
President of the Philippines

6

[On Western press reports critical of him]: The Western press sometimes chooses a target for itself, like [the late Nicaraguan leader Anastasio] Somoza, or like [South African leader Pieter] Botha. They choose a target and then continue to hit . . . In the end, they behave like the Communists, in a schematic way: those who are right on one side, those who are wrong on the other.

Interview/
The New York Times, 1-29:14.

Bill Moyers
Commentator, CBS News

1

[Criticizing CBS News for allowing entertainment and trivialization to encroach on its broadcasts]: Not only were those values invited in, they were exalted. The line between entertainment and news was steadily blurred. Our center of gravity shifted from the standards and practices of the news business to show business . . . Tax policy had to compete with stories about three-legged sheep, and the three-legged sheep won . . . Once you decide to titillate instead of illuminate, you're on a slippery slope.

Interview/Daily Variety, 9-9:2.

Jim Murray
Sports columnist,
"Los Angeles Times"

2

[On sportswriting]: Especially with major events, you have to assume that everyone who's interested already knows who won, knows the score, and probably saw the whole game on TV better than you did. So I, as a columnist, and I suppose even the reporters doing the game story, have to dig deeper. You can't sit up in the press box and write, "Outlined against a blue-gray October sky" today, like Grantland Rice did. Today's readers don't need to be told the score or who caught the big touchdown pass. They want to know what Dan Marino *felt* like after throwing a key interception. I can *ask* someone what happened. I'm after something else—some *essence* of the guy who made the play.

Interview/Writer's Digest, June:28.

Allen H. Neuharth
Chairman, Gannett Company

3

At 50 cents, a newspaper is the biggest bargain in town. That's no more—generally less—than people pay for an ice cream cone or a Coke. And it certainly gives them much more pleasure for a longer period of time.

Interview/
USA Today, 9-15:(A)13.

Richard M. Nixon
Former President of the United States

4

Some of you get the idea I don't like the press. Individually . . . I meet with them occasionally. I like individual members of the press. They are, most of them, liberals, but they're highly intelligent creatures. They're interesting. We have some good ones. But, you get them in a pack, and they're obnoxious.

Speech, Parsippany, N.J., Dec. 9/
Los Angeles Times, 12-10:(I)25.

Robert B. Oakley
Director,
Office of Counterterrorism,
Department of State of the United States

5

[Criticizing NBC's interview with Arab terrorist Abu Abbas]: When a media outlet makes deals with a terrorist not to divulge his whereabouts, the news organization is saying, in effect, "We've become his accomplices in order to give him publicity."

Broadcast interview/
Cable News Network, 5-6.

John O'Sullivan
Associate editor,
"The Times," London

6

Is there some compensating advantage that justifies television interviews with [international] terrorists? I do not believe there is. The justification commonly advanced is that "we need to know what these people think." But that is nonsense. To begin with, we invariably know what they think long before they appear on television to tell us. Second, what they say on television is not necessarily what they think, which is much more accurately conveyed by what they do—kneecapping, amputations, point-blank murder and the like. It is sugared propaganda.

At conference on terrorism,
Washington/Time, 4-14:51.

WHAT THEY SAID IN 1986

Neil Postman
Professor of communications arts
and sciences, New York University

1

Because it's television, the availability of film footage will [always] be crucial in what is defined as news. Because it's advertiser-supported . . . there has to be some sort of ratings war . . . Because that is the case, there has to be a conception of news that is not easily separable from entertainment. Because, in the ratings competition, celebrity is a key factor, all network news will try to amplify or heighten the celebrity value of their anchorman . . . Those things will be more or less constant as long as you have this sort of system.

Los Angeles Times, 12-29:(I)16.

Jody Powell
Former Press Secretary to
the President of the United States
(Jimmy Carter)

2

Journalism in this town [Washington] is much more likely, for a variety of reasons, to be tough on a President when he's dragging one leg and bleeding from one nostril than if he's riding high.

Time, 11-17:88.

Alan Protheroe
Assistant director general,
British Broadcasting Corporation

3

[On Western news media coverage of international terrorist incidents]: [My] journalistic assessment goes like this: Does what I am reporting actually enhance and add to the sum of information available to the viewer so that he may make up his mind? I still have the highest regard for the three [U.S. commercial] networks. I have to say that I'm a great fan of the American technology and a lot of the journalistic practices that you have. [But] I think a national broadcaster of that caliber, of that importance or relevance to the community, has got imposed upon him . . . certain standards and certain concepts and precepts that you don't run

from. You draw a line and say, "No, I am sorry, there are standards of taste and standards of decency and standards of journalistic behavior" . . . You draw a line and nobody crosses it.

Interview/
The Christian Science Monitor, 5-16:19.

Austin Ranney
Political scientist, University of
California, Berkeley; Former president,
American Political Science Association

4

Compared to the ineptness of the [Jimmy] Carter Administration in dealing with the press, and the hostility of the [Richard] Nixon and [Lyndon] Johnson Administrations, the Reagan Administration has been remarkably shrewd and successful. The news media are not enemies to them. They've tried to use the media to promote their goals, to advance their own ends. Whether they've been able to use news policy in a less-defensible way than other Administrations, by leaking false information, for example, is another question. F.D.R. did it in World War II, and L.B.J. during Vietnam. But that was war. Of course it's different now; we're not in a war.

The New York Times, 10-3:4.

Dan Rather
Anchorman,
"Evening News," CBS-TV

5

To be the [news] broadcast that every other [news] broadcast is measured by is something to be proud of. I would rather be Number 3 [in the ratings] and have the reputation of being a quality broadcast than be Number 1 and have the reputation of being crummy. The ideal, of course, is to be both—best and first . . . Somebody once said, "The first law of television is that nothing lasts," and it's true. Somebody once said, "It's a crazy business," and somebody was right . . . Nobody in this business can be King Canute. You can control some things, but the great forces of nature, and ratings madness, nobody can control.

Interview/The Washington Post, 3-4:(B)4.

(DAN RATHER)

1

[On CIA Director William Casey's criticism of the news media for reporting certain intelligence information revealed during a recent espionage trial]: We try very hard not to tell Mr. Casey how to catch spies, and I hope he'll understand that we're not going to take it too seriously when he tells us how to cover trials. The only position for a journalist in this case must be one of respectful defiance.

The Washington Post, 5-30:(A)12.

2

[Criticizing U.S. TV stations that give the impression that their news anchors are involved in the preparation of the news when all they really do is read it on the air]: [On the BBC,] they clearly say, "Make no mistake, we hire this guy to come in every night and read this stuff, and he shows up here and rehearses just as an actor does, and he puts it on." I think that's cleaner than blurring the line. I'm not on any high horse about it, [but] I'm looking for a little truth with the viewer . . . Increasingly what happens with a local station [is] they try to get the viewer to believe that the person who's on the air with the newscast is somehow involved with the news— when in too many cases, that person has about as much to do with the newscast as King James did with writing the Bible.

Interview,
Los Angeles, Sept. 14/
Los Angeles Times, 9-16:(VI)7.

Charles E. Redman
Spokesman for the Department
of State of the United States

3

[Criticizing NBC's interview with Arab terrorist Abu Abbas]: Obviously, terrorism thrives on this kind of publicity. This is the type of interview that gives terrorists the platform that they seek. Such publicity may, in fact, encourage the terrorist activities which we are all seeking to deter.

May 6/
The Washington Post, 5-7:(A)21.

George E. Reedy
Professor of journalism,
Marquette University;
Former Press Secretary to the President
of the United States (Lyndon B. Johnson)

4

Everybody [in government] gets mad at the press. That's easy. Who else can they get mad at? Their constituents? There is no virtue in getting mad at the American people. Themselves? Very few of them can ever admit they are wrong.

The Washington Post, 12-3:(A)17.

Donald T. Regan
Chief of Staff to the
President of the United States

5

[On whether the media should be prosecuted for revealing classified government information]: This is a complicated question. Not only by tradition, but also by law, we have freedom of the press. We also know that publishing top-secret material, particularly anything that endangers human life, is dangerous and really subversive. It's against our government . . . The leaker of this information, if it is highly classified information, should be prosecuted. If we have knowledge that the media are going to report such things, if we find out they're going to report it, we try to contact them and explain what they're going to do to national security by reporting that material. Usually, the media cooperate with us, and we're very grateful for that. They are responsible . . . I said that the leaking of this information was subversive. Not the publication. The publication of it depends upon whether or not they know the results of their acts, they know that in so doing they might cause harm to American lives and American interests, and then persist in doing it. I think that's something that should be referred to the Attorney General.

Interview/USA Today, 6-24:(A)7.

Gene Roberts
Executive editor,
"Philadelphia Inquirer"

6

Editors are more interested in what their papers look like than at any time in the past. And

WHAT THEY SAID IN 1986

anything that makes the newspaper . . . easier and more inviting to read is a good thing to do . . . especially . . . when what you make easier to read is worth reading . . . when it's part and parcel of a good, comprehensive journalistic effort to improve the paper substantively. But, in some cases, all these design techniques have been used as a substitute for substance.

Interview/Los Angeles Times, 3-13:(I)29.

A. M. Rosenthal
Executive editor,
"The New York Times"

1

I always talk about *The Times* either in terms of food or sex; I just realized that. I either say it's a smorgasbord or I say it's like a spouse or a lover: You can argue with it; you can quarrel with it; but, in the end, you have to love it or at least like it very much.

Interview, New York/
The Washington Post, 1-8:(C)2.

2

There should be a serendipity about the news sections [of newspapers] . . . I don't want everything . . . nice and neat and squared off . . . That's not the way the news happens. I think a certain unexpectedness or even awkwardness in the news sections is much more interesting.

Interview/
Los Angeles Times, 3-14:(I)20.

Timothy J. Russert
Vice president,
National Broadcasting Company

3

[Defending NBC's interview with Arab terrorist Abu Abbas]: If [critics of the interview] are suggesting that this interview is a favorable one and put him [Abbas] in a favorable light with the American public, that doesn't appear very likely. It is also indeed ironic that the [U.S. State] Department that said to the Soviets, "Let there be a free flow of information" [on the recent Cherno-

byl nuclear-plant accident] suddenly suggests that there should be censorship . . . If we are only going to cover the good news or only cover people who say things that we as a country hope they are going to say, then we don't have a free press.

May 6/The Washington Post, 5-7:(A)21.

Harrison Salisbury
Former associate editor,
"The New York Times"

4

What bothers me in journalism in general is that as the great newspaper chains come in, the idiosyncratic editor goes out . . . They are more and more corporate people who speak through the corporate spokesman . . . and the editor's voice is gone. The generation after the Abe Rosenthals [of *The New York Times*], the Ben Bradlees [of *The Washington Post*] and the Tom Winships [of *The Boston Globe*]: I hope to Christ they have as much crust as these other guys have. Don't make it out that I agree with them necessarily, but, in some ways, I will certainly miss them.

The Washington Post, 1-9:(B)2.

John Scali
Correspondent, ABC News

5

News organizations have a responsibility to help maintain the nation's vital secrets in a world where nuclear weapons can incinerate a hemisphere. But this doesn't mean we have to stand mute and salute everytime somebody [in government] demands a story be killed.

TV Guide, 2-15:6.

Helmut Schmidt
Publisher, "Die Zeit" (West Germany);
Former Chancellor of West Germany

6

In their fields, both journalists and politicians learn a great deal. But both run the risk of superficiality. Both are tempted to make up their minds too quickly. Only a person of character can resist that temptation. In both fields there is a continuum of people ranging from statesman to

(HELMUT SCHMIDT)

criminal. In 35 years in political life, I have learned much and received a great deal of intellectual advice from first-class journalists. I even brought two or three of them into the government . . . There are other journalists who do not have the characteristics of statesmen but who pose such intelligent questions that they are helpful in presenting ideas and answers to the public. This is a skill much esteemed among politicians, because it is not easy.

Interview/World Press Review, April:58.

John Seigenthaler
Editorial-page editor, "USA Today"

1

[On criticism of NBC's interviewing Arab terrorist Abu Abbas and its promise to Abbas not to reveal the site of the interview]: We as journalists don't see ourselves as an extension of any law-enforcement agency. What the journalist has to consider is whether the information to be gained is so vital that it tips the scale in favor of granting protection to a fugitive.

Time, 5-19:90.

Gerald Seymour
Author; Former journalist,
Independent Television News (Britain)

2

The television reporter is something special— I went to the best news places, getting up before dawn with the camera crew, seeing a little more than newspaper reporters. Then came a terrible frustration. My newspaper colleagues were able to write a thousand words while I was allowed 200 words as the voice describing the film. That meant I could not talk about what I was seeing. At the end of the day, you want to know who the real guys are in a story and what they thought. But you haven't got the air time. Another thing: The success formula of the television reporter can be binding—you learn how to do what is necessary pictorially.

Interview, Bath, England/
The New York Times, 1-22:19.

George P. Shultz
Secretary of State of
the United States

3

[Saying those in the press who publish secret government information should be prosecuted if they violate the law]: But I think they can properly be talked to—and journalists are talked to regularly—and I think there is a tradition of responsibility in the journalistic community, and it still exists and it should be encouraged. Nobody wants to undermine the national security.

Broadcast interview/
"Meet the Press," NBC-TV, 6-1.

Howard Simons
Curator, Nieman Foundation,
Harvard University; Former managing
editor, "The Washington Post"

4

Newspapers were put on earth, in the United States at least, to illuminate dark places, not to reflect sunlight, and to keep people honest, not to write about honest people.

Interview/USA Today, 7-24:(A)7.

Frank Sinatra
Entertainer

5

Those people in the press who write gossip and who always seem to be negative and who are always looking to dig up dirt about other people are nothing but parasites. They live off the real or imagined misfortunes of people more famous.

USA Today, 11-3:(D)2.

Larry Speakes
Principal Deputy Press Secretary to
the President of the United States

6

[On charges that the Reagan Administration "manages" the news]: Any organization, government or corporate, tries to present its message in the most favorable light. That doesn't mean managing the news. Look at those libel suits against *Time* magazine and CBS. There

(LARRY SPEAKES)

were an awful lot of "no comments" by them, which we would get criticized for. This Administration, no more than any other, has tried to present its message in the most effective way, and that doesn't mean lying or misrepresenting the facts. We don't do that.

The New York Times, 10-3:4.

David A. Stockman
Former Director, Federal Office
of Management and Budget

1

The press takes sides. There's a mythology that the press is totally objective, disinterested, neutral. But for the editorialists, the columnists and a lot of the reporters who indulge in what they call advocacy journalism, they're taking sides.

Interview/USA Today, 4-25:(A)13.

Tom Stoppard
Playwright

2

I would say, don't give interviews [to the press]. Once you give one, you're trapped. You have to keep living up to the last one. You present a version of yourself that you think will gratify the interviewer, and the next day you read about this person who puts himself forward in ways that you don't. It's embarrassing. And strangely enough, the more accurate the interview is, the more you're embarrassed.

Interview, London/
Los Angeles Times, 6-2:(VI)6.

Howard Stringer
President, CBS News

3

The press are the watch guardians [over the government]. It is part of the relationship between government and the press. It always brings out concerns on the part of the government that we are going too far too fast.

Los Angeles Times, 12-7:(I)18.

Arthur Ochs Sulzberger
Publisher,
"The New York Times"

4

We in the United States operate the only truly free press in the world. No one can hold a candle to us. And let me hasten to add that when I talk about the press, I include radio, television, magazines, advertising—the whole lot. We prove every day that we honor and cherish our freedom by extending its covering and protective wing to those with whom we disagree. We are free and we are good. And all of us together in our diversity will keep it that way.

Accepting Communication Award of Center
for Communications, New York, April 15/
The New York Times, 4-16:20.

Hycel B. Taylor
President,
Operation PUSH
(People United to Serve Humanity)

5

The media control the minds of people—white and black—in this country and the world. It can alter attitudes, distort reality and assassinate through the power of the pen.

Los Angeles Times, 4-22:(VI)1.

William F. Thomas
Editor, "Los Angeles Times"

6

[On the increasing use of color photographs by newspapers]: Color on the news pages of all newspapers is inevitable. But until color photos can be used with the same facility as can the present black-and-white, and until we can be confident of its quality, I think it would be a mistake for a serious newspaper to commit to it on a regular basis. [If you do] . . . you are forced to build your front page—and your public image—around whatever color photographs are available, whether or not they meet the test of news or reader values. To me, that's a distortion of priorities.

Interview/
Los Angeles Times, 3-14:(I)20.

Barbara Tuchman
Author, Historian

1

I think journalism has to try and make good actions . . . more newsworthy. When you see some group which has cleaned up its local river and brought the salmon back, or a family that has brought up six sons on no kind of income, all of whom turn out to be effective citizens—that sort of thing can be made more attractive to the public.

Interview, Cos Cob, Conn. /
The Christian Science Monitor, 10-7:19.

Sander Vanocur
Journalist; Host,
"Business World," ABC-TV

2

I've often had trouble with the term "investigative reporting." I came out of print journalism, and my whole training was that everything's investigative, whether you're going through records in a courthouse or using the phone . . . I would think that if there's any complaint that can be measured against the media, it's how easily we're manipulated by the White House. And not just this [Reagan] one. It goes back to the beginning of television, back to the [Dwight] Eisenhower years.

Interview/
USA Today, 12-1:(A)13.

Richard Wald
Senior vice president, ABC News

3

[Saying broadcast technology may alter the role of the TV news anchorman]: [The equip-

ment] is getting lighter, quicker, easier to move. It may be that if things really get small enough, easy enough, cheap enough, you will change the shape of what anchoring is. But it won't be because some brilliant person designed it that way. It will be because the technology drives it.

Interview/The New York Times, 2-27:26.

Caspar W. Weinberger
Secretary of Defense of
the United States

4

[Criticizing the press for printing sensitive military information]: Sometimes there seems to be little or no thought given to whether publication of facts will harm the national security; whether it will give aid and comfort to our enemies; whether it will complicate the conduct of our foreign policy; or, most important, whether it will endanger American lives.

The New York Times, 1-29:18.

Byron R. White
Associate Justice, Supreme
Court of the United States

5

[On press coverage of Supreme Court cases]: Abortion, sodomy, affirmative action, etc., these are cases people are going to be interested in, and the press is doing its job well. People should know as much as they can about a high-profile case. They should analyze, evaluate, criticize, etc. The better job of reporting that is done, the more people will understand.

Before Western judges and lawyers,
Sun Valley, Idaho, Aug. 22/
Los Angeles Times, 8-23:(I)24.

Literature

Kobo Abe
Japanese author

1

. . . I think the fundamental attitude of a writer should be a stoic one. Rather than putting everything I know into a novel, I try to eliminate everything that is not indispensable. It is all a process of erasure, an expression only of the necessary, not of loose memories and thoughts. And it's important for me to make sure I have made all the right choices.

Interview, New York/
The Washington Post, 1-20:(C)12.

Isabel Allende
Chilean author

2

In Latin America, if you have to survive earthquakes, a dictatorship, prison, it takes you over, and you are forced to write about those things rather than a small personal experience. It's practically impossible to ignore politics when I write.

At International PEN Congress, New York/
U.S. News & World Report, 1-27:65.

Isaac Asimov
Author

3

I can't explain why I am so productive. I know I've published well over 300 books and I guess that seems amazing, but it doesn't to me. There's nothing I like better than writing . . . I see a typewriter, I have thoughts, I type.

USA Today, 1-27:(D)2.

Ann Beattie
Author

4

Writing is not a "hands-on" skill. It's all in your head. Private. There isn't anything you can do if you feel helpless. I imagine that at least as

a photographer you can strap a camera around your neck, go out and *get* into it. Maybe I'm wrong. But I can't go out and find a story. And I can't just sit at a typewriter tapping keys. It would be the best thing in the world if that worked.

Interview/Publishers Weekly, 9-19:121.

Peter Benchley
Author

5

When I was 16, my father [the author, Nathaniel Benchley] said to me, "You've been rolling tennis courts, mowing lawns all these summers. I'll give you the same wage you would have made if you will write 1,000 words a day. Sit in a room, alone, minimum four hours. You don't have to show it to me; it never has to be published, or even submitted. But I want it written. And you'll get a taste for the discipline, because it's a lonely life, and I don't know if you want to do it." He did that for a couple of summers. It was wonderful. It gave me taste for the discipline and for seeing that it's something that I could do, and it was a life I could endure.

Interview/USA Today, 6-25:(A)7.

Daniel J. Boorstin
Librarian of Congress
of the United States

6

[On proposals to cut the budget of the Library of Congress]: The greatest of republics has been served by the greatest of the world's libraries. But this will not continue to be possible unless the Congress takes measures to repair the damage to be done by the vast and unprecedented cuts in the Library's budget . . . Historians will not fail to note that a people who could spend $300-billion on their defense would not spend $18-million on their knowledge—and could not even keep their libraries open in the evening . . . Knowledge is not a rock that we inherit from the

(DANIEL J. BOORSTIN)

geological past; it is a living, growing organism constantly in need of nourishment and renewal. Knowledge is not simply another commodity. On the contrary, knowledge is never used up; it increases by diffusion and grows by dispersion. Knowledge and information cannot be quantitatively assessed as a percentage of the GNP. Any willful cut in our resources of knowledge is an act of self-destruction.

Congressional testimony, Washington, Feb. 20/
U.S. News & World Report, 3-10:74.

1

Reading has often been compared to sexual activity: Much of it takes place in bed, and few are prone to underrate the prowess they bring to the task.

USA Today, 5-12:(A)10.

Ray Bradbury
Author

2

[On his new novel]: I made a conscious effort to think about the novel before I went to sleep so that my subconscious would give me answers when I woke up. Then, when I was lying in bed in the morning, I would say: "What was it that I was working on yesterday in the novel? What is the emotional problem today?" I wait for myself to get into an emotional state, not an intellectual state, then jump up and write it . . . The trouble with a lot of people who try to write is they intellectualize about it. That comes after. The intellect is given to us by God to test things once they're done, not to worry about things ahead of time.

Interview, Beverly Hills, Calif./
Writer's Digest, February:28.

Leo Braudy
Professor of literature,
University of Southern California

3

Writers occupy an interesting category of fame. All through history they have been on the edge between visibility and invisibility. They wrote books

and usually put their names on the title pages. But the books were not really them; the books were intermediaries between the writers and their audiences. Then writers gradually started having their pictures in their books. With the rise of 19th-century show business, writers like [Charles] Dickens and [Mark] Twain began to develop a performing side. But it was confined to the stage until the publicity culture of the 20th century helped create a fame like that of Ernest Hemingway.

Interview/U.S. News & World Report, 10-6:86.

Jimmy Breslin
Author, Columnist

4

If I go back over 10 years of columns at the [New York] *Daily News,* a good 50 per cent would be about women. But most newspaper guys, when they come to write a novel, figure it's got to be about a man—a cop or somebody. Men don't write about women. [William] Styron had one, I suppose—Sophie. But I'd like to do my next novel in the first person from inside a woman's head.

Interview, Los Angeles/
Los Angeles Times, 6-7:(V)1.

Bryten Breytenbach
South African poet

5

There was a time when one sensed through [Ernest] Hemingway and [Norman] Mailer the American manhood. Then, such authors as James Baldwin and Ralph Ellison explored the black experience, and Bernard Malamud and Saul Bellow gave a clear sense of growing up Jewish in America. But now, except for maybe William Styron, nothing like that is being attempted.

At International PEN Congress, New York/
U.S. News & World Report, 1-27:65.

Gwendolyn Brooks
Poet; Poetry Consultant to the
Library of Congress of the United States

6

I try to use my eyes when I have an inspiration, when I have seen something and heard

WHAT THEY SAID IN 1986

something or felt something in my gut, and I try to get that on paper. Since I have read a lot and know that metaphors are part of literature, naturally there will be metaphors and similies. As for where my imagery comes from, I've certainly dealt with the sounds and smells and sights of the city. I've often wondered what my poetry would have been like if I'd grown up in the country on a farm. I imagine it would have mentioned vegetables and fruits and trees and pigs more. But I think the emphasis still would have been on people. I'm a people poet.

Interview, Washington/
Washington Review, Feb.-Mar.:4.

Robert Burchfield
Editor, Oxford English
Dictionary supplement

1

[On the just-completed supplement, which took 29 years to put together]: When we reached "zilch" and "zillionaire," it was like having the finishing tape in sight in a marathon.

Time, 5-19:85.

James Clavell
Author

2

There are so many other writers out there who are better than I am but who perhaps don't have my *joss*. Whenever I feel lonely or depressed, my God, I think of all those other poor buggers working their tails off—equally hard as I. So if I can't enjoy it, then, my God, who can?

Interview/
Publishers Weekly, 10-24:55.

3

I don't like talking about [books] that aren't finished because, in my mind, the thing doesn't exist unless it's got a bottom and a top, a front and a back.

Interview/
Publishers Weekly, 10-24:55.

Laurie Colwin
Author

4

Some writers feel they have a mission to rub people's nose in terrible realities, but I don't feel that's my mission. I don't know what my mission is. There's a German word meaning, "to charm and irritate." And I've heard there's a Hebrew word meaning, "to visit and criticize." I want to do all four.

Interview, New York/
The Wall Street Journal, 5-7:28.

Richard Condon
Author

5

My goal is: How can I tell you a jolly good story? A reader walks seven miles to the library and the novelist has to hold up his part of the deal—to entertain. The novelist is saying, I have a few things I'd like to disclose to you. Along the way, I entertain you to get you to finish the book. "Very interesting," the reader says to himself. "I didn't know that—it's a revelation to me." So it's a trade-off. If I entertain the reader, he'll stick with my disclosures.

Interview, New York/
The New York Times, 10-29:25.

Jacques-Yves Cousteau
Explorer, Environmentalist

6

[Poets] are the only ones who take the time to think and to imagine. I was baffled, for example, to see that a long time before [Isaac] Newton, the English poet John Donne was describing in one poem the influence of the moon and the sun on the tides. Poets have an insight into things, and scientists come after them. They are the only ones who did not damage their good sense.

Interview/USA Today, 6-5:(A)11.

Michael Crichton
Author

7

Books aren't written, they're re-written. Including your own. It's one of the hardest things

(MICHAEL CRICHTON)

to accept, especially after the seventh rewrite hasn't quite done it.

Interview, Writer's Digest,
September:30.

Sandor Csoori
Hungarian poet

1

[In] Eastern and Central Europe . . . literature is a very "personal concern" of the state—most often posing a problem not only for the power of the state, but also for its psychological condition, almost to the level of producing psychopathical complex in the mind of the state. It fears literature, loves it and envies it, in the same way as the domineering man is jealous of his lover who seeks liberation. Put differently, just as we [in Eastern Europe] are not allowed a court system independent from the power of the state, there exists no literature separate from the state power and the political realm.

At International PEN
Conference, New York/
The Wall Street Journal, 1-24:22.

Peter Davison
Poetry editor,
"The Atlantic" magazine

2

[Criticizing the idea of a U.S. poet laureate to be chosen every year or two]: In 52 years, you could have 52 poets laureate. It's like the Book-of-the-Month Club. There haven't been 52 great poets in the history of the United States.

The Christian Science Monitor,
2-24:10.

E. L. Doctorow
Author

3

I wish people would read books with as little self-consciousness as they buy groceries or rent videos.

Newsweek, 12-1:25.

Lawrence Durrell
Author

4

I always wanted to think of a great novel or a great poem as a kind of domestic appliance, something that you could use to grow up with, that the thrill it gave you really changed your personality and reoriented you toward evolving in your sensibility.

Interview, New York/
The Washington Post, 5-29:(B)4.

Clifton Fadiman
Editor, Critic

5

If more people read great books, as a society we might be politically more aware. We might elect people to high office that are more mature than the ones we do [now]. It would be a society in which judgments would be exercised more carefully. Also, a knowledge of good literature would change our society so that we would not accept cheap and vulgar as easily as we do now. Good reading unconsciously creates in us a higher standard of excellence; we reject the shoddy and dishonest.

Interview, Santa Barbara, Calif./
The Christian Science Monitor, 7-18:21.

Richard Ford
Author

6

[On being a Southern writer]: What it used to mean was that you wrote like [William] Faulkner. That's mostly all it has ever meant, because, before Faulkner, there was no such thing as an important, isolable tradition of Southern literature. And there is none now. There are just good writers, and not-so-good writers.

Interview/The Christian
Science Monitor, 7-30:19.

7

I believe that literature . . . is a curative. That's at least one of the things it is. It's a way for people of the world to see themselves, in a wider and more complex way. It presumes that if

(RICHARD FORD)

people can see and understand the world better, they will make it better. It doesn't mean that you yourself have to be an optimist. In the very least sense, if you give somebody something, it means that they will have something more to do, to look forward to. I give you a book.

Interview/The Christian Science Monitor, 7-30:20.

Carlos Fuentes
Author

1

The world is a mine of good stories that haven't been told. The novel is hardly dead. This is one of the most brilliant periods in the history of the novel. Now you can talk of the geography of the novel, which is a world-wide geography. You've got Nadine Gordimer and J. M. Coetzee in South Africa. And Salman Rushdie in India. Gunter Grass, [William] Styron, [Juan] Goytisolo, [Norman] Mailer, Philip Roth, the Latin Americans. It's a formidable spectrum and it covers the world. Finally, this is happening because you know that there are things that can only be said through the novel. And this is particularly true in a century when the traditional provinces of the novel have been taken away from it by television, the movies, journalism, psychology, sociology. But I think this creates the obligation of the novelist to ask: "What the hell can we say in a novel that can be said no other way?"

Interview, Chicago/ Mother Jones, January:51.

Theodor Geisel (Dr. Seuss)
Author of children's books

2

The problem of writing a [children's] book in verse is, to be successful it has to sound like you knocked it off on a rainy Friday afternoon. It has to sound easy. When you can do it, it helps tremendously because it's a thing that forces kids to read on. You have this unconsummated feeling if you stop. You have to go right through to the end—to the final beat. The main problem with writing in verse is, if your fourth line doesn't come out right, you've got to throw four lines away and figure out a whole new way to attack the problem. So the mortality rate is terrific.

Interview/Los Angeles Times Magazine, 5-25:40.

Allen Ginsberg
Poet

3

This week I have a cash-flow problem. It'll be tough paying for secretarial help. In ancient days, poets had patrons or were wandering minstrels. Milton was Cromwell's secretary. Blake was an engraver and a painter. In more recent times, Whitman was a newspaperman, Wallace Stevens an insurance-company executive. T. S. Eliot was an editor at a publishing house. And most poets today, like John Crowe Ransom, Allen Tate and Robert Lowell, teach.

Interview, New York/ The Wall Street Journal, 3-11:30.

Nadine Gordimer
South African author

4

It's a fact that writers are an intellectual force. [Without them,] all the ontological questions will be solved on a managerial basis. But don't put the line so fine. The very truth of language depends upon our fidelity to craft.

At International PEN conference, New York/ The Christian Science Monitor, 1-29:20.

Shirley Ann Grau
Pulitzer Prize-winning author

5

I've started another novel, [but] I'm rather superstitious—if you talk about a thing, you tend to lose the tension that is absolutely necessary to pull it out of you. If you talk about a book, you don't write. If you talk, you don't do. I don't even like to talk about books when they're done.

Interview/Publishers Weekly, 1-10:71.

Graham Greene
Author

1

No one forgets more easily than a novelist—it is his salvation to forget. An impression once snatched and put down on paper is no longer useful; it is dispatched into the unconscious. Even a character whom he has invented and lived with for more than a year may disappear completely into oblivion.

Interview/Airport, October:12.

Alec Guinness
Actor

2

[Saying the book he wrote is not an autobiography]: I don't like those rivulets of "I"'s running down a page. So I thought I'd write about people who had influenced me when I was very young. By doing that, I thought I could stop someone else from writing about me and getting it wrong. I rather resent that others can use your life while you're still here. I could be dying in the gutter and there might be someone doing not too badly off a book about me. I'll take the cash myself, thank you.

Interview, New York/People, 4-7:70.

David Halberstam
Author, Journalist

3

. . . there are a lot of "bean counters" in publishing now. And, just as in Detroit, they're not interested in the product per se—making better cars or better books. Their idea is to see what someone else has done that makes money, then go and do the same thing. The problem is when they go from being a necessary fiscally conservative force in publishing to being actual tastemakers, because they're simply not equipped to do it.

Interview, New York/
Publishers Weekly, 10-17:45.

Anthony Hecht
Pulitzer Prize-winning poet

4

[Criticizing the idea that an academic job is bad for poets]: It seems to me that this is a rather romantic notion about what real life is. Real life involves being married and having a family, being sick and recovering, paying your bills and having a mortgage on the house. Poets have all these things; they're not reserved for other people who participate in "real life."

Interview, Washington/
Publishers Weekly, 7-18:71.

Michael Hooker
Chancellor, University of
Maryland, Baltimore County

5

[The history of literature is] the history of pointing out that the world is not as simple as it seems, that life is filled with ambiguity and uncertainty, that we deceive ourselves right and left. Literature tells the truth. And if it doesn't tell the truth it's not literature, [it's] propaganda or something else.

Interview, Baltimore/
The Christian Science Monitor, 10-1:17.

Jesse L. Jackson
Civil-rights leader

6

[Criticizing Federal spending cutbacks that could affect public libraries]: We are here to fight for access to books because books represent the oxygen for our minds. Give us libraries, give us books, give us food, give us jobs, or give us death!

At Library of Congress, Washington,
March 24/The Washington Post, 3-25:(C)2.

P. D. James
Author

7

A book almost always begins with a place. You start with the setting and it grows from there. It incubates so very many months. The most recent one started when I visited a church in Oxford [England]. I had this visual image of the dead bodies in the vestry. Then you decide who's been killed and when and why and who the suspects are going to be and what their vari-

377

WHAT THEY SAID IN 1986

ous motives are going to be. It develops from that original visual image of a particular place, or reaction to a particular place.

*Interview, London/
Los Angeles Times, 11-6:(V)19.*

1

In times of depression and anxiety, when you may be blown up by a terrorist bomb at the next airport, detective stories are reassuring. They provide a firm moral code and affirm the sanctity of life. Mysteries say that even the victim, who usually is pretty unpleasant, has a right to live his life to the last natural moment. What's more, they offer a solution. And it isn't by supernatural means or good luck; it's by human intelligence, courage and endurance.

*Interview/U.S. News &
World Report, 11-24:78.*

Garrison Keillor
Author

2

I can't think of stories in formal terms until they're written. *Then* I can look at a story that I have written, or that someone else has written, and I can describe its form, as I did when I was in school and was asked to write term papers. Every story finds its *own* form. Finding that form is the great struggle of writing, for which there is no prescription. I would say that the essential element in story-telling is the passion to tell a story that will get you through that struggle of finding out how to tell it. If you don't have that passion to tell a story, you will settle for telling it not very well, which is almost worse than not telling it at all. But if you have the passion to tell a story, it becomes a wonderful problem in your life—a wonderful problem like being in love. It becomes an irritation, a splendid misery, that might get some work out of a person who will do his little part in adding to the world's knowledge, in adding to the life of the world.

*Interview, Chicago/
Writer's Digest, January:35.*

Stephen King
Author

3

If you work out with weights for 15 minutes a day over a course of 10 years, you're going to get muscles. If you write for an hour and a half a day for 10 years, you're going to turn into a good writer.

Interview/Time, 10-6:80.

Tadeusz Konwicki
Polish author

4

[On Polish government restrictions on what can be written and published]: My opinion is that books ought to be edited and published here in a normal way. But nobody's worked out a method yet. What I'm trying to do is find my own way. Writers in Poland, you know, we're like parachutists. We're always plunging out without knowing where we're going to land.

*Interview, Warsaw/
The Washington Post, 9-5:(B)2.*

Judith Krantz
Author

5

Even though I have high hopes [about a new book], I have no guarantees. I worry right down to the day I can see my book at number one on the best-seller list. I'll have to be senile to stop worrying. Publishing is a horse race. And you can't not worry whether your horse will win, place or show. The rate of sale counts. I respect my competition. Being number one can mean the difference between selling 49 and 50 copies in a single bookstore.

*Interview, Los Angeles/
Publishers Weekly, 5-16:59.*

6

Trash to me is garbage. In my books, there is no garbage. I turn out, with great difficulty—believe me, it just doesn't happen—something that millions of people want to read in 19 languages. Trash it is definitely not.

*Interview, Washington/
The Washington Post, 5-20:(B)4.*

Louis L'Amour
Author

1

[On the fact that he's published 95 books]: I wish people wouldn't keep mentioning the total. That big number can give a wrong impression. Critics forget that Dickens and Balzac were prolific and that Noel Coward wrote one of his best plays [*Hay Fever*] in 24 hours. There are some, you know, who don't think I write fast *enough*.

Interview/Newsweek, 7-14:68.

John Le Carre
Author

2

[On how he writes]: According to simple principles. Like a professional athlete, I devote to writing the best hours of my day: early in the morning. I wrote the last six chapters of *A Perfect Spy* between 4 a.m. and 10 a.m., before the rest of the world had awakened. It is a habit I formed when I was a diplomat. The embassies rarely open before 10 a.m. You can thus gain half a day of work. I always write by hand. I cannot type; I cannot find the letters on the keyboard. I like the rhythm of a written manuscript, the pen and paper. When you alter something it is instantaneous. There is something purely physical in this process of artistic creation. When one writes slowly, one self-censors, and with a glance one can see the archeology of the manuscript.

Interview/
World Press Review, August:60.

Lu Wenfu
Chinese author

3

The present literature [in China] is marked by its ideological depths, and also by its variety in topics, style and form. And this is a landmark of prosperity of literature, because I think if there is only one style, then that means it is not flourishing.

Interview,
New York/The Christian
Science Monitor, 2-3:27.

Spark M. Matsunaga
United States Senator,
D-Hawaii

4

[Supporting the establishment of a U.S. poet laureate]: I've long held to the view that if the lessons of human experience are put into verse, we might better learn and remember them. The experiences of a democratic nation ought to be put into verse . . . Of all the industrialized nations, the United States is the only one without a laureate . . . The whole idea is not to set someone up for life, but to give other poets an opportunity to aspire to the position. This is an encouragement of the creative arts. The thing that survives civilization is the arts; and poetry is an art.

The Christian Science Monitor, 2-24:10.

5

[On the designation of the first U.S. poet laureate]: The poet laureate of the U.S. will raise the prestige and respect of the poet to the point where youngsters will aspire to become poets, just as politically minded youngsters aspire to the Presidency.

Time, 3-10:48.

Gregory Mcdonald
Author

6

Writing is not a profession, occupation or job; it is not a way of life; it is a comprehensive response to life.

Interview/
Writer's Digest, September:24.

Daniel Moynihan
United States Senator,
D-New York

7

[Arguing against Federal budget cuts affecting the Library of Congress]: If knowledge is power, its absence is weakness. Our nation can ill afford the price we will pay by limiting our access to information.

USA Today, 4-10:(A)4.

WHAT THEY SAID IN 1986

Alice Munro
Author

1

I no longer feel attracted to the well-made novel. I want to write the story that will zero in and give you intense, but not connected, moments of experience. I guess that's the way I see life. People remake themselves bit by bit and do things they don't understand. The novel has to have a coherence which I don't see any more in the lives around me.

Interview/Publishers Weekly, 8-22:76.

Jim Murray
Sports columnist, "Los Angeles Times"

2

I think writers are born, not made, and a born writer is not easily discouraged. It's easy to discourage a guy who shouldn't be writing. [A born writer,] oh, I guess it's when you look at something, seeing it in a different light, or at a different depth, from the way most people would. Of course, a writer can be improved if he's got what it takes to start with. He'll improve himself, the way Ted Williams, a born [baseball] hitter, did.

Interview/Writer's Digest, June:26.

Richard M. Nixon
Former President of the United States

3

When I was a student at Whittier College, an English professor persuaded me to spend one of my summer vacations reading the works of [Leo] Tolstoy. It was the best advice I had ever received. These two novels [*War and Peace* and *Anna Karenina*] left a number of indelible impressions on me. The greatness of Russia was one; the virtuosity of this greatest of writers was another.

U.S. News & World Report, 4-14:75.

Joyce Carol Oates
Author, Poet

4

In a phase of poetry-writing, I feel that I am most at home in poetry. There is something truly enthralling about the process—the very finitude of the form, the opportunity for constant revision—an incantatory solace generally missing in fiction. Poetry requires no time in the reading as prose fiction always does, particularly the novel; the demands of the novel on both reader and writer are considerable, after all. After finishing a long, difficult novel, I always enter a phase of poetry. It can last for perhaps six or eight weeks. Of course, this phase is by no means without its own difficulties, but its pleasures are more immediate and forthcoming. One can even *see* a poem in its entirety—a source of amazement to the novelist.

Interview/Writer's Digest, April:32.

5

The character on the page determines the prose—its music, its rhythms, the range and limit of its vocabulary—yet, at the outset at least, I determine the character. It usually happens that the fictitious character, once released, acquires a life and will of his or her own, so the prose, too, acquires its own inexplicable fluidity. This is one of the reasons I write: to "hear" a voice not quite my own, yet summoned forth by way of my own.

Interview/Writer's Digest, April:32.

6

Poetry tends to be more personal [than fiction] . . . I use it for convalescent reasons. When I feel very [spiritually] weak, I read a lot of poetry. Music and poetry, they bring you back, they fill up the soul, like a well that has to be replenished.

Lecture, Chapman College/
Los Angeles Times, 11-7:(V)6.

Philip Roth
Author

7

At one point [in his book *The Counterlife,* the character Nathan] Zuckerman says, "All my audacity derives from masks." He means that the best of his vividness, daring, originality and flair surfaces only through artistic posturing. Well, if that's the case, you had better become

(PHILIP ROTH)

either an actor or a novelist. The actor wears the mask for public performance; the writer dons the mask all alone in a room. He dons the mask of Humbert Humbert, the mask of Stingo or Herzog or Holden Caulfield. Unmasked, he lives, like everybody, primarily with "what is." As a masquerader, he is generally more curious about "what might have been." and "what could be."

Interview, New York/
The New York Times, 12-17:25.

Ernesto Sabato
Argentine author

1

I'm essentially a novelist. The novel has the advantage of expressing the total reality of man. The novel brings ideas, dreams, symbols, myths. And it brings together logical thought and magical thought . . .

Interview, Washington/
The Washington Post, 1-22:(C)9.

Mary Lee Settle
Author

2

Fiction is that raw material of memory, of research, of personal observation, of all the reading you've done, sunk down into a semiconscious field and then transmuted into something new. I can read a piece of fiction years after writing it and see cropping up in it a gesture or memory that was autobiographical, but it has been transmuted so much that I wasn't conscious of the personal element when I wrote it.

Interview/U.S. News &
World Report, 12-22:64.

Gerald Seymour
Author; Former journalist,
Independent Television News (Britain)

3

In fiction, it's the little guy who matters rather than some general or high public official. If you find yourself explaining the way the Pentagon works in a novel, it's boresville. Plot and background don't count if you fail in characterization. I like to start with a central character or a situation but try, at first, to suppress who that character will be. Journalists are obsessed with the information they've gathered. But in a novel you are not just imparting information. It's not how you research but how you use the research that is vital in a novel. You have to have your mind open to ideas and people. An overheard phrase, a paragraph at the end of a news story, can sometimes be built up into a whole chapter.

Interview, Bath, England/
The New York Times, 1-22:19.

Isaac Bashevis Singer
Author

4

I've always felt I've never done well. I've always felt I should have done better. It was true when I was 30. It is true at 81. If I'm famous, I cannot stop it or enhance it. Only today I know better what I'm doing when I write. When I was 20 years old, I didn't know what I was doing.

Interview/The New York Times, 1-22:16.

Sol Stein
President, Stein & Day, publishers

5

The intention of a book publisher should be to publish books that will have long-term value. Too many "instant books" are either superficial or rehashes of newspaper stories.

The New York Times, 5-15:21.

6

[Saying it is becoming difficult for publishers to obtain liability insurance]: We are uninsured as of June 1 . . . because we occasionally publish controversial books . . . Public service and controversial books are an integral part of a publisher's operation, as long as they are vetted very carefully. But now the insurance companies are saying they will insure us only if we publish innocuous books.

Interview, New York/
The New York Times, 6-23:15.

WHAT THEY SAID IN 1986

Gay Talese
Author

1

Never write anything that you think is "best-seller" material, because nobody really knows what makes a book a best-seller—and no good writer ever cares whether or not his book is a commercial success. What is important is always to do your best work.

Interview/Writer's Digest, September:27.

Henry Taylor
Pulitzer Prize-winning poet

2

[On his recently winning the Pulitzer Prize]: The Pulitzer has a funny way of changing people's opinions about it. If you haven't won one, you go around saying things like, "Well, it's all political" or "It's a lottery," and stuff like that. I would like to go on record as saying that, although I'm deeply grateful and feel very honored, I still believe that it's a lottery and that nobody deserves it . . . I have never gone so far as to say that the prize is so meaningless that if it ever comes to me I'll turn it down. Why should one turn it down? It's like finding money in the road. If you can't tell whose it is, keep it. And I can't tell whose the prize is, so I'll take it with great gratitude.

The Washington Post, 4-19:(D)9.

Peter Taylor
Author

3

My sister once met [author William] Faulkner at a dinner party, and she asked if he had any advice for a brother who was trying to be a writer. Faulkner said, "Tell him to read *Anna Karenina, Anna Karenina* and *Anna Karenina*." That's still about as good advice as you can get.

Interview/The New York Times, 5-7:25.

Jim Trelease
Author, Lecturer

4

It's really never too early to start reading to a child. If the child is old enough to talk to—and parents talk to their children from Day 1—then he or she is old enough to be read to as well. It doesn't matter that infants can't understand the words; the English language inside the covers of books is frequently a whole lot more organized, colorful and coherent than "koochie, koochie, koochie." Setting even a tiny child in front of a book and reading to him or her is intellectual stimulation . . . Next to hugging your child, reading aloud is probably the longest-lasting experience that you can put into your child's life. You will savor it long after they have grown up. Reading aloud is important for all the reasons that talking to children is important—to inspire them, to guide them, to educate them, to bond with them and to communicate your feelings, hopes and fears. You are giving children a piece of your mind and a piece of your time.

Interview/U.S. News & World Report, 3-17:65.

John Updike
Author

5

A writer comes into the world in his or her twenties usually with a certain amount of childhood and youthful *Sturm und Drang* behind him, and so his material is there ripe to be plucked. And that maybe lasts up to the age of 35; but you gradually run out of that initially magical material. Somehow, the impressions you gather when young are magical and self-evidentially important, and very worth telling. And one of the ingredients you ought to have if you're going to write fiction is the illusion that what you're telling is worth telling . . . But in your fifties, you should, I suppose, compensate for youthful energy by being in some way wiser, or at least having more reach, more variety, maybe turning out a more thoughtfully polished product . . . But what excites me is producing these books every year. Somehow, the smell of the binding glue and the look of the crisp print is terribly thrilling. Unduly thrilling, perhaps. The world is choked with books already.

Interview, New York/ The Washington Post, 9-30:(D)9.

(JOHN UPDIKE)

1

There is danger for a writer in doing too many interviews. Too much talk can make you fatheaded: You get the idea that everything you say is worth being recorded and that you are in some sense a wise man and an interesting person. The more an author thinks of himself in that way, the less attentive he's going to be to the business of trying to transcribe reality. We [authors] really are servants, basically, of reality, aren't we? We're trying to get a little piece of it into print. And so—partly to avoid more attention than I can absorb—I have spent my life in small towns where I'm more or less accepted as another citizen and householder and not made much of as a writer, as I might be if I lived in New York.

Interview/U.S. News &
World Report, 10-20:67.

2

Some people think of me as a prolific writer. I'm sorry that I give that impression, because I distrust prolific writers. I think that if they'd write half as much, they might be twice as good. I think of myself as writing at a stately pace—a few pages a day. That's really less than a thousand words—a very modest quota compared with that which many writers have set for themselves. Evelyn Waugh was once asked how long a novel should take, and he said, "Six weeks." I take about a year.

Interview/U.S. News &
World Report, 10-20:68.

Leon Uris
Author

3

The complete novelist would come into the world with a catalog of qualities something like this: He would own the concentration of a Trappist monk, the organizational ability of a Prussian field marshal, the insight into human relations of a Viennese psychiatrist, the discipline of a man who prints the Lord's Prayer on the head of a pin, the exquisite sense of timing of an Olympic gymnast, and, by the way, a natural instinct and flair

for exceptional use of language. Obviously, no man or woman has all of this. Yet unless he has some of it, dished out solely by the grace of the Lord, he cannot become a writer.

Interview/Writer's Digest, September:25.

Mario Vargas Llosa
Peruvian author

4

There is a widespread belief that writers have a monopoly on lucidity on political matters and that the statesman has a monopoly on political blindness. But even great writers can be totally blind on political matters and can put their prestige and their imagination and fantasy at the service of a policy, which, if it materialized, would be the destruction of what they do. [In Latin America,] we can effectively pass from [Chilean leader Augusto] Pinochet to the gulag. To be in the situation of Poland is no better than to be in the situation of Chile. I feel perplexed by these questions. I want to fight for societies where perplexity is still permitted.

At International PEN Congress,
New York, January/Time, 1-27:77.

5

[On PEN, the international writer's group]: PEN was founded on the hope that if writers can show how to coexist in a civilized way, the world will follow. That was very naive. But it is important to join together people from different countries, ideologies and religions because, whatever their differences they at least agree on the need to defend literary activities. We don't always make an impact on governments that disagree with that, but it is important for writers to try.

Interview/The New York Times, 1-11:13.

Kurt Vonnegut
Author

6

I've experienced the deaths of several world-class writers now who were friends of mine. When they're dead, it's the end of their careers, really. There's very little that's going to live after them . . . [Truman] Capote—wasn't he that

383

WHAT THEY SAID IN 1986

(KURT VONNEGUT)

funny little guy on the telly you don't see any more?

Interview, Dallas/
The Saturday Evening Post, May-June:39.

Irving Wallace
Author

1

Don't enter the world of book publishing expecting interest only in art and creativity. There *is* such an interest, especially among the younger editors. But little of it exists in their bosses. Most publishers are basically commercial-minded. They have no time for literary idealism.

Interview/Writer's Digest, September:31.

Wang Meng
Chinese author

2

My image of America seen through fiction doesn't compare with my own experience of visiting here. I get perplexed because American authors don't really write about America, but more about personal feelings.

At International PEN Congress, New York/
U.S. News & World Report, 1-27:65.

3

Just before the [Chinese] Cultural Revolution, literature was influenced too much by politics, so it didn't have its own characteristics. Now the development of writing reflects the reality of the society. And it reflects the writer's point of view of society and reality.

Interview, New York/
The Christian Science Monitor, 2-3:27.

Robert Penn Warren
Poet laureate of the United States

4

[Saying he decided to accept the honor of being named the first U.S. poet laureate because it does not carry the trappings that the title encompasses in Britain]: The idea of an official poet goes against our [American] system. We aren't English. Over there, the laureate becomes a member of the government. Over here, I will just be an employee of the Library of Congress.

Time, 3-10:48.

5

Almost all poems are fragmentary autobiography. Sometimes I can trace an idea back to some fragment of memory. But I couldn't start making sense out of the events that gave rise to the fragment. It has to make its own sense, years later. A line or two may exist in your head and suddenly it goes somewhere. Something makes it click again. Every poem is in one sense a symbol. Its meaning is always more than it says to you—the writer—and more than it specifies directly to a reader. Otherwise, it doesn't exist as a poem. It's just a statement of some kind which provokes the reader into his own poem.

Interview/U.S News &
World Report, 6-23:73.

6

There's no education in poetry in schools any more. Memorization doesn't exist. Doesn't exist. I remember a long generation ago, on a Friday afternoon [reciting] a long poem—a good poem, not a jingle. Memorization's the only thing that counts—*knowing* a poem, and hearing it in your head, even if you don't like it . . . You can't know anything about poetry unless you *know* it.

News conference, Washington/
The Washington Post, 10-7:(D)1.

Jerome Weidman
Author

7

The instinct to write was always there. From the beginning, I made a conscious formulation to sit down and write a story. You read a lot of stuff and you form judgments. You think, "I can do as well as that." Many writers who are enormously successful are terrible writers. But if they pluck a chord with the reader, the book will sell. On the other hand, sometimes I've written something that I thought was very difficult, some-

(JEROME WEIDMAN)

thing that I was really proud of, and no one else cared.

Interview, San Francisco/
Publishers Weekly, 9-12:72.

Eudora Welty
Author

1

Writing has gotten different and more interesting to me over the years—and it has probably gotten harder. When I first began, I wrote straight through and then stopped. The stories had a direction and a destination. I didn't revise at all; I didn't have enough sense to. Now that I know that you can write something in many different ways, I'm tempted to do so. I write a first draft and revise a lot as I see ways I can show something better. I'm sure that has slowed me down, and I don't care about that. But it may have taken some of the spontaneous quality out of my work. I know I can never get it perfect. You just have to know when you've done it the best way. A friend of mine who is a writer said he kept 13 drafts of a story and put them all in a drawer. Years later he went back, and it was Number 7 that was the right one. That taught me a real, true lesson.

Interview/U. S. News & World Report, 8-18:54.

2

What interests me is communicating a good story. Of course a story has to be personal, but it is not the putting on the page of "me, myself and I" . . . Even a frivolous story is based on a serious subject, some kind of backbone. And the most essential element is human truth.

Wellesley, Mass./
The Christian Science Monitor, 10-27:8.

Yevgeny Yevtushenko
Soviet poet

3

I don't like solitude. I like to see eyes [of the audience] while I read poetry from the stage. Even when I am alone and I write . . . I see those eyes expecting my words. I couldn't imagine myself in an ivory tower. Some very good poets are created by solitude . . . but I am a different man!

Interview, New York/
The Christian Science Monitor, 2-10:32.

Medicine and Health

George Allen
*Former football coach, Los Angeles "Rams"
and Washington "Redskins"*

1

Most of today's adults had a taste of fitness from their phys-ed classes in school before phys-ed was dropped by many schools. But today's kids don't get that taste of fitness now when they're young. My concern is that they might not be inclined to pursue it later on . . . One hundred million adults exercise regularly. There are 72 million who own bicycles, 55 million who walk seriously, 40 to 45 million who play softball, 35 million who run or jog. In this country [the U.S.], $30-billion is spent annually on exercise-related things. And, since 1970, there's been a 26 per cent decline in heart-disease deaths, a 40 per cent decline in stroke deaths. Our life expectancy is now 74 years. All this adult fitness is great. But the kids aren't fit enough.

The New York Times, 5-17:17.

Derek C. Bok
President, Harvard University

2

[There is a] lack of attention paid to the non-scientific side of medicine. [Doctors should] understand the emotional, psychological and cultural underpinnings of human behavior, including the interweaving of mind and body in illness and health.

The New York Times, 4-8:18.

Otis R. Bowen
*Secretary of Health and Human
Services of the United States*

3

Experts have estimated that anywhere from 5 to 15 per cent of practicing physicians would be candidates for some kind of disciplinary action, many because of drug or alcohol problems . . . Speak up when you see poor medicine being practiced. Not to do so is to render a grave dis-

service to patients and the profession alike.

*At New York University School of
Medicine commencement, June 5/
The New York Times, 6-6:9.*

4

[Calling for an expansion in Medicare and more incentives for people to buy health insurance]: A catastrophic illness can be a short-term condition requiring intensive acute services or a lingering illness requiring many years of care. It can affect anyone: the young, the middle-aged, the elderly. A catastrophic illness is financially devastating and requires personal sacrifices that can haunt families for the rest of their lives.

*News conference, Washington, Nov. 20/
The New York Times, 11-21:13.*

Cyril Brickfield
*Executive director, American
Association of Retired Persons*

5

[On the new "prospective payment" system Medicare uses to pay hospitals]: We've received hundreds of complaints [from patients]. Prospective payment, in which hospitals are paid a lump sum per illness, creates an incentive for hospitals to discharge people quicker. In too many cases, these earlier discharges happen to patients who continue to need hospital care. They cannot obtain nursing-home care because Medicare doesn't pay for it. In many places, community services are inadequate. We are most concerned about patients discharged to the home of another elderly person, usually a spouse, who is not capable of taking care of the person during convalescence.

Interview/U.S. News & World Report, 4-14:66.

Lonnie Bristow
*Physician; Trustee,
American Medical Association*

6

Whenever we have an illness with no effective cure, it becomes fertile ground for charlatans of-

(LONNIE BRISTOW)

fering treatments which have no beneficial effect.

Los Angeles Times, 12-11:(I)30.

James Burke
Chairman, Johnson & Johnson

1

[On the recent discovery of Tylenol capsules to which poison had been added]: If you look at this country and its ability to move masses of merchandise on free and open shelves, it's remarkable how few incidents we've had. People don't like it, and it's one more anxiety-producing part of their lives, but they understand the odds. About 3 billion capsules of all sorts have been sold since [the first poisoning incident some time ago in] Chicago; this is the first incident [since then]. It is still the safest system in the world.

Interview/U.S. News & World Report, 3-3:47.

Joseph A. Califano, Jr.
Former Secretary of Health, Education and Welfare of the United States

2

[Saying smoking should be restricted in public places]: People—whether they're children, workers or pregnant women—should not be forced to breathe other people's smoke. Maybe you can drink alone or eat alone, but it is not possible to smoke alone in an enclosed space with other people. Studies show that 5,000 Americans die each year because of secondhand smoke. A Japanese report concluded that non-smoking wives of heavy smokers had an 80 per cent higher risk of lung cancer than women married to non-smokers. Study after study has associated involuntary smoking and lung cancer, pneumonia, asthma and bronchitis. A recent study has linked secondhand smoke to heart disease . . . Why should the non-smoker have to protect himself against breathing smoke any more than a customer should have to inspect the kitchen of a restaurant to see if it is sanitary? . . . Smoking is slow-motion suicide. The point here is to

prevent secondhand smoking from becoming slow-motion murder.

Interview/U.S. News & World Report, 7-21:65.

Eunice Cole
President, American Nurses' Association

3

We've [nurses] been characterized as a profession of women—and it's women's work. One of the good things among many that came out of the women's movement was more men coming into the nursing profession. We're seeing that in the number of students graduating each year. Interestingly enough, many of those men going into nursing are men who have degrees in biology; they're going into nursing with another degree behind them, and they really do want to be nurses. They don't want to be health-care-type workers. We will continue to see a slow gain in terms of more men coming in. But the low salary has been a deterrent to some men coming in.

Interview/USA Today, 5-1:(A)9.

Shirley Coletti
Chairman, National Federation of Parents for a Drug Free Youth

4

As long as there is a permissive attitude in [the U.S.] regarding [illegal] drugs and drug usage, we can't possibly win the war on drugs. We are slowly turning those attitudes and those values around, but there are still a lot of people in the media, in entertainment, in industry, people with high visibility, who still have the attitude that "recreational" drug use is okay.

The Christian Science Monitor, 8-28:6.

Norman Cousins
Adjunct professor, School of Medicine, University of California, Los Angeles; Former editor, "Saturday Review"

5

The body moves down the path of its expectations. There are vast psychological factors at work in health, illness and the treatment of ill-

(NORMAN COUSINS)

ness. And these have to be respected. The healing system is tied to the belief system.

Interview, Beverly Hills, Calif./
The Christian Science Monitor, 11-12:29.

Mario M. Cuomo
Governor of New York (D)

1

[Proposing that all doctors be required to pass periodic competency reviews in order to keep their licenses]: Many citizens are disturbed by reports of misconduct among doctors. This reform effort will put in place the strongest system of quality control anywhere in the country . . . Other professions undergo recertification, requiring retraining or similar continuing education. Although most responsible physicians keep themselves abreast of rapidly changing medical technology, there is absolutely no continuing requirement now in place for members of this life-and-death profession.

New York, May 28/
The New York Times, 5-29:1,20.

William E. Dannemeyer
United States Representative,
R-California

2

[Calling for restrictions on certain rights of homosexuals and AIDS victims as a method of preventing the spread of AIDS]: AIDS is a public health crisis of epidemic proportions, not a civil-rights battle. If we do not take definitive action now, even actions which will compromise some of the rights of some in our society, we risk disaster. While we await a cure for this deadly disease, we are faced with difficult issues and public policy choices . . . We must find a way to change the approach of this nation's public-health officials. They have not treated AIDS like other epidemics, or even like other venereal diseases. The role of public-health authorities is to contain AIDS. They should not bow to powerful public pressure and coercive lobbying efforts to alter the course of appropriate and necessary public policy in the name of civil rights . . .

AIDS is a virus, and viruses do not have civil rights.

At Stanford University/
USA Today, 4-1:(A)6.

Henry Desmarais
Acting Chief, Health Care Financing
Administration of the United States

3

Hospitals are much more efficient than they ever were. That can't help but be good. Before the Federal government shifted to a system of prospective payment, there was little incentive to be efficient because the Medicare program simply paid the costs. Now hospitals are paid a fixed amount set in advance according to a system of diagnosis-related groups, or DRGs. That means hospitals have to operate at full capacity. They are specializing in the types of services they do best. As we know, practice makes perfect. So there's definitely an improvement in the quality of care from this kind of specialization.

Interview/U.S. News & World Report, 4-14:66.

Paul Dince
President, American
Academy of Psychoanalysis

4

Most of us [psychoanalysts] are a lot like the Judd Hirsch character in [the film] *Ordinary People*. We care about our patients. We're not rigid, pompous oracles and we work very hard with people who are suffering mightily. We're in the trenches with people who have severe disturbances and wish to overcome them so they can live an ordinary life. We do what we can, and I would insist that we can do a great deal.

Washington/
The Washington Post, 5-12: (B)9.

Alain C. Enthoven
Professor of public and private
management, Graduate School of Business,
Stanford University; Former adviser to the
Department of Defense of the United States;
Specialist in economics of health care

5

When I got involved in health care, I realized that doctors were a lot like Admirals. In both

(ALAIN C. ENTHOVEN)

groups you have a technological elite of highly trained people with a very distinct point of view. They go around in white coats and they say: "What I am doing is too important to be contaminated with considerations of money. Your job is to get me the money so I can go on doing this important and wonderful thing." And in both cases I had the reaction that when it gets *so* expensive, considerations of value for money have to be brought in. It's a very exciting challenge to figure out how to do that. It's not simple or obvious or easy.

Interview/American Heritage, Feb.-Mar.:94.

Frank Gawin
Director, cocaine treatment program,
School of Medicine, Yale University

1

Early in use, all of the positive things that are said about cocaine are true. As use continues, all the negative things become true.

The New York Times, 11-17:12.

Terence Golden
Administrator, General Services
Administration of the United States

2

Smoking has begun to infringe on the health interests of non-smokers in the workplace. No longer is it the right of the individual to smoke without regard for the health concerns of those who work in the same area. The official regulations I have proposed for [curbing smoking in] Federal buildings are a positive step toward the total wellness of Federal employees.

Speech sponsored by President's Council
on Physical Fitness and Sports, Seattle,
May 22/Los Angeles Times, 5-23:(I)4.

Toni Grant
Radio psychologist,
Mutual Broadcasting System

3

[On radio psychology programs]: Market research has indicated that the average person who

calls has listened to my program for about a year. These people are not capriciously picking up the phone to talk to a strange lady. They're picking up the phone to talk to someone they feel they know . . . They've listened; they trust me. In addition, there's the element of anonymity, which is part of the magic of radio . . . My intent is not to solve anybody's life issue in a small amount of time. I try to give them a little different focus, to give them a sense that they have options, another way of thinking about something. I think the major benefit of the program is not to the caller, but to the listener.

Interview/USA Today, 4-17:(A)9.

Derek Humphry
Executive director, Hemlock Society

4

[Saying doctors should be allowed to help terminally ill patients die and that the Hippocratic oath does not apply]: The reality is that most doctors never even read the Hippocratic oath. Most medical schools don't even answer to it nowadays because it's totally out of synchronization with modern life. For example, under the Hippocratic oath no abortions can be permitted. Nowadays, good doctors, particularly young doctors, realize that dying well is part of good medicine. Since 80 per cent of us die in the hospital, then the doctors must have an awful lot to do with death. Death is part of a doctor's business. It's also part of his business to try and prevent it. But it's also part of his business to sign the death certificate and to help patients to be as comfortable as possible in their last moments.

Interview/USA Today, 1-17:(A)11.

Daryl Inaba
Authority on biochemical
addictions, Haight-Ashbury
Medical Clinic, San Francisco

5

In reality, if you look at historical drug use, our worst drugs are basically our legal ones. There's no greater problems from a health perspective than those posed by alcohol, nicotine and caffeine.

Los Angeles Times, 11-23:(I)3.

Jesse L. Jackson
Civil-rights leader

1

Whether it's in San Diego or Phoenix or Albuquerque or Washington, D.C., drugs may be the most universal phenomenon in our schools today. The combination of drugs and alcohol and access to guns has made our schools the most dangerous places in the country to be between 9 and 3 during the day.

Interview/USA Today, 2-10:(A)9.

Erica Jong
Author

2

The AIDS plague has so fed into America's current need to disown the sexual revolution that it has been hard to determine whether the new disease is just a convenient excuse or truly a new Black Death.

Newsweek, 6-23:25.

Gail J. Koff
Founding partner,
Jacoby & Meyers, attorneys

3

In terms of medical malpractice, people are quicker to think about it. They might not act on it, but certainly they're thinking about it. But it works both ways. I think it's put a lot of doctors on their toes who weren't necessarily before. But medical malpractice has really gotten overblown . . . Doctors are only human, and because an operation isn't 100 per cent successful does not mean it's malpractice. People are a little confused about that. Basically, all doctors can do is what they can according to accepted medical standard practice and procedures. They're not magicians.

Interview/USA Today, 7-2:(A)9.

C. Everett Koop
Surgeon General of the United States

4

[Warning against the use of snuff and chewing tobacco]: My message is the same as it is with smoking: If you chew, quit. And if you don't, don't start. But I would go further with young people and say that it is not a sign of a macho personality. It is not a sign of virility. The white outline of a circular snuff can showing through your jeans pocket does not mean that you can lick the world.

News conference, Washington, March 25/
Los Angeles Times, 3-26:(I)4.

5

[On how the AIDS illness will affect sex education in schools]: There is now no doubt that we need sex education in schools and that it must include information on heterosexual and homosexual relationships . . . We have to be as explicit as necessary to get the message across. You can't talk of the dangers of snake poisoning and not mention snakes.

October/Time, 11-24:54.

6

The right of a smoker to smoke stops at the point where his or her smoking increases the disease risk in those occupying the same environment . . . If this evidence [that breathing of cigarette smoke by non-smokers can cause lung cancer] were available on another environmental pollutant—other than environmental tobacco smoke—we would have acted long ago. To fail to act now [to establish smoke-free workplaces] on the evidence we currently have would be to fail in our responsibility to protect the public health . . . It is now clear that disease risk due to inhalation of tobacco smoke is not solely limited to the individual who is smoking, but can also extend to those individuals who inhale tobacco smoke in room air . . . Involuntary smoking can cause lung cancer in non-smokers.

News conference, Washington, Dec. 16/
The New York Times, 12-17:14;
Los Angeles Times, 12-17:(I)1.

Hillel Laks
Director, cardiac transplantation
program, University of California,
Los Angeles, Medical Center

7

With heart transplantation and artificial hearts, all these questions, such as the quality of life,

(HILLEL LAKS)

the cost of medical care, become enormously important. We're living in a time now when there are people who are excellent candidates, with a 70 or 80 per cent chance of living five years, but who are being denied heart transplants because they do not have the insurance or the funds to pay for it. And at the same time, we're seeing $300,000 or $400,000 spent for a very experimental approach in a newborn who has to go through quite extreme suffering in the next few years. And the benefits they might receive are not the same that an adult would receive, who lives for two or three years, who has the joy of seeing his family grow up or his children graduate from school or college. The questions as to the importance of that quality of life are not purely medical questions.

Interview/USA Today, 7-9:(A)9.

Arthur Larson
Associate professor, Duke University

1

[On the potential for fraudulent claims for job-stress workers' compensation]: We have to get away from the concept that, if it's mental, it's just a ploy. Maybe there are abuses, but most people do not fake this kind of thing to get half or two thirds of their wages in benefits. It is true that stress cases have been mushrooming in the past few years, but that is partly because it has taken so long to catch up to the idea that mental trauma is real. There is no question that there is stress in almost every kind of work. The question is, at what point does stress get to be so bad that you can say it is the cause of psychological injury?

Interview/U.S. News & World Report, 3-24:76.

Louis Lasagna
Dean, Sackler School of Graduate Biomedical Sciences, Tufts University

2

[On whether generic drugs are as safe as brand-name drugs]: The problem is usually not one of

toxicity, but of inferior performance . . . The FDA lists a number of generic drugs that they say are suspected of not producing the same effect as the brand-name drug—that's what bioequivalent means. As a result, they do not recommend that these be substituted. The bioequivalence problem really stems from a lack of standards. It's not enough to just have the same amount of active chemical in the drug. Studies in people now show that things judged to be interchangeable on the basis of some of the standards actually act differently in the body.

Interview/USA Today, 12-8:(D)4.

John C. Lawn
Administrator, Drug Enforcement Administration of the United States

3

The cocaine user can be a 9-year-old child or a 76-year-old grandmother. That has aroused community awareness. Do you use an airplane? Do you fly commercially? Do you use a doctor? Do you use a lawyer? If you do any of those things, the cocaine problem should be a problem for you.

To "New York Times" editors, New York, Sept. 18/The New York Times, 9-19:17.

Jeffrey W. Levi
Executive director, National Gay and Lesbian Task Force

4

We [homosexuals] just happen to be different from other people. And the beauty of American society is that ultimately we do accept all differences of behavior and viewpoint . . . . the predominant scientific viewpoint is that homosexuality is probably innate; if not innate, then formed very early in life. All the responsible medical community no longer considers homosexuality to be an illness but rather something that is just a variation of standard behavior.

Before Senate Judiciary Committee, Washington, July 31/ The New York Times, 8-2:7.

Halfdan Mahler

Director General,
World Health Organization

1

[On the spread of AIDS disease]: We're running scared. [One cannot] imagine a worse health problem in this century. We stand nakedly in front of a very serious pandemic as mortal as any pandemic there ever has been. I don't know of any greater killer than AIDS, not to speak of its psychological, social and economic maiming.

News conference, United Nations,
New York, Nov. 20/
The New York Times, 11-21:1.

William E. Mayer

Assistant Secretary for Health Affairs,
Department of Defense
of the United States

2

I am convinced that the over-all quality of care in military medicine is equal to, if not better than, care over all in the civilian sector despite a relatively small number of highly visible, tragic instances of medical mischance. But the fact remains that there has been no precise way to compare quality of care.

Washington, Jan. 31/
The New York Times, 2-1:6.

Walker Merryman

Vice president,
Tobacco Institute

3

[Criticizing the U.S. Surgeon General's statement that second-hand cigarette smoke can cause disease in non-smokers]: The evidence does not support the conclusion that environmental tobacco smoke represents a health hazard to non-smokers. The National Research Council's report of a month ago noted repeatedly that more and better research needs to be done, and they were looking at the very same body of scientific literature the Surgeon General's people were.

The New York Times, 12-17:14.

David F. Musto

Professor in the Child Care Center,
psychiatry and the history of medicine,
School of Medicine, Yale University

4

[Saying drug abuse goes in cycles over the decades]: Public memory for a public problem is very important. When there is no clear-cut solution, you have these ups and downs and swings of the pendulum. Once you reintroduce a substance like cocaine, which causes people to feel happy, or at least not down, it really has an effect. It's like reintroducing it to a population which has forgotten. But you do know what they did the last time around. They eventually became very fearful of it. The cycle started with extreme enthusiasm, then uncertainty, then a feeling that this is an extremely dangerous substance. Each of these stages takes a decade or more . . . As long as we're human and there is no other cure except hard experience or religious conversion, or something like this, then you're not going to have steady progress. There are certain areas of life in which there is perhaps no progress over hundreds of years. We'd like to believe there is progress, and we're frustrated that there isn't.

Interview, New Haven, Conn./
Los Angeles Times, 7-31:(I)18,20.

5

Societies tend to react against drugs slowly, and the reaction usually comes just after the popularity of drugs has peaked. Learning to hate drugs comes not so much from a government brochure as from repeated observation of the damage to acquaintances and society.

The New York Times, 11-17:12.

G. Robert O'Brien

Executive vice president, Cigna Corporation;
President, Cigna employee-benefits
and health-care group

6

The trend in health care is toward integration, both horizontal and vertical. Everyone—insurer, HMO and hospital-management company—wants to expand geographically and offer the full

(G. ROBERT O'BRIEN)

array of financing and delivery choices. So it is likely that the HMO-only chains will have to affiliate with insurers or other broad-based organizations to compete effectively in the future, just as insurers in the hospital chains want to acquire, start or set up joint ventures with HMOs. The major competitors who survive the next decade will probably look very similar in terms of what they offer, regardless of their starting point.

Interview/The New York Times, 4-8:30.

Nancy Reagan
Wife of President of the
United States Ronald Reagan

1

You cannot separate polite drug use at a chic Los Angeles party from drug use in some back alley somewhere. They are both morally equal. You have the responsibility of forcing the issue to the point of making others uncomfortable and yourself unpopular. In all likelihood this will cost you some friends. But if a friendship is based on nothing more than condoning drugs, it's not much of a friendship anyway.

Before Los Angeles World Affairs Council,
June 24/Los Angeles Times, 6-25:(I)12.

Ronald Reagan
President of the United States

2

[On the current drug-abuse problem]: . . . the time has come, as it did once around the turn of the century in this country, and again cocaine was the villain, we had a great drug epidemic around the turn of the century. And it really was eliminated simply by the ranks of the people who suddenly said enough already. And then, whether it was peer pressure, whether it was friend helping friend or whatever, that disappeared for a very long time. Well, now we have the thing back again . . . Since we've been here, we have increased by 10 times over the seizure of narcotics with our drug enforcement. But that isn't going to do it. The only answer is going to

be taking the customer away from the drugs—turning them away from the drugs—turning them off.

News conference, Chicago, Aug. 12/
The New York Times, 8-13:8.

3

The American people want their government to get tough and go on the offensive [against drug abuse]. And that's exactly what we intend, with more ferocity than ever before . . . Our goal in this crusade is nothing less than a drug-free generation. America's young people deserve our best effort to make that dream come true . . . Drug use extracts a high cost on America. The cost of suffering and unhappiness, particularly among the young, the cost of our lost productivity at the workplace and the cost of drug-related crime. This legislation is not intended as a means of filling our jails with drug users. What we must do as a society is identify those who use drugs, reach out to them, help them quit, and give them the support they need to live right.

Signing anti-drug legislation, Washington,
Oct. 27/The New York Times, 10-28:9.

Uwe E. Reinhardt
Professor of political economy,
Princeton University

4

Patients obviously have a tolerance for sustained increases in [medical] fees. I tell physicians: "You can play this game like OPEC, the oil cartel, for a few more years, but the more physicians raise their prices, the more attractive will be the services of pediatric nurse-practitioners and other paramedics who charge half as much.

The New York Times, 7-26:18.

Arnold S. Relman
Editor, "The New England
Journal of Medicine"

5

[Saying there is an over-supply of doctors in the U.S.]: All over the country, doctors are more

(ARNOLD S. RELMAN)

concerned about their economic future than I can ever remember. There is more pressure on the doctor to maintain his income than is good for the public or the profession. Everything depends on whether the medical educational establishment and the medical schools are going to respond to what is clearly a growing glut of physicians by reducing the number of places in the entering class.

The New York Times, 6-14:8.

David Rogers
President, Robert Wood Johnson Foundation (health philanthropic organization); Former president for medical affairs, Johns Hopkins University

1

I hope it's a rare hospital that refuses to care for somebody who's critically ill and doesn't pay, but it seems to me they're skating fairly close to the margin with some people, and that's troublesome. I think hospital administrators are in this terrible dilemma: I'll do what I can to help people, but if I do too much of it I go belly up as an institution, and then I'm certainly not serving any good social purpose. They're walking kind of an uncomfortable line there, for which I have great sympathy.

Interview/USA Today, 6-17:(A)9.

John W. Rowe
Director, aging division, Harvard Medical School

2

In caring for sick old people, we've tended to compare them with healthy young people and to see the difference as disease . . . [But] we still know very little about the difference between a healthy young person and a healthy old person.

The New York Times, 6-10:18.

Albert Sabin
Medical researcher; Developer of Sabin polio vaccine

3

In a civilized, compassionate nation, there can be no place for depriving people who are un-

insured or under-insured from access to the same quality of health care that is the privilege of those who can afford the best.

Before House Select Committee on Aging, Washington, Sept. 12/ The Washington Post, 9-13:(A)4.

Oliver Sacks
Professor of clinical neurology, Albert Einstein College of Medicine

4

In looking at the brain there is a great danger in taking too exclusively physiological an approach. On the one hand, human beings are a set of organs—but we're also ourselves. We're the sum not only of our physiology but of our experiences, impulses, feelings, relationships and actions. We may be biologically similar, but we are each of us biographically unique. The physician must be equally sensitive to both.

Interview/U.S. News & World Report, 7-14:57.

James H. Sammons
Executive vice president, American Medical Association

5

To say that physicians would entice people to have things done that are medically unnecessary is untrue. Physicians are honorable people, ethical people. They are concerned about their patients.

The New York Times, 7-26:18.

Paul Screvane
Former President, New York City Council

6

[Arguing against restricting smoking in public places]: Such laws would establish two classes of citizens—smokers and non-smokers—and would be very confrontational. They give the non-smoker virtual dictatorial power to determine where smoking may not be permitted. And such laws are unenforceable. Health departments and the police are already overworked . . . I can find no evidence that second-

(PAUL SCREVANE)

ary smoke is a danger [to non-smokers]. At three separate workshops on this very issue, scientists concluded that health hazards to non-smokers could not be established . . . Passive [secondhand] smoke is a subterfuge. They [proponents of restriction laws] are really trying to make it difficult to smoke in public. They think many young people will say: "Well, if it's that inconvenient, why even get started on it? Forget it." They can't point to any scientific danger to non-smokers. It's a sham, a fraud.

Interview/U.S. News & World Report, 7-21:65.

Ronald K. Siegel
Psychopharmacologist,
University of California, Los Angeles

1

This is a drug society. We have prescription drugs, over-the-counter drugs and drugs you can buy in the grocery store. We have to understand that the drive to intoxication is irrepressible, unstoppable. It functions almost like hunger and sex. Our species has always gotten high on something, long before we were fully civilized primates.

Time, 9-15:64.

2

[On the movement toward testing of employees for drug use]: There are some very real problems here with what is being asked of these tests and what they can deliver. The widespread testing and reliance on telltale traces of drugs in the urine is simply a panic reaction invoked because the normal techniques [of controlling drug use] haven't worked very well. The next epidemic will be testing-abuse.

Los Angeles Times, 10-27:(I)1.

Mark Siegler
Director, Center for Clinical
Medical Ethics, University of Chicago

3

[Criticizing the withholding of food and water from seriously ill and comatose patients]: I

worry about causing such deaths by starvation and dehydration and developing a policy to cause it, because that would deprive the most helpless persons in our society of the most basic kinds of human care . . . The coming together of two laudable movements—death with dignity and cost containment—concerns me. You start with those in a permanent vegetative state. Then you move to the mentally retarded, the permanently senile, seriously ill defective newborns and the physically handicapped. Patients have a right to die. But do they have a duty to die?

The New York Times, 8-18:9.

Mervyn Silverman
President, American
Foundation for AIDS Research

4

It's obscene to attach a stigma to any illness. We don't do it with people dying from cancer because they smoked even when they were warned in time that smoking is dangerous. The vast majority of the people who have been exposed to the AIDS virus contracted it before we knew there was such a virus or how it spread. How can we hold them responsible for their fate?

Los Angeles Times, 11-28:(I)34.

Stephen J. Solarz
United States Representative,
D-New York

5

[Calling for fast-food restaurants to be required to publicly list the ingredients of their products]: Americans have the right to eat healthy or unhealthy food, but they also have the right to know what they're consuming.

USA Today, 6-12:(A)8.

Scott Stapf
Assistant to the president,
Tobacco Institute

6

[Criticizing the U.S. Surgeon General's statement that second-hand cigarette smoke can cause disease in non-smokers]: The science is not there to support [that thesis]. It's easy to see how his politics could have blinded him to the science. He is hell-bent on getting to his goal of a smoke-free society and has made it clear he's not going to let science stand in his way of getting there.

Los Angeles Times, 12-17:(I)16.

John Stephenson
President, Forum for Death
Education and Counseling

1

Computers may begin to take over more and more of the diagnostic, technical and scientific aspects of medicine, but there will always be a need for physicians practicing the art of medicine. In this context, the physician will be treating the whole person—not just a collection of symptoms—but a person who has feelings and dreams and fears.

The New York Times, 4-8:18.

Lewis Thomas
President emeritus,
Sloan-Kettering Cancer Center

2

. . . when we do succeed in making progress in either the prevention or the treatment of human disease, each advance is based necessarily on a preceding advance in basic science. We've got to understand how normal tissues and cells work before we do get an understanding of what happens in disease, before we can learn how to intervene . . . I think the most exciting things going on in biomedical science are indeed the events in basic research. Our understanding of living processes has not only been transformed within the last 40 years, it is still undergoing one astonishment after another . . . I think we can look forward to one overwhelming surprise after another, if the national effort in basic science continues and is given enough stability so that young scientists can take on long-range problems. It's easy enough to get quick answers to sure-fire, safe-and-sound scientific questions.

What we need for the years ahead is support for the big hunches, the important guesses, the ventures into the unknown.

Interview/USA Today, 1-6:(A)9.

James S. Todd
Senior deputy executive vice president,
American Medical Association

3

The practice of medicine is both an art and a science. While we tend to emphasize the scientific end, the art is to get along with people, to fulfill their psychological needs, to be supportive and understanding. All those things go into the proper practice of medicine . . .

Los Angeles Times, 12-26:(I)39.

Carlton E. Turner
Director, White House Office
of Drug Abuse Policy

4

Here's where a misperception is: If you believe only Federal dollars will help solve the [drug-abuse] problem, then you're dead on this issue, because it wasn't Federal dollars that turned this country [against] drug abuse . . . The Federal government doesn't hold a pistol to someone's head and make them use a drug. The Federal government didn't bring that child into the world . . . and somewhere along the way the community has to accept some responsibility. You've got to have an approach: no drugs in my family, no drugs in my school, no drugs in my community, no drugs in my workplace, no drugs in my country. Until you get that commitment, you can throw billions of dollars at the problem and you're not going to solve it.

Interview, Washington/
The Christian Science Monitor, 8-15:32.

Henry A. Waxman
United States Representative,
D-California

5

[Criticizing President Reagan for reducing Federal funding of AIDS research]: It's really

(HENRY A. WAXMAN)

outrageous. I can't understand how the President can propose this kind of budget when he talks as if he believes that AIDS is a national emergency. He's proposing to cut the 1986 funds by almost 22 per cent. And without the basic research and educational work, things we should have been doing for years now, the epidemic will continue to grow. Whatever they're saying about priorities for AIDS, the Administration's proposals for spending show they're treating it like a shell game. More people will get sick and die.

Feb. 5/The New York Times, 2-6:19.

Lowell P. Weicker, Jr.
United States Senator,
R-Connecticut

1

[Criticizing Reagan Administration attempts to cut government funds for the disabled]: Instead of advocating genuine opportunity for the disabled, this Administration pushes nothing but photo opportunities [with disabled people]. Despite glamorous displays of partnership with handicapped children, this Administration's true partnership is with the past, when the disabled were locked in institutions and out of the nation's schools and workplaces.

At Senate subcommittee hearing, Washington,
Feb. 21/Los Angeles Times, 2-22:(I)10.

Arnold Werner
Professor of psychiatry,
Michigan State University

2

College should teach students how to adapt and adjust to new situations. Most people who experience depression and other mental illness later in life lack that capacity to adapt.

USA Today, 5-15:(D)5.

Ralph Whitehead
Associate professor of journalistic studies,
University of Massachusetts, Amherst

3

[On drug-abuse]: The new morality of young America is success, the high-performance ethic.

Pot [marijuana] bred passivity. On alcohol, you can't perform well; you smell; people can tell when you've been drinking. But cocaine fits the new value system. It feeds it and confounds it. Young adults walk a tight line between high performance and self-indulgence, and cocaine puts the two together.

Time, 9-15:66.

Sidney Wolfe
Director, Public Citizen
Health Research Group

4

Most states are doing a grossly inadequate job of disciplining doctors, which means that doctors are loose in the community practicing medicine who shouldn't be, and these doctors are too often injuring or killing patients. Doctors who are found to repeatedly injure patients, because of negligence, are criminals and should be put in jail.

Interview, Washington/
USA Today, 3-19:(D)4.

Frank E. Young
Commissioner, Food and Drug
Administration of the United States

5

[On the Federal approval of a type of interferon for use against hairy-cell leukemia]: Further clinical testing will be needed to determine how effective interferon will be for any of these indications, but I am confident that this new approved treatment for hairy-cell leukemia is the forerunner for many other successful and life-saving applications of biotechnology. This is a milestone, a breakthrough—a sign of what is likely to come. It provides new hope not only to those who suffer from hairy-cell leukemia, but to all of us.

News conference, Washington, June 4/
Los Angeles Times, 6-5:(I)6.

6

[On the current wave of criminal tampering-poisoning of over-the-counter medicines]: I'm not convinced there's any way, unless we put a

(FRANK E. YOUNG)

cop in each person's house, we can prevent an adulterated bottle from getting there. If someone takes a bottle and throws in a poison at point of purchase, that's beyond what the FDA can protect you against. Regretfully, we've assumed all our medicines are safe and we don't look at them. Nothing is absolutely safe, whether it be capsules, tablets or caplets. I'd be misleading the American people if I implied otherwise . . . This kind of terrorism is just like a burglary—in this case, the burgler burglarizes our trust. I get angry that someone would do this to us as citizens.

Interview, Washington, June 22/
Los Angeles Times, 6-23:(I)1.

The Performing Arts

BROADCASTING

Alison Alexander
*Associate professor and
director of the graduate program,
Department of Communication,
University of Massachusetts*

1

I've observed a lot of families, and I see people using [TV] and using programming as a topic of conversation, as a way to bring the family together. I think that's excellent. If people can do their viewing within a family context—rather than letting their viewing push out everything else, including talking to other people—that kind of television can be a positive force. But it requires individuals to be selective and communicative.

The Christian Science Monitor, 9-22:27.

Steve Allen
Entertainer

2

If you think television is doing anything wrong or having any kind of negative effect on your child . . . turn the damn set off for a while . . . Human beings are more important than their images on television.

*Broadcast spot, "NBC, Tuned in to America"/
Los Angeles Times, 6-18:(VI)12.*

Danny Arnold
Writer, Producer

3

The movement of comedy in television has been the transition from a direct relationship between performer and audience to performer and performer. That's why it's hard for most comics to adapt to this medium. They're so audience-oriented that they never learn how to relate to another actor within a dramatic context. It mini-

mizes their own importance, and they don't realize it.

*Interview, Los Angeles/
Emmy Magazine, Jan.-Feb.:12.*

Lynne V. Cheney
*Chairman, National Endowment for
the Humanities of the United States*

4

[Criticizing a PBS documentary on Africa, funded in part by the NEH, which she says is anti-U.S. and anti-West propaganda]: You cannot have government agencies underwriting propaganda of any kind. If government agencies can underwrite propaganda unremittingly critical of the United States, then government agencies can underwrite propaganda unremittingly praiseworthy of our policies, and neither of these situations is correct . . . There's an important point to be made about freedom of expression, the First Amendment, this whole issue. Which is, that anybody can produce any sort of television that he or she might desire, as biased a production as he or she wants, and that has always been . . . But when you have the taxpayer doing the underwriting, then it seems to me that you defend the Constitution, you defend the First Amendment certainly, by asking, by demanding, balance.

*Interview, Washington/
Los Angeles Times, 10-28:(VI)10.*

Bruce L. Christensen
*President,
Public Broadcasting Service*

5

[On criticism by the National Endowment for the Humanities of a PBS program on Africa, which NEH funded and said turned out to be anti-West propaganda]: We don't allow anyone

(BRUCE L. CHRISTENSEN)

in the editing room who is a funder of public television. We don't allow Exxon, we don't allow Mobil, we don't allow anybody—IBM or whoever it is. I think NEH and NEA and the whole educational system of our country have an obligation to see that different points of view are made available . . . They aren't responsible for deciding what is or is not propaganda . . . To PBS, balance means that over the course of the broadcast schedule, you take the programs that we put on the air, you find the diversity of points of view and opinion expressed . . . It's not a balancing within every program, every series . . . From our perspective we look to see that no single point of view is dominant, or dominates to the exclusion of others.

Interview/Los Angeles Times, 10-31:(VI)1,24.

Barbara Corday
President,
Columbia Pictures Television

1

I am not one of the people who thinks that laugh tracks [in TV comedy shows] are a terrible idea. I have seen comedy shows alone in my house without a laugh track. It's deadly. Laugh tracks are awful in many ways, but not as awful as seeing a comedy in silence. Laughter is one of those things that's very hard to do all alone. People think laugh tracks are to tell the audience when something is funny because they're stupid. I believe that they're there to make the audience comfortable enough to laugh in their own houses.

Interview/USA Today, 5-9:(A)11.

2

I think that the public has as much responsibility as the television industry has to let the broadcasters know that they want to see something different [on TV]. As long as they make successes out of the ordinary, the broadcasters will continue to give them the ordinary. When they make successes out of the extraordinary, there will be more that is extraordinary.

Interview/USA Today, 5-9:(A)11.

Norman Corwin
Visiting professor,
School of Journalism,
University of Southern California;
Former radio dramatist

3

[Today's young people] have grown up in an environment of television—the great leveler. Let's not kid ourselves. It's a very powerful medium. And it has created something which never existed before in the home. That's a dilemma for parents. In the days of radio, no one had to say, "Stay away from that radio. You're listening too much" . . . Radio is the poet of the senses. It does engage the ear, the most sensitive of the senses in that the highest abstraction in art is sound. And also the subtlest. Words and music enlist the collaboration of the audience. Whereas, too often, the eye, the image, is simply mental chewing gum. It's literal, and one doesn't have to give much to it.

Interview/USA Today, 8-18:(A)9.

Bette Davis
Actress

4

If the motion-picture companies had bought into the [TV] networks in the beginning, they could have owned television. Tragically, they believed television was just a passing fancy. How wrong they were! In all our studio contracts written 1,000 years ago, there was a little last line: "You must have permission to go on television." None of us—even the agents—paid attention to that funny little line that ended up a great, big line for actors.

Interview/U.S. News & World Report, 12-8:76.

Federico Fellini
Motion-picture director

5

Television seems to me a bombardment of images which ultimately don't have any style. Unlike movies, people watch them with the lights on, while they are talking, eating dinner, and even switching channels.

Interview, New York/USA Today, 5-22:(D)4.

Fred W. Friendly
Professor emeritus of journalism,
Columbia University;
Former president, CBS News

1

A [TV] station I know in Los Angeles was [recently] bought for $530-million. Now, when you start paying that kind of money for stations, you've got to make a lot of money or you can't pay your mortgage. This new generation of station owners—not all, but a lot of them . . . they think they have a commodity like pork bellies.

TV Guide, 10-11:11.

Frederic Glazer
Literacy lobbyist

2

[On watching TV]: A three- to four- to five-hour experience with nothingness.

Newsweek, 12-1:25.

B. Donald Grant
President, CBS Entertainment

3

The quality of entertainment that's available to the public on TV today is better than it is anyplace. The level of the material that is on TV, in series and in made-for-television movies, is far more substantial than the material that is generally offered to the kids going to the movies. I think we go for a more substantial, literate, intelligent audience than films . . . The discriminating television viewer has more to see than the discriminating movie viewer.

Interview, Los Angeles/
The Christian Science Monitor, 1-16:19.

Jim Henson
Puppeteer, Writer, Director

4

[On TV violence]: There's a certain amount of violence in all of us. The kind of violence I object to is the kind that says it's a part of our lives. I disagree with that. That's portrayed in those "non-violent" violent shows where they don't show the knife going into the person's body

but where violence is somehow a part of the structure of things, where violence is an option you have as a person. I don't believe I have such an option. I've spent 49 years here with hardly any violence. I never get into fights or car chases. But I see hundreds of thousands of them on television. And our lives are not like that. The lives of my friends are not like that. We've pushed it quite far in the wrong direction. There's just an over-all lack of responsibility.

Interview, Beverly Hills, Calif./
Emmy Magazine, Jan.-Feb.:32.

John Jay Iselin
President, WNET-TV, New York

5

[On his public-TV station's recent co-productions arrangements with the NHK public-TV system of Japan]: The NHK 10 years ago was insular, indifferent to the need for co-production. They were so well funded that the economic imperative for international co-production was difficult to comprehend. Today, their Parliament is looking for ways to cut public-television costs there. In addition, four commercial networks are competing with NHK. There is a new phenomenon in the television universe. Commercial networks and state-supported systems, communication in general, are being subjected to the tests of the marketplace. Those of us who never rowed together are now going to have to row in the same boat.

The New York Times, 5-28:16.

Sonia Landau
Chairman, Corporation for
Public Broadcasting

6

One of the major reasons for CPB is ensuring that the guidelines for objectivity and balance of the Public Broadcasting Act are met. I believe that those who receive Federal funds should follow the guidelines across the board. First in our contract process . . . and in the objectivity and balance in programs of controversial nature . . . We cannot ignore such programs as *When the Mountains Tremble, The Africans,* and *Cuba in*

WHAT THEY SAID IN 1986

(SONIA LANDAU)

the Shadow of Doubt [which have been criticized for political bias]. These are not our finest hours.

Farewell address before
CPB board, Nov. 13/
The Christian Science Monitor, 11-20:55.

Richard Levinson
Writer

1

[On TV dramas that focus on real-life incidents and issues]: Here's a nun who left the church and became a cop, or a cop who became a centerfold, euthanasia, incest . . . The trouble with issue dramas is producers and writers tend to scan the newspapers instead of their imaginations. And it becomes pure polemics—just grab an issue and run around bragging about how risk-taking you are and never mind if the drama done is done in a quality way.

Interview, Los Angeles/
Emmy Magazine, July-Aug.:30.

Yegor K. Ligachev
Chief ideologist, Politburo,
Communist Party of the Soviet Union

2

All television and radio programs [in the Soviet Union] must be subordinated to one aim—explaining and implementing [Communist]Party policy.

U.S. News & World Report, 6-9:35.

Warren Littlefield
Vice president,
programming, NBC-TV

3

What has worked in television recently has been what is different. For a while, we had a plethora of six-foot-two-inch actors wearing mustaches. Now the trend may be toward more mature stories and characters. But I believe anything that succeeds will be unique.

Emmy Magazine, July-Aug.:54.

Susan Lucci
Actress

4

[On her being primarily a daytime soap-opera actress]: It seems to me that people on a prime-time show, particularly with a long run, are congratulated on it and asked the secret to their success. But somebody on daytime is constantly asked—*I'm* constantly asked—"how can you be on the show so long? Isn't it a wonderful steppingstone [to bigger and better] things?" There seems to be a vicious cycle within the industry—that the people on daytime want to be on prime-time series and, once anyone's on a prime-time series, they seem to want to be in movies. So nobody's happy anywhere. I guess that's just human nature.

Interview/
The Washington Post, 2-10:(B)1.

Vanessa Redgrave
Actress

5

[Saying she prefers acting in television to acting in motion pictures]: For me, there's no difference in terms of the work, and I'd choose always to work in television. It's now the more important of the two forms. Television is doing subjects you could trot around to film offices for three years and not find financing.

Interview, Los Angeles/
Los Angeles Times, 2-22:(V)1.

John Reynolds
General manager of co-productions,
British Broadcasting Corporation

6

[On the importance of co-productions among the world's public TV broadcasters]: Without co-finance from around the world, no major documentary series, especially one involving overseas filming, no major drama series, no substantive TV film and at least half of our music and arts programs would not happen. We've made over 100 co-production arrangements in the past year at the BBC.

The New York Times, 5-28:16.

Lloyd Richards
Dean, School of Drama, Yale University

1

All of the startling events of our time will happen on television. [Because of TV,] we've [already] seen war, which used to be a mythic thing that people did someplace else . . . We've seen assassinations, we've seen murder, we've seen starving—whatever the monumental events of our time are, we've been there, we've seen them. [Through TV,] I can instantly be in Reykjavik [at the U.S.-Soviet mini-summit meeting], right outside the door, waiting to see up close the look on the face of my President . . . I can make my assessment of just what has happened. I didn't get through the door, but I can be the first to see. Television has that power. It isn't just the words. Now, as we both look, the reporter and I, at that face, I can have a different interpretation. Without the ability to look at that face, I'm stuck with [the reporter's interpretation] . . . Just how are we responding as human beings to being placed in all of these events as they're happening? We certainly have to be conscious of [TV] as a very potent force, and its use has to be understood . . . We have to be very careful and very smart to deal with it.

Interview, New Haven, Conn./
The Christian Science Monitor, 11-4:19.

Howard Rosenberg
Television critic, "Los Angeles Times"

2

Today's television is just flat-out better than it used to be. When you have more old people, as well as more black people, more women represented, it improves television, gives it more texture, more depth, brings it closer to reality.

Emmy Magazine, July-Aug.:54.

Jonathan Sanders
Assistant director, W. Averell Harriman
Institute for Advanced Study of the
Soviet Union, Columbia University

3

Soviet television has a purpose far beyond simple entertainment. The state sees for television an important role of enlightenment and education. Soviet television is commercial to the extent that it advertises one product: U.S.S.R., Inc.

U.S. News & World Report, 6-9:35.

George Schaefer
Director

4

[On TV today]: The public wants and deserves better than special effects, car crashes, in-one-ear-and-out-the-other shows. In days of live TV, we had people who worked out of personal conviction. Now that impulse is diluted through network departments until it's lost. You'll have scripts bounced up through echelons and rewritten at each stop; by the time they get to the head man, they're stripped of the harshness and excitement of the ilk of [the late writer] Paddy Chayefsky. Everyone says, "Well, the money's great," and leaves it at that. Whether it's networks, movies, cable or theatre, that shouldn't be. It's a shame that people can't take advantage of their talent. What's [actress] Julie Harris doing on [TV's] *Knot's Landing*, when she should be on Broadway every year?

Interview, Studio City, Calif./
Los Angeles Times, 3-6:(VI)3.

Bob Schiller
Writer

5

The toughest part of writing a show is putting the story together. If you're a comedy writer, you can write jokes or you wouldn't be doing it. Writing a story is the tough part. There aren't a hell of a lot of people who can write the stories . . . Producers who don't know what they're doing will say, "We've got to change the jokes." Well, that's not going to make it any better. You'll laugh, but you won't like the show, and you won't know why you don't like the show. It's because the story is weak.

Interview,
Universal City, Calif./
Emmy Magazine, March-April:11.

Cybill Shepherd
Actress

1

You have to be an iron butterfly to survive in this [the TV] business. You have to have an iron side to yourself, to be strong and confident, and survive. But you won't be any good if you lose that sensitive side, that butterfly side. And doing a series is the hardest. You never know. You might wake up one day and you're all iron and no butterfly.

Interview, Encino, Calif./
Emmy Magazine, Sept.-Oct.:17.

Aaron Spelling
Producer

2

I love television and I think every time I get bored with it a new form comes along. I was bored before movies-for-television came in, and that was tremendous excitement. Then it went from 90 minutes to two hours, then a thing called the miniseries came in. We're going to try some things this year that have never been done . . . I think television will always be a tremendous business. It's tougher now. There have to be new forms. The action-adventure shows are going to be very hard to do. I think the day of saying every show has to have three car chases is out. I think it's going to go more to character development. Right now, comedy is a hot thing, but it will cycle and they'll be looking for action-adventure.

Interview, Los Angeles/
Los Angeles Times, 9-15:(VI)5,6.

Brandon Stoddard
President, ABC Entertainment

3

Some [TV] network executives have convinced themselves that it's okay if we think our program is dumb and boring, because the little old lady in Peoria will love it. I'm going to bet my job that the little old lady in Peoria thinks it's dumb and boring, too . . . I'd like to see a schedule that emphasizes the behavior of human beings versus car chases. I'd like to see shows and episodes that are *about* something.

News conference, Los Angeles/
USA Today, 1-9:(D)3.

Brandon Tartikoff
President, NBC Entertainment

4

It is not just a coincidence that, as the competition for our audience gets stronger, our [TV] programming gets better. The competition [from cable, pay-TV, etc.] has made extinct some of our lesser efforts . . . —the more derivative, lowest-common-denominator, least-objectionable programming. You can't get away with just putting on another show and figure you'll get a 30 share [of audience] just because you are dividing up the pie and there are only three [network] players. What it has forced us all to do is focus on the programming that is the most resilient to the competition, and that generally is programming which is well written, well acted, that is about something relevant.

Interview, Los Angeles/
The Christian Science Monitor, 1-16:18.

Arthur Unger
Television critic,
"The Christian Science Monitor"

5

I think we're dealing not so much with television as a *medium* these days; it is an *environment*. And it's something that you cannot shut off by simply turning the set off, just as you cannot shut off air pollution by closing the windows. Television is much more than just a communication or entertainment medium. It's become an integral part of everybody's environment.

Roundtable discussion/
The Christian Science Monitor, 8-21:18.

Dick Van Dyke
Actor

6

I've talked to producers about [doing] sitcoms . . . [but] nowadays, the writing seems to

(DICK VAN DYKE)

come not so much from life but from other sit-coms.

USA Today, 9-22:(D)3.

Michael Weisman
Executive producer, NBC Sports

1

It's the age-old problem of commercial television: We don't see enough ballet, culture or opera in prime time, because not enough people watch it, sponsors don't support it and we lose money. And *until* you start to show opera, ballet and sports journalism, the public can't show its

fondness. That's true, but who can afford to take the losses?

USA Today, 10-1:(C)3.

Jim Wright
United States Representative,
D-Texas

2

One of the unfortunate by-products of the television age is the short attention span of the American public. We walk along fat, dumb and happy until a crisis grabs us by the throat. Once it is off the front burner of nightly television coverage, we go back to sleep.

The New York Times, 11-17:12.

MOTION PICTURES

F. Murray Abraham
Actor

1

Acting is relating to people with love, and I don't mean either the usual adage of an actor being someone who wants to be loved, nor the even more simplistic approach of saying that in order to give something to an audience you must love it. At the end of the day, I think it is really something even more difficult: a search for someone who will agree to let you give them something, whether you call it love or not; in other words, to find someone who needs you.

Interview, Rome/Film Comment, October:17.

Woody Allen
Actor, Director, Writer

2

[On his film-making]: It happens this way: I'll be sitting at home and I'll get this great idea. In your mind's eye, it's perfect. Then you cast it and find the locations, and they're not quite so wonderful. By the time I shoot it, I think, "This isn't what I wanted to do." But it's too late to change, too expensive to make over again. And, by the time it comes out, it's so far off the mark of my original conception. And I'm so sick of it. I've never done a film . . . that's satisfied my original conception. I always see them much more beautiful and much more amusing.

Interview, New York/
Saturday Review, June:32.

3

[Criticizing the colorization of old black-and-white films]: To change someone's work without any regard to his wishes shows a total contempt for film, for the director and for the public . . . What they are really saying is that the public are morons, brainless people who can't enjoy a film if it's in black and white; they need colors be-

cause they don't have the brains to respond to content . . . It is not true. The world has responded to *Citizen Kane* and will continue to respond to it.

Los Angeles Times, 9-12:(VI)10,11.

Alan Arkin
Actor

4

Other people have nervous breakdowns when their jobs go away. Actors know the job ain't gonna last, so they only get *depressed* when the bottom falls out.

Interview, New York/
USA Today, 3-18:(D)5.

Richard Attenborough
Actor, Director

5

I *love* directing actors. That's my fun; that's my satisfaction; that's what I can do. How good or how significant a director I am I have no idea. But I do know that I can direct actors. And I do know that, in the movies I make, the performances are *bloody* good.

Interview, New York/
USA Today, 1-7:(D)4.

James T. Aubrey
Former president, CBS, Inc.;
Former president,
Metro-Goldwyn-Mayer,Inc.

6

The major difference [between TV and] movie-making is that everything here [in the movies] is manufactured from dreams. TV did not work that way. Movie producers and directors are told that every picture is going to be a smash and get Academy nominations. The mo-

(JAMES T. AUBREY)

ment a movie begins shooting, the dream machinery proclaims it a hit. I find that attitude unrealistic. Some movies are not going to turn out well. Yet very few directors will stand up and say, "I did my best, but it didn't work." So the executive becomes the heavy.

Interview, Los Angeles/
Los Angeles Times, 4-27:(Calendar)28.

Hector Babenco
Brazilian director

1

A completed movie never has anything to do with the one you set out to do. Absolutely *nothing*. It's like a dream; you can't organize the dream that you are going to have when you fall asleep. When you wake up, you have to try to recall as much as you can.

Interview/American Film, April:13.

John Badham
Director

2

[On what is the major problem facing the film industry]: The easy availability of television. The corrosive, destructive effect of video on motion pictures. There is no worse way to watch many movies than on video. It is not just that you are looking at the small screen, which is, in itself, not a terrific way to see something that was designed to be seen on a 60-foot screen. It is that your attention is totally split. The most common way to watch the video is to watch about 15 minutes and then wander off to the kitchen, or start talking to your friends. And the video becomes just part of the background, like your stereo.

Interview/USA Today, 5-30:(A)11.

Lucille Ball
Actress

3

The whole business is in chaos right now. The people being fired from networks and stu-

dios, the upheavals, the mergers and the takeovers by people who are not creative people. This is all very detrimental to something that we once looked at as a huge creative community with five or six umbrellas [major studios]. But the papas are all gone. MGM lost Papa [Louis B.] Mayer. Columbia—well, not that anybody ever called [Harry] Cohn a papa. They were people who took an interest in your career, who gave you a chance to build and learn and grow. I feel sorry for the young people today, terribly sorry. Now everybody has to do everything on his own.

Interview/TV Guide, 10-4:15.

Peter Bogdanovich
Director

4

I think a lot of directors put us in bad shape because they spent too much money on pictures that didn't do any business. And you can't expect an industry to be run for pictures that lose money. [Director] John Ford said to me, "There's two things that're important making pictures—one of them is that you have fun making it, and the other is that the picture makes money." And [director] Howard Hawks was even more succinct; he said to me, "Just remember, make pictures that make money." Now, if you make nothing but pictures that make money, you're probably not much of an artist—I don't know why, it just turns out that way. But in order to be a functioning artist in this business, you've got to have a few movies that make some money.

At American Film Institute seminar/
American Film, June:15.

5

It isn't just that pictures were better crafted then [in the old days], with a dexterity and flexibility that was extraordinary, but they also told more. Not like today, [when] most movies are 30-minute stories told in two hours. When you go to the movies now, you're lucky to get the hors d'oeuvres, much less the meal. Maybe you get hors d'ouevres and a soup, sometimes you get a salad, sometimes you get nuts, sometimes you get just nachos. I think it's important to give an audience a full meal.

At American Film Institute seminar/
American Film, June:15.

Klaus Maria Brandauer
Austrian actor

1

Life is sometimes boring but, in acting, you have the chance to kiss, to caress the audience. You must not make one second like another, because that could be boring. When I act, I want to do it with blood! Otherwise, why waste the time.

Interview,
Beverly Hills, Calif./
Los Angeles Times, 3-4:(VI)6.

2

If you're only going to make movies that have the stamp of greatness on them, then you're going to spend an awful lot of time not working.

Interview,
Los Angeles/Los Angeles Times,
11-23:(Calendar)28.

Marshall Brickman
Director, Screenwriter

3

The most difficult part [of film-making] is the editing. I like pre-production and photography a lot, also writing, because nothing is at stake but your own time. But editing forces me to confront my choices and their immutability . . . No matter how many times you run the damn thing through the Steenbeck or Moviola [editing machines], the guy is not going to say the line any better, and he's not going to say the line *before* he picks up the fork, either.

Interview/Film Comment, June:26.

Beau Bridges
Actor

4

. . . there are other actors who get more action—or more money—but I can't complain.

I've been in successful projects. And I'm blessed with a solid family life. There's a mystique in Hollywood that in order to be happy you must be on the order of Sylvester Stallone—that there's only this mythical superstar level, or failure. Well, that's simply not true. I feel quite fulfilled.

Interview, Los Angeles/
USA Today, 2-28:(D)3.

Robert Brustein
Artistic director, American
Repertory Theatre, Cambridge, Mass.

5

The actor is the tragic animal in our culture. He is the victim of a system that offers him tremendous [financial] goodies in exchange for a pitifully small part of his talent.

The Christian Science Monitor, 6-4:21.

Michael Caine
Actor

6

Acting for me has become somewhat like performing delicate brain surgery, as opposed to opening somebody up with an ax. Or it's like going into the jungle. You start out with a machete, smashing your way through the trees. Now I'm at the stage where I've cleared the path, and I'm sitting here wittling away at smaller and smaller details on a twig. I keep trying to hone it down. Just to prove I can do it.

Interview, Sag Harbor, N.Y./
Cosmopolitan, May:256.

7

Movies are behavior. In movies, it's a real tree, so it better be a real person. In theatre, you see, it's a cardboard tree, so you accept "acting." In movies, you don't act, you behave. If the audience believes you're a person, you're a great actor. If they think you're a great actor, then you're bad for movies. You've fouled up.

Interview/McCall's, June:140.

8

. . . having been a beginning actor, there's no lower form of life. Nobody wants to know

(MICHAEL CAINE)

you. They have ads in [English] tobacconists' windows for rooms to let: They'd say "No blacks, Irish, dogs or actors." You couldn't even get ahead of the dogs. Can you imagine being a black Irish actor with a dog? That's why actors never go by society's rules.

Interview/Los Angeles Times, 12-9:(VI)4.

Barbara Carrera
Actress

1

[Good scripts are hard to find] because we have people in this industry who aren't really artists. They're clerks, most of them, who come to make the quick buck . . . I've lost all my illusions in this business. I'd like to have kept some of my innocence. [But in this industry] no one wants to see the other succeed. It's an industry where someone celebrates someone else's defeat.

Interview/USA Today, 2-21:(D)2.

Julie Christie
British actress

2

The [British] Thatcher government cuts [in funds for the film industry] have been very bad. Eady [Fund] money and the National Film Financing Corporation, which financed most of the stuff over the last five years, have been cut. The government contention is that if you don't make films which are going to make large amounts of money in the U.S. market, then you don't deserve to make films; so the whole idea of new talent, learning through the process, is up the creek. All the means by which independent film-makers were able to make films [in Britain] have been cut, left, right and center, so I don't know how long it can go on.

Interview, New York/
American Film, Jan.-Feb.:20.

James Clavell
Author, Director

3

[On the characterization of him as cold, hard and ruthless when directing a film]: The pro-

ducer who made that remark, by the way, was working with me as I was directing a film we were shooting in Ireland. In that kind of environment, where you're making 500 or 600 decisions every day that will affect what happens in the cutting room six months later, you've got to be that kind of person. If you're the director, you've got to be fairly strong and cautious. There's no way you can be a dilettante in that situation, so of course not everyone is going to like me, and I go in expecting them not to like me.

Interview/Publishers Weekly, 10-24:54.

Peter Cushing
Actor

4

[On the horror movies he made for Hammer Films many years ago]: I have done a lot of other films that had nothing to do with horror, but I am amazed at the popularity of the Hammer films. I still receive letters expressing people's appreciation of them. Modern horror films reflect the times we live in with their violence and sex. Hammer films scared and frightened people but were never repellent. All I ever did was remove the odd heart and gently plonk it in another body. The films still stand up although they were made 25 or 30 years ago. Young people who write to me think they were made a couple of years back. If I'm stopped in the street, I just say I'm Peter Cushing's dad.

Interview/Films and Filming, April:12.

Bette Davis
Actress

5

Every major studio in those [old] days made from 50 to 60 films a year, so there was a limitless amount of employment. We [actors] became part of the public; they knew us. That has disappeared now. No young actress today can have an opportunity like mine. Talented players, if they are fortunate, will get one fine part and then have to wait a long time for another. There's no continuity, no working month after month, year after year.

Interview/U.S. News & World Report, 12-8:76.

WHAT THEY SAID IN 1986

Kirk Douglas
Actor

1

[On acting]: To me, making movies is exciting. Every movie is a new adventure. When we made *Tough Guys* it reminded me [of] when I was a poor kid. I always wanted a set of trains, but I never had any. Well, here [in the film] I have a *big* set of trains, and I can ride the locomotive, and run across the top of the speeding train, and have fun! So there's a childish element to being an actor that you always have to retain. I don't know what will be the next movie I do. It'll be a new adventure. It may take me to a far-off place, a whole environment that's different from anything else. That's what's exciting.

Interview, New York/
The Christian Science Monitor, 10-17:23.

Robert Duvall
Actor

2

[The executives] in Hollywood aren't film-makers, they are money-makers. There is a big difference. The film-maker thinks of quality first. The money-maker doesn't. I am very disappointed with what's going on now. It's just a business like any other business. That's sad.

USA Today, 10-6:(D)2.

Jules Feiffer
Writer, Cartoonist

3

Screenplays are not art. Nobody, especially playwrights, would write screenplays unless it was to earn money. The better, more serious they are, the less chance they have of ever being produced [on film]. Occasionally there is a glitch, and someone [at the major Hollywood studios] screws up, and a good script gets produced . . . [*Carnal Knowledge* was produced because] nobody could say no to [director] Mike Nichols.

Interview, New York/
Los Angeles Times, 5-8:(VI)8.

Federico Fellini
Director

4

Cinema is like a ritual. In its communication of a message, it respectfully leaves more interior space for the viewer. To have gone there [to the theatre], leaving the others outside in the street, is a testament to personal choice—"I want to go see this"—rather than succumbing to invasive dependency. The individual remains alone with the message, walks out of the dream and returns to his life. The ritual has a religious moment. It's not senseless, disrespectful and dangerous like tele-dependency, where you watch [TV] while you're on the phone, yelling at your children or switching from channel to channel while eating. The best way to watch TV is while you're asleep.

Interview, New York/
Los Angeles Times, 4-4:(VI)1.

Nina Foch
Actress; Acting coach

5

As an actor, you're servicing the writer, the playwright—which is our business, of course. The actor has to know the story absolutely and decide what the movement of the piece is, how the character changes from beginning to end and in each scene. You're preparing to play a grandmother; not that many lines, perhaps. As homework, you have to discover where she is at that moment, where she may have been. You have to prepare a context in your head for your movements and your postures. I never tell people what to do. But I ask them every possible question, and I get them to ask themselves every possible question. When they leave me, it's unlikely they'll be asked any questions they're not prepared to answer. They're *prepared*.

Interview, Los Angeles/
Los Angeles Times, 5-15:(VI)1.

Harrison Ford
Actor

6

The business of film-making is so demanding, so exhausting, that you find you give up com-

(HARRISON FORD)

pletely on regular life until the film is over, so you go back to it with a real vengeance when you have the chance. I do. To recoup my energies and to maintain some stable mental platform, and also just to get away from the introspection and the self-examination that's a part of acting. I try and get away from the movie business on a regular basis for as long as possible, and do ordinary things.

Interview, Los Angeles/
The Washington Post, 12-24:(C)3.

Milos Forman
Director

1

Art is struggling to rise above commercialism today, as always, and I am afraid for the future. Especially for film. Because film is sitting on two chairs which are pretty far from each other, so you have to develop a pretty big bottom to be comfortable. On one side, you have film as business. On the other side, film is indisputably the top art-form of the 20th century. But this is because business is always seeking for a strict discipline, for proven things, for profits, for planning, and everything like that. Art is always asking for courage, for risks, for emotional involvement—things which are in total contrast to the business requirements. So this always was, is, and will be a big struggle.

Interview/USA Today, 7-7:(A)9.

2

[Criticizing the colorization of old black-and-white films]: I might see a colorized film and not be offended by it. That's not the point. The point is creative rights. Coloring films is like putting aluminum siding on a 17th-century castle.

Los Angeles Times, 9-12:(VI)10.

Melvin Frank
Director

3

I know [film is] a young person's medium today. But I still think we old poops have got something to offer. It took [British director] John Schlesinger to come from London to make *Midnight Cowboy* here and put in things we Americans take so much for granted we don't even notice them. In the same way, I think we older movie-makers can provide a better perspective on the young than a lot of youthful directors. At least I hope so. Personally, I'd still use Billy Wilder, if it needed three men to carry him on the set each day.

Interview/Los Angeles Times, 6-22:(Calendar)33.

Sidney Furie
Director

4

. . . today you've got to aim for mass entertainment; a movie has got to be an event or it just won't work. It's a sad thing for any creative film-maker to have to sit down and think, "Is this the kind of thing millions of people will want to see?"—but what's the alternative?

Interview, Los Angeles/
Los Angeles Times, 2-2:(Calendar)17.

Hal Gaba
Vice chairman, Colorization, Inc.

5

[Arguing against those who criticize the colorization of old black-and-white films]: To tell the public that they can't watch it in color, to have the audacity to try to legislate this form of censorship, is really shocking. To carry their thinking out logically, they shouldn't allow color films to be shown on black-and-white television or films made for the big screen to be shown on television at all.

Los Angeles Times, 9-12:(VI)10.

Richard Gere
Actor

6

It's very bizarre to me that actors want to play real villains. I knew myself when I was younger that playing a crazy, a scumbag, a disgusting creature, was always the most attractive thing. I asked a younger actor about this recently: Why would you

(RICHARD GERE)

rather play a villian than a saint? He said, "Well, a saint is boring." I said, "Why?" I find that idea very curious. If I am going to be destructive, then I've got to know it's for a good reason.

Interview, New York/Ms., February:80.

Alec Guinness
Actor

1

I'm as irritated by a setback as anyone, but so often in the long run it's turned out well or luckily. And so I've often found that if I've done something for the wrong motive—accepted a film or play because I thought it could be very good commercially—I don't often think in those terms, but when I have it's always been a disaster. But when I've thought, "This is hopeless, I can't earn enough money at this to keep me a month, but I like it, so to hell with it"—it's been a success, at least in the sense that I've been happy I've done it.

Interview/The New York Times, 3-11:27.

2

People often ask if theatre provides feedback that performers don't get in films. I don't find that so. On a film set there are nearly always 80 people or more hanging around, and they're professionals in their own right. They know whether something is lousy or good. They can't be vociferous about it, but you sense it. You know roughly what they're thinking. As for television, I don't like to go to the [TV] studios. Those curious cameras come creeping up on you. I'm not relaxed. I always feel that if something goes wrong, they can't put it right. With film, you can cut and start again.

Interview/U.S. News &
World Report, 3-31:63.

Gene Hackman
Actor

3

There aren't any consummate performances [in his career]. There are a few moments in

Scarecrow and in *Conversation* and the withdrawal scene in *French Connection II,* but I've never come away from seeing one of my films without thinking I could have given more. I've yet to give it all. I'm afraid to commit myself too much. It's something I'm working on, something I've got to look forward to. But you know . . . maybe in the end, that's one of the things which keeps me in this game!

Interview/Films and Filming, May:27.

Mark Hamill
Actor

4

The only people who should become professional actors are people too crazy, stupid or talented to do anything else. If you can be talked out of the profession, it's not for you.

Interview, New York/
The New York Times, 3-7:17.

Goldie Hawn
Actress

5

When I think about my roles, I have to ask myself one question: How do you not abandon a certain kind of feeling you might give an audience while still branching out to other movies? There are certain things people want to see me do and certain other things I'd like to do. The reason I get a lot of money to do pictures is not because I do what I want to do but because what I do has a tendency to lift the spirits—and you don't want to pull that out from under anybody. I am, after all, in a business. And because I'm practical and someone of my word, I can't very well go in and say, "I want five million dollars to do *A Trip to Bountiful,*" because the studio isn't going to make any money back. It's ridiculous for me to work my price up to an exorbitant amount of money and then say to the studio, "Okay, now I'm going to make *my* movie, but you still have to give me the money." That's like saying, "How about doing me a favor?"

Interview,
Pacific Palisades, Calif./
Cosmopolitan, July:149.

Katharine Hepburn
Actress

1

What is interesting about an actor, in the last analysis, is if they can arrest your total attention. Can their concentration make you concentrate enough to identify something which they're doing with something in your own life—which is why one is moved, and usually why one laughs.

Interview, New York/
The New York Times, 3-3:16.

2

The [old-time movie moguls] Sam Goldwyns, Louis B. Mayers, Harry Cohns, and that bunch, were all romantics. They were tough men, but they were pushovers for this business. They wanted to make money, too, but they had a romantic attitude toward the people who made movies and the movies themselves. Now, for the most part, it's a money-making business. The money behind the business today is *cold* money. Theirs [the earlier moguls] was *hot* money.

Interview, New York/
Los Angeles Times, 3-29:(IV)9.

Charlton Heston
Actor

3

One of the things about acting or painting or writing or composing music, you're doing something you screw up at every day. You never get it right. You can spend a lifetime, and if you're honest with yourself, never once was it perfect. Never once was it the way I imagined it lying awake at 4 o'clock in the morning thinking about the next day. People say to me, "Well, what is your ambition now? You've got the awards and the parts and the money. What are your goals now?" I say, "To get it right one time."

Interview, Los Angeles/
The Washington Post, 5-2:(D)1.

4

American film exports the American dream, which is achievable, not a fantasy. What film has done to the developing world is to change its sense of possibility.

Time, 6-16:72.

Gerry Hogan
Vice president,
Turner Broadcasting System

5

[Defending his company's use of a new process to make color films out of old classic black-and-white films]: We're not destroying the black-and-white print. The classic picture lives on. If you turn the color knob [on your TV set] off, you'll see it in perfect black and white. The option is there for anyone who doesn't appreciate the color version to see it in black and white. But we are taking advantage of new technology to freshen these films. We're giving them a more contemporary look which we think will appeal to a new generation of viewers.

The New York Times, 8-5:21.

John Houseman
Director, Actor

6

It's very nice to have become a celebrity late in life. I've been in and around theatre, radio, television and film for as long as I remember, and now I finally realize why I always envied actors so much. They are pampered and catered to and get all the exterior rewards. It's wonderful.

USA Today, 10-20:(D)2.

Hu Qiaomu
Member, Politburo,
Communist Party of China

7

In today's artistic circles, there are some people who don't bear the masses in mind, nor do they bear in mind art—only money. Films which are healthy and beneficial to socialism should get the green light—and bad films should get the red light.

The New York Times, 1-13:4.

William Hurt
Actor

8

Acting is basically characterization in ensemble. You take your body and you shape it and you

413

WHAT THEY SAID IN 1986

(WILLIAM HURT)

change it. You treat it just like you would putty or paint, with the same underlying principle as putty or paint or clay or stone—you adapt the body to the theme of the piece in an atmosphere that is trusting and enlightened, and hopefully, eventually—if you work hard enough and sincerely enough—transcending. Remember that phrase that people went to the movie "to get away from themselves for awhile"? Well, the idea behind acting is not to make them forget; it is to help them accept. There's a real difference in those two activities. Acting is a compassionate thing. It's not about telling someone else what to be or how to be different. It's simply trying to see what you are.

Interview, New York/
American Film, July-Aug.:30.

James Ivory
Director

1

You don't have to spend a lot of money to make a film. Not if you make them the way we do. We don't travel first-class; we don't stay in grand hotels; we don't waste a lot of money on lawyers. And we use locations whenever possible.

Interview/
Los Angeles Times, 3-30:(Calendar)12.

Glenda Jackson
Actress

2

It always strikes me as ironic that when a woman gets to an age where she's fairly experienced both as a woman and, if she's an actress, as an actress, there's nothing to capitalize on that combined experience in a continuum of roles. I've had to hunt them out, and I'm very lucky in that they've either come to me or I've found people who would be prepared to put them on.

Interview, Paris/
Los Angeles Times, 9-7:
(Calendar)21.

David Jacobs
Producer, Director

3

[Comparing TV directing with directing feature films]: I think everybody knows television is much harder because of the time pressures, and as far as feature films are concerned, the brilliant directors in any medium are not the ones with the technical knowledge but the ones that have a vision. There are many episodic television directors that I work with who have more knowledge of the feat of film-making and the technical aspects than scores of theatrical film directors; and at the beginning I used to ask myself: Why isn't this guy out there directing features? And there's always a logical answer: They really lack a single governing vision. What they have to say doesn't have any consistency about it. There's no governing consciousness. I think that's what makes a wonderful film director.

Interview/The New York Times, 5-23:16.

Akira Kurosawa
Japanese director

4

I am constantly accused of making my films with a Western audience in mind. I've never had any intention other than to make movies in Japan as a Japanese. As a very normal part of my upbringing and education, I have studied not only the Japanese classics but also the Western classics and music. There is nothing unusual about this for a person of my generation. But there is some misunderstanding of my work in Japan, probably because contemporary Japanese have not studied their own cultural background to the extent that I do for my films. I am trying to get as close as possible to the historical and cultural truth of Japan. I can only say that I am very pleased that this seems to be appreciated outside Japan.

Interview, New York/
The Washington Post, 2-3:(B)4.

5

I don't make films to send a message. My views are, of course, in a finished work, simply because I am, as a human being, living now. But

414

(AKIRA KUROSAWA)

I don't conspicuously intend to express any philosophy or political views in a film. It's just me . . . my film.

Interview, London/
Films and Filming, May:18.

Sherry Lansing
Producer

1

[On violence in motion pictures]: There is so much random violence in the world, and everyone feels very impotent to deal with it. [Actors] Sylvester Stallone, Charles Bronson, Chuck Norris, Clint Eastwood and Arnold Schwarzenegger take away this sense of impotency. They are mythical figures, bigger than life, who solve all problems. You feel you can't do anything, and then you go to a movie where somebody just takes the law into his hands, righting all wrongs, almost like cowboys used to do.

Interview/U.S. News & World Report, 6-30:54.

Jerome Lawrence
Playwright

2

. . . people in Hollywood—and even more so in France, where the directors are the *auteurs*—look down their noses at the screenwriters. Occasionally, a screenwriter has cut through and had some clout, like Paddy Chayefsky had with *Hospital* and *Network* and a couple of other great movies. He lost it again on *Altered States* and, he was so frustrated by it, it killed him. Writers, contractually, have no control. They're often asked to stay off the set. Being a member of the Dramatists Guild, you know about the dignity that writers have, and use responsibly, in the theatre. If (screenwriters) get that much dignity, I think the scripts are going to improve.

Interview/Writer's Digest, March:34

Jack Lemmon
Actor

3

[On acting]: I found out that success breeds unemployment. A *Mister Roberts* comes along right away, and you just can't take any film afterwards. You look for something as good. In any career, you're going to end up doing enough bad films as it is. But if you do a film just for the sake of working, you're in trouble. Your popularity goes down—and that's all it's based on out there: how popular you are, not how good an actor you are. And all of a sudden you're not offered the better scripts. So you have to be choosy. And you wait. It's like telling an athlete, "Don't exercise for two years. Just show up for the big race."

Interview, Durham, N.C./
The Washington Post, 3-24:(C)1.

4

You never know which parts may or may not really grab you [as an actor] and leak over during the hours when you are not performing . . . [In *Save the Tiger*,] that really began to get to me, and I didn't realize it. I started behaving like the character. I'd be driving along in my car, and all of a sudden I'd start to weep and shake, and I didn't know what in the hell was happening to me. The character was right on the edge of having a nervous breakdown, and he was beginning to leak over . . . It scared the hell out of me for about two days. I'd be sitting at home thinking about the film, and I'd just start to go. It is a danger if a part begins to take over the acting. A lot of young actors think that the ideal would be if you, in a sense, became the character. However, when you lose control, you're no longer an actor. There is nothing to be gained by having the character take you over, and it does not matter what you feel like.

Interview/USA Today, 8-8:(A)13.

Cleavon Little
Actor

5

Where are the blacks [in acting]? Why aren't they chosen for more parts? Why don't the producers and directors put them in everyday parts that don't involve race? When blacks do get a part in a movie or a play, it's usually to show how black people suffer. But they don't all suffer. I don't suffer. We can play all kinds of parts,

(CLEAVON LITTLE)

but we have to get the chance . . . The producers operate out of fear. They're afraid of losing the white audience. But what people want is to be entertained. If you give them the best, they'll buy all the tickets you can sell.

Interview/The Christian
Science Monitor, 3-27:25.

Norman Mailer
Author
1

[On his currently directing a film he wrote for the screen from one of his novels]: No one will believe me, but it hardly feels that it's my own book at this point. The real separation is not when you go to direct it, but in the screenplay. A screenplay is really abstracting a novel. Movies are made through long tunnel-like tubes called lenses, and not everything fits. There are parts you can translate from the book and others that won't make it . . . There is a fundamental rule—almost a law—if you have a vivid imagination when you read a book, then you are seeing as you are reading a movie that goes on for many, many hours, so a two-hour feature will always disappoint you.

The New York Times, 12-12:26.

David Mamet
Playwright
2

To me the great American art-form is the movies. It's the movies that really express our culture. That's what throws us all together, as the theatre might have at one time but doesn't any more. We all know what "Make my day" [a line from a Clint Eastwood film] means or who E.T. [the character from a science-fiction film] is.

Newsweek, 12-15:73.

Rouben Mamoulian
Director
3

[Film] is such a rich, polymorphic form. It has such power. It can be used for so many things. You realize that we went through thousands of years without inventing an art and then, 90 years ago, the scientists, of all people, gave us the possibility of a new art. And [director] D. W. Griffith changed that cheap little toy into an art . . . The essence of film is imagery in motion. A blind man can get a lot out of a play from the language, but much less from a film with its visual imagery, the possibility which never existed before for arresting life and movement. All the other elements are secondary, including dialogue and sound.

Interview, Beverly Hills, Calif./
Los Angeles Times, 1-19:(Calendar)25.

4

The authority of the director is not like authority in the army; it's *not* authoritarian. The most important word in pictures is love. If you can create a family, you can do anything. You try to get the best people to work with you. Then you have three tough days. But if you give good ideas and you get good performances, thereafter you get great performances. You give love, you get love back. You achieve your authority on the set.

Interview, Beverly Hills, Calif./
Los Angeles Times, 1-19:(Calendar)25.

Walter Matthau
Actor
5

[Today's films are] just more trashy and more violent; and the films we used to make, with witty dialogue and classy characters, simply aren't being made today. Instead, you've got junk like *Rambo* and *Cobra*. But then I think there's something deep down in a lot of people that's attracted to cheap trash and violence.

Interview, Los Angeles/
USA Today, 8-20:(D)4.

Alberto Moravia
Author
6

. . . the cinema can . . . do marvellous things that literature can't. It can and does change re-

(ALBERTO MORAVIA)

ality, often in an overpowering, arrogant way. Maybe more so than other arts can. In literature and painting, that which changes reality is above all the style of a work. It's style that introduces change. But the cinema changes reality itself. In other arts, style is mysterious and personal in imposing itself upon an existing reality, but in the cinema the artist—the director, in this case— uses the camera in order to create a totally new reality, to create a new reality in the place of the old one; and that, too, is part of the chemistry of the camera, which lends itself to manipulation. Style is not a manipulation, it is an expression. But with the camera, dealing with reality becomes manipulation.

Interview/Film Quarterly, Spring:32.

Mike Nichols
Director

1

The best actors are those who love acting— and they know they love it, which is the most liberating thing of all. They're rid of all this crap about how painful and difficult it is. So they're free to go a lot of different places—literally, physically, metaphorically. It's like what [novelist] Milan Kundera said of his characters. They're sent to him across borders that he can't cross himself, into places he would like to go. They allow him to have experiences that are unavailable to him in life or might destroy him.

Interview, Washington/
The Washington Post, 3-21:(B)8.

2

Making a movie is starting a snowball rolling. After a week or so, you can't stop it. All you can hope is that it is rolling in the right direction. There's no going back. Whatever you learn about a scene, you've learned too late. You did that scene yesterday. So everyone, including the director, has the feeling that something is happening which is vaguely out of control. This is embarrassingly semi-mystical, but you have to have the sense *not* to try to control it.

Interview, Washington/
The Washington Post, 3-21:(B)8.

Chuck Norris
Actor

3

The key to my movies is that we do things everybody wants done against evil but you just can't get done. We save the hostages. We slaughter the terrorists. It's fighting back. It's fantasy, sure, but at least it's fighting back . . . Look, I don't know whether violence in films is good or bad. I do know that you don't avoid violence by ignoring it, by pretending it isn't there. If my films help people to *understand* violence, then it's probably a good thing.

Interview, Los Angeles/
Cosmopolitan, February:66.

Geraldine Page
Actress

4

I have learned a thousand different ways to work from all my teachers over the years. I think I've weeded out the work I don't approve of and slowly gotten closer to where I want to be as an actress. I have always tried to take the long view. It always seemed obvious to me that if you try to take the short route to "stardom," you'll be quickly [rooted] out . . . My concept as an actress has been to build a big, broad base, and always to go for quality. I have always thought that the rewards of life would make it all pay off, and now I think I am seeing the nice results of a very slow process. I'll probably never be rich, but I'd rather be happy.

Interview, New York/
Los Angeles Times, 1-7:(VI)6.

Arthur Penn
Director

5

[From the mid-1960s to mid-1970s,] the studios had come out of that phase where they felt they knew how to make movies and were taken up with those of us who were making them. They [studio bosses] were on a different edge. They were looking for things to startle us, shock us, something that wasn't conventional. In fact, conventional movies were harder to get made

(ARTHUR PENN)

then. It was a more adventuresome time at the studios. There was diversity. If your idea didn't fly at one place, you could take it someplace else and get a totally different response. Today, you get pretty much the same response from all the studios. Essentially, the same breed of executives are running all of them . . . On an I.Q. test, the guys running things now . . . are a lot brighter than the old guys. But they're smart in a different way. They are corporate smart. They know how to use the capitalist system to the teeth. They just don't know how to make movies.

Interview, New York/
Los Angeles Times, 1-24:(VI)24.

Sydney Pollack
Director

1

You can beat around the bush about directing. You can say it in a lot of nice ways. But the final objective is to get everybody to do what you want. And there are a lot of ways to do that. Sometimes you can do it without anybody knowing, and that's the best way. The people who run around barking orders and yelling "Quiet" all the time are usually very insecure people who don't feel like they're directing unless they're telling somebody what to do. The truth of the matter is a lot of directing is knowing when to shut up and stay out of the way of what's working by itself. If you've done the preparation properly, and you've hired the best production designer and the best costume designer, and you've talked about the characters with the actor and actress, and you've picked out every bit of the wardrobe, and you've got the right cinematographer and the right sound man, and you get on the set, you don't have to run around doing a lot of screaming. You just don't.

Interview/American Film, December:15.

Vincent Price
Actor

2

Everybody in Hollywood is typecast. The American mind is so departmentalized that if

you *don't* fit into a department, you're in trouble. Robert Redford is more typecast than any of them, because he only plays himself. Al Pacino is the gangster, Robert De Niro is the fugitive or some punk. John Wayne was always the cowboy. Cary Grant wanted to play in drama, but he couldn't—they thought of him only as a drawing-room comedian. Hollywood has the imagination of a flea!

Interview, New York/
The Christian Science Monitor, 8-11:32.

Bob Rafelson
Director

3

If nothing else, I've learned that, in order to survive, a director must always remember that the film industry is fickle and is in a state of constant ignorance, that his fate is being dictated by guesswork and that nobody endures forever. You will be subject to the whims of the public at all times—and so will the people who hire you.

Interview, Los Angeles/
Los Angeles Times, 9-28:(Calendar)21.

Ronald Reagan
President of the United States

4

[Criticizing films for a cavalier attitude toward drugs]: [The motion-picture] industry has started down a road they'd been on before once, with alcohol abuse. I can remember when it was rather commonplace in films . . . to portray drunk scenes and so forth as being very humorous. And the motion-picture industry decided some time ago that that wasn't right for them to do . . . and they stopped. And yet, recently, there have been some pictures in which there was a gratuitous scene in there just for a laugh [about] drug use, that it made it look kind of attractive and funny, not dangerous and sad.

Interview, Washington/Newsweek, 8-11:18.

Robert Redford
Actor

5

Unfortunately, my career as an actor has been somewhat weighted by that "movie star" cate-

(ROBERT REDFORD)

gory . . . Suddenly, when you're considered a star, you start feeling like a type, an object, rather than just an actor.

Interview, Truchas, N.M./
USA Today, 10-29:(D)1.

Martin Ritt
Director

1

The whole psyche of the world is turned on to fast foods and comic books and teen-aged excitement and instant gratification. The country is conditioned to accept predigested food and prefabricated houses; the [TV] networks believe action-adventure is the best way to attract an audience. The [film] studios partly believe that— along with horror films and teen-age films. They are looking to make a size 12 dress the country will buy, and the only criterion they have is last year's hit, insufficiently realizing that a really good film is the individual impulse of some creative person.

Interview, Burbank, Calif./
Film Comment, February:42.

2

It's naive to assume that any film is not political; they're all social, at least. They're either selling escape or they're selling reality. Even the Disney films at one time were considered totally without message. That's childish. They certainly weren't without message. They were selling a different parcel of food . . . which the American public and the world public was prepared to buy.

Interview, Burbank, Calif./
Film Comment, February:42.

Paul Schrader
Director

3

Critics are always crying, "Give me something new. We never see anything innovative." Then you do something they've never seen the likes of before, and they howl, "What is it?"

They refuse to take the time to understand the developments you're proposing . . . The critic decides to side either with the art-form and my innovations . . . or he decides to go with his constituency who buys newspapers to have things confirmed that they basically already know. Where's the critic who's up to making this film or other so-called difficult films accessible to his readership? Is he leading taste or hiding behind what he thinks his readers want? And how does he know? Popular criticism in this country, like everything else, is becoming extremely conservative, or just lazy.

Interview/Film Quarterly, Spring:12.

Run Run Shaw
Hong Kong producer

4

My motive was always entertainment. I'm here to make people happy. Good action, good musical, good picture. Still good. How do you call it good? Nobody can tell. Good becomes what the box-office does. It's the only way to measure.

Interview/American Film, June:39.

Ally Sheedy
Actress

5

The playfulness of film is the most important part of the process. You can't take it so seriously that you start worrying about whether this character is going to make or break you. You lose all the joy that way. I really blossom when I'm making a movie. I love figuring out what my character should look like, what should she wear, what does she like to eat. It's like being in a warm, wonderful cocoon. When I'm between shots on the set, I feel as if I'm in suspended animation.

Interview, Los Angeles/
Los Angeles Times, 5-13:(VI)1.

Cybill Shepherd
Actress

6

Oscar Wilde said a wonderful thing about actresses. He said, "Actresses are a little more

419

(CYBILL SHEPHERD)

than women and actors are a little less than men." I think he meant that there's an inherent vanity to being an actor. The way you look is very important, the way you move is important, the way you sound, your makeup, your hair. And, because of our culture, women are more comfortable with these things than men; the vanity sits more comfortably on women.

Interview, Encino, Calif./
Emmy Magazine, Sept.-Oct.:14.

George Sidney
Director

1

[On the days of the studio moguls]: It was a wonderful, magical time. The studio was your home. Everything you wanted was there and, for film-makers, everything we needed we were given . . . In the old days, we negotiated with principals, the heads of studios. They knew what film-making was about . . . [Now], all of a sudden, the studios were being sold and the people who came in knew nothing about movies. Then they would send lawyers who knew even less to deal with us . . . Say whatever you want about [the moguls] Mr. Mayer, Harry Cohn, Jack Warner and the others who ran the old studios, but they wanted to make movies and that made the business exciting. The conversations in this town [Hollywood] used to start out with, "Hey, I've got a great story." Today, they start with, "Hey, I've got a great deal."

Interview, Los Angeles/
Los Angeles Times, 1-21:(VI)1,3.

Dorothy Singer
Psychologist; Co-director,
Family TV Research and Consultation
Center, Yale University

2

[Criticizing the violence in motion pictures]: The film industry says that it is there simply to entertain, and that social responsibility is for social scientists and educators. But they do have a responsibility. Films are a very powerful con-

veyor of messages. One of the messages in these films is never to use reasoning or discussion, but to use force. TV- and film-makers are the first to admit the media can get a message across effectively . . . Why is it that those in the industry give themselves praise for positive effects, yet deny that the constant showing of negative films will have an impact? We know from TV research that heavy doses of violence can make young people behave more aggressively. I don't see why the effect of film would be any different.

Interview/U.S. News &
World Report, 6-30:55.

Steven Spielberg
Director

3

Now it's time to spend time away from the grind of picture-making. If you're here working every day, you tend to start Xeroxing your own style. It gets incestuous.

Interview, Universal City, Calif./
Los Angeles Times, 2-2:(Calendar)12.

4

[On directing]: I have to create a world in which the actors as well as the audience feels safe—where actors and audience can allow themselves to be vulnerable, to experiment, to drop all their armor and play like kids. I have to make them feel like they can trust their own imagination.

At Scopus award dinner, Los Angeles,
Dec. 14/USA Today, 12-16:(D)2.

Sylvester Stallone
Actor

5

I'm in the business of trying to please—through films that have a bit of social significance, but that are usually in an overblown, over-dramaticized format. I happen to think that's why people go to the movies. If everything [in the movies] was for real, all you would do, basically, is sit in front of your window all day, and say, "This is life, in actual scale." So everything is scaled up in my films—everything. The

(SYLVESTER STALLONE)

tension, the dramas, the dilemmas. I tend to play characters whose quests are a little larger than life—so I also tend to get more overblown criticism. It's all in proportion to the kind of work I do. I reach out—I go out on that limb.

Interview, Las Vegas, Nev./
Los Angeles Times, 9-14:(Calendar)39.

George Stevens, Jr.
Co-chairman,
American Film Institute

1

If motion pictures are this tremendous medium of communication that have great potential to enrich the world, you have to accept that they have the opposite potential if misused. I'm fond of [the late author] William Faulkner's speech when he accepted the Nobel Prize. He said that the artist's duty is to lift up men's hearts and help them endure. I've always thought that was a good touchstone for people in any medium. It's with decreasing frequency I see new films that do that. But, in the end, it's the films which last that really matter. We can ask: Will people be looking at [the violent film] *Cobra* on videocassette 10, 20 or 30 years from now? I would say that's unlikely.

Interview/U.S. News &
World Report, 6-30:55.

2

[Criticizing the new process by which classic black-and-white films are being changed into color films]: If this process were to flourish, I think it would represent a vulgarization of some of the most important creative works of this country in this century. A generation from now, no young person would ever see the world in the way it was seen by John Ford, William Wyler, Alfred Hitchcock, Orson Welles or Charlie Chaplin . . . Classic films are going to be principally accessible over television and in video cassette. People can't go to the archive and see the original print. They'll see the film the way it's marketed, so therefore the films will be essentially inaccessible in black and white. Here

you've got some computer technician who's going to tell us what color some scenery was in *Rebecca,* as if Hitchcock had not expressly chosen to make the film in black and white, which he did. If someone is not familiar with *The Treasure of Sierra Madre* or *Citizen Kane,* do you want to see the film that the film-maker created, or do you want to see somebody playing with creative-coloring-by-numbers? It becomes a distinctly different experience, and those of us who are around have some sense of protecting the work of people who made films but are no longer here to protect them.

The New York Times, 8-5:21.

James Stewart
Actor

3

[Criticizing the use of a new process to turn old black-and-white films into color]: I think it's wrong. I don't like the idea. We should leave things like that alone. What are they going to do next? Add talk to silent movies? Everything we do in film means something for that particular era. Those movies were special in black-and-white. Leave them alone.

Interview/USA Today, 4-21:(D)2.

Robert Stone
Author, Screenwriter

4

Movies are, above all, photography. You don't need dialogue; movies got along fine without it for years. It means, for writers, that writing for movies is not very much fun. It's not rewarding.

Interview, New York/
The Washington Post, 4-3:(B)2.

Barbra Streisand
Actress

5

Women film-makers can play a special role in times like these, because the world is in an upheaval . . . Women have a unique vision of the world. It is our instinct to nurture, to create life,

(BARBRA STREISAND)

not to destroy it. We must see that vision realized. We need to believe in our own sensibilities and our own power—but we need to do more . . . I think we will always have obstacles, not only because we are women but because we are artists as well. Sometimes one feels grateful for the struggle, because it can strengthen, motivate and inspire. The enormity of making a film can be frightening but, then, taking any risk is frightening, and it's even more frightening not to take one.

At Women in Film Week ceremony, New York,
May 1/Los Angeles Times, 5-3:(V)1.

Ted Turner
Chairman, Turner Broadcasting System

1

[On his selling most of the Metro-Goldwyn-Mayer film company]: The theatrical motion-picture business is not really a sound financial business. It's like baseball or basketball. They're hobby businesses. We can't play that game any more.

To TV critics/
Los Angeles Times, 6-7:(V)1.

Jack Valenti
President, Motion Picture
Association of America

2

Sure, the motion-picture business faces problems today it couldn't have imagined 20 years ago, but I still have faith . . . With all the VCRs and with cable [TV] and all the rest, there is still nothing like seeing a good movie with a bunch of other people in a theatre.

USA Today, 1-27:(D)2.

Agnes Varda
French director

3

In France, culture has historically been as important as commerce, and in this respect I [a woman director] have always been taken seri-ously in France as a film-maker. But never before now have so many women *made money* with their films, and that is the nitty-gritty, even in France.

Interview, Paris/
Los Angeles Times, 6-25:(VI)7.

Sam Waterston
Actor

4

Acting serves different purposes at different times. When you're young, it's one thing—for me it meant that I could be with my father, who was an amateur director, and that I could stay up late. When you're excrutiatingly shy, it's a way of getting you through that. And when you're assaulted with a huge cargo of feelings, it's a place to put it.

Interview, New York/
The New York Times, 1-24:17.

Richard Widmark
Actor

5

Today, when a kid doesn't know what he wants to do, he becomes a film-maker. Down the street, every other house has a budding young film-maker. Now—especially with self-focusing, self-loading cameras—anyone can do it. It's attracted a lot of very untalented people . . . Movies has so much hype, so much garbage, so much non-sense written about it. Directing, in the first place, is not that mysterious a thing. "A film by Joe Blow" really gets so pompous and pretentious! I've always felt that the minute they started calling movies "films," things started going downhill.

Interview/Films in Review, April:225,226.

6

[On the people running the major studios today]: The historical background of these idiots who are working now is just incredible! The head of production of one studio, the vice president in charge of production at another, are kids who don't know a damn thing! They think because they're kids, they know what kids are go-

(RICHARD WIDMARK)

ing to want when they make a movie. They're the last to know! The kids themselves don't know—until they see it. What's going on now is absolutely unbelievable!

Interview/
Films in Review, June-July:327.

Billy Wilder
Director, Writer, Producer

1

I would just like to write good parts, to make pictures where, after the people leave the theatre, they can go to the drugstore and talk about it for 15 minutes. I'm very happy if there is just something worth discussing. They say, "Well, you're very funny"—big deal. But if I smuggled in a little something that adds to their makeup, to their knowledge, I'm the happiest man in the world. I'm not the man who wrote the Ten Commandments. Just the Ten Suggestions.

Interview, Los Angeles/
American Film, March:24.

2

There are no studios any more. In the olden days, you went to see an MGM picture, you *knew* it was an MGM picture. It had its own handwriting. Or you knew it was a Warner Brothers picture—Cagney and Bogart and the small actors that were under contract there. Now studios are nothing but the Ramada Inn: You rent space, you shoot, and out you go . . . Nobody talks about the picture [any more], just about what kind of deal: who presents? whose picture is it? and all that totally idiotic crap! It's a world with ugly terrifying words like "turnaround" and "negative pickup" . . . People meet and spend a year on a deal, and I want to spend a year *making the picture*. People don't even *talk* about making movies. They are not obsessed with celluloid.

Interview, Los Angeles/
American Film, March:28.

3

My father told me once, nobody's an alche-

mist. But if I was, I'd make a thriller. There was never one kind of picture I made. I went from *Witness for the Prosecution* to *One, Two, Three*. [Alfred] Hitchcock, he made only thrillers, and magnificently. But you know what a thriller is to me? It's the movie where the boss chases the secretary around the desk . . . That's a thriller—and that's alchemy!

Interview, Los Angeles/
Los Angeles Times,
3-2:(Calendar)18.

4

[On the burgeoning technological advances in entertainment delivery systems that will increase the volume of films and programs available to people around the world]: What about the software [the films and programs]? Who is going to write it, direct it, act it? For all I know, these [technology] guys are trying to replace the human element. Relax, fellow picture-makers. The bigger they get, the more irreplaceable *we* become. Theirs may be the kingdom, but ours is the power and the glory.

At American Film Institute's Life
Achievement Award dinner in his honor,
Beverly Hills, Calif., March 6/
Daily Variety, 3-10:42.

5

[Criticizing the colorization of old black-and-white films]: Those fools! Do they really think that colorization will make *The Informer* any better? Or *Citizen Kane* or *Casablanca*? Or do they hope to palm off some of the old stinkers by dipping them in 31 flavors? Is there no end to their greed?

Los Angeles Times,
9-12:(VI)1.

6

The language that has been established between the picture-maker and the onlooker has been tremendously refined. Today, they [the audience] outthink you, outguess you all the time. You had better not underestimate them. Let people reach for it. Let them add it up. Don't spell it out. They're not stupid.

Variety, 9-24:10.

WHAT THEY SAID IN 1986

Joe Wizan
Producer

1

Nobody knows what a picture is going to do [at the box-office] until you get it done. It's like playing poker. The good poker players know which hands to throw out. The good production people know which movies *not* to make.

Interview, Los Angeles/
Los Angeles Times,
4-4:(VI)1.

Peter Yates
Director

2

[On violence in motion pictures]: To the studios, violence is an insurance policy of sorts. They feel that if you have violence two thirds of the way through, if a film seems to be lagging, maybe you'll pick the audience up for the last third. It's like the way they used to do nudity until they so wore it out that no one became excited by it.

Interview/U.S. News &
World Report,
6-30:55.

Yevgeny Yevtushenko
Soviet poet

3

[On the opening of his first motion picture]: I don't want to dedicate the rest of my life to cinema, and it *is* certainly a struggle [getting a film made]. But cinema does have the advantage of reaching a very wide audience. I *do* believe in the power of art, and the art of the cinema can show peoples' real faces.

At Film Forum, New York, Feb. 5/
Los Angeles Times, 2-8:(V)9.

Fred Zinnemann
Director

4

The studios by and large are run by people who don't know anything about show business because they're primarily moneymen. Whereas, in the old days, the studio heads were people who had enormous practical experience and were showmen. That is what's missing to a great extent today in the upper echelons. But more important and more dangerous, I think, is the uniformity of stuff that's coming out. Our only defense is, I think, to remember the standards of our forefathers and the kinds of pictures they made.

Interview, Los Angeles/American Film, Jan.-Feb.:67.

MUSIC

Licia Albanese
Former opera singer

1

I had timing and luck in my career but, most important, I had *qualita*. I listen to young singers all the time. Most of them can do anything. But the sound! Where is the *qualita*? I don't know if I could do it today. I'm not sure Beniamino Gigli and Schipa could. Why? The conductors. All the conductors in my day could adjust to the voices in a cast. Now they can't or won't. Toscanini could adjust. That, plus my technique, is why I could do some of the parts I did. That beautiful smile of Tullio Serafin looking up at you from the pit, supporting you, encouraging you . . . The ability of a conductor to realize the difference between an orchestral forte for a light voice, like Tito Schipa's, as opposed to the stentorian one of a [Giacomo] Lauri-Volpi. Adjustment meant achieving transparency in the supporting sound from the pit, the simple knowledge that a wind instrument using a round tone is enough to eat up even a substantial voice.

Interview, New York/
Los Angeles Times, 6-1:(Calendar)44.

Christian Badea
Conductor, Columbus (Ohio)
Symphony Orchestra

2

At some point, you have to get through all of the crust and get to the core of music. There was one very precise moment when Klaus Tennstedt conducted *Fidelio* at the Met when it suddenly came out very pure. He was taking himself away, saying, "I'm not here, I'm just presenting the music to you." Many artists obtain this sincerity, this fusion, at one time or another. Very few attain it quite often. And nobody can do it all the time.

Interview/Opera News, May:22.

Pierre Boulez
Orchestra conductor

3

[Music is] a bit like architecture. In previous centuries, people built marvels of stone and wood . . . when there were no other materials. One can see the material is not completely apart from the thought and design. The history of music is not just the history of sounds but the history of materials. Every culture reinvents its own. There's a deep relationship between what you want to express and the materials you want to express it with.

Interview, New York/Ovation, July:29.

Jimmy Bowen
Head of Nashville
operations, MCA Records

4

[On charges that country music has been diluted and doesn't really exist any more]: Well, neither does big-band music. Pop music used to be big-band music. It doesn't exist as it once did, either, but it was part of a time. Country music hurt itself at one point by staying one way too long. Music does not create the times; it's a mirror of the times. And if you don't stay a mirror of the times, you fall clear out of the picture.

Interview/USA Today, 3-6:(A)9.

Grace Bumbry
Opera singer

5

Of course I enjoy being a prima donna—why not? I worked very hard for it. But it is not something that I worked toward, really. I worked toward doing a good job, toward satisfying an audience. You know, two days before an important performance I don't talk, I don't eat certain foods, I don't even dare think about drinking

WHAT THEY SAID IN 1986

(GRACE BUMBRY)

wine or anything like that. You've got to have your wits about you, and I can only do that if I know this little mechanism in my throat is working at its greatest capacity. I try to leave absolutely no stone unturned, no stone.

Broadcast interview/
Opera News, 1-18:19.

Semyon Bychkov
Music director, Buffalo (N.Y.)
Philharmonic Orchestra

1

[By performing the masterworks of the great composers,] an orchestra grows as an artistic entity. Each time you play this music you find new insights. [New music] enriches the audience and the orchestra. But if you play something for the first time, it's still only a first try—there's only so much you can dig into. From the "standards," an orchestra gets style and commitment. *They* make the orchestra and conductor better musicians.

Interview/Ovation, February:14.

2

I suppose conducting is the most unusual way of expressing music. You express it visually and silently, and try to communicate what you know about music to evoke other people who actually produce the sound to respond to it. You have to make people as possessed and seized by the music as you are.

Interview/Ovation, February:15.

Montserrat Caballe
Opera singer

3

In the past, maybe 20 or 25 years ago, to have a Serafin or a De Sabata—you know, conductors who showed the singers how to interpret their parts, how it was supposed to be; they were not only conducting the orchestra. Today it is not the same. Maybe we have many spectacular conductors now, but quantity does not mean quality to me.

Broadcast interview/Opera News, 1-18:19.

4

I am an opera singer, and opera is music with voice—with sound and words. I cannot do it like drama. The music is first, and then the drama falls into place. Everything is in the music—how you have to move; and even in a pause there is your cry.

Broadcast interview/
Opera News, 1-18:19.

Ray Charles
Musician

5

[On whether sexual and violent lyrics in today's music should be banned]: I don't see any point of making records which describe violence or pornography. I don't go for it. But I still don't believe that people ought to go around telling other people what they ought to listen to. If that's what they groove on, more power to them. As for those people who feel that it's bad for their kids—I came up from the old school, and the things that my mama didn't like just never got done. So a lot of parents [today] just have no control over their own children, and they want to make other people responsible for it. That's unfair.

Interview/USA Today, 6-23:(A)9.

6

I think a lot of the creative forces in music are leaving, and there are no replacements. You aren't going to have an abundance of Duke Ellington in the near future. I think these things run in 100-year cycles. I watch the kids now; one or two people come up with an idea and the whole industry jumps on it. When I was coming up, the artist grew out of the company. Now it's the other way around. When [singer] Michael Jackson does *Thriller,* *everybody* starts using the synthesizer. I have nothing against the new music. It's what's behind it. You can't have people making musical decisions who can't tap their feet. Nothing's wrong with being an accountant. Nothing's wrong with being a lawyer. But they can't groove. All they can do is say, "Gimme the financial report." If you don't make money right away, you're gone! G-O-N-E. When I was com-

(RAY CHARLES)

ing up, nobody told me what to do. Never! I made less money, but I had the leverage. Let the artist be creative. Let the company handle the marketing. When you're dealing with somebody who can't read a quarter note as large as a piano, I'm through.

Interview, Los Angeles/
Los Angeles Times, 12-24:(VI)9.

Dick Clark
Television and music
personality, and producer

1

Music has always been the mirror held up to what's going on. I'm sure as time goes by it can mirror things that become more popular or less popular. And it's usually a reflection of the times. The nonsensical, inane, mean-nothing lyrics of the 1950s were like the 1950s; nothing ever happened. The latter part of the 1960s—all the protests and anti-war lyrics were a reflection of the feelings of the young people. And the disco period was into: "Give me the beat, man. That's all I want."

Interview/USA Today, 1-24:(A)11.

Bruce Crawford
General manager,
Metropolitan Opera, New York

2

I have no desire to run this place [the Met] like a corporation. You *can* run it in a business-like manner, and if you run it wastefully, you squander resources you need. But there's always going to be more risk than you would take in a business.

Interview/Opera News, September:12.

Regine Crespin
Opera singer

3

For the prima donna, behind the facade of flowers, success, lights and all that, there is a life that is real and sometimes very painful. A prima donna is also a woman, like me, with un-happy family relations, with sad love affairs, a bout with cancer and other human tragedies . . . We artists have a fabulous life, doing a job we love. But there are sacrifices, like not having a child. Now I can talk about it. I was pregnant, and of course we wanted to have a child. But everyone said, "You're going to Bayreuth for the first time; such an opportunity you'll never find again. Have a child later." So I had an abortion, and then I was never able to become pregnant again. Not everybody could accept my kind of crazy life, because it is a crazy life. Singing is like a kind of drug.

Broadcast interview/
Opera News, 1-18:20.

Placido Domingo
Opera singer

4

[Saying his economic remuneration from doing opera is not as good as from doing concerts]: Opera is just not an economic solution to anything. I think of opera as a sickness. One must love it pathologically or one wouldn't make the sacrifice. When it's good, nothing is better. When it's bad, nothing is worse.

Interview, Los Angeles/
Los Angeles Times,
9-14:(Calendar)56.

Thor Eckert
Music critic,
"The Christian Science Monitor"

5

In music, opera has always been the medium that has been most responsive to the political situation of the time. Most of Verdi's operas were very specific responses to political situations. And I think of the new John Adams opera that's going to be done in Houston in October 1987, *Nixon in China.* It involves Mao and his wife engaged with Mr. and Mrs. Nixon in a sort of drama of wills and forces.

Interview,
New York/The Christian
Science Monitor, 7-22:16.

427

WHAT THEY SAID IN 1986

Larry Gatlin
Singer, Songwriter

1

The record companies killed the goose that laid the golden egg. When I first moved to Nashville [in 1972], artists ran the labels. Then the record companies realized it was big business, and all the lawyers started running things. The biggest mistake was having non-music people make musical decisions. I was at my record company [Columbia Records] and looked around the office and noticed there wasn't one person who has sung, written, played on, produced or had anything to do with a hit record . . . They do a great job and I respect their efforts in selling records, but [they] should leave the music to the artists.

Interview, Vallejo, Calif., July 9/
Los Angeles Times, 7-11:(VI)6.

Benny Goodman
Clarinetist

2

Young players have been brought up on the more contemporary big-band music. It's loud. Real swing ensembles are surprisingly gentle mechanisms. They don't depend on obvious virtuosity.

Interview, New York/
The Wall Street Journal, 3-13:22.

Jerry Hadley
Opera singer

3

The hardest thing about opera acting is learning to trust the music, learning that it's okay to stand still and sing. In an effort to overcome the stereotypical opera singer who is put on a wagon and wheeled out to hold his spear and sing, we've maybe gone over the edge with histrionics. What often happens in opera acting is that we are too worried about the movement per se, not enough about the reason *why* we move. If you watch the videos of [Maria] Callas, you see she doesn't move that much. You see the concentration on her face, so that when she does make a move it's so right, so motivated, that's riveting. In those performances I've given, in which

I've been brave enough to stand still and sing, thinking about what I'm saying, trying to communicate something I truly feel, I've found the audience drawn in a way that it is *not* drawn to you if you're running around the stage apologizing for being there. That happens too often, particularly if you're working with a director who doesn't know the piece well—and that's far too often the case.

Interview/Opera News, July:14.

Lionel Hampton
Jazz musician

4

These groups that play now and sing now— it's terrible. They call it metal rock, hard rock, and all that. It's a disgrace, because it's really a mockery of the type of music that we blacks are known for—the blues and the good swing music. But it had a lot of promotion. They had the media with them; they had the radio and the press. [But] there's nothing like getting a big jazz band and getting that swing and that feeling. Swing draws people together. When it's swinging, people can pat their feet; they can be happy with each other. But in a disco, there's no feeling at all. You've got to make the feeling, and you've got to get yourself interested in dancing, and the music is secondary.

Interview, New York/
The Christian Science Monitor, 6-25:23.

Lynn Harrell
Cellist

5

A pianist can expect that he's going to keep on learning new pieces through his entire career, maybe 60 years. Either that, or he'll have to specialize—that is, get down to a level of close detail and concentration on certain works or composers. Cellists, working with a smaller repertory, constantly keep re-evaluating the entire range of their music, bringing a greater scrutiny to it, trying to find something new, another aspect. And that seems to produce a greater variety of approach among us. I think that today there are more personality differ-

(LYNN HARRELL)

ences, more individual styles, separating cellists than separating violinists.

Interview/Ovation, March:9.

Woody Herman
Band leader

1

[On his constant traveling with his band]: Music is a great escape. As long as you're playing, nobody can get to you—about anything. If you're an independent kind of person who values freedom in music, the best existence is to be on the road. If you stay in one area you'll soon be playing the music somebody else wants you to play.

Interview, Atlanta/USA Today, 4-1:(D)4.

2

[Young musicians] have to be aware of [Louis] Armstrong and all the beginning forces—who they were and what they did—so that their ears aren't closed to everything before 1970. [If you don't learn about the roots,] all of a sudden you reach a brick wall, and you can't go beyond it. There are too many limitations when you try to make new material of your own doing, without any foundation, and without considering the great things that have already happened. That's why knowing and having a background of all great music is terribly important.

Interview, New York/
The Christian Science Monitor, 6-25:23.

Dick Hyman
Jazz pianist

3

Until be-bop, and even at the beginning of be-bop, jazz still played by the rules of songs. It was improvisations on themes people knew, and people could pick up on them, even if they had never thought songs could be done this way. In the newer music, you don't quite know what's going on until you learn the new language—it's a different repertory, a different length of solos and a different goal in performance. Formerly, it

was more fun. Not to be blunt, but the music takes itself too seriously now.

Interview/The New York Times, 7-22:22.

Billy Joel
Singer, Songwriter

4

It may sound crazy, but songs come to me in dreams. I hear the melody, the chords, the rhythm. Sometimes I hear sounds, vowel sounds. But I don't hear words. What happens is that, when I'm trying to write, I get into this creative frame of mind that's still there when I'm asleep. Stuff comes to me when I'm sleeping. I'll wake up at 4 or 5 o'clock and mumble something into a tape recorder or go to a piano . . . My best songs have come to me in dreams. You can always tell the ones I didn't dream—they sound labored. I've done a lot of labored songs, more than I care to admit.

Interview, Tucson, Ariz./
Los Angeles Times, 11-21:(VI)14.

Gwyneth Jones
Opera singer

5

On the best nights, I feel so much love flowing over both sides of the footlights. When an artist reaches beyond the notes and generates that special magic, the response is overwhelming. Singing means giving, and one day I'll teach that message in master classes. Starting with excellent vocal technique, the complete artist shapes his entire body into an impressive instrument. In my classes, I'll want clients to communicate life through their eyes, lips, even fingertips. That's the ongoing challenge and joy of the art.

Interview/Opera News, 3-29:32.

Ernst Krenek
Composer

6

The ability to perceive a [musical] work's emotional impact depends on musical literacy. And we don't have much of that. When I was a

WHAT THEY SAID IN 1986

(ERNST KRENEK)

young composer, the blame was always put on the fact that old audiences didn't understand new music. But now there are younger ones in the audiences and *they* don't understand either.

Interview, Long Beach, Calif./
Los Angeles Times, 4-22:(VI)6.

Katia Labeque
Pianist

1

I believe that [as a musician] if you stay too much attached to your original tastes, you don't progress that much. You limit yourself. The classical world is a beautiful world, but there is still plenty of music happening in the world that isn't classical, and it's beautiful music . . . I don't know enough about jazz. But jazz is not a question of words—it is a question of experience. It's not like classical music, where you can stay home and read your score. You need to go onstage and learn everything from the other musicians.

Interview/Ovation, August:14.

James Levine
Artistic director,
Metropolitan Opera, New York

2

[On his becoming artistic director of the Met, moving up from music director]: It won't change what people think. They've always said, "If that production, that performance, is there onstage and he's facing it, he must like it." But over the years I found myself too often with an intolerable situation. Take our recent *Simon Boccanegra,* where if I abandon the production because I can't stand it, I also abandon the chorus and orchestra and singers. That's why, when there is an impasse and someone has to say we will do it this way—whether the "it" is the staging, the sets, the costumes—I want to be the person contacted to make the decisions.

Interview/
Opera News, September:11.

Larry Livingston
Dean, School of Music,
University of Southern California

3

In the absence of an explanation for life, music is the best substitute I've found. At those moments when music exerts its greatest power, we recognize that this is the best it gets.

Interview, Los Angeles/
Los Angeles Times, 9-17:(VI)6.

Paul McCartney
Singer, Songwriter;
Former member of the Beatles

4

. . . you need some distance before you can really see [the quality of] a record. You can't be objective at the time you finish it. You're too close. Take *Back to the Egg,* which is kind of a minor record. At the time, I probably thought it was a good record. The situation is, if you've made a record, you put it out. It doesn't matter how big you are or how little you are . . . You do your bit and you put it out. I'm not that precious with it . . . I know there are lots of people who say that "you owe it to yourself, you owe it to us, to always make sure it's the finest quality." But I didn't promise a rose garden type of thing. It's not my whole thing to be that safe.

Interview, New York/
Los Angeles Times, 8-26:(VI)4.

5

[On offensive rock lyrics]: I think there is a point, like with newspapers, where you start to want to censor stuff.

Newsweek, 9-1:13.

Seth McCoy
Classical concert singer

6

When I go out onto the stage, I am there to *express,* not *impress.* Before the performance, I do everything I can to prepare myself. I read, I study, I rehearse and I make decisions. But when I walk on, I'm there to give the audience an ex-

(SETH McCOY)

perience, to let them go away with something, to make the music live.

Interview, Pasadena, Calif./
Los Angeles Times, 4-11:(VI)2.

Gian Carlo Menotti
Composer

1

I don't want to baffle my audiences. I don't try to simplify things, but I don't try to obfuscate them. When I hear some of today's music, I'm reminded of the man who burns down his house to fry two eggs. If a critic says, "The harmonies Menotti uses are those of 50 years ago," well, so what? So many young composers become very self-conscious about lyricism. They are a bit afraid.

Ovation/November:12.

Krzysztof Penderecki
Composer

2

I'm not a Chagall, who painted very nice pictures but always the same. My music goes zigzag, not in a straight line. In fact, it is impossible at the end of the 20th century to create as a Mozart did. Our times are too charged with the potential devastation of mankind.

Interview, Los Angeles/
Los Angeles Times, 3-27:(VI)2.

John Pritchard
Music director,
San Francisco Opera

3

As I move through the world's capitals, I now have a brief for looking at [opera] singers and conductors, especially slightly younger ones. The days when the opera could afford to engage [Riccardo] Muti and [Claudio] Abbado are far from past, but these conductors are being very difficult now with their demands, and opera companies don't like interference with their prerogatives by the great orchestra leaders. Also, I

want to look at the rehearsal-time allocation. However many operas are given, there is never enough time to rehearse them properly. I'm not sure people have the necessary technical knowledge [for this task]—perhaps they are advised by someone with an ax to grind. What is needed in this job is a certain detachment . . . We opera conductors have got to be very careful to realize the supreme responsibility we have. I put my nose outside the beautiful enclosure of Glyndebourne because I knew I had broad shoulders and was quite strong. But when you open any stage door, you immediately get into problems.

Interview/Opera News, October:79.

Bonnie Raitt
Singer

4

If I had to start all over again today [as a singer], it would be a lot tougher—now it's all image and leather underwear.

Newsweek, 9-29:13.

Leonie Rysanek
Opera singer

5

What is missing a little today is respect for the art, for doing, for the work, for good work, for your craft. It's not only money and fame. I mean, my God, what is fame? For a week you're famous, and the next you're forgotten. My goal is still a great performance. The ovations, I'll be very honest, are like a fur, like a warm breeze. It's not, "Ah, this was great, you deserve it." But I say to myself, "Yes, this was your night." And I'm very unhappy if that doesn't happen. I can never hide my emotions. I can't pretend I'm happy. Those great evenings—that's my life.

Interview/Opera News, 3-15:50.

Kurt Sanderling
East German orchestra conductor

6

Mostly, interpretation comes from the conductor. But the orchestra has a part in it, too. And the situation—the acoustics, the hall, the traditions in that place. But sometimes—even often—what the orchestra is offering me, I must, with pleasure, let them play the way they are playing.

Interview, Los Angeles/
Los Angeles Times, 4-3:(VI)2.

Ricky Schultz
Executive director,
MCA (Records) Jazz

1

[On the renewed interest in jazz among major record companies]: We know jazz is not a fad. It's been around in some form since the turn of the century. With the graying of America and the maturing of the baby boomers, there's a move toward quality on all fronts—better cars, better clothes, things of lasting value. I think that extends to the arts as well.

The New York Times, 5-5:20.

Andres Segovia
Guitarist

2

[On the guitar]: It is the most beautiful, poetical instrument ever devised by man. Being polyphonic, it has different, complicated factors. Everything is possible with a guitar . . . I try not to be the interpreter of compositions made just by guitarists. That's a narrow world. I have asked many symphonic composers to write for the guitar. At first they refuse. "I don't know how," they say. But then they learn. Castelnuovo-Tedesco, for example, came late to the guitar and wrote more than 100 compositions. They are captivated by the guitar. It has poetry, and always a little melancholy.

Interview, New York/
Los Angeles Times, 7-16:(VI)1,4.

Peter Serkin
Pianist

3

I can't imagine someone playing old music properly unless they're interested in new music.

I think those old composers are modern, too. They were rebels, involved in something brand new at the time, not in perfecting some museum piece. I feel that inherent in a lot of the music we play and think about is an audacity and eccentricity that we should bring out—not to promote ourselves but to express the music. People often don't have the courage to bring out what's there. That spirit must be understood by any performer.

Interview/Ovation, January:12.

Thomas Stewart
Opera singer

4

My advice to young singers today? If you are not blessed [with a legendary voice], a singer has got to be sharp, to know how to move around the stage; has got to know what it means to say something to an audience, not just as a singer but as a performer; has got to learn, in addition to his vocal talents, theatrical talent . . . You can't *make* a voice. You can destroy it; you can make it more beautiful; you can make it more effective by learning other things. But you cannot make a voice . . . You are either a good singer or a lousy singer. And if you are a lousy singer, you can maybe, if you are bright enough, and smart enough, and shrewd enough . . . make people not aware of your shortcomings as a singer. And a lot of times you will become a great performer and you will please the people listening to you.

Interview, San Francisco/
The Christian Science Monitor, 1-27:23,24.

Martii Talvela
Opera singer

5

[Saying young singers put too much emphasis on technique rather than interpretation]: We still have great voices, but the problem is to project what you have learned, what you feel, what you will give to others. Technique is a servant, nothing more. Behind this is the human being who can see something mystical. You don't need to sell yourself—just give your heart, and learn how to open your soul.

Interview, New York/Opera News, 2-1:33.

Yuri Temirkanov
Chief conductor,
Kirov Opera, Leningrad

1

There is no great difference between Soviet and English and American musicians. In Russia we play Brahms and Copland as well as Tchaikovsky. I don't know any pianist who plays the Beethoven sonatas better than Sviatoslav Richter. But I also don't know a better recording of the Shostakovich Fifth Symphony than the one by Leonard Bernstein and the New York Philharmonic.

Interview, New York, Jan. 7/
The New York Times, 1-9:18.

Virgil Thomson
Composer

2

The music world is not without its economic realities. But economics are not the sense that it makes. In sport we distinguish amateurs from professionals by financial criteria. If a tennis player takes money for playing tennis, he's a professional; if he doesn't, he has kept his amateur standing. This has nothing to do with the quality of his play. And so, as a musician, you may be a professional—that is to say, earn money—and still be irresponsible as a musician. Or you may be an amateur, not accept fees, and practice your art according to the highest standards known to your time. Any musician who practices his art, however modestly, in full acceptance of his obligation to maintain the highest standards that he is aware of, is a real musician.

At New England Conservatory of
Music commencement, May 18/
The Christian Science Monitor, 6-16:23.

Judith C. Toth
Maryland State Delegate

3

[Criticizing pornographic lyrics in rock music]: How does a parent respond to that? Yes, parents have a primary role, but it has been substantially eroded by the pressures of peers and the media . . . I don't believe that the industry is incapable of self-regulation. The movie industry cleaned itself up after the same kind of public and legislative pressure we are talking about today . . . Think of the children. Think of contaminated young minds. Think of kids growing up to the sound of glorified rape and sexual violence. Think of our obligation to protect our youth. Think of your 12-year-old listening to Judas Priest extolling oral sex at the point of a gun.

Before Maryland Senate Judicial
Proceedings Committee, Annapolis/
The Washington Post, 3-26:(A)18.

Benita Valente
Opera singer

4

[Doing a new piece of music is] like a crescendo. When I get into the first rehearsal I sing a certain way, and as we go on I do more. But there is always something left for the performance that I haven't done yet. That's the fascination of performing. There's always something else I want to uncover. Then with each performance there is even more. With each time you feel you've accomplished something. I've always done a lot of thinking. I like to have thought about everything beforehand. Then it's not like there's a fresh thought as I stand there onstage; but there are so many different ways you can do something. Each performance is different, simply from how you react to other singers, and how the music goes. I've had one pianist in recitals who would say, "Well, that's not the temp you took the last time," or "You didn't make the crescendo at that point like you did the last time." Well, that's not how I think of music. I see it as something you build each time you do a piece. I hate it when someone trails after me and points out, "Well, you didn't do this, you didn't do that." Well, get away from me. I don't want anything to do with you! The magic of making music—that's the wonderful thing. You're into the music. After you've thought about and decided on many, many things, there's always that magic that comes out, that creative thing inside you, that urge you to let it just pour out.

Interview, New York/Opera News, 2-15:14.

WHAT THEY SAID IN 1986

Jon Vickers
Opera singer

1

The opera world is in trouble today because it's being invaded by those techniques that are corrupting our society—big PR, the personality cult, techniques that create hysteria but do nothing for the intellect and do not elevate man. They degrade our art.

Interview, London/Opera News, 3-1:43.

THE STAGE

George Abbott
Producer

1

[On the high cost of producing a musical on Broadway today]: This makes things tough for the time being on those of us who work in [the theatre], and it is too bad we can't have good musicals for an affordable price. People are also less willing to take chances than they were before, because audiences want stars, as well as extravagance.

Interview, New York/
Los Angeles Times, 6-25:(VI)4.

Richard Armitage
British producer

2

[On the increase in British-originated musicals]: The Brits were nowhere to be seen for decades. Now that's all changed. But I don't think the supreme American talent for musical has gone away. It's just waiting to swing back. And it will.

USA Today, 6-12:(D)2.

Emanuel Azenberg
Producer

3

Costs [of producing a show on Broadway] are obscene. I grew up in the labor movement, and no one is more dedicated to it than I am. But what we need in the theatre is a [Carl] Icahn or a [Lee] Iacocca [both corporate leaders who turned their failing companies around]—someone to do what [U.S. President] Reagan did with the air controllers [fire those who were striking]. Does this mean that we [in the theatre] should take a strike if we have to? If it comes to that, yes. You could replace 65 per cent of the people who work in these jobs at no loss; there would be plenty of people ready to take their places. At $700 a week for a 40-hour week, people would be standing in line around the block. We're not talking about getting people to take less pay, but about productivity. Just let every man work the hours he's paid for; that's all I ask. We're like the railroads that kept the firemen long after there was no coal . . . Everyone has to be willing to clean house, to rip it all out, and the producers and theatre owners aren't ready for that yet. They still think one big hit will turn the whole thing around. I don't know what it will take before they wake up; I guess we'll have to hit bottom, and we may never do that. We'll just keep limping along.

Interview/The Wall Street Journal, 6-10:30.

Robert Brustein
Artistic director,
American Repertory Theatre,
Cambridge, Mass.

4

[On his winning a Tony award for outstanding regional theatre]: I'm very ambivalent about the award. I'm very proud of the theatre, but for the past 20 years I've been a critic of the Tonys as stimulating that lust for celebrity and stardom that is antithetical to the theatre . . . If we've done anything here [at the American Repertory Theatre], it's to establish a model, that if you stick with [your artistic goals] and the audience perceives that commitment, you'll come through.

Interview, Cambridge, Mass./
The Christian Science Monitor, 6-2:48.

5

We have never seen more first-rate artists entering the theatre field than right now. We will look back on this age as the golden one.

The Christian Science Monitor, 6-4:21.

WHAT THEY SAID IN 1986

(ROBERT BRUSTEIN)

1

The theatre must free the audience's imagination. To do this, it must unsettle the audience. It must shatter their usual way of looking at the world. I don't want to affect just what people think during the day. I want to affect their dreams.

Los Angeles Times, 10-5:(Calendar)35.

Martha Clarke
Choreographer

2

I'm mesmerized by things that develop slowly. I like impacted emotion that can't be done fast, although there are bursts of energy. When things happen fast, you're only working on what you're seeing onstage, whereas, if it's slow, the viewer has a chance to go into his or her own well of imagery and references. I have always been moved in the theatre by the things that happen between the lines, or, in wonderful dancing, by the movements that happen between moves. It's the things that slip into the cracks in the floorboards that I'm interested in.

Interview/Dancemagazine, April:74.

Gordon Davidson
Artistic director,
Mark Taper Forum, Los Angeles

3

Young people are the audience of tomorrow. They must be cultivated and led into the range of what live theatre can provide. It's really partly self-interest. If we don't talk to the next generation, they won't know what live theatre is. We have an obligation to young people to develop material that speaks very directly to their lives— honest material that expresses what they are thinking about.

The Christian Science Monitor, 6-3:44.

Daniel Duell
Principal dancer, New York City Ballet

4

Before, dancing had an immediate and glorious reward in the response of the audience, the response of fellow dancers. It was combined with a religious feeling, too. It was something good and pure and required enormous discipline. For a long time, that sustained me. Now I don't think of it in such pure and virtuous terms. I like big, dramatic, active movement. I like the opportunity it gives for expressing myself. I enjoy performing! I like being a ham. I like showing off in public. Now I'm not afraid to admit it. It's okay, and I think it's one of the biggest motivators for almost any performer. I used to condemn myself for it, saying, "No, no! I'd better be modest and upright and shy about those things." Now I can enjoy myself and let it show.

Interview/Dancemagazine, May:46.

Friedrich Durrenmatt
Swiss playwright

5

When I write, my public is myself and nobody else. I think only of my characters, of the play's form. I start with a vision of the whole work. Then the characters start to exist on their own. I talk and argue with them, even in my sleep. The curious thing is that my plays end as I wanted them to end, even though I don't know the scenes or the characters beforehand. They become clear to me as I write.

Interview/World Press Review, April:58.

6

Too many plays have too much of the playwright and director in them. And I am terrified at the idea of watching one of my own works. I come to blows with directors who are determined to transform them into something I am not in agreement with. I have written 19 plays, but I sometimes ask myself why I should bother to write a twentieth.

Interview/World Press Review, April:58.

Garth Fagan
Director, Bucket Dance
Theatre, Rochester, N.Y.

7

Technical wizards are a dime a dozen in the dance world. They can touch the sky with their

(GARTH FAGAN)

feet. Technique is barren unless it's at the service of the dance . . . If people just want craft from me, I can make 50 dances a day. But I want to make art. I want to make dances that knock me over.

Interview/The Wall Street Journal, 2-4:24.

Martha Graham
Choreographer

1

[On her old age and dancing]: I believe one thing: that today is yesterday and tomorrow is today and you can't stop. The body is your instrument in dance, but your art is outside that creature, the body. I don't leap or jump any more. I look at young dancers and I am envious, more aware of what glories the body contains. But sensitivity is not made dull by age.

Interview/The New York Times, 1-22:16.

2

[As a child,] the discipline, the professionalism, the mystery [of dance] caught me, and I was caught forever. [But] I had to have something else to dance *about*. I knew I was a rebel, and I was called a revolutionary—although I wasn't trying to shatter anything, only to build something else. I didn't set out as an evangelist seeking to send a message, but to simply make the great energy that is life pass through me as best I could. I had such confidence in myself. This is what I want from my dancers today, to be grounded firmly in a technique, but not to be imitations of me.

Interview, New York/
Los Angeles Times, 4-21:(VI)5.

Stephen Graham
Producer

3

Broadway has turned into a super-show thing, for musicals and big comedies. A serious play has a real uphill battle if it's going to play on Broadway. Look at *Glengarry Glen Ross*. It won a Pulitzer Prize, it never sold out a single week

here and it closed in the red. Ditto *'night, Mother,* another Pulitzer Prize winner. And *Ma Rainey's Black Bottom,* a play that got sensational reviews, just hung on by its fingernails until it ran out of steam and closed. By keeping *A Lie of the Mind* at the [off-Broadway] Promenade [Theatre], we'll have four times the length of a Broadway run.

Interview, New York/
The Wall Street Journal, 1-10:11.

Helen Hayes
Actress

4

. . . when I was a young actress, a very grand Boston hostess took me to lunch and told me I was too much of a plain, normal woman, and that if I was going to become a star, I need a real star image. That bothered me, until I realized that all an image would be worth to me would be more lunches with people like her . . . I do know that many people in the theatre world—not the public, God bless them—but the people in the theatre's so-called "inner circle," haven't taken me as seriously as I deserve to be taken as an actress. And that's simply because I haven't been *exciting,* or made many splashes as an individual. Their attitude hasn't hurt my feelings, believe me, because there's *nobody* so naive as the people who are the inner circle in show business.

Interview, Nyack, N.Y./
Good Housekeeping, March:240.

Glenda Jackson
Actress

5

[Comparing acting on the stage with acting in films]: [In films,] you're working for a camera and a camera is totally absorbed in what you're doing; you never have to work for its attention. It's not the same kind of fear as working in a theatre where, apart from everything else, you have to *make* an audience, which is just a crowd sitting down until you turn it into an audience.

Interview, Paris/
Los Angeles Times, 9-7:(Calendar)23.

WHAT THEY SAID IN 1986

Carol Jeschke
Founder, National Showcase
of Performing Arts

1

Much of [theatre for children in the U.S.] has been condescending, awful stuff that somebody thought was appropriate for children. There's still an awful American impression that children's theatre is tacky . . . The international companies are very often liberally funded by their governments. Their best actors perform in them. The productions are often just lovely, with excellent skills and good production values. The Canadian government gives great support—the same level as adult. They feel, as they should, that there is no difference between good theatre for adults and good theatre for children.

The Christian Science Monitor, 6-3:44.

Ted Kivitt
Artistic director, Milwaukee Ballet;
Former dancer, American Ballet Theatre

2

Being a dancer is very difficult. There is the desire inside—the thing that burns and pushes you—to bring yourself to a higher level each time you go onstage. You can never rely on your last performance to pull you through the next one. There is always something out there to stand in your way, so you must be prepared to conquer each of those obstacles all of the time.

Interview/Dancemagazine, May:53.

John Lanchbery
Principal conductor,
Royal Ballet, London;
Former music director,
American Ballet Theatre.

3

There is something about [ballet] dancers that draws me. They're so lovely to look at, of course. But it's their selfless discipline and grueling hard work I admire so. Once I stayed in the theatre watching Rudi [Nureyev] go over and over a dance phrase. He just couldn't get it right. The longer he tried, the worse it got and he just swore a blue streak. I gently suggested he sim-

plify the steps, but he waved me aside, saying, "Understand, Jack, I have to challenge myself."

Interview, Los Angeles/
Los Angeles Times, 7-18:(VI)2.

Jerome Lawrence
Playwright

4

We [he and his collaborator Robert E. Lee] always say that all our serious plays are funny and all our funny plays are serious. It's more important that a comedy have something really basic to say because then you can take off and be funny about it. There are, alas, so many young playwrights who take themselves so seriously that they are afraid of humor. Wit might trivialize their profound work. The best playwrights—Tennessee Williams, for instance—will puncture the most serious moment with an outrageous laugh. The audience delights in it. They need the relief. They need the laughter—or what Norman Cousins calls "inner jogging"—for the joy of life. The more an audience laughs, the more it feels. Shakespeare knew this—there's comedy in his most serious plays.

Interview/Writer's Digest, March:32.

5

Your play has to be *about* something. If someone says, "What's your play about?" and all you can answer is, "It's about two and a half hours long," then the only answer back is, "It's two and a half hours too long." It has to have a spine, it has to have some meaning, it has to offer some illumination.

Interview/Writer's Digest, March:34.

Robert E. Lee
Playwright

6

I think there's a marvelous plasticity to people who are approaching writing seriously for the first time. You hear them say: "Wow! You can do this, you can do that, you can play God. You can create these characters and make them do what you want them to do" . . . You see, a young playwright is a "terra incognita"—a new

(ROBERT E. LEE)

creative landfall to be sighted. On the other hand, a known playwright wears the albatross of his own reputation around his neck. He is a *target*.

Interview/Writer's Digest, March:32.

David LeVine
Executive director, Dramatists Guild

1

There is almost no playwright in the U.S. who does not write for another medium. They do it to make the bucks. At $35,000 to $40,000 for a screen assignment, you'd have to be crazy not to.

The Christian Science Monitor, 6-4:21.

Bella Lewitzky
Choreographer

2

I know there is no such thing as a virgin audience [for dance]. Most people come to see a couple of pirouettes, some jetes; you know, pretty movement, two dancers going off the stage whistling. But there are always others deeply affected by what I'm trying to say. The bottom line is that the dancer must learn *why* he is dancing. That will help him forget those in the audience who choose to see as far as the skin, but not the blood. The greatest gift a dancer gives his audience is to dance for himself, to measure up to his highest expectations no matter what the response, knowing he is creating an act of art.

Interview/Ballet News, January:23.

Hal Linden
Actor

3

[On directing]: You have to be an expert in dramaturgy—what the play is about, what each character means; a visual artist; an expert in psychology—how both actors and audience will react; an editor; a communicator who can talk to each actor; and, on top of it all, [be] incredibly

patient. You can't force people to do what they don't want to do, but still you want it done.

*Interview, New York/
The New York Times, 9-26:21.*

Lar Lubovitch
Choreographer

4

American dance has become overly technical, and we see the price that's been paid. *Movement* is an important subject that is not being taught by enough dance teachers working in America. Technique has superceded movement. Movement is what dance is about, but many people don't understand what movement *is* now, or how to put movement together. Typically, people will go from pose to pose, and have very little awareness of how they spent the time between the poses. That piece of time between the poses is what could be called the movement itself. Putting those things together, threading them together, is the movement, and people don't understand how to govern the transitions to turn them into movement.

*Interview, New York/
Dancemagazine, November:56.*

David Mamet
Playwright

5

Theatre has few new plays, and most of them are bad. Critics seem to thwart originality . . . Television buys off the talented.

*At Harvard University/
The Christian Science Monitor, 6-4:21.*

Jackie Mason
Comedian

6

Nothing creates a star like a Broadway show. In the theatre, you can show yourself off in an atmosphere that makes people of the highest level respect your accomplishments. They see you as an artist instead of a bum telling jokes in a toilet.

*Interview, Beverly Hills, Calif./
The Washington Post, 12-3:(G)1.*

439

Kevin McKenzie
Ballet dancer,
American Ballet Theatre

1

[Saying the star system in ballet is not dead]: People come to see individuals. They're fascinated by individuals. It's been said that [choreographer George] Balanchine never had a star system. What a joke! He created star after star after star. He just did it differently. He made masterpieces for his dancers, and that's what made them stars. Stardom is what theatre is all about. Playwrights write great plays. Composers write great music. But only when a great performer interprets their works do you realize what a work of art is all about. In the end, when the curtain goes up, it belongs to the performer. They can make or break a work of art. That's been the case forever—and it will continue to be the case forever.

Interview/
Dancemagazine, June:48.

Des McNuff
Artistic director,
La Jolla (Calif.) Playhouse

2

We [in the theatre] cannot afford to be a snob. Theatre has traditionally been a popular, not an elitist, art-form. There is a generation of new theatre artists emerging, and we have got to win this [artistic] battle.

Interview,
La Jolla, Calif./
The Christian Science Monitor, 6-4:20.

John A. McQuiggan
Producer

3

There's an alarming difference in attitude of audiences toward Broadway and Off-Broadway. With Broadway, they want to know who's in it. With Off-Broadway, they want to know what it's about.

Interview,
New York, Nov. 25/
The New York Times, 11-26:22.

Jonathan Miller
Producer, Director, Writer

4

If a play is readable only in light of the actual people that are involved, then it's simply a documentary, not a play. For its life—or after-life—to be guaranteed, it must eventually slip its anchor. Unfortunately, people's reactions to drama are something like what Konrad Lorenz discovered with the graylag goose. They become imprinted on the first thing they saw and anything else is wrong. But characters don't exist until you re-create them.

Interview, New York/
The Wall Street Journal, 4-11:22.

Mike Nichols
Director

5

Directing is like cleaning a floor. You clean one square, then the next one, and the next one, and finally the whole floor is clean. Then you decide if you want to change its color or give it another coat of polish. I don't know any other way to do it. There is no magic stroke that makes a play work.

Interview, Washington/
The Washington Post, 3-21:(B)1.

6

[On Broadway]: Everyone's tired of the whole process. Everyone's tired of spending $150 [for a ticket], once again, to be misled into seeing something that bores [them] for three or four hours . . . If Broadway has to go, it has to go. It just means that Broadway will rise in another shape. What is Broadway anyway? It's just some Shubert houses. There will be a phoenix somewhere else.

Interview, Washington/
The Washington Post, 3-21:(B)8.

Rudolf Nureyev
Ballet dancer;
Artistic director, Paris Opera Ballet

7

[On the playing down of the star system in ballet today]: When I danced with Margot [Fon-

(RUDOLF NUREYEV)

teyn] and with Ballet Theatre, ballet was very popular and going to performances was an exciting event. The public was caught up in this. Later, I felt there was a move to demote me, to let the cart run without the horse. It happened at the Royal Ballet and in New York . . . [Today,] although you have [Mikhail] Baryshnikov and [Fernando] Bujones, I don't think you have the same great motor. The public comes and fills the theatre, but you don't have an event. It is an every-day activity—and you can't blame people for skipping it.

Interview, New York/
The New York Times, 7-8:22.

Joseph Papp
Director, Public Theatre, New York

1

My basic desire is to create a theatre constituency in New York City and a three-state area for plays that have something to say, at affordable prices in Broadway houses that are empty and threatened with demolition. The way to attract new audiences to Broadway is first of all to get actors that are known to them—from films and television, but primarily films. There are no great stage actors any more that people instantly recognize.

Interview, New York, June 11/
The New York Times, 6-12:26.

2

[On playwrights who abandon the theatre to become writers for the movies]: Very few playwrights come back. You get into the California mode, life is easier, you get used to it, you make more money. Why go out of your way to court poverty? Man cannot live by art alone.

Newsweek, 12-15:74.

Lloyd Richards
Dean, School of Drama,
Yale University

3

Every year it is annually asked [in the media] whether theatre in America will survive. [How-

ever,] there never has been a time more needful of fresh vision [for American theatre] than right now.

The Christian Science Monitor, 8-19:26.

4

A theatre is an exciting place to be. It is [also] a dangerous place to be, because living people are there—there is communication that is going on in so many different ways. It isn't just from the stage to the audience; it's from each individual audience member to the stage and each individual member to each other. I don't think that [we] have devised anything to replace that [kind of communication]. I think as long as that exists, we will have theatre. We will have people telling stories and . . . having conversations. And the theatre is a conversation.

Interview, New Haven, Conn./
The Christian Science Monitor, 11-4:19.

Jason Robards
Actor

5

[Fredric] March and I once did a scene from *Count of Monte Cristo* at a benefit. Oh, he was terrific. You felt the surge. You accepted the fact that he was impassioned. I love that kind of theatre. Make-believe—that's what's fun. That's what it's all about. It's not a lot of self-analysis. And the better you make believe, the more the audience makes believe with you, and the more wonderful the evening is.

Interview, Los Angeles/
Los Angeles Times, 2-9:(Calendar)4.

Gerald Schoenfeld
Chairman, Shubert Organization

6

[On the fact that respected playwright Sam Shepard has had his plays produced off-Broadway, but never on Broadway]: It has nothing to do with Mr. Shepard's talent. We would love to have Mr. Shepard's play in one of our [Broadway] theatres. It's largely a matter of economics. People who work off-Broadway are content to work for less money. If the same scales existed on

441

WHAT THEY SAID IN 1986

(GERALD SCHOENFELD)

Broadway, Mr. Shepard would be produced on Broadway . . . [I blame the small audience for serious theatre in the U.S. on the] failure of the media, particularly the electronic media, and the educational system in this country to cultivate audiences for serious plays. If people were inculcated to the drama as they are in England, then we would have a wider audience for contemporary plays as well as for Shakespeare and Chekhov on Broadway.

Interview, New York/
The Wall Street Journal, 1-10:11.

Peter Sellars
Artistic director, American National
Theatre, Kennedy Center, Washington

1

Theatre has to reinvent itself in the next generation. Because traditional theatre is no longer relevant to a whole generation, and the most exciting developments today are electronic, theatre must remake itself, from an electronic standpoint.

The Christian Science Monitor, 6-5:22.

2

Every one of my productions hammers against the surface of materialism and forces the audience—either through total frustration, out of boredom, or whatever—to have a reaction that goes beyond the mundane. Why it's so hard to do theatre now is because theatre is about this confrontation with existence. And confrontation is, needless to say, not popular at this period in America, not politically or any other way.

Interview, Washington/
The Christian Science Monitor, 9-26:26.

3

I really dislike this cult of the director that has sprung up in recent years. It drives me crazy, because what you see on-stage are rarely my ideas. I've had some participation in them, I've organized them so they make sense and line up, but [they belong to] all the people I work with.

Interview, Los Angeles/
Los Angeles Times, 12-1:(VI)6.

Ron Silver
Actor

4

[Saying that when he takes on a new role, he first makes voluminous notes]: It's all totally lost when instinctual fusion starts. But there has to be a form at the back of the mind . . . What we [actors] do is a deliberate distortion of the truth to get at a greater truth.

Interview, New York/
The New York Times, 5-2:21.

Tom Stoppard
Playwright

5

[On whether writing gets easier or harder]: Harder. I look at stuff I wrote 10 years ago and I say, I wouldn't know how to do that today. Of course, I also look at stuff and wonder what I was thinking of. I saw *Jumpers* not too long ago in a provincial British theatre and I thought that we must have been mad to think that this was a Broadway play.

Interview, London/
Los Angeles Times, 6-2:(VI)6.

Paul Taylor
Choreographer

6

I'm not known for having a lot of theories about dancing, but I always recommend that audiences sit there and be sponges. Open up the pores of sensation rather than the brain. If you think too hard, sometimes you don't see any more. Thinking is what you do *after* seeing a piece.

Interview, New York/
The Christian Science Monitor, 4-28:27.

Robert Wilson
Director, Playwright

7

I think mystery . . . allows us time to dream. It allows for the knowledge within us to come

(ROBERT WILSON)

forth. Socrates said we were born with knowledge within us—it's just the uncovering of the knowledge we need. It's through the mysteries we do this. That's why I don't like [realistic] theatre. It kills the mysteries for me.

Interview,
New York/The Christian
Science Monitor, 3-12:25.

William P. Wingate
Executive managing director,
Center Theatre Group/
Mark Taper Forum, Los Angeles

1

Theatre has to be able to continually reinvent itself in order to survive. If it doesn't, it leads to mediocritization and trivialization of theatre, and then why should we exist?

The Christian Science Monitor, 4-17:29.

Philosophy

Mortimer Adler
*Educator; Director, Institute
for Philosophical Research*

1

It is more difficult to become morally virtuous under affluent conditions than under adverse conditions. Adversity is a better product of development of moral character than affluence. Take any family. Children of affluent families are often ruined by the affluence that surrounds them. Everything is too easy. I'm not recommending hardship. I'm only saying it's more difficult [to raise] morally virtuous young people [under affluent conditions]. If you said to many people today, "You really have to suffer stringent reductions of your standard of living for the sake of your grandchildren and your grandchildren's grandchildren, [since] we can't go on spending the way we're spending," they would be morally incapable of doing that.

*Interview, Aspen, Colo./
The Christian Science Monitor,
9-23:16.*

Maya Angelou
Author

2

Sometimes we think we have found the place, the niche, and my insight is that we should keep on our traveling shoes, that we are in process, every one of us, and we should keep on the traveling shoes and be ready.

*Interview/
Los Angeles Times, 6-12:(V)1.*

Alan Arkin
Actor

3

I believe it's man's natural state to be creative. The aberration is *not* being creative. It's walls that we put up in order to stifle ourselves. We're afraid of what's going to come out if we let go—if we start dancing! . . . Everybody has

talent for everything. I know it sounds like a Pollyanna-ish thing to say. But it's what I think.

*Interview, New York/
The Christian Science Monitor, 7-8:36.*

Danny Arnold
Writer, Producer

4

What's good comedy? It's not a matter of jokes. That's just a comment on a particular moment that you give a virtuoso performer who can make it funny. Too much of that is nonsense—*Kinderspiel*. True comedy comes out of tragedy. We are all dealing with the fundamental will to survive, because everything out there is conspiring to kill you—the water, the air, crazy drivers, drugs, terrorists, mistrust, aggression, hostility, religion . . . everything. And the best comedy is organic. It's something so personal that you don't have to fancify.

*Interview, Los Angeles/
Emmy Magazine, Jan.-Feb.:13.*

Jose Azcona
President of Honduras

5

There are no magic formulas to push development and conquer poverty. Since the origin of man, work has been the source of well-being and wealth.

*Inaugural address,
Tegucigalpa, Honduras, Jan. 27/
The New York Times, 1-28:3.*

Bruce Babbitt
Governor of Arizona (D)

6

It often takes more courage to brave the little things than to take the heroic, public step. I was thinking the other day, for some reason, about the second person to fly solo across the Atlantic. I mean the guy who did it after Lindbergh. And

(BRUCE BABBITT)

I thought—that's the hero. It's one thing to risk something for greatness. But it's the one who made it commonplace without the fame who deserves our more practical gratitude.

At Claremont McKenna College
commencement, May 18/
The Christian Science Monitor, 6-13:24.

1

I spent two years re-learning the truth about history—that real change comes slowly and incrementally, and that laws cannot change the heart and soul of people . . . We work for progress when we work to change a single person. And that is a task beyond none of us.

At Claremont McKenna College
commencement, May 18/
The Christian Science Monitor, 6-13:24.

James Baldwin
Author

2

I was born 21 years before the Atomic Age. I was born to live an ordinary life. I could dream of getting to be 70 or 80, if I should live that long. Behind me stretched, however disagreeably or however beautifully, a sense of time, of continuity. But I began to suspect that to anyone born after 1945, the sense of time which I had inherited was as remote for them, really, as ancient Rome is for me. That one whole generation, two generations, have come into the world under the threat of extinction. And this changes everyone's reality. It seems to me, in that case . . . it is probably going to be your generation—it is too late, I think, for mine—to reconsider everything.

At Hampshire College commencement, May 17/
The Christian Science Monitor, 6-16:24.

Marilyn Bergman
Songwriter

3

Interesting things, words. I've had a love affair with them for as long as I can remember . . . Words can be used to express or repress, to release or restrain, to enlighten or obscure. Through words we can adore each other or abhor each other. Nations can offend or befriend one another. Words can enslave and keep people in their place. They're easy prey for those who would tamper with the integrity of their meaning.

At Women in Film luncheon, Los Angeles,
May 30/Los Angeles Times, 6-2:(VI)4.

Rose Elizabeth Bird
Chief Justice,
Supreme Court of California

4

I think that no matter how much material success you may achieve, you pave the way to disappointment if you set up your five- and 10-year goals and say to yourself, "By then I want to be there." We are here, I believe, to achieve wisdom and live ethically. And if we can look upon the journey of life as a learning process, we will begin to perceive a lot of the difficult and disappointing things that happen along the way in a very different light—and perhaps grow from the experience, rather than turn bitter. You really can't control very much of what happens to you. But what you can control is how you react to the things that do happen. And there, I believe, is the key to finding out about life.

At University of California-Davis
commencement/Time, 6-9:62.

Allan Boesak
South African anti-apartheid activist;
President, World Alliance of
Reformed Churches

5

Violence destroys something in you. There is an element of uncontrollability in it. . . . the people who say violence will solve all problems, the total militarization of [President] Reagan in this country [the U.S.]—I think that is romantic, that by grabbing the gun and eliminating the enemy you solve the problem. I say to my people, "If we begin to put our faith in violence this way, don't you fool yourself, this is going to happen to us. Before you know it, the desire for vio-

WHAT THEY SAID IN 1986

lence, the lust for violence, the naturalness of violence, overcomes you. You never control it; it controls you." In Western society, it's the Rambos of the world who are the heroes. I think that's sick. It twists our values beyond almost any recognition of humanity.

Interview, Washington/
The Washington Post, 6-9:(C)8.

Sissela Bok
Social philosopher; Teacher
in humanities and ethics,
Brandeis University

1

Gandhi used the expression, I think, of "zones of peace." If one could make one's self into a more peaceful individual [and] if one could [then] try to extend that into one's family, one would already have done quite a lot. If one could do something within the community, and perhaps within one's society, and keep very much open to the possibility of trying, however hard it is, to do it for the entire world—it's this idea of forming a small zone and pushing outward that I think is very impressive.

Interview, Cambridge, Mass./
The Christian Science Monitor, 10-22:16.

Ray Bradbury
Author

2

When I started [selling newspapers as a young man], I was yelling, "Paper! Paper!" After about six months I was getting hoarse screaming the name of the goddamn paper. I experimented one day not yelling to see if it made any difference in the sales. There was no difference. I'd been yelling for nothing. That gave me my primary lesson: Don't worry about things. Don't push. Just do your work and you'll survive. The important thing is to have a ball, to be joyful, to be loving and to be explosive. Out of that comes everything, and you grow. All you should worry about is whether you're doing it every day and whether you're having fun with it.

If you're not having fun with it, find the reason. You may be doing something you shouldn't be doing.

Interview, Beverly Hills, Calif./
Writer's Digest, February:28.

Klaus Maria Brandauer
Austrian actor

3

For me, Hamlet was a decent, innocent, fantastically well-educated man who realized that the moment you made a decision it would be wrong for someone—that no decision can be right for everybody. He was a man who reflected. It would not be useful for society if we were all Hamlets. There would be no progress because no decisions would be made. But people like Hamlet are necessary for the perspective they provide.

Interview, Beverly Hills, Calif./
Los Angeles Times, 3-4:(VI)6.

Leo Braudy
Professor of literature,
University of Southern California

4

America has taught the world about both the dissemination and power of fame. In the U.S., fame has been democratized. As a result, it is now the performer—not the monarch or the Roman general—who is the model for fame. Fame is no longer restricted to a dynastic, political elite; it is open to everyone. But immortality doesn't last as long as it used to.

Interview/U.S. News &
World Report, 10-6:86.

Carol Burnett
Entertainer

5

. . . children are the best actors in the world. They become whatever the costume they are wearing *tells them* they are. This happens with adults as well. Go to a black-tie dinner and watch. They would all act differently if they had on sneakers.

Interview/The Saturday
Evening Post, November:48.

Vinicio Cerezo
President of Guatemala

1

Authority is not power. They are two different concepts, and we must see the difference between them, because power without authority is tyranny.

Inauguration address,
Guatemala City, Jan. 14/
The New York Times, 1-15:3.

Lynne V. Cheney
Chairman, National Endowment for
the Humanities of the United States

2

The Founding Fathers made this point often: A free people, if they are to remain free, must be able to think critically, as the humanities teach us to do. We must be able to judge truth from falsehood and right from wrong, to distinguish what abides from what is merely passing. Above all, we must be able to judge wisely, a capacity that grows as we gain the broad perspective that the humanities encourage.

At rededication of Buffalo Bill
Historical Center, Cody, Wyo./
The Washington Post, 7-25:(A)18.

Dick Clark
Television personality and producer

3

The real truth of it is, the money stopped being the motivation about 25 years ago. It's the activity; it's the play. That's the same reason a lot of people do what they do. Once you get enough money to live on, that's all you need. But the money does change your attitude a little bit. It's not an extraordinarily easy business. It's very competitive. When I was a lad I was very competitive, and I still am. But now it doesn't hurt so much to lose something, or give something away. It's not laziness, it's maturity, to know that you just can't do everything, nor are you equipped to do it. That sometimes takes a little time to figure out.

Interview, New York/
The Christian Science Monitor, 1-27:32.

Jacques-Yves Cousteau
Explorer, Environmentalist

4

The best way to approach happiness is expansion of yourself . . . with creation . . . with love . . . with sharing . . . with knowledge. And they are the only ways that lead to a form of happiness. If you concentrate on yourself, you're doomed, you're miserable, you're neurotic.

Interview, Mexico/
The Washington Post, 5-30:(C)8.

5

I think that anybody living close to nature cannot be bored. I think that the peasants that were actually working on the ark, without factories, without the noise of the motors, without television, when they came home they must have been bedazzled by sunsets and sunrises. But people today don't see that. If they see the sun rise or the sun set, it's on television. As soon as you are cut off from nature, I think you are losing enthusiasm.

Interview/USA Today, 6-5:(A)11.

William Crowe
Admiral and Chief of Operations,
United States Navy;
Chairman, Joint Chiefs of Staff

6

Freedom is not free—and that message must be passed on year after year from generation to generation if our way of life is to survive.

Veterans Day commemoration,
Nov. 10/USA Today, 11-11:(A)4.

Mario M. Cuomo
Governor of New York (D)

7

When you get that second car in your garage, that Jacuzzi installed in your beach house in the Hamptons, and when you have your Nathan's hot dogs delivered by courier, you may well ask, "Is this where the dream ends?" Just remember, there are those who work hard, are successful, and never look back; and there are those who make it, look back and lend a helping hand.

At Brooklyn (N.Y.) College commencement,
June 10/The New York Times, 6-11:19.

447

Marian Wright Edelman
President, Children's Defense Fund

1

Democracy is not a spectator sport. I hope you will not run away or refuse to get involved because issues are often complex and controversial. The world, Albert Einstein said, "is in greater peril from those who tolerate evil than from those who commit it."

At Rutgers University commencement/
USA Today, 5-29:(A)11.

Deborah Eisenberg
Author

2

I don't think things are ever exactly the way one expects, and I don't think things are ever the way one assumes they are at the moment. What I actually think is that one has no idea of what things are like, ever.

Newsweek, 5-5:17.

Marvin Feldman
President, Fashion
Institute of Technology

3

If you succeed in all you do, it's a sure sign you're not reaching high enough. Learn to be reckless. The way to find yourself is to lose yourself—completely, without hesitation, without resistance—to the things you believe.

At Fashion Institute of Technology
commencement, New York, May 30/
The New York Times, 5-31:9.

David Gardner
President, University of California

4

I've never believed that any job is worth sacrificing one's personal life for. I have never believed that any success outside the home can compensate for failure within it. It's important to hold on to your own values, or you will surely lose them.

Interview/
USA Today, 10-30:(A)11.

John Gavin
Former United States
Ambassador to Mexico

5

I do encourage you to maintain an active and healthy skepticism. That, after all, is what a university preparation is about—learning to judge, learning to think. I am constantly amazed by the distortions and untruths I find in reports and comments about subjects on which I am informed. I therefore cannot help but have a healthy skepticism. I encourage you to adopt the same attitude. It is wise to remember, as my father says, that some people so treasure the truth that they use it with great economy.

At Pepperdine University-Malibu
commencement/Time, 6-9:63.

Richard Gere
Actor

6

. . . I used to think my work had a theme, that I was expressing all the possibilities inside me. By the end of my life, if you put all the roles together, they would be me. But now I'm not so sure. I think less about my career than I used to. I try to remember that I'm a worker. I have a craft. But I've been to countries where people have discovered that a few hours of daily labor can assure all their needs and security. That leaves the rest of the day for activities more worthy of a human being.

Interview, New York/Ms., February:80.

A. Bartlett Giamatti
President, Yale University

7

As I think back and look forward, I see how nothing is unambiguous; nothing is without risk. Salvation does not come through simplicities.

At Yale University commencement,
May 25/Time, 6-9:62.

Jackie Gleason
Entertainer

8

There are lots of people funnier than me. You see them at cocktail parties and conventions all

(JACKIE GLEASON)

the time. They are really funny, tell a good story, mimic their faces well and have timing. The only difference is that they don't have the confidence or ego or whatever it takes to go on stage or on television and do it there. And when you can do that and say "I'm funny," then you are a talent.

USA Today, 11-3:(D)2.

Andy Griffith
Actor

1

Most people go along saying, "Well, if this would only happen, or if that would just come true, then my life would be fulfilled, everything would be great." But that ain't the way it works. Now, I'm tickled silly to be playing [on a new TV series] and having producers and a network think I'm back in fashion. But even if the show's successful, it doesn't mean I'm going to live happily ever after. What you do is, you approach everything realistically and give it the best caring effort you know how, and then maybe things will turn out.

Interview/
TV Guide, 10-4:35.

Alec Guinness
Actor

2

It's a pity if the people who are celebrities or near-celebrities let it go to their heads and think they are great people, because one knows only too well that may last only six months or a few years. I have seen people fall for quick success and not know how to deal with it. They take to the drink or, nowadays, to the drugs. It's as if it's too much for them. There's something pathetic about people who have overnight success and huge amounts of money and take off into a fantasy world and have their entourage of henchmen around them. I've seen it too often.

Interview/U.S. News &
World Report, 3-31:64.

Philip C. Habib
Special Envoy for the
President of the United States

3

In my profession, optimism is a necessity. But I think there is a cause for optimism. Why should we try to educate a generation of pessimists? . . . Any problem that can be created by human beings can be solved by human beings. That's a basis for optimism.

At California State University-San Diego
commencement, May 25/
Los Angeles Times, 5-26:(I)5.

Katharine Hepburn
Actress

4

I don't think you should spend this life preparing for the next. Life *is* very hard, isn't it? But we're all going to die, and we must not be afraid to die. *Life's* what's important. Walking, beauty, family. Birth and pain and joy—and then death.

Interview/Ladies' Home
Journal, September:165.

Thor Heyerdahl
Anthropologist, Explorer

5

We in the so-called developed world should learn a lot from developing people, as we call them, before we have developed so much that none of us will know what life is on this planet . . . As one who travels as much as I do, I'm struck by the fact that some of these people, whom we want to force a new civilization on, receive you with a smile. They are laughing; they show every sign of being happy. But walk on the streets in a big city [in the developed world]. Do you see any person laughing or smiling at you? There must be something they have which we shouldn't take away from them.

Interview/USA Today, 9-2:(A)9.

Michael Hooker
Chancellor, University of
Maryland, Baltimore County

6

When I was a kid, I worked. I came home; I worked after school. I worked weekends—had a

(MICHAEL HOOKER)

part-time job and, if I wasn't at my part-time job, I was mowing the lawn or taking out the garbage or doing something around the house. I was occupied. Kids today don't have that necessity of occupation. So an emptiness creeps in. That doesn't mean that my life was more meaningful than their lives. It's just that I had activity to fill it, so I didn't have time to dwell on the meaninglessness of my life, if you will . . . Dwelling on the meaninglessness of your life is a meaningful activity. What I'm concerned about is the people who *don't* dwell on the meaninglessness of their lives, or the meaningfulness of it—who just pursue mindless entertainment. The shopping mall [where many young people spend much of their time] is a contemporary opium. Half of the kids that are there are stoned anyway, but the other half are stoned by the mall. The mall provides a kind of transfixing environment which takes their mind off of whatever their issues are. They walk around—you look in their eyes, and there's nobody home.

Interview, Baltimore/
The Christian Science Monitor, 10-1:16.

John Paul II
Pope

1

Man resigns himself to death when he aspires only to the things of the earth, when he seeks only those things. The earth alone does not conceal within itself the leaven of immortality. Man not only resigns himself to death, but he has often made death the method of his existence on earth. Is not the method of death found in the method of violence, the method of the bloody conquest of power, the method of selfish accumulation of wealth, the method of the struggle against poverty that thrives on hatred and the longing for revenge, the method of intimidation and the abuse of power, the method of torture and terror?

Easter message,
Vatican City, March 30/
The New York Times, 3-31:3.

A society crumbles when marriages become fewer and fewer and more unstable, and when a person's first concern is to satisfy his or her own selfishness and to seek easy pleasures, when infidelity and breakup of marriages becomes acceptable.

Homily, Seychelles, Dec. 1/
The New York Times, 12-2:7.

Janos Kadar
First Secretary,
Communist Party of Hungary

3

I have never been interested in rank and to a certain extent even in popularity. In my view, anyone who thinks he creates history is stupid. Everyone should attend to the job at hand. If it becomes a part of history, so be it . . . Ordinary men do not spend a lot of time looking at themselves in the mirror. But it is important that when you *do* look in the mirror, you should not feel ashamed.

Interview, Budapest/Time, 8-11:31.

Jack Kemp
United States Representative,
R-New York

4

I think despair is defeatism, and I am not a defeatist. And I don't think defeatism is anything other than accepting it. I don't accept it. That isn't to say I couldn't be defeated in my attempt to overcome the forces that are opposed to some of the things I am in favor of. But even that would not be an ultimate defeat. I definitely would have a longer-run view.

Interview/Esquire, January:77.

Stephen King
Author

5

People of my generation, 25 to 40, we were obsessive about our own childhoods for a long time. We went on playing for a long time, almost feverishly. I write for that buried child in us, but

(STEPHEN KING)

I'm writing for the grown-up, too. I want grown-ups to look at the child long enough to be able to give him up. The child should be buried.

Interview/Time, 10-6:80.

Jeane J. Kirkpatrick
Former United States Ambassador/
Permanent Representative to
the United Nations

1

I'll tell you what I'm really like. I'm basically shy and introverted. I make a loyal friend. I have a problem-solving temperament. And it isn't that I am a depressive, but I must say I don't always look at the bright side. I am strong. I am not opinionated. Opinionated means having an unchanging, narrow frame of reference. I form opinions slowly and revise my analysis along the way . . . I've been married 31 years. I've kept the same friends over 30 years. I've had one of my jobs—teaching at Georgetown University—for 15 years. I've lived in one house 27 years and had the same little Iranian hairdresser 10 years—and for that short a time only because my old hairdresser died. Such stability is not compatible with being temperamental. That label shows the chauvinism of my enemies.

Interview, Washington/
Ladies' Home Journal, May:108.

Leszek Kolakowski
Professor of philosophy,
University of Chicago

2

We got used to shrugging off many horrors of our world by talking about "cultural differences." "We have our values, they have theirs" is a saying which we frequently hear when dealing with the atrocities of totalitarianism or of other forms of despotism . . . To put it crudely, shall we say that the difference between a vegetarian and cannibal is just a matter of taste?

Jefferson lecture,
Washington, May 7/
The New York Times, 5-13:9.

Ted Koppel
Anchorman, "Nightline," ABC-TV

3

How much of what is said publicly these days is recorded? Almost everything. How much of what is said is worth remembering? Almost nothing.

At Stanford University commencement/
The Wall Street Journal, 7-28:14.

Katia Labeque
Pianist

4

To me, success is like when you go out into the sun. A little bit of sun is good but, if you stay too long under the sun, you become an idiot. Success is like a jacket. You put it on and, if you take off your jacket, you still have to be the same person.

Interview/Ovation, August:16.

Konrad Lorenz
Nobel Prize-winning zoologist

5

The importance of pets . . . has grown [as] an urbanized mankind has become alienated from nature. Pets for most people are the most important—if not the only remaining—contact with living nature.

Newsweek, 9-1:65.

Robert MacNeil
Co-host,
"MacNeil/Lehrer News Hour,"
PBS-TV

6

H. L. Mencken, through that creativity in language in the 20th century, up till the 1940s, compared well with the creativity in the language in Elizabethan times, the other great growth era. So, while strict grammarians . . . may be distressed that there is a popular disregard for a lot of the niceties of the English grammar, at the same time the language grows richer and stronger all the time . . . The language has thrived on change over the centuries. It is impos-

(ROBERT MacNEIL)

sible to think that it can stand still. Change should not dismay us.

Interview, New York/
The Christian Science Monitor, 9-12:25.

Norman Mailer
Author

1

No matter what brutalities men have exercised upon women, they've obviously lived in sufficient awe of women. They didn't destroy women. But if you ever reversed it, if women had all the power, there would be very little to keep men safely on earth, I can tell you that. That's probably why men are so desperate about maintaining their position. Beneath this comedy of New York middle-class women screaming at every outrage that's perpetrated upon them— these little privileged creatures—there's a real biological drama going on, a sense of biological superiority that women feel.

Interview/Esquire, June:244.

Sanford N. McDonnell
Chairman,
McDonnell Douglas Corporation

2

Ben Franklin said, "Only a virtuous people are capable of freedom." He meant that the leaders in government, the leaders in industry, and the majority of people have to be committed to certain absolute values . . . if our freedom can survive. Because without those values being practiced by at least the majority of the people, well then, you start losing trust. And when you lose trust, then laws and regulations and red tape rush in to force people to be trustworthy.

Interview/USA Today, 5-27:(A)11.

Daniel Moynihan
United States Senator, D-New York

3

Capitalism is not just the way you do business here [in the U.S.]. It is a way you ought to

live. It has the right virtues. It is the source of republican—small "r"—virtue. It makes freedom possible, it makes culture thrive. It is good, and anything that inhibits it is bad.

At Graduate School of Public Administration,
New York University/
The Christian Science Monitor, 4-24:4.

Mike Nichols
Motion-picture and stage director

4

More and more I'm finding, both in life and art, the secret at the core of things is that women are more generous than men. They have a network of support that men don't have. They're more for one another than men are. Men keep beating up on women in various ways, and the women keep responding with life-giving things . . . if that doesn't appear hopelessly sentimental.

Interview, Washington/
The Washington Post, 3-21:(B)8.

Joseph O'Hare
President, Fordham University

5

Anybody who is going to break new ground in any field, be it theology or science, has to be given the freedom to be wrong.

U.S. News & World Report, 11-17:67.

James E. Olson
Chairman, American Telephone
& Telegraph Company

6

My message is a simple one. In five words: Stand up and be counted. In two words: Get involved. In one: Care. "Be not simply good," wrote Henry Thoreau. "Be good for something." He said, in short, take a stand. Personally. Professionally. And, as citizens. From this day forward, your opportunities multiply. Take full advantage of them. Doing so will enrich your lives, and enrich all of our lives. You will find wide opportunities to take stands, to get involved, to be good for something. Don't shy

(JAMES E. OLSON)

from those opportunities. Seize them.

*At University of North Dakota commencement/
USA Today, 5-29:(A)11.*

Geraldine Page
Actress

1

All the great books of the world and every wise person has said the same thing: put in the work and you will get the reward. But very few people seem to listen to this and, instead, think they can skip the work and go through the eye of the needle. Then they're surprised when they go nowhere.

*Interview, New York/
Los Angeles Times, 1-7:(VI)6.*

Javier Perez de Cuellar
*Secretary General of
the United Nations*

2

In charting a wise course toward the next millenium, the first task is to identify the many goals which most countries, including the most powerful, have in common. No country can be harmed by the eradication of hunger. All countries will gain from advancing global development. All countries will gain from a reduction in armaments, especially nuclear arms. All countries require peace. We have the competence, the technological skill to ensure a world safe from nuclear annihilation and environmental disaster, provided governments perceive the necessity of working together, of sharing their resources and their experience.

*At University of Michigan commencement/
USA Today, 5-29:(A)11.*

H. Ross Perot
*Financier; Chairman,
Electronic Data Systems Corporation*

3

Most people don't have the stomach for the fight. If you don't have the stomach to develop a

plan, develop a strategy, take the hits and win the fight, I say you're just kind of a morning glory: You're going to wilt by noon.

*Interview, Dallas/
Los Angeles Times, 5-11:(I)1.*

Ronald Reagan
President of the United States

4

The only thing produced in abundance by Marxism-Leninism has been deprivation and tyranny. From Ethiopia to Cuba, from the Soviet Union itself, which is beginning to fall even further behind the Western democracies, to Vietnam, throughout the Communist world, the cupboards are empty and the jails are full.

*Human Rights Day address,
Washington, Dec. 10/
Los Angeles Times, 12-11:(I)6.*

William H. Rehnquist
*Associate Justice, and
Chief Justice-designate,
Supreme Court of the United States*

5

There are other very important things in life besides earning a living, even if you earn a living by practicing law . . . If you don't have a hobby, you should develop one. You should set aside enough time to keep physically fit. Literature, painting, the theatre, all beckon with their own peculiar ways of enriching your life . . . Do not give up what you can do today with the thought that there will be plenty of time . . . later in life. Unfortunately, there isn't. The moving finger writes and, having writ, moves on.

USA Today, 6-19:(A)5.

Lloyd Richards
*Dean, School of Drama,
Yale University*

6

If you read, as I read a few weeks ago, [that] we now believe that we can depart this planet and set up existence elsewhere—what a fabulous thing that is. [But] what a tremendous and hor-

(LLOYD RICHARDS)

rendous thing that is, because it relieves us of a certain responsibility. If we do succeed in destroying the earth, there are some of us who need not be destroyed with it—and who can depart, observe it from afar, and start something else someplace else. A couple of years ago, we were worried about destroying the earth—which meant destroying ourselves and the future. And that responsibility for the future—that big thing that weighs on us all, which is our responsibility to future generations—that was an aspect of our concern about the destruction of the earth. But now, we can even be relieved from *that*. We can go someplace else. The earth can be discarded like any other product—disposable rubbish.

Interview, New Haven, Conn./
The Christian Science Monitor, 11-4:18.

Chi Chi Rodriguez
Golfer

1

My philosophy is to live like a millionaire and die poor. I don't want to live poor and die a millionaire.

USA Today, 5-5:(C)13.

Ralph Rossum
Professor of government,
Claremont (Calif.) McKenna College

2

We tend to think of democracy as a naturally good thing, but the framers [of the U.S. Constitution] were suspicious of it. It was a problematic concept in 1787. Democracy in many other cases had degenerated into anarchy or tyranny.

Los Angeles Times, 9-8:(I)20.

Dorothy Rubin
Professor of education,
Trenton (N.J.) State College

3

It used to be thought that history never changes. However, we now know that past events are reinterpreted in the light of current events.

Many times, terrible things are buried, and they tend to be forgotten or are assumed to have never taken place. And leaders who were thought to be monsters become heroes because of a reinterpretation of past truth. Does history change? No. It's the person who's writing it.

Interview/USA Today, 12-22:(A)15.

Arthur M. Schlesinger, Jr.
Historian

4

I think every country ought to know its history. History is to a country the way memory is to an individual. Just as an individual cannot function without memory, so really a nation can't function intelligently without a national memory, which is embodied in its history. We ought to know our traditions, and the kind of perspective we can get from that enables us to meet present and future crises better.

Interview/USA Today, 11-25:(A)11.

George C. Scott
Actor

5

. . . I believe in suicide. In classical times, suicide was the honorable way to go. The Judeo-Christian ethic doesn't believe in that, but I'm an atheist. I can name to you 50 actors who have taken their own lives in the last 30 years. I'm not saying that's a good thing or a bad thing, but it's not necessarily anathema to morality. Why hang on until 85 and be incapacitated, deaf and blind and have to be taken care of by somebody that you don't even know? It will happen to all of us. Either you die in a car crash, or you live to be too bloody old.

Interview, Los Angeles/
The New York Times, 8-13:20.

Mary Lee Settle
Author

6

My view of life has been helped by the fact that I have lived in places and with people who were dirt poor. Growing up in the coal country

(MARY LEE SETTLE)

of West Virginia, I saw real poverty. That experience is very different from that of writers whose whole world is a narrow track of suburbs and city. All they need do is open their eyes and look at parts of New York to find out what the world is like. Hemingway's view of grace under pressure has to do with going out and becoming a world correspondent or hunting big game. But to see real grace, you just have to look next door to see what happens when illness or poverty hits.

Interview/U.S. News & World Report, 12-22:64.

B. F. Skinner
Psychologist

1

Western democracies have gone a long way in seeing to it that everyone enjoys the right to security and access to goods. But in many ways they have gone too far . . . . we have moved toward a way of life that is free of unpleasant things. We escape not only from painful extremes of temperature and exhausting work but from mild discomforts and annoyances . . . There is very little left to escape from. The strengthening consequences of negative reinforcement—that we enjoy as relief—have been lost . . . People look at beautiful things, listen to beautiful music and watch exciting entertainments, but the only behavior reinforced is looking, listening and watching. It may seem that one would enjoy a life spent looking at beautiful things, eating delicious foods, watching entertaining performances, but it would be a life in which almost nothing else was done, and few of those who have been able to try it have been notably happy.

Interview/USA Today, 3-24:(A)11.

Margaret Chase Smith
Former United States Senator, R-Maine

2

I've never held grudges because, for one thing, I feel the other fellow has a right to pretty much do and think what he wants, and I want him to let me do the same.

Interview, Skowhegan, Maine/
The Washington Post, 8-4:(B)1.

Thomas Stewart
Opera singer

3

I'm firmly convinced that we, as human beings, in every facet of our lives, are being desensitized so horribly. Anything that requires you to have a fine touch, or a fine ear, or to be aware of something happening inside of you—those things are being manhandled. That is the reason the world has become so violent. All forms of entertainment . . . look for the startling, the shocking. It's screamed at you.

Interview, San Francisco/
The Christian Science Monitor, 1-27:23.

Peter Taylor
Author

4

To me, the most interesting commune in the world is the family. I grew up in an extended family, full of parents, siblings, uncles and aunts and other characters. I'm one of those people who think the world will end not because of the Bomb or the death of God, but because of the family giving out.

Interview, Charlottesville, Va., April 21/
The Washington Post, 4-22:(B)10.

Edward Teller
Nuclear physicist; Senior research fellow,
Hoover Institution, Stanford University

5

My experience has been in a short 77 years, of which 49 years I spent in the U.S., that in the end when you fight for a desperate cause and have good reasons to fight, you usually win. I have experienced that more often than once, and you may object to my statement by calling me an optimist . . . A pessimist is a person who is always right but does not get any enjoyment out of it. An optimist is one who imagines that the future is uncertain, and it is a duty to be an optimist because, if you imagine that the future is uncertain, then you will do something about it.

At Institute for Advanced Political
and Strategic Studies, Israel/
The Wall Street Journal, 8-8:14.

455

WHAT THEY SAID IN 1986

Barbara Tuchman
Author, Historian

1

[Sometimes] I say to myself, "If we could change the rewards—if instead of status and power, people got their reward in life through some other satisfaction." But I don't think that's possible, either, because what does move people to really energetic action is doing something for themselves. [In the Middle Ages,] they used to call it greed.

Interview, Cos Cob, Conn./
The Christian Science Monitor, 10-7:18.

Jack Valenti
President, Motion Picture
Association of America

2

I've always, in both business and politics, felt like you learn by whatever mistakes are made. I often repeat the saying that he who does not read history is doomed to repeat it. John Kennedy learned from the Bay of Pigs, Lyndon Johnson learned from Vietnam and Richard Nixon learned from Watergate. There is no question there will be lessons learned as long as people have hospitable memories.

Los Angeles Times, 12-10:(V)12.

Mario Vazquez Rana
Mexican newspaper publisher;
Owner, United Press International

3

In my country, if you say somebody is ambitious, it has a negative connotation. But ambition is a desire to improve yourself. Whatever I get involved in, I like to come out triumphant.

Interview, Washington/
USA Today, 6-11:(B)4.

Kurt Vonnegut
Author

4

I don't console myself with the idea that my descendants and my books and all that will live on [after his death]. I honestly believe, though, that we are wrong to think that moments go away, never to be seen again. This moment and every moment last forever.

Interview, Dallas/
The Saturday Evening Post, May-June: 39.

Barbara Walters
Broadcast journalist

5

[Addressing graduating college students]: This is not only the day when you are most confident, it is also the day when you are most vulnerable. Look at me. I sound like someone who really knew what she wanted and got it. Baloney. When I was graduating from college, I hadn't a clue. You don't have to know now, and you probably shouldn't know exactly now. The next time somebody says, "And what are you going to do?" try saying, "I don't know yet." What a relief. You may not even want a career. You may want a job and something else: more time for yourself, more time to write, paint, explore, create, have babies, stay home . . . The hardest thing you will ever have to do is to trust your own gut and find what seems to work for you.

At Hofstra University commencement/
Time, 6-9:63.

Elie Wiesel
Author, Historian

6

If I shall be insensitive to one pain, I shall be insensitive to all pains. Never be neutral in any situation where human dignity is concerned. The world out there is not always sunny. There is so much suffering, it is easy to give up hope. But if we are not aware and sensitive, then your children will inherit the ruins of the world.

At Long Island University Brooklyn
Center commencement, June 6/
The New York Times, 6-7:11.

7

If there is one word that describes all the woes and threats that exist today, it's *indifference*. You see a tragedy on television for 3 minutes and then comes something else and something else. How

(ELIE WIESEL)

many tragedies have we had recently? The *Challenger* [space shuttle disaster], Chernobyl [Soviet nuclear plant accident], the earthquake in El Salvador. And then there are the wars and those still in jail in the Communist countries. Because there are so many tragedies, a sense of helplessness sets in. People become numb. They become indifferent. Indifference, to me, is the epitome of evil. The opposite of love is not hate, it's indifference. The opposite of art is not ugliness, it's indifference. The opposite of faith is not heresy, it's indifference. And the opposite of life is not death, it's indifference. Because of indifference, one dies before one actually dies. To be in the window and watch people being sent to concentration camps or being attacked in the street and to do nothing, that's being dead.

Interview/U.S. News &
World Report, 10-27:68.

Elie Wiesel
Author; Winner,
1986 Nobel Peace Prize

1

. . . how naive we were [about Nazi atrocities against Jews in the 1930s and '40s], that the world did know and remain silent. And that is why I swore never to be silent whenever and wherever human beings endure suffering and humiliation. We must always take sides. Neutrality helps the oppressor, never the victim. Silence encourages the tormentor, never the tormented.

Accepting Nobel Peace Prize, Oslo,
Dec. 10/The New York Times, 12-11:8.

Andrew Young
Mayor of Atlanta

2

Salvation does not come through simplicities, either of sentiment or system. The gray, grainy complex of existence and the ragged edges of our lives as we actually lead them defy hunger for a neat, bordered existence and for spirits unsullied by doubt or despair.

At Senior Class Day ceremony,
Yale University, May 25/
The New York Times, 5-26:11.

Franco Zeffirelli
Motion-picture and stage director

3

I am a person who needs hope, which is why I despair of the way socialism is creeping in everywhere, leaving no room for fantasy and dreams. Look at Sweden. Do you want to go there? Even their films are gray. I need to be where there is life and color—places like Rio and New York. Places like Positano [Italy]. If I ever have to leave there, I will be sad indeed.

Interview, Los Angeles/
Los Angeles Times, 8-17:(Calendar)42.

Religion

Nancy T. Ammerman
Assistant professor of the sociology
of religion, Chandler School
of Theology, Emory University

1

We're finding that the [religious] fundamentalists are madder, they're more discontented, more alienated, and by virtue of that discontent have a little more momentum behind their efforts at the political convention. What fundamentalism offers is a very orderly world, a set of answers, a clear sense of right and wrong, a clear sense of who should be in authority. And that's very attractive in a world that looks very disorderly, where nobody knows what's right or wrong.

The New York Times, 6-9:13.

William J. Bennett
Secretary of Education
of the United States

2

If students grow up ignorant of the role of religion, of religious freedom and religious faith in American life, then surely we will have badly failed them.

Speech/The New York Times, 6-3:22.

3

All of the [U.S. Founding Fathers] intended religion to provide a moral anchor for our liberty in democracy. Yet all would be puzzled were they to return to America today. For they would find, among certain elite circles in the academy and in the media, a fastidious disdain for the public expression of religious values, a disdain that clashes directly with the Founders' vision of religion as a friend of civic life.

At University of Missouri, Sept. 17/
The New York Times, 9-18:16.

Warren E. Burger
Chief Justice of the United States

4

[On school prayer]: A moment of silence is a right to thoughts. As long as there is no specification that it be a moment of prayer, I think it's a good idea to have a moment of silence.

Interview, Washington, June 13/
Los Angeles Times, 6-14:(I)25.

Jimmy Carter
Former President of the United States

5

I'm a Southern Baptist, and I have always believed in a total separation of church and state. And I think the injection of religion into politics is not good for this country. The Moral Majority trying to say if you voted for the Panama Canal treaty, you are not a Christian; if you negotiate with the Soviet Union, you're not a Christian. Those kinds of things to me are ridiculous. I think you've seen a tremendous loss of popularity for people like [evangelist] Jerry Falwell who's now had to change the name of his organization from the Moral Majority to something different. My belief in Christ is so important in my life, that it's unshakable. I don't accept human definitions of what I have to believe, you know, to be a Christian.

Interview/
USA Today, 5-12:(A)11.

Norman Corwin
Visiting professor,
School of Journalism,
University of Southern California;
Former radio dramatist

6

Religion is suffering from a recrudescence of extremism, which takes the form of intolerance for dissenters, which takes the form of erosion of the strength of our First Amendment. In this country [the U.S.], where religious freedom is one of the original tenets, we have more to lose than other countries where state religion is in effect.

Interview/
USA Today, 8-18:(A)9.

458

Charles E. Curran
Professor of moral theology,
Catholic University of America

1

[Defending his controversial views on birth control, abortion and other issues, which are counter to traditional Catholic teaching and which have drawn criticism from the Vatican]: What I've always tried to do in my theology is in the light of an age-old axiom that says, "in necessary things unity, in doubtful things freedom, in all things charity." In the Catholic Church, we have to learn to be big enough to disagree with one another but not to be disagreeable about it . . . The Roman Catholic tradition has never said that the Bible alone is enough. In the 4th, 5th and 6th centuries, we said the Bible must always be understood in terms of the thought pattern of contemporary times. The Bible says nothing about nuclear weapons; the Bible says nothing about many of the problems we're facing today . . . Therefore, you just can't appeal to what's said in the Bible, because there's a different reality going on. And if God speaks to us in human words and in human conditions, those words and conditions can change over time.

Interview/USA Today, 3-18:(A)9.

2

[On the Vatican's ruling that he can no longer teach theology at Catholic University because of his dissenting views on sex, abortion and divorce]: The theologian has to play the role of the loyal opposition . . . I am a theological moderate. In my judgment and in the judgment of my peers, I have been and am suitable and eligible to exercise the function of a professor of Catholic theology . . . I remain convinced that the hierarchial teaching office in the Roman Catholic Church must allow dissent on these issues and ultimately should change its teaching. According to Catholic theological tradition, the word and work of Jesus must always be made present and meaningful in the contemporary historical and cultural circumstances.

News conference, Catholic University,
Washington, Aug. 20/
The New York Times, 8-21:8.

Billy Graham
Evangelist

3

To be honest with you, there are too many times when I feel I'm preaching from an empty well. Really, I feel far more humble now than when I began 40 years ago. You take my upcoming Washington Crusade. The numbers don't really matter, do they? And what can you really hope to accomplish in eight days? If just one person changes his ways because of me, then maybe in God's sight I'll be a success. Forty years ago, I thought I was going to change the whole world. I don't think that any more. You know, Jesus was here only three years with his public life. He went about from town to town. And then he said, "I have finished the work the Father has given me to do."

Interview, Montreat, N.C./
The Washington Post, 4-28:(B)1.

Germain Grisez
Professor of Christian ethics,
Mount St. Mary's College,
Emmitsburg, Md.

4

[On the Vatican's disallowal of dissent from Catholic principles in teaching theology at Catholic universities]: In case of theology, one has a particular difficulty because the principles themselves depend on a pre-supposed position of religious faith, and consequently what looks like reasonable moves to someone who has a particular faith may not look reasonable to someone who doesn't share that faith. The proper norms of a Catholic theologian are to go back to the Christian faith and moral teachings as the Catholic Church believes and teaches it.

The New York Times, 8-21:8.

Irwin Groner
Rabbi; Treasurer,
Rabbinical Assembly

5

[On the re-confirmation by Conservative rabbis of the traditional tenets of Conservative Judaism]: We no longer consider ourselves all things

(IRWIN GRONER)

to all people. There are times when we emphasize the need for the Conservative movement to respond to change, but there are issues so fundamental to the existence of the Jewish people that we feel the necessity to reaffirm this historic principle.

At Rabbinical Assembly meeting,
Kiamesha Lake, N.Y./
The New York Times, 5-22:16.

Monika Hellwig
President, Catholic Theological
Society of America

1

The major problem the [Roman Catholic Church] hierarchy faces may be that Catholics simply don't believe in hell and eternal punishment the way they used to. The American laity, especially the college-educated, is well aware that the hierarchy doesn't have many sanctions against them. It's harder to frighten them.

The New York Times, 12-24:4.

Arthur Hertzberg
Rabbi; Professor of religion,
Dartmouth College

2

[An] essentially materialist notion [has taken hold in the U.S.]: Even Judaism in America has been bent, by some, away from transcendence and toward centering on man's well-being . . . Even in religion, man, not God, has become the measure of all things.

At World Jewish Congress
convention, Washington/
Los Angeles Times, 3-29:(I-A)6.

Donald Hodel
Secretary of the Interior
of the United States

3

It's no accident that [U.S. President Reagan] ends every speech with "God bless you." But he understands that a leader of a free society cannot

give religious speeches. The last thing Christians ought to want is theocracy. If government identifies with the church, both go wrong. History shows neither can survive the process.

Interview/
Christianity Today, 4-4:37.

John Paul II
Pope

4

[Defending church involvement in social and political affairs, including "liberation theology," as long as it doesn't deviate from central Church doctrine]: I want to confirm that a theological reflection on liberation can and must exist, founded on solid doctrinal elements pertaining to the most authentic magisterium of the Church. The Church considers it her duty to continue, put into practice and deepen this reflection more and more. Purified of elements that could adulterate it, with grave consequences for the faith, this theology of liberation is not only orthodox but necessary.

To hierarchy of Brazilian Catholic Church,
Vatican City, March 13/
The Washington Post, 3-14:(A)25.

5

[On Christian-Jewish relations]: Today's visit [to this synagogue] is meant to make a decisive contribution to the consolidation of the good relations between our two communities, in imitation of the example of so many men and women who have worked and who are still working today, on both sides, to overcome old prejudices and to secure ever wider and fuller recognition of that bond and that common spiritual patrimony that exists between Jews and Christians . . . The Jewish religion is not "extrinsic" to us, but in a certain way is "intrinsic" to our own religion. With Judaism, therefore, we have a relationship which we do not have with any other religion. You are our dearly beloved brothers and, in a certain way, it could be said that you are our elder brothers.

At central synagogue, Rome, April 13/
The New York Times, 4-14:4.

Richard Long
Professor of English and chairman,
Afro-American studies department,
Atlanta University

1

Unfortunately, the black church has never risen to its full potential as a force for uplift. [The late civil-rights leader and reverend] Martin Luther King certainly was a leader from the church; but the church typically had simply religious entertainers rather than religious leaders. Nevertheless, the church provided a focal point for blacks. Today, most black people are beyond the pale of the church. They have no involvement with, no connection to, and no particular respect for the church.

Interview/USA Today, 2-4:(A)7.

Barry W. Lynn
Legislative director,
American Civil Liberties Union

2

The arena of public institutions, such as schools, is not the place for the dissemination of religiously based values. I don't think there is any basis for saying that the [U.S. Founding Fathers] believed that religion should be the foundation of democracy.

Sept. 17/The New York Times, 9-18:16.

Roger M. Mahony
Roman Catholic Archbishop
of Los Angeles

3

[On criticism of the Vatican's recent denouncing of a U.S. Catholic educator who dissented publicly from the Church's doctrine]: The Church is not a democracy, but many tend to see the Church as valid only when it reflects the American democratic experiment . . . Freedom of speech and academic freedom in the American college or university tradition is supposed to be the criterion for how the American Catholic Church is to teach. But that is not the beginning of the Church . . . It's been formed in a different context.

Interview/Los Angeles Times, 8-23:(I)1.

James W. Malone
Roman Catholic Bishop of Youngstown,
Ohio; President, National Council
of Catholic Bishops

4

No one who reads the newspapers of the past three years can be ignorant of a growing and dangerous disaffection of elements of the Church in the United States from the Holy See. Some people feel that the local Church needs more freedom. Others believe that more control is in order. Some feel that appeals to authority are being exercised too readily. Others applaud what they perceive to be a return to needed central control. Wherever you stand, this division presents the Church in the United States with a very serious question: How will we move to address this developing estrangement, to strengthen the . . . bonds between the Church here and the Holy See.

At National Conference of Catholic
Bishops meeting, Washington, Nov. 10/
Los Angeles Times, 11-11:(I)19.

Martin E. Marty
Religious historian

5

[On Pope John Paul II]: This Pope is very good at being Pope in the Third World. He's the Pope for the poor and oppressed, he's the Pope for people just getting their act together. [But] I don't think he likes Northwest Europe, and I don't think he likes a lot of things about America. Trained as he is in Poland, where the regime is always forcing unity upon the Church, he is not really ready for the wild, free pluralism we have in America.

U.S. News & World Report, 11-17:69.

John May
Roman Catholic Archbishop of
St. Louis; President-elect,
National Conference of Catholic Bishops

6

The Church feels it is not free to leave it up to majority rule in our good old American way. That's not the way the Church is run. We believe

(JOHN MAY)

that the primary life of the Church is not determined by us, but by the gospel of Jesus Christ and his teaching. And that we just cannot change. Now, as to parish councils and school administration, there's a lot of room for major decision-making.

USA Today, 11-17:(A)13.

Anthony T. Podesta
President, People for the American Way

1

[Saying religion is given poor coverage in U.S. school textbooks]: The two themes, which have been in tension since the earliest colonial times—religious intolerance and religious idealism—are not recognized as essential to an understanding of the American character. When religion is mentioned, it is just that—mentioned. While history textbooks talk about the existence of religious diversity in America, they do not show it. Jews exist only as objects of discrimination. Catholics exist to be discriminated against and to ask for government money for their own schools. There is no reflection of the diversity within American Protestantism . . . The poor coverage of religion is not the result of any ideological bias—left and right in the world of religion are ignored equally. When there is no [evangelist] Billy Graham, there is no National Council of Churches. In fact, more often than not, when Moral Majority is mentioned, it is treated as virtually the only religious development since World War II. [Publishers] fear pressure from both militant atheists and militant fundamentalists.

The New York Times, 6-3:22.

2

I think the [U.S.] Founding Fathers clearly intended religion to flourish freely among the people. But it is historically dubious to suggest one needs the Judeo-Christian ethic to have a democratic form of government. Many people who are committed to the separation of church and state, including most clergy, are very much believers in religion.

Sept. 17/The New York Times, 9-18:16.

Ronald Reagan
President of the United States

3

[On his support for prayer in schools, and the criticism of it that says the Constitution prohibits such prayer]: There are only 16 words in the Constitution, and those 16 words are very simple and plain. The Congress shall—I may not be able to quote accurately the words of the Constitution—the Congress make no laws or provisions—whatever the word it used there—regarding the establishment of religion or the prohibition of the practice of religion. And whatever it is comes out to just 16 words, and that's it. Well now, if you tell somebody they can't pray, aren't you violating those 16 words? And are you violating those 16 words with regard to establishment of religion if somebody's allowed to pray? . . . To this day, the [U.S.] Congress opens with prayer. And on our coins it says, "In God We Trust." And, to me, the decision that prevented voluntary prayer by anyone who wanted to do so in a school or in a public building is just not in keeping with the Constitution at all.

Interview, June 23/
Los Angeles Times, 6-24:18.

4

No one can hold this office without noticing that prayer is something deep woven into the fabric of our history, that, indeed, spiritual values are essential to the successful life of a democracy.

Proclaiming May 7 as National
Day of Prayer, Washington, Dec. 22/
The Washington Post, 12-23:(A)9.

Adrian Rogers
President,
Southern Baptist Convention

5

We are not trying to tell any [seminary] professor what he must believe, or any denominational employee; that is between him and God. But we are saying that those who work for us and those who have their salaries paid by us ought to reflect what we want taught.

The Washington Post, 6-14:(A)4.

(ADRIAN ROGERS)

1

[Saying seminary professors should not stray from teaching according to the basics of the Bible]: I think that the goal of responsible conservative leaders is that all of our seminary professors would reflect in their teaching what the vast majority of the people feel and believe. That does not mean that we're trying to practice mind control, or that we are trying to force anyone to believe anything. I would fight for the right of a man to be an atheist if he wished to be. All we're saying is, that if they work for us and are paid by us, then they ought to fairly represent us. That's not mind control, because they're free to work anywhere they wish.

Interview/USA Today, 6-16:(A)13.

2

I don't believe that the state need interfere in the internal workings of the church, nor should the church interfere in the internal working of the government. But I don't believe for one moment in the separation of God and government. I believe it was Daniel Webster who said that whatever makes a man a good Christian makes him a good citizen at the same time.

Interview/USA Today, 6-16:(A)13.

Ismar Schorsch
Chancellor, Jewish Theological
Seminary, New York

3

The laity are the shapers of Judaism, along with the rabbis. The vast changes in modern Judaism did spring up from pressure from below—the introduction of the sermon, the use of music, the transformation of the role of the rabbi, the use of mixed seating. Conservative Judaism has a message for our time and for all times. In its struggle for balance, integrity and moderation, Conservative Judaism is most authentically Jewish. Firmly planted in the soil of tradition, Conservative Judaism is capable of withstanding the blandishments and absorbing the wisdom of its surroundings.

Speech, Dec. 2/
The New York Times, 12-4:19.

Ronald F. Thiemann
Dean-designate,
Harvard Divinity School

4

Harvard Divinity School has pioneered the integration of the study of comparative religion into professional preparation for the ministry. Every student who goes through the master-of-divinity program at Harvard must take a series of courses in comparative religion. That means that people who are being prepared for the ministry will bring to their parish ministry both sensitivity to and understanding of other religious traditions . . . No longer is the study of religion simply [the teaching] of the great literary texts produced essentially by high culture. Now we've developed the methods whereby we can understand religious practices—what religion was like as it was practiced by the people who were most directly influenced by it. While the study of the great textual tradition goes on, where explosions have taken place in terms of what we learned is at a level of a kind of combination of history and sociology.

Interview, Boston/
The Christian Science Monitor, 1-28:1,32.

Barbara Tuchman
Author, Historian

5

I don't know how much less people really relate to religion or church-going [these days], because . . . I've never been a religious person. But I do think that there's a kind of absence of common understanding, particularly with the young as they grow up, of what's good behavior and bad behavior, and what's right and what's wrong. That is disappearing.

Interview, Cos Cob, Conn./
The Christian Science Monitor, 10-7:19.

John Updike
Author

6

. . . I find that just to be human I really seem to need a dose of church now and then. I need some sort of otherworldly point of refer-

463

(JOHN UPDIKE)

ence . . . All church services have this wonderful element: People with other things to do get up on a Sunday morning, put on good clothes and assemble out of nothing but faith—some vague yen toward something larger. Simply as a human gathering I find it moving, reassuring and even inspiring. A church is a little like a novel in that both are saying there's something very important about being human.

Interview/U.S. News & World Report, 10-20:67.

Paul C. Vitz
Professor of psychology,
New York University

1

[Saying religion is given poor coverage in U.S. school textbooks]: Secular humanists have been able to dominate and control education. Those who write and publish the textbooks are of a relatively homogeneous, secular and anti-religious mentality. Individual principals or superintendents who select textbooks are of the same attitude.

Interview/The New York Times, 6-3:22.

Elie Wiesel
Author, Historian

2

I have always believed in God, though I have my quarrels with Him. In the Jewish tradition, one may say no to God if it is on behalf of other people. Sometimes I ask Him questions and He doesn't answer—and I go on asking questions. I believe that one can be a good Jew or Christian or Buddhist and be with God or against God, but not without God.

Interview/U.S. News & World Report, 10-27:68.

Science and Technology

Joseph Allen
Former American astronaut

1

[On the recent explosion of the space shuttle *Challenger* just after take-off, in which seven astronauts were killed]: This was the day that everybody in the business knew was going to come. As [former astronaut] Chuck Yeager says, "Progress is marked by great smoking holes in the ground." This is how knowledge moves forward. That has to be the legacy.

U.S. News & World Report, 2-10:20.

Jack Anderson
American journalist

2

. . . the industrial powers of the future are going to be exotic, faraway, obscure places like India, South Korea and Taiwan. And the warning to the United States that I hope to report in dramatic fashion is that we must do something about it. We are going to lose our industrial base whether we wish to or not. And our only hope is to retain a superior technology. That superior technology right now is based on a small elite . . . About 10 per cent of our people are contributing to our technological superiority. And the base is very narrow. Our potential rivals— the Soviet Union, West Germany, Japan— are building a broad base. From 70 per cent to 90 per cent of high-school graduates in those three nations are proficient in science, math and technology. Of our high-school graduates, only 6 per cent have the same proficiency . . . The people in our base are perhaps smarter than anyone else in the world but, since we have a narrower base to draw from, there is a great danger that we could be surpassed. I would encourage our business managers to think in global terms and gain control of the industrial plants around the world and to furnish the technological know-how. That is going to have to become our greatest export—technology and information. Manufactured goods, whether we like it or not, will be produced elsewhere.

Interview/USA Today, 1-8:(A)9.

Isaac Asimov
Science-fiction author

3

[Supporting manned space exploration]: Robots are by no means as capable as humans in many respects. It will be a long time before they are. We have to have human beings in space to do the things robots can't do. There has been many an unmanned vehicle in space that went wrong because there was no man—or woman for that matter—who could tighten a bolt or replace a compartment. We can't do everything from down here. And if we don't do it, the Russians will. If we want the Russians to take over while we sit and watch and wave our hands, okay.

Interview/USA Today, 2-3:(A)9.

Max Baucus
United States Senator, D-Montana

4

For years, the Japanese government and Japanese companies have been putting enormous effort into learning from American technological advances. The United States, on the other hand, has done little to keep track of Japanese technological developments. Much of the first-rate work being done in Japan is not available in the United States because it hasn't been translated into English.

The New York Times, 4-9:12.

James M. Beggs
Former Administrator, National Aeronautics and Space Administration of the United States

5

[On the recent run of failures and tragedies in U.S. space launches]: The successes breed a good deal of confidence in the hardware. What tends to happen in a program like this [is] you have a string of successes and then a succession of failures. What you find generally is that somebody changed something in the hardware stream along

465

WHAT THEY SAID IN 1986

the way. It could be a fairly small change in the method by which you assemble and test a component and, bang, you have a problem.

Los Angeles Times, 5-5:(I)16.

Daniel J. Boorstin
Librarian of Congress
of the United States

1

[On the recent explosion of the space shuttle *Challenger* just after take-off, in which seven astronauts were killed]: I have a terrible feeling of sadness; I want to weep. [But] in the long run, this shows us that the best things in life are not free. It makes us more grateful to the people who have been taking these risks all along without our knowing it. I hope this won't stop the space program; I don't think it will. Sir Francis Drake, Magellan, countless other great explorers lost their lives; this happens in any great adventure. It's sad it has to happen, but somebody has to take these chances if we're to do things that have never been done before. It does affect us deeply; something like this brings the nation together. The space program in general has done that. People understand the grandeur even if not the technology; and to share that grandeur is what makes a great nation.

Interview/
The New York Times, 1-29:8.

Frank Borman
Chairman, Eastern Airlines;
Former American astronaut

2

[On the recent explosion of the space shuttle *Challenger* just after take-off, in which seven astronauts were killed]: These launches are right on the cutting edge of technology. And although NASA's success has somehow caused the public to treat them almost as everyday events, anyone who's been in or around the program knows each one has an inherent degree of risk, which in my mind is very great.

USA Today, 1-29:(A)2.

3

Space research not only is very important for military surveillance but it also paces our technology. It exacts the best of our scientific and engineering community, and the work filters down to everything from airplane electronics to computers and biomedical applications.

Interview/U.S. News &
World Report, 2-10:19.

Cleanth Brooks
Author, Critic; Professor emeritus
of rhetoric, Yale University

4

It seems to me more and more clear that science always deals with *how* it happens, [with] process. It is dealing not with "Why?" or "What is the meaning of it?" but [with] "how." [The difficulty arises] when you start asking the questions, "Yes, but to what end? Why are we alive? What values should we seek?" I don't think we can get very many answers in science. We wanted to put a man on the moon. We did it. And it was a wonderful achievement, a staggering achievement. But *why* put a man on the moon?

Interview, New Haven, Conn./
The Christian Science Monitor, 11-3:25.

William Carey
Executive officer, American
Association for the
Advancement of Science

5

Science rarely travels into the Oval Office [of the U.S. President] these days under its own flag. Most of the time science gets there because it is embodied in some other very large policy question, such as defense policy, space policy, fiscal policy, energy policy and so on.

The Christian Science Monitor, 5-27:6.

Eugene A. Cernan
Former American astronaut

6

[Supporting manned spaceflight]: Our insatiable desire for knowledge would never be satisfied

(EUGENE A. CERNAN)

by the simplicity of a picture or some remote sensors that give us some information back. Exploration without man is not exploration at all.

Broadcast interview, "Nightline,"
ABC-TV/The New York Times, 1-30:14.

Thomas M. Donahue
Chairman, Space Science Board,
National Research Council

1

The Board, and scientists in general, have been worried for years about the devastating effect of [NASA's] decision to phase out unmanned launched vehicles—so-called expendable launch vehicles—for launching scientific missions. We are calling for a drastic change in policy that would once more make expendable launch vehicles the primary system for launching scientific spacecraft. We want the National Aeronautics and Space Administration to get involved in designing and contracting for such spacecraft the way the Department of Defense is involved on behalf of national-security payloads . . . We are simply recommending that the United States reserve manned flight for those missions in which human resources are clearly needed, and diversify our launch capabilities to assure that a single tragic accident [such as the recent explosion of the *Challenger* space shuttle, in which seven astronauts were killed] cannot again cripple the entire space program, civilian and military.

To reporters, Washington, May 21/
Los Angeles Times, 5-22:(I)8.

Oriana Fallaci
Journalist

2

[Saying she would still want to take a flight on the space shuttle despite the recent shuttle explosion which killed seven astronauts]: I have been a war correspondent for so many years—and still am—and maybe it is because I have a certain habit. You know, when you go to war—and I think I have covered all the possible wars of our time—you get kind of used to the fact that you

can die. You don't wish to die. You don't want to die. Who wants to die? But it can happen. But, in this particular case, it's more than worthwhile. If you risk your life to follow a war, you can risk your life to go into space.

Interview/
USA Today, 2-7:(A)13.

Richard P. Feynman
Member, Presidential commission on
"Challenger" space-shuttle disaster;
Physicist, California Institute of Technology

3

[Calling for the establishing of an independent safety organization to aid in prevention of future space-shuttle disasters, such as the recent explosion of the *Challenger*]: The problem is communication and that communication will be fixed if you have the safety panel, if there is a member of the astronauts on the safety panel, because then you'll be fully aware of all the things that are unsafe. An argument is always given that the last time it [the shuttle] worked. It's a kind of Russian roulette. There was a risk, but you got away with it. But it shouldn't be done over and over again. When I look at the reviews, I find perpetual movement heading for trouble.

At meeting of shuttle commission,
Washington, April 3/
Los Angeles Times, 4-4:(I)12.

James C. Fletcher
Administrator, National Aeronautics
and Space Administration
of the United States

4

We have to set our sights on the future. But make no mistake, that future could be in jeopardy if we do not respond effectively to our immediate challenge—to restore this nation's launch capabilities in the wake of the [explosion of the space shuttle] *Challenger* and the expendable-rocket accidents . . . The space station [serviced by the space shuttle] will enable the United States to continue to explore and use space for peaceful purposes and for the benefit of mankind. We have

(JAMES C. FLETCHER)

traditionally excelled at this, and, I believe, the space station is essential to that pursuit of excellence.

News conference, Cape Canaveral, Fla.,
May 14/The New York Times, 5-15:13.

1

The NASA you and I know made mistakes in the past, corrected them and moved on . . . But sometimes I wonder if the NASA you and I know is the same organization that some in the media portray since the *Challenger* [space-shuttle] accident. [Although most of the news media] has striven to be accurate, thorough and fair, I believe that a small number of reporters have acquired a deep and unwarranted suspicion of NASA, its organization, its motives and its people. They have sought to question every action, and to uncover its every perceived blemish and wart . . . [The NASA portrayed in those media reports is] not a NASA that has done magnificent and creative things, but a NASA that has always been poorly managed, a NASA that has always made mistakes and a NASA that never got its act together . . . I believe it creates a distorted image of who we are and what we are about.

To aerospace industries group,
Williamsburg, Va., May 22/
The Washington Post, 5-23:(A)3.

2

I have accepted the President's call to make this agency as vibrant and careful as it can be, to help it earn the respect it deserves and the excellence that has been its hallmark. We will achieve those goals in a more restrictive atmosphere than we have been accustomed to. Like other departments and agencies of government, we work under the severe budget limitations and restrictions of our time . . . But we cannot and will not sacrifice safety concerns to budget limitations. We are going to behave like a family which has suffered a tragic event [the recent explosion of the space shuttle *Challenger*]. We are going to deal responsibly with our loss, without needless recrimination, and we are going to move forward, facing and conquering the challenges that

face us. Where management is weak, we will strengthen it. Where engineering or design or process need improving, we will improve them. Where our internal communications are poor, we will see that they get better. This is an agency whose excellence and commitment to new frontiers drew to it seven exceptional Americans [the astronauts killed in *Challenger* explosion]. Our response must be to overcome our errors, not to quit, to stop or to cave in. To stumble now in hesitation is to mock their commitment to reaching for distant horizons and their willingness to take a chance in seeking knowledge and understanding.

News conference, Washington, June 9/
Los Angeles Times, 6-10:(I)10.

3

I think there are some important policy questions that have to be answered by the White House and the Congress, and that is to what extent do we want America to retain its leadership in space? I think it's been pointed out that we are losing a great deal of that leadership. Now, that's not on all fronts. We still have a [space] shuttle, and nobody else has one. We still launch to the outer planets, and nobody else has. But, on the other hand, other countries are beginning to build their own shuttles.

Interview/USA Today, 9-4:(A)9.

John Glenn
United States Senator, D-Ohio;
Former American astronaut

4

Some people believe the space race ended when Neil Armstrong walked on the moon. But the race for space is a marathon. It's not a sprint. And we must be prepared to go the distance.

USA Today, 6-11:(A)4.

5

[Criticizing cutbacks in government spending for scientific research]: The President [Reagan] says that if research is worth doing, private industry will do it. I say nonsense. Cutting back on basic research is like eating your seed corn. We're playing Russian roulette with our future.

The Washington Post, 11-26:(A)19.

Clark Glymour
Professor of philosophy,
Carnegie-Mellon University

1

[Saying there is an increased demand for philosophy majors]: It may seem odd. What happened is that some years ago philosophy grew closely connected to logical theory, which, in turn, was the genesis of computer algorithms involved in the development of digital computers. Programmers for computers are a dime a dozen, but what is needed are people who can take vaguely formed problems and find ways to make them precise enough to be programmed. This is what philosophers can do and they are planning a major role in artificial intelligence. For the past 40 years American philosophy has been closely tied to the logical and mathematical study of knowledge and inference. The theories produced in these areas have been precise enough to be used in the design of artificial-intelligence programs.

The New York Times, 3-4:54.

Albert Gore, Jr.
United States Senator,
D-Tennessee

2

[On the recent explosion of the space shuttle *Challenger* just after take-off, in which seven astronauts were killed]: Something has gone wrong with the absolute commitment to quality control and discipline that we've come to associate with NASA. It seems that some of the memos in NASA files should have raised all kinds of red flags and set off warning bells [about the safety of the *Challenger* flight], and yet they didn't.

At Senate Space Subcommittee hearing,
Washington, Feb. 18/
U.S. News & World Report, 3-3:6.

Jerry Grey
Publisher,
"Aerospace America" magazine

3

[Warning against the U.S. retreating from space exploration]: Britain . . . made a compara-

ble decision back in the early part of this century when they . . . relinquished their marine dominance of the world at that time. We are in the same position now in regard to space. We could relinquish our dominance of space by simply proceeding with budgets as they have been . . . In our view, the next major industry really is in space, and a revolution comparable to the microelectronics revolution is coming. It's still in the early stages, to be sure. But unless we acquire [space leadership] and maintain that lead, . . . those large lucrative markets will go to other nations who are at present actively pursuing a strong commitment to space activity.

Interview/The Christian
Science Monitor, 8-28:3.

Robert Jastrow
Former Director, Goddard Institute for
Space Studies, National Aeronautics and
Space Administration of the United States

4

[On whether the recent explosion of the *Challenger* space shuttle is a major setback to U.S. technology]: No, this country has invented everything that enhances the productivity of human labor in this world in this century—television, lasers, radio, computers, semiconductors, all of it. This is the most hazardous occupation that we now have, but it is no more hazardous than railroad trains were in the 19th century, no more hazardous than airplanes were in 1915. Flying was a really dangerous job then, and there were a lot of deaths—many more deaths than we have experienced in the space program in the early years of aeronautics. But the image of America as the leader of the world has not suffered from this one disaster.

Interview/USA Today, 3-12:(A)9.

John W. Kiser III
President,
Kiser Research, Washington

5

[On U.S. utilization of Soviet technology]: Keeping up with Soviet technical achievements is not easy. There's a language barrier, there are

469

WHAT THEY SAID IN 1986

(JOHN W. KISER III)

political problems and trade barriers, there's a disparity between our economic systems, and there's an immense bureaucracy to maneuver through. But, from our standpoint, the U.S.S.R. represents a vast, underutilized intellectual asset that we should be tapping. We tend to forget that Russians pioneered the science of chemistry and the development of lasers, put the first satellite and the first man in space, built the fastest, deepest-diving submarine, and so on. Why shouldn't we take what we can from them?

Interview/
The New York Times, 12-16:18.

Herman Krier
Rocket propulsion authority,
University of Illinois

1

[On the recent U.S. space shuttle disaster and two other rocket explosions]: It's crazy for a scientist to say it's a jinx; we're not supposed to talk that way. But this is queer . . . If you would have asked me, as an engineer, to calculate the probability of there being a major accident on any of these rockets, I would have put down $1,000 against it. That all three should fail like this, I would have said the odds are in the millions.

The Washington Post,
5-5:(A)13.

Richard D. Lamm
Governor of Colorado (D)

2

[Saying it is important for people to be familiar with technology]: I guess you don't have to be a scientist or a technician to be able to vote. But, on the other hand, I sure do think that it is extremely important to the long-term health of democracy that people know those basic trends that are affecting our society.

At National Technological Literacy
Conference, Baltimore, Feb. 14/
Los Angeles Times, 2-15:(I)7.

Kenneth C. Laudon
Sociologist, New York University

3

We're living in a dossier society where ultimately everyone may be judged by his data image. We've got big, powerful computers collecting information about all of us, but no one's managing the data—how it's used, its accuracy.

Interview/Los Angeles Times, 7-29:(I)1.

Yegor K. Ligachev
Chief ideologist, Politburo,
Communist Party of the Soviet Union

4

To keep up with the requirements of this day, Soviet science, and especially academic science, is to undergo a serious restructuring. The point at issue is not minor, partial improvements, but a radical change in the way of acting, a radical change in all spheres of activity . . . The bitter lesson of [the Soviet nuclear-plant explosion at] Chernobyl was a reminder to us all that complacency is inadmissible.

Before Soviet Academy of Sciences/
The New York Times, 10-17:7.

Joseph Loftus
Assistant to the Director, Johnson Space Center

5

What's been achieved in space is extraordinary. If you laid out a proposal to do in the next 25 years what has been done in the past 25, no one would believe you.

Time, 6-9:14.

John P. McTague
Acting Director, Federal Office of
Science and Technology Policy

6

We [the U.S.] need a new national science-and-technology strategy as we begin to approach the 21st century. Unless we respond to this challenge, we face a certain loss of technological and economic leadership in the world, with consequences which are not measured in dollars alone.

The Christian Science Monitor, 5-15:3.

John P. McTague
Former Acting Director,
Federal Office of Science
and Technology Policy

1

This country [The U.S.] is at an era of absolutely unsurpassed creativity in . . . every field of science. There isn't a field of science now which doesn't have an aura of being in an absolute renaissance. It's incredible. Even fields which should have died 50 years ago . . . We have deliberately decreased [Federal] funding in the areas close to commercialization with the viewpoint that that is much more efficiently done by the private sector. On the other hand, we have emphasized the unique Federal role in supporting fundamental basic research that is of such long-range nature and such distributed impact that one cannot expect the private sector to make a major role in it.

Interview/The Christian
Science Monitor, 5-27:6.

Jon D. Miller
Director,
Public Opinion Laboratory,
Northern Illinois University

2

A substantial majority of Americans do not have a sufficient vocabulary or comprehension of concepts to utilize a wide array of scientific communication . . . If terms like molecule and DNA are not acquired during formal schooling, it is unlikely that they will be acquired later through the media or other informal educational channels.

Before American Association for the
Advancement of Science, Philadelphia, May/
The Washington Post, 6-2:(A)8.

Jesse W. Moore
Associate Administrator,
National Aeronautics and Space
Administration of the United States

3

[On the explosion of the space shuttle *Challenger* just after take-off, in which seven astro-

nauts were killed]: We always strive in every flight that we perform to be as reliable and as safe as we possibly can, and to do everything we can to insure that the vehicle and the systems are all ready to fly. Flight safety is our Number 1 priority in the space-shuttle program. And certainly, when you see an event like this this morning, we are going to have to do a very detailed assessment of the set of circumstances to try to understand what occurred, and we will then, in turn, assess the impact from that to determine where we go in the future.

News conference,
Cape Canaveral, Fla., Jan. 28/
The New York Times, 1-29:4.

Gerard K. O'Neill
Professor emeritus of
physics, Princeton University

4

[On U.S. space technology]: In terms of entrepreneurial technology, the tremendous advantage that America has is its irreverence. You just don't find that in a place which has a long, settled tradition, in which the people in authority are never questioned, and new ideas are not free to develop. The enterprise system is also key. Almost all of these ideas are realized first by entrepreneurial, high-risk start-up companies.

Interview, The New York Times, 11-12:32.

David Packard
Co-founder,
Hewlett-Packard Company;
Former Deputy Secretary of
Defense of the United States

5

Despite the fact that the Federal government has provided a very large level of support for [science], we do not have a rational national policy on research and development. [Lacking such a policy,] our government tends to support things that are glamorous but [that] don't contribute very much to the solution of basic problems.

Interview, New York/
The Christian Science Monitor, 11-21:23.

Thomas O. Paine
*Chairman, National Commission
on Space of the United States;
Former Administrator, National Aeronautics
and Space Administration
of the United States*

1

The last time we really had a Presidential policy in space was when [U.S. President] Jack Kennedy set our sights on the moon. All decisions since then have really been about hardware, without a real sense of direction.

U.S. News & World Report, 6-16:16.

2

[On estimates that the Soviet Union has a 10-year lead over the U.S. in the practical utilization of space]: I had been waiting for that shoe to drop. There is no question whatever that the relative movement forward, the relative thrust in space, is getting quite out of whack. The Soviets are conducting a very bold program, doing very sophisticated work in projects such as life support and closed ecology systems that have very long-range implications . . . We haven't had an objective to crystallize our efforts since President [John] Kennedy set the objective of the landing on the moon in the 1960s. What we must remember is that he said the United States must be pre-eminent in space and, in order to demonstrate that, we would go to the moon.

*Interview, Los Angeles, June 16/
Los Angeles Times, 6-17:(I)6.*

Linus Pauling
*Winner, 1954 Nobel Prize in chemistry;
Winner, 1962 Nobel Peace Prize*

3

I don't think that a scientist could be President [of the U.S.]. I know one chemist who managed to become elected to the House of Representatives, and then he ran for the Senate and was defeated. The basic principle of science is respect for the truth. You can't get elected if you have respect for the truth. Scientists have difficulty in compromising because of the feeling that the truth is the important goal.

Interview/USA Today, 3-11:(A)7.

H. Ross Perot
*Financier; Chairman,
Electronic Data Systems Corporation*

4

If we did not have such a thing as an airplane today, we would probably create something the size of NASA to make one. It's a good thing the Wright brothers didn't know any better when they made the machine fly.

*At Fall Joint Computer Conference,
Dallas/The New York Times, 11-19:36.*

Ronald Reagan
President of the United States

5

[On the explosion of the space shuttle *Challenger* just after take-off, in which seven astronauts were killed]: I know it's hard to understand that sometimes painful things like this happen. It's all part of the process of exploration and discovery; it's all part of taking a chance and expanding man's horizons. The future doesn't belong to the fainthearted. It belongs to the brave. The *Challenger* crew was pulling us into the future and we'll continue to follow them. I've always had great faith in and respect for our space program, and what happened today does nothing to diminish it. We don't hide our space program; we don't keep secrets and cover things up. We do it all up front and in public. That's the way freedom is and we wouldn't change it for a minute. We'll continue our quest in space. There will be more shuttle flights and more shuttle crews and, yes, more volunteers, more civilians, more teachers in space. Nothing ends here. Our hopes and our journeys continue . . . The crew of the space shuttle *Challenger* honored us by the manner in which they lived. We will never forget them, nor the last time we saw them this morning as they prepared for their journey and waved goodbye and "slipped the surly bonds of earth to touch the face of God."

*Broadcast address to the nation, Washington,
Jan. 28/The New York Times, 1-29:9.*

6

[On the explosion of the space shuttle *Challenger*, in which seven astronauts were killed]:

(RONALD REAGAN)

We think back to the pioneers of an earlier century, the sturdy souls who took their families and their belongings and set out into the frontier of the American West. Often, they met with terrible hardship. Along the Oregon Trail, you can still see the grave markers of those who fell on the way. But grief only steeled them to the journey ahead. Today, the frontier is space and the boundaries of human knowledge. Our nation is indeed fortunate that we can still draw on immense reservoirs of courage, character and fortitude, that we are still blessed with heroes like those of the space shuttle *Challenger*.

At memorial service for the "Challenger"
astronauts, Houston, Jan. 31/
The Washington Post, 2-1:(A)6.

1

[On the recent explosion of the space shuttle *Challenger,* in which seven astronauts were killed]: I don't believe that there was any deliberate or criminal intent in any way on the part of anyone [to cause the explosion]. I think that with the great record of success that NASA has had, all the way back to when men circled the earth in those capsules, and then to men on the moon, and now 24 successful shuttle flights—I think there was a complacency there. And yes, it's something that has to be corrected before ever one of those takes off again. But I think it was just a carelessness that grew out of success. And I think that it's time for us, also, to remind ourselves of the tremendous record that NASA had, and help now in the restoration of the [shuttle] program and their going forward, and to see that this cannot happen again.

News conference, Washington,
June 11/The New York Times, 6-12:10.

William P. Rogers
Chairman of commission investigating
space shuttle "Challenger" disaster

2

[On the explosion of the space shuttle *Challenger* earlier this year in which seven astronauts were killed]: We can't afford to have another accident involving humans. We can't be so enthusiastic about space as such that we lose sight of the fact that, if accidents happen that are so tragic it sets the program way back; it is better to go slower and be safer.

Newsweek, 6-16:64.

Alex Roland
Professor of history,
Duke University

3

[Arguing against manned space-shuttle flights, such as the recent mission of the *Challenger* shuttle which exploded just after take-off, killing seven astronauts]: The relative cost of sending humans into space is so much higher than sending machines. I'm not convinced that all the things we are doing in space today require humans to be up there. The astronauts are aware of the dangers, but most taxpayers aren't.

U.S. News &
World Report, 2-10:18.

Carl Sagan
Professor of astronomy and
space science, Cornell University

4

[On the setback to the U.S. space program caused by the *Challenger* space-shuttle disaster]: The U.S. is in desperate shape. If we continue as we're doing, the mantel of leadership in the exploration of the solar system will pass. While the U.S. is opting out, the Soviets, Japanese, Europeans, and by the end of the year the Chinese, are picking up the slack.

USA Today,
10-29:(A)1.

Abdus Salam
Director, International Center
for Theoretical Physics (Italy)

5

[Scoffing at the idea that peaceful scientific spinoffs result from military research]: The statement that defense expenditures have "fallout" is rubbish, total rubbish. And the statement

473

WHAT THEY SAID IN 1986

(ABDUS SALAM)

that since you invest in "Star Wars" [the proposed U.S. space defense system] you will do your toothpaste better is [also] total rubbish.

Interview, Trieste, Italy/
The Christian Science Monitor, 12-9:28.

Russell L. Schweickart
President, United States branch,
Association of Space Explorers;
Former American astronaut

1

[Saying recent space failures should not prevent the U.S. from continuing its space plans for the future]: If we shy away from these tough decisions, we would be like the Portuguese who developed navigation and sailing ships and shied away from using them. Spain and England became the naval powers, and Portugal was never heard from again. We cannot afford to become the Portugal of the Space Age.

U.S. News & World Report, 6-16:16.

Richard G. Smith
Former Director, Kennedy Space Center,
Cape Canaveral, Fla.

2

[On the recent explosion of the space shuttle *Challenger*, which killed seven astronauts]: I am convinced that, coming out of the accident, NASA is showing signs of being too conservative. I believe that it's beginning to affect morale. I think the agency should be more aggressive, more assertive, in getting back to flying . . . Over the long haul, you should be getting that launch rate up to the maximum extent that you can, consistent with high morale. And high morale comes with people sensing they are accomplishing something difficult, not easy. [A high launch rate] does not necessarily mean taking risks. In fact, I would say that if you're launching too slow, you may run a chance of people becoming more complacent and less challenged, and create an environment of greater risk than one of being very demanding.

Interview, Cape Canaveral, Fla./
The Christian Science Monitor, 8-4:3.

Weston Stacey, Jr.
Director,
Fusion Research Center,
Georgia Institute of Technology

3

In basic science, such as physics, they're [the Soviets] unsurpassed. They have been and probably still are the best. We [the U.S.] approach them, the Europeans approach them, in certain aspects; but I would say, over-all, in basic science, the Soviets are very, very good. I know this to be true not only in plasma physics but in other areas . . . [But] the Soviet Union, as far as I can tell, is very uneven in its technology. Those things that the government gives priority to, they do quite well. I think Americans tend to misjudge the Soviets and say, "Oh, they're clumsy and awkward in their technology." That's not true over-all. In areas where they don't have priority, then they don't follow through on their technology and manufacturing processes.

Interview/
USA Today, 7-15:(A)11.

Richard H. Truly
Rear Admiral,
United States Navy;
Director, space shuttle program,
National Aeronautics and Space
Administration of the United States

4

[Saying the space shuttle program will resume under very conservative rules in the wake of the recent shuttle explosion which killed seven astronauts]: I do not want you to think this conservative approach, this safe approach, which I think is the proper thing to do, is going to be a namby-pamby shuttle program. The business of flying in space is a bold business. We cannot print enough money to make it totally risk-free. But we certainly are going to correct any mistakes we may have made in the past, and we are going to get it going again just as soon as we can under these guidelines.

News conference,
Houston, March 25/
The New York Times, 3-26:11.

James Van Allen
Professor of physics, University of Iowa

1

[Opposing the building of a new space shuttle to replace the *Challenger,* which exploded earlier in the year]: I'm not intrinsically opposed to manned flight. But, within a frozen space budget, NASA is emphasizing things that don't work and neglecting those that do. Research in communications, weather forecasting and all fields of space science is suffering severely. The shuttle is nowhere meeting promises that its commercial and military projects will allow it to pay for itself.

Interview/U.S. News & World Report, 8-25:61.

Albert Wheelon
Executive vice president,
Hughes Aircraft Company

2

[Saying it has become difficult for U.S. industry to launch satellites because of the setback to the U.S. space program after a series of NASA launch disasters]: Last July, no sane person would have forecast the state of affairs in which we find ourselves today. No one would have conceived that our communications-satellite industry would face extinction because the government may deny it access to the launch vehicles that only it supplies.

Los Angeles Times, 7-21:(I)1.

Sports

Henry Aaron
Former baseball player,
Atlanta "Braves"

1

The drug problem has been here [in professional sports] a long time. Unfortunately, it has been swept under the rug. Nobody wanted to face it. One way to get rid of them [drug users] is on the first offense to knock them out of the game. There should be no second chance . . . You're talking about grown men. You're not talking about babies.

Before Durham (N.C.) Sports Club/
The Washington Post, 2-19:(D)2.

George Allen
Former football coach,
Los Angeles "Rams" and
Washington "Redskins"

2

[On whether there is too much emphasis on winning in both college and professional sports]: You have to remember that coaches, and in some cases athletic directors, have to win to keep their jobs. So there's nothing wrong with demanding winning, stressing winning, because that's really what life is. Either you're going to be a success in life and achieve something, or you're going to fall by the wayside and complain and say you didn't get a good break.

Interview/
USA Today, 8-14:(A)9.

Sparky Anderson
Baseball manager,
Detroit "Tigers"

3

To me, the biggest change [in baseball] is the media. It used to be that they never looked for any dirt. They'd seen all that, or were doing it themselves. Today, that's all a lot of guys look for. They want sidebars on the player's love life, who's getting along with the manager. I don't

see what that's got to do with baseball. To me, baseball's the game. It's only what he does on the field that counts to me.

Interview, Lakeland, Fla./
Los Angeles Times, 3-23:(III)1.

4

[On high player salaries]: I don't think the owners knew what they were doing until they opened their books. I think they were shocked at what they saw. This was a toy to them. Even the players were laughing about $400,000 going to mediocre players. There's a carload of them. In three years, you'll see it totally backward, but the [Kirk] Gibsons, the [George] Bretts, the [Dwight] Goodens—they'll still make good money.

The New York Times, 4-7:33.

Ray Arcel
Former boxing trainer

5

We have an old saying in boxing: "To rest is to rust" . . . After four years of idleness, the rust [in a boxer] piles up. Your reflexes aren't the same, your coordination isn't the same and, once they're gone, they're gone forever. Time erodes the skills. You can never regain them, no matter how hard you try . . . You can work out all you want, but it doesn't replace a real fight, and the experience of fighting regularly. In the gym, you're just shaking your can, doing a little shimmy.

Interview/The New York Times, 8-20:20.

Arthur Ashe
Tennis player

6

A [John] McEnroe, somebody with that much talent, comes around once every half-century. What we need [in the U.S.] are better athletes to play tennis. We need to broaden the base. Other countries are enticing their best athletes to play

(ARTHUR ASHE)

tennis and subsidize them at a young age. Our best athletes are in the NBA, NFL and playing major-league baseball.

USA Today, 5-28:(C)2.

Eva Auchincloss
Executive director,
Women's Sports Foundation

1

Boys and girls alike learn so much through playing sports. They learn to work together to achieve a goal. Sports is fast becoming part of the regular, accepted way of life, and women deserve the opportunity to grow and to challenge themselves the same as men do . . . We're looking toward the parents and the educators, letting them know that sports are important to girls and women, too. It is up to them, and to the kids themselves, to continue the forward progress. Women are getting into the mainstream of life, and sports are a major influence in our society. Sports are a way of competing— they teach you to be a team player, let you learn to take risks.

The Christian Science
Monitor, 2-10:26.

Red Auerbach
President, Boston
"Celtics" basketball team

2

In the old days, every [basketball] team used to start its best players and then come in with the players of lesser ability. I wanted to change the concept of the game so that the finishing lineup became a team's best. The biggest problem involved in having a "sixth man" often created an ego problem. Maybe that's why coaches didn't buy the idea right away. That extra starter, the sixth man, has to be a special player; more importantly, a special person.

Interview, Boston/
The New York Times, 5-16:24.

Ernie Banks
Former baseball player,
Chicago "Cubs"

3

[On why baseball is so popular]: People come to baseball games to study the quantitative method of optimum decision-making under conditions of uncertainty. It ameliorates the classic polarization between the self-motivated individual and the collective ideology.

Vero Beach, Fla./
USA Today, 2-24:(C)2.

Red Barber
Former sports announcer

4

Jim Turner was the pitching coach of the New York *Yankees* when I was at the [Yankee] Stadium, and he used to say that a timid man can't pitch—that a pitcher can't stand on the mound, face a great batter, and wish he didn't have to pitch to this man at this time. George Sisler, who once batted .420 and taught batting for years, told me that an afraid man can't hit—that a batter can't stand at the plate and worry about a fastball coming at his head . . . that he must concentrate on the ball, decide whether to swing at it or not and, should the pitch be at his head, then allow his reflexes to take him away from the ball.

At Lincoln High School
commencement, Tallahassee, Fla./
The Christian Science Monitor, 6-25:18.

Raymond Berry
Football coach,
New England "Patriots"

5

You can overwork as an individual and a football team. I've been on football teams where you're kept on the field too long, and it's a mistake. The object is to get your football team on the field at a peak. It's an art. I want them out of the gate fresh. If I'm going to make a mistake about it, I'd rather underwork than overwork them.

New Orleans, Jan. 24/
The New York Times, 1-25:16.

477

WHAT THEY SAID IN 1986

(RAYMOND BERRY)

1

[On his team's losing the Super Bowl]: I don't believe in apologizing. Only when you don't give it all you've got do you apologize. We had nothing more to give. When your players give everything they've got, folks, there's nothing more you can ask.

To reporters, New Orleans, Jan. 27/
The Washington Post, 1-28:(D)3.

2

Our product [professional football] involves affecting people's spirit. It's elusive trying to define it, but when you read the mail these people write, you realize the staggering dimension of pro football's influence. We all have spheres of influence. It's in the path that every one of us walks, and too often we walk totally oblivious to this fact. It's important to me that the influence factor of a professional football team be used properly. It's a responsibility.

Interview, Foxboro, Mass./
The Christian Science Monitor, 9-3:18.

Steve Boros
Baseball manager,
San Diego "Padres"

3

I like to think of myself as a patient man, but firm. Players now are more intelligent, more articulate, better disciplined and more self-motivated than when I was a player. They just have to be told what the manager wants.

USA Today, 2-26:(C)1.

Omar Borras
Soccer coach, "Los Celestes"
(Uruguayan national team)

4

A team is like a clock. If one piece, just a small piece, is wrong, the clock won't work. In a team, that small piece may be a matter of having a great player—but using him in the wrong position. Players must be understood and used properly—they are not machines.

Miami/The New York Times, 5-2:48.

Christopher Bowman
Figure skater

5

Ninety per cent of this sport is a beauty contest, and don't let anyone tell you different. It matters how you look, act and present yourself. I try to be warm toward an audience. I try to skate aggressively. It's a sport, but it's more. It's like dance. It's a show, too.

Interview, Uniondale, N.Y./
The New York Times, 2-5:20.

Terry Bradshaw
Former football player,
Pittsburgh "Steelers"

6

[On playing on Super Bowl-winning teams]: The thing that happens is that it loses its flavor [after time passes]. As an athlete and now as an ex-athlete, people no longer think much of it. It's like the astronauts: I meet them now, and they've been on the moon, and for a year or two they were the hottest thing going. Now you see them out there just like everybody else. They don't have the glow around them that they once had. I feel the same way now. I don't feel particularly different or anything special. But when people mention playing in the National Football League and did you play for a championship and you say, "Yes, I played on a team that won four Super Bowls," that has a little clout to it.

Interview/
The New York Times, 1-20:42.

George Brett
Baseball pitcher,
Kansas City "Royals"

7

[On clutch hitting]: You can't be emotional at all, because when you are emotional you tend to try so hard that you go beyond your fundamentals. It's the guys who know exactly what they are doing and stay within themselves that are so tough in the clutch.

Interview/The Christian
Science Monitor, 5-5:30.

Jimmy Connors
Tennis player

1

[On hecklers at tennis matches]: The crowds are part of the game. If they sit on their hands and say nothing, it makes it boring for us. But they've got to take it back when they give it, otherwise they're wimps. They say something, I say something back and, if they can take it, that's what keeps the rapport going.

Interview, Boca Raton, Fla./
USA Today, 2-21:(C)7.

2

[On the importance of ego to a tennis player]: At times it's very important, as long as you know when it is and when it's not. Ego on the court is knowing that you're going out there knowing who you are, what you've done and what you can do. As long as that's where it stops, having a reputation can win you some tennis matches.

Interview/USA Today, 6-20:(A)11.

Howard Cosell
Sports commentator

3

[On team owners who threaten to move their franchises to other cities]: We see a continuing saga of carpetbagging sports franchises, holding cities hostage for greater personal gain either by the threat of removal or actual removal . . . The kind of wrongdoing the NFL has been guilty of should not be rewarded with what would in effect be a blanket antitrust exemption [as is being proposed]. There are proper grounds for franchise removals: loss of money over a continuing period—say three years—plus other factors listed by the appeals court in the *Raiders'* [football-team relocation] case. But there is no need for a wider antitrust exemption. In fact, there should be *no* exemptions—baseball's exemption is totally unreasonable today. Let the moguls of sports run their businesses like any other, fully accountable to the antitrust laws. Lord knows major-league sports are a big business.

Before Senate Judiciary Committee,
Washington/USA Today, 8-4:(A)6.

John C. Danforth
United States Senator, R-Missouri

4

[Saying professional sports teams should not be allowed to easily move to other cities]: A lot of a city's self-image is based on its sports teams. It's something that brings people together, something that well-to-do businessmen and the poorest blue-collar workers have in common. It's something they can talk about. If you lose that, you lose your pride, and part of your economy, and a cohesive force in the community. People like to root for something.

The New York Times, 5-23:10.

Mike Davis
Football player,
Los Angeles "Raiders"

5

[Criticizing NFL Commissioner Pete Rozelle's plan for mandatory, random testing of players for drug abuse]: I just think he's wrong in doing it the way he's doing it. We're dealing with an educational and morality issue. We're opposed to drug use. We're not playing tough guys in saying we don't want random testing, but ultimately we want to be the ones to decide what we do and what we won't do.

Los Angeles Times, 7-8:(III)4.

Dave DeBusschere
Former basketball player,
and former executive vice president,
New York "Knicks"

6

[Criticizing the ownership of teams by corporate conglomerates, as the *Knicks* are owned by Gulf and Western]: Upon reflection, no team has ever been successful when operated as part of big business. This is true in all professional sports. The way it works inhibits and prohibits immediate action, quick decisions and the necessary decision-making that has to be done at one level and one level only.

News conference,
New York, Jan. 7/
The New York Times, 1-8:23.

Don Denkinger
Baseball umpire,
American League

1

I have never, ever looked for celebrity status, or wanting people to know who I was. That's not part of my profession. My profession is to go out there and do an objective job. You slip in and slip out. Nobody knows where you come from. Nobody knows where you're going when it's over. You just go out and officiate.

Interview, Phoenix/
The New York Times, 4-7:38.

Jerry Diamond
Former executive director,
Women's Tennis Association

2

[Saying the USTA is neglecting its job]: Too often, it has concentrated on the profits of the U.S. Open rather than spend substantial money on the development of young players. That's where we're missing the boat and that's why U.S. women pro players are not developing. They need a chance to develop on the secondary level and earn some good bucks at the same time. Instead, they jump up and play top events and get beaten in the first round.

USA Today, 5-28:(C)2.

Mike Ditka
Football coach,
Chicago "Bears"

3

[Supporting mandatory drug-testing of players]: If you have a product that you're proud of, then you keep that product as clean as possible. If that means that you have to test mandatory, then I think you do it. I'd get in line first every week, every day, whenever it has to be done. I think everyone else in our organization would, too. I don't feel that it's an infringement on my private rights. My private rights don't mean a whole heck of a lot if the game of football weren't there. I owe everything I have to football, as do most of the people playing the game. Football does owe some things to some of the

people because of their contribution. But I think that's a cop-out to say that's an invasion of your private rights.

To reporters, March 10/
Los Angeles Times, 3-11:(III)8.

Brian Downing
Baseball player, California "Angels"

4

The great thing about baseball is that you can do something wrong early on and still get center stage at the end. Or vice versa.

Interview, Anaheim, Calif./
Los Angeles Times, 4-15:(III)1.

Fred Dryer
Former football player,
Los Angeles "Rams"

5

[On Super Bowl XIV, in which he was a player]: When all the over-coaching, over-preparing and over-writing is done, the Super Bowl is a goddam game. We played well. I let the event *in* completely and enjoyed the whole thing tremendously. The loss was gone the second I walked out of the stadium . . . To put [football] aside, you almost have to give up the fact of who you were. I couldn't be an athlete in my mind the rest of my life, so I left the football player behind. Within a year, it was like I never played sports.

Interview/Time, 1-27:54.

Don Drysdale
Former baseball pitcher,
Los Angeles "Dodgers"

6

I've been on the major-league level for 30 years, and today's players may be big and strong, but I've never seen so many injuries. I know one thing for sure—they're not any better than we were. They don't know the game as well, but nowadays they don't have to. The era of the '50s and '60s may never be equalled for talent. I don't know how good the players were before that period, but I know it's not like that today.

Interview/Los Angeles Times, 3-23:(III)17.

Carl Ekern
Football player,
Los Angeles "Rams"

1

[Criticizing NFL Commissioner Pete Rozelle's plan for mandatory, random testing of players for drug abuse]: It's witch hunting. And in America, we don't do those types of things. There are enough avenues so that if a player screws up he can be approached, tested and helped in whatever fashion is set up. We don't need to go searching for people; we don't need to invade everyone's privacy by spot checking. In America, it's innocent until proven guilty. People fought and died to maintain those rights.

Los Angeles Times, 7-8:(III)4.

Sean Farrell
Football player,
Tampa Bay "Buccaneers"

2

[On player objections to women sports reporters being allowed in team locker rooms]: I don't think you can sacrifice the boundaries of human decency for the sake of someone being a journalist. I've got no problem being nude from time to time, but I'd like to choose the people I'm nude with.

Los Angeles Times, 1-5:(III)12.

Don Fehr
Executive director, Major League
(baseball) Players Association

3

[Arguing against mandatory drug-testing of players]: I think you're talking about real important stuff here. You're talking about whether a society will operate on a premise that you don't accuse somebody without proof. You don't require him to testify against himself. That you don't invade his privacy, in this case by the search of bodily fluids, without a good reason to do so . . . or whether we are going to live in a society where the accepted behavior is to suspect everybody. To demand people to prove themselves innocent, and if somebody is unwilling to prove himself innocent, you assume . . . even

without evidence that he is, in fact, guilty. That's pretty serious stuff. It is interesting that this whole drama is being played out with baseball players . . . I think we are seeing the beginnings of the first serious national debate [on the issue]. Do we really want 220 million Americans tested for drugs all the time . . . Is that what we really want? Is that the kind of place you want to live in? I don't.

Vero Beach, Fla., March 10/
Los Angeles Times, 3-11:(III)3.

4

[Criticizing the change from a 25-man roster to a 24-man roster]: The bottom line is that it cheats the fans. Whether it's a pinch hitter in the sixth inning or a pitcher to face one hitter in the eighth, or a defensive replacement in the ninth, or whoever, you don't have the opportunity to use him because he's not in your dugout. Fans have a right to ask owners: Is it worth a few thousand dollars to you to put your best team on the field? And the owners have clearly answered, "No, it's not."

USA Today, 6-11:(C)2.

Bill Fitch
Basketball coach, Houston "Rockets"

5

[On the importance of a good relationship between players and coach]: Having one is nice, but it isn't what the job requires. I think it's more important that the players develop a relationship between themselves, a tight bond in which they have great respect for one another and aren't selfish. That's what a coach should be responsible for. The easy thing would be to be a popular coach, but what good is it if the players loved the coach and not each other?

The New York Times, 5-26:24.

Larry Fleisher
Director, National Basketball
Players Association

6

We feel there is no reason we [in basketball] can't operate under a free-agent system where a

WHAT THEY SAID IN 1986

(LARRY FLEISHER)

player can sign a contract and move wherever he wants to move and a player can come out of school and sign with whomever he wants. It's been ingrained in the minds of the public and some of the players that you have to have a draft to exist. We don't believe that.

Feb. 25/USA Today, 2-26:(C)4.

Raymond Floyd
Golfer

1

I have always prided myself with being able to handle pressure. I know about emotions, and many times that's the difference between winning and losing.

Southampton, N.Y., June 15/
USA Today, 6-16:(C)3.

Bill Frieder
Basketball coach,
University of Michigan

2

A lot of coaches, when they're picked to do well, worry about failing, about not living up to expectations. We have a good team; we've worked hard. I think we'll do well. But if we don't do as well as people expect, I'm still going to be the coach at Michigan next year, whether people like it or not. And the year after that.

Interview, Bloomington, Ind./
The Washington Post, 1-7:(E)1.

Gayle Gardner
Sports anchor,
ESPN "Sports Center"

3

[On the lack of female sportscasters on TV]: There's still a firm belief, by network executives and news directors, that a hard-core male viewing audience does not want to see a woman. They say, "If we could find one who really knew sports, with a background in TV, who looked great, we'd hire her in a second." Baloney. Granted, there's not hundreds of women across

the country who would fit that bill. But they're not delving into the people working who do. I hate to be discouraging, but there's just not jobs to be had for women. We're not welcome with open arms by any stretch of the imagination.

Interview/USA Today, 2-14:(C)3.

Steve Garvey
Baseball player, San Diego "Padres"

4

[On whether he understands fan anger when a well-paid sports star does not give his all during a game]: Oh, sure, because we who play the game are essentially living out a childhood fantasy, of being able to play a sport for a living and get paid very well for it. And the very least we can do, even with our God-given talents, is to hustle. Performance in itself is subject to the human elements. You know, some days we're on, and we can go four-for-four, and some days, no matter what we do, we can't get a hit, or we can't seem to pick up the yardage, or make a basket. So, the real foundation of the sport is the effort.

Interview/USA Today, 7-11:(A)9.

5

[On whether baseball players are over-paid]: Well, yes and no. Obviously, if·you go purely on performance, sometimes a player may be over-paid for a season. But I think, all in all, the players are paid according to a scale that was established by ownership. And I think that's the way you have to look at it. An owner won't pay somebody unless he thinks he can afford it. And that's his business decision. And the fan, although he sometimes can't understand it or can't relate to it, must understand that it is a short career for [a player], and [the player] must take as much advantage of it as possible.

Interview/USA Today, 7-11:(A)9.

A. Bartlett Giamatti
President-designate, National (baseball)
League; Former president, Yale University

6

Baseball is a business, but it is not only that. It grew up with the country and has been around

(A. BARTLETT GIAMATTI)

longer than any other major sport—amateur or professional. It still has the feel to it of the leisurely pace of an older time. People were playing it before the Civil War, and it became more popular during the Reconstruction period as waves of immigration began to hit these shores. One of the ways people became Americans was to grab onto this game, which did not exist in the old country. As the population went West, baseball did, too. It was almost like a banner that people planted.

Interview/U.S. News &
World Report, 10-13:66.

Dwight Gooden
Baseball pitcher,
New York "Mets"

1

[As a young boy, throwing rocks at passing cars,] I knocked out a lot of windows, got a lot of whippings. At night I'd lie in bed throwing a tennis ball up in the air and catching it, throwing it up in the air and catching it, throwing it up in the air and catching it, until I fell asleep.

Interview/Time, 4-7:56.

Albert Gore, Jr.
United States Senator,
D-Tennessee

2

[Saying professional sports teams should have more freedom to move to other cities, or that there should be more freedom for professional teams to be formed within the various leagues]: The older cities and older states have their teams and that's fine. But those areas that have been growing in the latter half of the century deserve a chance to participate and compete for a reasonable number of new teams. States like Tennessee are prevented from even competing for a team, so long as an artificial scarcity is enforced by the current arrangement.

The New York Times, 5-23:10.

Jack Hartman
Basketball coach,
Kansas State University

3

Every now and then people say there's not as much cheating going on [in college athletics] as you hear. That's hogwash. Television money has had such an impact. The non-revenue sports have to be funded, which puts such a burden on the revenue-producing sports . . . The pressure to win and fill the arena to make the money to operate the program—there you are. It's really disgusting, the state we're in.

News conference, Jan. 30/
USA Today, 1-31:(C)1.

Elvin Hayes
Former player,
National Basketball Association

4

[Saying players should think about their lives and careers after they finish basketball, and that education is an important element]: Athletes need to be what I call a balanced-life person . . . Guys playing now think they're going to play forever. It's an awful, fearful thing to retire. They need a school where they can sit these guys down and say, "You *used* to be." When you ask these players what else they can do, they come up with all kinds of things. But when you put all the bull aside, the answer is "nothing."

Interview/
USA Today, 1-3:(C)2.

Dave Henderson
Baseball player,
Boston "Red Sox"

5

[On when he was a high-school All American in football]: Pressure is when you've got to deal with college football coaches from all over the country when you're 18 years old. You grow up in a hurry then. I can remember a Southern Cal assistant coach shoving out a hand with four Rose Bowl rings on it. "Here, kid, you want one of these? Come to USC." That, I call pressure.

Los Angeles Times, 10-23:(III)2.

WHAT THEY SAID IN 1986

Whitey Herzog
Baseball manager,
St. Louis "Cardinals"

1

It really wasn't difficult getting over losing the World Series [last year]. [But] it's tough to lose the playoffs; for a manager, that's the toughest defeat you can have. Nobody remembers the team that lost the playoffs. I hate to say this, but sometimes today the World Series is anticlimactic.

Interview, St. Petersburg, Fla./
USA Today, 3-6:(C)6.

2

Basically, I like the designated hitter because it gives the fans a lot more offense, and that's what most people pay their money to see. On the other hand, it wouldn't bother me if they cut out the DH entirely. What I don't like is that one league has it and the other doesn't. Either they should both have it or nobody should have it. But I can tell you why baseball is dragging its feet on the designated hitter: It's because too many teams have the DHs signed through 1988, and getting rid of that rule now would be hitting American League club owners with a tremendous financial burden.

Interview/The Christian
Science Monitor, 5-30:20.

Ben Hogan
Golfer

3

Some of the [golf] clubs today don't look like clubs at all. They look like something out of a comic book. A golf club should be like a work of art, like a fine piece of jewelry.

Interview/USA Today, 12-18:(C)2.

Larry Holmes
Former heavyweight boxing
champion of the world

4

I don't have any good intentions about letting a person survive in a fight, because nobody wants *me* to survive . . . I want blood pouring down my face, like in [the film] *Rocky,* and blood pouring down his [the opponent's] face. I want my eyes closed; I want his eyes closed. I want to fight, man. I want to get hit in the mouth and get all my teeth knocked out. And I want to do the same thing to his ass.

Sports Illustrated, 4-28:25.

Hale Irwin
Golfer

5

There are so many good [golfers] now, not great players but dozens of really good players, that it's all but impossible for a man to win more than two or three tournaments a year. The days of a player winning six or seven or eight tournaments, like Johnny [Miller] did a few years ago, those days are gone forever.

Los Angeles Times, 1-5:(III)4.

Jesse L. Jackson
Civil-rights leader

6

[On drug abuse in college athletics]: Leaders in athletics must play a leading role. They must look at the pressures of professional athletics under an amateur and academic veneer. Professional is the only way to understand a situation where athletes are not going to school, not graduating but, instead, are being propped up and pumped up. The whole system is exploitative. Right now, the tail is wagging the dog. There are too many games, too much money involved and too much pressure on the coaches to win at all costs. It's not just one school, it's everywhere.

News conference, Washington, June 25/
The New York Times, 6-26:21.

Reggie Jackson
Baseball player,
California "Angels"

7

[On his being a 40-year-old player]: Physically, I could probably play three more years. But considering the mental strain, I don't see myself playing beyond next year. Then again,

(REGGIE JACKSON)

this could be it. You never know. If I don't hit, my manager is not going to play me. The end can come when you least expect it.

Interview, Detroit/USA Today, 5-19:(C)2.

1

There always seems to be a place in baseball for white stars after they retire. Apparently, the same isn't true for black greats. I'm not saying it's racism or discrimination, but the number of former black players dictates that there are some who are smart enough to make decisions. It's sad, but it seems that if you wake up in the morning with ash on your arms, you just aren't treated the same.

Interview/Ebony, July:111.

2

There's only one thing that matters if you play the game professionally, and that's "Do you help your team win games?" Nothing else matters, unless you're playing sandlot ball for a keg and trying to impress the pretty girls. Nothing else has any meaning to me at all. Some people criticize me, say I strike out too much, knock my fielding, say I was controversial, a clubhouse lawyer. Those comments never bothered me. To me—I won. Wherever I was. I was in six World Series and won five. That's all that matters.

Interview/Los Angeles Times, 7-1:(III)3.

3

I've probably hit a hundred [home-run] balls more than 400 feet, but to me the personal satisfaction is having the ball leave the park before you can take a step out of the batter's box. The awesome thing to me is not how far but how quickly the ball travels.

Los Angeles Times, 7-21:(III)13.

Dave Johnson
Baseball manager, New York "Mets"

4

I've never felt that you had to have a great glove at shortstop to win a pennant. If the man there is a good hitter and can make the routine

plays, then he's got a job with me. It never made much sense to me to start your best defensive team, get behind, and then have to pinch-hit. I'd rather have guys out there who can give me an early lead with their bats.

The Christian Science Monitor, 8-1:18.

Jim Kaat
Former baseball pitcher

5

Pitching was like being in a bubble. When you're in that bubble, you're in a world of your own. I always knew that even when there were fifty, sixty thousand people screaming in the stands, the most peaceful place in the universe was right on the pitcher's mound.

The New York Times, 5-19:36.

Al Kaline
Former baseball player, Detroit "Tigers"

6

Players today, in my opinion, don't want to pay the price to be good. The very top ones have the pride, but generally I don't believe today's players have the good of baseball at heart. They're not looking 10 or 15 years down the line to visualize what baseball will be like.

Interview/Los Angeles Times, 3-23:(III)17.

Harmon Killebrew
Former baseball player, Minnesota "Twins"

7

I'm all for the present-day athlete . . . they're better trained and physically more talented. But it seems to me players used to have more fun playing. In today's era, everyone knows what [salary] everyone else is making, and that creates problems.

Interview/Los Angeles Times, 3-23:(III)17.

Eugene Klein
Former owner, San Diego "Chargers" football team

8

[On the drug-use problem on NFL teams]: Any owner who says his team is clean is either

(EUGENE KLEIN)

naive or ignorant of what's going on around him. What's come out so far has only touched the surface. Players taking drugs is going on everywhere . . . I've always been an avid proponent of drug testing. The attitude of the players' association is ludicrous [in objecting to testing of players]. They have an obligation to the public to be clean and, if they're not, they should be banned from the sport.

Interview, Palm Springs, Calif./
Los Angeles Times, 1-31:(III)12.

Bob Knepper
Baseball pitcher,
Houston "Astros"

1

Winning on the road is the epitome of challenge in baseball.

The New York Times, 10-11:16.

Steve Largent
Football player,
Seattle "Seahawks"

2

There's a difference between being fast and being quick, and in pro football quickness is better because it can create openings for you. After that, it's hands and concentration, getting a feel for the ball, and then not letting anything the opposition does distract you.

Interview/The Christian
Science Monitor, 11-12:30.

Tom Lasorda
Baseball manager,
Los Angeles "Dodgers"

3

When a team wins, a lot of guys had good years or great years, they didn't get injured, the ball bounced your way. Look at the [New York] *Mets* and Houston *Astros* [who won this year's National League East and West championships]: Their guys had terrific years. But you try to win the next year, and everything might not work.

How many guys will have their "best" year twice in a row?

The New York Times, 12-10:52.

Sugar Ray Leonard
Former welterweight boxing
champion of the world

4

[On whether he worries about being injured in the ring]: No, I'm [not]. You know, that's what made me champion. We assume the risks. That's what makes a great champion; that's what makes athletes. We don't care [about injuries]. We care, but you can't let that be a burden to you. It's like certain businessmen who travel for weeks. They jeopardize their marriage, but get along. They want to better themselves financially. It's the same thing . . . Boxing to me is an art. I've always said that, and I'll always believe that. It's an art, and I try to beat you with scientific techniques. I'm not out there to hurt you or anything. I'm there to defeat you. It's a business.

Interview/USA Today, 5-16:(A)15.

Chris Evert Lloyd
Tennis player

5

[Criticizing the behavior of some tennis players]: Tennis players get away with a lot more than any other sports figures, and you've got to put a cap on it . . . There has to be more control over the behavior of players and how they treat umpires and officials. Half the people that come to matches are there to see tennis and half are there to watch [John] McEnroe arguing with the officials. People can relate to that, I guess. They can get all their frustrations out. But it's hurting the image of the game.

Boca Raton, Fla./USA Today, 2-24:(C)3.

Juan Marichal
Former baseball pitcher,
San Francisco "Giants"

6

You used to know that if you didn't win 20 games [in a season], you were going to get cut

(JUAN MARICHAL)

the next year. Now you can have a lousy year and get a raise. Today, you hit .260 or .270 and sign a big contract. I think you have the same caliber of players today, but if you sign a $1-million contract I don't think you're going to play as hard.

Interview/Los Angeles Times, 3-23:(III)17.

James A. Mathisen
Professor of sociology,
Wheaton (Ill.) College

1

[There are distinctive myths, beliefs and values in sports that] are accepted on faith by great masses of people . . . from the President of the United States down to the most humble bootblack. For example, if I believe the myth that "sport builds character," then I will guide my children toward youthful athletic participation with a virtual untestable certainty that, without experience as a shortstop or as a left wing, their lives will be morally deficient. Further, I will infer that the "character" of successful adult Americans who happen to have participated in sport at some point in their lives is what it is as a result of comparable participation in sport. Selective perception guarantees that I will interpret biographies in terms of the ideology and mythology of sport. Not to do so would be a demonstration of lack of faith and of irreligion.

Before Society for the Scientific Study
of Religion, Washington, November/
Los Angeles Times, 12-31:(I)3,15.

Gene Mauch
Baseball manager,
California "Angels"

2

Since you play the same teams season after season, everybody gets to know what the other fellow does best. Basically, there are no secrets in baseball. Even when an opponent uses a rookie pitcher or hitter against you, the front office will have already sent down a scouting report detailing what he did in the minors. However, some man-

agers do have a flair for capitalizing on this knowledge more effectively than others. They will do this by shading an infielder a step or two toward second base to nullify a certain hitter's strength. Or they might give the steal sign when they know that the opposing catcher has been having trouble throwing accurately. Sure they are little things, but sometimes they do win ball games.

Interview/The Christian
Science Monitor, 3-24:26.

3

I don't think I'll ever get managing out of my system. There have been times when I thought I could, but I've always known I'll be back. You're dealing with the greatest commodity in the world—human beings, people. The situation can never be boring because of the variables. The situations might look the same, but there's really no likeness because of the differences in the people involved.

Interview, Anaheim, Calif./USA Today, 9-9:(C)2.

John McEnroe
Tennis player

4

[On his reputation for being arrogant and the attention given it by the press]: The society we live in is so negative and maybe I've dwelled on the negative, too. But now, they'll do anything to try to sell newspapers. I think people who love tennis should look at this more carefully before criticizing one of the greatest players who ever played. If they come to see me throw a racquet, I want them to leave, saying, "God, can he play tennis!"

Interview, Stratton Mountain, Vt./
The New York Times, 8-6:21.

Al McGuire
Sports commentator, NBC-TV

5

Once you start keeping score, winning's the bottom line. It's the American concept. If not, it's like playing your grandmother, and even then you try to win—unless she has a lot of money and you want to get some of it.

Los Angeles Times, 6-3:(III)2.

487

WHAT THEY SAID IN 1986

Jim McMahon
Football player,
Chicago "Bears"

1

Football is not a nice game. It is a sick game. There are people out there trying to maim you for life.

Newsweek, 3-3:13.

Archie Moore
Former light-heavyweight
boxing champion of the world

2

[On critics of boxing who say the sport should be banned]: Don't those people have anything better to do than pick on boxing? Wouldn't they feel more useful to themselves if they put their energy into solving the awful problems we're having with drugs and our kids? Look at the awful things that have happened in the world lately—all those people who're going to die at Chernobyl [the Soviet nuclear plant disaster], the astronauts who died in that explosion [of the U.S. space shuttle] . . . and they're picking on boxing? What's boxing done, except to entertain millions of people, given so many people so many good memories?

Interview,
San Diego/
Los Angeles Times, 9-18:(III)12.

Brent Musberger
Commentator,
CBS Sports

3

[On drug use in the NFL]: To get the kids off dope, it's going to take spot urinalysis checks [of players]. I have a sympathy about individual rights but there's a much larger issue about our youth that uses these guys [the players] as role models. The laws of the country come before the NFLPA. It's illegal to use and distribute cocaine. People are saying the [Chicago] *Bears* beat up on a bunch of cokeheads [the New England *Patriots*] in the Super Bowl.

USA Today, 1-31:(C)3.

Martina Navratilova
Tennis player

4

I never really compare women's tennis to men's tennis. We are an entity of our own. We stand on our own two feet, make our own decisions, are in control of our game more than the men are. Any time you have people who can make $1-million a year doing anything, you've got it made.

Interview/USA Today, 1-16:(A)9.

Merlin Olsen
Former football player, Los Angeles "Rams"

5

The biggest change in professional sports in the last 25 years is in the business side of the game. I don't find that to be a very tasteful part of the game. I find that to be in many ways the ugly part of sport. There used to be an innocence, if you will, to the players. I was kind of on the cusp of this change. The athletes who played professional football before I did, for example, could have made just as much money being good butchers or driving an 18-wheeler or working as a salesman. They played football because they wanted to, not because they had a $3.5-million contract.

Interview/USA Today, 1-10:(A)9.

6

We don't bring the two teams to the Super Bowl who play the best football during the season. We bring the teams to the Super Bowl that survive the playoffs. And because of that, we sometimes end up with two teams in the Super Bowl who are not the two that played best during the year. You get a bad day and you get a couple people hurt, you drop the football or kick it away a few times, and you go home a loser.

Interview/USA Today, 1-10:(A)9.

Jesse Orosco
Baseball pitcher, New York "Mets"

7

[On being a relief pitcher]: In the big leagues, somebody loses every day . . . I hate losing, but

(JESSE OROSCO)

I've got to lose sometimes. I didn't always have a philosophy about the dangers of relief pitching. I developed one . . . I learned a lot about attitude from Neil Allen . . . Win or lose, he was always bouncing around with all that energy. And I learned from him that somebody's got to lose, and tomorrow everybody gets another shot.

Interview, San Diego/
The New York Times, 5-27:43.

Ferdie Pacheco
Boxing analyst, NBC-TV

1

The state of the heavyweight division [of boxing] is semi-critical and the prognosis is grave. It is not in optimum condition . . . What we have is a series of dog fights by a dreary succession of heavyweights who are incapable of holding on to the title for more than one or two fights. They are meaningless fights by overweight, untalented people. There's no hook to hang on to like [former champion Muhammad] Ali . . . In the world of reality, with the quality of the division deteriorated over the years and without a ruling body to decide what's good for boxing, it's virtually impossible to accomplish the unification of the heavyweight title and the return of the word "champion" to its rightful meaning.

Las Vegas, Nev./
Los Angeles Times, 4-20:(III)12.

Alan Page
Former football player,
Minnesota "Vikings"

2

[On the Super Bowl, in which he once participated]: It doesn't particularly interest me. To some degree, it's inescapable for everyone, but I won't go out of my way to watch it. For a football player, I guess I'm not much of a football fan. To tell you the truth, I never quite understood the whole magic vision people see around sports.

Interview/Time, 1-27:53.

Bill Parcells
Football coach, New York "Giants"

3

Some of the greatest mistakes in this business center around the emotional aspect of what you think you need [in terms of player personnel], then over-rating people who appear to fill the need and then doing something to acquire those people, and then not having it work out. You have to be very careful in speculation about other people.

Interview, East Rutherford, N.J.,
Aug. 24/The New York Times, 8-25:42.

Joe Paterno
Football coach,
Pennsylvania State University

4

[On the win-at-all-costs attitude of some coaches]: That kind of attitude is nonsense. We tell our players: "It's a game, enjoy it. Get yourself ready for a strong confrontation. Pull up your pants, look the other guy in the eye and give it your best shot. Either you can do it, or you can't. Either way, enjoy it." I think if it is just a question of winning and losing, football is a silly game. It's hard for me to picture myself in a situation where the only important thing is whether we won a game or not. College football doesn't mean that much to me. I think there's much more to a college football experience than winning or losing.

Interview, Miami/USA Today, 1-2:(C)3.

Lou Piniella
Baseball manager, New York "Yankees"

5

When you manage my particular ball club, you really get to know the true meaning of the word "pressure." Sometimes I fight back. Or laugh it off. Sometimes I even ignore it. There are plenty of ways to handle it. But I'd never turn to drugs. That's no way to deal with things. Unless you're into destroying yourself. And if you're that dumb . . . you'll never be a member of my club.

Anti-drug TV message/
The New York Times, 8-19:51.

Gary Player
Golfer

1

[Saying the decrease in dominance of American players in professional golf is attributable to a large extent on the U.S. top-125 system, in which the top 125 money-winners each year are excluded from the next year's tournaments]: I've traveled around the world and I've seen it coming for a long time. So it doesn't surprise me at all. And there are a lot of good [foreign] guys that are still capable of coming over [to the U.S.]. And I think as long as America—and I might be wrong—as long as America goes for this top-125 all-exempt system it has now, your golf is not going to improve at the rate that it should. Because now you've got guys who win X amount of money and say, "Oh, now I'm in the top 125!" When [Arnold] Palmer and [Jack] Nicklaus and I played, there was only one thought on our minds: You gotta win the tournament. Now there's a complacency, and I think it's a bad thing. The system is breeding complacency on the tour. And the one thing that made this country so great is competition!

Interview, Augusta, Ga./
Los Angeles Times, 4-9:(III)1.

2

[Golfer] Jack Nicklaus isn't the best striker of a golf ball that I've ever seen by any means. I think Sam Snead, Ben Hogan and Byron Nelson were the best golfers that ever lived, as far as striking the ball. But everybody says Nicklaus is the best golfer that ever lived, and nobody can deny that because he's the best scorer that ever lived. After all, it's the score that counts, and Nicklaus has got the best mind control I've ever seen in a golfer. That, to me, is the most important thing.

Interview/Los Angeles Times, 5-9:(III)2.

Darrell Porter
Baseball player, Texas "Rangers"

3

[On players who complain that their civil rights are violated by compulsory testing for drugs]: What rights? We're no different from anybody else. You hear guys crying about the invasion of their privacy and their rights, and to me it's a lot of noise. We've got to become responsible for what we do. We've got to quit worrying so much about our own rights and start doing what's really right for everyone else.

Los Angeles Times, 4-9:(III)2.

Bobby Rahal
Auto-racing driver

4

For a driver, winning at [the] Indianapolis [500 race] has the same effect as winning the Kentucky Derby has for a jockey, or winning the masters has for a golfer. The difference is that, in horse racing or golf, there are other major races or major tournaments. But in auto racing, there's only one major—the Indianapolis 500.

Interview, East Rutherford, N.J./
The New York Times, 6-27:21.

Willie Randolph
Baseball player,
New York "Yankees"

5

Just thinking about putting on a uniform every day, knowing what it means, going out every day and playing hard and playing winning baseball—that's how you stay around [in baseball]. Be consistent, be proud to put the uniform on; it means something.

Interview,
Fort Lauderdale, Fla./
Los Angeles Times, 3-23:(III)9.

Nolan Richardson
Basketball coach,
University of Arkansas

6

[On college sports recruiting]: The competition for players is greater than ever before There's been a change in players, too. Fifteen years ago, kids were playing for the joy of playing. Now you see 13- and 14-year-olds preparing themselves for NBA contracts. Winning has always been important, but now, with so much rid

(NOLAN RICHARDSON)

ing on success, there's more pressure to win and earn money. Whenever money gets involved, things change.

The New York Times, 6-9:37.

Pat Riley
Basketball coach,
Los Angeles "Lakers"

1

[On his team's not making it to the NBA championship series this year]: Our problem was, we suffered from complacency during the regular season. It's a disease, an insidious disease. Some of the players take the attitude that they'll wait until the playoffs to get it going. When you take that attitude, you're setting yourself up for a failure. If you are going to be mediocre for many months, you are going to be mediocre when it counts. The players have conned themselves for too long that the regular season is too tiresome, that they have to save themselves for the playoffs. They have to get that out of their minds and come back with a clean attitude. You learn nothing from success. You learn from failure.

Interview,
Thousand Oaks, Calif./
Los Angeles Times, 8-8:(III)3.

2

I have no problems with egos. Everybody assumes that I do, but my main problem coaching the *Lakers* is keeping these guys away from the burden of having to win every time. The public, the media, fans and even management have such unrealistic expectations about winning that I have to deal with the possibility that the players will get no joy out of the season. No one can win all the time. When you're not only expected to win, but to win and look great, you're put in a position where you can never be satisfied. I tell the team that it's okay to lose 25 games—that should be our goal.

Interview/
USA Today, 12-17:(C)6.

Pete Rose
Baseball manager and player,
Cincinnati "Reds"

3

While everybody seems to agree with the statement that pitching is 75 per cent of winning, that's not really true unless you've also got a team that is sound fundamentally and plays good defense. Pitching and defense are always going to keep you in a game longer than your offense, no matter how many good hitters you have.

Interview, Tampa, Fla./
The Christian Science Monitor, 3-18:24.

4

[On those who say he is too old to play]: It seems like they're always trying to put in on me, and I get tired of it. I mean, to say I shouldn't be playing because of my age is like saying Jack Nicklaus shouldn't be playing golf and Willie Shoemaker shouldn't be riding horses. I can remember a time in Cincinnati when people said we were too young. Make up your mind.

Interview,
San Francisco/
Los Angeles Times, 6-9:(III)11.

Patrick Roy
Hockey goaltender,
Montreal "Canadiens"

5

[Saying he talks to the goal posts during the game]: I started talking to the goal posts by accident. We were playing in Hartford, and I started talking to the goal posts during the anthem. They helped me, and I played a good game. In overtime, a guy took a slap shot and hit the post and we won. I say [to the posts], "Come on, guys, help me out." Before the game, I give them direction. I feel every goalie needs a superstition. The goal posts are always with me. Some nights they say "bing." But some nights they have a bad night, too.

Interview, Montreal/
Los Angeles Times, 5-20:(III)2.

WHAT THEY SAID IN 1986

Pete Rozelle
Commissioner, National Football League

1

[On the Super Bowl]: I would be satisfied to see it hold its present popularity. At the worst, I don't see it diminishing in popularity. One of the good things about the Super Bowl is the rotation with different cities. The teams themselves, and the cities of the teams, place such a premium on this one-day event: getting to the Super Bowl. Of course, that's the aim of all 28 clubs. There's tremendous dedication, that drive to do it, and it just builds the importance of the game.

Interview, New Orleans, Jan. 23/
USA Today, 1-24:(C)2.

2

The Super Bowl, a few people say, "Well, it's hype. It's something that's just overdone." But I think it's tremendous. I've often said, if the American public didn't have an entertaining, emotional outlet, we'd have trouble. We'd be a sick society. We don't say the Super Bowl is the end of the world. But, naturally, we feel it gives half the country a chance to think of something else, other than our domestic troubles and our international troubles. It's meant to be fun. We think it is.

News conference, New Orleans, Jan. 24/
Los Angeles Times, 1-25:(III)8.

Bill Russell
Former basketball player, Boston "Celtics"

3

When I was growing up, my mother wouldn't allow me to go near a golf course. She didn't think the people who played [golf] were very nice. Now I play [golf] every day, and you know what? She was right.

Los Angeles Times, 5-27:(III)2.

Buddy Ryan
Defensive coordinator,
Chicago "Bears" football team

4

You have to have intelligent [players]. I'd take intelligence first and toughness second; and

then, if they're a great athlete, that's a plus. If you're a great athlete and you don't know where to go and you won't hit anybody, it's not going to help you.

Interview, New Orleans/
Los Angeles Times, 1-22:(III)10.

Nolan Ryan
Baseball pitcher, Houston "Astros"

5

[On those games when a pitcher has everything working well]: I can't explain the feeling, but when it's been there you walk off the mound more satisfied than by any records you might have been honored for. Tunnel-vision is how I explain it. You get into a rhythm or a groove—whatever you want to call it. You know that everything is going right and you become isolated from all outside distraction . . . and there's only you, the hitter and the catcher. It's the most satisfying feeling I've known.

Interview, New York/The New York Times, 5-19:36.

Dan Schatzeder
Baseball pitcher, Montreal "Expos"

6

[On the change from a 25-man roster to a 24-man roster]: . . . I think it has made the game better over-all. Managers might not agree, but the 25th man is generally a utility infielder who plays once every two weeks or so, and I've watched these guys' talents diminish so much over the course of a season. Now [with a 24-man roster] you see right-handed hitters facing right-handed pitchers they don't normally get to face. You see guys playing positions they don't usually play. You see guys stretching themselves, and that makes things more interesting. I hope it stays this way.

USA Today, 6-11:(C)2.

Howard Schnellenberger
Football coach, University of Louisville

7

I worked for a long time for $6,000. I worked for a long time for $9,000. I worked for a long

(HOWARD SCHNELLENBERGER)

time for $13,000 . . . as have a number of other coaches who've developed good contracts. It took me about 22 years to get to the point where I was a head coach. I would say coaching is probably the most underpaid profession in the country.

Interview/
USA Today, 9-24:(C)2.

Tex Schramm
President,
Dallas "Cowboys" football team

1

[On the drug-use problem on NFL teams]: You hear all kinds of things about your own players and players on other teams, but when it comes down to proving it, that's where the whole system breaks down. So much of it is hearsay. That's why I say the only way to go is with mandatory unscheduled [drug] testing [of players].

Los Angeles Times,
1-31:(III)12.

2

[On objections by players to having them tested for drug use]: I don't buy that invasion of privacy. When you come into sports, you become a role model, a person who loses some of his rights of privacy.

USA Today, 1-31:(A)8.

John Schuerholz
General manager,
Kansas City "Royals"
baseball club

3

[On club owners' recent hard line on player salaries]: For 10 years, the owners heard the players say, "If they are dumb enough to give it [high salaries] to us . . ." It's simple. The owners are tired of being called dumb.

USA Today, 1-29:(C)5.

John Slaughter
Chancellor, University of Maryland,
College Park; Chairman, National
Collegiate Athletic Association
Presidents Commission

4

I have learned that a [college] president or chancellor has to be on top of everything in athletics if he or she is going to run an educational institution. You have to make sure the athletic director reports to you and that you get the information you need in a timely way. At least two presidents have lost their jobs because of problems in their sports programs. Intercollegiate athletics, even though it's a pitiably small part of the budget of an institution—less than 2 per cent at the University of Maryland—can be the tail that wags the dog.

Interview/U.S. News &
World Report, 9-15:64.

Jay Snider
President, Philadelphia
"Flyers" hockey team

5

[On why his team refused to play the visiting Soviet hockey teams]: The Soviet Union is an enemy of the United States. It is immoral to engage in cultural exchanges with the Soviet Union because to do so implies acceptance of the Soviet system and of the people who rule it. To engage in cultural exchanges with barbarians is to sanction their barbaric acts.

The Washington Post,
1-15:(D)8.

Warren Spahn
Former baseball pitcher,
Milwaukee "Braves"

6

I'm not sure the ballplayers around now are better than we were. The thing missing from today's players is pride, simple pride.

Interview/
Los Angeles Times, 3-23:(III)17.

493

WHAT THEY SAID IN 1986

Roger Staubach
Former football player,
Dallas "Cowboys"

1

Anybody who loses the Super Bowl is forgotten. It's like losing an election: What ever happened to [losing 1984 Presidential candidate] Walter Mondale anyhow? When we lost [the Super Bowl], I felt so bad I wished we hadn't even played the game.

New Orleans/
The Christian Science Monitor, 1-17:20.

Dick Steinberg
Chief scout, New England
"Patriots" football team

2

The single most important football quality is competitiveness. Film studies show that [it] determines far more sacks than skill or anything else. You get more sacks if you just keep coming—if you never give up—than if you have the best moves and techniques in the league.

Los Angeles Times, 4-29:(III)4.

Leigh Steinberg
Sports agent

3

There is no effective free agency in the NFL. The rule exists in the book, but the right of first refusal by the original team, and the compensation demanded by the team that would sign a free agent, are an overwhelming deterrent to any player ever switching teams by free agency.

Los Angeles Herald Examiner, 2-1:(C)7.

4

Too many of our athletes are inaccessible to other people. They're spoiled, self-indulgent playboys—hired Hessians who sadly skim the cream off the top of a city and never give any of it back. That's not in the best interest of the sport, the city or the player . . . The concept of the role of the lawyer-agent in the sports field is too narrow. It ought to involve more than just adding another dollar to the client's bank book. Athletes serve as role models. They can influ-

ence the quality of life off the field as well as on. They have an obligation to repay some of the good fortune they have enjoyed.

Interview, Los Angeles/
The Christian Science Monitor, 4-8:6.

George Steinbrenner
Owner, New York
"Yankees" baseball club

5

[Approving baseball commissioner Peter Ueberroth's tough stance on testing of players for drug abuse]: The commissioner, in my opinion, showed some real guts. He's got a program going and he's going to enforce it. The [players] union is trying to temper that, but I think his patience is wearing thin. The union is wrong when they say some guy is going to come forward and confess "I got a [drug] problem and please help me." Who are they kidding? We're not a bunch of sugar-plum fairies. We didn't just ride into town on a load of pumpkins. Neither did the American sports public. Anybody who believes that is crazy. I think baseball has taken the lead. Basketball—they suspend one for life so they got the problem licked? Are they kidding? How many people they think in basketball are on stuff? It's prevalent in all sports today and it's got to be cleaned up and they got to do it tough.

Interview, Tampa, Fla./
USA Today, 5-21:(C)6.

6

[Criticizing recent *Yankee* player performance]: It's time for our million-dollar employees to start looking like million-dollar employees. If you want to get paid like a champion, you've got to play like a champion. We're not playing to our potential. We are grading the players on a 1-to-5 scale. Everything outstanding, good or bad, they do will be written down. But for everything else they will be given a grade from 1 to 5 . . . If they [the players' association] say I don't have the right to do that, well, then I'll schedule meetings for every night of the week to watch game films. I sure have the right to do that.

June 18/Los Angeles Times, 6-19:(III)10.

494

(GEORGE STEINBRENNER)

1

Everybody criticizes me because I change managers so often. But I don't really fire my managers. Every guy that was ever with me knows that he has a place with me forever if he wants it. He can leave me and come back, or he can stay with me in another capacity. But when other owners fire managers, they're usually gone for good.

Interview/The Christian
Science Monitor, 8-11:20.

David Stern
Commissioner,
National Basketball Association

2

[On the problem of drug-abuse in the NBA]: Our goal is rehabilitation. It would be easy to say that we should give the druggies—as some commentators call them—one shot and they're out. We take a more compassionate view, but we also want to send the message that our patience has some limits.

Los Angeles Times, 2-23:(III)12.

Don Sutton
Baseball pitcher,
California "Angels"

3

Baseball people, like most people, are drawn more to the spectacular than the dependable, and I am not in that class . . . I've read there are 16 basic personality types, and mine wants to be dependable, accountable and responsible. I don't need trumpets and flags on the front end, but I do need a pat on the back on the back end.

Interview, Los Angeles/
USA Today, 4-2:(C)2.

4

[On his just winning his 300th career game]: Tom Seaver and Steve Carlton have been the dominant right-handed and left-handed pitchers of my era. I'm somewhere next to [Phil] Niekro and [Gaylord] Perry . . . mechanics who can grind it out and do their share, never spectacu-

larly. I'm an unspectacular grinder who stayed around for 21 years and did his part. It's nice to know, of course, that there's more than one way to do something.

Interview, Anaheim, Calif., June 18/
Los Angeles Times, 6-19:(III)1.

5

[Saying the New York *Mets,* who recently won the World Series, are an arrogant team]: I really didn't want the *Mets* to win. They project themselves, and the key word is *project,* as arrogant asses, and [manager] Davey Johnson did nothing to change my mind when the first thing he said when they handed him the trophy was: "Thank you, sir. We won 110 games. This is right where we deserve to be" . . . I don't think the Baltimore *Orioles* were [arrogant] when they were winning every year. I don't think [American League champion] Boston was this year. I believe consistently good teams don't have to say, "We win because we're good and we lost because you're lucky." But I think that's the image the *Mets* project. If they got beat it was because the umpire made a bad call or the *Cubs* were lucky. They never got beat; I never heard them say they got beat. Eighteen to nothing? "Hey, they just caught us on a bad day." Yeah, it was Monday. If you get beat, you get beat. If you win, you win and move on. Nobody's infallible, but I think they sounded that way.

Interview/Los Angeles Times, 11-20:(III)2.

Barry Switzer
Football coach,
University of Oklahoma

6

[On his players' saying they are "loose"]: Loose to me means a player has the leeway to cut his hair and express his personality the way he wants; not having to worry about how someone else perceives him or about stepping on someone else's toes. It means having fun and being yourself. That's our football team. But when game time comes, we're business-like. Our players will go out and hit you right in the mouth and play as hard for 60 minutes as we can play. We might not look the same or say the same things,

(BARRY SWITZER)

but inside we're football players. If people want to say something against me as a coach because my players are different, then that's their problem.

Interview, Miami/USA Today, 1-2:(C)3.

Harry Usher
Commissioner,
United States Football League

1

[On the recent verdict in the USFL's favor in its antitrust suit against the NFL, and the jury's award of $1]: I don't know how to say it more emphatically: We won. We set out to prove the NFL had violated the antitrust laws and injured us, and that's what the jury found unanimously. But what we're faced with now is confusion on the part of the jurors as to what and how should the damages have been awarded. It defies logic. It defies common sense to have an award of $1. We do not think the [award] verdict makes sense.

July 30/The New York Times, 7-31:20.

Chuck Tanner
Baseball manager,
Atlanta "Braves"

2

Baseball should be fun. It was never intended to be a 9-5 job that you left on your desk. For the people who play major-league baseball, it should be a life-style. I like the fellows who get to the ballpark early, who spend time playing cards, sharing a bucket of chicken. A baseball team should be a family, one that sticks together through the bad times as well as the good.

Interview, Atlanta/
USA Today, 6-6:(C)5.

Bill Terry
Former baseball player and
manager, New York "Giants"

3

[Comparing baseball today to when he played and managed in the 1930s and '40s]: No, I don't

miss baseball. I'm glad I'm out of it. The last time I was at Cooperstown, I was talking with Jim Campbell of the Detroit club. Jim said to me, "Bill, you couldn't manage in baseball today. You ran your team, did everything, called all the shots. You can't do that today. Today the players have a union, there is free agency, there are agents, there is too much money!" I never liked night games and wouldn't play them if I could help it. The designated hitter is terrible . . . it's not baseball . . . you can't maneuver your pitchers with the pitchers never batting. There are too many games . . . the season runs into football. I don't know how the clubs are going to pay all the money they owe certain players.

Interview, Jacksonville, Fla./
The Christian Science Monitor, 6-4:22.

Jeff Torborg
Baseball bullpen catcher and
coach, New York "Yankees"

4

[On relief pitchers]: The good ones I've seen all had that certain attitude when the phone rang in the bullpen. It's like in school, when the teacher asks a question. The good student throws up his hand right away, eager to answer. Others look away, hoping the teacher won't call on them. [When] the phone rings, [the good relief pitcher] looks at you as if to say, "Me?" His eyes light up. He's ready. All the good ones are like that.

Interview/
The New York Times, 4-7:31.

Gary Tranquill
Football coach,
United States Naval Academy

5

[On Navy's scheduling philosophy]: First you line up five teams you should beat. Then you get three or four tossups—teams you can beat if you play your very best. Then you get two who should beat you and, if you can steal one of these, you'll have a successful season.

USA Today, 8-25:(C)11.

Lee Trevino
Golfer

1

[On the drug-abuse problem in sports]: I wouldn't say 100 per cent of [golfers] don't try it, or haven't tried it, but golf is an individual sport and I don't think it's the place for it. No, I don't think you'll hear anything like that in golf. Golfers are self-motivated, and have a built-in discipline that goes against anything like that. Kids growing up in team sports don't have that kind of discipline because they haven't needed it. From the time they're in junior high school, they've been romanced, taken care of, told when to eat, what to eat, when to go to bed, when to get up. Someone takes them to the game, then takes them home. Everything they do is planned by someone else, so they have no concern except to play their game. A basketball player lives like this for 10, maybe 12 years, and then he's suddenly handed a million bucks bonus and turned loose in the world. What do they expect him to do? It's the first time he's been on his own, and he's rich. But he's a babe in the woods.

Interview, Long Beach, Calif., July 8/
Los Angeles Times, 7-9:(III)10.

Peter V. Ueberroth
Commissioner of Baseball

2

Drug-testing [of players] is not a cure-all and end-all for anything, but this is an emergency time for baseball. It [testing] allows for early detection and provides a far greater chance for recovery. You wait until a player is on his belly and everybody is a loser. I can show you examples in baseball, football and basketball.

News conference, New York, Feb. 28/
Los Angeles Times, 3-1:(I)28.

3

Drugs are over in baseball. It's flat over. It's done . . . because the players want it done . . . We're going to have a season that's virtually drug-free. We'll be the first sport that can say that . . . Maybe there will be a little incident one place or another . . . but I don't think there'll even be that. I've been in touch with

people on all sides, including the [players'] union. Everyone is in agreement that we've got to get rid of the problem. When you have that much intent and effort, the momentum is there.

News conference, April 7/
Los Angeles Times, 4-8:(III)5.

4

[On the drug problem in baseball]: We are going to lick this problem and do it this year. We are going to wipe drugs out of this game, and not because I want it. I don't count. The [players] union doesn't count. The [club] owners don't count. It's the players who know how bad this is for the game and it's the players who want it gone once and for all. And it will be gone.

USA Today, 4-14:(D)2.

5

[On club owners' calls for a moderation in player salaries based on the financial condition of the clubs]: We got them [the owners] to open their books for the [players] union, and it turned out the owners hadn't looked at them seriously for a long time themselves. It turned out to be a powerful tool. Those books had some surprises for them—and I think some surprises for people in your profession [journalism], too. Some of the teams that lost money were a surprise. And, over-all, they lost so much money it's embarrassing.

Interview, New York/
The Christian Science Monitor, 8-5:20.

6

[On drug use by players]: The most effective of all the things [to stop player drug use] is peer pressure. Basically, baseball players are not on drugs and were not in the past, but there were a few. And, as a part of society, we stood by and permitted it. But now you have a commissioner who won't permit it, you have a [players] union that won't permit it, you have a group of owners that won't permit it and, most importantly, you have players who put on group pressure—if they get somebody on their team who wants to play with that stuff, they get rid of him.

Interview/
USA Today, 10-10:(A)11.

WHAT THEY SAID IN 1986

(PETER V. UEBERROTH)

1

Almost every decision I make makes some [team] owners very unhappy. Very unhappy. I have made some decisions now that they will never forgive me for. Certain prominent owners will never forgive me for opening the books on baseball. But they're going to continue to be open. There are so many other things: I must fine owners; I must discipline them; when they behave badly, I have to tell them. To get favorable votes, you have to butter up people. That's just not my nature.

Interview/USA Today, 10-10:(A)11.

John Weistart
Professor of law, Duke University

2

There is tremendous psychological pressure on athletes. They are surrounded by people boosting their egos and telling them they're invulnerable to the ordinary pressures that we all face. An athlete has to deal with the disjunction between the outside world, which says he's exceptional, and what he feels inside, which is he's just as human as the rest of us.

Time, 8-25:54.

Hoyt Wilhelm
Former baseball pitcher

3

To throw a knuckleball effectively, you can't really concentrate on much else [in the way of pitches]. I know that sounds odd, but you have to learn to deliver the ball at such reduced speeds that this eventually fouls up your motion for standard pitches. The thing is, you always push the ball toward home plate more than you throw it.

The Christian Science Monitor, 8-11:20.

Billy Williams
Batting instructor, and former player,
Chicago "Cubs" baseball club

4

You hear fans saying that this star or that one was a "natural," but 99 per cent of the time they're wrong. Sure, you gotta have ability, but you also gotta work, and every good hitter I knew worked hard to get that way. You have to practice your swing all the time, just like a golf pro. And if you think golf's hard, try it sometimes with a guy throwing the ball at you.

Interview, Mesa, Ariz./
The Wall Street Journal, 3-14:20.

Edward Bennett Williams
Owner, Baltimore "Orioles" baseball club

5

The worst mistake you can make is to be happy with your team. I'm not happy, no. I'm hopeful, but we have some problems that have to be sorted out . . . When we won the world championship in 1983, everybody said, "You never tinker with a champion. Don't change a winning formula." You have to change.

Interview, Miami/USA Today, 4-4:(C)8.

Pat Williams
General manager, Philadelphia
"76ers" football team

6

I've been in sports for 25 years. And all that matters is whether you win. If you don't win, they have strange habits. My contract expires in six months. This is not a sympathy business. This is a results business.

The New York Times, 5-12:29.

Butch Wynegar
Baseball player, New York "Yankees"

7

[Saying he has re-signed with the *Yankees*]: I don't think the free-agent market is like it used to be. I had no offer from any other club. There were talks with other clubs, but not anything concrete. You have to admit the owners stuck together. We were sort of playing Russian roulette with the *Yankees*. I agree with the owners. I have said all along the [player] salaries had to stop somewhere. The players are paid too much.

News conference, New York, Jan. 13/
The New York Times, 1-14:25.

The Indexes

Index to Speakers

A

Aaron, David, 120
Aaron, Henry, 476
Abbott, George, 435
Abdul Kadir Sheikh Fadzir, 275
Abe, Kobo, 372
Abraham, F. Murray, 406
Abram, Morris B., 56, 294
Abrams, Elliott, 120, 245
Abrams, Floyd, 357
Abu Ghazala, Abdel Halim, 312
Acker, C. Edward, 210
Adams, Gerry, 294
Adedeji, Adebayo, 217
Adelman, Kenneth, 56
Adelsohn, Ulf, 294
Adler, Mortimer, 94, 152, 201, 345, 444
Akinyemi, Bolaji, 217
Alarcon, Ricardo, 246
Albanese, Licia, 425
Alexander, Alison, 399
Alexander, Lamar, 94, 111, 152
Alfonsin, Raul, 246
Allen, George, 386, 476
Allen, Joseph, 465
Allen, Steve, 399
Allen, Walter, 94
Allen, Woody, 406
Allende, Isabel, 372
Ammerman, Nancy T., 458
Anaya, Toney, 48
Anderson, Jack, 312, 465
Anderson, Sparky, 476
Andreotti, Giulio, 294
Angelou, Maya, 444
Anrig, Gregory, 94
Aquino, Corazon C., 11, 120, 275-278
Arafat, Yasir, 312
Arashi, Qadi Abdul Karim, 312
Arbatov, Georgi A., 294
Arce, Bayardo, 246
Arcel, Ray, 476
Ardabili, Abdulkarim Musavi, 312
Arias, Oscar, 246-247, 357
Arkin, Alan, 406, 444
Armey, Richard, 77
Armitage, Richard, 435

Arnold, Danny, 399, 444
Ash, James, 94
Ashe, Arthur, 476
Asimov, Isaac, 372, 465
Aspin, Les, 56
Assad, Hafez al-, 313
Asselstine, James K., 111
Astin, Alexander W., 184
Astorga, Nora, 247
Attas, Haider abu Bakr, 313
Attenborough, Richard, 406
Aubrey, James T., 31, 406
Auchincloss, Eva, 477
Auerbach, Red, 477
Azcona, Jose, 247, 444
Azenberg, Emanuel, 435
Aziz, Tariq, 313

B

Babangida, Ibrahim Badamasi, 217
Babbitt, Bruce, 152, 201, 444-445
Babenco, Hector, 407
Badea, Christian, 425
Badham, John, 407
Bailey, Ralph, 111
Baker, James A., III, 77
Baker, Raymond, 313
Baker, Ross K., 184
Baldrige, Malcolm, 31
Baldwin, James, 445
Baliles, Gerald L., 210
Ball, George, 31
Ball, George W., 120, 313
Ball, Lucille, 407
Balladur, Edouard, 294
Bani-Sadr, Abolhassan. 314
Banks, Ernie, 477
Barber, James David, 184
Barber, Red, 477
Barco, Virgilio, 248
Barry, Marion, 17, 201
Barry, Peter, 295
Barthelmey, Thomas, 57
Baucus, Max, 465
Bauer, Gary, 95, 201
Bazin, Marc, 248
Beattie, Ann, 372

E

F

I

J

M

Index to Subjects

A

Abbado, Claudio, 431:3
Abbas, Abu, 365:5, 367:3, 368:3, 369:1
Abortion—*see* Women
Acquired immune deficiency syndrome (AIDS)—
  see Medicine
Acting/actors, 406:4, 406:5, 408:5, 408:6, 408:8,
  409:5, 412:4, 413:1, 413:6, 413:8, 417:1,
  419:5, 420:4, 422:4
  age, 414:2
  audience aspect, 406:1, 408:1, 408:7
  blacks, 415:5
  childish aspect, 410:1
  mask, wearing of, 380:7
  men/women aspect, 419:6
  parts begin to take over life, 415:4
  perfect/consummate performance, 412:3, 413:3
  in politics, 197:7
  popularity, 415:3
  preparation, 410:5
  stage/theatre, 435:1, 437:4, 439:6, 441:1
    stage/motion pictures compared, 437:5
  stars, 408:4, 417:4, 418:5, 435:1, 437:4,
    439:6
  television, 404:1, 441:1
    TV/motion pictures compared, 402:5
  truth, distortion of, 442:4
  typecasting, 418:2
  villains, 411:6
Adams, John, 15:4, 427:5
Addams, Jane, 346:1
Adversity, 444:1
Advertising—*see* Commerce
Afghanistan:
  freedom fighters, 139:1
  foreign relations with:
    China, 285:3
    Soviet Union, 74:2, 123:2, 129:1, 280:6,
      281:1, 281:6, 283:2, 288:6, 289:1,
      292:5, 336:2
Africa, pp. 217-244
  black-on-black atrocities, 232:1
  Communism, 227:2, 237:3
  dictatorships, 217:5
  East/West, black aspect, 17:4
  economy, 217:1, 217:2, 232:3, 233:4

Africa *(continued)*
  liberation, 221:1
  nationalism, 129:2
  poverty/famine, 231:2, 231:3
  foreign relations with:
    Soviet Union, 134:6
    U.S., 134:6, 135:2, 236:2
  See also specific African countries
Agriculture/farming:
  cyclical, 41:2
  economic/financial problems, 79:3, 91:6
  government aspect, 42:1, 85:1, 204:1
    See also prices/supports, *this section*
  imports/exports, 32:5
  prices/supports, 41:2, 43:2, 46:3, 85:1
    subsidy for wheat to Soviet Union, 139:4,
      145:5, 282:1, 285:4
  soil erosion, 116:4
  surpluses, 41:2, 43:2
Air transportation—*see* Transportation
Albania, 305:8
Alcohol—*see* Medicine: drugs
Alfonsin, Raul, 261:2
Ali, Muhammad, 489:1
Aliens, illegal—*see* Foreign affairs: immigration
Allen, Neil, 488:7
Ambition, 456:3
America/U.S.:
  anything can happen, 13:2
  being an American, 15:5
  bragging, 11:6
  class status, 14:4
  common culture, 11:2
  community, sense of, 14:1
  contradictions in, 14:5
  democracy, 14:3
  disparate human resources, 12:4
  equality, 11:1, 11:3
  freedom/liberty, 11:4, 12:5, 15:5
  government, oldest, 14:6
  government, participation in, 12:2
  ideals/aspirations, 11:3
  immigrants, assimilation of, 14:2
  individual, importance of, 11:5
  openness, 15:1
  opportunity, 11:1, 13:2

D

Education/schools *(continued)*
college/university (continued)
degree, 104:5
drugs, 96:5
enrollment, cut in, 94:7, 103:1
land-grant, 204:1
for masses, 95:3
moral superiority, 97:1
not for everyone, 105:2
presidents, college, 95:4, 97:5, 98:6, 103:4, 493:4
professors, 102:2
public/private—*see* Education: public/private
quality, 106:1
renewing itself, 107:2
sports/athletics, 99:6, 100:4, 102:5, 105:2, 106:4, 107:4, 108:1, 109:4, 493:4
basketball, 490:6
cheating, 483:3
drugs, 484:6
football, 100:4, 106:4, 489:4
recruiting, 483:5, 490:6
students:
conservatism/liberalism, 184:1
maturity, 100:1
pool, size of, 94:7, 97:4, 103:1
radicals, 96:3
unprepared, 96:1, 105:2
think, learning to, 448:5
tuition/costs, 97:3, 98:2
U.S. intelligence, cooperating with, 102:3
Egypt:
economy, 326:1
foreign relations with:
Germany, West, 326:1
Israel, 142:3, 330:7
Japan, 326:1
Libya, 312:2
Morocco, 326:1
Saudi Arabia, 326:1
Sudan, 326:1
Tunisia, 326:1
U.S., 326:1
Ehrlichman, John D., 153:2
Einstein, Albert, 448:1
Eisenhower, Dwight D., 74:5, 89:6, 190:4, 209:2, 371:2
El Salvador:
Communism, 256:4, 273:6
democracy, 254:1, 256:4, 267:3, 270:3
governing of, 254:2
rebels, 254:1, 274:3
repression, 238:4

El Salvador *(continued)*
foreign relations with:
Cuba, 273:6
Nicaragua, 270:1, 274:3
U.S., 256:4
Elderly—*see* Social welfare
Elections—*see* Politics
Eliot, T. S., 376:3
Ellington, Duke, 426:6
Ellison, Ralph, 373:5
Employment—*see* Labor
Energy:
nuclear, 111:4, 116:7, 119:4
Chernobyl accident, 63:5, 64:1, 111:5, 112:1, 113:5, 114:3, 114:6, 115:2, 115:3, 117:3, 118:5, 127:7, 294:5, 297:4, 300:3, 302:5, 306:3, 308:4, 368:3, 456:7, 470:4
Nuclear Regulatory Commission (NRC), 111:2, 111:3
Three Mile Island accident, 111:2, 115:2
oil:
environmental aspect, 114:2, 115:5, 117:5, 118:3
Israel, 318:1
Japan, 317:3
Korea, South, 317:3
Middle East, 119:5, 317:3, 318:1, 334:1, 336:2
OPEC, 115:4, 116:5, 318:1
prices, 112:2, 112:3, 113:2, 114:4, 115:4, 116:5, 118:2, 118:4, 119:2, 119:6, 318:1
production/exploration/supply, 111:6, 112:3, 113:2, 114:2, 118:1, 118:2, 118:4, 119:6
Saudi Arabia, 114:1, 116:5, 119:2
Strategic Petroleum Reserve, 114:5
risks, 112:1
Environment, pp.111-119
acid rain, 116:2, 116:3, 118:6
air, 118:6
chlorofluorocarbons, 117:2
Alaska, 114:2
business vs. environmentalists, 112:4
cost of protection, 111:1
development vs. preservation, 115:1
government aspect, 113:1, 152:2
Interior, U.S. Secretary of the, 115:1
nature, 119:3, 447:5, 451:5
oil aspect, 114:2, 115:5, 117:5, 118:3
parks:
Everglades, 114:1

F

M

Social welfare *(continued)*
  poverty/the poor *(continued)*
    205:2, 205:5, 206:1, 206:3, 206:4, 208:2, 208:3, 209:2, 209:5, 444:5, 454:6
  religion/church aspect, 208:4
  Republican Party aspect, 206:1
  responsibility, 206:3
  retirement, mandatory, 80:7, 205:4
  safety/OSHA, 202:4
  safety net, 204:4, 207:1, 208:3
  Social Security, 174:3, 202:2, 202:6, 203:3, 205:6, 207:2, 207:4, 209:1
  street people, 208:2
  under-class, 14:4, 19:1, 49:2
  unemployment compensation, 207:3
  welfare, 27:5, 201:2, 201:6, 202:5, 202:6, 203:1, 203:5, 204:1, 204:2, 205:3, 206:3, 208:3, 208:4
  women, 201:4, 202:7, 206:4
    maternity leave/benefits, 201:4, 203:2, 207:2
Socrates, 442:7
Somoza, Anastasio, 247:5, 249:5, 258:1, 265:6, 271:5, 271:6, 364:6
South, the U.S., 16:2, 194:5
South Africa:
  apartheid/blacks/whites/racism, 218:1, 218:2, 218:3, 218:4, 219:2, 219:3, 219:4, 219:5, 220:1, 220:3, 220:4, 221:1, 221:4, 221:5, 223:1, 223:4, 224:1, 224:2, 225:2, 225:3, 225:5, 226:2, 227:4, 227:5, 228:3, 229:4, 230:5, 232:1, 232:2, 235:5, 236:1, 237:1, 237:4, 237:5, 237:6, 238:1, 238:2, 238:4, 239:2, 240:1, 240:2, 240:3, 240:4, 240:5, 241:2, 241:3, 241:4, 242:3, 242:4, 243:1, 243:2, 243:3
    African National Congress (ANC), 219:6, 222:2, 223:3, 225:5, 227:5, 228:3, 229:4, 230:4, 232:5, 234:2, 239:1, 239:3, 239:4, 240:3, 241:4
    Afrikaner Resistance Movement, 240:4, 240:5
    black-on-black violence, 223:3
    disinvestment, 224:3, 225:6, 236:3, 237:2, 243:2
    Jews aspect, 233:2
    raids on foreign anti-apartheid bases, 219:6, 225:5, 236:1
    sanctions, economic, 17:4, 217:4, 217:5, 219:1, 220:2, 220:5, 221:2, 221:3, 222:1, 222:2, 222:3, 222:4, 222:5, 223:2, 224:4, 224:6, 225:6, 226:3, 226:4, 227:1, 227:2, 227:3, 228:4,

South Africa *(continued)*
  apartheid *(continued)*
    sanctions, economic *(continued)*
      228:5, 228:6, 229:1, 229:2, 230:1, 230:4, 231:4, 232:6, 233:1, 233:2, 233:3, 234:1, 234:3, 235:6, 236:3, 236:4, 237:2, 238:3, 238:5, 239:4, 240:6, 241:1, 241:5, 242:1, 242:2, 244:1, 244:2
    state of emergency, 224:5, 232:4, 235:1
  Botha, Pieter W., 222:2, 223:4, 224:1, 228:3, 230:1, 232:6, 235:6, 237:4, 240:2, 240:5, 364:6
  Communism/socialism, 219:3, 223:3, 232:5, 234:2, 240:3, 243:1
  democracy, 217:4, 217:5, 219:2, 221:5, 223:3, 224:1, 225:6, 229:1, 235:2, 239:3, 240:3, 241:4, 241:5, 243:1, 243:3
  economy, 223:3, 237:1
    See also South Africa: apartheid: sanctions, economic
  education aspect, 225:1, 225:2
  gold/diamond miner strikes, 230:5
  human rights, 172:6
  loans, repayment of, 244:1
  press/media, 232:4, 238:2, 243:1
  Third World aspect, 220:5
  United Nations (UN), 219:6
  foreign relations with:
    Angola, 224:2, 228:2, 235:3
    Britain, 219:1, 225:6, 226:2, 226:4, 227:1, 227:3, 228:4, 228:5, 234:1, 242:1, 242:4
    Canada, 231:4
    Cuba, 224:2
    Germany, West, 219:1, 226:2, 242:4
    Israel, 233:2
    Lesotho, 228:1
    U.S., 217:4, 218:1, 218:2, 219:1, 221:3, 221:5, 222:2, 222:4, 222:5, 223:1, 223:2, 224:3, 225:4, 226:2, 226:3, 226:4, 227:2, 228:2, 228:5, 228:6, 229:2, 230:1, 232:6, 233:1, 233:3, 234:1, 234:3, 236:3, 237:2, 238:1, 238:5, 242:2, 242:4, 244:2
    Zambia, 228:3
Soviet Union/Russia/U.S.S.R.:
  aggressiveness, 300:2
  agreements, violation of, 131:1
  arts, 351:3
  Chernobyl nuclear accident—*see* Energy: nuclear
  colonial empire, 124:6

W

Y

Z